A History of Mathematics Education in the United States and Canada

Thirty-second Yearbook

WASHINGTON, D.C.
National Council of Teachers of Mathematics
1970

Correspondence relating to and orders for
additional copies of the Thirty-second Yearbook
and earlier yearbooks should be
addressed to

THE NATIONAL COUNCIL OF TEACHERS OF MATHEMATICS
1906 Association Drive
Reston, VA 20191-1502
(703) 620-9840; (800) 235-7566; www.nctm.org

ISBN 0-87353-535-9

First printing 1970
Second printing 2002

Library of Congress Catalog Card Number: 71-105864

The publications of the National Council of Teachers of Mathematics present a variety of viewpoints. The views expressed or implied in this publication, unless otherwise noted, should not be interpreted as official positions of the Council.

Printed in the United States of America

Preface

At a time when there seemed to be a slight lull in the "revolution" in school mathematics, it seemed appropriate to undertake a history of mathematics education. Accordingly, in December 1966 this book was proposed to the Editor by the Yearbook Planning Committee of the National Council of Teachers of Mathematics—a committee composed of M. Vere DeVault, John F. Devlin, Jack E. Forbes, Adrian L. Hess, Joseph N. Payne, and L. Doyal Nelson (chairman). They asked that it be ready for the semicentennial celebration of the National Council of Teachers of Mathematics in 1970.

The committee suggested: "The emphasis of the book should be on the historical origin of the content, methodology, and course sequences existing in the United States and Canada rather than on the chronological aspects of the topic. It is expected that the yearbook would also delineate the important issues and problems which need to be resolved in the coming decades."

The editorial committee for this book was then selected and met in Ann Arbor, Michigan, in June of 1967. It prepared a plan and budget which were approved by the Publications Committee and the Board of Directors of the National Council of Teachers of Mathematics. President Donovan A. Johnson notified the editorial committee of the Board's approval in October of 1967.

The editorial committee enlisted a few additional writers and together they met in Chicago in November of 1967 to elaborate and review the original outline and prepare a work schedule.

Many friendly, exciting, and vigorous debates developed. There is neither time for nor value in recounting most of these, but one in particular typifies our problems. The editorial committee originally planned that one Part of the book would be devoted to the development of major themes in content, such as number, proof, and function through grades K–12. A second Part was planned to trace a parallel story of the development of pedagogical problems and devices, such as the problems of individual differences and the use of laboratory and discovery techniques in teaching, again to cover the K-12 span.

This plan was initially accepted by the enlarged writing team because of their general agreement that it is a highly desirable trend to diminish the distinction between elementary and secondary school programs and to place great emphasis and stress on the need for articulation and continuity over the entire span, grades K-12. However, when our outlines were further elaborated and work was begun, difficulties were encountered. Practicality was given precedence over a desire to encourage articulation. These Parts were reorganized into the present Parts Two and Three, separated on the basis of grade level rather than on the basis of content and teaching problems. The motives for this change were several: (1) the elementary-secondary distinction has been significant in the history we were trying to write, and we were not trying to change the past; (2) the readers we seek are still strongly oriented this way and might be more able and inclined to follow our story than if it were consolidated; (3) the writers themselves tended to be better informed and more confident of their knowledge and views at one level or the other rather than over the entire K-12 range.

There were other caveats suggested by the authors as we discussed and wrote. For example: the distinction between "forces" and "issues" is rarely sharp and varies with the time and the topic; which forces and issues are more important or more inclusive is a function of the authors' viewpoints as well; and finally the amount of space allotted to each force or issue occasionally had to be dictated by an editor.

In a historical undertaking that tries to be analytical as well as factual it is particularly difficult to acknowledge, or even to define, all one's sources of aid and ideas. Our extensive bibliographies are intended to do this as well as to be an aid to persons with further interest in our story. There are two especially important sources not adequately covered by a bibliography, however—our own teachers and our students. The Editor, for example, profited more than the bibliography reveals from work with Raleigh Schorling and Louis C. Karpinski.

Several groups of graduate students have indirectly helped by stimulating thought and gathering data. At Ohio State University a group of graduate students in mathematics education prepared a paper, "The Evolving Mathematics Curriculum in the United States since 1890," which was interesting and helpful. This group included Carl V. Benner, Sister Lenora Carmody, Charles McNerney, Lloyd Merick, John

C. Peterson, Richard L. Price, H. Marks Richard, David Robitaille, and Susan Stock. A paper on the history of mathematics curricula in the United States, written by George P. Richardson for Professor E. G. Begle of Stanford University, was read by the Editor with interest and profit. Kristina Leeb-Lundberg sent us outlines of a thesis, "The History of Mathematics in the Kindergartens of the United States." Other persons, whose theses are listed at the end of our bibliography and who either corresponded or conversed with us, are Lewis J. Berenson, Robert G. Clason, and John D. Hancock.

Professor Jerry P. Becker of Rutgers University made available to us a manuscript, "A Historical Survey of Attempts to Improve School Mathematics in the United States," which he had prepared for a junior-senior high school teacher institute in the summer of 1968.

Professor Frederick L. Goodman of the University of Michigan read Part One critically and made helpful suggestions.

Finally, our appreciation goes to those persons who have made this book a reality: Charles R. Hucka, who directs the Council's publishing program; Julia A. Lacy, who supervised the editorial process; Dorothy C. Hardy, who did the major copy editing; and Colleen Clark, Karen Craig, and Lois G. Saunders, who gave substantial help at various stages of production.

The Editors and Authors

(Members of the editorial committee are indicated by asterisks.)

Arthur F. Coxford, Jr.,*
  Associate Editor
  The University of Michigan
Douglas H. Crawford
  Queen's University
F. Joe Crosswhite
  The Ohio State University
M. Vere DeVault
  The University of Wisconsin
Harold P. Fawcett*
  The Ohio State University
E. Glenadine Gibb
  University of Texas
Phillip S. Jones,* *Editor*
  The University of Michigan

Houston T. Karnes*
  Louisiana State University
L. Doyal Nelson*
  University of Alberta
Alan R. Osborne*
  The Ohio State University
Douglas J. Potvin
  Loyola College
Solberg E. Sigurdson
  University of Alberta
J. Fred Weaver*
  The University of Wisconsin
F. Lynwood Wren
  San Fernando Valley State
  College

Acknowledgments

Grateful acknowledgment is made for permission to reprint extracts from the sources named below. Individual articles are listed under the name of the journal or book in which each appears.

American Mathematical Monthly. "Recommendations concerning Preparation for Major Teaching of Secondary Mathematics," by the Commission on the Training and Utilization of Advanced Students in Mathematics. Also, review of David Eugene Smith's *Poetry of Mathematics*, by Eric T. Bell. Both are reprinted from vol. 42 (1935) by permission of the Mathematical Association of America.

"The Arithmetic of the Elementary Schools of Ontario," by J. D. Campbell. Dissertation, University of Toronto, 1943.

Canada, a Story of Challenge, by J. M. S. Careless. © 1963, 1965, by The Macmillan Co. of Canada Ltd.; reprinted by permission of The Macmillan Co. of Canada Ltd. and St. Martin's Press.

The Development of Education in Canada, by C. E. Phillips. © 1957 by W. J. Gage, Ltd.

Educational Psychology, by Peter Sandiford. © 1934 by Longmans, Green & Co.; reprinted by permission of Longman Group Ltd., London.

Education and the Cult of Efficiency, by R. E. Callahan. © 1962 by The University of Chicago Press.

Education for All American Youth. Published 1948 by the National Education Association.

An Emerging Program of Secondary School Mathematics, by Max Beberman. © 1958 by Harvard University Press.

Elementary School Journal. "The Place of Meaning in the Teaching of Arithmetic," by William A. Brownell. © 1947 by The University of Chicago Press.

General Education in a Free Society, by Harvard Committee. © 1945 by Harvard University Press.

General Education in School and College, a committee report by the faculties of Andover, Exeter, Lawrenceville, Harvard, Princeton, and Yale. © 1952 by Harvard University Press.

Goals for Mathematical Education of Elementary School Teachers, by Cambridge Conference on Teacher Training. © 1967 by the Education Development Center, Inc. Reprinted by permission of Houghton Mifflin Co.

Goals for School Mathematics, by Cambridge Conference on School Mathematics. © 1963 by Education Development Center, Inc. (formerly Edu-

ACKNOWLEDGMENTS

cational Services Incorporated). Reprinted by permission of Houghton Mifflin Co.

The High School Curriculum (3d ed.), edited by Harl R. Douglass. "Mathematics," by Lucien B. Kinney. © 1964 by The Ronald Press Co., New York.

Historical Highlights, 1891–1960, by the Ontario Association of Teachers of Mathematics and Physics. © 1962 by Copp Clark Publishing Co.

Journal of Experimental Education (1937). "Changes in Curriculum in Elementary Algebra since 1900 as Reflected by the Requirements and Examinations of CEEB," by Orlando E. Overn. Reprinted by permission of Dembar Educational Research Services, Inc.

Mathematical Education in the Americas. "The Reform of Mathematics Education in the United States of America," by E. G. Begle. © 1962 by the Bureau of Publications, Teachers College, Columbia University; reprinted by permission of Teachers College Press.

Mathematical Learning, Monographs of the Society for Research in Child Development, vol. 30 [ser. no. 99]. "Some Factors in Learning Non-Metric Geometry," by Robert M. Gagné et al. Published by The University of Chicago Press. © 1965 by the Society.

Mathematics and the Teacher: Report of a Conference, 1967. Reprinted by permission of the Canadian Teachers' Federation.

Mathematics in Canadian Schools, by the Canadian Association of Mathematics Teachers, 1967. Reprinted by permission of the Canadian Teachers' Federation.

Mathematics in General Education, by a committee of the Progressive Education Association. Published by D. Appleton-Century Co. (now Appleton-Century-Crofts, Educational Div., Meredith Corp.).

Newsletter No. 1, SMSG progress report, by School Mathematics Study Group. Published by Yale University Press, 1959. Used by permission of SMSG.

New Thinking in School Mathematics, by the Organization for Economic Cooperation and Development, 1961. Reprinted by permission of the OECD, Paris.

Offerings and Enrollments in Science and Mathematics in Public High Schools, by Kenneth E. Brown. U.S. Office of Education, 1956.

Outline of Report of Inaugural Conference on Mathematics (1962), by the Nova Scotia Teachers Union, which has granted permission to reprint.

Philosophies and Procedures of SMSG Writing Teams, by School Mathematics Study Group. Published by Stanford University Press, 1965. Reprinted by permission of SMSG.

The Psychology of Arithmetic, by Edward L. Thorndike. Published in in 1922 by The Macmillan Co.

Recommendations for the Training of Teachers of Mathematics, by the Committee on the Undergraduate Program in Mathematics of the Mathematical Association of America, 1961. Reprinted by permission of the MAA.

The Reorganization of Mathematics in Secondary Education, by the National Committee on Mathematical Requirements of the Mathematical Association of America, 1923. Reprinted by permission of the MAA.

Report of the Commission on Mathematics: Program for College Preparatory Mathematics. Published in 1959 by the College Entrance Examination Board, New York.

Report of the Society's Committee on Arithmetic, Twenty-ninth Yearbook of the National Society for the Study of Education. "Introduction," by F. B. Knight. Also, "The Grade Placement of Arithmetic Topics," by Carleton Washburne. © 1930 by the Society.

Research and Development toward the Improvement of Education. "Curriculum Research in Mathematics," by E. G. Begle. © 1969 by Dembar Educational Research Services, Inc.

The Revolution in the Schools. "The New Curricula," by Evans Clinchy. Published by Harcourt, Brace & World, Inc. © 1964 by Evans Clinchy.

School Science and Mathematics (1946). "The Preparation of High School Science and Mathematics Teachers," by a committee of the American Association for the Advancement of Science. Reprinted by permission of the Central Association of Science and Mathematics Teachers.

"Secondary School Curricular Change in Canada with Special Emphasis on an Ontario Experiment," by Harry Pullen. Dissertation, University of Toronto, 1955.

SMSG: The Making of a Curriculum, by William Wooton. Published by Yale University Press, 1965. Used by permission of the School Mathematics Study Group.

Strayer-Upton Arithmetics, Higher Grades, by George D. Strayer and Clifford B. Upton. © 1928 by the American Book Co.

The Teaching of Arithmetic, by Harry G. Wheat. Published by The University of Chicago Press. © 1951 by the National Society for the Study of Education.

"The Teaching of Mathematics in Ontario," by W. B. Gray. Dissertation, University of Toronto, 1948.

Teaching the New Arithmetic, by Guy M. Wilson, Mildred B. Stone, and Charles O. Dalrymple. © 1939 by McGraw-Hill Book Co.

The Transformation of the School, by Lawrence A. Cremin. © 1961 by Alfred A. Knopf, Inc.

Table of Contents

Preface *iii*

Acknowledgments *vi*

INTRODUCTION
Phillip S. Jones and *Arthur F. Coxford, Jr.*

1 The Goals of History: Issues and Forces *1*

    Our Goals *1*
    Our Themes: Forces and Issues *2*
    Progress by Periods *4*
    Summary and Preview *7*

PART ONE

Mathematics in the Evolving Schools
Phillip S. Jones and *Arthur F. Coxford, Jr.*

2 From Discovery to an Awakened Concern for Pedagogy: 1492–1821 *11*

    The Earliest American Mathematics *11*
    The Content and Processes of Colonial Instruction *13*
    The Latin Grammar School and the Academy *18*

    The Colleges and the Mathematical Community *18*
    Self-Instruction *20*
    The Teachers and Pedagogy *21*
    Summary *22*

3 From Colburn to the Rise of the Universities: 1821–94   *24*

    Forces at Work *24*
    The Elementary Schools *25*
    The Secondary Schools *27*
    The Colleges and the Mathematical Community *28*
    Teacher Training and Pedagogy *30*
    The Climate of Reform *33*
    Summary *34*

4 First Steps toward Revision: 1894–1920   *36*

    Forces at Work *36*
    The Elementary Schools *37*
    The Secondary Schools *39*
    The Colleges and the Mathematical Community *41*
    Pedagogy and Teacher Training *42*
    Summary *43*

5 Abortive Reform—Depression and War: 1920–45   *46*

    A Period of Unrest *46*
    The Elementary School *48*
    The Junior High School *51*
    The Senior High School *53*
    The War and Its Effects *58*
    The Junior College *60*
    The Colleges, Teacher Training, and the Mathematical
      Community *61*
    Psychological and Educational Theories *63*
    Summary *63*

6 Reform, "Revolution," Reaction: 1945–Present   *67*

    A Buildup of Pressures for Reform: Old Forces *67*
    New Forces *68*
    The Prelude to Reform *72*
    The Elementary School *76*
    The Secondary School *78*
    Teacher Training, Certification, and the Conversion to
      New Programs *79*
    Collegiate Mathematics *81*
    Reaction *81*
    Psychological and Educational Theories *83*
    Summary *86*

CONTENTS   xi

PART TWO
Forces and Issues Related to Curriculum and Instruction, K–6
M. Vere DeVault and J. Fred Weaver

7 Elementary Mathematics Education: An Overview   93

    The Major Periods *93*
    The Continuing Issues *94*
    The Continuing Forces *95*

8 From Settlement to the End of the Nineteenth Century: 1607–1894   *98*

    Introduction *98*
    Why Teach Mathematics? *98*
    What Mathematics Should Be Taught? *99*
    How Should We Organize the Mathematics We Teach? *103*
    How Should Instruction in Arithmetic Be Organized and Implemented? *104*
    Summary of the Period 1607–1894 *105*

9 Scientism and Changing Conceptions of Elementary Schooling: 1894–1923   *107*

    Evidences of Change *107*
    Why Teach Mathematics? *109*
    What Mathematics Should We Teach? *110*
    How Should We Organize and Implement Instruction? *114*
    Summary *116*

10 Mathematics Education during the Rise and Fall of Progressive Education: 1923–52   *118*

    Forces at Work *118*
    Why Teach Mathematics? *120*
    What Mathematics Should We Teach? *122*
    How Should We Organize the Mathematics We Teach? *125*
    How Should We Organize and Implement Instruction? *127*
    Summary *131*

11 Designing a Contemporary Elementary School Mathematics Program: 1952–Present   *133*

    Introduction *133*
    Why Teach Mathematics? *134*
    What Mathematics Should We Teach? *135*

How Should We Organize the Mathematics We Teach? *140*
How Should We Organize and Implement Instruction? *142*
Summary *144*

PART THREE

Forces and Issues Related to Curriculum and Instruction, 7–12
Alan R. Osborne and *F. Joe Crosswhite*

12 Emerging Issues: 1890–1920   *155*

Introduction *155*
Mathematics Education in 1890 *155*
Arithmetic *157*
Algebra *158*
Geometry *161*
Other Forces *162*
The Committee of Ten *163*
Impact of the Report of the Committee of Ten *167*
College Entrance Requirements *168*
The Unified Mathematics Movement *173*
Reactions to the Unification Movement *177*
Geometrical Developments *179*
The International Commission *182*
Practical Utility in Mathematics Education *183*
The Changing School Population and Vocational Education *184*
Psychologizing Secondary School Mathematics *185*
The Cult of Efficiency and Secondary School Mathematics *188*
The Educational Generalists' View of the Curriculum *192*
The Founding of the NCTM *194*
Overview: 1890 to 1920 *196*

13 Mathematics Education on the Defensive: 1920–45   *197*

"The 1923 Report" *197*
Aims and "The 1923 Report" *202*
Psychology and the Report *204*
The Function Concept *205*
Model Curricula of the Report *206*
Immediate Reactions and Responses to the Report *208*
The Dominant Forces—1920 through 1940 *209*
Individual Differences Become an Issue *212*
Objectives, Psychological Theories, and Progressive Education Become Issues *213*

CONTENTS xiii

　　　　The Curriculum in Grades 7 and 8 *218*
　　　　Algebra and General Mathematics *220*
　　　　Geometry *222*
　　　　The Reports of the Progressive Education Association
　　　　　　Committee and of the Joint Commission—1940 *225*
　　　　Gearing Up for War *231*
　　　　Summary *233*

14　Reform, Revolution, and Reaction　　　　　　　　　　*235*

　　　　Introduction: Forces and Issues *235*
　　　　The Educational Policies Commission *239*
　　　　The Harvard Report *241*
　　　　Commission on Post-War Plans *243*
　　　　"General Education in School and College" *246*
　　　　Technological Needs and Education of the Gifted *248*
　　　　The University of Illinois Committee on School
　　　　　　Mathematics *251*
　　　　The Coalescence of National Support *256*
　　　　The Commission on Mathematics of the CEEB *259*
　　　　The NCTM's Support of the Reform Movement *266*
　　　　Early Curriculum Development Projects *268*
　　　　The School Mathematics Project *269*
　　　　A Summary of the Curriculum Reform Projects *281*
　　　　Criticisms of Reforms *284*
　　　　Similarities among Reform Movements *287*
　　　　The Cambridge Conference *291*
　　　　Reactions to the Cambridge Report *295*
　　　　New Directions *296*

PART FOUR

The Education of Teachers of Mathematics

*E. Glenadine Gibb, Houston T. Karnes,
and F. Lynwood Wren*

15　Teacher Education in the United States through 1945　　*301*

　　　　Introduction *301*
　　　　The First Normal School *302*
　　　　The Normal School Program *304*
　　　　The First Two Decades of the Twentieth Century *308*
　　　　In-service Teacher Education *314*
　　　　"The 1923 Report" and Its Consequences *316*
　　　　Further Developments: 1923–45 *320*

16 The Modern Era: 1945–Present — 327

    Introduction *327*
    Status Surveys *328*
    In-service Education *329*
    Recommendations for Improvement
      in Teacher Education *334*
    The Implementation of Recommendations *341*
    What of the Future? *345*

PART FIVE
School Mathematics in Canada

17 Mathematics Education in French-speaking Canada — 353
    Douglas J. Potvin

    Two Cultures *353*
    The Historical Development *354*
    The Classical Colleges *358*
    Mathematics in New France *359*
    Mathematics in the English Schools *364*
    New Trends in Mathematics Education *365*
    Uniformity in the Curriculum *367*
    Forces and Issues *370*

18 School Mathematics in Ontario, 1763–1894:
    From Settlement to System — 371
    Douglas H. Crawford

    Introduction *371*
    The Pioneer Period: 1790–1841 *372*
    The Ryerson Regime: 1841–76 *374*
    McLellan and Subsequent Reaction: 1876–94 *380*
    Summary *384*

19 School Mathematics in Ontario, 1894–1959:
    Expansion and Moderate Reform — 385
    Douglas H. Crawford

    Introduction *385*
    The Period of Reform Movements: 1894–1920 *387*
    Adapting Curricula to Life: 1920–45 *392*
    Postwar Reform and the "Rebirth" of School Mathematics:
      1945–59 *399*

CONTENTS

20 Mathematics Education in Western Canada — 412
    Solberg E. Sigurdson

    A Survey *412*
    Elementary School Arithmetic *415*
    Intermediate School Mathematics *419*
    Unifying Mathematics *421*
    The Decline of High School Arithmetic *424*

21 Rethinking School Mathematics: 1959–Present — 426
    Douglas H. Crawford

    The Socioeconomic Status of Canada in 1960 *426*
    The Commissions on Education *427*
    The 1960 Ottawa Seminar *428*
    The Canadian Association of Mathematics Teachers *430*
    Alberta *431*
    Ontario *434*
    Nova Scotia *440*
    An Overview *444*

PART SIX

Epilogue: Summary and Forecast

22 Present-Day Issues and Forces — 453
    Phillip S. Jones

    Persons and Personalities *453*
    Research in Mathematics Education *454*
    Recurring Issues and Continuing Themes *455*
    Forces *460*
    Teacher Education *463*
    Similarities and Differences *463*
    "L'Envoi" *464*

Appendix A—Members of Committees Cited
and National Council of Teachers of Mathematics
Officers, Directors, and Editors — 467

    Cited Committees *468*
    National Council of Teachers of Mathematics *480*
    Index of Names *487*

Appendix B—A Survey of Research in Mathematics Education   *493*

Bibliography A—The United States of America   *501*
    Committee Reports and Status Studies   *501*
    Books and Pamphlets   *506*
    Journal and Yearbook Articles   *518*
    Dissertations   *526*

Bibliography B—Canada   *528*
    Reports, Status Studies, Programmes   *528*
    Books and Pamphlets   *530*
    Journal and Yearbook Articles   *533*
    Theses and Dissertations   *535*

Index   *537*

Illustrations

"Both Puzzled"	*xviii*
Pages from a Copybook in the Archives of Dartmouth College	*xx, 10*
First Arithmetic Printed in the United States	*Facing pages 14, 15*
First Arithmetic Written and Printed in the United States	*Facing pages 18, 19*
First English Work on Descriptive Geometry	*Facing page 28*
First Advanced Mathematical Work Published in the United States	*Facing page 29*
Pages from Colburn's *Arithmetic*	*90, 92*
More Pages from Colburn's *Arithmetic*	*Facing pages 102, 103*
Pages from *The Reorganization of Mathematics in Secondary Education*	*199–201*
First Book on the Teaching of Mathematics Published in the United States	*298*
First Book on the Teaching of Arithmetic Published in the United States	*300*
Egerton Ryerson	*Facing page 380*
James A. McLellan	*Facing page 381*
Ontario Algebra and Geometry Examination, 1914	*Facing pages 410, 411*
Alberta Matriculation Examination, 1939	*Facing pages 414, 415*

BOTH PUZZLED
"But, Sir, if wanst nought be nothin', then twice nought must be somethin', for it's double what wanst nought is." (Henry Graves & Co., London.)

Reproduced in Edwin C. Guillet's *In the Cause of Education*, a centennial history of the Ontario Educational Association, founded in 1861.

Introduction

Phillip S. Jones
Arthur F. Coxford, Jr.

A COPYBOOK IN THE ARCHIVES OF DARTMOUTH COLLEGE, showing arithmetic as a college subject in 1769. At right, part of an extended treatment of weights and measures. (See also illustrations on page 10.)

CHAPTER ONE

The Goals of History: Issues and Forces

1. *Our goals*

There are many kinds of history directed toward many goals. The chronology of events may serve for some as an end in itself, and for others as the basis of forecasts or of the search for causes and effects. Patriots or chauvinists may seek with history to revive feelings of nationalism, to justify past actions, to create or enhance a national image. The history of a special field may seek to clarify its boundaries, content, or methods and to increase understanding of the present nature and values of the discipline. Our chief goal in this history of mathematics education is to direct the thoughts of mathematicians, educators, and even the public at large to the issues of today, by showing that although the content and methods of mathematics education have changed significantly over the years, strong continuing forces imply that further change is imminent and important. The continuing development of new mathematics, new uses of mathematics, new pedagogical devices, and changing goals for a changing society all demonstrate the need for continued change in mathematics education.

However, a thoughtful view of history shows that many apparently new ideas are actually old and that they merit a revival only after the lessons of the past have been studied. The old approaches and materials should be examined in the light of both old experience and a new situation. For example, Colburn's "inductive approach" to arithmetic and algebra has many elements in common with the "discovery teaching" of today; and attention to numeration systems and geometry in the elementry school has been urged on many occasions since the beginning of the nineteenth century. History suggests that past innovations have been adopted in response to changing needs and philosophies, although rarely with a speed that could be called revolutionary, and that they have often failed to be as magically effective as their proponents expected. It is hoped that steadier progress will result from a survey of the causes and effectiveness of past proposals and projects. For this reason our plan is to stress issues, and the forces leading to action on these issues, throughout this book.

2. *Our themes: forces and issues*

We would like this book to be not a mere catalog of facts about mathematics education in North America, but a description of forces and issues related to mathematics education based upon such a catalog of facts. We regard *issues* as questions with reference to which there has been or may be some debate. Many issues exist in mathematics education today. Many of these are the same as, or slight modifications of, issues that have occurred frequently in our history. The emergence both of these issues and of proposed answers to them is due to a variety of *forces*—in mathematics itself, in educational theory and psychology, and in our changing culture. Our ultimate goal, then, is to provide a better understanding of the issues of today and the forces which gave rise to them, and to suggest answers for them. We believe that this may be achieved through a tracing over the past centuries of emerging issues and changing forces.

We believe that the major issues and forces relating to mathematics education can be considered under two headings: *curriculum* and *instruction*. The former, of course, includes both the content and the grade placement of materials taught. The latter is chiefly concerned with the method of teaching but also includes provisions for individual differences. This means that a complete separation of these two headings, curriculum and instruction, is not possible, since questions on individual differences are certain to involve questions of mental maturity which are related to the grade placement of materials in the curriculum.

Although we shall treat the evolution of mathematics education chiefly under these two headings, two other categories will frequently appear as the sources of issues and forces. These are the changing views of *mathematics* itself and of the newly developing fields of *educational philosophy* and *psychology*. During the period of our story mathematics first developed in association with studies of the physical world, becoming a major tool in the scientific and technological revolution of the seventeenth, eighteenth, and early nineteenth centuries. Then, in the nineteenth and twentieth centuries, it became a collection of man-made, axiomatic structures rooted in the interests and intuitions of its builders but not in the physical world. Connections of mathematics with the physical world often developed later out of the work of persons other than mathematicians. As this view of mathematics developed, rigor, abstraction, and generalization increasingly characterized the work of the professional mathematician.

Educational psychology developed in somewhat the reverse manner. From the musings of educational philosophers it moved first into laboratories in which behavior was studied and then out to share in the redesigning of textbooks and the development of teaching procedures to embody the ever-changing views of the learning process and problem solving.

Further, although the authors believe in minimizing the distinctions between elementary and secondary education and in stressing continuity and articulation rather than differences in grade placement or course content, we have found it convenient to divide our discussion of forces and issues emerging through history in accord with the elementary and secondary levels of education. The extent and manner to which this distinction is being blurred today is a current issue, but we are writing history. We cannot deny that in the past one could differentiate rather sharply both the curriculum and instructional procedures according to grade level. For this reason we think that under today's circumstances our audience may be larger and more understanding if we heed this separation but try to point out both the issues involved in eliminating it and the forces tending to drive us in this direction. Along with this, we shall point out the issues and methods that are common to instruction at both levels.

These considerations have led us to design a book in six parts:

Part 1: Mathematics in the Evolving Schools
Part 2: Forces and Issues Related to Curriculum and Instruction, K–6
Part 3: Forces and Issues Related to Curriculum and Instruction, 7–12

Part 4: *The Education of Teachers of Mathematics*
Part 5: *School Mathematics in Canada*
Part 6: *Epilogue: Present-Day Forces and Issues*

→»→» 3 *Progress by periods*

In Part One we will present the facts of the history of mathematics education, stopping occasionally to indicate themes that will be further developed in later parts. Our aim has been to clarify issues and identify forces which may both produce issues and help resolve them.

We have divided the story into five periods. Although time is a continuum which can be uniquely and sharply separated by specifying a single point, educational and cultural forces and issues are always overlapping and intermingling throughout all periods of time. However, it seemed sensible to us to begin with only a brief reference to the period prior to the first settlement in the United States and Canada (1607) and to extend the early history of mathematics education across the period of the beginnings of schools to the time of Warren Colburn, whose first book was published in 1821. We have selected Warren Colburn as representative of the beginning of a new concern for pedagogy. Although Colburn's arithmetic (125) and algebra (126)* written on "inductive principles" are neither the first mathematical books written or published in the Western Hemisphere nor the first to give thought to pedagogy, they represent a new and more general concern for pedagogical processes in this country.

For our second period we have chosen 1821 to 1894. The latter year dates the beginning of three new forces in mathematics education in North America. This was the year of the founding of the American Mathematical Society (AMS), which was derived from the New York Mathematical Society initiated in 1888 (244, pp. 105–6). The AMS itself has probably not been a significant factor in secondary and elementary education. However, certain early members of the society, notably Professor E. H. Moore, were much concerned with the problems of secondary school mathematics and gave time and attention to them, as well as giving this area of investigation the prestige that came from their interest in innovation in the teaching of mathematics. The year 1894 also saw the publication of the *Report of the Committee of Ten*

---

* Numerals in parentheses, as they appear here, refer in the Introduction and Parts One through Four to items in Bibliography A, for publications in the United States; in Part Five, to items in Bibliography B, for Canada.

GOALS OF HISTORY: ISSUES AND FORCES 5

on Secondary School Studies (72), the committee having been appointed two years earlier by the National Education Association (NEA). The appointment of this committee typifies two forces in American mathematics education: (1) the concern of persons with a major initial interest in education as a whole for the specialized subject-matter field of mathematics and (2) the influence of national committee reports as stimulators of reform.

The founding of the AMS and the role of the NEA in appointing the Committee of Ten represent another significant force that affected education during the latter part of the nineteenth century and the first part of the twentieth. This force was the rapid development of many professional organizations, both those associated with the organization and administration of the schools and those associated with scholarly research. The *Report of the Committee of Ten* will be discussed later, but it is interesting to note how many still-current issues received its attention: the introduction of more geometry of an intuitive sort into the elementary schools; the earlier beginning of algebra; the incorporation of solid geometry with plane; and the development of what later was called a "double track" program after the first year of algebra, with one syllabus for those planning to continue into college and another for those not so bent. This last provides an example of an issue and a related force. The issue is this: For what students and for what goals should the school program be defined? The force is the pressure on the secondary schools to plan curricula and guide students with college entrance requirements and examinations in mind.

We have chosen to terminate our third period with 1920, the date of the founding of the National Council of Teachers of Mathematics (NCTM) and of the issuing of the preliminary report of the National Committee on Mathematical Requirements, *The Reorganization of the First Courses in Secondary School Mathematics* (57). This committee had been appointed by the Mathematical Association of America (MAA) in 1916, prior to the entry of the United States into World War I. The major concern of the MAA, itself only recently founded (1915), was for the undergraduate mathematics curriculum in the colleges. Its sponsorship of this committee emphasizes the effect of college requirements and ideas on the secondary school curriculum and also the continuing concern of many mathematicians at the college level for improvement in the schools. A number of persons with close relations to the secondary schools—both persons training teachers and persons teaching in the schools—were sought out and included on the committee. The committee was spoken of with great approval by the first president of the NCTM, C. M. Austin, in his initial note to the members of that organization at the time it took over the *Mathematics Teacher* as its official journal in 1921 (289, p. 1). This period, 1894-1920, might then be labeled "The Growth of College and University Influence," or perhaps "First Steps toward Revision."

Our fourth period, 1920-45, introduces the effect of two strong forces outside the control of school or college personnel: economic depression and war. We have chosen 1945 as the terminal year of this period because it marked the end of World War II and the appearance of two of the reports of the Commission on Post-War Plans of the NCTM (16; 17). This committee was the first of a number of committees, commissions, and studies to be set up as a result of concern for the inadequacies in mathematics education that were brought out during the war.

The reports of the Commission on Post-War Plans may be regarded as one of the links between the issues of the prewar period and the reforms that began to get under way about 1952. Prior to the war mathematics educators had struggled to answer many criticisms. There were two major types: (1) The mathematical (arithmetical) competence of high school graduates was viewed as inadequate for many occupations such as business, elementary school teaching, and the armed services. (2) Much of secondary school mathematics, even extending to long division, was regarded as of questionable value for general education by many educational philosophers, psychologists, and guidance specialists. The Commission on Post-War Plans clearly exposed fallacies in this view. Other educators began to stress that the war had not only demanded mathematical competencies at many levels but had also led to the development of many new applications with postwar, peacetime significance. Both the applications of mathematics and much of the actual mathematics were new. This led to the view that to be prepared for unforeseen needs one must know and understand the structure of mathematics, not merely its facts and operations.

Two major issues of the prewar period persisted after the war: (1) Does school mathematics instruction serve the needs of individual students? (2) Does school mathematics instruction contribute effectively to the solution of the problems of our society? Before the war many people would have answered both questions with a no. The answer remained the same; but the reasons behind it, the remedies called for, and even the persons giving the answer changed during the war and the years immediately following it when proposals for extended experimentation and reform were developed.

This led to our definition of the years from 1945 to the present as our fifth and last period, a period of experimentation and reform which some termed a "revolution." Naturally, changes so extreme as to be called revolutionary brought forth some protests and reaction.

⇶⇶ 4. *Summary and preview*

In Part One, then, we will seek to provide the factual framework from which emerge the *issues* that have called for concern and change and the *forces* that have given rise to these issues and given direction to the changes.

In our introductory remarks we have passingly focused on such issues as these:

1. *What should be the goals of mathematics education?* Providing for personal and vocational practical needs? Providing "mental discipline"? Training in logic and problem solving? Preparing for further study?

2. *How can mathematical education in both content and instruction be adapted to the varied needs, capacities, and interests of students?* By "double tracks"? Self-instruction?

These are perhaps the *only* issues in the sense that perhaps all others are in some way subsidiary to them. However, we have also noted, implicitly at least, these additional issues:

3. *What mathematics should be taught?* "Facts" and operations—or structure?

4. *What students should take mathematics?* Everyone? All college preparatory students? Only would-be scientists and engineers?

Some issues which will arise in later chapters are:

5. *What persons or groups should direct mathematics education?* Professional mathematicians? If so, should they be the pure or the applied mathematicians? Educators? Psychologists? Mathematics educators? The general public?

6. *How can one provide for the experimentation needed to guarantee continued tested progress in both curriculum and instruction?*

7. *What levels of rigor are sound and desirable at different stages of a student's development?*

8. *What is the role of applications and mathematical models in motivating and clarifying instruction?*

9. *How do we teach so that students perceive the excitement and beauty of mathematics as well as its facts and theorems?*

10. *Can we teach so that students will "discover" and be more creative?* If we can, should we?

Forces that have been mentioned in our introductory remarks include:

1. *Practical needs*—of explorers, soldiers, navigators.

2. *The research and beliefs of psychologists and philosophers*—with reference to the goals and methods of instruction.

3. *College entrance examinations and requirements.*

4. *The presence in the schools of increasing numbers of students with increasingly varied interests and abilities, but all needing to be retained and educated.*

This list is incomplete, and some of these forces are subsidiary to others in conception or importance. However, it is hoped that this introductory list may make the reader more alert to perceive our theme and goal: the presentation of the history of mathematics education as the story of changing issues and forces as they affect practices which, in turn, provide a series of approximations to changing educational goals. We hope that such perceptions may stimulate, prepare for, and help determine the best directions for future changes.

*Mathematics in
the Evolving Schools*

PART ONE

Phillip S. Jones
Arthur F. Coxford, Jr.

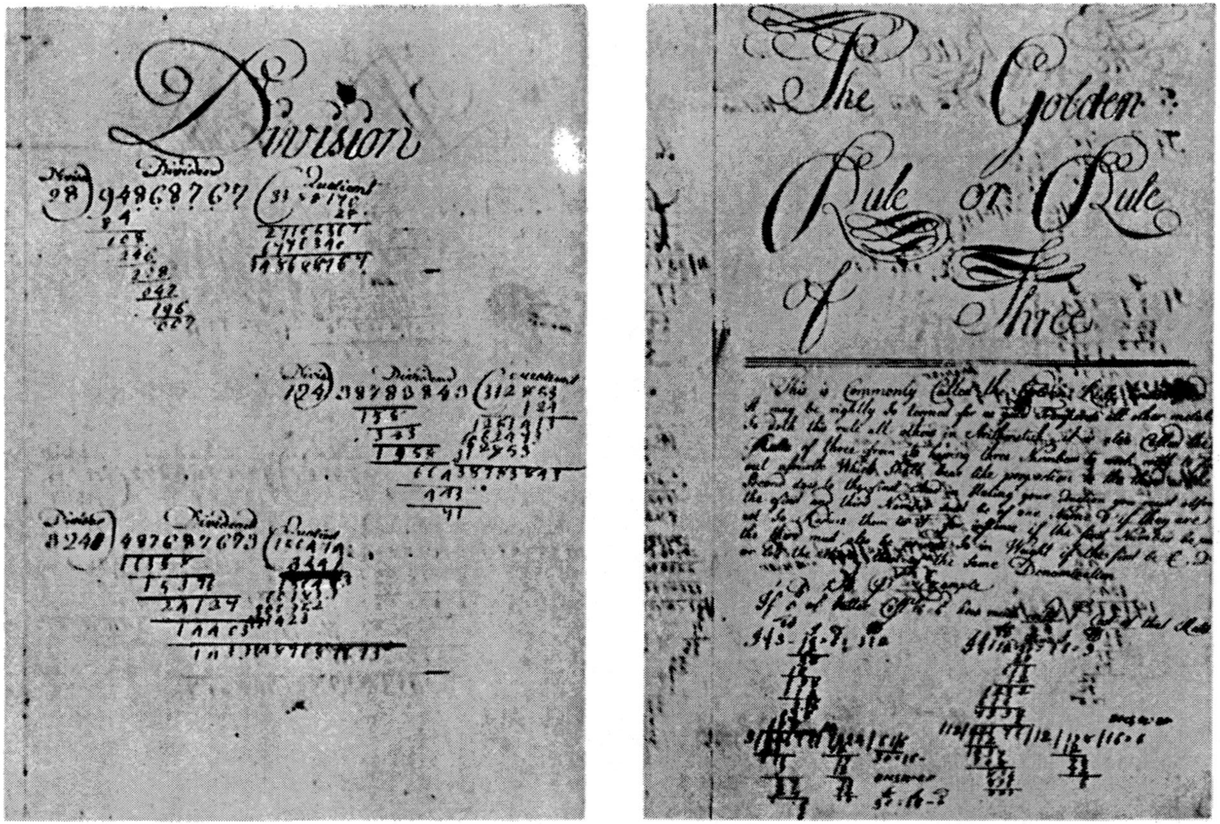

A COPYBOOK IN THE ARCHIVES OF DARTMOUTH COLLEGE. These leaves illustrate the stress on rules and lengthy computation. The flowery description of the Rule of Three suggests verbatim copying of dictated material. (See also page xx.)

CHAPTER TWO

From Discovery to an Awakened Concern for Pedagogy 1492–1821

1. The earliest American mathematics

Few people realize that the Mayans of Yucatan in Mexico and Central America had a remarkably well-developed numeration system containing a zero symbol and utilizing place-value concepts but based on twenty rather than ten, long before the Spanish explorers came to the Western Hemisphere. In fact Cajori even suggests that the Mayan use of zero is the earliest use of such a symbol anywhere in the world (120, p. 11). This is a little uncertain because of the difficulties of dating Mayan hieroglyphics and also because it is debatable whether a special symbol used as a separatrix in the Seleucid period of Babylonian mathematics should be regarded as the use of a zero in that system. In any case, this was a rather remarkable prehistoric development in the Western Hemisphere, as was the somewhat similar development of a numeration system by the Aztecs.

There is also some evidence of the existence of genuine prehistoric mathematics in this hemisphere, or at least of number words in the languages studied by anthropologists who have worked with North American Indians. However, we shall pass quickly from these earliest periods to our major concern, the story of developments since 1492.

A little-known fact about the earliest mathematics in the Americas is that the first book of mathematical content printed in the Western Hemisphere was the *Summario Compendioso de las quentas de plata y ore*, published by Juan Diez Freyle in Mexico City in 1556. Although the major concern of this book was the conversion of gold ore into value equivalents in different types of coinages of the Old World, a problem requiring chiefly the use of ratio and proportion or what was called "the rule of three," it also contained a short chapter on algebra. In addition to this book, there were seven Mexican and four Peruvian books with substantial mathematical content published prior to 1700 (164, pp. 25-35). None of these books was devoted solely to mathematics. Their major concerns in fact were chiefly military matters such as the design and construction of camps and fortifications; surveying and navigation; and the calculation of the calendar, especially to determine various feast days and religious holidays. An educational sidelight on the times is suggested by the title of Pedro Paz's book, published in Mexico City in 1629, *Arte para aprender todo el menor del arithmetica sin maestro.*

Its theme of home study, or study "without a master," is typical of the time and of a land being newly exploited and settled. This is reflected also in the first book with mathematical content in the English language published in the Western Hemisphere. Published in Boston in 1703, this was a reprint of an English book by John Hill entitled *The Young Secretary's Assistant*. It included arithmetical ideas needed by the young businessman along with discussions of letter writing, bookkeeping, etc. This book represents several of the forces operating in a new land—the influence of foreign authors, of vocational needs, and of commercial demands—and again the role of home study and self-teaching in the educational system of newly settled territories.

The first English-language mathematical book both written and published in North America was entitled *Arithmetick, Vulgar and Decimal*. It was written by Isaac Greenwood and published in Boston in 1729. Greenwood, who served as the first Hollis Professor of Mathematics at Harvard from 1728 to 1738, had studied in England. Mathematics books in German, Dutch, and French appeared in 1774 (Germantown, Pa.), 1730 (New York), and 1775 (Quebec), respectively.

These facts further illustrate the continuing effect of foreign influences upon the mathematics taught from the time of the earliest settlements to the middle of the nineteenth century. Other forces led to change and development, and some of them continue up to the present:

1. *Practical needs.* The needs of exploration, navigation, and trade are dominant in a developing frontier community; later the needs of developing technology and science become important.

2. *Church and religion.* In the Spanish books cited above they influenced the content of the books; later they influenced the content and purpose of all education, especially higher education.

3. *Intellectual curiosity.* The existence and role of intellectual curiosity are suggested by the inclusion of unrelated work in algebra in Juan Diez Freyle's earliest book.

⇢⇢⇢ 2. *The content and processes of colonial instruction*

At the outset, the earliest settlements had no schools at all. When schools did develop, their chief objective was the teaching of reading and writing. Reading and writing usually included the reading and writing of numerals and therefore counting. The famous hornbook of early American schools and homes included arithmetic only in the sense that on one side roman numerals were listed for memorization. Commercial arithmetic was often taught in special schools called reckoning or writing schools. Bronson Alcott's description of the schools in Massachusetts as late as the beginning of the nineteenth century included the note (121, p. 9):

> Until within a few years no studies have been permitted in the day school but spelling, reading and writing. Arithmetic was taught by a few instructors one or two evenings in a week. But in spite of the most determined opposition, arithmetic is now being permitted in the day school.

It was rare for a young student of the seventeenth or eighteenth century to possess an arithmetic book. As Robert Clason points out (441, p. 54), "Pupils were provided with books of blank pages, called ciphering books, given a rule and a problem, and set to work." A pupil of about 1810 described his experience thus (181, p. 45):

> Printed arithmetics were not used in the Boston schools till after the writer left them, and the custom was for the master to write a problem or two in the manuscript of the pupil every other day. No boy was allowed to cipher till he was 11 years old, and writing and ciphering were never performed on the same day. . . . Any boy could copy the work from the manuscript of any further advanced than himself, and

the writer never heard any explanation of any principle of arithmetic while he was at school.

Although students did not use printed texts in the ciphering-book approach to arithmetic, texts were available for teachers. These early arithmetic books were self-contained, complete, single volumes with no internal spiraling—each topic in its turn was treated completely and then dropped. The same book would be used over several years of study at different age levels, in or out of school. The most popular eighteenth-century arithmetic in America was Thomas Dilworth's *The Schoolmaster's Assistant: Being a Compendium of Arithmetic Both Practical and Theoretical*, a reprint of an English text. The first American edition (1773) was labeled the seventeenth edition. Its only concession to the new locale seems to be the addition in the preface of the book's fifty-first endorser, Nathaniel Wurteen, "Schoolmaster at Philadelphia." Karpinski (164, p. 73) lists fifty-eight American printings and editions through 1832. The topics listed in its table of contents were:

1. Arithmetic in whole numbers, ...
2. Vulgar Fractions ...
3. Decimals, in which, among other things, are considered the Extraction of Roots; Interest, both Simple and Compound; Annuities, Rebate, and Equation of Payments
4. A large collection of questions, with their answers, serving to exercise the forgoing rules; together with a few others, both pleasant and diverting
5. Duodecimals, commonly called Cross Multiplication

All this is encompassed in 192 small pages, and preceded by a "Preface Dedicatory" addressed to "Schoolmasters in Great Britain and Ireland" and an essay "On the Education of Youth" addressed to parents. Some extracts from the former will give some idea of the pedagogical problems and concepts of the day:

> I believe it is confessed by All, that it is a Task too hard for *Children* to be made compleat *Masters of Arithmetic;* and therefore the best Way of instructing them in it is, most certainly, first to give them a general Notion of it, in the easiest Manner, and next to enlarge upon it afterward, if there be Time; otherwise it must be done by themselves, as their increase in *Years* and Growth in Understanding will permit. ...
>
> In all Places where it could be done conveniently, I have given Directions for varying the *Examples* by Way of *Proof;* because it not

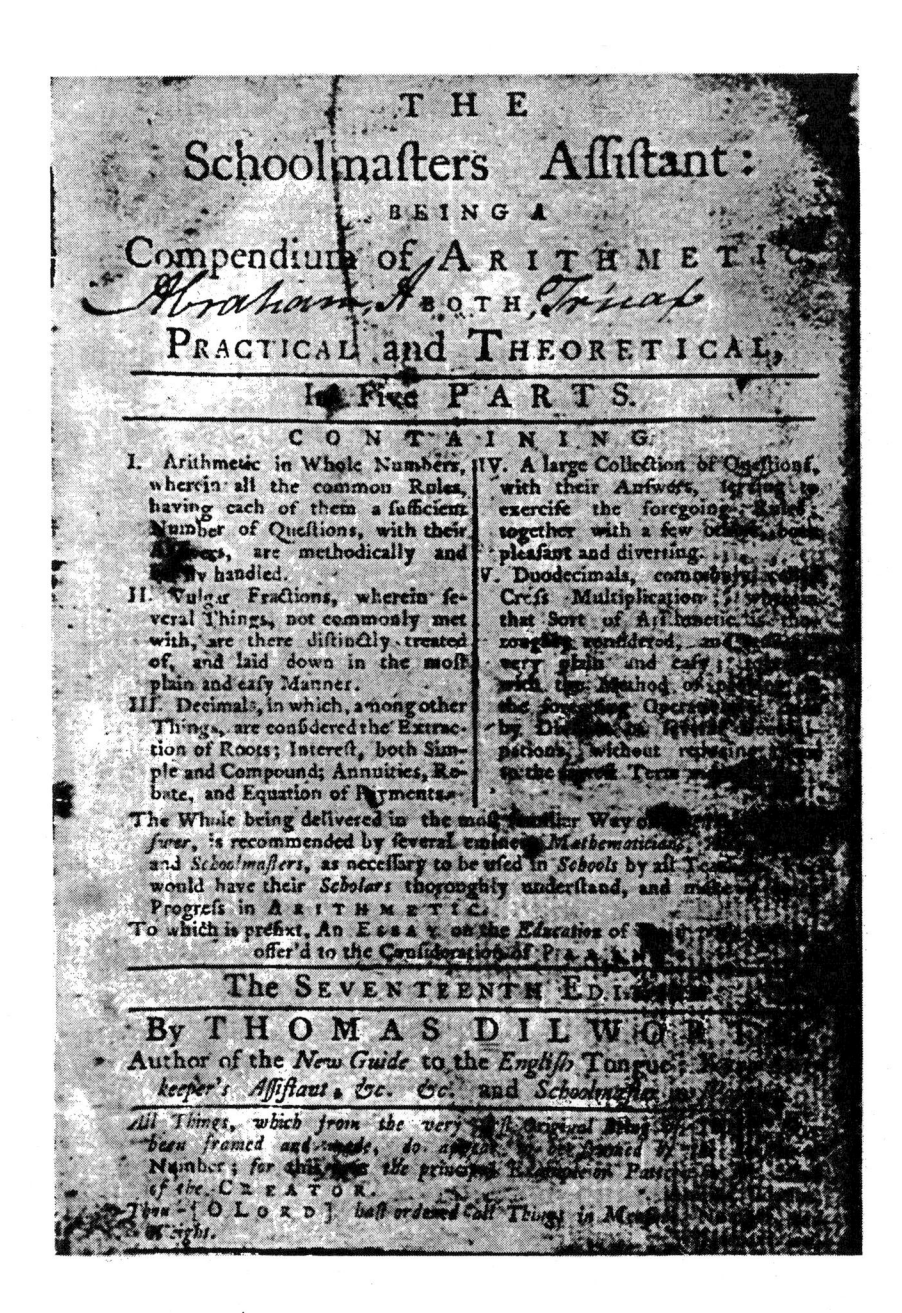

THE
Schoolmasters Assistant:
BEING A
Compendium of ARITHMETIC
BOTH,
PRACTICAL and THEORETICAL,

In Five PARTS.
CONTAINING

I. Arithmetic in Whole Numbers, wherein all the common Rules, having each of them a sufficient Number of Questions, with their Answers, are methodically and ... handled.

II. Vulgar Fractions, wherein several Things, not commonly met with, are there distinctly treated of, and laid down in the most plain and easy Manner.

III. Decimals, in which, among other Things, are considered the Extraction of Roots; Interest, both Simple and Compound; Annuities, Rebate, and Equation of Payments.

IV. A large Collection of Questions, with their Answers, serving to exercise the foregoing Rules; together with a few others, both pleasant and diverting.

V. Duodecimals, commonly called Cross Multiplication; wherein that Sort of Arithmetic is thoroughly considered, and the very plain and easy; with the Method of proving the foregoing Operations by Different Methods of Operations, without requiring the ...

The Whole being delivered in the most familiar Way of ..., is recommended by several eminent Mathematicians and Schoolmasters, as necessary to be used in Schools by all who would have their Scholars thoroughly understand, and make Progress in ARITHMETIC.

To which is prefixt, An ESSAY on the Education of ... offer'd to the Consideration of PARENTS.

The SEVENTEENTH Edition.

By THOMAS DILWORTH,
Author of the *New Guide* to the *English Tongue*; Bookkeeper's *Assistant*, &c. &c. and Schoolmaster ...

All Things, which from the very ... Original Being, been framed and made, do appear ... denied by Number; for this ... the principal Foundation Part of the CREATOR.

Thou [O LORD] hast ordered all Things in Measure ...

FIRST ARITHMETIC PRINTED IN THE UNITED STATES. From the University of Michigan's collections.

THE Schoolmasters Assistant

PART I.

Of Arithmetic in Whole Numbers.

The INTRODUCTION.
Of Arithmetic in general.

Q. WHAT is Arithmetic?

A. *Arithmetic* is the Art or Science of computing by Numbers, either whole or in Fractions.

Q. *What is Number?*

A. *Number* is one or more Quantities, answering to the Question, *How many?*

Q. *What is Arithmetic in* Whole Numbers?

A. Arithmetic *in whole Numbers* or *Integers*, supposes its Numbers to be entire Quantities, and not divided into Parts.

Q. *What is Arithmetic in* Fractions?

A. Arithmetic in *Fractions*, supposes its Numbers to be the Parts of some entire Quantity.

Q. *How do you consider Arithmetic with Regard to Art and* Science?

A. Both in *Theory* and *Practice*.

Q. *What is* Theoretical Arithmetic?

A. *Theoretical Arithmetic* considers the Nature and Quality of Numbers, and demonstrates the Reason of Practical Operations. And in this Sense Arithmetic is a *Science*.

Q. *What is* Practical Arithmetic?

A. *Practical Arithmetic* is that which shews the Method of working by Numbers, so as may be most useful and expeditious for Business. And in this Sense Arithmetic is *an Art*.

Q. *What is the Nature of all Arithmetical Operations?*

A. The Nature of all *Arithmetical Operations* is, by some Quantities that are given, to find out others that are required.

Q. *Which are the fundamental Rules in Arithmetic?*

A. These Five; *Notation, Addition, Subtraction, Multiplication* and *Division.*

B

DILWORTH'S *SCHOOLMASTERS ASSISTANT*. English arithmetics in dialogue and catechetical form date back to Robert Recorde, c. 1540.

only discovers the *Reason* of the operation, but at the same time both produces a new *Question*, and proves the *old One*. ...

I have thrown the subject of the following pages into a *Catechetical Form*, that they may be the more instructive; for *Children* can better judge the Force of an *Answer*, than follow *Reason* through a Chain of *Consequences*. Hence also it proves a very good *examining Book;* for at any time in what Place soever the *Scholar* appears to be defective, he can immediately be put back to that *Place* again.

The note to parents is also fascinating in its reflection of modern pedagogical problems such as tardiness and homework. In particular, parents are urged to "never let their own Commands run counter to the Master's"; and a substantial paragraph is devoted to lamenting that "the fair Sex" are either not sent to school before they are eighteen or twenty years of age or that they do not stay at their "Writing Schools" long enough (more than a year).

The most popular arithmetic in America prior to 1850 was *Daboll's Schoolmaster's Assistant, Being a Plain Practical System of Arithmetic; Adapted to the United States*, first printed in New London, Connecticut, in 1800. This English text by Nathan Daboll and a revision by David A. Daboll had appeared in eighty editions by 1841. Daboll's book is much like his countryman Dilworth's: short (240 small pages with a six-page appendix on bookkeeping by Samuel Green in the edition examined), it is limited to arithmetic and stresses commercial topics and problems. Many of its problems involve large numbers and extended computation. Although dollars and cents appear, more problems involve pounds and shillings. Extended computations with varied units of measure and their "reduction" are included. It does not use a catechetical method but in each section gives a rule, a worked example, and problems.

The most popular American-written arithmetic text of this early period was Nicholas Pike's *A New and Complete System of Arithmetic Composed for the Use of the Citizens of the United States*, published in Newburyport, Massachusetts, in 1788. Together with an abridgment made in 1792 it appeared in nineteen printings and editions by 1822. The first edition was endorsed by B. Woodward, professor of mathematics at Dartmouth University; S. Williams, Hollis Professor of Mathematics and Natural Philosophy at Harvard University; and by the presidents of those two schools and Yale College. It was of a different character from Dilworth's book, much more extensive both in length (512 pages) and in subject matter, and clearly aimed at more mature students. Something of its range may be revealed by citing a few topics and summarizing its major categories:

> Rules for Reducing all the Coins, from Canada to Georgia (pp. 111–23)
> Tare and Trett [sic] (pp. 192–94)
> Extraction of the Biquadrate root (p. 210)
> Annuities (pp. 264–66, 300–323)
> Circulating Decimals (pp. 323–28)
> Permutations and Combinations (pp. 339–45)

A great deal of space was given to mensuration, the calendar, and related astronomical problems, with less space devoted to such topics from mechanics as falling bodies, the pendulum, lever, and screw. A summary of Pike's second edition (1797) shows the following distribution of materials: arithmetic, 396 pages; geometry, 4 pages; trigonometry, 11 pages; mensuration (including the area and volume of an eicosaiedron [sic] and the volume of a mash tub), 46 pages; algebra, 33 pages; conics, 10 pages.

This tabulation of contents makes it quite clear that Pike's book was not a textbook for elementary school students. It was, in fact, adopted immediately as a textbook by Harvard, Yale, and Dartmouth (240, p. 64). Pike's book has also been listed as the third book published in the American colonies to include algebra. The first was Freyle's, mentioned in the first section of this chapter. The second was *Arithmetica of Cyffer-Konst . . . Als Mede Een kort ontwerp van de Algebra*, by Peter Venema, printed by J. Peter Zenger in 1730 in New York (240, p. 58).

In geometry, of the fourteen books published in America prior to 1820, only three could be classified as dealing with demonstrative geometry. The remaining were works dealing with mensuration and surveying, such as *Hawney's Complete Measurer* (1801), the first book dealing with geometry printed in America. This, like the three demonstrative geometries, was written abroad. The geometries included two English books, Simson's and Playfair's; and one translation from French, A. M. Legendre's *Elements of Geometry*. This latter book's first appearance in 1819 was followed by forty-two later editions and translations, the last in 1890. It was used as a text at Yale University as late as 1885. The popularity of Legendre's book and an analysis of its unique features (such as its departure from Euclid's axioms and sequence of theorems, its inclusion of some formulas, and its use of algebraic symbols and processes in proofs) show the strength of the French influence on early American mathematics.

The introductions to these books also document the goals judged proper for mathematics education at the time. Legendre said the value of the "method of the ancients" is "to accustom the student to great strictness in reasoning," and also cited its value in mathematical research. Simson asserted that geometry was "of great use in the arts of peace and war" (358, p. 5).

In summary, even though a few books delayed or deleted the presentation of formal definitions and rules, especially at the elementary level, and a few used a catechetical question-and-answer format, the net effect was a heavy reliance on set exercises and texts with the result that the teaching process was "State a rule, give an example, and set exercises to be followed (or, in geometry, give proofs to be memorized)."

The content of mathematical education laid a heavy stress on practical applications—especially those related to exploration, commerce, and settlement (mensuration, bookkeeping, navigation, and surveying).

Instruction in mathematics was often minimal. It was irregular (or at least not daily), and it was often given by a private tutor outside of a formal day school.

However, the seventeenth century was notable for the early emergence of one of the strongest continuing forces in American education: the belief that education is necessary for the welfare of society. For example, a Massachusetts law of 1642 required the instruction of children in reading and catechism and also their apprenticeship in a trade. There was no mention of mathematics in this. In 1647 Massachusetts law required every town of fifty families to provide an elementary school teacher and every town of a hundred families to provide a Latin grammar school. The chief function of the Latin grammar schools was preparation for college; the college in turn taught Latin as a preparation for the ministry, law, and the teaching of Latin. These occupations and college attendance being limited, there was only limited popular support for the schools. The grammar schools had their effect on mathematics education somewhat negatively, since reading but not mathematics was required for entrance into the Latin grammar school.

The belief in the important of education for a society, its religion, and its government has continued to be a strong force up to the present moment. But as the early neglect of mathematics suggests, it necessarily leads to an important issue: *What* is the education that is necessary to the welfare of society?

3. The Latin grammar school and the academy

Although the Latin grammar schools had some public support, they tended to be modeled after the English grammar school, to be attended by children from wealthy families, and to direct their instruction toward preparation for college—which in turn was directed toward the preparation of gentlemen, ministers, lawyers, and doctors. The Boston Latin Grammar School was founded in 1635. By 1700 about thirty New England towns had such schools. Their curriculum was chiefly Latin and literature, with some attention to writing. Later some arithmetic was introduced, in response to public demand. But the cost and aristocratic nature of the grammar schools, together with a need for a practical education for a growing group of merchants, artisans, navigators, and surveyors, led to a decline in the Latin grammar school. This was accelerated by opposition to taxation and by the American Revolution.

Academies developed in response to the forces listed above. The first academies, beginning with the one founded by Benjamin Franklin in 1749–51, were privately supported. The extensive development and spread of academies did not get under way until the nineteenth century.

The academy aimed at preparation both for life and for college. Its broader curriculum included mathematics for its practical utility and also for its mental discipline. The broadened curriculum and growing number of academies ultimately made necessary the institution of college entrance requirements.

4. The colleges and the mathematics community

The colleges founded prior to the Revolutionary War—Harvard (1601), William and Mary (1693), Yale (1701), Princeton (as the College of New Jersey, 1746), Pennsylvania (as Philadelphia, 1755), Columbia (as Kings, 1754), Brown (1764), Rutgers (1766), Dartmouth (1770)—differed somewhat in their origins and goals, but in mathematics none had extensive requirements or offerings at first. Arithmetic was made an entrance requirement at Yale in 1745, at Princeton in 1760, and at Harvard in 1807. Harvard, though starting late, moved ahead rapidly, requiring "the whole of arithmetic" in 1816 (only the four operations, "reduction," and the "rule of three" were required in 1807) and then moving on to become in 1820 the first to require

ARITHMETICK
Vulgar and *Decimal*:

WITH THE

APPLICATION

THEREOF, TO

A VARIETY of CASES

IN

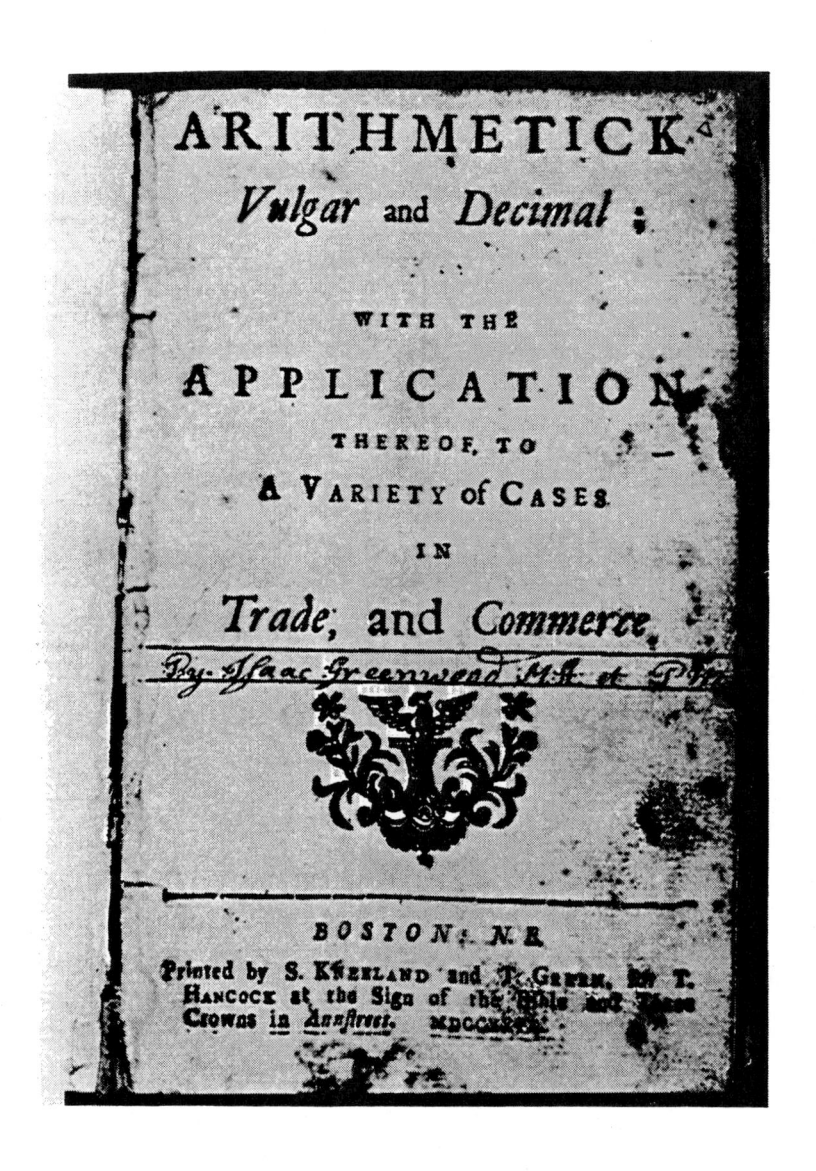

Trade, and *Commerce*

By Isaac Greenwood M.A. et P.

BOSTON: N.E.

Printed by S. KNEELAND and T. GREEN, for T. HANCOCK at the Sign of the Bible and Three Crowns in Ann-street. MDCCXXIX.

FIRST ARITHMETIC WRITTEN AND PRINTED IN THE UNITED STATES. From the Plimpton Collection of Columbia University. A second copy there bears the autograph of Samuel Adams. (See also illustration on following page.)

Pages from Greenwood's *Arithmetic*, showing his use of "billion" for a million million, and also the older forms of Roman numerals. (See also illustration on previous page.)

algebra. Geometry was not required for entrance until after the Civil War.

The early college mathematics curriculum was pretty scanty. As late as 1726 the only mathematics taught at Yale was a smattering of arithmetic and surveying in the senior year. In 1748 Yale required some mathematics in the second and third years. Something of conics and fluxions was taught as early as 1758, and by 1766 a program might have included arithmetic, algebra, trigonometry, and surveying.

At Harvard, whose program originally extended through only three years, the mathematical course began in the senior year and consisted of arithmetic and geometry during the first three quarters of the year and astronomy during the last quarter (121, p. 19). At that time each class concentrated for a whole day on one or two subjects. Mathematics or astronomy was studied on Monday and Tuesday.

Smith and Ginsburg (244, p. 32) quote a report to King George III, given after England's acquisition of Canada at the end of the French and Indian War in 1763 to the effect that there was "a pitiful contrast between the intellectual culture in the newly acquired Canada and the uncultured backwardness of the older English colonies." These historians then remark, "Whether or not the comparison was just, it is certain that the work in the new republic, judged by their curricula, was of a low grade."

Lecture notes show that Isaac Greenwood taught a formal sort of algebra based on the work of John Wallis during his period as first Hollis Professor of Mathematics and Natural Philosophy (1728-38). Greenwood's successor, John Winthrop, also taught calculus (fluxions), but his major interests and contributions were in astronomy (244, pp. 20, 52). The inclusion of astronomy with mathematics—and as a major part of mathematics—was typical of the times and resulted from both practical forces and the intellectual climate. The practical need for astronomy in connection with navigation and surveying is obvious. At the same time, the European intellectual revolution stemming from the rise of science and the work of Copernicus, Galileo, Descartes, Newton, and many others was communicated to the colonies rather rapidly. Witness to this is borne by the term "natural philosophy" as it recurs in the titles of courses and professional chairs at the colleges of the eighteenth century. By 1776 six of eight colonial colleges supported professorships of mathematics and natural philosophy (225, p. 29).

Mathematics had become a tool of science as well as of commerce, and science required more advanced mathematics than did commerce.

This force, the rise of science, was displayed in new curricula set up early in the nineteenth century in such older colleges as Pennsylvania and Princeton and in the plans for such post-Revolutionary War colleges as West Point (1802), Virginia (1818–24), and Rensselaer Polytechnic (1824).

Reference to the University of Pennsylvania and the University of Virginia brings to mind two prominent early American intellectual and political leaders who did much for American education: Benjamin Franklin (1706–1790) and Thomas Jefferson (1743–1826). Franklin, although he did no mathematics himself, wrote "On the Usefulness of Mathematics," which appeared in the *Pennsylvania Gazette*, 20 October 1735; and he included a school of mathematics along with schools of English and Latin in the design of his academy, influencing the design of the University of Philadelphia, which became the University of Pennsylvania. Thomas Jefferson published several mathematical articles about surveying, almanacs, astronomy, and Napier's theories on spherical triangles (244, pp. 58, 61). He was a major influence in setting up the University of Virginia with an orientation that was classical and humanistic but included such popular and practical new subjects as mathematics (225, p. 125).

5. Self-instruction

The "mathematical community" of this early period included not only a few professors and sponsors but also some remarkable self-taught mathematicians whose major activities were outside the academic world.

We have noted that in the earliest days, lack of formal mathematical instruction made self-instruction a necessity for all. Economic, familial, and cultural pressures often denied to eager and able students what formal instruction was available. Three outstanding examples of such students are Benjamin Banneker (1731–1806), David Rittenhouse (1732–1796), and Nathaniel Bowditch (1773–1838).

Benjamin Banneker, a Negro, was sent to an obscure school where he learned to read and do arithmetic "as far as double fractions"; but the school was open only during the winter, and he was allowed to attend only until he became big enough to help his father on the farm (383, pp. 32–37). His work, like that of the other two self-taught men, was largely in astronomical computations and the preparation of almanacs.

David Rittenhouse progressed from watchmaker to instrument

maker, surveyor, and astronomer. He served as vice-provost of the University of Pennsylvania, and George Washington appointed him director of the mint (244, p. 56; 218, pp. 21-28).

Nathaniel Bowditch is best known today as the original author of *The American Practical Navigator*, still published by the United States government. At the age of ten he was apprenticed to a ship's chandler, but he was allowed to read in the private Salem Philosophical Library. While sailing for many years he progressed from supercargo to captain; after his retirement from the sea he ultimately became president of an insurance company. His translation of Laplace's *Mécanique Céleste* (1829-39) contained many added explanations and commentaries and was the first book of substantial or advanced mathematics published in this hemisphere (356, pp. 333-38).

⇶⇶ 6. *The teachers and pedagogy*

There was a wide range in background and competence among teachers, especially in the earliest days. It was an exceptional teacher who possessed a fair knowledge of "fractions" and "the rule of three," according to Cajori (121, p. 9). The best-trained ones were very young college graduates and ministers who often engaged in teaching for only a short time early in their careers—and did that in the Latin grammar schools. For example, John Adams, later to become president of the United States, taught at the grammar school at Worcester for a time after graduating from Harvard and before beginning the study of law (p. 9). On the whole, the status of grammar school teachers was not high—it was about that of skilled laborers (118, p. 253).

The college teachers had somewhat stronger backgrounds. Both Isaac Greenwood and John Winthrop, who succeeded Greenwood at the age of twenty-four, had studied in England. Walter Minto (1753-1796) was appointed to Princeton in 1788 on the recommendation of the Earl of Buchan. He had studied at the University of Pisa, had translated the *Cours de Mathématique* of Bossut, and had published some original work (244, p. 30).

The dominant pedagogy of this period, as mentioned earlier, was to state a rule, give examples, and provide problems. However, the development of new educational views and procedures abroad soon had an effect in this country. In particular, a debt to the ideas of J. H. Pestalozzi (1746-1827) was explicitly recognized in the title of the first edition (1821) of Warren Colburn's *An Arithmetic on the*

Plan of Pestalozzi with Some Improvements. (The acknowledgement was later dropped.) Daniel Adams, whose first arithmetic appeared in 1801, tried to reconcile older procedures with Pestalozzi's concept of mental discipline as a goal for instruction and with his teaching methods. These methods placed a heavy emphasis upon concrete experiences as the basis of an induction from many examples to an understanding of rules. Adams's attempt is reflected in the title of his 1827 text, *Arithmetic in which the Principles of Operating by Numbers are Analytically Explained, and Synthetically applied; thus combining the advantages to be derived both from the Inductive and the Synthetic Mode of Instruction.*

7. Summary

Issues

In this chapter we have seen the following issues arise:

1. Should a free education be provided for all children?
2. Is the same amount of education appropriate for boys and for girls? For the children of the wealthy and for the children of tradesmen and workers?
3. Is the proper character and content of public education the humanities? The practical arts? The sciences? Is the goal of instruction mental discipline? Practical skills? Knowledge?
4. Does arithmetic (mathematics) have a place in the public school program?
5. Is rule-example-practice the best pedagogical procedure, or should inductive processes be used?
6. How can teaching processes be embodied in texts? Does a catechetical text embody teaching processes?

Forces

We have also seen the following forces at work:

1. The practical needs of exploration, pioneering, settlement, war, and a developing commerce
2. The church's need for trained ministers and missionaries
3. The belief that education is necessary to the welfare of society
4. The institution of college entrance requirements, including mathematics

FROM DISCOVERY TO A CONCERN FOR PEDAGOGY

5. The rise of "natural philosophy"—science, especially physics and astronomy
6. Individual initiative and self-instruction
7. Foreign texts and foreign-trained teachers
8. Intellectual curiosity and the scholarly interests of political leaders

CHRONOLOGY

1556 Juan Diez Freyle's *Summario Compendioso* published in Mexico City
1629 Pedro Paz's *Arte . . . arithmetica sin maestro* published in Mexico City
1635 Elementary schools established in Quebec
1635 Boston Latin Grammar School founded
1642 Harvard College founded
1647 Massachusetts law requires towns to have schools
1655 A Jesuit college for secondary education established for Quebec
1703 John Hill's *The Young Secretary's Assistant* printed in Boston
1728 Isaac Greenwood becomes Hollis Professor of Mathematics and Natural Philosophy at Harvard
1729 Greenwood's *Arithmetick, Vulgar and Decimal* published in Boston
1745 Yale requires arithmetic for admission
1749 Franklin's academy founded
1788 Nicholas Pike's *A New and Complete System of Arithmetic* published in Newburyport (Mass.)
1801 Hawney's *Complete Measurer* printed in Philadelphia
1802 U.S. Military Academy founded at West Point
1803 Robert Simson's *The Elements of Euclid* printed in Philadelphia
1807 District Public Schools Act passed in Canada
1816 Common Schools Act passed in Canada
1820 Harvard requires algebra for admission
1821 English High School founded in Boston
1821 Warren Colburn's *An Arithmetic on the Plan of Pestalozzi* published in Boston

CHAPTER THREE

From Colburn to the Rise of the Universities: 1821–94

1. Forces at work

The period from 1821 to 1894 was one in which formal instruction at all levels developed and spread but was subjected to a number of conflicting forces. Practical, theoretical or philosophical, and scientific forces all influenced mathematics education. To the practical needs cited earlier, one might add the demands of a rapidly developing technology, engineering, and westward expansion. Manufacturing that used interchangeable parts, the telegraph, steamships, canals, railroads —all made some use of measurement and simple mathematical ideas. These forces led to a recognition of the need for useful knowledge and the development of practical and engineering programs even in the colleges.

At the same time the rapid rise of science, especially mechanics and astronomy, called not only for *more* mathematics but for *more advanced* mathematics.

We have already noted the early effect of Pestalozzi's educational ideas. His work was preceded by the philosophical writings of Locke and Rousseau. Pestalozzi's stress on adapting instruction to the individual, beginning with motor skills and object lessons, and motivation by appeal to natural interests and instincts, led to new and more modern teaching methods. He was followed, chronologically, by J. F. Herbart (1776–1841) and Friedrich Froebel (1782–1852). Their methods coexisted with a belief in mental discipline as a goal and, later, an associated faculty psychology.

Two foreign wars had led to a growth of French influence in the United States, especially in mathematics.

Jacksonian democracy and waves of immigration led to newly franchised lower- and middle-class voters who favored government support for roads, railroads, and westward expansion. These forces stimulated both a contempt for purely intellectual activities and a demand, especially in the North, for free public education in "the three R's." In the South, wealthy planters wanted education for their children, with the result that until 1850 the South was ahead of the North in providing private academies and colleges (182, pp. 502, 530).

The Civil War further stimulated interest in engineering, manufacturing, and westward expansion, while at the same time retarding the growth of education in the South.

This was a period of general ferment and concern for such social reforms as abolition, women's rights, child labor, property qualifications for voting, and penal reform. Near the close of this period, several very strong forces for reform in education began to be felt. These included psychological experiments and theories discrediting the mental discipline goal; rapid growth of the school population; and the beginnings of advanced study, learned societies, and professional journals.

2. *The elementary schools*

During this period arithmetic largely passed from the secondary school to the elementary school. Colburn's first book was intended for five- and six-year-olds. His primary method was to use carefully sequenced series of questions, leading a child to discover his own rules or principles. Colburn's avoidance of formalized rules was attributed by one writer to his "natural aversion to every kind of rule" (362, p. 163); another criticized the method for leaving "the child to work out his own salvation" (399, p. 270).

Colburn's method was emulated in the "mental" or "intellectual" arithmetics that were commonly attached to arithmetic series as a supplement. These were problem books but not mere drill books. They proposed problems that were to be reasoned out, often orally, rather than solved by direct application of rules. The stress on reasoning rather than rule is illustrated by the use of "analysis" or "unitary analysis." To illustrate:

What is $\frac{3}{4}$ of $\frac{2}{5}$?

Answer: We first get $\frac{1}{4}$ of $\frac{2}{5}$. Now $\frac{1}{4}$ of $\frac{1}{5} = \frac{1}{20}$; $\frac{1}{4}$ of $\frac{2}{5}$ is, then, twice as much, or $\frac{2}{20}$, which equals $\frac{1}{10}$. Therefore $\frac{3}{4}$ of $\frac{2}{5}$, which is 3 times $\frac{1}{4}$ of $\frac{2}{5}$, is $\frac{3}{10}$.

This example is from the 1884 revision of *Colburn's First Lessons*. Such exercises were seen as an important means of exercising the mind. As a practical technique of problem solving they outlived the era of mental discipline.

The inductive discovery approach of Colburn was overshadowed in the middle of the nineteenth century by the introduction of a deductive structure. Whereas pre-Colburn texts had given rules for solving specific problems, the texts of this period stated general definitions and principles which were developed into a deductive system that made arithmetic the "science of number." In this system, numbers were defined and classified as concrete or abstract, like or unlike, simple or compound, and even as natural or artificial. The processes and applications of arithmetic were fitted to the system. For example, in multiplication, principles were enunciated which allowed the multiplicand to be either concrete or abstract but demanded that the multiplier always be abstract and the product be "like" the multiplicand. Thus 3 times 4 inches was 12 inches. Such rationalizations contrast with the earlier rule-example-exercise approach in which a student "never heard any explanation of any principle" (181, p. 45). They also contrast with Colburn's disinclination to formalize. Although Colburn was praised by historians and authors of texts, the "science of number" approach came to dominate the major texts, and sections of definitions and principles were often inserted even into the supplementary mental arithmetics. Edward Brooks, whose texts were widely used in the second half of the nineteenth century, likened arithmetic to synthetic geometry, maintaining that "in arithmetic we have the same basis, and proceed by the same laws of logical evolution" (106, pp. 165–66).

Both the deductions of the "science of number" and the reasoning of the mental arithmetics were viewed as exercising specific psychological faculties, a purpose that justified the inclusion of large amounts of arithmetic in the elementary curriculum. Brooks stated the mental discipline thesis as follows (104, p. 37):

> *The mind is cultivated by the activities of its faculties.* . . . Mental exercise is thus the law of mental development. As a muscle grows strong by use, so any faculty of the mind is developed by its use and exercise. An inactive mind, like an unused muscle, becomes weak and unskillful. Hang the arm in a sling and the muscle becomes flabby and loses its vigor and skill; let the mind remain inactive, and it acquires a mental flabbiness, that unfits it for any severe or prolonged activity. An idle mind loses its tone and strength, like an unused muscle; the mental powers go to rust through idleness and inaction.

⇢⇢⇢ 3. *The secondary schools*

During this period grammar schools continued to decline. Academies rose in prominence from 1820 to 1845 and began a decline after 1850. A new type of secondary school, the high school, developed. The English High School was founded in Boston in 1821. Seven years later Girls High School got under way. There was a period of rapid expansion of high schools from 1840 to 1860, and by 1875 they were quite well established, at least in the North.

Morison (182, p. 532) states that by 1850 three basic principles not only had been formulated but were fairly well established: free elementary and secondary education should be available for all; attendance at school should be required; and teachers should have some professional training. However, only in New England were primary schools free and open to all. In other regions plans and theories gave way to practical necessities. In Ohio, for example, free school for grades K–12 was planned as early as 1850, but it was not possible to have it actually available everywhere in the state.

Arithmetic moved from the academies and high schools to become an elementary school subject by the end of the nineteenth century.

Algebra was on its way to becoming a mainstay of the high school curriculum when Harvard required it for admission in 1820, with Yale and Princeton following in 1847 and 1848 respectively.

Geometry moved down from the college level a little later. Yale made geometry an entrance requirement in 1865. Princeton, Michigan, and Cornell required it in 1868, and Harvard required geometry *and* logarithms for entrance in 1870.

Algebra and geometry had the good fortune to be espoused by both of two groups whose programs sometimes were in conflict. A faculty psychology and the need to prepare for further study combined with a belief in the mental disciplinary value of languages and mathematics to make mathematics required of the college-bound students. On the other hand, the practical utility of mathematics in the newly developing science and technology as well as in the older fields of surveying and navigation made persons planning non-college-preparatory programs speak out for algebra, geometry, trigonometry, and mensuration.

Although Harvard set up the first elective courses after an undergraduate rebellion in 1823, an extended elective system did not take hold there until the presidency of Charles William Eliot, beginning in 1869. He was motivated by a belief in individual differences and the difficulties being experienced with student motivation (225, pp. 118, 290–95). A little later this change came to academies and high schools as the result of additional forces such as the decline of religious and humanistic goals in favor of informational, social-civic, vocational, and practical aims (118, p. 497). By the end of the nineteenth century the high school curriculum was becoming more varied, and elective courses and programs were set up as a result of the changing and growing population of high schools, which motivated the changes in goals. Vocational, commercial, and manual training programs began to be established, sometimes in separate schools, during the latter part of the nineteenth century. These led to varied demands for mathematics and even to the development of special courses.

4. *The colleges and the mathematical community*

As mentioned in our introduction, this was a period when technical institutes and midwestern and western colleges were being founded. They included such "new" subjects as mathematics, science, English, and history in their programs; and even the older schools were debating the desirability of introducing these subjects. A famous Yale report of 1828 restated the case for the classical curriculum and the disciplinary values of mathematics. However, Harvard granted a bachelor of science degree in 1851, and in 1852 Yale introduced a bachelor of philosophy degree that originally had lower admission standards and required only three instead of four years, but admitted these new subjects as part of a degree program!

The first technical institute in the United States, the Military Academy at West Point, was founded in 1802. In its early days it was regarded as a center for mathematics and innovative ideas. It brought teachers, books, and ideas from France. These included descriptive

A

TREATISE

ON

Descriptive Geometry,

FOR THE USE OF THE

CADETS OF THE UNITED STATES
MILITARY ACADEMY.

BY C. CROZET,
PROFESSOR OF ENGINEERING IN THE ACADEMY.

PART I.

CONTAINING THE ELEMENTARY PRINCIPLES OF DESCRIPTIVE
GEOMETRY, AND ITS APPLICATION TO SPHERICS
AND CONIC SECTIONS.

New-York:
PUBLISHED BY A. T. GOODRICH AND CO. 124, BROADWAY,
CORNER OF CEDAR-STREET, OPPOSITE THE CITY HOTEL.

Wm. Grattan, Printer, 4, Thames-street

1821.

FIRST ENGLISH WORK ON DESCRIPTIVE GEOMETRY. Claude Crozet, one of Napoleon's engineers, was brought over to teach at the U.S. Military Academy. He later served as a consultant in railroad engineering.

MÉCANIQUE CÉLESTE.

BY THE

MARQUIS DE LA PLACE,

PEER OF FRANCE; GRAND CROSS OF THE LEGION OF HONOR; MEMBER OF THE FRENCH ACADEMY, OF THE ACADEMY OF SCIENCES OF PARIS, OF THE BOARD OF LONGITUDE OF FRANCE, OF THE ROYAL SOCIETIES OF LONDON AND GÖTTINGEN, OF THE ACADEMIES OF SCIENCES OF RUSSIA, DENMARK, SWEDEN, PRUSSIA, HOLLAND, AND ITALY; MEMBER OF THE AMERICAN ACADEMY OF ARTS AND SCIENCES; ETC.

TRANSLATED, WITH A COMMENTARY,

BY

NATHANIEL BOWDITCH, LL. D.

FELLOW OF THE ROYAL SOCIETIES OF LONDON, EDINBURGH, AND DUBLIN; OF THE ASTRONOMICAL SOCIETY OF LONDON, OF THE PHILOSOPHICAL SOCIETY HELD AT PHILADELPHIA, OF THE AMERICAN ACADEMY OF ARTS AND SCIENCES; CORRESPONDING MEMBER OF THE ROYAL SOCIETIES OF BERLIN, PALERMO; ETC.

VOLUME IV.

WITH A MEMOIR OF THE TRANSLATOR,

BY HIS SON,

NATHANIEL INGERSOLL BOWDITCH.

BOSTON:
FROM THE PRESS OF ISAAC R. BUTTS;
CHARLES C. LITTLE AND JAMES BROWN, PUBLISHERS.
M DCCC XXXIX.

FIRST ADVANCED MATHEMATICAL WORK PUBLISHED IN THE UNITED STATES.   The first volume appeared in 1829.

geometry as a subject and the blackboard as a teaching device. Charles Davies, chairman of its mathematics department, translated many French texts for use there and in other American schools. In 1850 Davies published the first American methods book, *The Logic and Utility of Mathematics with the Best Methods of Instruction Explained and Illustrated* (133). The academy introduced the study of analytical trigonometry and encouraged learning and research through the founding of the Military and Philosophical Society, which collected materials and books and at whose meetings papers were presented.

The French influence in American schools and colleges is dealt with in other works (244, pp. 76–81). The role of West Point and of Davies's ideas and work in spreading this influence is apparent in the list of mathematics texts adopted at the University of Michigan in 1837 for its seven students: Davies, *Arithmetic*; Davies, *Bourdon's Algebra* (translated from the French); Davies, *Legendre's Geometry* (translated from the French); Davies, *Surveying*; Davies, *Descriptive Geometry*; Bridges, *Conic Sections*; Gregory, *Mathematics for the Practical Man*.

The scientific and technological trends of the period are also typified by the vigorous and nontraditional development of Rensselaer Polytechnic Institute (founded in 1824) under Amos Eaton, a Yale-trained botanist and geologist who was its first "senior professor." Among his contributions were an interesting practical textbook on trigonometry and surveying titled *Art without Science* (357, p. 421) and the setting up on a canal boat of a summer laboratory course in surveying.

The new colleges, especially those west of New England, had both peculiar advantages and peculiar problems. They did not have the classical humanistic tradition to impede progress, but neither could they count on their students having had adequate secondary school preparation. Many of them set up associated academies in which they enrolled students who, due to the lack of or inadequacy of secondary schools near their homes, were unprepared to enter college. To ameliorate these conditions, the acting president of the University of Michigan set up a system for the accreditation of high schools in 1870, and in 1871 President James Burrill Angell appointed a commission to inspect schools. This led to the founding of various regional accrediting associations, of which the first was the New England Association of Colleges and Secondary Schools, established in 1885 (118, p. 503). However, the increase in elective courses and programs in both high schools and colleges was creating entrance and articulation problems requiring more than regional associations for their solution.

Toward the end of this period there was a further collegiate development that, eventually, had several significant effects on school mathematics. This was the introduction in this country of the idea of modern graduate education. Master's degrees had been awarded by many of the early colleges, but the concept of extended advanced study and specialization associated with research and the creation of new mathematics can largely be dated from three related events: the founding of the Johns Hopkins University in 1875 and the tenure of J. J. Sylvester as professor of mathematics there (1877–83); the founding of the *American Journal of Mathematics* there by Sylvester and W. E. Story; and the founding of the American Mathematical Society (AMS) in 1894. Its forerunner, the New York Mathematical Society, had been founded in 1888 and had begun to publish its *Bulletin* in 1891 (244, pp. 105–6, 121). The Chicago section of the AMS was established in 1896 (244, p. 107).

As the nineteenth century passed, it became increasingly true that with very few exceptions those Americans who had had advanced mathematical training or who were doing research in mathematics had studied abroad and were largely employed as college teachers. However, the U.S. Coast and Geodetic Survey and Nautical Almanac Office supported the endeavors of such largely self-taught mathematicians as Benjamin Peirce (1809–80) and Simon Newcomb (1835–1909). Peirce spent most of his life as a professor at Harvard after having studied there as an undergraduate and having assisted Nathaniel Bowditch in the preparation for the press of his translation of Laplace's *Mécanique Céleste*. His most famous work was *Linear Associative Algebra*. This pure mathematical work was developed from lectures given at the National Academy of Sciences and was issued in 1870 in a small edition through the "labors of love" of persons in the U.S. Coast and Geodetic Survey (86, p. 2). The tendency for American mathematical research to be very pure, and in the general area of the foundations of mathematics rather than in applied mathematics, continued into the twentieth century, becoming a real national handicap at the time of World War II.

5. *Teacher training and pedagogy*

This period saw the rise of preservice and in-service teacher training and of a group of professional educators. The first public normal school was founded in Massachusetts in 1839 under the leadership of Horace Mann. Formal teacher training was instituted in universities as early as 1832 at New York University, 1850 at Brown University, and 1860 at the University of Michigan. Teachers College, Columbia University, was founded in 1888 (118, p. 468). Courses in methods of teaching were offered in 1893 at the University of Michigan and at Michigan State Normal School. Louis Agassiz held a summer session at Harvard as early as 1873. In 1891 methods courses were also to be found in Kansas, California, Indiana, and Minnesota.

Horace Mann, who became chairman of the new Massachusetts Board of Education in 1837, had studied German educational ideas and translated Victor Cousin's report on Prussian education. The state of Ohio in 1836 sent Calvin E. Stowe to study European education systems (182, pp. 530–32). Such men as these not only spread word of the work of foreign educators including Pestalozzi, Herbart, and Froebel, but were active in initiating changes at home. The educational interests and theories of such European philosophers as John Locke (1632–1704), Immanuel Kant (1724–1804), and Herbert Spencer (1832–1903) were known and discussed in the books and periodicals on pedagogy which began to appear late in this period.

As noted above, Davies's methods book appeared in 1850. It was the first book in the United States for secondary school teachers of mathematics. Today it might be regarded as a mixture of foundations of mathematics and professionalized subject matter.

Nineteenth-century arithmetic texts, including those written for use in the normal schools, had many notes to teachers. However, the first book that can be viewed as a "methods" text for the elementary schools was Edward Brooks's *The Philosophy of Arithmetic* (1880). It seems to have been thoughtful, extensive, and based on considerable familiarity with pedagogical and mathematical literature. At that time, as today, there was considerable thought given to the nature of number by mathematicians, philosophers, and educators. Brooks discusses Hamilton's conception of algebra, and thereby arithmetic, as the science of time.

This interest in the nature of mathematics and its fundamental concepts, mentioned earlier in connection with American research interests, is further evidenced by the publication of several books. Albert Taylor Bledsoe, professor of mathematics at the University of Virginia, wrote *The Philosophy of Mathematics,* published at Philadelphia in 1868. It was largely concerned with the basic concepts of analytic geometry and calculus, discussing the work of Cavalieri, Descartes, Leibnitz, and Newton. In 1871 W. M. Gillespie of Union College published *The Philosophy of Mathematics, Translated from the Cours de*

Philosophie Positive of Auguste Comte. Again, although this was far from a methods book, many of its section headings have both a modern and a pedagogical ring: "The Object of Mathematics," "The True Definition of Mathematics," "Concrete Mathematics," "Abstract Mathematics," "The True Idea of an Equation," "Two Methods of Introducing Angles."

The rise of psychology as an offshoot from philosophy is perhaps typified by the writings of Herbert Spencer (1820–1903). His father was a schoolmaster who had written an inductive, laboratory-type, secondary-school text in geometry. Spencer wrote an introduction for its American edition (247), telling how fascinated the girls in his father's school had been with his inductive approach to geometry, which was a carefully sequenced series of questions and instructions. Today it would be termed a "discovery" or "heuristic" approach.

The inductive method of Colburn had neither the stress on objects advocated by Pestalozzi, whom he professed to follow, nor as well developed a sequence of questions and activities as in Spencer's book. However, Colburn did reduce formalism and definitions and strive to lead the student to understanding by means of questions and explanations. Colburn extended this approach to algebra in 1825 with the publication of *An Introduction to Algebra on the Inductive Method of Instruction.* He said his object was

> to make the transition from arithmetic to algebra as gradual as possible [by] beginning with practical questions in simple equations, such as the learner might readily solve without the aid of algebra. . . . The most simple combinations are given first. . . . The learner is expected to derive most of his knowledge by solving the examples himself. . . . This method, besides giving the learner confidence, by making him rely on his own powers, is much more interesting to him, because he seems to be constantly making new discoveries.

In summary, then, this period saw the rise of teaching procedures stimulated by changing philosophical-psychological ideas of the goals and processes of education. Mental discipline as a viable goal of education, and drill as a procedure, were retained along with other newer goals and processes for more than thirty years after 1894, but the three-step process of "state a rule, give an example, practice" was yielding to inductive, reasoning, and discovery-teaching processes. Both goals and processes were being questioned, and new psychological bases for learning and teaching were being sought.

⇛⇛ 6. *The climate of reform*

The many forces enumerated in the previous sections include the problem of high school–college articulation and the problem of "psychologizing" both the content and the methods of the secondary school curriculum to improve learning for all student groups but especially to adapt to the changing high school population with its many non-college-bound students.

These two related problems were studied by two committees appointed at the conclusion of this period and the beginning of the next. The appointment of these committees typifies several significant forces at work at this time.

The first of these was the Committee on Secondary School Studies. This group, often referred to as the Committee of Ten, was appointed in 1892, and it published reports in 1893 and 1894 (71, 72). The fact that it was appointed by the National Education Association (NEA) demonstrates the growing influence of professional organizations at this time. The NEA had been formed in 1870 out of the National Teachers Association, which had been founded in 1857. The subcommittee on mathematics of the Committee of Ten was the first national group to consider the goals and curriculum for mathematics education (306). This subcommittee was composed of leading mathematicians. Its recommendations were quite radical and forward-looking, even though it was largely oriented toward the goals of college preparation and mental discipline. Some of its recommendations, particularly the recommendation that the mathematics program be unified or integrated rather than compartmentalized, are still to be put into effect. However, the recommendation that introductory work in algebra and geometry come earlier and be more psychologically designed preceded the introduction of informal and intuitive geometry into the junior high program of the early twentieth century. This began a trend that is being revived today with the inclusion of more geometry in the elementary school and the movement of algebra into the eighth grade, together with even earlier introduction of preliminary algebraic concepts.

The other committee referred to is the Committee on College Entrance Requirements of the NEA, appointed in 1899, with some of the members named at the suggestion of the AMS. Its report (74) affected the period covered by our next chapter, but the problem and the forces and organizations associated with it had their roots in the 1821–94 period we have just discussed.

7. Summary

Issues

Several issues were prominent in this period:

1. Should education be free for all? If so, what should be the extent and content of free education?
2. What are the goals of mathematics education?
3. How should teachers be trained?

Forces

The following forces were particularly strong in this period:

1. Demands for a practical education growing out of war, industrialization, and western expansion
2. Rapid growth in the strength of middle- and lower-class segments of the population, accompanied by very rapid growth in the school population, with a corresponding variety of goals, backgrounds, and capacities; rise of the public high school
3. The influence of European ideas with respect both to educational philosophies and to the content of mathematical curricula
4. The rise of educational philosophers, practitioners, and psychologists
5. The need for more mathematics to accompany the development of science as well as technology, in higher education as well as in industry
6. The founding of the U.S. Military Academy and technical institutes
7. The instituting of graduate study and research in universities
8. The founding of professional and scholarly societies and journals
9. The development of training in pedagogy

Chronology

1821   English High School founded in Boston
1824   Rensselaer Polytechnic Institute founded
1828   Girls High School founded in Boston
1839   Massachusetts sets up the first public normal school
1847   First Canadian normal school founded in Toronto
1850   Charles Davies's *The Logic and Utility of Mathematics with the Best Methods Explained and Illustrated* published in New York
1852   Massachusetts passes the first compulsory-school-attendance law
1857   National Teachers Association founded

- 1870 National Education Association founded
- 1871 College accreditation of high schools is provided for
- 1876 Johns Hopkins University founded
- 1878 The *American Journal of Mathematics* begins publication
- 1880 Edward Brooks's *The Philosophy of Arithmetic* published in Lancaster (Pa.)
- 1888 New York Mathematical Society founded
- 1888 Teachers College, Columbia University, founded as New York College for the Training of Teachers
- 1893 Felix Klein lectures at Northwestern University Colloquium
- 1894 Report of the Committee of Ten on the secondary school syllabus published
- 1894 American Mathematical Society founded

CHAPTER FOUR

First Steps toward Revision 1894–1920

1. *Forces at work*

The issues in mathematics education tend to endure, to change slowly if at all. However, the prominence of various issues tends to change with the shifting of the nature and direction of the forces exerted to change the educational program. The major force during the period of 1894 to 1920, resulting from the growth in school enrollments, was the pressure to provide an education for all children. Added to this were forces generated by psychological research and changing theories of learning. Mental discipline as an achievable goal of instruction was being questioned. Both educators and mathematicians were calling for an integration of content and a shift to newer methods using concrete, developmental, and intuitive approaches to this content.

This period (1894–1920) is characterized by a somewhat intensified consideration and refinement of the issues formulated in the previous period. One should also note the similarity of the problems and proposals of this period to those of the following period. For example, World War I diverted concern and energies from education while at the same time leading to some support for the continued education of returning veterans. Later, World War II gave a far greater push to mathematics and its applications as well as providing greatly expanded higher educational facilities for veterans. The pressure to enroll in college in this later period paralleled the earlier pressure to complete a high school program.

In the period covered by this chapter much of the teacher training, especially for elementary school teachers, was done in normal schools. As a result, colleges and universities had much less concern for or contact with elementary and secondary education than they have today. In 1894–1920 the chief concerns common to the secondary schools and the colleges were the setting and administering of standards for the admission of high school graduates to college. Both the traditional college requirements and the then-new elective undergraduate college programs, along with developing graduate programs, exerted pressures for college preparation on the high schools. However, these pressures were not uniform. They varied with the colleges and with new college curricula. Further, these pressures often opposed the forces implicit in a growing high school population, much of which was non-college-bound and had immediate vocational-personal needs. The prominent issues became these: What are the goals of high school mathematics education? How can the school adapt to the varied needs, backgrounds, interests, and abilities of its students?

2. *The elementary schools*

The elementary schools underwent a terrific expansion, from 16 million to 24 million pupils in the interval from 1900 to 1930. The dominant organizational pattern of schools was beginning to change toward the end of this period. The "8-4" pattern, eight years of elementary school followed by four years of high school, was changing to "6-3-3," with a three-year junior high school inserted between a six-year elementary school and a three-year high school.

Arithmetic, once a college and secondary school subject, had moved to the elementary school. Now, in the elementary school, separate texts for early arithmetic work were disappearing. It was proposed that primary number ideas be treated incidentally and informally. The NEA's Committee of Fifteen on Elementary Education, which reported in 1895 (68), suggested that grades 2 through 6 complete basic arithmetic and that number work be continued into grades 7 and 8 where some algebra would be introduced, along with a reduction in the amount of time per day devoted to mathematics. This introduction of some algebra was to serve as a "transitional step to algebra proper" (p. 58), an idea in keeping with the purposes of the newly developing junior high school.

The arithmetic pedagogy of the latter half of the nineteenth century had tended to stress what Clason (441, pp. 72, 115–16) calls the "science of number," after the definition of arithmetic often given in the texts of this period. In this approach, as was noted in the previous chapter, considerable discussion was devoted to distinguishing different types of numbers such as "concrete," "abstract," and "denominate." These definitions associated number with units and collections of objects for the purpose of rationalizing the operations with numbers.

The early part of the period 1894–1920 saw substantial innovations in the approach to numbers. Herbert Spencer's dictum that number is *relation* led William Speer to stress number as the directly perceived ratio of quantities, lengths, areas, and volumes rather than as an abstract concept or a collection of discrete objects (441, pp. 135, 210, 302). Spencer's emphasis on the spiral nature of learning affected both the presentation and the organization of arithmetic texts, which in the earlier period had presented each new topic in its turn, once and for all (441, p. 62).

Later John Dewey (1859–1952) viewed number as originating through measurement. The text for teachers of arithmetic written by him and James A. McLellan, and the school books based on it, therefore stressed measurement activities, problems, and units (441, pp. 129, 205–10).

Following these innovative approaches there was a reaction typified by the eclecticism and avoidance of extremes to be found in the writings and texts of David Eugene Smith, according to Clason (441, p. 63).

Clason suggests that the next period in elementary school mathematics spanned the years 1917–35 and should be termed the period of connectionism. This term largely refers to the stimulus-response psychology so strongly presented by Edward L. Thorndike after the psychologists of the day thought they had thoroughly discredited the concepts of mental discipline and transfer of training. *The Thorndike Arithmetics* appeared in 1917. In *The Psychology of Arithmetic* (1922) and *The Psychology of Algebra* (1923) Thorndike stressed the importance of establishing many "bonds" by means of much practice (265; 266). This psychological approach led to the fragmentation of arithmetic into many small facts and skills to be taught and tested separately. This theory even led to the avoidance of teaching closely related facts close in time to one another for fear of establishing incorrect bonds. Thus Clason says, "For good or ill, it was Thorndike who dealt the final blow to the 'science of arithmetic' " (441, p. 64).

3. The secondary schools

There were several approaches to "psychologizing" secondary school mathematics during this period. Perhaps the "Perry movement" in England should be mentioned first, since it was well publicized in this country by the efforts of Professor E. H. Moore, one of the leading mathematicians of the United States. Moore took the unusual step of devoting a major portion of his 1902 address on retiring as president of the AMS to a discussion of needed improvements in American schools (381). He urged that schools abolish the "watertight compartments" in which algebra, geometry, and physics were taught. He also suggested a stress on the interrelationships of mathematics with science. This latter was one of the three major proposals vigorously advocated by John Perry in addresses given in 1900–1902. Perry also urged that mathematics be made concrete by use of laboratory-teaching techniques and applications and by bringing into lower grade levels many simple ideas usually postponed to later grades. Moore endorsed all of this and further stressed the desirability of developing in the United States junior colleges, junior high schools, and improved subject-matter training for teachers in these schools and in the high schools. He also noted a forthcoming article in which "John Dewey, calling attention to the evolutionary character of the education of the individual, insists that there should be no abrupt transition from the introductory, intuitional geometry to the systematic, deductional geometry" (p. 48).

The National Committee of Fifteen on the Geometry Syllabus was appointed in 1908–9 under the joint auspices of the American Federation of Teachers of the Mathematical and Natural Sciences and the NEA. Its "Provisional Report" (66) appeared in 1911 in *School Science and Mathematics*, journal of the Central Association of Science and Mathematics Teachers. This report showed some effect of Moore-Perry views as well as a reaction to rising failure rates in algebra and geometry, which were still required courses in many high schools. This report called for the use in geometry of some informal proofs and for the exclusion of materials dealing with limits and incommensurables—with, however, continued stress on logical structure. It called for more use of concrete examples and graded "originals."

Many of these same pedagogical emphases were discussed in the *Report of the American Commissioners of the International Commission on the Teaching of Mathematics* (49) issued in 1912. The International Commission was set up at the Fourth International Congress of Mathematicians held in Rome in 1908. It reported at the 1912 congress held in Cambridge, England. The final report of the American commissioners was based upon the reports of many subcommittees (39–48). As a continuation of this project and based on some later reports as well as those given at the congress, I. L. Kandel and R. C. Archibald prepared comparative studies of the training of teachers here and abroad. These appeared in 1915 and 1918 (163; 5).

The American commissioners in 1912 noted tendencies in this country to omit difficult or obvious geometric proofs, to postpone difficult topics, to reduce the stress on manipulation in algebra while increasing the stress on solution of equations and applications.

Archibald stated in 1918 (5, p. 4):

> At the present time superintendents . . . [in] the United States have been forced by public opinion to consider numerous radical changes in methods of secondary school education. If a high minimum standard of preparation were required on the part of each teacher, and the position of the teacher were made such as to attract in sufficient numbers the best talent in the country, other difficulties would disappear. Most countries considered in this bulletin have far higher standards than we with respect to teachers of mathematics in the secondary schools.

The most influential committee dealing with the teaching of mathematics appointed in the United States prior to the recent (1956–59) Commission on Mathematics was the National Committee on Mathematical Requirements, whose final report, *The Reorganization of Mathematics in Secondary Education* (59), was published in 1923. A preliminary report appeared in 1920 and a summary in 1922 (57; 58).

The committee was appointed by the MAA in 1916, before the United States entered World War I. The committee contained several persons with special interest in and experience with the secondary schools, in addition to the mathematicians who represented the association's major concern with the undergraduate college program. Its preliminary report was circulated through the U.S. Bureau of Education with a call for criticisms and comments to be submitted for consideration before preparation of the final report. The committee was also remarkable for having some financial support from an outside source for its staff and activities.

Its final report stressed many of the ideas mentioned above, such as the reduction of elaborate manipulations in algebra and of the memorization of theorems and proofs in geometry by decreasing the number "required" theorems and increasing the number of "originals." It also advocated a general mathematics program for grades 7–9 which would include topics from arithmetic, algebra, intuitive geometry, numerical trigonometry, graphs, and descriptive statistics. An entire chapter was devoted to the importance and unifying nature of the function concept.

This period, 1894–1920, can be partially typified by a concern for goals and curriculum revision. Several regional educational organizations and state education departments also prepared reports and syllabi.

4. *The colleges and the mathematical community*

An emphasis on the function concept and on interrelationships within mathematics had been strongly advocated since the middle of the nineteenth century by Germany's famous mathematician Felix Klein. He and a number of other foreign mathematicians attended the international conference held in conjunction with the Chicago World's Fair of 1893. Klein stayed on after the fair to participate in a colloquium at Northwestern University. This colloquium had a very stimulating effect upon mathematical research in the United States. Klein's summer lectures to German mathematics teachers were translated by E. R. Hedrick and C. A. Noble and published in this country in 1932 under the title *Elementary Mathematics from an Advanced Standpoint*.

A number of translations of important foreign treatises were published in this country around the turn of the century. G. B. Halsted translated source materials related to non-Euclidean geometry by Bolyai and Lobachevsky (translated in 1891 but published in 1914), and Saccheri (1920). E. J. Townsend's translation of Hilbert's *Foundations of Geometry* was published in 1902. Halsted, feeling that the high school geometry of his day was out-of-date and too full of errors, wrote *Rational Geometry* as a high school text based on Hilbert's axioms (151).

Axiomization became a major American research interest. E. V. Huntington and Oswald Veblen published a new set of axioms for geometry in 1904. Huntington axiomatized elementary algebra in 1905. Later continuing this American interest, G. D. Birkhoff devised a new set of axioms for geometry in 1933. This system, involving "ruler and protractor postulates," was later incorporated into a high school text, *Basic Geometry*, by Birkhoff and his mathematics-educator colleague at Harvard, Ralph Beatley (97).

Several books were written or compiled to convey the then-"modern" ideas of mathematical foundations to teachers. J. W. Young's

Lectures on Fundamental Concepts of Algebra and Geometry appeared in 1911 (284), and J. W. A. Young edited *Monographs on Topics in Modern Mathematics* (1911), which included articles by Veblen, Huntington, Birkhoff, and David Eugene Smith (286). J. W. Young of Dartmouth College is probably better known among mathematicians for his extensive axiomatic treatise on projective geometry written with Oswald Veblen. J. W. A. Young, after writing a dissertation in group theory at Clark University in 1892, was listed as "Associate Professor of the Pedagogy of Mathematics at the University of Chicago" in the 1920 edition of his book *The Teaching of Mathematics in the Elementary and Secondary School* (285). This book was first published in 1906. It was the second American book to deal extensively with the teaching of secondary school mathematics. Although Davies's earlier book purported to be for teachers, David Eugene Smith's *The Teaching of Elementary Mathematics* (241), which appeared in 1900, was the first book to resemble a modern methods text.

Another strong collegiate influence upon secondary school mathematics developed during this period. The College Entrance Examination Board (CEEB) was established in 1911. It included mathematics in the set of tests it administered for its member colleges, and it published syllabi defining the high school mathematics content upon which its tests would be based. The development of the board came after long concern for the problems of articulating the high school and college curricula and selecting high school graduates who were capable of succeeding in college. The Committee on College Entrance Requirements reported to the NEA in 1899 (69). This committee also advocated concrete geometry and introductory algebra in the seventh grade.

5. Pedagogy and teacher training

David Eugene Smith and J. W. A. Young may be regarded as representing an interesting development in this period—the appearance of "mathematics educators." Smith was professor of mathematics at Teachers College, Columbia University, from 1901 until his retirement in 1922. He played important roles in the AMS (86), MAA, and the NCTM. He served on many important committees, including the National Committee on Mathematical Requirements. He was one of the American commissioners on the International Commission on the Teaching of Mathematics. He was also a founder of the History of Science Society, a prolific writer, and the director of many studies in the teaching and history of mathematics.

A number of persons who were primarily mathematicians also maintained an interest in school programs. For example, the National Committee on Mathematical Requirements was appointed by E. R. Hedrick, president of the MAA. The committee included Smith and mathematicians J. W. Young, A. R. Crathorne, C. N. Moore, and H. W. Tyler. Vevia Blair of the Horace Mann School and Raleigh Schorling of the Lincoln School, New York City, were from experimental or "laboratory" schools. Both the existence of these schools and the appointment of persons from them to the committee were manifestations of the development of professional mathematics educators. Miss Blair also represented the Association of Teachers of Mathematics in the Middle States and Maryland. W. F. Downey was added to the committee later as a representative of the Association of Teachers of Mathematics in New England, and J. A. Foberg represented the Central Association of Science and Mathematics Teachers. The remaining members of this committee were A. C. Olney, commissioner of secondary education for California, and P. H. Underwood and Eula A. Weeks, mathematics teachers from Texas and Missouri.

Local and then national organizations concerned with the teaching of mathematics began to be formed along with the general growth of scholarly and educational societies. Three of these were cited in the previous paragraph. The MAA was founded in 1915. The NCTM was incorporated in 1920. It was largely stimulated by the interest and planning of the Chicago Men's Mathematics Club. The Council's journal, the *Mathematics Teacher*, was taken over in 1921 from the Association of the Teachers of Mathematics in the Middle States and Maryland.

Research pertaining to mathematics education was also carried on by general educators, especially by persons in the rapidly growing field of tests and measurements. We have already cited, for example, the work and influence of E. L. Thorndike.

6. *Summary*

Issues

In addition to a continuing stress on the issues cited in previous chapters, three new issues began to evolve. The continuing older issues were these:

1. What are the goals of mathematical instruction?
2. How can the mathematics curriculum and teaching methods be

adapted to the needs, backgrounds, interests, and abilities of students?

The newer issues were these:

3. What is the proper role of inductive and intuitive approaches to mathematical teaching and learning as compared with a rule-giving and theorem-memorizing approach?
4. How much logical rigor is appropriate for the different levels of the schools?
5. Should mathematics instruction be compartmentalized or integrated in some manner within itself or with instruction in science?

Forces

Many of the forces operative in this period should be familiar from our earlier discussions:

1. The growth and changing socioeconomic status of the population
2. Technological, industrial, and scientific developments
3. The resulting growth and change in the school population
4. The development of varied college programs and college entrance requirements together with the College Entrance Examination Board and its syllabi
5. The beliefs (more than the texts) of foreign authorities such as John Perry, Felix Klein, Herbert Spencer

   However, several essentially new drives were developing during this period:

6. The growth of psychology into a recognized and separate discipline with a particular interest in learning theory
7. The associated development and exposition of educational theories and philosophies
8. The appearance of a group of specialists, educators, and even more highly specialized mathematics educators
9. The related development of specialized professional organizations
10. Associated particularly with forces 7 and 8, but motivated by concerns stemming from forces 5 and 6, the preparation and dissemination of committee reports recommending changes in syllabi and methods
11. The beginnings of research in mathematics education
12. The growth of the junior high school

Chronology

1895 Report of NEA Committee of Fifteen on Elementary Education
1899 Report of the Committee on College Entrance Requirements
1900 David Eugene Smith's *The Teaching of Elementary Mathematics* published in New York
1901 John Perry's address to the British Association for the Advancement of Science
1902 E. H. Moore's retiring presidential address to the American Mathematical Society, stressing pedagogical problems
1902 Central Association of Physics Teachers founded
1903 Central Association of Physics Teachers enlarged to become the Central Association of Science and Mathematics Teachers
1911 "Provisional Report of the National Committee of Fifteen on the Geometry Syllabus" published
1911 College Entrance Examination Board founded
1912 Reports of the International Commission on the Teaching of Mathematics
1915 Mathematical Association of America founded
1917 Smith-Hughes Act passed
1920 National Council of Teachers of Mathematics founded
1920 Preliminary report of the National Committee on Mathematical Requirements

CHAPTER FIVE

Abortive Reform—Depression and War: 1920–45

1. *A period of unrest*

The period from 1920 to 1945 was a turbulent one that included many frustrations for mathematical education in America. This period encompassed a humbling depression and a tragic war, each of which materially affected education. The number and percentage of school-age youth attending school continued to increase dramatically. Both the role of mathematics in secondary education and the effectiveness with which it was taught were seriously questioned.

The previous period had seen the beginning of a reform movement in mathematics education. The Committee of Ten (1894), Committee on College Entrance Requirements (1899), International Commission on the Teaching of Mathematics (1911–18), and National Committee on Mathematical Requirements (1916–23) had made recommendations for improving the secondary school mathematics curriculum. As well-reasoned and appropriate to the times as the reports of these groups were, they did not fully recognize the needs of the changing public school population. There was little hint in the reports of the need to vary mathematics programs to accommodate the varied interests and capacities of the increasing number of students being retained in the secondary schools. In fact, the report of the National Committee on Mathematical Requirements found no conflict between the needs of college preparatory students and those of non-college-aspiring students, stating (59, p. 43):

> The separation of prospective college students from the others in the early years of the secondary school is neither feasible nor desirable.... Fortunately, there appears to be no real conflict of interest between those students who ultimately go to college and those who do not, so far as mathematics is concerned.

In this period the varied needs and capacities of school pupils brought into focus two vital issues: What should be the contribution of mathematics to general education for all children? How can mathematical instruction be redesigned to accommodate individual differences?

Some efforts at reform recommended earlier did attain at least partial success in the period 1920–45. The junior high school, whose beginnings can be traced to the turn of the century, was quite well established by 1920 and had become the pattern rather than the exception by the late 1930s (341). Within these schools the mathematics program was beginning to be less dominated by arithmetic. Instead it was turning to the general mathematics concept, that is, to an integrated study of arithmetic, informal geometry, elementary algebra, statistics, and numerical trigonometry as recommended by the National Committee on Mathematical Requirements in its final "1923 Report" (169, pp. 21–28, 245). Furthermore, manipulation and memorization were reduced, and the "function concept" and other recommendations of the "1923 Report" were widely discussed in texts, at least in their prefaces (152).

Other problems remained virtually untouched by reform during this period, and new difficulties developed or became matters of concern. Simple mathematical competency continued to elude many graduates and undergraduates (388, p. 91). In 1925 Schorling wrote:

> Many European visitors to our schools, though they may be enthusiastic about many excellent characteristics, are vigorous in their indictment expressed in such phrases as: "You foster half learning"; "You are satisfied with low standards"; "You do not fix habits."

He cited considerable data gathered by himself and others that showed a very low level of mastery to exist at the seventh-grade level (231, pp. 20–44). Thorndike published similar data and conclusions for ninth-grade algebra (266, chap. 12).

Not only was the effectiveness of the teaching of mathematics questioned, but the desirability of teaching much of the classical content was also questioned. The pragmatism of John Dewey and others led to a heavy stress on utility as a goal of education. This in turn led to numerous investigations of the occurrence of mathematics in newspaper and magazine reading, in student activities, and in adult social and business activities (231, pp. 45-85). The conclusion was that many topics taught had little or no utility for the general student. In other words, school mathematics, especially as taught in grades 7-12, was under rather severe attack.

These conditions led to decreasing enrollments in mathematics relative to the school population. For example, 57.51 percent of the students in public high schools were enrolled in algebra in 1905. The percentage dropped continually; there were 40.15 percent enrolled in 1922 and only 30.14 percent enrolled in 1934. Other mathematical areas exhibited similar declines (161, pp. 28-29).

Several factors undoubtedly contributed to the general failure to enact sweeping reform in mathematics teaching in the years between 1920 and 1945. First, there was resistance to change on the part of teachers and administrators. Very few schools had the liberty or the leadership to innovate extensively. A second reason was the depression. The scarcity of money reduced opportunities for experimentation and the production of text materials. Moreover, the increased total enrollments that came with the depression left little time for teachers to consider and work with new programs. Finally, the outbreak of World War II distracted attention from school reform.

➢➢➢ 2. *The elementary school*

With the increase in the number of junior high schools, the elementary school came to focus its attention on the K-6 program. In mathematics this program consisted, in the main, of arithmetic. The major emphasis was on the computational aspects of that subject. As a result the critical issues in the elementary school did not develop around the question of what to teach, but rather about *when* and *how* to present the agreed-upon arithmetic concepts. The issues centered about (1) the *readiness* of youngsters to learn mathematical ideas and manipulative skills, (2) the *postponement* of instruction in arithmetic based on an assumed lack of readiness, (3) the dependence upon *incidental learning* of mathematics mainly via projects, (4) a new psychologically based stress on teaching for *meaning* and *understanding*, and (5) the role of *drill*.

This latter was particularly stressed in the early part of the 1920–45 period. Long practice, often with involved problems, had characterized nineteenth-century arithmetic. In the early twentieth century, drill was justified by the connectionist school of psychology and E. L. Thorndike's theory of bonds. This theory was described as follows (305, p. 118):

> Whenever there is a response of the learner to a stimulus, a "bond" is formed. This "bond" is conceived as involving changes in the nervous tissue . . . the strength and the permanence of a "bond" are largely a matter of repetition, of "exercise." That is, the "trace" left in the nervous organism by each response is strengthened by repetition, by drill.

The impact of this theory on the schools was such that algebra as well as arithmetic was taught by drill techniques. Each problem was analyzed into a great many isolated units or elements of knowledge and skill. The student was then drilled on the mechanical mastery of these units with little regard for understanding.

Under the influence of these theories children learned, for example, one hundred addition facts, with no stress on structural number properties, such as commutativity, which might have reduced the number of facts to be memorized.

Later in this 1920–45 period two new theories of arithmetic instruction, partially supplementing each other, strongly influenced texts and teaching. These were the *meaning* theory and the *readiness* theory. The former was most clearly and extensively advocated by William A. Brownell, who planned and conducted careful research to support it. He explained the theory in the lead article in the Tenth Yearbook of the NCTM, in which he said (312, p. 28):

> According to the *meaning* theory the ultimate purpose of arithmetic instruction is the development of the ability to *think* in quantitative situations. The word "think" is used advisedly: the ability merely to perform certain operations mechanically and automatically is not enough. Children must be able to analyze real or described quantitative situations.

This theory seems to be closely related to Gestalt psychology, although Brownell did not appeal directly to it. In the schools a stress on meaning and understanding was used to support slightly inconsistent content and procedures. One can detect in Brownell's statement a possible paradox in the interpretation of "teaching for meaning." Some persons associated the accent on *thinking* with *mathematical* thinking and the understanding of mathematical structure and reasoning. On the other hand, Brownell's statement that "children must be able to analyze . . . situations" suggested to others the importance of the social setting of the problem to be thought about. Thus the same word "meaning" might lead to significantly different stresses in instruction: *mathematical* meaning or *social* meaning.

The latter emphasis was most closely related to the second theory of arithmetic learning to play an important role in the period 1920–45. This is the *readiness* theory which grew out of the studies of Gesell and other child development psychologists as expounded and applied by Leo J. Brueckner in the Thirty-eighth Yearbook of the National Society for the Study of Education (318, pp. 275–98).

The conclusion that children would not learn and hence should not be taught until they are ready for learning each particular skill and concept led to studies of readiness. These were followed by analyses of the grade placement of particular topics and by the postponement of formal instruction in many arithmetic topics to grades later than those in which they had been introduced previously (84, pp. 309–13).

This tendency to postpone formal instruction was accompanied by the development of a theory of teaching that gained some prominence as an alternative to drill techniques, namely, *incidental learning*. In this approach, which was used mainly in elementary schools, arithmetic was not taught as a separate system. Rather, the number facts were to be acquired through incidental experience. In discussing an experiment by Hanna, Betz concluded that "incidental learning will not produce results in arithmetic" (305, pp. 122–26). However, as late as 1945 the Commission on Post-War Plans of the NCTM found it necessary in its second report to include in the recommendations for the improvement of the mathematics program the following "theses" that were directed toward excesses developing out of the principles of readiness, postponement, and incidental learning (16):

> *Thesis 5.* We must abandon the idea that arithmetic can be taught incidentally or informally.
>
> *Thesis 6.* We must realize that readiness for learning arithmetical ideas and skills is primarily the product of relevant experiences, not the effect of merely becoming older.
>
> *Thesis 7.* We must learn to administer drill (repetitive practice) much more wisely.

In theses stated earlier this commission took stands on two other issues suggested above:

Thesis 3. We must conceive of arithmetic as having both a mathematical aim and a social aim.

Thesis 4. We must give more emphasis and more careful attention to the development of meanings.

3. *The junior high school*

According to Koos the junior high school began and gained acceptance because the 8-4 school organization did not (1) adequately provide for differences in student capacities, interests, and needs, (2) provide adequate occupational training, (3) stem the high mortality rate in grades 6–12, or (4) provide for the physical changes of adolescents. Moreover, the four-year high school building was crowded and removal of the ninth grade decreased the congestion (169, p. 1). Betz noted that "the depression . . . brought an even greater influx into our secondary schools, while at the same time available funds were sharply reduced" (305, p. 85). The youngsters who previously had left school to engage in gainful employment now remained in school and met an academic curriculum that was not designed for their talents or their interests. It became abundantly evident through failure rates and by means of the newly developed achievement and intelligence tests that individuals differ, and the question of how to provide for individual differences became a critical issue. Orleans reported that in 1929, in New York City, from 38.6 percent to 43.2 percent of all pupils at the proper grade level enrolled in elementary algebra, but that 30 percent of them failed (395).

The rise of the junior high school was accompanied by opportunities for improving mathematical education. Breslich stated (310, p. 1):

> The development of the junior high school offered a real opportunity for the reorganization of secondary school mathematics, making it possible to extend downward the period of secondary education, to give instruction in algebra and geometry at an early period, and to distribute the content of these courses over a period of several years.

In the 1920s a great many people, mathematicians and others, advocated what was called "general mathematics" for grades 7–12. The general mathematics concept was based on a reorganization of school mathematics that de-emphasized compartmentalization. In essence it was to consist of a sound, gradual development of algebra, geometry, trigonometry, and introductory statistics throughout the six years of secondary school, a development that would stress interrelationships.

For grades 7 and 8 the general mathematics concept was extensively accepted, probably because it conformed to the philosophy that the junior high school was to be exploratory in nature and because text materials were available. For the grades above the eighth, general mathematics as defined here, although repeatedly urged, has never been generally accepted.

It is easy to oversimplify and overgeneralize this situation. Both the type of school organization (8-4, 6-3-3, or 6-6) and the offering of general mathematics varied with the geographic region and with the size of the school. For example, a sample study in 1952 of mathematics enrollments showed 47 percent of eighth-grade students in New England enrolled in general mathematics, but only 1 percent of the students in the Mountain States (108, p. 4). However, another study, made at an earlier date (1932), showed that the "arithmetic" label frequently included much of the general mathematics content. In the seventh grade, "arithmetic" syllabi called for more time with fractions and graphs and made more mention of ratio, proportion, and computation. "General mathematics" syllabi gave more time to measurement, geometric constructions and forms, and the meaning and use of formulas (171, p. 24).

At the ninth-grade level some form of mathematics was required in 55 percent of the schools included in the 1932 survey. The number of schools requiring mathematics in this grade was growing as a result of the recommendations of the National Committee on Mathematical Requirements and also those of the mathematics committee of the Department of Superintendence of the NEA. Algebra was the course offered most often in the ninth grade, but the proportion of pupils taking it had been decreasing since 1905, and between 1922 and 1928 the percentage of public school pupils in algebra decreased from 40.15 to 35.22. At the ninth-grade level, general mathematics was often planned and taught as a lower-level alternative to algebra rather than as the continuation of a broadly planned general mathematics program. Other alternatives were commercial arithmetic or some form of applied mathematics. The report of this survey concluded:

> ... The adaptation of ninth grade mathematics to the interests and needs of the student body is the chief problem faced in the three grades being considered.
> In at least three of the cities [of the study] the conclusion of the National Committee that "there appears to be no conflict of interest during this period between those pupils who ultimately go to college

and those who do not" has not worked out in practice to the extent that they feel able to offer a single course in the ninth grade that will meet the demands of both groups.

Since the junior high school accepted general mathematics and the senior high school remained quite traditional in its offerings, there was a disparity that created a problem of articulation between junior and senior high schools. The problem was magnified by the scarcity of appropriately trained junior high school teachers, the tendency for distinct faculties to develop, and the lack of continuity in instruction and emphasis (310, pp. 2-3).

4. *The senior high school*

The major problems of the senior high school from 1920 to 1945, whether it contained grades 9-12 or 10-12, are implicit in the discussion in the previous section: rising failure rates, criticisms of the value and effectiveness of instruction in mathematics, and problems of articulation with the lower schools.

From the turn of the century to 1920, although there had been efforts to change the secondary school mathematics curriculum, the offerings remained mainly college preparatory in nature. During the depression years, however, college attendance decreased sharply. Thus there was an added impetus to stress the importance of vocational and personal needs in school mathematics and to de-emphasize the sequential courses. Combine this emphasis with the nonuniform college entrance requirements and the elective principle, and the once-firm position of mathematics in secondary education becomes insecure. School mathematics became an elective subject, and enrollments sharply decreased as shown in the table on the following page.

Algebra continued to be the most common ninth-grade course. However, a type of general mathematics not contemplated by the National Committee on Mathematical Requirements began to develop out of the increasingly common requirement that everyone take at least one year of mathematics in grades 9-12. This new general mathematics developed as the most popular alternative to algebra in the ninth grade. Down to the present day this course has been ill-defined and often poorly, or at least unwillingly, taught. The mode of selection of the students for this course has led to such common problems as students with little interest and a wide range of ability—mostly low—and teachers who by their choice of field and their training in it are neither prepared for nor interested in it.

TABLE 5.1
PUPILS IN THE LAST FOUR YEARS OF PUBLIC HIGH SCHOOL
IN CERTAIN MATHEMATICS COURSES
1889/90 THROUGH 1954/55

YEAR	PERCENTAGE OF PUPILS		
	Algebra	Geometry	Trigonometry
1889/90	45.4	21.3	1.9
1899/1900	56.3	27.4	1.9
1909/10	56.9	30.9	1.9
1914/15	48.8	26.5	1.5
1921/22	40.2	22.7	1.5
1927/28	35.2	19.8	1.3
1933/34	30.4	17.1	1.3
1948/49	26.8	12.8	2.0
1952/53	24.6	11.6	1.7
1954/55	24.8	11.4	2.6

Adapted from table on p. 16 of entry 109 in Bibliography A

Geometry continued to be a popular subject under the pressure of college entrance requirements, but the percentage of students taking it declined throughout the period. This continued beyond the 1920–45 interval; in 1954 the actual number of students taking geometry was less than it had been in 1934.

Since second-year algebra, solid geometry, and trigonometry were taken almost solely by persons planning to continue in technical or scientific college programs, the enrollments in these courses were small. In fact, as late as 1954 only 23 percent of the schools with a twelfth grade offered solid geometry and 26 percent offered trigonometry (p. 15). However, since these included the larger schools, only 11 percent of the high school students attended schools where these courses were not available (p. 3).

These facts account for a number of the recommendations of the Commission on Post-War Plans of the NCTM, such as a double-track program in grade 9 and a better mathematics program in small high schools by cycling of courses, use of extension courses, or teaching of two courses simultaneously (16, pp. 211–13).

Two important committees had reported earlier, in 1940. The Joint Commission to Study the Place of Mathematics in Secondary Education was finally constituted in 1935 when a committee of the NCTM joined one appointed by the MAA. A 1934 meeting of the MAA committee had been supported by the Commission on the Secondary School

Curriculum of the Progressive Education Association (PEA), which had formed its own mathematics committee in 1932. A. A. Bennett and M. Hartung were members of both committees. Both committees had some support from outside sources and published preliminary reports that were widely circulated and discussed before being revised into the final forms published in 1940.

The report of the Joint Commission, *The Place of Mathematics in Secondary Education* (50), was published as the Fifteenth Yearbook of the NCTM. This report recommended that mathematics be required of all students through grade 9 and that there should be a "two track" program in grade 9. It suggested two possible curricula for the college-bound track in grades 9-12. One proposal was that the standard algebra and geometry for the ninth and tenth grades be followed by a merger of algebra and trigonometry in the eleventh grade, with further work extended to include analytic geometry and some calculus in the twelfth.

The alternate proposal called for a more integrated program. It contained a general mathematics course in the ninth grade that was less technical than a pure algebra course, and included some review and maintainance of arithmetic, graphic representation, some geometry, numerical trigonometry, and logarithms. This course was thought to be suitable for all students, whether or not bound for college, but it was suggested that larger schools might offer an algebra course, too. The tenth-grade geometry course in this curriculum plan contained more algebraic and trigonometric applications than was normally the case. Intermediate algebra was proposed for the eleventh grade, and the twelfth was to include two of the following four courses: trigonometry, solid geometry, social-economic arithmetic, and college algebra. The Joint Commission emphasized the spiraling of instruction by including a grade-placement chart that displayed the attention given in each grade to each of what were called major subject fields, namely: number and computation, geometric form and space perception, graphic representation, logical thinking, relational thinking, and symbolic representation and thinking.

Several chapters in this report are particularly indicative of problems or trends of the time. Actually the introduction and first four chapters discussed the goals of mathematics in the secondary school. The chief stresses were on utility and on training in clear thinking with some attention to desirable work habits, attitudes, and mathematical appreciations. Although written positively, the approach gives the impression that mathematics was on the defensive.

Another significant aspect of this report was its recognition of educational problems and developments that went beyond a concern for the mathematics to be taught. For example, it displayed an acute awareness of individual differences among students and of emerging and varying curricular organizations. This is illustrated by its recommendations for a two- or even three-track program in the ninth grade and alternative curricula for college-bound students. There was an appendix outlining a program for slow pupils which supplemented chapter 7, "The Problems of Retardation and Acceleration." The report also discussed enrichment materials and programs, exhibits, films, and historical materials. These were thought of as largely motivational; the report stressed the importance of "dramatizing the role of mathematics in modern life" (p. 70), a popular concern of the time.

Another appendix, "The Transfer of Training" (pp. 217–22), recognized the importance for the teaching of mathematics of the then-current debates and research in psychology.

A chapter entitled "The Education of Teachers" included a program for training junior college teachers, as an earlier chapter had discussed a mathematics program for these colleges.

The second report to appear in 1940 was associated with one of the most powerful and controversial influences on the secondary school in the 1930s. This was the emergence of an educational philosophy-psychology that stressed the importance of a felt *need* as a motivation and as a condition for learning-readiness. As was noted in our earlier discussion of this new force in elementary education, it was interpreted in various ways. By some it was interpreted to mean that greater emphasis should be put on socioeconomic topics and applications and on vocational needs in mathematics courses. This emphasis was exhibited in such courses as consumer mathematics, business mathematics, and shop mathematics. This type of interpretation was enhanced by the concern with practical considerations engendered by the depression. A broader interpretation was presented by a committee of the Progressive Education Association in its 1940 report, *Mathematics in General Education*. It first stated (24, p. 9):

> Changes in mathematics instruction have not kept pace with the changing interests and concerns of the student body or with emerging conceptions of the proper aims and purposes of secondary education. The teacher has been made increasingly aware of the inappropriateness of traditional courses by the indifference of many students to the subject, or their outspoken dislike for it.

ABORTIVE REFORM—DEPRESSION AND WAR 57

This last statement may have referred to a poll by *Fortune* magazine which showed mathematics to be at once both the most disliked and the most liked high school subject (15, p. 231). The committee report continued. Excerpts follow (pp. 19-46):

> How, then, shall the educational needs of the learner be defined? In this Report they are taken to be the resultant of his present inclinations and quests, on the one hand, and the demands of desirable social living on the other. . . . Any field of study deserves a place in the curriculum only insofar as it has a unique role to play in meeting the educational needs of the students. . . .
>
> Adolescents encounter certain problems as they strive to meet their needs in the basic aspects of living. . . . [Mathematics makes its] special contribution whenever quantitative data and relationships of space and form are encountered. The highly effective special symbolism and methods of mathematics have been developed in order to treat just such aspects of experience. . . . The teacher of mathematics bears the responsibility of equipping students to solve problems with the aid of mathematical concepts and methods as they seek to meet their needs throughout life. In this process he also has the responsibility of throwing light on the nature of problem solving.

The report did not rely upon a mental-discipline psychology to argue that mathematics provides training in problem solving, however. This committee analyzed the problem-solving process and then urged that mathematical instruction stress problem-solving methods and skills at all levels of instruction. The report listed (1) formulation and solution, (2) data, (3) approximation, (4) function, (5) operation, (6) proof, and (7) symbolism as the concepts that both enter into problem solving and play a unifying role in mathematics. It asserted that these concepts were "of inestimable value to the teacher in helping the student to learn the nature of both mathematics and the problem-solving process, and to appreciate the values of a democratic society" (p. 59). Thus the concept of continuing themes in the mathematics curriculum, which had been initiated by the stress on functional thinking in the 1923 report of the National Committee on Mathematical Requirements, was extended and reemphasized in these two reports of 1940, even though the forces influencing mathematics education in this latter year were of a somewhat different nature. This concept of continuing themes and spiraled learning was picked up again, in 1959, in the Twenty-fourth Yearbook of the NCTM (200) and reinforced once again, in 1963, in the Cambridge Conference report, *Goals for School Mathematics* (11).

However, any claim that mathematics instruction teaches problem solving or logical reasoning reopens the psychological question of "transfer of training." This was recognized by the inclusion of an appendix on this topic in the report of the Joint Commission (50, pp. 217-22). Probably the most extensive classroom experiment related to the transfer of training was that by H. P. Fawcett published as the Thirteenth Yearbook of the NCTM in 1938 under the title *The Nature of Proof* (141). Fawcett reported a two-year experiment to lead students to develop their own system for Euclidean geometry while exploring the importance and nature of definitions and assumptions in logical thinking in general—including politics, advertising, and school problems. This was a most important study. Many teachers tried versions of it in their own geometry classes as geometry textbooks began to include units on these topics; and others, many of them Fawcett's students, tried similar approaches in algebra and other classes.

The notion of mathematics' playing an important role in general education and in the vocational and personal needs of students, the decline in enrollments, and the criticisms of the mathematical achievement of junior and senior high school students led the teachers to rally about the slogan of "functional competence" for graduates. Functional competence was gauged by a checklist of twenty-nine items compiled by the Commission on Post-War Plans. In essence, this competence was thought of as the mathematical literacy necessary for a person to be an effective citizen in a democracy; and the list was included as a preface to the *Guidance Pamphlet in Mathematics for High School Students* (18), first published in 1947 and widely circulated by the NCTM.

⇶⇶ 5. *The war and its effects*

World War II broke out in Europe in 1939. Although this country did not enter it until December 1941, a concern for our possible involvement developed quickly among mathematicians. The AMS and the MAA appointed a joint War Preparedness Committee in 1940. Marston Morse, its chairman, reported on its activities and those of its subcommittees at the February 1941 meeting of the NCTM (54, pp. 195-202). "On Education for Service" (36), William L. Hart's report of the Subcommittee on Education for Service which he chaired, was printed in 1941 in the *Mathematics Teacher*, the *American Mathematical Monthly*, and *School Science and Mathematics*.

Admiral Nimitz, who at that time was in command of the

Great Lakes Region Naval Training Program, spoke strongly of the mathematical weaknesses of navy volunteers and would-be officer candidates (388).

In December 1942 the U.S. Office of Education (USOE), in cooperation with the president of the NCTM, appointed a committee to report on what the schools could do in an emergency to prepare students for induction into the armed services. Its report, "Pre-Induction Courses in Mathematics," was printed in the *Mathematics Teacher* and widely circulated as a reprint (76).

Analyses of training manuals used by the armed forces provided evidence that men needed the kind of simple mathematical training that they should have received in the secondary schools. Recognizing the inadequacies revealed by these statements and studies, individuals and organizations requested specific remediation plans that could be implemented in the schools. The NCTM responded to these requests by publishing, in 1943, "Essential Mathematics for Minimum Army Needs" (34), the report of further study by another committee appointed by the USOE and the NCTM.

The war had a vitalizing effect on mathematics in the schools, as at all levels. Old uses of mathematics in quality control, aerodynamics, and electronics were publicized, and such new fields as operations analysis and communication theory were developed and perceived as having extensive peacetime uses also. The army and navy set up many specialized training programs, and acronyms for them abounded (ASTP, V-12, RONAG). Some, such as that for electronics technicians based in the former Stevens Hotel (now the Conrad Hilton) in Chicago, were at the technician level. Some, such as the Army Specialized Training Program, the Navy V-12 Program, and the intensive language training programs, were at the college level and were based at colleges. Many made extensive demands for advanced mathematical training and included intensive "refresher" and new training in mathematics, often at the graduate level. The Reserve Officer Naval Architecture Group, the army's Guided Missiles Program, and the air corps's meteorological training programs were of this type. The basic outcome was that to mathematics and science there returned a prestige that had not been theirs for several years.

However, thoughtful persons recognized the need not merely to avoid a return to the prewar status of mathematics but also to remedy prewar deficiencies in curriculum and instruction and to provide for anticipated shortages of men with the background and insight to apply both old and new mathematics to new situations. In response to this concern, the board of directors of the NCTM appointed the Commission on Post-War Plans on 25 February, 1944 (15, p. 226). This commission was to make recommendations concerning the mathematical education appropriate for *all* youth in the schools. The results of the commission's work were contained in four reports (15-18). Many of its major recommendations have already been cited. It asserted the need for (1) functional competence on the part of graduates, (2) offering revitalized sequential courses appropriate to changing needs, (3) a two-track system, (4) improved teaching in all areas—elementary, secondary, and junior college, (5) mathematics in general education, (6) mathematics in consumer education, and (7) the guidance of pupils, teachers, counselors, and administrators in the varied opportunities open to those interested in mathematics. There were also glimmerings of the massive reform to come in the next decades when, in its first report, the commission noted that the sequential courses were woefully out of date and that changes in pupils, teachers, and materials would be needed to remedy the situation (15, p. 232).

A somewhat different problem was anticipated by a report prepared in July 1945 by the War Policy Committee of the AMS and MAA. This report, "Universal Military Training in Peace Time" (82), anticipating the passage of legislation for a continuation of the draft, urged a liberal interpretation of "military training," deferments but no exemptions for persons continuing in technical study, proper placement within the armed services of persons with special training, and encouragement of continued education during military service.

The conclusion of the war brought not only the anticipated peacetime draft, but even more immediately a postwar enrollment boom due to the influx of veterans studying with government support under the "GI Bill." Many special and technical schools, some private, grew up under the pressures of this boom; but the greatest pressures were on the staffs and facilities of the colleges. As enrollment in mathematics grew even more rapidly than enrollment in college, the pressure to find effective college teachers of mathematics increased at the same time that unprecedented demands developed for mathematicians in non-teaching jobs and in consultation with government and industry.

⋙⋙ 6. *The junior college*

Almost concurrently with the development of the junior high school, a second organizational change had taken place in public school systems. The new unit was the junior college. It was often close to the high school physically and administratively, and it even, on occasion, shared the high school staff. The report of the Joint Commission to Study the Place of Mathematics in Secondary Education included a chapter entitled "Mathematics in the Junior College." This chapter dated the growth of such schools from 1902 (50, p. 149). By 1920 the junior college movement was well established in American education. Even though at first the junior college provided training equivalent to the first two years of a college or university, it moved rather rapidly into also offering courses of a terminal nature (142, pp. 19, 34, 296). The Joint Commission discussed this double role of the junior colleges briefly, and then, assuming that the preparatory function of the junior college with respect to mathematics was determined by the four-year colleges, the Joint Commission discussed junior college courses for semiprofessional groups and, especially, for general education. At all levels of instruction, general education was a popular educational term and concern at this time.

The junior college introduced additional and continuing articulation problems—with both the high school and the four-year college. This problem, also, was discussed by the NCTM's Commission on Post-War Plans in 1945 (16, pp. 213–14).

7. *The colleges, teacher training, and the mathematical community*

Secondary school and collegiate mathematics education have two interfaces: the first is the mathematics required for admission to college, and the second is the collegiate program for preparing secondary school teachers. Throughout this period, 1920–45, there was a trend to reduce college entrance requirements in mathematics. This was in part an outgrowth of the elective system in the colleges, as a result of which it became possible to select many undergraduate programs that included neither mathematics per se nor any courses, such as physics, for which mathematics was a prerequisite. This situation, which led to college admission for persons who had much less than a complete high school mathematics background, was recognized by the College Entrance Examination Board in 1935 when it established three new mathematics examinations, "alpha," "beta," and "gamma" (!), correlated with three levels of high school preparation and expected later use of mathematics. These new examinations were designed to test understanding and appreciation of mathematics as well as skills and information (311, pp. 61-62).

The National Committee on Mathematical Requirements seems to have been the first to make recommendations for the training of teachers in mathematics, although E. H. Moore had expressed concern for it in his presidential address of 1902. The Mathematical Association of America appointed a Commission on the Training and Utilization of Advanced Students of Mathematics in 1933. Its report in 1935 included "Report on the Training of Teachers of Mathematics" (77). The Joint Commission to Study the Place of Mathematics in Secondary Education prepared recommendations for the training of high school teachers, both of mathematics alone and of mathematics in addition to a second subject, and for the training of junior-college teachers of mathematics. Their recommendations for high school mathematics teachers included college algebra, analytic geometry, calculus, a critical examination of Euclidean geometry with brief introductions to other geometries, theory of equations, history of mathematics, advanced calculus, some modern algebra, and cognate work in a science. Their recommended professional preparation included a course in methods "given by a person who has had a good mathematical education and also experience in high school teaching" (50, p. 202).

The Cooperative Committee of the American Association for the Advancement of Science (AAAS) was founded in 1941. It was to have a considerable effect on teacher training, but its first report on this topic came out in 1946 and will therefore be treated in our next chapter.

The colleges themselves were on the verge of curricular changes. The general education movement, which began at Columbia University in 1919 (225, p. 455) and extended for some years—witness the "Harvard report" of 1945 (37)—was an attempt to regain some of the intellectual and spiritual heritage that had been lost to the elective principle. In mathematics, general courses for nonspecialists in mathematics began to appear in the late 1930s amid strong criticisms of educators who would no longer require mathematics for college graduation. At first many general courses were highly criticized, but such courses became more numerous and more acceptable after the publication of the report of the Harvard Committee, *General Education in a Free Society* (37).

The *American Mathematical Monthly* published in 1941 "Mathematics Instruction for Purposes of General Education" (52), the report of a committee of the AAAS. A variety of freshman courses were being developed and written about. Three broad categories of general education mathematics courses emerged. The first type stressed "functional competence" for all adults. This often consisted of a mixture of practice in arithmetic skills together with simple algebra and geometry or mensuration. A second type stressed "cultural" values, with chapters on many more-or-less modern topics such as set theory, transfinite numbers, non-Euclidean geometry, simple analytic geometry, and polynomial calculus. Both the first and second types stressed applications of mathematics. The third type of general education mathematics course stressed a modern view of the foundations of mathematics—displaying abstract structures and giving careful proofs.

A course called "Fundamental Mathematics" was developed by E. P. Northrop and other members of the college staff of the University of Chicago. The college accepted bright high school students who had finished the eleventh grade. This course foreshadowed later reforms. Not only was it "modern" in content, stressing structure, proof, logic, and careful definition, but it was taught to high-school-age students. This course was already under way when Northrop described it in 1944 at a meeting of the MAA (389). He was asked to speak about it again in 1947 (390).

8. *Psychological and educational theories*

It should be noted that this chapter began as the previous one ended, with discussions of the influence of educational and psychological theorists. The social-need goals of educational philosophers and the felt-need motivation of the psychologists affected both elementary and secondary school mathematics education in this period. The concept of a general education affected collegiate mathematics courses as well. Further discussion of these matters is reserved for the later parts of this book.

9. *Summary*

ISSUES

During this period old issues became more clearly defined, and some of their subsidiary questions came into view. These might be outlined as follows:

1. What are the goals of mathematical instruction?
    a) General education or preparatory or technical education?

b) "Functional competence" or utilitarian skills and concepts or problem solving and critical thinking processes?
  c) Knowledge or understanding or appreciation of the nature and beauty of mathematics?
2. Do we teach the same mathematics in the same way to all students?
3. How much mathematics should be required of all students—and in what grades should it be required?
4. What is the most effective organization of the curriculum?
  a) Compartmentalized or integrated?
  b) "Complete" teaching of each topic as introduced or a spiraled sequence?
  c) How do we provide for the articulation of the programs of the elementary school, junior high school, senior high school, junior college, and college?
5. What are the implications of psychological theory and research for mathematics instruction?
  a) Can readiness be taught or stimulated?
  b) Is drill or developing understanding the basic technique for teaching mathematics?
  c) What is meant by "meaning"? Is "meaning" an important prerequisite to learning mathematics?
6. Is there such a thing as transfer of training? If so, when does it occur and how can one teach to facilitate it?
7. How can one help students to select the mathematical studies essential to their own future interests and goals?

Forces

The following major forces were operating during this period:

1. Psychological research and changing theories about learning and the conditions required for it
  a) Stimulus-response psychology and Thorndike's theory of bonds, followed by a stress on child development, readiness, and need, and then by a "meaning" theory of learning
  b) Testing of intelligence and achievement, underscoring existence of individual differences and a low level of achievement
2. A high failure rate in the classical high school mathematics courses
3. A declining enrollment in the classical high school mathematics courses
4. The depression and its effect on school enrollment and student goals
5. The rapidly growing and changing school population

6. A questioning of the utility of mathematics to the general student, and of his interest in mathematics
7. A changing school organization, with the addition of the junior high school and the junior college
8. The reports of study committees appointed by professional groups
9. Changing college entrance and graduation requirements
10. The concept of continuing themes in the curriculum—themes that are taken up each year and advanced a little further in a spiral fashion
11. The wartime needs for mathematics
12. The war-stimulated expansion of both mathematics and its uses

Chronology

1920 National Council of Teachers of Mathematics founded
1921 NCTM takes over publication of the *Mathematics Teacher* from the Association of Teachers of Mathematics in the Middle States and Maryland
1923 Final report of the National Committee on Mathematical Requirements
1926 First Yearbook of the NCTM published
1932 Committee on the Function of Mathematics in General Education appointed
1933 Mathematical Association of America appoints forerunner of the Joint Commission
1935 College Entrance Examination Board announces three new mathematics examinations
1935 "On the Training of Teachers of Mathematics," report of a subcommittee of the Commission on the Training and Utilization of Advanced Students of Mathematics (appointed by the MAA in 1933)
1935 Joint Commission of the MAA and the NCTM to Study the Place of Mathematics in General Education appointed
1939 World War II breaks out
1940 Report of the Committee on the Function of Mathematics in General Education
1940 Report of the Joint Commission to Study the Place of Mathematics in Secondary Education
1940 War Preparedness Committee appointed by the AMS and the MAA
1941 "On Education for Service," report of a subcommittee of the War Preparedness Committee

1941 Letter by Admiral Nimitz published
1941 United States enters World War II
1941 Cooperative Committee on the Teaching of Science and Mathematics appointed by the AAAS
1941 "Mathematics Instruction for the Purposes of General Education," report of a committee of the AAAS
1942 "Pre-Induction Courses in Mathematics," report of a committee of the U.S. Office of Education
1943 "Essential Mathematics for Minimum Army Needs," a second report of the USOE committee
1944 NCTM appoints Commission on Post-War Plans, which publishes a first report
1945 Second and third reports of above NCTM commission
1945 World War II ends
1945 "Universal Military Training in Peace Time," report of a subcommittee of the War Policy Committee of the AMS and the MAA

CHAPTER SIX

Reform, "Revolution," Reaction: 1945–Present

1. *A buildup of pressures for reform: old forces*

It may be that this period is harder to describe and seems significantly different from earlier periods because we are so close to it. However, the forces critical of mathematics education and, indeed, of all education have never been so varied nor so strong at any other time. Likewise, the range of innovations actually attempted and the energies poured into educational reform in this period—especially 1952–62—have never before been even approximated.

In 1945 there was a backlog of criticisms and recommendations from the prewar and wartime studies and reports. The Commission on Post-War Plans of the NCTM urged the need for reconsideration of such prewar policies as postponement of formal instruction and reliance on incidental learning and a narrow interpretation of utility as a basis for curriculum design. Its call for reform in the curriculum and in the traditional courses showed some appreciation of the potential effect upon the schools of the changes that had taken place in the nature and role of mathematics. Its *Guidance Pamphlet* (18) foreshadowed the concern for the manpower problem which was soon to become general. The NCTM also recognized the continuation of concern for concreteness and utility in teaching through its yearbooks and journals. Its Seventeenth, Eighteenth, and Nineteenth yearbooks, published in 1942, 1945, and 1947, dealt with applications of mathematics, multisensory aids, and the history and classroom use of surveying instruments. The *Mathematics Teacher* began monthly departments on teaching aids and applications of mathematics in 1948.

The declining enrollment and negative attitudes of the prewar years were reflected in the Symposium on College Entrance Requirements held at the January 1948 meeting of the MAA. A. J. Kempner (363) outlined the problem of colleges that were abandoning all entrance requirements while at the same time an increasing number of courses and curricula within the college were setting mathematical prerequisites. C. N. Shuster (413), president of the NCTM, followed Kempner with a call for reform in high school mathematics. He called for decompartmentalization, elimination of deadwood, and introduction of newer, more interesting, and more practical material. He stressed, as had Raleigh Schorling (409) and others, that a committee of experts with adequate financing would be necessary to effect the needed changes.

Other powerful forces that had been building up over the war years were to provide the impetus and financing for such committees—although the motion finally generated in mathematics education was not in precisely the direction called for. These additional forces were a generally recognized manpower problem, a related concern for superior students, a general attack on the professional education establishment, a changed prestige for mathematics and science, and a changed view of both mathematics and its utility.

⇶⇶ 2. *New forces*

One of the first activities of the newly founded Cooperative Committee on the Teaching of Science and Mathematics of the AAAS was to assist in the preparation of volume 4 of the so-called Steelman report (80). John R. Steelman was chairman of a committee on manpower appointed by and reporting to the president of the United States. Volume 4, *Manpower for Research*, included data on mathematical manpower needs, chiefly in relation to research and to the other sciences. Such needs can be met only by students who have come from our secondary school programs.

The report pointed out the need for redirection of earlier guidance programs. Throughout the 1940s the major efforts of mathematics educators had been directed toward ensuring functional competence for high school graduates. Clearly the definition of functional competence in the guidance pamphlet was concerned almost entirely with the mathematical training of all youth for life in a democratic society (18). World War II made manifest the fact that, for some, this level of competence was not sufficient to meet the demands of a postwar, scientifically oriented society. The demand for people highly trained in mathematics was present in many areas: government (374), engineering, skilled trades, retail business, and all facets of industry. For example, Orth cited the need in 1952 for 60,000 engineers to fill existing jobs, with only enough trained personnel entering the labor market to fill approximately 20 percent of the positions (396, p. 417); and the entire January 1953 issue of the *Mathematics Teacher* was devoted to the mathematical needs of business and industry.

Certainly the manpower shortage was one stimulus to provide adequate mathematical training in the schools. However, the type of mathematical training necessary to cope with the newer applications was not being provided in the schools. Beberman (91) cited the following deficiencies in the mathematical preparation of freshmen entering the College of Engineering at the University of Illinois: (1) poor computational facility, (2) poor conceptual background, (3) ignorance of proof and structure except in geometry, and (4) ignorance of contemporary applications in natural science, social science, and technology. In other words, the mathematics curriculum was extraordinarily out of date. It did not reflect the predominant view concerning the nature and role of mathematics. In this more modern view mathematics was not considered a mere tool subject. Mathematics was interesting in and of itself and not merely because it could be used to solve a problem in the physical world; that is, the study of mathematics was, or could be, intrinsically motivated.

Structure, proof, generalization, and *abstraction* were seen as the essence of modern mathematics. Emphasizing these ideas required *precision* and *care* in all mathematical statements. In teaching mathematics, then, these four essentials should be clearly evident to the learner because of their importance, but also for another reason. To make mathematics applicable the problem solver must perceive the structures inherent in both the application and in the mathematics to be used. From this viewpoint the first essential in applying mathematics is the perception of a mathematical structure or system that has abstract properties corresponding to the physical system's properties. Thus abstraction and application are not antithetical, but essential companions. Only if he understands the structures of mathematics and of the application can the user of mathematics choose a mathematical model whose structure most nearly satisfies the requirements of the problem situation. This conception implies that students well prepared in mathematical theory should be able to apply mathematics to completely novel situations with more facility than persons trained otherwise. This conviction was not a mere rebirth of a belief in mental discipline but a pragmatic view of transfer of training which had been born out of the greatly accelerated expansion in both mathematics and its applications. During the war both mathematics and its uses had expanded at a tremendous rate. Many persons had been forced to do and think things that they had never been specifically taught. A backward look suggested that this must also be the case for the future.

This unprecedented growth in mathematics can be partially documented for a younger person or a nonmathematician by looking at *Mathematical Reviews*, an international abstracting journal. It was founded in 1940, and it contained 334 pages in 1945, 870 pages in 1950, 1,338 pages in 1955, 1,652 pages in 1960, and 2,664 pages in 1965. In fact, the development of new mathematics had been so rapid that "the university mathematician has been forced to continue his in-service training throughout his entire career" (210, p. 2).

The rapid growth of new applications of mathematics can be illustrated in many ways. For example, the theory of games dates from 1944 with the work of John von Neumann and Oskar Morgenstern in *The Theory of Games and Economic Behavior*. Other new applications beginning during the war or shortly thereafter included linear programming, operations research, and quality control. Moreover, mathematics became more important in psychology and sociology as statistical techniques and mathematical models were more widely employed.

The increasing prestige of mathematics and science stemmed from many sources, peacetime as well as war-related. However, atomic energy, guided missiles, and radar were much in the popular view. It was vaguely appreciated that they were born out of mathematics and were developed and controlled through mathematical theory and computation. The solution of complicated problems in these areas was not merely made easier but was, in fact, made possible by automatic digital computers (210, p. 4). All of these forces reinforced two general feelings: (1) that more advanced training should be provided for more students at an earlier time and (2) that the complexity of the mathematical applications and the rapidity with which they were being developed and changed signified that advanced training should be carried out with attention to meaning and understanding. Thus teaching for meaning and understanding, which had started as an issue in the thirties, had become a goal of mathematics instruction in the sixth and seventh decades of the century.

Before 1950 preoccupation with a narrow interpretation of the democratic ideal had stifled the development of creative ways of providing for superior students (166, p. 21). As America became more scientifically and technologically oriented, concern grew for providing more substantial programs for them (349; 355; 400). The two most commonly suggested procedures were *enrichment* and *acceleration*.

Acceleration of superior students was given a lift when the report of a joint study of high school–college articulation by three eastern universities and three preparatory schools appeared in 1952 (35). The subcommittee on mathematics made recommendations for saving time in the secondary school program: (1) abandon systematic, deductive solid geometry and (2) decrease time spent on determinants, logarithmic solution of triangles, and the geometry of the circle. Following these recommendations, it was argued, would allow more time to teach superior students some analytic geometry and calculus or, if more valuable to the student, probability and statistics.

Added impetus was given to the acceleration movement when the report of the School and College Study of Admission with Advanced Standing was published in 1954 (6). The agitation for acceleration and advanced collegiate standing culminated in 1955 when the Committee on Advanced Placement of the CEEB assumed responsibility for administering advanced standing programs that included an advanced standing syllabus and examination in analytic geometry and calculus. The result was the Advanced Placement Program of the CEEB, which is now a well-established part of many high school programs.

Another factor that contributed to the reform movement was the sharp criticism of secondary education as a whole by several influential persons from the academic community, such as Arthur E. Bestor. In 1952 he published an article in the *Scientific Monthly* (301) in which he bitterly attacked schools, state departments of public instruction, and professors of education. In essence, his argument was that achievement of intellectual pursuits in school was no longer of high priority. Rather, social goals were predominant. Bestor blamed professional educators for eliminating "the established disciplines of science and scholarship" and claimed that professors of education were fostering antiintellectualism. This type of criticism was rather widely publicized, especially in professional circles. For example, Stewart Cairns expounded his colleague's views and applied them to mathematics in a later article in the same journal (322). These protests were symptomatic of the frustrations of many college teachers and perhaps suggested to some content specialists that they should become more concerned with public school education.

⇛⇛ 3. *The prelude to reform*

The committee reports and symposia noted in the previous section all helped to set the stage for experimentation and the development of new course content. There were, moreover, several specific events that directly preceded the outburst of new programs. It is difficult to date some of these because their roots lie in the discussions, preliminary plans, and proposals that preceded the granting of funds, the appointing of committees, and the writing of materials. For example, a committee with members from the Engineering and Education schools and the department of mathematics at the University of Illinois prepared a pamphlet, *Mathematical Needs of Prospective Students in the College of Engineering of the University of Illinois*, which was published in 1951. This was partly an extension of an earlier program for so accrediting high school courses and teachers that their students would not be required to take preparatory courses in trigonometry and algebra after arriving at college. Out of the questions raised during this collaboration came the impetus for the appointment in December 1951, by the University of Illinois colleges of Education, Engineering, and Liberal Arts and Sciences, of the University of Illinois Committee on School Mathematics (UICSM), "to investigate problems concerning the content and teaching of high school mathematics in grades 9–12" (60, p. 57). The Carnegie Foundation of New York provided financial support, and additional monies were later obtained from the NSF and the USOE.

UICSM was the first large-scale project begun to prepare materials for secondary school mathematics which expressed the modern view and role of mathematics. From the beginning UICSM was guided by several tenets (166, p. 27): (1) A *consistent* presentation of high school mathematics can be devised. (2) Students *are* interested in ideas. (3) *Manipulative* tasks should be used mainly to allow insight into basic concepts. (4) The *language* should be as unambiguous as possible. (5) The organization of materials should provide for student *discovery* of many generalizations. (6) The student must *understand* his mathematics. (91, p. 4.)

UICSM produced, tested, and revised units for grades 9–12. It conducted institutes to train teachers in the use of the materials and, in fact, would not let the units be used without adequate previous teacher preparation. It obtained a set of cooperating schools in which the materials were used. The precedents set by UICSM became a pattern for later projects.

In 1954 the Educational Testing Service (ETS) undertook a status study of mathematics education problems—especially those related to the college preparatory program. Although the results of this study were not published until 1956, they were available earlier to the CEEB. These results led the CEEB to appoint the Commission on Mathematics in 1955.

The CEEB is always faced with a dilemma. Its examinations do influence high school programs. If the examinations are radically changed, the board is accused of trying to dictate curricula from without the school. If the examinations are not changed, the board is accused of being a stultifying influence, holding back progress. The establishment of the commission was an overt attempt on the part of the board to influence the secondary school curriculum in mathematics. However, rather than exert the pressure directly, it chose to select a commission of professionals which was representative of the three groups most immediately concerned with mathematics in the schools: collegiate mathematicians, high school teachers, and teachers of teachers of mathematics.

The purpose of the Commission on Mathematics was "to review the existing secondary school mathematics curriculum, and to make recommendations for its modernization, modification, and improvement." Although the commission acknowledged the school's role in serving all students, its main concern was with the "college-capable" students, and its program was designed for such students (12).

The major recommendations of the commission emphasized the modern nature and role of mathematics and were summarized in a nine-point program. This program emphasized a balanced preparation in concepts and skills, deductive reasoning throughout high school, the display and use of mathematical structure, correlation of equalities and inequalities, stressing of unifying ideas in mathematics such as set and function, and special suggestions for reorganizing geometry, trigonometry, and twelfth-year mathematics. In order to clarify the recommendations, the commission prepared a supplementary volume, *Appendices*, "to provide information, instruction, and enrichment that will assist teachers in preparing themselves to translate the recommendations of the *Report* into action, as classroom materials become available" (13).

The *Report of the Commission on Mathematics* was not formally published until 1959, but it had been widely circulated and discussed in a preliminary form. The revised version was available to the School Mathematics Study Group (SMSG) when it began operation in 1958. SMSG largely followed the commission's recommendations as it prepared new course-content material.

To tell the story of SMSG, it is necessary to go back in history a little and to discuss the National Science Foundation. Assuredly UICSM could have done little without the support of the Carnegie Foundation, the NSF, and the USOE, and it is unlikely that SMSG would ever have been undertaken without NSF support. Whereas in the twenties and thirties financial support was lacking, when reform was imminent in the fifties, money was available. The availability of support must be included as a major force leading to reform.

The NSF was established in 1950 by an act of Congress as an independent agency of the executive office of the president and given a small appropriation ($225,000). The expressed purpose of NSF was to develop a national policy for the promotion of basic research and education in the sciences (175, p. 16).

Until 1957, NSF's major contribution to elementary and secondary education was support of summer institutes in mathematics and science. The first mathematics institute was designed to upgrade and modernize well-trained instructors in liberal arts colleges who had been somewhat outside the mainstream of recent developments. It was held at the University of Colorado in the summer of 1953. Since then NSF has supported many in-service, summer, and academic-year institutes for secondary school and elementary school teachers. In 1957 NSF broke its pattern of support by granting $245,000 to the Physical Science Study Committee (PSSC) for the purpose of planning and writing teaching materials for high school physics. PSSC, under Jerrold R. Zacharias of the Massachusetts Institute of Technology, was successful not only in writing materials but also in producing PSSC teachers, the teachers being trained in summer institutes sponsored by NSF.

The PSSC and UICSM patterns for improving high school courses were similar, even though PSSC had a broader base because it used specialists from other institutions as consultants more extensively than did UICSM. Each in its way verified that the way to improve science education was "to create better teaching materials for science courses" (175, p. 86).

SMSG grew out of two conferences of mathematicians sponsored by NSF. The first, the Chicago Conference on Research Potential and

Training, convened on 21 February 1958. The major recommendation of that conference was that the president of the AMS appoint a committee whose charge it would be to solve the problem of the existing state of the school mathematics curriculum. A week later the Mathematics Meeting of the NSF convened in Cambridge on the campus of the Massachusetts Institute of Technology. It supported the prior recommendation to the AMS and, in the pattern of PSSC, recommended that the AMS-appointed committee (1) hold a four- or five-week writing session in the summer to prepare a detailed syllabus for school mathematics and (2) arrange for the preparation and publication of mathematical monographs for the use of students in schools. After conferences with Harold Fawcett, president of the NCTM, and G. Baley Price, president of the MAA, AMS president Richard Brauer on 3 April 1958 appointed a committee of eight mathematicians to implement the recommendations of the two conferences (282).

Edward G. Begle of Yale University accepted the responsibility of directing the work of the organization that was called the School Mathematics Study Group. The initial support of SMSG came from NSF on 7 May 1958, in the amount of $100,000. It was decided by the Committee of Eight that an advisory committee would aid Begle in his direction of SMSG and that each activity in which SMSG engaged would be under the supervision of a panel. The first advisory committee consisted of twenty-six members drawn from all areas of mathematics education: college, high school, experimental programs, the NCTM, and the Commission on Mathematics. This composition reflected the aim to make SMSG aware of the concerns of every professional segment interested in school mathematics.

The first major problem facing Begle and SMSG was the summer writing session to be begun 23 June 1958, at Yale University. Forty-five persons agreed to participate: twenty-one from colleges, twenty-one from secondary schools, and three from other sources. As it turned out, the summer writing session at Yale was successful. It produced outlines in varying degrees of completeness for grades 9–12, and it wrote thirteen units for grades 7 and 8 which were tried out the following year (1958/59). In addition, the writing session showed that mathematicians and secondary school teachers and supervisors could work successfully together. This was a success and a strength of SMSG (282, pp. 17–43). Since the history of SMSG has been well covered by William Wooton in *SMSG, The Making of a Curriculum* (282), and its texts are available in many places, we shall merely note that ultimately it produced sample textbooks for grades K–12, teacher's manuals and surveys, enrichment materials, and tested programmed materials; and, in 1962, it initiated a National Longitudinal Study of Mathematical Abilities.

This listing is by no means complete, but it serves to indicate the far-reaching and diversified interests of SMSG. Even though SMSG faced criticism of its work from many sectors (282, pp. 135–44), it was instrumental in continuing the revolution in mathematics education. Its work served as a model for authors of commercial publishing houses to build and improve upon.

UICSM, the Commission on Mathematics, and SMSG were only a few of the many projects developing improved materials for school mathematics. Ball State Teachers College (Indiana) in 1955 began a course-content-development project in geometry, headed by Charles F. Brumfiel, with NSF support. In September 1957 the University of Maryland Mathematics Project (UMMaP) undertook the task of preparing materials for grades 7 and 8, under the direction of John R. Mayor. This project was supported originally by the Carnegie Foundation and later by NSF. Projects proliferated so rapidly that a pamphlet published in 1960 to summarize them listed six projects for grades K–6, twelve projects under the heading of "Secondary Mathematics," two under "College Mathematics," eight under "School Mathematics (K–College)," and two under "Teacher Training" (250).

A detailed listing of these does not seem appropriate here, but some analysis of the later projects can be found in two NCTM publications, *The Revolution in Mathematics* (64) and *An Analysis of New Mathematics Programs* (60).

4. *The elementary school*

During the period 1945–68, two issues were particularly prominent: *What mathematics should be taught in the elementary school?* and the corollary question, *How should mathematics be taught in the elementary school?* By 1955, partly as a result of the unrest growing out of World War II, the lay public throughout the country had been told in magazine articles and in books that the academic substance of the school curriculum was grossly inadequate. It was said that the content not only of mathematics but of other subjects as well had for too long been determined by professional educators with little or no impact from the scholars of the various disciplines. Aroused both by these reports in the mass media and by personal concern, academicians turned their attention to the school curriculum.

Mathematicians were among the first scholars from the various disciplines to give critical attention as well as time and energy to the improvement of elementary school programs. But where to begin? Across the land efforts in at least three directions were in evidence. Sometimes in consort with professional educators and sometimes without their cooperative support, some mathematicians began to work to improve teachers' understandings of mathematics through single speeches or through extended in-service education programs. The NSF supported summer institutes as well as in-service institutes, especially for elementary school mathematics supervisors. Other mathematicians focused their attention more directly on the task of improving the content of the elementary school program through the preparation and testing of new text materials. Still others went directly to children in the classroom, sometimes because of dissatisfaction with the mathematics education their own children were getting. Out of this general and, apparently, spontaneous activity came many new projects.

In 1958 UICSM spawned the University of Illinois Arithmetic Project under David A. Page, which later moved to Cambridge (398). The Greater Cleveland Mathematics Program under B. H. Gundlach began in 1959 with a teacher-training program for first-grade teachers. Experimental classroom materials were introduced in January 1960 (294). The outcome of an SMSG conference on elementary school mathematics in February 1959 was the Panel on Elementary School Mathematics that met in January 1960 and began planning new materials for grades 4, 5, and 6 (427). These materials later expanded into a K–6 program.

Individual mathematicians who had earlier ventured into elementary school classrooms included Newton S. Hawley and Patrick Suppes in Palo Alto, California; Robert B. Davis of Syracuse, New York; and W. W. Sawyer of Middletown, Connecticut, as well as Page. The first two began in 1958 with an experiment that involved teaching geometrical notions and constructions to first-grade students (351). Davis began by using supplementary materials of an algebraic character with fourth graders (328).

Commercial publishers, public school personnel, and teacher educators assumed much of the burden of continuing the content-improvement efforts others had gotten under way. PTA groups discussed "modern math," and books on "modern math" for parents appeared. While this went on some mathematicians turned to the second question, *How should mathematics be taught?* They were intrigued with this question—first, because many were disappointed that changes in content had not resulted in the direct increase in understanding and appreciation of mathematics which had been anticipated; and, second, because psychologists and mathematicians were beginning a long-delayed dialogue. Although at times it seemed difficult for them to communicate with each other, each realized the other was saying something of importance which should be heard.

By the end of the sixties it was apparent that the forces exerted by society through the mass media and by the mathematics community had made a substantial impact on the content of the elementary school mathematics program. Much work was yet to be done. The *Cambridge Report* (10) suggested that extensive additions to mathematical content were still needed, and there was general recognition that to change the content of textbooks and to talk about the need for reform did not necessarily mean that the mathematics content and instruction met by children in classrooms was substantially improved.

The revolution moved on as mathematicians increasingly talked about the need for integration among subject areas and especially between mathematics and science. They were experimenting with discovery approaches to learning and with instruction. Dienes (330), Page, and others advocated the use of multisensory materials. In these matters they sounded much like the progressives of an earlier era, in which mathematics was to be made a part of the child's world of experience. However, another aspect of the "revolution" appeared as a major reversal of the trend toward postponement. Not only was a formal mathematics program developed for the early years, but such topics as negative numbers and intuitive geometry were being brought down from the secondary school. A stress on the structure of arithmetic provided some increase in abstraction and distraction from social applications. These trends were further stimulated by a general and spreading concern among mathematics educators for spiraling, continuity, and articulation in grades K–12 such as was stressed in the Twenty-fourth Yearbook of the NCTM (200).

5. *The secondary school*

As we have seen in earlier sections, the secondary schools in this period, 1945–68, were subjected to pressures to teach more advanced topics and courses (analytic geometry and calculus); to teach entirely new courses (modern algebra and matrices, probability and statistics); to combine plane and solid geometry, second-year algebra and trigonometry; to enrich instruction with clubs, contests, and readings.

Teachers more or less frantically went to conferences, workshops, and institutes. They participated in experimental teaching of new materials. Many of them found a new excitement as well as hard work in new learning and new teaching. The question became: What will substitute for the stimulus of experimentation and change when the "revolution" of the time has taken place? The answer was, in part, that there is no end to change. The schools must not assume that once having "modernized," they can settle back into their former lethargic state. SMSG continued to experiment with courses woven around or stressing the applications of mathematics—and with further integration of course material. A new group, the Cambridge Conference, brought together concerned persons, largely pure mathematicians, who outlined greatly accelerated programs as goals for the distant future (3). Their proposals called for a high school program for able students that would include the equivalent of the first two years or more of college work. To do this they had to meet again, to plan the extension of many high school topics down into the elementary grades (10). They felt that this would be possible through a spiraling of the curriculum and a stress on discovery teaching; their assumption was that more meaningful teaching and intrinsic motivation and practice would reduce the time needed for pure drill.

However, it was still true that the greatest concern and the greatest changes had been in the programs for the average and superior college-bound students. Of course the elementary and junior high school programs were intended for all students, but even here less consideration had been given to the slower students. Beyond the ninth grade there had not even been any general discussion of programs for non-college-bound students.

6. *Teacher education, certification, and the conversion to new programs*

There was general agreement on the basic and all-pervading importance of the teacher at all times, whether the curriculum is new or traditional. The problem of improving the quality of teachers had two aspects, their preservice and their in-service education. The MAA, with support from the NSF, sponsored a Symposium on Teacher Education in Mathematics at the University of Wisconsin in August 1952. This was chiefly aimed at defining an ideal program for the preservice training of high school teachers.

Probably the most influential report on this topic came later. It was *Recommendations for the Training of Teachers of Mathematics* (26), by the Panel on Teacher Training of the Committee on the Undergraduate Program in Mathematics (CUPM) of the MAA, which appeared in 1961 and was revised in 1966.

In the meantime, other groups had become concerned with the problem, not only in mathematics but in all fields of science. Studies of teacher certification were undertaken, and recommendations for improved teacher training were prepared by the AAAS Cooperative Committee on the Teaching of Science and Mathematics (4) and as part of a Carnegie Foundation–financed study sponsored by the National Association of State Directors of Teacher Education and Certification (NASDTEC) and the AAAS (55).

The problem of in-service training for teachers who were to use the new curricular materials was even more immediate. The first of the course-content projects, UICSM, laid heavy stress not merely on teacher training, but on specific training of teachers to use their materials.

SMSG prepared extensive teacher's guides to go with each of its texts. In addition, teacher institutes were widely supported and were often designed to deal directly with new classroom materials. The NSF's fine support of institutes for teachers has been noted earlier. However, it should be mentioned that general institutes for mathematics teachers had been held at Duke University in the summers of 1941–52 under the directorship of Professor W. W. Rankin. Several other universities (University of California at Los Angeles, Louisiana State University, University of Michigan) had sponsored summer programs of this type before the advent of the NSF. The New England Association of Teachers of Mathematics had also operated summer conferences for its members.

Through the efforts of the Conference Board of the Mathematical Sciences, television courses in modern algebra and in probability and statistics for teachers were broadcast nationally in 1960 on "Continental Classroom."

The problem of introducing new mathematical programs into the schools also included a need to persuade principals, supervisors, superintendents, school boards, and parents of both the need and the value of "new mathematics." Several major steps in this direction were taken by the NCTM. With support from the NSF and under the direction of Frank B. Allen, it sponsored eight Regional Orientation Conferences in Mathematics for key educators in different sections of the country.

The booklet *The Revolution in School Mathematics* (64) presents the case which was the subject of these conferences. Later the NCTM also prepared a film for showing to such audiences as school boards and PTAs.

7. Collegiate mathematics

Changes somewhat similar to those in the secondary schools, but perhaps not so revolutionary, were taking place at all levels of the college program.

Partly as a result of wartime applications of mathematics in operations research, a committee of the Social Science Research Council studied the new uses of mathematics in the social sciences, issued a report (418) describing them, and in 1953 and 1954 sponsored summer institutes in mathematics for graduate students and postdoctoral faculty members in the social sciences.

The MAA set up its Committee on the Undergraduate Program (CUP) in 1953. With money from the NSF it prepared *Universal Mathematics*, a college textbook for a modern freshman mathematics course. This committee was later (1959) reorganized as CUPM, already referred to, and it has continued to develop course specifications for many types of undergraduate mathematics programs.

Mathematics enrollments in college during these years increased much more rapidly than college enrollments as a whole. Both the level and the mathematical quality of the beginning undergraduate courses rose during this period. This tends to show that the reforms in the secondary school were having a beneficial effect on the guidance, motivation, and learning of high school students.

8. Reaction

By 1962 the revolution in school mathematics was in full swing. This is most graphically documented by the status of SMSG textbooks, which are the major examples of learning materials reflecting reform. In 1962 the textbooks for the sequential course covering grades 7–12 were available. Each had gone through a preliminary edition, been used in cooperating schools, and been revised using the evaluations of teachers. Moreover, SMSG was producing text materials for the elementary school, versions of their materials for grades 7–9 that had been modified for average students, an alternate geometry book using coordinates, and various other supplemental and teacher education materials.

Most mathematicians, teachers, and mathematics educators were positively disposed towards the work of SMSG and the basic tenets of the reform movement. However, the reform was not without its critics, and Morris Kline of New York University stood "as the spokesman for hosts of doubters—superintendents, parents and others" (329, p. 297). Although he had published criticisms as early as 1958 (365), substantial notice began with the appearance of his October 1961 article in the *New York University Alumni News* (366).

This article criticized many aspects of the reform in mathematics but concentrated on the SMSG program. It contended that much of algebra, geometry, and trigonometry were replaced by set theory, symbolic logic, matrices, and Boolean algebra; that all the material was arranged in a formal structure; that recommendations were made casually; that the work was done helter-skelter; and that the reformers asserted they had the correct curriculum.

In the judgment of the writer of that article, the problem of mathematics education was not that the curriculum was outmoded, but rather that the presentation of materials was very bad—that there was little motivation, little intuitive development before generalization, no inclusion of applications, and little active participation on the part of the student in creating the material he was to learn. To Kline the remedy was clear (366, p. 3):

> It is to build a better corps of teachers. . . . These teachers must not only be better informed in mathematics, but they must also acquire a far better idea of why mathematics is important, why particular topics in mathematics are taken up, and what values mathematics offers to our civilization and culture. The primary value of mathematics . . . is that it is the language and essential instrument of science.

In 1962 a group of mathematicians published a lengthy list of objections to the reform movement in mathematics (394). E. G. Begle published an evaluation of these criticisms in the same issue of the *Mathematics Teacher* (297). Since then the two reports of the Cambridge Conference, also largely composed of mathematicians, have suggested further extensions of the reform program.

On another front some educators were critical of the reform movement, but for different reasons. In one case, in a personal letter distributed to school administrators, Paul Elicker, executive secretary emeritus of the National Association of Secondary School Principals, criticized SMSG on the grounds that it was developing a national curriculum and was thus usurping the responsibility of state and local agencies. His tactics called for a write-in campaign to congressmen, who would then cut off SMSG's financial support (140).

The examples of Kline and Elicker demonstrate that, however general the criticism of education and however unanimous the demand for change, there is never agreement, let alone proof, that any one direction or method is the proper one. In contrast, there is more agreement on underlying philosophies than appears at a first reading of criticisms. No group has advocated a national curriculum. All writers believe in progress from concrete to abstract, from particular to general. No group wants sloppy and imprecise proofs as an end product, but no group denies the role of intuition in the processes both of understanding old mathematics and of inventing new mathematics. The questions are when, how, and at what pace does one proceed to encourage and develop both intuition and rigor, concrete real-world models and their ultimate abstractions and generalizations?

9. *Psychological and educational theories*

This period, beginning in 1945, has been remarkable for a new quality of interest in the psychological processes of learning mathematics. The Swiss developmental psychologist Jean Piaget was publishing the results of his research on the mental development of young children as early as 1921 (143, p. 454). However, two of his major books dealing with mathematical concepts, *La Représentation de l'Espace Chez l'Enfant* and *La Géométrie Spontanée de l'Enfant*, were not published until 1948, and English translations did not appear until 1956 and 1960 (157, p. v). A book entitled *The Child's Conception of Number* appeared in 1952 (208), and *The Growth of Logical Thinking from Childhood to Adolescence* was published in 1958 (160). Although Piaget's views of the various stages in the development of mathematical concepts, of "conservation" and "reversability," and of the ages at which children are ready for them, have been questioned, they have also significantly influenced the early approaches to numerical, geometrical, and logical ideas in American texts.

From the outset, the University of Maryland Mathematics Project incorporated psychologists and concern for both psychological principles and evaluation in their plans. One of their consultants was Robert M. Gagné, then at Princeton. Although his major concern is the broad area of learning theory, he has published a number of articles dealing with the teaching of mathematical concepts (145, pp. 300, 301). His theory, that knowledge is organized psychologically in hierarchies of principles (145, pp. 142–56) and that subordinate concepts and principles must be learned before principles of higher order can be learned, has affected texts and research in mathematics education.

Gagné's theory also stresses the role of instruction in learning. His two highest forms of learning, principle learning and problem solving, differ essentially "only in the nature and amount of guidance provided by verbal instructions" (145, p. 164). Problem solving requires the learner to discover a principle without specific verbal instruction, whereas principle learning makes use of verbal aid. Gagné warns that "problem solving must be based on knowledge and recall of the principles that are combined in the achievement of the solution" and that without these there is little chance of successful solution (145, p. 165). These notions imply that his theory of transfer of training is quite specific.

Another psychologist who has publicly discussed instructional problems is Jerome Bruner. It is unfair to Bruner, who has worked broadly in the field of learning psychology and concept formation, to associate him quickly with only a few groups or to categorize him by catch phrases. However—he has worked with Piaget, was a member of the steering committee of the 1963 Cambridge Conference, and is known for both his support of "discovery" teaching and his dictum, "The foundations of any subject may be taught to anybody . . . at any age in some form" (112, p. 2).

In addition to listing general theorems in his "Theorems for a Theory of Instruction" (115, pp. 196–211), Bruner often uses mathematical illustrations in his more general works (113, pp. 55–72), and he has written directly on the learning of mathematics (114, pp. 50–59).

In his book *The Process of Education* he stresses the importance of structure in all teaching and associates it with the changing theories of transfer of training. As the psychologists' concept of the learning process shifted "from an emphasis upon the production of general understanding to an emphasis on the acquisition of special skills," studies of transfer of training shifted from studies on the transfer of formal discipline and the training of "faculties" to the transfer of identical elements or specific skills. Bruner concluded that "while the original theory of formal discipline was poorly stated . . . it is indeed a fact that massive general transfer can be achieved by appropriate learning, even to the degree that learning properly under optimum conditions leads one to 'learn how to learn' " (112, pp. 5-6).

Bruner stresses four themes in addition to *structure*. These are *understanding*, *readiness* for learning (which, however, he believes calls for earlier and spiraled teaching rather than for postponement), the nature of *intuition* ("the intellectual technique of arriving at plausible but tentative formulations"), and the *desire to learn*, including ways of stimulating this desire. He believes that "interest in the material to be learned is the best stimulus to learning rather than such external goals as grades or competitive advantage" (112, pp. 11-14).

Bruner believes in discovery teaching but points out that it would be too time-consuming for presenting all of what a student must cover in mathematics.

A psychologist who disagrees somewhat with the emphasis on discovery teaching is David Ausubel, of the University of Illinois. He believes it has limited applicability. In his articles discussing discovery teaching he suggests that "in the early, unsophisticated stages of learning an abstract subject matter, particularly prior to adolescence, the discovery method is invaluable" (290, p. 22), that "the discovery method also has obvious uses in teaching problem solving techniques [but that except in these instances] subject matter content can be both transmitted and illustrated much more efficiently by means of exposition, demonstration, and schematic models" (290, p. 24). For mathematics learning, Ausubel suggests that verbal exposition supplemented by appropriate problem-solving experience is the most meaningful and efficient method to use in teaching secondary-school and college students (292, p. 296).

A pair of related modern developments are mathematical theories of learning which are not necessarily or directly tied into the teaching of mathematics, and theories of the learning of mathematics. Patrick Suppes and his colleagues at Stanford University have been associated with both of these (248; 260). In addition to developing theories, this group has been developing, and using with children, related texts, equipment, and processes.

Much more experimentation is needed. Further, even when valid conclusions can be drawn from experimentation, the translation of such conclusions into school and classroom procedures will still remain a difficult task. However, we may be on the way toward developing more insights into the instructional process than we have ever had before.

10. Summary

Issues

The issues in mathematics education during this period are more nearly new, or at least have a newer emphasis, than those of any other period of our history. This is especially true of the first two issues of our list:

1. What incentives and activities of the future can continue to impart to schools and teachers the excitement and feeling of aliveness in teaching that came to them with the materials, experimentation, and debate of the "revolution"?
2. For what students, if any, is it appropriate to stress the concern for *structure, generalization,* and *abstraction* which characterizes today's advanced mathematics?

The remaining issues center around old problems (the aims of instruction, individual differences, and the psychology of learning), but they take a somewhat new form. For example, projected manpower shortages made utility an important goal, but the utility sought became associated with the needs of society more than with the personal and vocational needs of individuals. These issues are the following:

3. Can one teach the direct applications of mathematics to "real world" problems, or can one teach the process of applying mathematics? If so, how should this be done—and should it be done at the expense of a stress on structure, precision, and proof?
4. Is intrinsic motivation as effective as extrinsic motivation? For all people?
5. What is the role of drill? Can it be replaced by understanding? Can it be partially or entirely programmed into developmental or problem-solving work?
6. What is the role of discovery teaching?
7. Can one so arrange mathematical instruction that *creativity* in mathematics is fostered by it?
8. Is a "unified" and "spiraled" curriculum superior to one that stresses courses in arithmetic, algebra, geometry, etc.? If so, how is it constructed? Around central themes?
9. What should be the scope and sequence of the curriculum for superior students? For non-college-bound students?

Forces

Similarly, the forces tending to direct the changes in mathematics education in 1945–70 were initially similar to those existing prior to World War II:

1. A skeptical attitude toward the utility of the classical sequential high school mathematics courses (but, though the skepticism remained, the reasons for it changed from the classical courses' lack of stress on applications to their lack of generality and modernity)
2. The relaxation of college entrance requirements
3. The continuing effect of child development psychology and a pragmatic philosophy of education
4. A declining enrollment in the sequential courses

However, these forces were soon reinterpreted and new ones were added to them:

5. Forecasts of manpower shortages
6. An argument that not only does mathematics have high utility because of its practical applications but it has the greatest utility because its theoretical and structural aspects have potential transfer or problem-solving values
7. The new prestige of science and mathematics gained through World War II developments and new applications in many fields
8. The resulting establishment of the National Science Foundation
9. Unprecedented support (from the NSF and other foundations) for new and experimental course-content material
10. Similar support for teacher-training institutes
11. The attention given by psychologists to intrinsic interest, the importance of structure in learning, the role of discovery teaching, and a new view of transfer of training
12. Attacks by various prominent persons on professional educators for nonintellectualism and corresponding arguments for a new stress on deepening and accelerating content programs in many fields

These new emphases, and the manpower studies, tended particularly to stimulate:

13. New concern for superior students
14. Much publicity to manpower needs, new materials, and such reports as those of the Commission on Post-War Plans and the Commission on Mathematics (given through journals, meetings, and special conferences sponsored by the NCTM and the USOE)

The tremendous growth of pure mathematics itself had two effects:

15. The insistence of some mathematicians that only by relying on the organizing aid of structure and generalization could men continue to comprehend and use mathematics
16. A related insistence that more mathematics must be learned earlier, with the result that more professional mathematicians spent more time and thought on school mathematics than ever before

Chronology

1947 Publication of *Guidance Pamphlet* of the Commission on Post-War Plans of the National Council of Teachers of Mathematics
1947 Publication of John R. Steelman's *Manpower for Research*
1948 Symposium on College Entrance Requirements of the Mathematical Association of America
1950 National Science Foundation established by act of Congress
1951 Appointment of the University of Illinois Committee on School Mathematics (UICSM)
1952 UICSM receives Carnegie grant
1952 Publication of *General Education in School and College*
1952 Arthur Bestor leads attacks on the educational establishment
1952 Symposium on Teacher Education in Mathematics, held by MAA at University of Wisconsin
1953 NSF's first summer institute, for college teachers
1953 Organization by MAA of Committee on the Undergraduate Program (CUP)
1953–54 Social Science Research Council sponsors summer sessions and a report on mathematics for social scientists
1954 Report of School and College Study of Admission with Advanced Standing
1954 NCTM begins publication of the *Arithmetic Teacher*
1954–56 Educational Testing Service supports a study published as *Problems in Mathematics Education*
1955 College Entrance Examination Board Advanced Placement Program begins after a considerable period of experimentation and planning
1955 Ball State Program work in geometry begins
1955 Appointment of CEEB Commission on Mathematics
1957 PSSC supported by NSF to prepare secondary school materials in physical science
1957 University of Maryland Mathematics Project begins

1957 Publication of *Insights into Modern Mathematics*, Twenty-third Yearbook of the NCTM
1957 October 4, Sputnik orbits the earth
1958 Initiation of School Mathematics Study Group through the concern of professional mathematicians, with NSF support
1959 Publication of *Program for College Preparatory Mathematics* and *Appendices*, CEEB Commission on Mathematics
1959 Publication of *The Growth of Mathematical Ideas: Grades K–12*, Twenty-fourth Yearbook of the NCTM
1959 "Secondary Mathematics Curriculum," report of the Secondary School Curriculum Committee of the NCTM
1959 CUP reorganized as CUPM
1960 NCTM, with NSF support, sponsors Regional Orientation Conferences
1960 "Continental Classroom" nationally televises two courses for training teachers in modern algebra and probability and statistics
1960 The Ottawa Seminar held in Canada
1961 Publication of *The Revolution in School Mathematics* by the NCTM
1961 Publication of *Guidelines for Preparation Programs of Teachers of Secondary School Science and Mathematics*, based on studies by the National Association of State Directors of Teacher Education and Certification and the American Association for the Advancement of Science
1962 A group of mathematicians summarizes concern that there may have been undesirable aspects of the reform movements
1963 Publication of *Goals for School Mathematics*, report of the Cambridge Conference on School Mathematics
1966 Publication of *The Training of Teachers of Elementary Mathematics*, Cambridge Conference
1967 Founding of the Canadian Association of Teachers of Mathematics

AN
ARITHMETIC

ON

THE PLAN

OF

PESTALOZZI,

WITH SOME IMPROVEMENTS.

BY WARREN COLBURN.

BOSTON:
PUBLISHED BY CUMMINGS AND HILLIARD.
Hilliard & Metcalf, printers.
1821.

From the Plimpton Collection of Columbia University. Manuscript notes on the catalog cards state that this book introduced the use of "billion" in the sense of one thousand million and was an "unmathematical work" which injured the mathematics of the country and was even "inflicted on poor heathen by the perversity of missionaries." (See also illustrations on page 92 and those facing pages 102 and 103.)

*Forces and Issues
Related to Curriculum
and Instruction, K-6*

PART TWO

*M. Vere DeVault
J. Fred Weaver*

ARITHMETIC.

PART I.

SECTION I.

A. 1.* James has two apples, and William has three; if James gives his apples to William, how many will William have?

2. George has three cents, and Joseph has four; how many have they both together?

3. Dick had five plums, and John gave him four more; how many had he then?

4. David had seven nuts, and gave three of them to George; how many had he left?

5. Three boys, Peter, John, and Oliver, gave some money to a beggar; Peter gave seven cents; John, four cents; and Oliver, three cents; how many did they all give him?

6. How many did Peter give more than Oliver?

* For the manner of solving question, and the explanation of the plates, see the key at the end of the book.

Sect. II. ARITHMETIC. 11

7. A man owed fifty-six dollars; at one time he paid seventeen dollars; at another, eight; at another, five; at another, seven; at last he paid the rest of the debt, wanting four dollars; how much was the last payment?

8. Six men bought a horse for seventy dollars; the first gave twenty three dollars; the second, fifteen; the third, (twelve; the fourth, nine;) the fifth, seven; how much did the sixth give?

9. A man bought a horse for forty-five dollars, and paid fifteen dollars for keeping him; he let him enough to receive twenty dollars; and then sold him for forty-three dollars; did he gain or lose by the bargain? and how much?

SECTION II.

A. 1. What cost three yards of tape, at two cents a yard?*

2. What cost four apples, at two cents a piece?

* The pupil should be made to observe that three yards will cost three times as much as one yard; and say, if one yard cost two cents, three yards will cost three times two cents. He should be made to give this reason for the solution of each question, varying the numbers according to the question

---

THE BEGINNING OF COLBURN'S *ARITHMETIC*. (See also illustrations on page 90 and those facing pages 102 and 103.)

CHAPTER SEVEN

Elementary Mathematics Education: An Overview

1. The major periods

The American elementary school and its contribution to the mathematics learning of the citizens it has served and continues to serve can best be viewed by focusing, in turn, on a succession of four historical periods. For most early colonists there was little dependence on the arithmetic instruction of schools. Not only were a very small percentage of the children in school, but arithmetic was not thought to be a subject as appropriate for school study as were religion, reading, and writing. Arithmetic as a school subject grew from this low position to one of substantial importance by the end of the nineteenth century. The first period, then, extends from the beginnings of this country to a time near the end of the nineteenth century.

Scientism in education had a major impact on the schools beginning with the turn of the century. Arithmetic instruction was very much influenced by this force. As a result the period from 1894 to 1923 represents a second period in the history of elementary school mathematics instruction.

The rise and fall of progressive education (1923–52) had a profound effect on instruction in all subjects of the elementary school, but in none more than arithmetic. This third period in elementary mathematics education was, then, dominated by new educational philosophies. The hopes of a new day in education, spawned by the philosophy of John Dewey and heralded by his many followers, were found wanting in respect to practical application as World War II came to a close and there was time to review the needs and expectations our society had for its schools. With a wave of criticism throughout the popular press typified by articles such as "Why Johnny Can't Add" (332; see also 424), it became increasingly obvious that the demands for substantial changes in school programs and practices required a response.

This response was made in a variety of ways, and the mathematics community exerted considerable leadership in this response. The last period, then, beginning in 1952, focuses on the contemporary elementary mathematics program, which resulted from forces of many kinds and dimensions. These forces have caused changes in the mathematics curriculum as substantial as any, for a comparable period of time, in the history of the elementary school.

2. *The continuing issues*

From the colonial school to our present curriculum emphasizing new content and new methods, there have been many changes in response to a quest for resolutions of four major issues:

1. Why should we teach mathematics in the elementary school?
2. What mathematics should we teach in the elementary school?
3. How should we organize and sequence the mathematics we teach?
4. How should we organize and implement instruction?

These have been continuous, interrelated issues, as is shown in figure 7.1. In every period those whose responsibility it has been to determine the nature of instruction in the school have responded to these issues. In some periods certain issues have seemed to be more at the focal point of our concern than others; indeed, there have been times when we have seemingly been satisfied to ignore one or more of these issues and to focus the major portion of our efforts on the resolution of others. This is perhaps true in more recent years, as we appear to have been much more concerned with the issue of what mathematics to teach than we have with the issue of why teach mathematics.

These four issues, then—why, what, how to sequence, and how to instruct—have continuously confronted us for several decades and

ELEMENTARY MATHEMATICS EDUCATION 95

```
┌─────────────────┐
│ 1. Why should we │
│    teach mathematics │
│    in the elementary │
│    school? │
└─────────────────┘
         │
┌─────────────────┐
│ 2. What mathematics │
│    should we teach │
│    in the elementary │
│    school? │
└─────────────────┘

┌─────────────────┐    ┌─────────────────┐
│ 3. How should we │    │ 4. How should we │
│    organize and se- │    │    organize and │
│    quence the mathe- │←→│    implement in- │
│    matics we teach? │    │    struction? │
└─────────────────┘    └─────────────────┘
```

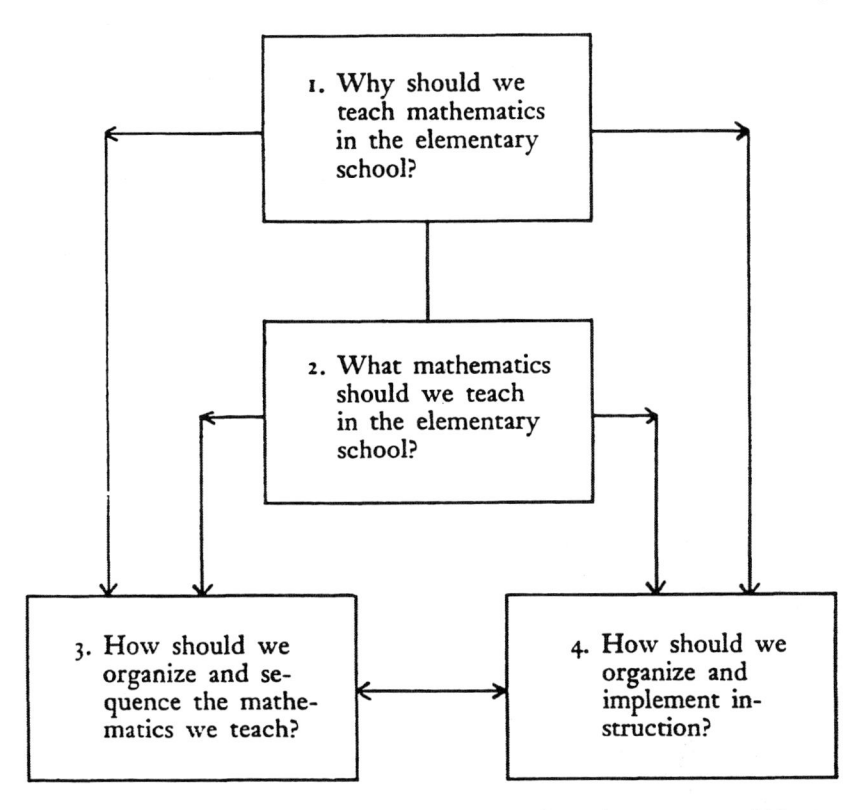

Fig. 7.1. Recurring major issues pertaining to mathematics programs within the elementary school setting

will continue to represent the major questions for us in the decades ahead.

→»→» 3. *The continuing forces*

Just as these issues are persistent, so are the forces that give direction to the manner in which educators and mathematicians have responded and continue to respond to these issues.

The needs of society constitute one persistent force which provides direction to the way issues are resolved. This force has been more compelling in some periods than in others, as when arithmetic in the early days of this country was directed essentially to commercial utility.

A second force which has persistently influenced the response to the issues in mathematics instruction in the elementary school is the discipline of mathematics. Perhaps the period through which we have most recently passed or are passing is one in which the discipline of mathematics has been as important a force as at any time in our past history. Certainly the role of mathematicians in current reform and improvement in elementary school mathematics instruction has been continuous throughout a period of fifteen years. It has been particularly profound in its effectiveness in creating new responses to two of the continuing issues: What mathematics should be taught? How should this mathematics be organized?

A major force which, during the present century at least, has

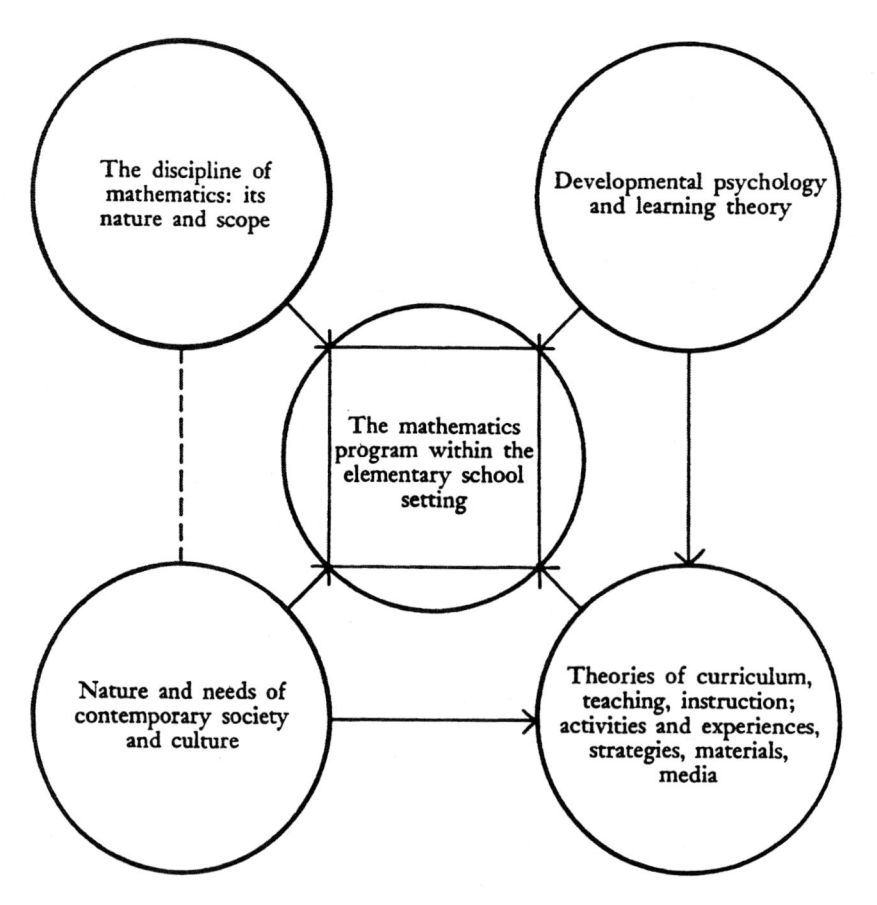

Fig. 7.2. Principal forces influencing the mathematics program within the elementary school setting

affected school programs has been knowledge derived from the discipline of psychology. The nature of the child and the nature of learning have influenced, to varying degrees within different historical periods, the response to each of the issues.

Finally, forces generated from theories and practices in curriculum and instruction have had an impact on the issues which have persistently shaped the nature of instruction in elementary school mathematics. A Pestalozzian influence, the Lancasterian system for a time, and more currently the attempts to individualize instruction and the new organizational patterns for elementary schools have all shared in the shaping of elementary school mathematics instruction. The impact of the forces on the mathematics program in the elementary school is shown in figure 7.2.

The influence of these forces on the four continuing issues and on decisions about the elementary school program will be discussed, in the remaining chapters of Part Two, for the major time periods already described.

CHAPTER EIGHT

From Settlement to the End of the Nineteenth Century: 1607–1894

1. *Introduction*

In the early colonial period, schools for young children included instruction in religion, reading, and writing. The only things we might call arithmetic that might have been included in the curriculum of that time were some copying of numerals and perhaps some rote counting experience. Throughout the colonial period and through the nineteenth century, arithmetic became an increasingly essential part of the elementary school curriculum. It was not until late in this period, however, that a textbook for elementary arithmetic instruction was provided. Until that time a single text served for arithmetic instruction throughout the public school. This period, then, spans a time during which the elementary school arithmetic program emerged as an entity of its own.

2. *Why teach mathematics?*

In the early colonial period the needs of society were such that arithmetic was seen as necessary primarily for clerks and bookkeepers.

The study of arithmetic was beneath the dignity of some of those who attended the earliest schools, which were formed largely after the manner of the European schools the settlers knew best. Arithmetic in some instances was taught in separate schools supported by the early colonies. As business and commerce increased, however, the need for a corresponding increase in the number of citizens capable of doing much simple arithmetic became apparent. For this reason schools began to add arithmetic to the required subjects of religion, reading, and writing. Arithmetic became a required subject in the schools of Massachusetts and New Hampshire in the year 1789. With industrialization in the eighteenth and early nineteenth centuries adding to the mathematical needs of business and commerce, arithmetic took an important place among elementary school subjects.

Psychological theories also had a profound effect on arithmetic instruction throughout the nineteenth century. Emerging from a philosophy that can be traced from Plato, Aristotle, and the medieval scholastics, the theory of mental discipline has had many adherents in every period up to and including the present age. At no other time, however, has faculty psychology, an aspect of mental discipline, been as great a force on the issue of why mathematics should be taught as it was during the latter half of the nineteenth century. The development of faculty psychology is credited to Christian Wolff (1679–1754), a German philosopher and mathematician. His *Psychologia Rationalis* (280), published in 1734, described the mind as consisting of several distinct faculties. Imagination, memory, perception, and reasoning are but a few of the faculties he identified. Each of these faculties was thought of as being analogous in some ways to a muscle that could be trained with the appropriate exercise. One of these faculties was will, and it was believed that the will was strengthened as the student learned increasingly to assume and complete difficult and distasteful tasks. Arithmetic instruction seemed particularly suited to the development of reasoning and the will, among other faculties. Thus it was that faculty psychology contributed to the rather wide acceptance of the idea that mathematics was taught to strengthen the mind.

➢➢ 3. *What mathematics should be taught?*

In the colonial period the needs of society dictated that those computational skills necessary to the clerk and the bookkeeper were to be taught. Much of the computation was with denominate numbers representing the kinds of measures in use at any particular time.

The following tables are selected from the fourteen given in the chapter "Denominate Numbers" in George R. Perkins's *The Practical Arithmetic* (207, p. 112). They are preceded by the statement, "The following are the most important tables of weights and measures, &c., and must be thoroughly learned by the pupil."

Avoirdupois Weight

16 drams (dr.)	make	1 ounce,	oz.
16 ounces	"	1 pound,	lb.
25 pounds	"	1 quarter,	qr.
4 quarters	"	1 hundred weight,	cwt.
20 hundred weight	"	1 ton,	T.

Note 1.—By this weight are weighed all things of a coarse or drossy nature, as bread, butter, cheese, flesh, groceries, and some liquids; all metals, except gold and silver.

Note 2.—Formerly 28 pounds were estimated as 1 qr., 112 pounds 1 cwt., and 2240 lbs. 1 ton. These weights are still used for cheap and heavy articles, such as iron, coal, plaster, &c.

Note 3.—The pound Avoirdupois contains 7000 grains Troy, while the Troy pound contains only 5760 grains.

Long Measure

12 inches (in.)	make	1 foot,	ft.
3 feet	"	1 yard,	yd.
5½ yards	"	1 rod, perch, or pole,	rd.
40 rods	"	1 furlong,	fur.
8 furlongs	"	1 mile,	mi.
3 miles	"	1 league,	L.
69⅙ miles, nearly,	"	1 degree,	deg. or °

Note 1.—4 inches make 1 hand; 9 inches, 1 span; 18 inches, 1 cubit; 6 feet, 1 fathom; 3 feet, 1 pace.

Note 2.—The inch is subdivided sometimes into tenths; sometimes into halves, quarters, eighths, sixteenths, and sometimes into twelfths, called lines or primes.

Note 3.—A nautical or geographical mile is 1/60 of a degree of the earth's circumference. And since one degree is 69⅙ statute or legal miles, we have 1 nautical mile equal to 1 11/72 = 1·1527 statute miles = 6086⅔ feet.

Mensuration was a topic consistently included in textbooks of this period, and with this study certain geometric topics were included. In an 1870 text the following topics are listed and their definitions given as quoted (277, pp. 100–102).

SURFACES—Definitions

A *Line* is length.

A *Straight Line* is a line having the same direction throughout its whole extent.

An *Angle* is the divergence of two lines meeting at a common point. The point of meeting is called the *vertex*.

An *Obtuse Angle* is greater than a right angle, and an *Acute Angle* is less than a right angle.

A *Surface* is that which has length and width, but not depth or thickness.

A *Plane Surface* is a surface such that all possible straight lines connecting each two points of it, lie wholly within the surface. It is also called a *Plane*.

A *Rectangle* is a plane figure bounded by four straight lines and having four right angles.

A *Square* is a rectangle with its four sides equal.

A *Square Inch* is a square each side of which is an inch in length.

A *Triangle* is a plane figure bounded by three straight lines and having three angles.

A *Right-angled Triangle* is a triangle having a right angle.

A *Circle* is a portion of a plane bounded by a curved line, all points of which are equally distant from a point within, called the *center*. The curved line which bounds a circle is its *Circumference*.

The *Diameter* of a circle is a straight line passing through the center and terminating on both sides in the circumference. One-half of a diameter is a *Radius*.

The *Area* of a plane figure is its extent of surface, or superficial contents. It is expressed by some unit of measure as a square inch, a square foot, etc.

Interestingly enough, the impact of the discipline of mathematics on the issues of *why* mathematics should be taught or *what* mathematics should be taught was negligible at this time. Throughout the three-hundred-year period a great deal of mathematics was being created, but the new developments were not represented in any way that influenced the issue of what mathematics should be taught. Although the content varied considerably in the time from the early colonial period to the end of the nineteenth century, the domain from which this content was drawn had been available for a number of centuries.

The discipline of psychology, however, came to have a profound effect on what mathematics was to be taught. Its influence on what would be taught was felt indirectly, as decisions were made concerning the extension of the content of mathematics instruction downward to younger children. These shifts followed changing perceptions of both the nature of instruction and the nature of the child. The most dramatic impact of psychology, however, came with the advent of faculty psychology, and the result was both difficult computational content and a heavy reliance on mental arithmetic. In both instances the changes were designed to add content that would provide exercises designed to strengthen the mind.

Brooks in 1883 wrote (105, p. 342), "Arithmetic, for the purpose of instruction, may be divided into two parts: *Mental Arithmetic* and *Written Arithmetic*. In Mental Arithmetic the problems are solved without the aid of written characters." "Oral arithmetic" and "intellectual arithmetic" he recognized as less useful terms than "mental arithmetic" to convey the same idea.

Mental-arithmetic exercise was based on the concept of the unit as the fundamental idea of arithmetic. Brooks said, "We reason to the unit, from the unit, and through the unit." Two examples (pp. 384-85) will suffice to illustrate both the emphasis on the unit and "the analytical and inductive treatment of the science of numbers."

> If 4 apples cost 12 cents, what will 5 apples cost? Here the *cost of 4 apples* is the known quantity, the *cost of 5 apples* is the unknown quantity; the object is to determine the unknown by comparing it with the known. This comparison cannot be made immediately, since the mind does not readily perceive the relation between *five* and *four;* we therefore pass from *four* to *one*, and then from *one* to *five*. Thus the analysis is: "If *four* apples cost 12 cents, *one* apple cost ¼ of 12 cents, or 3 cents; and if *one* apple costs 3 cents, *five* apples cost 5 times 3 cents, or 15 cents."
>
> If ⅔ of a yard of cloth cost 8 cents, what will ¾ of a yard cost? The solution is as follows: "If 2 *thirds* of a yard cost 8 cents, *one-third* of a yard costs ½ of 8 cents or 4 cents, and three-thirds, or one yard, cost 3 times 4 cents, or 12 cents; if *one* yard costs 12 cents, *one-fourth* of a yard costs ¼ of 12 cents, or 3 cents, and *three-fourths* of a yard cost 3 times 3 cents, or 9 cents."

ARITHMETIC.

PART II.

KEY.

The Key contains an explanation of the plates, and the manner of using them. The manner of solving the examples in each section is particularly explained. All the most difficult of the practical examples are solved in such a manner, as to show the principles by which they are performed. Care has been taken to select examples for solution, that will explain those which are not solved. Many remarks with regard to the manner of illustrating the principles to the pupils, are inserted in their proper places.

Instructers, who may never have attended to fractions, need not be afraid to undertake to teach this book. The author flatters himself that the principles are so illustrated, and the processes are made so simple, that any

ANOTHER PAGE FROM COLBURN'S *ARITHMETIC*. There were separate plates accompanying the first edition of this book. The plates are very rare today. This page and the two following pages, from the "Key" at the back of the book, explain how the plates were to be used. (See illustrations on pages 90 and 92 and those facing page 103.)

KEY. Part II.

one, who shall undertake to teach it, will find himself familiar with fractions before he is aware of it, although he knew nothing of them before; and that every one will require a facility in solving questions which he never possessed before.

The reasoning used in performing these small examples is precisely the same, as that used upon large ones. And when any one finds a difficulty in solving a question, he will remove it much sooner and much more effectually, by taking a very small example of the same kind, and observing how he does it, than by recurring to a rule.

Explanation of Plate I.

This plate, viewed horizontally, presents ten rows of rectangles, and in each row ten rectangles.

In the first row, each rectangle contains one mark, each mark representing unity or one. In the second row each rectangle contains two marks, in the third, three marks, &c.

The purpose of this plate is, first, to represent unity either as an unit, or as making a part of a sum of units. Secondly, to represent a collection of units, either as forming an unit itself, or as making a part of another collection of units; and then to compare unity

Part II. KEY.

and each collection of units with another collection, in order to ascertain their ratios.

All the examples, as far as the eighth section, can be solved by this plate. The manner of using it, is explained in the key for each section in its proper place.

The pupil, if very young, should first be taught to count the units, and to name the different assemblages of units in the following manner;

The instructer showing him the first row, which contains ten units insulated, requests the pupil to put his finger on the first, and say *one*; then on the second and say, *and one are two*, and on the third and say, *and one are three*, and so on to ten; then commencing the row again, let him continue and say, *ten and one are eleven.*

After adding them, let him begin with ten, and say, *ten less one are nine, nine less one are eight*, &c. Then taking larger numbers, as twenty or thirty, let him subtract them in the same manner.

Next let him name the different assemblages, as twos, threes, &c. Afterward, let him count the number of units in each row.

Note. The sections, articles, and examples, are referred to by the same marks which distinguish them in Part I.

MORE PAGES FROM COLBURN'S *ARITHMETIC*. (See illustration facing page 102, where discussion of Colburn's "Key" is begun. See also pages 90 and 92.)

⇢⇢⇢ 4. *How should we organize the mathematics we teach?*

Neither the needs of society nor the discipline of mathematics had much of an impact on the changing nature of the organization of the mathematics taught throughout this long period of the developing elementary school mathematics program. Historical patterns of organizing mathematics content seemed to provide the essential direction contributed by mathematics.

The discipline of psychology, however, did influence the manner in which the issue of the organization of mathematics was resolved during this period. This was particularly true in the latter decades of the nineteenth century as the force of faculty psychology became clearly focused on the developing school program. Perhaps the work of Pestalozzi was most influential in changing the organization of the mathematics taught in the elementary school. His emphasis on the use of concrete materials and real experiences made it possible to move the initial teaching of arithmetic from the age of eight, nine, or ten years to the age of five or six. A trend in this direction was evident early in the nineteenth century with the publication of Emmoc Kimber's *Arithmetic Made Easy to Children* (1805) and Samuel Temple's *An Arithmetic Primer for Young Masters and Misses* (1809). In 1821 Warren Colburn's book *An Arithmetic on the Plan of Pestalozzi* (125) was published. This text included work designed for five- and six-year-olds. From this time on to the end of the nineteenth century there was an ever-increasing attention to the organization of arithmetic content for young children. The organization of text material during the nineteenth century progressed from extensive use of the ciphering book, through the single-text pattern of Colburn's books, to three texts suitable to present-day grading equivalents of primary, intermediate, and seventh and eighth grades. A separate text for each grade was not available until early in the twentieth century.

The Grube system, developed on the principles of Pestalozzi, influenced in two ways the organization of mathematics content in the last fifteen years of this period. First was the slow introduction of natural-number ideas. The numbers one through ten were presented in the first year, and eleven through one hundred in the second. Each number was to be mastered before proceeding to the next. Second, all four operations were presented at the outset, and all combinations of a number were taught before proceeding to the next number. This system resulted in one text series by Wentworth and Reed (273) which presented the numbers for the first year's work in the order of one, four, seven, nine, six, five, two, three, eight. In a companion teacher's book (272), the chapter concerned with the teaching of the number eight was 34 pages long (441, p. 199).

5. How should instruction in arithmetic be organized and implemented?

Instructional methods in the schools were inherited from those of the church in the early colonial period. Catechetical, rote procedures were the order of the day, and much of the early arithmetic instruction was in this mode. As the United States became an increasingly recognized world power, society influenced the drive to relate educational developments in this country to those in others. The German influence through Pestalozzi was particularly important.

Increased industrialism resulted in growing urban centers and large numbers of learners and, associated with a shortage of teachers, brought forth the Lancasterian system, which made it possible for a single teacher assisted by a number of advanced students to instruct a large number of younger students.

The issue of how instruction should be organized and implemented was an active one throughout the period from colonial days to the end of the nineteenth century. The major force having impact on this issue was our knowledge of psychology. Our understanding of the nature of the child and of the nature of learning underwent profound changes throughout this period of time. In the seventeenth and eighteenth centuries the child was thought of as a young adult and was treated as one. This attitude placed a major emphasis on the child as an inactive learner. Instructional attention focused specifically on the mental functions, and the concept of the whole child—which was not to be emphasized until the early twentieth century—was far from the vision held by those who influenced the nature of instruction in the schools. Gradually in the nineteenth century, however, with the impact of writing by Rousseau, Froebel, and particularly Pestalozzi, many questions were raised about instructional methods.

Pestalozzi emphasized the fact that the foundation of all knowledge is "sense impressions." He emphasized the importance of the child's development of "clear ideas." Mental arithmetic was viewed as excellent training for development of the power to form these clear ideas. Counting was the essential practice in instruction. Children were encouraged to use "fingers, peas, stones, or other handy objects" for obtaining the necessary sense perceptions. Later in the children's work a units table consisting of many rows of ten marks each were used for counting. Shortcuts in determining numbers, sums, or number relations were not permitted until sense perceptions had permanently fixed clear ideas (181, pp. 57–58).

With the writings of these three, principles of curriculum and instruction began to take shape and to become important influences on the nature of instructional materials for children. Until the nineteenth century the instructional material for arithmetic was essentially a ciphering book. This was simply a set of blank pages, or what today would be considered a pad of paper, on which the pupil took dictation from the teacher. Often the teacher was dictating from "a ciphering book which he had made when he learned to cipher" (181, p. 44). This instruction was usually individual, as the student copied sums and rules in his ciphering book. Following the rules and using his knowledge of memorized sums, the student made a series of computations that demonstrated his ability to perform a given mathematical exercise.

With Colburn's *First Lessons* (125) in 1821 a number of significant changes were implemented almost immediately in schools throughout the country. Arithmetic instruction was initiated at an early age, made possible through Colburn's advocacy of the use of concrete and manipulative materials for "object lessons," after the writing of Pestalozzi. He also emphasized the postponement of drill until after understanding (an instructional goal, it might be added, that we continue to pursue 150 years later).

6. *Summary of the period 1607–1894*

THE NEEDS OF SOCIETY

Societal needs changed drastically in this period. The separation of church and state replaced the earlier emphasis on religion in education. The early need by a few for arithmetic instruction related to business and commerce gave way to the need by many for arithmetic instruction as a large proportion of our citizens participated in an increasingly industrialized America.

THE DISCIPLINE OF MATHEMATICS

During this period the discipline of mathematics was not a force that gave significant direction as various issues were resolved in the ever-changing spectrum of elementary school mathematics instruction. The mathematics content of elementary school programs was drawn from a period well before the colonization of America.

Knowledge of Psychology

As our understanding of psychology changed, profound forces were exerted in the schools affecting, especially, the resolution of issues relating to what mathematics we should teach and to how instruction should be organized and implemented. It was during this period that psychology grew out of philosophy into a discipline in its own right. Changing understandings of the nature of the child and of child development, together with new theories of learning, had much influence on the nature of elementary school arithmetic as it was taught in the schools of this country.

Curriculum and Instruction

The implications of psychologies of learning gave rise to a wide variety of questions concerning the sequence of topics and the instructional procedures to be used in presenting them to learners. The application of these theories of learning heralded not only the discipline of psychology but also a field of inquiry into curriculum and instruction which may yet arrive at such a state that it may be generally conceded to be a discipline.

One senses the beginning signs of a scientism in education, growing out of the developments of the late nineteenth century, as this period comes to a close. The next period opens with what many proclaim as the initial scientific investigations in education. These were to influence profoundly the continuing issues that are of concern to us in the study of the development of the elementary school mathematics program.

CHAPTER NINE

Scientism and Changing Conceptions of Elementary Schooling: 1894–1923

1. Evidences of change

Committee reports, papers read at national meetings, and individual books have seldom provided a significant impetus for change in American schooling. These reports, meetings, and books rather should be viewed as representative of trends that are under way or of thoughts that are giving direction to efforts in the schools. Several things combined just prior to the turn of the century to represent rather clearly the changes that were taking place.

The elementary school during the latter part of the nineteenth century had become increasingly a formal environment dedicated to the task of transmitting to the child subject matter selected and organized on principles related to the nature of the discipline. The science of number had given the direction to thought about the desired nature of the elementary school arithmetic program. Extensive attempts to establish arithmetic instruction on a scientific definition of number were evidenced in many texts. These attempts were directed toward the establishment of a formal system that related the idea of number to the physical world. Systems were based on definitions of number as units in the real world. Attention was directed to distinctions between concrete and abstract, concrete and denominate, or natural and artificial units. From a variety of sources there seemed to be a growing uneasiness about these concepts of number in relation to the physical world.

A review of events at the turn of the century reveals several signs of change which provide evidence of direct action resulting from this uneasiness.

An early sign of change and a very important one is represented by G. Stanley Hall, the recipient in 1878 of the first Harvard doctorate in psychology.

Cremin writes the following (129, pp. 101-2):

> Hall's basic thesis—the "general psychonomic law," which he borrowed from Haeckel and Spencer—was that ontogeny, the development of the individual organism, recapitulates phylogeny, the evolution of the race. The thesis assumes that psychical life and individual behavior develop through a series of stages that correspond more or less to the stages through which the race is supposed to have passed from presavagery to civilization. Moreover, the normal growth of mind requires living through each of the stages, since the development of any one stage is the normal stimulus for the emergence of the next. Herein lies the link between Hall's general psychology and its application to pedagogy. For he was ready to judge a civilization by the way its children grew, and a school system by the way it adapted itself to the natural growth of individuals. Nature was right, he insisted, particularly in the lives of children. To a nation about to celebrate "the century of the child," his doctrines had enormous appeal.

In 1883 Hall published a monograph, "The Contents of Children's Minds" (345). The research he reported included data collected via questionnaire. This study and other early works by Hall were part of the slowly unfolding development of the child-study movement. This movement grew to such proportions that in 1894 the NEA established the Department of Child Study. In 1895 the NEA's Committee of Fifteen reported, "Modern education emphasized the opinion that the child, not the subject of study, is the guide to the teacher's efforts. To know the child is of paramount importance." (67, p. 242.)

At about this same time Joseph Mayer Rice, a pediatrician concerned about the plight of children in school, turned his attention from medicine to education. Rice, hailed as a founder of the progressive education movement and as a pioneer educational researcher (342, p. 129; see also 420), was

> the second son of German immigrants to Philadelphia, . . . born in 1857. Reared in Philadelphia and New York City, he attended public schools in those two cities and graduated from the Columbia University College of Physicians and Surgeons in 1881. After seven years

of practice during which he was particularly concerned with prevention of disease, he decided to study psychology and pedagogy in Germany, then recognized as the center of those studies in the western world. In a recent letter his son reported that his father had found the practice of medicine "distasteful." Returning to the United States in 1890, he deplored the teaching in the New York City schools, asserting [407] "the entire public school system of the city of New York is conducted upon unscientific principles, not far in advance of those existing in the middle ages before the science of education came into existence."

In a series of articles, Rice reported on his observation of schools he had visited in a number of cities throughout the country. Not only did he collect examples of excellent lessons from those few schools whose practices he approved, but he also initiated some of the early school achievement studies in spelling and other school subjects. He developed tests—including arithmetic in 1902—for use in the schools, and in 1903 he published in the *Forum* an article entitled "Educational Research: Causes of Success and Failure in Arithmetic" (405; see also 406).

These events, then—G. Stanley Hall's initial work, the establishment of the NEA Department of Child Study, and Rice's research on schools and school achievement—are here used to illustrate the dramatic change which, over a period of a decade or two, was to have a profound effect on the schools in the first quarter of the twentieth century.

→→→ 2. *Why teach mathematics?*

On all sides, novelty confronted the American citizen as the new century got under way. Science, industry, and transportation were all poised to make amazing strides in this period, and the stage was ready for new demands on the schools. The American Federation of Labor in 1900 included half a million workers but by 1914 claimed more than two million. Compulsory attendance laws brought more and more children into the schools, with greater diversity—diversity in background as well as diversity in expectation. Compulsory attendance laws were passed in Massachusetts in 1852; Vermont in 1867; New Hampshire, Michigan, and Washington in 1871; and all but six southern states by 1910. Mississippi was the last of the states in 1918. With such widespread compulsory education, it seemed natural that schools should turn to the needs of society to determine anew why mathematics should be taught. It also seemed natural that that answer should come from the new industrialism—we teach mathematics because adults use mathematics in their everyday work requirements.

Johann Herbart (1776–1841), although of an earlier period, had a number of American followers who had studied in Germany and returned to introduce many of his concepts into American education. The National Herbartian Society was founded in 1892, and in 1902 it was renamed the National Society for the Scientific Study of Education. To Herbart, education was concerned essentially with man's character. He emphasized the importance of history and literature. These concerns were a prominent force in education at this time, but they did not provide answers to the questions involved in the issue of why mathematics should be taught. As we will see later, however, he did significantly influence how mathematics was taught.

⇶⇶ 3. What mathematics should we teach?

If few forces during this period provided answers to the question of why mathematics should be taught, the set of needs of society was a force that strongly influenced the resolution of the issue of what mathematics should be taught. The main concern was the use adults made of mathematics. In the 1904 NEA meeting of the Department of Superintendents Frank McMurry read a paper titled "What Omissions Are Desirable in the Present Course of Study?" (379). This report initiated two decades of extensive research designed to determine the mathematics used by adults in the society the schools serve. Guy Wilson directed a study, in cooperation with teachers of Connersville, Indiana, in which they used a questionnaire technique to determine the portion of mathematics normally taught in the schools for which adults had no use. In a course of study for the Connersville schools of 1911 (279, p. 9), the purpose of instruction in arithmetic was stated as follows:

> Purpose: While not denying the cultural and disciplinary value of arithmetic (in common with any subject systematically studied), this course of study is dominated by the idea that the chief purpose of arithmetic in the course of study is its utility in the common affairs of life. We learn the multiplication table not primarily to sharpen the wits or comprehend a beautiful system, but in order to figure our salaries, our taxes, or the interest on a note.

The Connersville study was but one of many conducted during this period for the purpose of determining, as a guide to what should be taught in the schools, what mathematics was used in adult life.

Brooks's idea of number as a unit is, in a way, characteristic of the basic idea that gave direction to content in arithmetic texts up to about 1900. In the late nineties, three different bases for number were proposed by various writers, and these ideas gradually replaced the "number as a unit" idea of Brooks. The three concepts might be categorized as (1) sense oriented, (2) ratio through measurement, and (3) rote counting (441, pp. 302-11).

The sense-oriented concept was espoused by Speer (246, pp. 24-25) as follows:

> Mathematics deals with realities. —However divergent may be the lines of mathematical thought, their beginnings are sensible intuitions —that is, the ideas of magnitude must be based on perceptions; and however long the line, its extension is in all cases by means of successive acts of comparing and inferring.

John Dewey's impact on arithmetic—in both content and instruction—was the result of cooperative effort with James A. McLellan, with whom he collaborated on a text for teachers, *The Psychology of Number*. They present this concept (178, p. 61):

> *The method of things*—of observing objects and taking vague percepts for definite numerical concepts—treats number as if it were an inherent property of things in themselves, simply waiting for the mind to grasp it, to "abstract" it from the things. But we have seen that number is in reality a *mode of measuring value*, and that it does not belong to things in themselves, but arises in the economical adaptation of things to some use or purpose. *Number* is not (psychologically) got *from* things, it is put *into* them.

Finally, rote counting was encouraged as fundamental by Phillips in the following excerpt (399):

> This is essentially the counting period, and any words that can be arranged into a series furnish all that is necessary. *Counting is fundamental, and counting is spontaneous, free from sensible observation, and from the strain of reason.*

Although the publication in 1930 of the *Twenty-ninth Yearbook, National Society for the Study of Education* postdated this historical period by a few years, the *Yearbook* clearly reflected the tenor that prevailed during the latter part of the period. F. B. Knight, in his introduction to the *Yearbook* (370, pp. 3-5), said the following in regard to the why and what of mathematics instruction in the elementary schools of the day:

> The spirit in which this Yearbook was written, while not extreme, assumes the desirability of a liberal school in contrast to the lock-step, teacher-driven school of the 90's. It recognizes the child as the center of interest. The final criterion of all values is considered to be the effect any technique of teaching or any content of instruction has upon the child. The Committee has held in mind, however, that it is the whole child, not a part of him, which is the reality to be kept constantly in mind. A child's present life is but a part of himself, and educational philosophy based upon the assumption that the present interests, needs, strengths, weaknesses, whims of the child comprise the sole or dominating aspect of the child will in practice render but limited service. The child's future is a part of him. In a sense, that the child will soon become an adult is a reality of childhood which must not be forgotten. . . .
>
> It is not enough to cast education in terms of children's present interests and desires alone. A child's life at the moment is not a thing in itself, nor is it at all self-sufficient and self-contained. His life is a continuum; his future is more real than his present. He is essentially an organism which is becoming something other than a child. Hence the education of the child must be cast in terms of his becoming an adult as well as in terms of his present status. The child must, of course, learn (and be taught) in ways which utilize the principles of child psychology, but the aims of his education must be influenced by two considerations: (a) his real nature, a potent part of which is his rapid leaving of his present status and his constant becoming an adult, and (b) the demands which life will place upon him tomorrow. These demands are not those of our wishing, but those which will exist in the United States in the next generation, many of which can be predicted with reasonable certainty. . . . Present society is changing in its technicalities, but the fundamentals of competent and useful living are not changing so rapidly that reasonable predictions of demands a generation or two in the future are either impossible or undesirable. . . .
>
> The philosophy of this Yearbook, then, finds aims in the future as well as in the present. It suggests the desirability of preparation for adult living and holds it to be evident that a prediction of the demands of the future is feasible to a reasonable and useful degree of certainty. We should teach, then, those skills, informations, judgments, attitudes, habits, ideals, and ambitions which the child will find adequate and satisfying to the most important part of his whole self; that is, to his future adulthood as well as to his present childhood. How to teach

the child can be separated, in discussion, from what to teach—and how to teach is fundamentally more a matter of psychology based on research and investigation than a matter of philosophy.

Scientism in education, as it is represented by the beginnings of research and the testing movement, has been a part of the force that is psychology. Psychology has been a force wherever research in these early decades provided direction for the organization of content in the curriculum. The research of E. L. Thorndike and R. S. Woodworth, reported in 1901, was designed to test the validity of the concept of mental discipline, or faculty psychology. Their study, reported in a series of papers titled "The Influence of Improvement in One Mental Function upon the Efficiency of Other Functions" (423), concluded that the idea of mental discipline was scientifically untenable.

In the years folowing, Thorndike went on to develop his theories in the camp of the behaviorists. His own work was known as connectionism or stimulus-response (S-R) bond theory. This theory assumes that, through conditioning, specific responses are linked with specific stimuli —a position considerably distant from that of faculty psychology, which sought to improve a general faculty that would then serve the learner in a variety of situations far removed from the stimulus situation that provided the initial learning.

Thorndike's work, in general, was especially important to the behaviorists. In addition, Thorndike was particularly interested in mathematics instruction and in 1922 published *The Psychology of Arithmetic* (265). His contribution to the organization of the mathematics we teach is related to his insistence on the very direct relation between stimulus and response. This theory resulted in identifying each small segment of the curriculum (almost) as disjoint from all other segments. Instruction was focused on a given objective or bit of content, and that objective was to be achieved in considerable isolation from other content in the curriculum. Indeed, there was an attempt to combine dissimilar items of content in sequence, in order to reduce the possibility of intereference between similar stimuli.

Let us cite two instances of this specificity of learning. First, Thorndike in his *Psychology of Arithmetic* listed (265, p. 52) the following S-R bonds involved in "simple two-column addition of integers":

1. Learning to keep one's place in the column as one adds.
2. Learning to keep in mind the result of each addition until the next number is added to it.
3. Learning to add a seen to a thought-of number.

4. Learning to neglect an empty space in the columns.
5. Learning to neglect the o's in the columns.
6. Learning the application of the combinations to higher decades may for the less-gifted pupils involve as much time and labour as learning all the original addition tables. And even for the most gifted child the formation of the connection "8 and 7 = 15" probably never quite ensures the presence of the connections "38 and 7 = 45" and "18 and 7 = 25."
7. Learning to write the figure signifying units rather than the total sum of a column. In particular, learning to write o in the cases where the sum of the column is 10, 20, etc. Learning to carry also involves in itself at least two distinct processes, by whatever way it is taught.

Sandiford indicated that each of these bonds "is psychologically distinct, and requires separate educational treatment" (227, p. 365). With reference to Clapp's study (124) of the relative difficulty of number combinations, Sandiford asserted (227, pp. 367–68) the following:

> These lists, comprising 390 basic bonds in the fundamental operations with integers, seem to give undue prominence to the number of elementary habits which have to be formed by pupils before they may be regarded as facile in arithmetic. As a matter of fact they grossly under-state the number. No mention, for example, is made of addition combinations in higher decades, of linguistic habits necessitated by arithmetic, of habits of eye-movements during arithmetical operations, of tables of lengths, areas, volumes, and money which even very elementary arithmetic involves, etc. If these were included, the number of separate habits, instead of being 390, would run into many thousands. And it must be remembered that these habits are, for the most part, quite specific, showing little or no transfer from one to the other. Children, for example, cannot transfer their knowledge of 9 and 7 to 19 and 7 and higher decades without specific guidance.

4. *How should we organize and implement instruction?*

Although the needs of society were as diverse as the learners who came to the schools from that society, little was done to differentiate instruction or the curriculum. Perhaps the most important societal force affecting instruction is best represented by the survey and reports of J. M. Rice in the late nineteenth century and in the early decades of the twentieth. Rice's attack was directed in large part against the formalism that prevailed and to the unchildlike environments he found in most of the schools he visited.

The organization of the National Herbartian Society in 1892 reflected the impact the ideas of Johann Herbart had on American education during the final decades of the nineteenth century. His influence on the nature of instruction was to continue well into the twentieth century. The popularity of the inductive method employed in most texts at the turn of the century stems from Herbartian method, which emphasized organization of instruction in four steps: (1) preparation, (2) presentation, (3) comparison and abstraction, and (4) generalization. Such instruction was designed to develop understanding of the general processes and consequently the ability to apply skills to practical and theoretical contexts requiring arithmetical solutions (181, p. 141).

Another psychological force influencing the resolution of issues related to the organization and implementation of instruction was embodied in Thorndike's work. He established three primary laws of learning as a part of S-R bond theory: the law of exercise or repetition, the law of effect, and the law of readiness. According to the first, the more times a stimulus-induced response is elicited, the longer the learning (response) will be retained. This resulted in a heavy emphasis on many practice exercises for each stimulus-response bond that was to be established. The law of effect simply states that responses associated with pleasure are strengthened and those associated with pain weakened. The law of readiness associates satisfaction or annoyance with action or inaction in the face of a bond's readiness to act or not act.

Thorndike's general principles have implications both for the organization of content and for instructional method. He indicates (265, pp. 152-55) that only the first one is an "absolutely" general principle and that the list is only illustrative.

Take the order that works best for arithmetical learning.
Other things being equal, one new set of bonds should not be started until the previous set is fairly established, and two different sets should not be started at once.
Other things being equal, bonds should be formed in such order that none will have to be broken later.
Other things being equal, arrange to have variety.
Other things being equal, use objective aids to verify an arithmetical process or inference after it is made, as well as to provoke it.
Other things being equal, reserve all explanations of why a process

must be right until the pupils can use the process accurately, and have verified the fact that it is right.

Arrange the order of bonds with due regard for the aims of the other studies of the curriculum and the practical needs of the pupil outside of school.

The development of graded textbooks came first as a separation between elementary and secondary school texts. Later a separation of the elementary school mathematics books into two texts developed, and finally a completely graded series. New approaches to the sequencing of mathematics and to instructional procedures came with these texts. The spiral curriculum, with a presentation of content at one grade level and further development of that content at another, increasingly became the practice throughout the first quarter of the twentieth century.

The reaction against the formalism of the school in the late 1890s and the impact of the child-study movement tended to encourage instructional methods that were less harsh in teacher-pupil interaction and less definitive in the separation of various subject areas. This is reflected in John Dewey's statement that mathematics is like a piece of literature, art, or music, in that unless it is appreciated in its own right it will not be utilitarian when it needs to be used. Thus teaching for appreciation became a means that served the utilitarian focus of this period.

5. *Summary*

The Needs of Society

Changes in the elementary school mathematics program were to a very large extent a reflection of the changing needs of society. America had reached a kind of midpoint in its drive toward industrialization, and with partial industrialization came new expectations for the role of the school. Thorough investigations of the uses of mathematics by adults provided the schools with a direct image of the task that needed to be accomplished if mathematics instruction was to prepare students for life in industrial America.

The Discipline of Mathematics

New developments in the discipline of mathematics during this period did not influence what mathematics was taught in the elementary school, nor did they affect thinking about why mathematics should be taught there.

Knowledge of Psychology

New developments in psychology at the turn of the century had considerable influence on the question of why teach mathematics—in a kind of negative fashion. During the nineteenth century, faculty psychology had motivated the teaching of mathematics because it was regarded as an excellent discipline for the training of specific faculties. With the decline of faculty psychology the teaching of mathematics was no longer justifiable by arguments emanating from the discipline of psychology.

The psychology of Thorndike did prove to be a force that gave direction to the organization of the mathematics content to be taught. Specifically, the effect of the S-R bond theory was to emphasize the importance of each small bit of the mathematics and to encourage its teaching in isolation from other bits of content which from a mathematics point of view might be regarded as quite related. Thorndike's laws of learning—the law of exercise, the law of effect, and the law of readiness—had considerable influence in providing direction to some aspects of the nature of instruction. This is reflected in the following contention by Sandiford (227, pp. 370–73):

> The teacher's problem is to identify the separate elements, to devise economical ways of teaching them to children, and to arrange the elements in such a way that each receives an adequate amount of practice. Above all, he should teach in such a manner that the pupils start each new habit in the right way and do not drill themselves on uneconomical procedures. . . .
>
> When the course of study has been selected, it is necessary to secure adequate practice for the pupil in each of the bonds we desire him to form. Drill has been frequently shown to be the most important factor in securing facility in arithmetic. The amounts of drill provided in any text for each of the bonds of the four fundamental operations can easily be calculated.

Curriculum and Instruction

As a force, curriculum and instruction drew its power from a variety of sources. The impact of Hall, of Thorndike, and of Dewey influenced the quality of schooling experienced by children at the turn of the century in different ways. The child-study movement perhaps best exemplifies the changing focus, which was to have a profound influence on the school during this period and in the ensuing period of progressive education.

CHAPTER TEN

Mathematics Education during the Rise and Fall of Progressive Education: 1923-52

1. Forces at work

Many forces out of the preceding several decades combined to produce, on 4 April 1919, the Progressive Education Association (PEA). Lawrence A. Cremin identifies three of these forces as having impact on the schools during the twenties and thirties. In his chapter "Scientists, Sentimentalists, and Radicals" he effectively portrays these three forces as having a major impact on the educational milieu of the day (129, pp. 179-239).

Among the "scientists," E. L. Thorndike is represented in this period as an active participant in the testing movement that had been initiated with the early work of the French psychologists Alfred Binet and Theodore Simon and was then followed by the work of Terman just prior to World War I. The 1918 Yearbook of the National Society for the Study of Education, *The Measurement of Educational Products*, edited by Charles H. Judd, gave considerable impetus to the testing movement in education. The work of Robert M. Yerkes, president of the American Psychological Association, who was in charge of the U.S. Army testing services, contributed much to the emphasis given the movement and to the research activities made possible by it during the early decades of the progressive education era.

Sentimentalism in this period was represented by some interpreters of Dewey, Rousseau, and Freud. The child-study movement initiated several decades earlier by the work of G. Stanley Hall grew during this period into a force that created schools for young children and at all levels of schooling placed an emphasis on child-centeredness. The belief was that innate powers of youth should be released to provide the creative direction for schooling. Expressionism became the fad of the day, and for education the result was too often a mere shell of the structure that many of the philosophers of progressivism had envisioned as the product of their influence on the schools.

The radicals found their primary champion in George S. Counts. His position was that educators should assume responsibility for the design of schools, which would change the nature of society. This position was forcefully stated in 1932 in his small pamphlet *Dare the School Build a New Social Order?*

These were the forces at work, then, as the period of the PEA got under way. Officially organized in the spring of 1919, the PEA was founded largely as an organization of concerned parents with membership open to teachers. The principles espoused by the founders of the organization included the following:

1. Freedom to develop naturally
2. Interest the motive of all work
3. The teacher as a guide, not a taskmaster
4. Scientific study of pupil development
5. Greater attention to all that affects the child's physical development
6. Cooperation between school and home to meet the needs of child life
7. The progressive school as leader in educational movements

Progressive Education, the journal of the PEA, was initiated in 1924 and served as an effective instrument in promoting the principles of the organization among both parents and teachers. By the early thirties the association had become an important force in American education, and what had been predominantly a parents' organization became during the thirties a most important professional education forum. Nonetheless, the hopes expressed by many when this period opened were seldom heard by the time World War II had come to a close. Cremin comments (129, p. 185) that "had the Russian Sputnik never illuminated the Western pedagogical skies, the movement would have died of its own internal contradictions. Sputnik may well have dramatized the end; but even so there were few mourners at the funeral."

➢➢➢ 2. *Why teach mathematics?*

During the first half of this period, the needs-of-society, or social-utility, doctrine continued to have a strong influence on answers to the question, Why teach mathematics? In *Teaching the New Arithmetic*—a popular methods text of the times—Guy M. Wilson and his associates stated (279, p. 7) their unequivocal belief that "the basic and dominating aim of arithmetic in the schools is to equip the child with the useful skills for business."

But in the second half of the period there were strong expressions of equally unequivocal beliefs of an opposing nature, such as the statement in the influential "Second Report" of the Commission on Post-War Plans (16, p. 199) that "we must discard once and for all the conception of arithmetic as a mere tool subject."

Who contributed significantly to this change in point of view in this period? The genesis of this change may be found in the paper "The Fallacy of Treating School Subjects as 'Tool Subjects'" prepared by Charles H. Judd of the University of Chicago and published in the Third Yearbook of the NCTM (359). But it was one of Judd's former students, William A. Brownell, who wrote the first comprehensive statement of the "meaning" theory of arithmetic in his now classic chapter "Psychological Considerations in the Learning and the Teaching of Arithmetic" in the Tenth Yearbook of the NCTM. Brownell characterized this point of view in the following way (312, p. 19):

> The "meaning" theory conceives of arithmetic as a closely knit system of understandable ideas, principles, and processes. According to this theory, the test of learning is not mere mechanical facility in "figuring." The true test is an intelligent grasp upon number relations and the ability to deal with arithmetical situations with proper comprehension of their mathematical as well as their practical significance.

As one outgrowth of the meaning theory, during the second half of this period there was constantly increasing recognition and acceptance of two principal phases of arithmetic instruction: the mathematical phase and the social phase. Leo J. Brueckner epitomized these phases in the Sixteenth Yearbook of the NCTM as follows (319, p. 141):

> [In the preliminary report of the Committee on Arithmetic] the Committee took the stand that "the functions of instruction in arithmetic are to teach the nature and use of the number system in the affairs of daily life and to help the learner to utilize quantitative procedures effectively in the achievement of his purposes and those of the social order of which he is a part." This point of view recognizes two major mutually related and interdependent phases of instruction in arithmetic, namely, the *mathematical* phase and the *social* phase. Full recognition of both phases is essential. Emphasis on the social phase to the neglect of the mathematical phase will not develop in the pupils the quantitative concepts, understandings, and insights that should be the outcomes of a well-rounded program of instruction in arithmetic. On the other hand, emphasis on the mathematical phase to the neglect of the social phase will not lead the learner to sense completely the social significance of number in the institutions and affairs of daily life. A balanced, well-integrated treatment of both phases is essential. Arithmetic should be both *mathematically meaningful* and *socially significant* [italics added].

But there were some persons who decried this dichotomization of arithmetic into the mathematical and the social phases, notably, Harry G. Wheat, who stated the following (430, pp. 32–33):

> The practical situation, and the number relations that we commonly describe as "involved" in it, are but a single item of experience. True, we can abstract, or take out, the number relations abstracted, because then there is no practical situation. In fact, the number relations of a situation are what make it a situation. This is the reason why there is really no such thing as social arithmetic per se, however active our minds as we imagine it. . . . We could go on naming all the practical situations in which we erroneously think we *apply* our arithmetic . . . and in each and every instance we have no situation except such as the numbers and number relations, that are its warp and woof, make it a situation. In short, the pupil does not first learn his arithmetic and then apply it, as separate items of experience; he does not develop his skill, get his meaning, acquire his attitude, make his application, and become independent, either at separate times or along separated pathways at the same time. He does them all at once, or rather as one act, as he moves along the *single* [italics added] road of number thinking.

For Wheat there was but one phase, one principal aim associated with arithmetic—and that was mathematical in nature.

⇾⇾⇾ 3. *What mathematics should we teach?*

There were at least three quite different kinds of answers to this question in evidence during this period.

Some persons "would limit arithmetic as taught to children to the needs of children and . . . urge that the needs of adults are too far removed from childhood" (279, p. 7). These persons believed that "children will learn as much arithmetic as they need, and will learn it better, if they are not systematically taught arithmetic. . . . The learning is through incidental experience" (312, p. 12). Epitomizing this kind of answer to the question of what mathematics should be taught was the investigation by Harap and Mapes, "The Learning of Fundamentals in an Arithmetic-Activity Program" (346).

Other persons answered the question principally in terms of adult usage rather than child usage. The surveys conducted by Wilson and his students led him to conclude (279, p. 7) that

> 90 percent of adult figuring is covered by the four fundamental processes; addition, subtraction, multiplication, and division [of whole numbers]. Simple fractions, percentage, and interest, if added to the four fundamental processes, will raise the percentage to over 95 percent. Mastery of these essentials becomes the drill load in arithmetic for the grades. Beyond that, the work is informational problem work adjusted to child interests.

The following adaptation of Wilson's "grade curriculum" (p. 36) is more specific:

A. Drill:
Grade 1. None.
Grade 2. None.
Grade 3. Addition, possibly subtraction also, completely covered as to facts and steps, perfect mastery.
Grade 4. Addition and subtraction checked and taught as necessary. Multiplication added, complete coverage, perfect mastery. Short division as reverse of multiplication, if taught.
Grade 5. Addition, subtraction, multiplication. Long division added, complete coverage, perfect mastery.
Grade 6. Review and reteach the above, according to pupil needs as revealed by inventory tests that give complete coverage. Simple fractions as the new process, but only on an objective non-manipulative basis, applied to halves, fourths, thirds, and in special situations, eighths and twelfths.

Grade 7. Thorough check on individual needs in the fundamentals, reteach as needed. Percentage and interest as the new processes.

Grade 8. No new drill processes. But in the average school today, less than 20 per cent of pupils are letter perfect in the simple fundamentals. These should receive first consideration.

B. Problem work:
Meaningful [i.e., socially significant] problem units. No work on isolated textbook verbal problems of the usual type.

C. Appreciation work:
Appreciation units.

D. Incidental learning and teaching:
There will be much incidental learning. Pupils will learn to count. They will learn to read numbers; some teaching will take place when needed. They will encounter roman numbers on the clock face and in chapter headings. They will learn most of the needed fractions in actual usage before systematic teaching in the sixth grade. They will learn all that is needed in manipulation of decimals from United States money. Measures will be understood through usage.

In an attempt to reconcile a child-usage focus and an adult-usage focus, Wilson stated the following (p. 8):

> The start is on the child level; the work is carried forward on the child level; common adult usage comes in to set the limits on drill-mastery requirements. The number needs of adults in the common affairs of life do not go so far beyond child needs as to prevent cordial cooperation between progressives and ultraprogressives.
>
> In practice, children can be easily motivated to go into arithmetic the necessary distance to cover common adult usage, for in the average American home, the problems of the home and the father's business are discussed enough so that children early acquire an interest in adult problems.

The third kind of answer to the question of what mathematics should be taught is reflected in Brownell's various discussions of the nature of the meaning theory of arithmetic. For instance, he states the following (316, p. 481):

> Some advocates of what *they* call meaningful arithmetic disregard or minimize arithmetical meanings in favor of social applications, holding that experience in using arithmetical skills will make them meaningful. The fallacy in this thinking has been pointed out several times:

experience in using skills may produce some awareness of the usefulness of number (that is, of its significance), but it cannot produce meanings. Meaning is to be sought in the structure, the organization, the inner relationships of the subject itself.

He discusses the theory again (317, pp. 257–58) as follows:

> "Meaningful" arithmetic ... refers to instruction which is deliberately planned to teach arithmetical meanings and to make arithmetic sensible to children through its mathematical relationships. ...
> The meanings of arithmetic can be roughly grouped under a number of categories. I am suggesting four.
> 1. One group consists of a large list of basic concepts. Here, for example, are the meanings of whole numbers, of common fractions, of decimal fractions, of per cent, and, most persons would say, of ratio and proportion. ...
> 2. A second group of arithmetical meanings includes understanding of the fundamental operations. Children must know when to add, when to subtract, when to multiply, and when to divide. They must possess this knowledge, and they must also know what happens to the numbers used when a given operation is employed. ...
> 3. A third group of meanings is composed of the more important principles, relationships, and generalizations of arithmetic, of which the following are typical: When 0 is added to a number, the value of that number is unchanged. The product of two abstract factors remains the same regardless of which factor is used as multiplier. The numerator and denominator of a fraction may be divided by the same number without changing the value of the fraction.
> 4. A fourth group of meanings relates to the understanding of our decimal number system and its use in rationalizing our computational procedures and algorisms.

Such characterizations of "meaningful arithmetic" demanded an obviously different kind of content than was the case under a social-utility theory of arithmetic.

There is a very real sense in which the emphases of meaningful arithmetic were in the spirit of the modern mathematics of the period to follow. It is defensible to consider the modern-mathematics programs in elementary schools of the 1960s to be refinements and extensions of the meaningful-arithmetic programs that were initiated in the 1930s, grew in popularity through the 1940s, and were the commonly accepted programs of the 1950s.

But this common acceptance did not come without opposition, especially during the earlier years of the period 1930–50. Wilson, for instance, was outspoken in his opposition (279, pp. 52–53):

> Any theory may at times be used to cover wrong procedures. The "meaning" theory is being so used at present by those who would attempt to have third-grade children understand the rationale of the number system, and this illustrates the fallacy of attempting to guide practice by nothing more than theory. It were better to study the child and his interests on the one hand and the needs of adults in the community on the other hand.

But meaningful arithmetic was based on more than theory alone, and it influenced answers to questions other than what mathematics should be taught. This will be seen in the sections that follow.

4. How should we organize the mathematics we teach?

One answer to this question was embedded within the "activity," or "incidental learning," theory of arithmetic instruction. The introduction, development, maintenance, and extension of mathematical content and skills were a function of the incidental need for them in connection with an activity unit. Since there was no systematic program of mathematics instruction per se, the arithmetic that was taught was unorganized at best. Not all persons shared the belief, however, that "child need" was the most defensible basis upon which to organize mathematics instruction.

A very different answer to this question came from the work of Carleton Washburne and the Committee of Seven. In their initial set of investigations (83, p. 641) the committee sought to answer the following two questions:

> 1. At what stage of a child's mental growth, as measured by intelligence tests, can he most effectively learn the following phases of arithmetic: addition facts, subtraction facts, subtraction process, multiplication facts, simple long division, meaning of fractions, graphs, and Case-I percentage?
> 2. What degree of mastery of more elementary facts and skills is necessary for the effective learning of each of the above topics?

Washburne reported (p. 643):

The results show, in general, (1) that there is a definite mental level below which the attempt to teach any given process is usually futile; (2) that there is a degree of mastery of the prerequisite elements of a process without which that process cannot be efficiently learned; and (3) that if a child has reached a specified mental level and a specified skill in prerequisite topics, he is reasonably sure to learn the new topic adequately and to retain it well. These mental levels and prerequisite skill levels have now been determined for the topics herein reported and are being determined·for more.

It is entirely possible that the degree of effective mastery could be raised and that the mental level at which it can be attained could be lowered if the teaching conditions as a whole were improved.

Specific findings were reported as follows (p. 670):

Topic	Minimal Mental-Age Level	Minimal Arith. Foundations Test Score (in Percent)
Addition Facts		
Sums 10 and under	6 yr. 5 mo.	—
Sums over 10	7 yr. 4 mo.	—
Subtraction Facts		
Easier 50	7 yr. 0 mo.	84
Harder 50	8 yr. 3 mo.	96
Subtraction with Carrying	8 yr. 9 mo.	57
Multiplication Facts	8 yr. 4 mo.	
	or 10 yr. 2 mo.	96
Simple Long Division		
1- and 2-place Quotient	10 yr. 9 mo.	81
Meaning of Fractions		
Non-Grouping	9 yr. 0 mo.	—
Grouping	11 yr. 7 mo.	—
Graphs, Simple Bar	10 yr. 5 mo.	—
Percentage, Case I	12 yr. 4 mo.	
	or 13 yr. 4 mo.	100

The work of the Committee of Seven continued, but not without some severe criticism—notably, from Brownell (313; 314)—and some extensive debate, as was acknowledged and discussed by Washburne in his 1939 report of the committee's work (84).

Despite such criticism and debate, the Committee of Seven's investigations attracted much favorable attention and had an unquestioned influence on the organization of the arithmetic curriculum. In particular, there was a push upward in the grade placement of topics, each of which embraced a relatively large block of work associated with the development of computational skill—for example, "long division with a [two-place divisor and a] two-place quotient involving naughts, remainder, and trial-divisor difficulties" (84, p. 313). For each such topic there was determined the mental age at which at least 75 percent of the pupils could demonstrate at least 80 percent mastery on a retention test, and that mental-age level was translated into a grade level by many persons who were developing arithmetic curricula. Such curricula were, very obviously, highly skill-oriented.

Furthermore, the mental-age basis for determining placement of topics often led to a separation of things that were closely associated mathematically. Washburne's 1939 report stated (p. 309): "The addition facts with sums of 10 and under are all learned at this level [mental age seven to eight], and there is little gain in further postponement. . . . The easy subtraction facts can be successfully learned at this age, but there is a definite gain in postponing them to the next level [mental age eight to nine]."

But just as the meaning theory represented an opposing force to certain answers to the question of what mathematics should be taught, so the meaning theory represented an opposing force to certain answers to the question of how the mathematics taught should be organized. A basic tenet of the meaning theory was the contention that meanings are not all-or-none affairs; this implied a spiral rather than a block form of organization of mathematical content.

Also, a basic tenet of the meaning theory rejected the view of arithmetic content as a multitude of unrelated facts and relatively independent skills, and it insisted that the content of arithmetic be organized in a way to take advantage of and highlight its inherent relationships.

By the end of this period the organization of arithmetic programs was influenced more by such tenets of the meaning theory than by the opposing points of view, which were held more widely during earlier years of the period.

5. *How should we organize and implement instruction?*

This period was a significant one pedagogically, reflecting the peak and decline of one psychology of learning and the rise of another. At the beginning of the period the organization and implementation of arithmetic instruction was dominated by "association" learning theory —in particular, by Thorndikean connectionism. But by the end of the period, the organization and implementation of arithmetic instruction was influenced more by "field" learning theory (closely allied with Gestalt psychology).

Certain yearbooks of the NCTM and of the National Society for the Study of Education characterized admirably this change in pedagogical point of view. Every serious student of mathematics education at the elementary school level, if he has not already done so, should trace through the following sequence of yearbook chapters:

Knight, F. B. "Some Considerations of Method." In *Report of the Society's Committee on Arithmetic*. Twenty-ninth Yearbook, National Society for the Study of Education, 1930.

Brownell, William A. "Psychological Considerations in the Learning and the Teaching of Arithmetic." In *The Teaching of Arithmetic*. Tenth Yearbook, NCTM, 1935.

McConnell, T. R. "Recent Trends in Learning Theory: Their Application to the Psychology of Arithmetic." In *Arithmetic in General Education*. Sixteenth Yearbook, NCTM, 1940.

Buckingham, B. R. "What Becomes of Drill?" In *Arithmetic in General Education*. Sixteenth Yearbook, NCTM, 1940.

Buswell, G. T. "The Psychology of Learning in Relation to the Teaching of Arithmetic." In *The Teaching of Arithmetic*. Fiftieth Yearbook, pt. 2, National Society for the Study of Education, 1951.

And to this list the following yearbook should be added *in toto;* it is not restricted in its coverage to mathematics at the elementary school level:

Fehr, Howard F., ed. *The Learning of Mathematics: Its Theory and Practice*. Twenty-first Yearbook, NCTM, 1953.

How may we characterize mathematics instruction under a connectionistic theory of learning such as that which prevailed in the early years of this period? Brownell has given the following succinct characterization (315, p. 147):

> All learning consists in the addition, the elimination, and the organization of connections—this, and nothing else. These connections are

formed, or broken, or organized, between situations and responses. The process of teaching, then, comprises the following steps:

1. Identify for the learner the stimuli (or the situation) to which he is to react,
2. Identify the reaction (or response) which he is to make,
3. Have the learner make this response to the situation under conditions which reward success and which punish failure,
4. Repeat step (3) until the connection has been firmly established.

Brownell goes on (p. 148) to identify "four instructional weaknesses to which," he feels "connectionistic theory has contributed directly or indirectly":

1. Our attention as teachers is directed away from the processes by which children learn, while we are over-concerned about the product of learning,
2. Our pace of instruction is too rapid, while we fail to give learners the aids they need to forestall or surmount difficulty,
3. We provide the wrong kinds of practice to promote sound learning,
4. Our evaluation of error and our treatment of error are superficial.

In contrast to Brownell's characterization of learning by association or under connectionistic theories, McConnell cited (376, pp. 269, 277, 280) the following three characteristics of learning under what might be termed field theories:

1. Learning is not the acquisition of items of information or skill, or of a multitude of discrete reactions, but is a *change in the organization of behavior* which gives the individual more effective control over the conditions of experience. . . .
2. Learning is a process of development. . . . Association theories confused the *end* or the product of learning with the process; they treated learning as the fixation of responses. . . .
3. *Learning is a meaningful rather than a mechanical process.* Fundamentally, meaning inheres in relationships. Relationships are established by the control which some organization or system exercises over the parts. The "meaning theory" of arithmetic instruction, therefore, emphasizes the importance of teaching children to understand our decimal number system and the ways of manipulating it. This system provides the basic pattern for understanding and relating the many specific items which are included in it and controlled by it.

Research interests changed during this period. The kind of research that was supportive of connectionistic learning theory began to wane, and a different research emphasis emerged which was supportive of field learning theory. Noteworthy investigations included the following:

Brownell, William A. *The Development of Children's Number Ideas in the Primary Grades.* Supplementary Educational Monographs, no. 35. University of Chicago, 1928.

McConnell, T. Raymond. *Discovery vs. Authoritative Identification in the Learning of Children.* Studies in the Psychology of Learning, vol. 1. University of Iowa, 1934.

Thiele, C. Louis. *The Contribution of Generalization to the Learning of the Addition Facts.* Teachers College, Columbia University, 1938.

Brownell, William A., and others. *Learning as Reorganization.* Duke University Research Studies in Education, no. 3, 1939.

Anderson, G. Lester. "Quantitative Thinking as Developed under Connectionist and Field Theories of Learning." In *Learning Theory in School Situations.* University of Minnesota Studies in Education, no. 2, 1949.

Brownell, William A., Harold E. Moser, and others. *Meaningful vs. Mechanical Learning: A Study in Grade III Subtraction.* Duke University Studies in Education, no. 9, 1949.

Swenson, Esther J. "Organization and Generalization as Factors in Learning, Transfer, and Retroactive Inhibition." In *Learning Theory in School Situations.* University of Minnesota Studies in Education, no. 2, 1949.

Van Engen, Henry, and E. Glenadine Gibb. *General Mental Functions Associated with Division.* Educational Service Studies, no. 2. Iowa State Teachers College, 1956. (Although this study is reported in our next time period, it is closely allied with the preceding investigations in its concern for meaningful learning and instruction.)

In general these and other investigations brought an increasing body of evidence in support of the meaning theory of arithmetic instruction and tended to confirm the following observations, which McConnell cited (376, p. 279) as "significant facts" derived from studies early within this period:

> (1) Abstract ideas of number develop out of a great amount of concrete, meaningful experience; mature apprehension of number relationships can be attained in no other way. Furthermore, the adequate development of number ideas calls for systematic teaching and learning.

(2) Drill does not guarantee that children will be able immediately to recall combinations as such.

(3) Habituation of number combinations is a final stage in learning which is preceded by progressively more mature ways of handling number relationships.

(4) Repeating the final form of a response from the very beginning may actually encourage the habituation of immature procedures and seriously impede necessary growth.

(5) Drill as such makes little if any contribution to growth in quantitative thinking by supplying maturer ways of dealing with number.

(6) Intermediate steps, such as the use of the "crutch" in subtraction, aid the learner both to understand the process and to compute accurately. With proper guidance, these temporary reactions may be expected to give way to more direct responses in the later stages of learning.

(7) Reorganization of behavior occurs as the child's understanding grows, and results in the emergence of more precise, complex and economical patterns of behavior.

(8) Understanding the number system and the methods of operation it makes possible facilitates both quantitative thinking and, ultimately, rapid and accurate computation.

6. *Summary*

THE NEEDS OF SOCIETY

The content of the mathematics curriculum during part of this period reflected the social utilitarian point of view that had been initiated in the first two decades of the century. Studies of adult usage were continued at least through the thirties, but their influences in the selection and organization of content had diminished by 1952. Although the two World Wars and the intervening depression had substantial impact on the design of the curriculum at the secondary school level, direct influence at the elementary school was slight. The progressive education movement, to the extent that it was a reflection of a larger, societal progressive movement, did represent an influence from society on the elementary school mathematics program. The child-centered curriculum, with its attendant emphasis on the selection and organization of content as it is needed by the child, represented one major shift to and fro throughout this period. Content well established at the opening of the period in 1923 was questioned in a period when there was considerable debate about the influence of the child-centered movement on education. By the end of the period in 1952 the content of the program was different from that at the beginning of the period, due principally to the rise of the meaning theory. To what extent the schools really did reflect the child-centered curriculum during the thirties and forties has been a moot point and probably will remain so in the future.

The Discipline of Mathematics

This period probably represents a low point in the involvement of mathematicians in the elementary school program. Mathematicians were not involved in the preparation of text materials or in major research of the period, which was directed chiefly by educational psychologists. Insofar as the discipline of mathematics was represented, it seemed to be so in the determination of the nature of mathematics not so much as a tool subject but rather as a part of the cultural heritage which required educational attention in its own right, not necessarily because it was useful in other endeavors.

Knowledge of Psychology

The scientism in education which was initiated in the previous period flowered during the period of progressive education, although it was not necessarily directly related to that movement. The testing movement and its progress prior to and during the twenties and thirties made much of the research possible. Many of the specific questions relative to mathematics education derived from this testing movement. Psychological theories were often tested in mathematical settings. Indeed, a sizable number of educational psychologists became substantially involved in mathematics education either before or following, or in direct relation to their research in mathematical settings. Within the period there clearly was a shift away from connectionism and a drill theory of arithmetic instruction to field theory and a meaning theory of arithmetic instruction.

To the beginnings of the fifties, the period had seen much rhetoric and hope for the new school which failed in any large sense to materialize. In retrospect it appears that although many of the efforts were sufficient in themselves, much was left to be hoped for in another day. The role of the mathematicians particularly was to be sought in another time. Adequate funding of research and of development activities was lacking, and society's support for rather full-scale research was needed. The fifties and the sixties provided an opportunity to hope again for a better school tomorrow.

CHAPTER ELEVEN

Designing a Contemporary Elementary School Mathematics Program: 1952–Present

1. Introduction

Throughout the history of mathematics education, debate punctuated with proposals and counterproposals has characterized the scene at the highest theoretical levels. Philosophers, psychologists, educators, and—especially about the turn of the century—superintendents have proposed faculty psychology, S-R bond theory, child-study foci, concepts of social utility, and other points of departure for program planning and implementation. These conflicting ideas have been promoted consecutively and, on occasion, concurrently. But what has been the impact on the learner in the classroom? Perhaps the learner and too often his teacher have been oblivious to the debate, as fish swimming in deep water may be serenely oblivious to a storm raging above. At best, the impact of new ideas, new content, and new methodology often has been slow in influencing the school life of the learner.

At midcentury and beyond, American life moves at a rapid pace. Social, economic, and political demands rapidly change. If the life of the school is to reflect the larger life of the society, it too must change at a pace never previously achieved.

The feverish pitch at which mathematicians went to work on the task of improving school mathematics programs following World War II, first at the secondary school level and then at the elementary school level, was in tune with the temper of the times. Post–World War II reports had provided clear evidence that all was not well in our schools. The mass media were ever eager to document the inadequacies of school programs in the early fifties, just as many self-styled educational experts were eager to offer remedies.

The 1950s brought criticism of the schools from diverse individuals such as Arthur E. Bestor (94), Robert M. Hutchins (159), Albert Lynd (172), Rear Adm. Hyman Rickover (219), and Paul Woodring (281). Ruth Dunbar, education writer for the *Chicago Sun-Times*, contended (332) that "in many classrooms teachers still rely exclusively on the drill-and-memory system of the past. Others teach arithmetic 'incidentally,' as it is needed in other subjects and school activities."

The academicians in various disciplines, including mathematics, became acutely aware of the extent to which they had ignored, over a period of several decades, the needs of schools. Organizations and individuals committed time and energy to the improvement of mathematics education at the elementary school level as well as at the secondary school level, not uncommonly resorting to crash programs.

Mathematicians from colleges, universities, and industry became actively involved in the preparation of text materials that illustrated the kinds of mathematical content they felt should be included in an elementary school mathematics program. Again, there was hope that a new approach to a continuing set of problems would provide a major and immediate breakthrough. Anything less than such a total effort was deemed inadequate for the task they faced. Perhaps more than during most previous periods, those theorists who were directing the debates centered on the major issues were also those who were directly responsible for the implementation of the ideas they were generating. Now one might hope that the rapidity with which society was changing would be paralleled by a rapid transition from theory to practice in the classroom.

2. Why teach mathematics?

A major factor contributing an answer to the question "Why teach mathematics?" in the elementary school grew out of our experience in World War II. It became abundantly clear to America that the schools had not provided the quality education to which it had dedicated its

A CONTEMPORARY PROGRAM							135

efforts for more than a hundred years. That service recruits in such large numbers failed to exhibit minimal competence in many subjects including mathematics pointed the finger directly at the giant that is the American elementary school. By the opening of this period in 1952 there were signs that the lumbering giant was beginning to stir and that increased attention was being given to the mathematics curriculum.

The shock of Sputnik in October 1957 gave impetus to the drive to improve education, for it was avowed again that only through education could the American dream become a reality. This time, however, as an ever-increasing period of technology has unfolded during the years from Sputnik to the present, mathematics has been a vital part of the patterns being designed to assure our future safety and welfare.

Technology had a tremendous impact on the question of why mathematics should be taught. For both the average citizen and the worker employed in the expanding economy, mathematics was an essential. Increasingly it was recognized that the man on the street needed to be knowledgeable in mathematics if he was to understand the world in which he lived. If extended mathematical education was to be provided for a larger proportion of our citizens, the elementary school was called upon to strengthen its contribution to this education.

There was much discussion during this period concerning the role of computers in everyday life. Would not a day soon come when computers handled personal financial transactions, simple accounting tasks, and most computation? Did this not mean that new reasons for teaching mathematics were generated? An understanding of mathematics is needed if we are to understand our technological society, and mathematics has a cultural aspect that is the heritage of all citizens.

The discipline of mathematics contributed to these discussions mainly through the involvement of mathematicians. Their concern for an ever-growing body of mathematical knowledge, for the importance of providing America with a mathematically informed citizenry, and for those students capable of doing advanced work in mathematics were all factors that had substantial impact on our commitment to teach mathematics.

3. *What mathematics should we teach?*

In a rapidly changing society, how does one answer the question of what mathematics should be taught? Certainly one cannot look to the past. The mathematics taught a generation earlier is hardly a guide; indeed, there is a question about the utility of the mathematics taught or used today as a guide to selection of content. It is no longer possible to specify what will be needed. In the year 2000, those youngsters who enter school in the 1970s will be in the middle of their productive years. What mathematics will they need in that year and on into the twenty-first century?

The message has consistently been that we teach those things that are universal. Thus we have come a full turn from the identification of highly specific and relatively independent bonds or connections, each to be established, practiced, and maintained so as to be ready for use when needed. Within the discipline of mathematics there have been identified sets of characteristics which give that discipline certain unifying structures. The following properties provide an example:

Consider the set of integers $J = \{\ldots, ^-4, ^-3, ^-2, ^-1, 0, ^+1, ^+2, ^+3, ^+4, \ldots\}$ and the familiar operation of addition, $+$. For this set of numbers (the integers) and this operation (addition), the following four things (among others) are true:

1. For any integer a and any integer b, $a + b$ is an integer (i.e., $a + b$ is an element of J).

2. For any integer a, any integer b, and any integer c,

$$(a + b) + c = a + (b + c).$$

3. There exists a particular integer, i, such that for every integer a,

$$a + i = i + a = i.$$

4. For any integer a, there exists in J a second integer, a', such that $a + a' = i$. More specifically, since $i = 0$,

$$a + a' = a' + a = 0.$$

These four properties illustrate a particular mathematical structure known as a group. There are other sets of elements (that may or may not be numbers) and other operations (that may or may not be number operations) for which the same four properties are valid. Each such system (set of elements and a binary operation defined on the set) which has these four properties is said to have the same structure (in this instance, a structure called a group), regardless of how dissimilar the sets of elements or the operations may appear to be. The group is but one of various mathematical structures that serve to unify many things that otherwise often appear to be quite diverse.

Jerome Bruner, in his report of the Woods Hole Conference (112), emphasized the importance of teaching the fundamental structure(s) of any subject. He identified clearly his reasons as follows, with particular reference to mathematics:

(a) Understanding fundamentals makes a subject more comprehensible.
(b) Unless details are placed into a structured pattern, they are rapidly forgotten. The learning of general or fundamental principles ensures that memory loss will not mean total loss, and that what remains will permit one to reconstruct details when needed.
(c) Understanding of fundamental principles and ideas appears to be the main road to adequate "transfer of training."
(d) By constantly re-examining material taught in elementary and secondary schools for its fundamental character, one is able to narrow the gap between "advanced" knowledge and "elementary" knowledge.

The reader may be interested to note the similarity between several of Bruner's reasons and some of the following values for the pupil which, more than ten years previously, Brownell (317, pp. 263–64) had cited as advantages of teaching arithmetic "meaningfully":

1. Gives assurance of retention.
2. Equips him with the means to rehabilitate quickly skills that are temporarily weak.
3. Increases the likelihood that arithmetical ideas and skills will be used.
4. Contributes to ease of learning by providing a sound foundation and transferable understandings.
5. Reduces the amount of repetitive practice necessary to complete learning.
6. Safeguards him from answers that are mathematically absurd.
7. Encourages learning by problem-solving in place of unintelligent memorization and practice.
8. Provides him with a versatility of attack which enables him to substitute equally effective procedures for procedures normally used but not available at the time.
9. Makes him relatively independent so that he faces new quantitative situations with confidence.
10. Presents the subject in a way which makes it worthy of respect.

Elementary school mathematics programs within this period have not attempted to teach mathematical structures per se. But these programs have emphasized the recognition and use of those properties that, in the study of mathematics at secondary school and higher levels, are used to characterize particular structures explicitly.

This concern for including within an elementary school mathematics program some of the building blocks for mathematical structures led to two related practices that pertain to the question of what mathematics should be taught: (1) an emphasis upon unifying mathematical ideas and (2) the inclusion of certain content that was new at the elementary school level.

The Twenty-fourth Yearbook of the NCTM (200) was organized around the following unifying mathematical ideas:

1. Number and operation
2. Relations and functions
3. Proof
4. Measurement and approximation
5. Probability
6. Statistics
7. Language and symbolism
8. Mathematical modes of thought

The preface stated (p. v): "These modes are not quite mathematical concepts themselves, but are rather understandings and procedures which are implicit in the study of all mathematical topics."

A similar organization in terms of unifying "strands" was suggested in the report of the California State-wide Mathematics Advisory Committee (9) as follows:

1. Numbers and operations
2. Geometry
3. Measurement
4. Applications of mathematics
5. Statistics and probability
6. Sets
7. Functions and graphs
8. Logical thinking
9. Problem solving

Concern for such unifying mathematical ideas or strands led to a reinterpretation, from a contemporary point of view, of much familiar content. Not uncommonly this reinterpretation was a refinement of content considerations that were reflected earlier in less precise ways in the "meaning" theory of arithmetic. For instance, the contemporary interpretation of whole-number operations in terms of appropriate set operations was a refinement of earlier, less precise characterizations of these operations.

Concern for unifying mathematical ideas or strands also led to the inclusion of new content at the elementary school level. Some of this new content involved an introduction from a contemporary viewpoint of content that earlier had been introduced at higher grade levels. This new content included things such as the following:

1. A substantial amount of intuitive, nonmetric geometry

A CONTEMPORARY PROGRAM

2. Nondecimal systems of positional notation
3. Expanded notation and its application to algorithms
4. Exponential notation
5. Open sentences using placeholders
6. Inequalities
7. Coordinate geometry
8. Number theory, particularly primes

It is important to recognize that through most of the 1950s elementary school mathematics programs were in a stage of consolidating and reinforcing the changes that had been effected through an increasingly wide acceptance of the meaning theory of arithmetic. Although concerted efforts to modernize the mathematics of secondary school programs began early in the 1950s, similar efforts to modernize the mathematics of elementary school programs did not begin until late in the 1950s. When such efforts were directed to the elementary school level, they originated principally from projects that were supported in the main from federal sources—notably, the National Science Foundation—and to a lesser degree from state and private sources.

Projects that had varying degrees of direct influence upon the modernization of elementary school mathematics programs include the following:

School Mathematics Study Group (SMSG) project, Mathematics for the Elementary School, grades K–6 (E. G. Begle, director)

Project, Experimental Teaching of Mathematics in the Elementary School, stemming from the work of the Stanford University Institute for Mathematical Studies in the Social Sciences (Patrick Suppes, director)

Project of the Educational Research Council of Greater Cleveland, which led to the Greater Cleveland Mathematics Program (GCMP; this project had several different directors during the course of its work)

Syracuse University–Webster College Madison Mathematics Project, grades 1–9 (Robert B. Davis, director)

Minnesota School Mathematics and Science Teaching Project (MINNEMAST), grades K–9 (this project had several different directors during the course of its work)

Project, Patterns in Arithmetic, grades 1–6 (Henry Van Engen, director)

University of Illinois Arithmetic Project (David A. Page, director)

Newton S. Hawley's Geometry Project, with an emphasis upon reading and construction

Projects such as the preceding ones differ in a variety of details. But all have exerted a greater or lesser degree of influence upon an answer to the question of what mathematics we should teach. Initially there was some strong resistance to attempts to modernize the traditional content of elementary school arithmetic programs and introduce new content that would provide mathematics programs rather than arithmetic programs for elementary schools. But by the end of the 1952-69 period, the general spirit and intent of these contemporary programs was as commonly accepted as was the meaning theory of arithmetic during the first half of this period.

As we shall see in subsequent sections of this chapter, the influence of certain of these projects was felt on answers to other questions as well.

4. How should we organize the mathematics we teach?

Both the discipline of mathematics and that of psychology have given direction since 1952 to the organization of the mathematics we teach. One hears little of the activity unit so important in the period of progressive education. Now the organization of content is determined by interpretations of the nature of mathematics as a discipline. The structure of mathematics and the organization of ideas around unifying mathematical strands have provided the direction. Mathematics-text series during the period have been organized around content strands, and emphasis has been placed upon the interrelatedness of mathematical ideas.

From psychology, the task analysis of Gagné (340) has encouraged the search for the organization of content along hierarchical lines. Each concept or skill, according to the task analyst was to be analyzed into subordinate concepts and skills which, in turn, were to be similarly analyzed until the most basic learning entities were determined for any particular hierarchy. This kind of analysis is illustrated by Gagné's report "Some Factors in Learning Non-Metric Geometry" (146), which includes the diagram shown in figure 11.1. (In a superficial way this resembles the analyses of skills which were of interest to some researchers in the preceding period, 1923-52.)

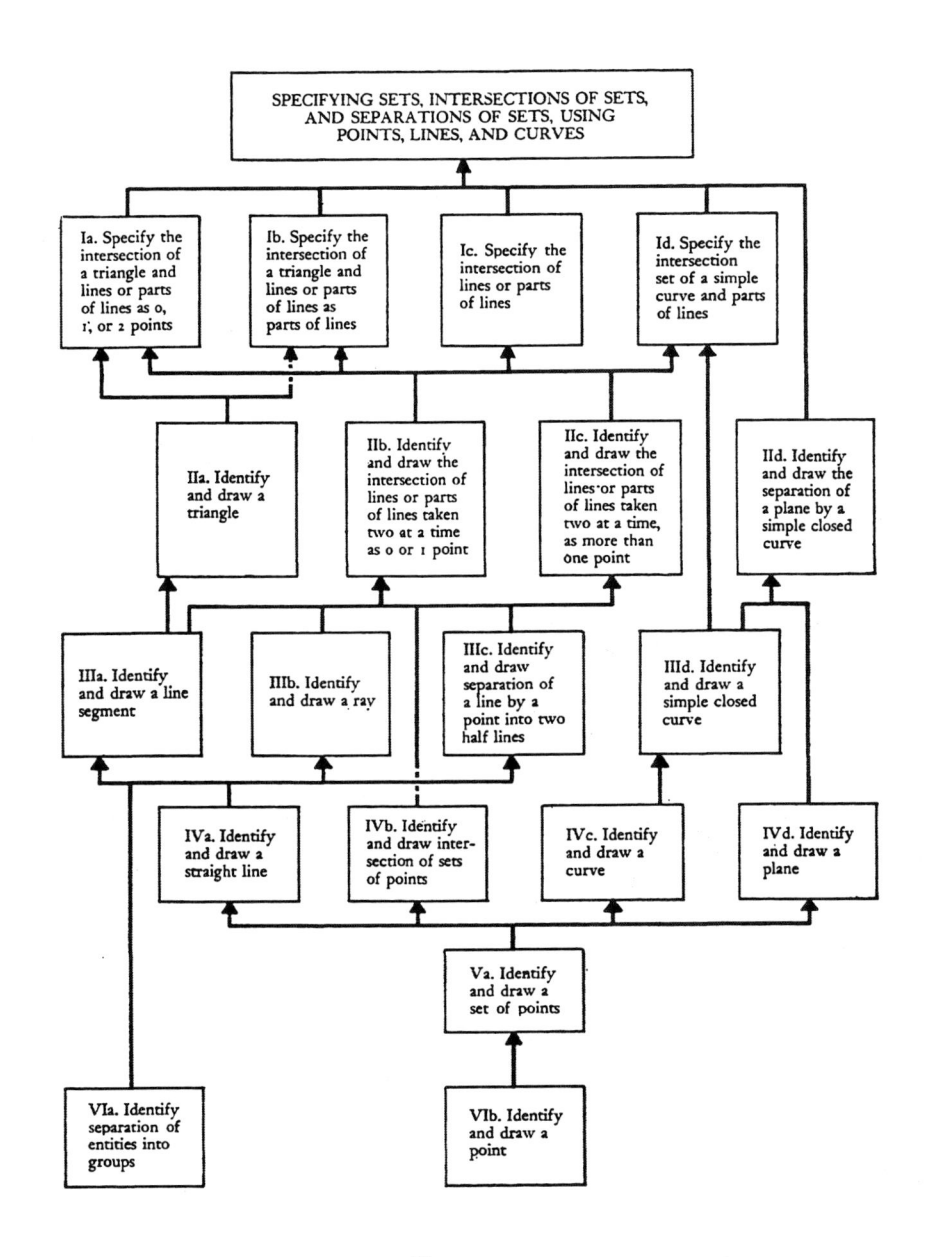

```
┌─────────────────────────────────┐
│ SPECIFYING SETS, INTERSECTIONS OF SETS, │
│    AND SEPARATIONS OF SETS, USING       │
│       POINTS, LINES, AND CURVES         │
└─────────────────────────────────┘
```

| Ia. Specify the intersection of a triangle and lines or parts of lines as 0, 1, or 2 points | Ib. Specify the intersection of a triangle and lines or parts of lines as parts of lines | Ic. Specify the intersection of lines or parts of lines | Id. Specify the intersection set of a simple curve and parts of lines |

| IIa. Identify and draw a triangle | IIb. Identify and draw the intersection of lines or parts of lines taken two at a time as 0 or 1 point | IIc. Identify and draw the intersection of lines or parts of lines taken two at a time, as more than one point | IId. Identify and draw the separation of a plane by a simple closed curve |

| IIIa. Identify and draw a line segment | IIIb. Identify and draw a ray | IIIc. Identify and draw separation of a line by a point into two half lines | IIId. Identify and draw a simple closed curve |

| IVa. Identify and draw a straight line | IVb. Identify and draw intersection of sets of points | IVc. Identify and draw a curve | IVd. Identify and draw a plane |

Va. Identify and draw a set of points

| VIa. Identify separation of entities into groups | VIb. Identify and draw a point |

Figure 11.1

Diagram from Robert M. Gagné (entry 146 in Bibliography A)

By the time of the most recent years of the present period there was beginning to be evidence that the task-analysis work of psychologists was having some impact on elementary school mathematics programs. This was particularly so in connection with initial efforts in computer-assisted instruction.

The work of Jean Piaget (probably best summarized in J. H. Flavell's *The Developmental Psychology of Jean Piaget*) had a substantial impact on thought, if not on classroom practice, during this period. Although Piaget has been writing for several decades, it was not until the early 1960s that his work was recognized by the mathematics-education community in this country. Then his impact came as a discovery. His developmental stages were of special interest to researchers and curriculum workers. The former set out to perform dozens or perhaps hundreds of related studies that either tested or extended his ideas. In general, the work of Piaget seems to have been substantiated. Developmental stages do exist, and those who would plan for the organization of mathematics content have been aware of the futility of teaching topics at one stage before prerequisite understandings have been developed.

Piaget's developmental stages may be identified as follows (258, p. 4):

(1) Sensorimotor stage (0 to 2 years)
(2) Preoperational stage (2 to 7 years)
    (a) preconceptual thought (2 to 4 years)
    (b) intuitive thought (4 to 7 years)
(3) Operational stage (7 to 16 years)
    (a) concrete operational thought (7 to 11 years)
    (b) formal operational thought (11 to 16 years)

It is understandable that the implications of Piaget's developmental stages for the organization of elementary school mathematical learning have been investigated particularly with respect to stages 2b and 3a.

Thus, within this period there have been both mathematical and psychological influences that have had a bearing upon attempts to answer the question of how the mathematics we teach should be organized.

5. *How should we organize and implement instruction?*

At all levels of American society during the period from 1952 to the present a commitment to the improvement of education has been

A CONTEMPORARY PROGRAM 143

evidenced. Initially the commitment was to the improvement of the content taught in the schools, but as content changes were implemented attention turned to the whole school. Nothing less than a total revolution was to produce the changes required. Federal enactment of the National Defense Education Act of 1958 initiated a level of funding previously unknown to American education. Supplemented with funds from various foundations (federal and private) and with business and local tax money, all aspects of the elementary school were subject to experimental redesign. Although funding increased manyfold in the years that followed 1958, it became increasingly obvious that the designated task required ever greater amounts if a really significant change was to take place. Nonetheless, the context in which mathematics was taught by the end of this period was beginning to change. Team teaching, nongraded primary schools, flexible scheduling, specialists in various areas, aides as teacher assistants, and increased reliance on media were all a part of the innovative school of the sixties.

At the beginning of the period, as mathematicians first turned their attention to the elementary school program, that attention was directed almost exclusively to the improvement of content. Some projects such as the SMSG very deliberately espoused no doctrinaire methodology.

But there were some noteworthy exceptions. In particular, reference may be made to the Madison Project, whose final report is entitled *A Modern Mathematics Program As It Pertains to the Interrelationships of Mathematical Content, Teaching Methods and Classroom Atmosphere* (136). Throughout the work of the Madison Project there was a commitment to investigating a discovery approach to instruction which was akin to the philosophy often attributed to Bruner. Discovery approaches to instruction were not restricted to the Madison Project, and there were honest differences of professional opinion regarding the role of discovery in mathematical learning, as summarized by Bittinger in the *Arithmetic Teacher* (308).

In any event, by the mid-sixties there was growing recognition on the part of many mathematicians that content alone would not solve the problem of improving mathematics instruction in the elementary schools. The significant role of instructional methodology was more widely recognized, whether the methodology was based on a discovery approach to instruction or on a strictly behavioral theory of conditioning (as developed by Suppes and his associates).

The relevance of media and technology to mathematics instruction also was an issue of significance. These techniques ranged from the use of sets of unique manipulative materials such as Cuisenaire rods to the use of computers. The most extensive explorations of computer-assisted instruction in elementary school mathematics have been conducted by Suppes and his associates (261).

Concern for instructional methodology, media, and technology stems in no small way from a broader concern for individual differences in mathematical learning among elementary school children. Attempts to differentiate effectively or to individualize instruction have utilized variations in the content and in the administrative organization of instruction as well as in methodology and the use of media and technology (429). Answers to the question of how instruction should be organized and implemented were being sought from a wide variety of potentially relevant sources. Some of these sources came from outside the United States. Considerable interest has been evidenced in two things: (1) the work of Z. P. Dienes (138) in Australia, England, and Canada, which emphasized the discovery approaches to mathematical structures through the use of manipulative materials, and (2) the Nuffield Mathematics Project in England, which emphasized a laboratory approach to learning.

The Nuffield Project has been responsible in no mean way for an accelerating interest in the development of mathematics laboratories in elementary schools here. These laboratories initially received attention as a result of activities associated with the Madison Project.

6. *Summary*

The Needs of Society

Throughout the period from 1952 to the present, the needs of society have been focused on the elementary school mathematics programs as never before. In a technological world, moving toward the twenty-first century envisioned by many as a new concept of life on this globe, it is thought that mathematics must play a major role involving appreciation, understanding, and advanced applications. Finding the role of the elementary school in the achievement of that assignment was never more difficult.

The Discipline of Mathematics

It was often said at the beginning of this revolutionary period that the mathematics content of the schools, both elementary and secondary, had not changed in three hundred years. No one seemed to voice an objection to this opinion. All of that changed in the years beginning with 1952 as set theory, new algebras, and new geometries had an impact on the content of elementary school mathematics programs. Tentatively at first, but with increased assurance as the period progressed, educators, psychologists, and mathematicians began to work together, increasingly confident that each had an essential role to play in the shaping of the elementary mathematics program.

Initially the mathematicians had turned their attention almost exclusively to matters of content improvement. In the later years of the period, however, many were convinced that the improvement of content alone was not enough. Integration of mathematics with other subject areas, laboratory experiences for learners, wide use of concrete materials, and a relation to the child world were increasing concerns of the mathematicians. Ultimately, mathematicians were sounding many of the phrases that had been popular with the progressives twenty or thirty years earlier. Now, however, those who would design such programs were armed with mathematical competence—an ingredient often lacking in the arsenal of the progressive educator.

Knowledge of Psychology

Some of the major experimental mathematics projects of this period were implemented by staffs that included a blending of mathematicians, educators, and psychologists. Conferences in which mathematicians and psychologists exchanged ideas were not always productive of immediately useful results, but they did much to make each group aware of the contributions that could come from the other discipline. The studies made by Gagné, Bruner, Piaget, and Suppes are primary examples of the work that was contributing to the design of elementary school programs.

As the fifties got under way there was a major dedication to the improvement of elementary school mathematics education from many sections of our society. How shall we evaluate our accomplishments as of this date? Certainly there is reason to believe that again much has been achieved at a theoretical level. Indeed, textbooks today differ substantially from those experienced by learners prior to 1952. However, there is considerable evidence to indicate that until teachers, parents, and school personnel understand more clearly the improvements that have been wrought through major innovative efforts, and until expectations, texts, and curriculum guides represent these improvements, the learner may still benefit only partially from the best that we know about the teaching and learning of mathematics in the elementary school.

The Future

One significant assessment of the things that have happened in mathematics education during this present period comes from E. G. Begle, director of SMSG, as follows (92):

> I am sure that many of our teachers look on our new curricula as a revolution in school mathematics. In a sense this is correct, but it is merely a small aspect of a revolution in mathematics itself which has been going on for a century and a half. . . . There are two important observations that need to be made. The first is that this revolution has been successfully concluded. The second is that no new revolution is clearly in sight. Even if the first stirrings of a new revolution might be taking place in mathematical research, its effects could not appear in the pre-college program for generations. Consequently we can agree on the broad outline of the content of the mathematics curriculum for the schools. This content is well enough known that we need not spell it out here in detail. Suffice it to mention that the mathematical topics included in the curriculum are, with few exceptions, those included in the pre-revolutionary curriculum. Only a few new topics, such as inequalities, have been added because of their intrinsic importance, and only a few other topics have been given lesser emphasis than before.
>
> On the other hand, the new curriculum differs radically from the old in that it includes the structure of the common mathematical systems, the basic mathematical concepts and their interrelationships, as well as the basic mathematical facts and techniques.

Now as we look to the future we can expect various interpretations of the details which should reflect this "broad outline of the content of the mathematics curriculum for the schools." One such interpretation is given in the Cambridge Conference report (11). To what extent is the report's content outline accepted and implemented at present? To what extent will it be accepted and implemented during the 1970s? To what extent will it be tempered by reactions voiced by persons such as Marshall Stone (422) and Irving Adler (287)?

The following items are quoted from the outline given in the Cambridge report (pp. 31–41):

The Earliest Grades, K through 2

The Real Number System

Early experiences in studying numbers should be designed to give insight into the mathematical properties of the real number system. *They probably should not focus on the learning of algorithms, which will come considerably later in the curriculum.*

Experiences with numbers using concrete objects which can be counted, measured, and arranged in various ways should have a prominent place in the first years of school. . . .

(1) Experiences with "grouping" that will establish the idea of place-value numerals to various bases, including base 10.

(2) Extensive use of zero as a number, not merely as a symbol.

(3) The idea of inequalities, and the symbols < and >.

(4) The idea of transitivity of <. (This can be built into game situations where the child is asked to guess a "secret" number from a set of carefully devised clues, and so on.)

(5) The number line, including negatives from the beginning.

(6) Use of rulers with 0 at the center.

(7) Use of the number line in the "transitivity" games mentioned above.

(8) Use of fractions with small denominators to name additional points on the number line.

(9) Use of the idea of "the neighborhood of a point" on the number line; relation to inequalities.

(10) Use of the number line to introduce decimals by change of scale.

(11) The use of "crossed" number lines to form Cartesian coordinates; various games of strategy using Cartesian coordinates.

(12) Use of an additive slide rule, including both positive and negative numbers.

(13) Physical interpretations of addition and multiplication, including original interpretations made up by the children themselves (such as 2 × 4 represented by 4 washers on each of 2 pegs, or 2 stacks of 4 washers each, or a 2 × 4 rectangular array of washers [or dots, or pebbles, etc.], of 2 washers of each of 4 different colors, 4 washers of each of 2 different colors, and so on).

(14) Questions that lead the children to "discover" the commutative nature of addition and multiplication.

(15) Multiplication of a number "a little bit more than three" by a number "a little bit less than five."

(16) Division with remainder using, for example, the pattern: "20 ÷ 8" means

"If we have 20 dots, how many rows of 8 will there be?"

. . . .
. . . .
. . . .

Answer: "2 whole rows and 4 left over."

(17) Division with fractional answers. 20 ÷ 8 = 2½.

(18) Recognition of inverse operations.

(19) Use of □ as a variable in simple algebraic problems.

(20) Experience with Cartesian coordinates, including both discrete and continuous cases, graphs of linear functions, graphs of functions obtained empirically, simple extrapolation ("When will the plant be seven inches tall?"), and so on. Various games of strategy played on Cartesian coordinates, etc. Graph of □ + △ = 10, in connection with learning "addition facts," etc.

Geometry

Geometry is to be studied together with arithmetic and algebra from kindergarten on. Some of the aims of this study are to develop the planar and spatial intuition of the pupil, to afford a source of visualization for arithmetic and algebra, and to serve as a model for that branch of natural science which investigates physical space by mathematical methods. . . .

The earliest grades should include topics and experiences like these:

(1) Identifying and naming various geometric configurations.

(2) Visualization, such as cutting out cardboard to construct 3-dimensional figures, where the child is shown the 3-dimensional figure and asked to find his own way to cut the 2-dimensional paper or cardboard.

(3) The additive property of area, closely integrated with the operation of multiplication.

(4) Symmetry and other transformations leaving geometrical figures invariant. The fact that a line or circle can be slid into itself. The symmetries of squares and rectangles, circles, ellipses, etc., and solid figures like spheres, cubes, tetrahedra, etc. This study could be facilitated with mirrors, paper folding, etc.

(5) Possibly the explicit recognition of the group property in the preceding.

(6) Use of straightedge and compass to do the standard geometric constructions such as comparing segments or angles, bisecting a segment or angle, etc.

(7) Similar figures, both plane and solid, starting from small and enlarged photographs, etc.

Logic and Set Theory; Function

. . . .

The ideas of *set* and *function* should be introduced as soon as possible. In the earliest grades:

(1) Number as a property of finite sets.

(2) The comparison of cardinals of finite sets with emphasis on the fact that the result is independent of which mapping function is used.

A CONTEMPORARY PROGRAM 149

(3) Numerical functions determined by very simple formulas.

(4) The use of logical statements to determine certain sets. For example, games like Twenty Questions in which the set of possibilities is successively narrowed through the answers to yes-no questions.

(5) Familiarity with both true and false statements as a source of information.

Applications

The work with real numbers, described above, can be closely related to work in "science" and "applications," such as:

(1) Measurement and units, in cases of length, area, volume, weight, time, money, temperature, etc.

(2) Use of various measuring instruments, such as rulers, calipers, scales, etc.

(3) Physical interpretations of 1/2, 1/3, 1/4, 2/3.

(4) Physical interpretations of negative numbers in relation to an arbitrary reference point (as 0° Centigrade, or altitude at sea level, or the lobby floor for an elevator, etc.).

(5) Physical embodiments of inequalities in length, weight, etc., again using games where the child must use the transitive property, or the fact that $a > c$ implies $a + b > c + b$.

(6) Estimating orders of magnitude, with applications related to physics, economics, history, sociology, etc.

(7) Visual display of data on Cartesian coordinates, such as recording growth of seedlings by daily measurement of height, or graph of temperature vs. time for hourly readings of a thermometer.

Grades 3 through 6

In these four grades we should continue pursuit of the main objective, familiarity with the real number system and geometry. At the same time we must start pre-mathematical experiences aiming towards the more sophisticated work in high school.

The Real Number System

(1) Commutative, associative, and distributive laws. The multiplicative property of 1. The additive and multiplicative properties of 0.

(2) Arithmetic of signed numbers.

(3) For comparison purposes
  (a) Modular arithmetic, based on primes and on non-primes.
  (b) Finite fields.
  (c) Study of 2 × 2 matrices; comparison with real numbers; isomorphism of a subset of 2 × 2 matrices with real numbers; divisors of zero; identities for matrices; simple matrix inverses (particularly in relation to the idea of inverse operations and the nonexistence of a mul-

tiplicative inverse for zero). Possible use of matrices to introduce complex numbers.

(4) Prime numbers and factoring. Euclidean algorithm, greatest common divisor.

(5) Elementary Diophantine problems.

(6) Integral exponents, both positive and negative.

(7) The arithmetic of inequalities.

(8) Absolute value.

(9) Explicit study of the decimal system of notation including comparison with other bases and mixed bases (e.g. miles, yards, feet, inches).

(10) Study of algorithms for adding, subtracting, multiplying, and dividing both integers and rational numbers, including "original" algorithms made up by the children themselves.

(11) Methods for checking and verifying correctness of answers without recourse to the teacher.

(12) Familiarity with certain "short cut" calculations that serve to illustrate basic properties of numbers or of numerals.

(13) The use of desk calculators, slide rules, and tables.

(14) Interpolation.

(15) Considerable experience in approximations, estimates, "scientific notation," and orders of magnitude.

(16) Effect of "round-off" and significant figures.

(17) Knowledge of the distinction between rational and irrational numbers.

(18) Study of decimals, for rational and irrational numbers.

(19) Square roots, inequalities such as $1.41 < \sqrt{2} < 1.42$.

(20) The Archimedean property and the density of the rational numbers including terminating decimals.

(21) Nested intervals.

(22) Computation with numbers given approximately. (E.g., find π^2 given π.)

(23) Simple algebraic equations and inequalities.

. . . .

Geometry

In the later grades of elementary school, relatively little pure geometry would be introduced, but more experience with the topics from K–2 would be built up. . . . New topics might include:

(1) Mensuration formulas for familiar figures.

(2) Approximate determination of π by measuring circles.

(3) Conic sections.

(4) Equation determining a straight line.

(5) Cartesian coordinates in 3 dimensions.
(6) Polar coordinates.
(7) Latitude and longitude.
(8) Symmetry of more sophisticated figures (e.g. wallpaper).
(9) Similar figures interpreted as scale models and problems of indirect measurement.
(10) Vectors, possibly including some statics and linear kinematics.
(11) Symmetry argument for the congruence of the base angles of an isosceles triangle.

Logic and Foundations

(1) The vocabulary of elementary logic: true, false, implication, double implication, contradiction.
(2) Truth tables for simplest connectives.
(3) The common schemes of inference:

$$\frac{P \to Q \text{ and } P}{Q} \qquad \frac{P \to Q \text{ and } \sim Q}{\sim P}$$

(4) Simple uses of mathematical induction.
(5) Preliminary recognition of the roles of axioms and theorems in relation to the real number system.
(6) Simple uses of logical implication or "derivations" in studying algorithms, more complicated identities, etc.
(7) Elements of flow charting.
(8) Simple uses of indirect proof, in studying inequalities, proving $\sqrt{2}$ irrational, and so on.
(9) Study of sets, relations, and functions. Graphs of relations and functions, both discrete and continuous. Graphs of empirically determined functions.
(10) Explicit study of the relation of open sentences and their truth sets.
(11) The concepts of isomorphism and transformation.

. . . .

Theory of Real Functions

(1) Intuitive consideration of infinite sequences of real numbers.
(2) The logarithm function, built up by interpolation, from approximate equalities like $2^{10} \approx 10^3$. . . .
(3) Trigonometric functions.
(4) Partial and linear orderings, with applications.
(5) Linearity and convexity.

. . . .

Applications

Because a good deal of science can, and probably will, be introduced into primary school, more applications of mathematics will be possible in the upper grades.

Some of the most important applications involve probability and statistics, which we conceive as purely empirical subjects at this level. The study should begin with

(1) Empirical investigation of many-times-repeated random events.

(2) Arithmetic study of how the ultimate stabilization of observed relative frequency occurs through "swamping."

These investigations should be applied to the problems of measurement in connection with all science experiments.

*Forces and Issues
Related to Curriculum
and Instruction, 7–12*

PART THREE

Alan R. Osborne
F. Joe Crosswhite

CHAPTER TWELVE

Emerging Issues: 1890-1920

1. Introduction

Goethe remarked that "every emancipation of the spirit is pernicious unless there is a corresponding growth of control." The period from the Gay Nineties to the Roaring Twenties provides an example in mathematics education of this poetically perceptive statement. Chapter 4 of this yearbook, "First Steps toward Revision," sets the stage for the exploration of the issues and forces of this period. The story of this chapter is one of freeing mathematics teaching from the constraints of the mental-discipline theory of learning and the associated narrow aims for secondary schooling. The story is also one of the seeking of adequate replacements for the mental-discipline theory and of the exploration of suitable goals for learning mathematics. The period approaches its close with a potentially deadly and deleterious state existing in mathematics education. No well-developed philosophic base comparable to mental discipline was developed. What the aims of education were and what were the most effective ways of accomplishing these aims remained open questions, and little controlled guidance towards acceptable alternative answers was available to school people and the people whom they served.

2. Mathematics education in 1890

Today mathematics education faces issues much like those that were being explored in the 1890s. During the 1890s the issues were treated for the first time by groups reflecting a national purpose. School systems, colleges, and universities were well enough established to look beyond themselves to questions of effectiveness rather than to struggle for mere existence. Schools at all levels were viable and ongoing.

What would a person concerned with the teaching of mathematics see in examining the schools of the 1890 era? Which issues and forces would appear most crucial? What mathematics was being taught, and why was it being taught?

The typical teacher in 1890 was guided by the philosophy of mental discipline. The basis of this prevailing concept of learning and transfer was a nonempirically based psychology that smacked of Cotton Mather and Calvinism. Text materials seemed to be organized according to each author's notion of mental discipline. Mental disciplinarians held that the best materials and methods were those that trained the faculties of the mind to the utmost capacity. Activities to train for perception, reasoning, will, attention, and the like were the heart of the study in geometry, arithmetic, and algebra. It was felt that these capacities would automatically transfer to another discipline. George A. Wentworth's *Grammar School Arithmetic*, published in 1889, indicates the climate of the day in the preface as follows (270, p. iii):

> Whether arithmetic is studied for mental discipline or for practical mastery over the everyday problems of common life, mechanical processes and routine methods are of no value. Pupils can be trained to logical habits of the mind and stimulated to a high degree of intellectual energy by solving problems adapted to their capabilities. They become practical arithmeticians, not by learning special business forms, but by founding their knowledge on reasoning which they fully comprehend, and by being so thoroughly exercised in logical analysis that they are independent of arbitrary rules.

The teacher would have found little help in deciding which exercises would best train specific faculties, for there was little professional literature and little professional education, and there were few professional organizations.

Textbooks in the three subject areas of school mathematics (arithmetic, algebra, and geometry) provide evidence that the operant philosophy in determining curricular content was mental discipline. Little attention was given to the use of mathematics as a tool. Indeed, mathematics was learned primarily for its own sake and for the purpose of training the faculties of the mind. Subjects were compartmentalized,

EMERGING ISSUES 157

and within a given subject little or no effort was made to establish interrelationships of ideas. The concern for logical organization took precedence over the immediate utility of mathematics. Little effort had been made to adjust college-oriented mathematics to less mature students.

⇢⇢⇢ 3. *Arithmetic*

Some authors of texts in arithmetic did indicate a concern for the practical and vocational in their books. Perhaps this reflected the attempts of people like Woodward to found manual-training schools and the concern of fledgling labor unions for vocational education. Lawrence Cremin (129, pp. 22–57) documents the post-1870 reawakening concern for the practical and for the vocationally oriented curriculum. For example, Joseph Ray (1807–1857), whose book *The Little Arithmetic* was first published in Cincinnati in 1834, sold his copyright to the publishers of the McGuffey Readers (164, p. 19). Later books and editions appeared, under many different titles, as late as 1877. The primary objective of his *Intellectual Arithmetic*, published in 1857 (212) was "to train and develop the mind by the science of numbers. Numbers are the instruments employed to strengthen the memory, to cultivate the faculty of abstraction, and to sharpen and develop the reasoning powers." However, the *New Practical Arithmetic*, published under his name in 1877, stated that "changes . . . in the modes of transacting business" made it necessary to change the content of the book. In addition to whole and rational number arithmetic, the content included money, billing, weights and measures, metric system, discounts, profit, loss, stocks, interest, discounts, exchange, insurance and taxes, partnership, bankruptcy, and square and cube roots. As was typical, "The arrangement is strictly philosophical; no principle is anticipated; the pupil is never required to perform any operation until the principle on which it is based has first been explained" (213, p. iii). The book was self-contained. The learner could proceed from first principles of arithmetic to the sophistication required for understanding compound interest. The material was appropriate for the older students, probably at least of junior high school age. Each section began with definitions, moved to examples and rules, and was completed by problems (answers given). One problem typifying the content as well as the level of sophistication required was the following (p. 275):

> 4. A bookseller imports a case of books; their cost in Germany was 1317.04 marks, case and charges 34.36 marks, and commission 6%.

158   HISTORY OF MATHEMATICS EDUCATION

What was the duty at 25% in U.S. money, the mark being estimated at 23.8 ct.?

Joseph Ray was the McGuffey of mathematics. Thirty-eight different arithmetics and nineteen algebras were published under his name (183, pp. 173-77). His writings were organized on the tenets of mental discipline but showed awareness of vocational needs. His arithmetic texts provided the teacher with a choice. He could choose a text directed toward vocationalism, or he could choose an approach that was more general, more directly based on the concept of mental discipline.

4. *Algebra*

The teacher of the 1890s saw little in algebra books that indicated concern for the practical. Algebra was studied primarily to fulfill college entrance requirements. Algebra was first made a requirement in 1820 by Harvard. Orlando Overn (397, p. 374) makes the case that it preceded geometry as an entrance requirement. He indicates that the original impetus for algebra in the secondary school curriculum was the result of practical rather than disciplinary considerations. However, algebra was moved from the colleges to the secondary schools with little or no modification.

During the nineteenth century, as mathematics became a part of the secondary school curriculum, algebra attained an important position in this curriculum. Once established as a secondary school subject, it began to have an impact on the rest of the mathematics curriculum. It forced a reconsideration of arithmetic teaching in the elementary school as preparation for algebra.

Amy Olive Chateauneuf's study (440) of 257 algebra textbooks published during the period from 1820 to 1928 indicates that algebraic techniques (factoring, roots, powers, and fundamental operations) occupied the major portion of texts during the 1890s. Equation solving, problems, and the study of functions and their graphs were apparently of less importance. Figure 12.1, taken from Overn's study of the effect of college entrance requirements on algebra textbooks, shows the relative balance of topics in textbooks by decades. Indeed, the peak of attention to technique was attained during the 1890s. By Chateauneuf's criteria, 64 percent of the text material was concerned with technique (p. 151). She also claimed that the problem material in this era was more difficult than that of other decades. David Eugene Smith (416) wrote in 1926 of this period that "the subject [algebra] was usually

EMERGING ISSUES 159

GRAPH NO. 1 SHOWING DISTRIBUTION OF MATERIAL IN TEXTBOOKS IN ELEMENTARY ALGEBRA, 1820-1928 (AFTER CHATEAUNEUF)

GRAPHS
LITERAL EQUATIONS AND FORMULAS
NUMERICAL EQUATIONS AND PROBLEMS
FUNDAMENTAL OPERATIONS WITH RATIONAL EXPRESSIONS
POWERS AND ROOTS
FACTORING, FACTORS AND MULTIPLES

NINETEENTH CENTURY | TWENTIETH CENTURY

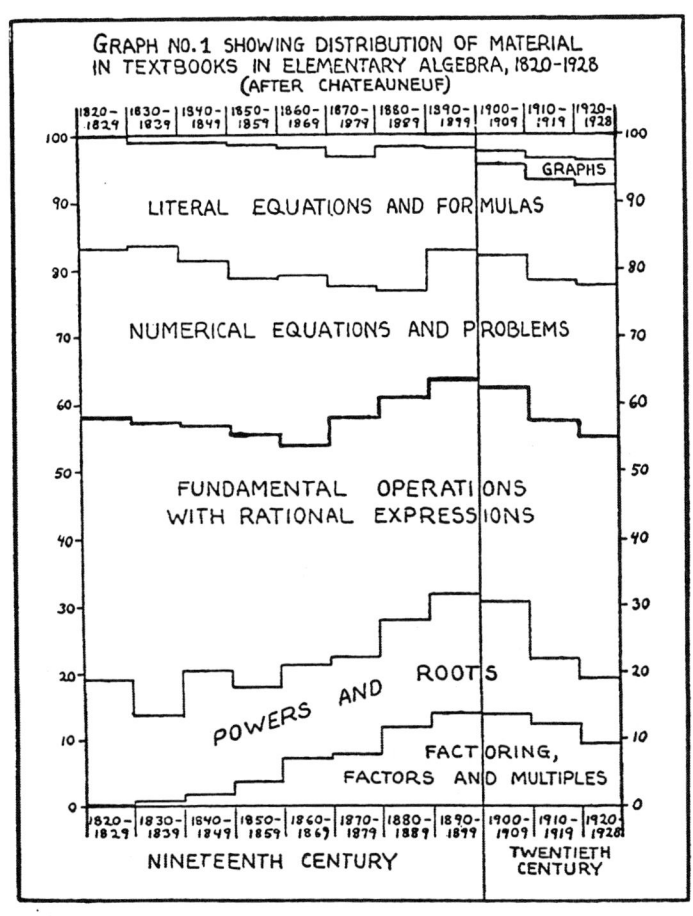

Figure 12.1. From Overn (397, p. 375)

taught as if it were a purely mathematical discipline, unrelated to life except as life might enjoy the meaningless puzzle."

Examination of typical algebra texts shows that writers assumed that one text would encompass all of the secondary school experience with algebra. For example, William J. Milne's *High School Algebra* in 1892 (179) ended with developments of logarithms, the binomial theorem, partial fractions, and the theory of equations. The organization of texts was logical, with ideas usually being developed from definitions. A few rare authors attempted an axiomatic development of some theorems. Chateauneuf indicated that only 0.1 percent of text material in the 1890s contained work with graphs. Most authors treated variables as unknowns, accepting the idea that algebra was a generalized arithmetic. However, very few authors attempted to provide an inductive basis for concepts. Little or no attention was given to what are today called unifying concepts. Significant concepts such as variable, function, and data analysis were not given the honor of special treatment. Few authors attempted to help students tie ideas together.

The progression of difficulty of problems was consistent with the assumption that one text would be used. Most authors treated simultaneous equations with three or four unknowns immediately after work with two unknowns. Most authors used literal notation for some of the work because of the generality of solution. Work progressed rapidly to the relatively difficult. Milne (pp. 180–86) progressed in a short seven pages on evolution to finding the square root of

$$\frac{c^4}{4} + \frac{x^2}{2} + \frac{c^3}{x} - cx + \frac{c^2}{x^2} - 2$$

and to finding the first four terms of the square root of $1 + x$. This was preceded by a worked example and by a rule.

Algebra would seem, to the teacher of the 1890s, generally consistent with the concept of mental discipline. It was difficult. It made little pretense of practicality. Manipulative skills were emphasized. The content of elementary algebra was relatively well standardized. It was quite abstract.

Florian Cajori surveyed teachers of mathematics in 1890. The Cajori report indicated that the teacher in 1890 was crying out against the emphasis on the manipulative skills in algebra and was beginning to ask for a treatment of the subject which would bring more meaning and understanding. Typical of the responses to the question "What reforms are needed in the teaching of algebra?" were the following (121, p. 330):

> More of the spirit and reason and less of mechanical solution.
>
> Rattle the bones of the algebraic skeleton, as exhibited in this country, and show it in its living, breathing continuity and beauty of form.
>
> Anything to make it less a collection of dry bones and more a living and beautiful science.

Perhaps it is typical that two-thirds of these same teachers who were quick and biting in their commentaries still relied almost exclusively upon the textbook as a teaching device, and that only 2 of

EMERGING ISSUES 161

168 reporting were bold enough to assert that they used the lecture more than the text.

➛➛➛ 5. *Geometry*

The teacher of high school geometry in 1890 typically provided his students with an introduction to rigorous, axiomatic thinking. Although noteworthy attempts to introduce geometry in the elementary school had been made, there had been little success. For example, as early as 1859 Thomas Hill, in "The True Order of Studies" (354, p. 12), suggested that experiences in geometry in the early elementary grades provide a basis for arithmetic and that youngsters aged eight to twelve should learn theorems as facts before proceeding to their demonstrative geometry in high school. In this essay, Hill remarked that Sir William Hamilton's argument against geometry as a basis for mental-discipline experiences was not altogether appropriate because it overlooked the training of faculties of observation and imagination, which are "as important as those of reasoning" (p. 21). The geometry teacher would find that, aside from mensurational work in the practical arithmetics, there would be little geometry taught previous to his course.

Before the Civil War geometry had been a college subject. The most widely used texts of the 1880s were the first attempts of writers to provide geometry for secondary school students rather than college-age students. Chapter 3 indicates that texts were generally based on the geometry of Legendre, which provided the following three differences from the traditional Euclid which Jabir Shibli (238, p. 22) maintains were aids to the teacher who did not have a background in the work of Euclid:

1. Numbers were associated with line segments. Consequently, arithmetic and algebra could be used to simplify work in mensuration and ratio.
2. The degree of rigor demanded of students was decreased.
3. Legendre changed Euclid's sequence of theorems. Charles Davies's translation of Legendre (134) separated propositions by topic.

A fourth difference from Euclid appearing in these first secondary school geometries was not attributable to the influence of Legendre's book. Both Euclid and Legendre proved every proposition that was stated. Greenleaf's *Geometry* was the first to include exercises, called "originals," for which the student was to supply the proofs. This innovation was to be widely accepted. Wentworth claims in the preface of his *A Textbook of Geometry* (rev. ed.) to have introduced more than seven hundred exercises that were "carefully graded and specially adapted for beginners" (271, p. vii). The number of proved theorems versus the number of originals was to become an issue. Most of the exercises in the geometry texts were originals requiring proof rather than applications and problems.

The geometry course in the 1890s was also based primarily on the concept of mental discipline. Geometry seemed eminently suited for the training of the faculties of logical thinking, observation, and concentration. Wentworth suggests to the teacher (p. v) that pupils write the proofs on their first reading of the geometry:

> This method will furnish a valuable exercise as a language lesson, will cultivate the habit of neat and orderly arrangement of work, and will allow a brief interval for deliberating on each step. After a book has been read in this way, the pupil should review the Book, and should be required to draw the figures freehand. He should state and prove the propositions orally.

The content of texts generally included work on solid geometry. This was not integrated with the content of plane geometry. Wentworth's book closes with fifty-one pages devoted to the geometry of the conic sections. Authors attempted to treat incommensurability by means of limit arguments. Students were started on the processes of proof almost immediately in most texts.

6. *Other forces*

The pedagogical world of the secondary school mathematics teacher has been incompletely reflected in the preceding examination of the state of the curriculum in arithmetic, algebra, and geometry. The vantage point of eighty years of experience makes the issue of mental-discipline and subject-centered aims versus vocationally practical-child-centered aims stand out clearly. Other forces and issues might have been clearer to the teacher in the 1890s.

The number of secondary schools had increased dramatically after the Civil War. Most communities in the northern states had established public high schools, and increasing numbers of youths of high school age were enrolled (although in 1890 the proportion was still extremely small by modern standards—approximately 7 percent). Many of the students did not have as their goal the usual mid-twentieth century aim of continuing to college. This contributed to the diversification of the curriculum. Several new subject-matter areas were recognized as appropriate to the secondary school. Courses in psychology, political economy, chemistry, metereology, and modern language had been foreign to the typical secondary school curriculum of the Civil War era. Curricular offerings expanded with little or no design. Teacher shortages developed. Not only was there little uniformity in course offerings, there was little standardization of what was meant by algebra or geometry from school system to school system. Indeed, this diversity characterized the secondary school program prior to 1890. Further, if the percentage of failures is taken as the measure, mathematics and Latin shared the dubious distinction of being the most difficult subjects in the secondary school. (392, p. 21.)

7. *The Committee of Ten*

The dissatisfaction with the state of secondary education reached a peak in 1890, prompting the National Council on Education (a part of the National Education Association) to appoint a committee on the problems of secondary schools. This committee, reporting in 1892, suggested that there was a need for a massive study looking toward reconstruction of the secondary school curriculum. The NEA then appointed the Committee of Ten on the Secondary School Studies. During this committee's first meeting in November of 1892, ten-member subject-matter subcommittees were appointed for the nine areas of (1) Latin, (2) Greek, (3) mathematics, (4) English, (5) modern languages, (6) physics, (7) astronomy and chemistry, (8) biology, botany, zoology, and physiology, and (9) history, civil government, and political economy.

The original Committee of Ten, in considering the problems of secondary education, addressed itself to issues that were of great import to the special committee on mathematics. The original committee, composed largely of people from eastern private schools, held training to be the primary aim of education. Three words were of particular significance: observation, logic, and judgment. Discriminating observation was promoted by the study of languages and natural sciences, comparative judgment by history, and the "logical faculty of following an argument from point to point" by mathematics. The Committee of Ten is significant in American education because it opened the way for subsequent modifications of the theory of mental discipline. Although the committee talked in terms of training, faculties, and mental power, the members were strong in taking the stand that the cultivation of mental powers is not the unique function of any particular part of the curriculum. Indeed, perhaps because of the influence of Charles W. Eliot, the president of Harvard, an elective approach to curriculum building was deemed appropriate.

A subject should meet the criterion of being taught "consecutively enough and extensively enough" to warrant inclusion as an elective. The committee was concerned that a student might not get the most from school if his attention was spread too thinly. Consequently, it recommended limiting students to three or four courses at a given time. As shall be seen, this was slightly at variance with the recommendations of the subcommittee on mathematics (72, pp. 21–22). The courses offered by a school were to be based on the subject-matter content. Instruction for a given subject was "to be in the same way and to the same extent" for all pupils. The committee recognized that students would have differing aspirations by stating "Not that all students should pursue every subject for the same number of years; but so long as they do pursue it, they should all be treated alike" (72, p. 17). In saying this, the committee specifically recognized that for most students secondary school was terminal, and yet it recommended studies oriented to the college-bound students. This could only serve to perpetuate the existing curriculum pattern in mathematics. Freeman Butts and Lawrence Cremin suggest that the report was clearly dominated by "the more conservative spirit of the colleges and universities of the time" (119, p. 390).

The committee's statements concerning mathematics had more direct relevance to the elementary school curriculum than to that of the secondary school. The committee found the elementary school programs inadequate for the students entering secondary school. It was recommended not only that the study of arithmetic be completed by grade 8 but also that algebra and geometry be informally introduced in the upper elementary school. Comparable recommendations were made for other subject-matter areas. More generally, the committee suggested, as an alternative to the way schools were being organized, that the secondary program begin two years earlier, "leaving six years instead of eight for the elementary period" (72, p. 45).

The subcommittee of ten persons appointed by the Committee of Ten to study the mathematics curriculum was known as the Conference on Mathematics. It agreed with the general committee that the teaching of mathematics was in need of change. However, the confer-

EMERGING ISSUES 165

ence was much more specific in its set of recommendations. The conference, in addressing itself primarily to the three areas of arithmetic, algebra, and geometry, supported the committee's views on mental discipline. Arithmetic, for example, should be "abridged by omitting entirely those subjects which perplex and exhaust the pupil without affording any really valuable mental discipline" (72, p. 105). Some subjects fitting this criterion were compound proportion, cube root, abstract mensuration, and denominate quantities.

The conference's position concerning the utility of mathematics, however, was not entirely consistent with the committee's position. The committee had suggested that the grade placement of topics in the arithmetic of commerce was crucial. The principles of business operation were beyond the understanding of students in arithmetic because of their youth and inexperience. Topics such as profit and loss, bank discounts, and compound interest were offered as examples "not easily made intelligible to the pupil." Consequently, they should be omitted from the prealgebra arithmetic experience. But the conference made the following significant statement concerning commercial arithmetic (p. 45):

> The Conference is of the opinion that up to the completion of the first year's work in algebra the course should be the same, whether the students are preparing for college, for scientific schools, or intend their systematic education to end with the high school. In the case of those who do not intend to go to college, but to pursue a business career, the remainder of the term which has been allotted to algebra might well be devoted to bookkeeping and the technical parts of commercial arithmetic.

Thus, much of the then-traditional content of higher arithmetic was to be delayed until after completion of algebra (if it were to be taught at all).

The Conference on Mathematics issued a five-section report, one section of which was concerned with algebra. Assuming a basic curriculum in arithmetic during the first eight years, the report recommended the inclusion of the simple algebra of algebraic expressions, symboling, and simple equations in grades 5–8. This "generalized arithmetic" (72, p. 105), so foreign to the spirit of modern algebra generated in the nineteenth century by such notables as H. G. Grassmann, W. R. Hamilton, Benjamin Peirce, and J. J. Sylvester, was to provide an inductive base that could be extended and used in the secondary school. The inductive method was to be continued in the elementary ninth-grade algebra. "Rules should be derived inductively instead of being stated dogmatically" (p. 105). Mastery of topics through quadratic equations could be assured by concentrating the study of algebra in grade 9 to the extent of five periods per week.

The writers of the conference report demonstrated their concern for the teaching approach. An orientation toward generalized or literal arithmetic pervaded the comments concerning proofs and rigor. Verification of theorems typically proved today, such as $(-a)(-b) = ab$, was to be delayed beyond grade 9. Advanced topics, such as the binomial theorem, were also to be delayed. Rigor was to take at least second place to the inductive approach. Theorems were to be presented with enough illustrations and concrete examples to convince the learner —much in the fashion of Hill's approach to geometric propositions in the later elementary school. Oral work was recommended, as it was by Wentworth (quoted in the section on geometry), to help provide for acquisition of speed and accuracy. The conference followed the spirit of the times in stressing that skill and accuracy were important in the techniques associated with literal coefficients and exponents (p. 112). The concept of equation—the solution of equations and their use in problem solving—was sufficiently important to the committee to be labeled by today's commentators as a unifying concept. The concept of proof could be acquired in the two and one-half days per week devoted to algebra in the tenth and eleventh grades. This is evidence of a European influence, for this pattern of the simultaneous offering of algebra and geometry was common in some European school systems. No recommendation was made either for any concept to serve as a unifying idea or for a fusion of related concepts of algebra and geometry. The conference's approach was often referred to as correlated mathematics. This issue of how the ideas of algebra and geometry should be related was to become important during the next two decades.

Supporters of the theory of formal discipline would probably have found the section dealing with geometry more acceptable than the rest of the report. Instruction was to be for two and one-half hours per week throughout grades 10 and 11, paralleling the instruction in algebra. No other suggestion for interrelating the concepts of geometry and algebra was made. The position that mathematics was uniquely suited for training the faculty associated with logical argument was supported by the commentary on teaching style and by the nature of the geometry course. The conference recommended that the level of rigor in geometric demonstrations be raised. Elegance in both written and oral proofs was important: the conference stated that lack of "oral elegance" was a flaw that made the recitation of proofs practically valueless. It added that "it prevents the discipline for which this exercise is chiefly prized" (p. 113). The conference recommended that ample opportunity for recitation should be provided and that all proofs that were not formally perfect be rejected. Original exercises were deemed important (p. 115). The feeling communicated is that students cannot become original, creative thinkers unless they have opportunity to be original.

A goal of the course in geometry was to establish an axiomatic description of space. The role of undefined terms and axioms in defining space was to be made clear. The conference recommended the use of formal logic in geometry. Specific attention was to be given to the logical relations between a statement and its negative, contrapositive, inverse, and converse statements (p. 114). Attention was given to the use of the analytic method for discovering strategies for proof. This method, first used extensively by Eudoxus, requires the student to work backwards from the conclusion to the hypothesis by asking what he needed to know to establish each step. Then the student can write down his synthetic proof in the appropriate order. This approach was recommended but was not to distract students from the essential, synthetic character of proof. It was further recommended that some advantage might be obtained from the combination of plane and solid geometry into the same course. This defined another issue that was to prevail for several years. Inclusion of some projective and/or modern synthetic geometry was discussed.

8. *Impact of the report of the Committee of Ten*

Reactions to the report were generally positive, for the report could hardly be labeled revisionist. This is not to say that dissenting and/or quizzical reaction papers are not to be found (447). James Greenwood, for example, held that the capabilities of children for learning arithmetic were underrated, that too much time was suggested for the teaching of algebra given the available texts, and that many of the pedagogical ideas were already in use (343). Most commentary on education during the remainder of the decade alluded to the report.

An impact on the schools was slow to be realized. Solberg Sigurdson's collection of evidence relating to the report indicates that by 1900 little change had been made in the topics normally covered in arithmetic (447). In 1911 the International Commission, referring to the recommendations for arithmetic, stated that 38 percent of the fifty largest school systems had put them into practice (47, p. 17). The Committee on the Economy of Time in Elementary School Studies (1911) considered many of the same topics for inclusion in the curriculum, but for different reasons.

Informal, concrete-geometry texts were written for the upper elementary grades. D. E. Smith lists nine such geometry books, published between 1895 and 1907, whose authors paid homage to the report in their prefaces (416). Most high schools did not follow the report's recommendation that they change their practice of completing the study of algebra before beginning the study of geometry. Townsend's 1902 survey of Illinois schools, for example, established that 70 percent of the schools were finishing algebra in grades 9 and 10 before undertaking geometry (425).

The primary purpose in convening the Committee of Ten was to provide a national force for standardizing the secondary school curricula. The success of the committee in accomplishing this goal is difficult to ascertain. The impact of the report is in part measured by the fact that the NEA convened the Committee of Fifteen on Elementary Education and the Committee on College Entrance Requirements as a direct result of the deliberations related to the report. The latter committee had a profound effect in that it contributed to the establishment of the CEEB and the definition of the standards first used by this board.

Any attempt to measure the impact of the Committee of Ten must be made with the awareness that the committee was appointed in a period of profound social unrest. Richard Hofstadter ably documents the growing economic and social pressures that gave rise to Hull House, increasing power for labor unions, and trustbusting and eventually led to progressivism in our political structure (156). Further, this pressure for reform encompassed schools and schooling (129). The work of the Committee of Ten may be looked upon as evidence of the first of many activities in education demonstrating an activist orientation. Psychologists, mathematicians, and schoolmen all were to be part of optimistic moves toward self-betterment, many of which were distinct from the endeavors of the Committee of Ten.

9. *College entrance requirements*

The College Entrance Requirements Committee was appointed by the NEA in 1895 in response to a paper by W. C. Jones entitled "What Action Ought to Be Taken by Universities and Secondary Schools to

EMERGING ISSUES 169

Promote the Introduction of the Programs Recommended by the Committee of Ten?" The committee was recognized in the twenties and thirties as having had some of the most profound influences on the secondary school mathematics curriculum (416, p. 4; 232, p. 90). Many of the ills in mathematics for the inner-city schools today are blamed on the cumulative effects of the college entrance requirements. The College Entrance Requirements Committee cooperated quite closely with committees of the newly founded accrediting agencies: the North Central Association of Colleges and Secondary Schools, the New England Association of Colleges and Secondary Schools, the Association of Colleges and Secondary Schools of the Middle States and Maryland, and the Southern Association of Colleges and Secondary Schools. The aid of professional organizations such as the American Historical Association, the American Philological Association, and the American Mathematical Society (AMS) was enlisted by the Committee on College Entrance Requirements in preparing the final report in 1899. (It had not been requested for the two preliminary reports.) This cooperativeness has been a continuing characteristic of entrance examination work.

J. W. A. Young chaired the ten-member advisory committee appointed by the AMS. It was largely made up of members in the Chicago area, but it included two high school principals, one from New York.

The following "Summary of Principal Conclusions" was submitted to the NEA committee before it received consideration by the Society, but it received after-the-fact approval of the total Society at its 1898 annual meeting (69, pp. 135–49; 397, p. 384). A whole series of issues is involved in these eleven points:

1. To the close of the secondary-school course the required work should be the same for all pupils.
2. The formal instruction in arithmetic as such should terminate with the close of the seventh grade.
3. Concrete geometry should be a part of the work in arithmetic and drawing in the first six grades.
4. One half of the time allotted to mathematics in the seventh grade should be given to the beginning of demonstrative geometry.
5. In the eighth grade the time allotted to mathematics should be divided equally between demonstrative geometry and the beginning of algebra.
6. In the secondary school, work in mathematics should be required of all pupils throughout each of the four years of the course.

7. Wherever, from local conditions, it is necessary to defer the beginning of geometry and algebra to the secondary school, here, likewise, geometry should be begun before algebra.
8. When once begun, the subjects of geometry and algebra should be developed simultaneously, insofar, at least, that both geometry and algebra should be studied in each of the four years of the secondary school course.
9. The unity of the work in mathematics is emphasized, and the correlation and interapplication of its different parts recommended.
10. The instruction should have as its chief aim the cultivation of independent and correct thinking on the part of the pupil.
11. The importance of thorough preparation for teachers, both in mathematical attainments and in the art of teaching, is emphasized.

This first cooperative venture with school people is notable for (1) the assumption that the same mathematics is appropriate for all students, (2) the indicated terminal character of the study of arithmetic, and (3) the emphasis in five of the eleven recommendations on the concomitant development of algebraic and geometric concepts.

The AMS committee made recommendations about content and pedagogy relating to arithmetic, algebra, demonstrative geometry, and trigonometry. The recommendations and concerns were quite similar to those of the mathematics conference of the Committee of Ten. The equation was taken as the important concept in algebra. A very strong concern was stated for the danger of mechanical, haphazard manipulation of symbols. The committee stressed the cultivation of independent thinking—the student's task was to think for himself and not to learn proofs but to make proofs.

The NEA College Entrance Requirements Committee was in substantial agreement with the advisory committee of the AMS. It recommended concrete geometry with introductory algebra in grade 7, rather than demonstrative geometry (69, p. 21). The curriculum outlined by the committee was the following:

Grade	Content
7–8	Concrete Geometry and Introductory Algebra
9–10	Demonstrative Geometry and Algebra
11	Solid Geometry and Plane Trigonometry
12	Advanced Algebra and Mathematical reviews

The committee pointed out the importance of applications and maintained that skill in accurate reckoning with integers and common and decimal fractions should be kept alive throughout the high school course.

The Association of Colleges and Secondary Schools of the Middle States and Maryland established the College Entrance Examination Board in May of 1900 to bring uniformity to the then chaotic state of college entrance requirements and, interestingly, to set a uniform standard that might serve to guide the work of the secondary school. The requirements in mathematics were based on the recommendations of the above committee of the NEA, according to the CEEB's own statement (75, p. 387).

For example, the description of the algebra content to be tested for was as follows:

Testing Level	Description
Mathematics A_1	Elementary Algebra to Quadratics
Mathematics A_2	Elementary Algebra to Quadratics and Beyond
Mathematics B	Advanced Algebra

Colleges and universities outside of the eastern states made only limited use of the CEEB tests until after World War II, yet it would be inaccurate to assume that the CEEB had a limited influence on the secondary schools outside of the eastern states. The North Central Association of Colleges and Secondary Schools used the CEEB course descriptions in defining acceptable course units for purposes of accreditation. A unit course of study was defined in the 1902 appendix report of the Commission on Accredited Schools of the North Central Association as a "course of study covering a school year of not less than 35 weeks with four or five periods of at least 45 minutes per week" (75, p. 8). Two such units in mathematics were to be required for graduation if the high school were to be accredited. Four such units had to be available for the student. The following states minimal descriptions of courses as found in the reports of the commission (75) in 1902 (pp. 11–13) and again in 1908 (pp. 14–15):

> In mathematics the commission adopts the statement of the College Entrance Examination Board, except that a somewhat smaller portion in algebra is assigned to the first year, and a review of essentials is recommended in connection with the advanced course in algebra.
> 1. Algebra. The four fundamental operations for rational expressions, factoring, highest common factor, lowest common multiple, complex fractions, the solution of equations of the first degree containing

one or more unknown quantities, radicals, including the extraction of the square root of polynomials and numbers, and fractional and negative exponents. Quadratic equations and equations containing one or more unknown quantities that can be solved by the methods of quadratic equations, problems depending upon such equations.

2. Plane geometry, including the solution of simple original exercises and numerical problems.

3a. Algebra. A review of the essentials to be followed by ratio and proportion, and the binomial theorem for positive integral exponents. The progressions, the elementary treatment of permutations and combinations, and the use of four and five place tables of logarithms.

3b. Solid geometry, including properties of straight lines and planes, of dihedral and polyhedral angles, of projections, of polyhedrons, including prisms, pyramids, and the regular solids, of cylinders, cones and spheres, of spherical triangles, and the measurement of surfaces and solids.

4a. Algebra. Undetermined coefficients, the elementary treatment of infinite series, the binomial theorem for fractional and negative exponents, and the theory of logarithms.
Determinants, and the elements of the theory of equations, including Horner's method for solving numerical equations.

4b. Trigonometry. Plane trigonometry, including the definitions and relations of the six trigonometrical functions as ratios, proof of important formulae, theory of logarithms and use of tables, solution of right and oblique plane triangles. Spherical trigonometry, including the proof of important formulae and the solution of right and oblique spherical triangles with the proper interpretation of the ambiguous cases.

The writers of the 1908 description appended a remark stating that "colleges make no formal entrance requirement in arithmetic." It recommended that the introduction to proof should be gradual and informal. The following plea is made:

> In the secondary school arithmetic, algebra, geometry, and trigonometry should be regarded and treated, as different phases of one subject, mathematics, and not as different and mutually exclusive subjects. The geometric, the arithmetical, the algebraic, and the physical phases of mathematics should be presented from the beginning to the end of the secondary school course. To do this best and most freely would require some reshaping of curricula, which should come gradually. But the individual teacher can do much, pending this readjustment, by letting down the barriers, by using geometry in algebra, and algebra

EMERGING ISSUES 173

in geometry, by concrete physical, graphical, arithmetical work, by free use of whatever material or methods will help towards the main end.

With the systematic restoration of the close relations between mathematics and the physical sciences, so long unnaturally severed in the instruction of the secondary school, it is well to consider the methods of instruction in the physical laboratory. Some of these methods, suitably modified, may be of value also in the instruction of mathematics.

Given the use of the CEEB course descriptions in defining accreditation criteria and the importance for school districts of being accredited, one must conclude that the NEA's Committee on College Entrance Requirements had significant impact.

→»→» 10. *The unified mathematics movement*

The commitment to the unified character of mathematics represents a profound modification of the Committee of Ten's perception of the nature of mathematics. The evolution from the concept of parallel courses (2½ hours per week for algebra and 2½ hours per week for geometry) to this position was a significant change. Implicit in this evolution was a continuing dialogue concerning the issue of the aims of teaching mathematics. Many of the major figures in this dialogue were located in the Chicago area. Solberg Sigurdson traces the origin of this dialogue to controversy between the advocates of Legendre's geometry and the advocates of Euclid's geometry (447, pp. 109-10). The controversy concerning the nature of course offerings extended the dialogue down through elementary school even to kindergarten. The dialogue was to contribute to the definition of mathematics for the junior high schools and to provide a significant issue in the evolving concept of general mathematics.

The concept of correlated mathematics was first formulated in a form that could be applied in the schools by Truman Safford in 1887 (226). His belief that some demonstrative geometric content should precede algebra stimulated discussion at the 1893 Committee of Ten meetings. The concept of formal discipline tended to keep separate the parallel branches of algebra and geometry. But some commentators on the report of the committee felt that the concept of parallel courses was not sufficient. Henry Coar (327) and H. H. Seerly (412) considered it a mistake to teach arithmetic, algebra, and geometry as if they were unrelated. Sigurdson indicates, however, that at the turn of the century the most influential educators and committees were advocating distinctly parallel rather than integrated courses (447, p. 120).

Some efforts were made in text materials to provide integration. Griffin's *Grammar-School Algebra* (1899) states the following problem (148, p. 45):

Find the perimeter of [the figure identified here as figure 12.2].

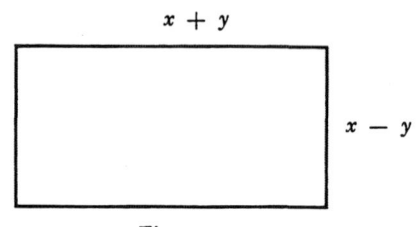

$$x + y$$

$$x - y$$

Figure 12.2

Many examples based on geometric concepts, some more complicated than this, were given. Geometry texts only rarely included arithmetically based exercises. The innovation of including graphs in algebra texts may be construed as an incorporation of geometry into algebra. J. A. Izzo found that not one of the thirteen algebra texts incorporating graphs (of forty-seven published) made use of graphs for anything other than solving equations (445).

Commentators on the history of mathematics education have cited the E. H. Moore presidential address to the AMS in 1902 as a particularly significant point or force in the evolution of mathematics education and of unified mathematics particularly. The speech (381) is significant for two reasons:

1. A broad perception of school mathematics is communicated. It neither totally rejects the axiomatic nature of mathematics nor represents a commitment to totally utilitarian mathematics.

2. The topic of the speech was not typical of the selection of most outgoing presidents.

Moore combined the ideas of Felix Klein (the function concept as a unifying idea permeating all mathematics) and John Perry (a practical, laboratory approach to mathematics learning). Moore rejected the totally axiomatic approach as unreasonable at the secondary school level. Perhaps he was familiar with the fact that the average and below-average students were having difficulty with a Peano-motivated axiomatic approach in the Italian schools (66, p. 344). At the same time that he was admonishing the professional mathematicians to be activists in school mathematics, he was undoubtedly aware that many members of the Society were already performing a labor of love in school mathematics. J. W. A. Young, D. E. Smith, E. R. Hedrick, G. B. Halsted, Florian Cajori, and many other members of the AMS were making and would continue to make significant contributions to mathematics education. The North Central Association's 1906 eighteen-member mathematics committee had ten college professors of mathematics in addition to schoolmen.

D. E. Smith offered the following commentary on how the Society received the speech (415, p. 136):

> It is now nearly a year and a half since Professor Moore gave his presidential address before the American Mathematical Society. . . . It was a fact apparent to all who heard it that the address was not favorably received by many of those present. Whatever opinions may have been publicly expressed, in private there were two adverse criticisms, (1) that a man who stood among the few recognized leaders in higher mathematics in this country should lose the opportunity offered to consider the great problems of the science per se and (2) that one whose field had been so peculiarly one of research should presume to enter the realm of education and to criticise existing methods.

The idea of unification was not new. The Society's committee, cooperating with the NEA's Committee on College Entrance Requirements, had strongly suggested the idea. The uniqueness of Moore's plea was that it was based on the concept of function. This concept, from his point of view, served the purpose of motivating students by showing the practicality of the ideas being learned. Other writers were committed to equation and equation-solving as the unifying idea. Moore clearly did not accept the concept of formal discipline. He incorporated science into his discussion of the teaching of mathematics. Moore helped to refine a major, recurring issue of mathematics education. Shall it be pure or applied mathematics that is taught? He stated (381) that

> by emphasizing steadily the *practical* sides of mathematics [italics added], that is, arithmetic computations, mechanical drawing and graphical methods generally, in continuous relation with the problems of physics and chemistry and engineering, it would be possible to give very young students a great body of the essential notions of trigonometry, analytic geometry, and the calculus.

The ideas of Moore were not particularly innovative in the Chicago area. The Central Association of Science and Mathematics Teachers developed into a significant professional organization there. Its original constitution of 1900 contained a commitment to the exploration and exploitation of the relation of science to mathematics. This was during a period in which most high school mathematics teachers were also teaching subjects other than mathematics. John Dewey's Laboratory School and the Parker School incorporated a child-centered orientation into a curriculum that was entirely consistent with the Moore position.

More significant for the development of the unified- or fused-mathematics movement was the development of unified materials under the primary authorship of George Myers. Myers and the mathematics department of the University of Chicago Laboratory School, including Ernest Breslich, with the cooperation of the mathematics department of the university also, produced a mimeographed text for ninth-grade classes in the 1903/4 school year. The text was revised twice before being published commercially in 1906. This fusion text was revised in 1915 and again in 1928 by Breslich. In the 1928 edition (102) Moore, Myers, and the psychologist Charles Judd wrote statements supportive of the "twenty-five year experiment."

A second-year fusion text followed. It evolved essentially from a book entitled *Geometric Exercises for Algebraic Solution*. Myers had originally held, as had J. W. A. Young, that correlation was a tenable approach. The fusion books are an outgrowth of his reaction to the discontinuities implicit in the correlation approach (447, p. 532).

The first-year text was primarily algebra, whereas the second-year text was primarily geometry. The authors felt that a more thorough coverage of quadratic equations was given than was usual in one year of algebra, and they introduced students to trigonometry in addition to the typical coverage of algebra and geometry. The following description of the second-year text indicates the nature of the fusion (384, p. 68):

OUTLINE OF CHAPTERS AND ASSOCIATED ALGEBRAIC WORK

Chapters	*Associated Algebra*
I. Congruency of Rectilinear Figures and Circles	I. Use of Algebraic Notation and of Equations
II. Ratio, Proportion, Similar Triangles	II. Graphing Circles

EMERGING ISSUES 177

 III. Measurement of Angles by Arcs of Circles
 IV. Similarity and Proportionality in Circles
 V. Inequalities in Triangles and Circles

 VI. Areas of Polygons

 VII. Regular Polygons in and about a Circle

 III. Use and Reduction of Radicals
 IV. Quadratic Equations; Solution by Formula
 V. Inequalities; Indeterminate Equations; Discussion of Roots; Simultaneous Quadratics
 VI. Use of Algebraic Formulas and Equations
 VII. Radical Equations

Myers incorporated problems from science and everyday life. This was consistent with the spirit of the times. The Central Association had a committee on real, applied problems in mathematics, which had a section in the problem department of *School Science and Mathematics* (see vol. 11 for examples). Myers's methods sought the evolution of concepts by proceeding from concrete situations to abstract generalizations, often using a laboratory approach. He reported fewer failures, greater enchantment with mathematics, and greater understanding by students. Myers believed and stated emphatically that algebra served to simplify geometry.

⇛⇛ 11. *Reactions to the unification movement*

 Both science and mathematics teachers were enamored with the fusion of science and mathematics at the turn of the century. The scientists did not retain this feeling. The thrust in science education became oriented to a descriptive study of nature. A national commission on physics, which included such prestigious names as those of Nicholas M. Butler, G. Stanley Hall, H. N. Chute, A. A. Michelson, and Robert H. Millikan, rejected too much mathematizing of physics (447, p. 162).

 The mathematics-education community retained an enchantment with the concept of the unification of science and mathematics which has continued even to the present day. Perhaps this is because, for many mathematics teachers, mathematics is a science. In the era of the move toward unification, many articles in *School Science and Mathematics* used the phrase "the science of mathematics" and were written almost in the Kantian sense. Mathematics was the queen of the sciences rather than the handmaiden of the sciences. Numbers and variables were often defined in the texts of the era in terms of quantities, as if they must have a measure in the scientific sense (255, pp. 218–19). The generalized-arithmetic concept of algebra was consistent with this view of the nature of mathematics. This indicates the timeliness of G. B. Halsted's translation of Bolyai's and Lobachevsky's non-Euclidean geometries, of the publication of a Hilbert-based geometry, and of J. W. A. Young's editorship of *Monographs on Topics in Modern Mathematics* (286).

Sigurdson ably documents the growing disenchantment of both Myers and Moore with the correlation of physics and mathematics (447, p. 169). Each of these gentlemen possessed a much broader perspective of unification than was entailed in the correlation of science and mathematics. They realized the value of using the concrete as a starting point in the learning process, together with an experimental, try-it-out methodology. Moore's more sophisticated idea of the function as a unifying concept was not the basis Myers used to organize his fusion texts. Myers simply taught geometrical and algebraic ideas together without organizing them around a single concept.

The writers of other texts incorporated some unification ideas in their writing. John Stone and James F. Millis claimed for their 1911 *Elementary Algebra* (255, pp. iv–v) that

> algebra has been correlated with arithmetic and geometry. . . . The graph has been used as a natural means of solving certain types of problems and of interpretation of algebraic principles, rather than as an exercise in the form of topics of analytic geometry.

Geometrically based real, applied problems appeared throughout. Most dealt with the use of formulas and measurement. There was an attempt to show the utility of the algebra through the use of problems at the beginning of many of the chapters (p. iv).

> The pupil is led to see the subject [algebra], not merely as a system of exercises to be pursued for the purpose of mental discipline, but rather as a scientific instrument for solving certain types of problems such as are actually encountered in the world's work.

The law of distribution was explained in an exercise (p. 79) by reference to a diagram for $a(x + y + z) = ax + ay + az$, shown here as figure 12.3.

EMERGING ISSUES 179

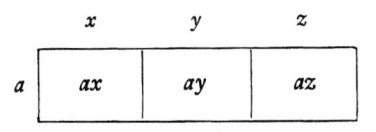

	x	y	z
a	ax	ay	az

Figure 12.3

The identity $x^3 - y^3 = (x - y)(x^2 + xy + y^2)$ was explained (p. 151) by use of a rectangular solid. The axioms for equation solving were rationalized by explanation in terms of pictures of balances (p. 23). E. H. Moore's squared-paper procedures were used for studying variation (pp. 218–29) as well as for the solution of equations. One interesting graphic method of solving quadratic equations, which is seldom used in first-year algebra texts today, was the following (p. 293):

1. Solve $2x^2 + 3x - 20 = 0$.
   Solution. This equation corresponds to the system

$$x^2 = y \qquad (1)$$

$$2y + 3x - 20 = 0 \qquad (2)$$

Draw a large perfect parabola ($x^2 = y$), and by use of it and a ruler [find the roots by finding the abscissa of the points of intersection of the two curves].

This text was meeting, in more than an incidental manner, the demand for real, applied problems and for incorporation of geometry into algebra. However, it did not go as far as the fusionists desired.

The writers of ninth-grade algebra texts found that geometric ideas provided a good problem source and that a geometric rationale was useful in some explanations. The texts could not be labeled as unified texts, but most exhibited the influences of the unified-mathematics movement and of the movement calling for a stress on real, applied problems.

⇛⇛ 12. *Geometrical developments*

The Perry movement in England had been a frontal attack on geometric content and teaching methodology. Change in content and methodology was realized more slowly in the United States. The influence of the college entrance examinations and of state examining bodies such as the New York regents (who specified the geometrical material tested by specifying theorems rather than broad concepts as they did in algebra) may have contributed to this inflexibility. Perhaps teachers and authors felt some kind of cultural responsibility to the geometry of Euclid or that of Legendre. Apparently curriculum designers did not feel it appropriate to steal the thunder of the analytic-geometry teacher. In the generation of this set of teachers, geometers such as Pieri, Veblen, Russell, Huntington, and Peano developed alternative sets of axioms for geometry. Perhaps teachers just could not imagine other approaches to geometry because they were unfamiliar with these recent mathematical developments. The typical quantity or magnitude approach used was not the careful treatment found in Euclid but incorporated the Legendrian relaxation of rigor. However, the tacit assumptions involving the real numbers in this loose manner were apparently more comfortable than a step toward the higher geometry of coordinatizing the lines in the plane.

The NEA and the American Federation of Teachers of Mathematical and Natural Sciences cooperated in 1908 in establishing the National Committee of Fifteen on the Geometry Syllabus. The committee's 1911 report exhibited the prevailing mind-set of the teaching community. Algebraic approaches and notations were repeatedly and strongly emphasized throughout the report, which was 74 pages long and was published in *School Science and Mathematics* (66). The committee felt (p. 512) that

> the use of algebraic forms of expression and solution in the geometry courses may well be extended, with advantage to both algebra and geometry, and that this may be done without in any way encroaching upon the field of analytic geometry, which belongs to a later stage of development. . . . Many of the theorems of geometry may be stated to advantage in algebraic form, thus giving definiteness and perspicuity and especially emphasizing the notion of functionality.

The committee, chaired by H. E. Slaught, contained such individuals as D. E. Smith, E. R. Hedrick, F. Cajori, W. Betz, and W. W. Hart. The first third of the report was a historical review of attempts to reform the teaching of geometry during the eighteenth and nineteenth centuries. The second section was entitled "Logical Considerations." The nature and use of axioms and definitions were discussed. Concerning axioms to be used, it stated the following (p. 434):

EMERGING ISSUES

> As to the nature of quantities, positive quantities, are to be understood. . . . It would not be desirable to confuse beginners in geometry by the question of dividing unequals by negative numbers.

The committee did not deem it desirable to postulate the existence of points, lines, and angles, to assume Pasch's postulate, or to postulate continuity. It was recommended (p. 436), however, that teachers "mention incidently that tacit assumptions are *always* made" (italics added). This second section concluded with a statement of the values of using the history of mathematics in the classroom and a discussion of the value and reasons for incorporating solid geometry into the tenth-grade course. Essentially, the committee's pleas were in terms of the increasingly utilitarian features of solid geometry and of the cultivation of space intuition (p. 446).

The next section was concerned with special courses for particular student populations. It was recommended that no special courses be suggested (p. 446). This section made a strong plea for informal geometry in the grades.

The major thrust of the report concerned the use and nature of exercises and the number and character of theorems. The committee indicated two concerns: (1) the "growing tendency in the last two decades to increase *abnormally* the number of exercises" that possessed "at best a remote connection with any uses . . . of the ordinary high school student" and (2) the unrealistic distribution of exercises and grading of difficulty of exercises. The concerns were clearly pedagogical, as indicated by the following statement (p. 451):

> On the basis of distribution we have all extremes in the various texts, including: (1) the purely logical presentation, that is, the continuous chain of theorems with practically no applications in concrete setting in connection with them and almost none at the end of the books; (2) the same as the foregoing, except that the long sets of exercises are placed at the end of each book, where they loom up before the pupil as great tasks to be ground through, if, indeed, they are not omitted altogether; (3) the psychological presentation in which the more difficult exercises are either postponed to a later part of the course or are omitted altogether, and the easier ones are brought into more immediate connection with the theorems to which they are related.
>
> The time and space made available by the third method of presentation provides an opportunity for the pupil to gain some acquaintance with the uses of the theorems as he proceeds and to become genuinely interested in the development of the subject.

This section of the report concluded with a discussion of the sources of problems and included many real, applied problems, but it cautioned on the danger of using too many problems in any narrow field.

The final section listed theorems that the committee felt constituted a basic set for a geometry course. An effort was made to state the theorems algebraically wherever possible. For plane geometry, 106 theorems were listed, but many included several cases that, it was indicated, were to be regarded as separate theorems. Valid converses were not listed. For solid geometry, 75 theorems were listed. The basic ratio ideas of trigonometry were included with the statement (p. 523) that they

> should have a place where time for their discussion can be secured, which will doubtless be the case except under pressure from examining bodies.

It was recommended that the style of proof could be "that of any mathematical textbook." The most notable feature of the listing was the omission of theorems concerning limits and incommensurability. The committee recommended that some theorems be treated informally.

The committee retained a Legendrian orientation but urged a watering down of the geometry course. It made a plea for more algebra and for real, applied problems. Teachers and authors were willing to drop incommensurability, but the plea for algebraic approaches was slow to be realized. The CEEB limited tested propositions to the committee's listing of basic theorems.

13. *The International Commission*

The Committee on the Geometry Syllabus was not as successful in accomplishing its goals as the committees that, as participants in the International Commission on the Teaching of Mathematics, contributed reports to the International Congress of Mathematicians. Perhaps the success of the latter reports was due to the fact that the goal was of a less ambitious nature. Rather than attempting to reform the teaching of mathematics, the International Congress decided to survey the status of mathematics and the teaching of mathematics in various countries. D. E. Smith, who had influenced the congress to undertake this study at its 1908 meeting in Rome, chaired the American committee. Thirteen committee and subcommittee reports were widely circulated in the United States from 1912 to 1917. Four major tendencies were noted:

EMERGING ISSUES 183

1. Some geometric content was being omitted.
2. The sequence of topics in algebra was being rearranged.
3. Utilitarian aims were becoming increasingly more important.
4. The formal-discipline concept of education was being questioned.

The first tendency indicates that the Committee of Fifteeen on the Geometry Syllabus had some effect on the writers of texts. The committee had indicated a pressing need for improving teacher education. The United States was found to be behind most European countries. It should be noted that in Europe the concept of education for all did not possess the same impact for secondary education as it did in the United States (49).

A major concern of the commission was the patchwork pattern of the curricular efforts of individual school systems. The curricular revisions took place at the local level as independent efforts of county, city, and, in some cases, state systems. The issue of local versus national control is still present today. This first attempt at national assessment served further to explicate this issue, which had led to the founding of the CEEB, accrediting agencies, and state boards of education.

⇢⇢ 14. *Practical utility in mathematics education*

The tendency towards emphasizing utilitarian aims noted by the International Commission became a force of greater strength and complexity as the twenties approached. At the turn of the century teachers were realizing the potential for motivating students implicit in practical problems. Klein, Perry, and Moore incorporated pleas for the practical into their commentaries on the mathematical curriculum. Klein's *Elementary Mathematics from an Advanced Standpoint: Geometry*, in discussing the mathematics of geographic mapping, notes the following (167, p. 102):

> It will interest every boy to hear from what point of view the maps in his atlas were drawn. The teacher of mathematics can put more feeling into his instruction, if he can give the desired information, than he can if he discusses only the abstract questions.

This concern for motivation was a major facet of the real-applied-problems movement as shown in the report of the Committee of Fifteen on the Geometry Syllabus (66).

15. *The changing school population and vocational education*

Three new forces developed during the first two decades of this century which supported the increasing emphasis on utilitarian aims. These three forces developed outside of mathematics education and, in their interrelationship, acquired an impact upon educational thought which is potent to this day. One force was the changing nature of the school population. Not only were many more people attending school, but they were expecting schools to prepare them for a useful life in American society. A second force was generated by the new and burgeoning field of psychology, which was beginning to flex its muscles and look to related fields for application of newly explicated and powerful concepts. The third force grew out of an attempt to transfer to education the concepts of the cult of efficiency which had recently developed in the business community.

The number of students graduating from high school increased by a factor of eight from 1890 to 1918, although the number of school-age children in 1918 was less than five-thirds the number of school-age children in 1890 (188, p. 146). Laws establishing a minimum age for leaving school were only beginning to be considered. The large number of immigrants provided the United States with a need for a program of assimiliation, which to reformers included not only an inculcation of the American way of life but also an education that would ensure a contributing member of American society.

W. D. Reeve, in 1929, stated a principle for curriculum design which he undoubtedly evolved before laws about the age for leaving school were passed (188, p. 167): "The subject matter selected should be that material which will be most valuable to the pupil, *provided that he leaves school at the end of that year*" (italics added). In addition to having profound implications for what is now called the junior high school program, this point of view was evidenced by the growing pressure for specialized vocational mathematics courses. One contributing force was the increasing importance of vocational schools. Cremin opined that 1910 marked a turning point in the thrust for vocational education in that the NEA, the American Federation of Labor, the National Association of Manufacturers, and the Grange began intensive lobbying campaigns not only in Washington but in state capitals. State laws provided for some form of industrial education in twenty-nine of the forty-six states. Only four states had given legislative attention to industrial education prior to 1900 (129, pp. 50–51). Continuing legislative attention culminated in the Smith-Hughes Act in 1917.

The movement for vocational education created special needs for mathematics. Although generally supportive of the move for unified mathematics, books appeared that were, for the most part, quite similar to those of the more typical curricula (447, p. 290). The primary difference was in the type of problems. C. I. Palmer's *Practical Mathematics* texts encompassed arithmetic, algebra, geometry, and trigonometry. Written for young adults, both the first (1912) edition and the second (1918) edition of the algebra text stressed the engineering problems, some quite geometrical, that would be helpful to shop foremen (206). More typical is the *Vocational Arithmetic* of C. E. Paddock and E. E. Holton (205), which was a segmented approach to arithmetic with many problems concerning interest, plane and solid mensuration, carpentry and foundry work, and the mathematics of gears and pulleys. Most vocational mathematics was of a unified nature. The fact that better students tended to elect college-preparatory mathematics contributed to the downgrading of unified mathematics in the minds of teachers during the second decade of the century.

⇛⇛ 16. *Psychologizing secondary school mathematics*

Psychology was a relatively new field of endeavor in 1900. The incorporation of psychological principles into curricular and instructional planning was a slow process during the first twenty years of this century. Acceleration of the process of incorporation is perhaps more appropriately attributed to the youthful nature of the field of psychology and its eager practitioners than to individuals whose livelihood was mathematical instruction. Edwin Boring, in his monumental *History of Experimental Psychology*, includes the following statement made by Edna Heidbreder, who completed her Ph.D. in psychology at Columbia in the early twenties. She indicated the spirit that permeated psychology as follows (101, p. 561):

> Psychology at Columbia is not easy to describe. It stands for no set body of doctrine, taught with the consistency and paternalism found

in more closely organized schools.... A graduate student cannot spend many weeks at Columbia without becoming aware of the immense importance in that atmosphere of curves of distribution, of individual differences, of the measurement of intelligence and other human capacities, of experimental procedures and statistical devices, of the undercurrent of physiological thought. He discovers immediately that psychology does not lead a sheltered life; that it rubs elbows with biology, statistics, education, commerce, industry and the world of affairs.

Boring carefully argues that the American temper fostered a functional approach to psychology which would result in such a view. European psychologists were, in his opinion, concerned with the description of the structure of the mind and with taxonomical descriptions of what happens and how it happens. American psychologists concentrated on the "why" of the mind. A functional orientation developed which was futuristic, predictive, and basically applied. This approach to psychology was uniquely American around the turn of the century, having evolved under the ministration of John Dewey, William James, and the Columbia group (101, pp. 550–60).

The functionalism of American psychology is evident in the type of experiments that profoundly changed the nature of the mathematical curriculum. The work of William James in the 1890s questioned the theory of mental discipline. E. L. Thorndike, his student, reported an experiment in 1901 which some authorities designate as dealing the death blow to the concept of mental discipline (168, p. 31). The experiment, reported as "The Influence of Improvement in One Mental Function upon the Efficiency of Other Functions," was the first of many conducted by Thorndike and his students which explored the why of transfer. The mental-discipline theory implicit in the report of the Committee of Ten could no longer provide a basis for defending the inclusion of mathematics in the curriculum for purposes of utility and practicality.

Experimental psychological evidence contributed to the increasingly vociferous dialogue concerning transfer in mathematics. For example, in 1910 Earle Hedrick felt compelled to talk and write of the purposes for which a student studied algebra (352). Although not referring specifically to Thorndike's experiment, Hedrick demonstrated an awareness of the need for more precise analysis of the psychological rationale for teaching mathematics: "We have been led to believe by eminent psychologists that the training of broad powers cannot be the function of any one branch of learning, that the power to think precisely means only power in the realm of the topic concerned." Indicating that therefore the algebra course should include "as wide a range of topics . . . as is consistent with proper intensiveness of the subject," Hedrick stated there were "direct" reasons for the study of algebra. The first "direct" ground for the study of algebra listed is the solution of problems. "The problems must exist and need solution, it is not sufficient to invent them arbitrarily. . . . Direct values of this kind are not the only reason for selection in our required curriculum." Hedrick continued to discuss the study of variable quantities and "the acquisition of the ability to control and to interpret such relations" as the raison d'être for algebra in the curricula. He strongly argued the power of symbolism in algebra as the chief basis for algebra's claim to a place in the curriculum.

Hedrick's article demonstrates the growing professional awareness of psychology. The impact of psychology was not limited to attacks on the mental-discipline basis for transfer. By 1910 the mental-measurement movement was sufficiently well established that a manual describing fifty-four tests was published. As early as 1903 Thorndike was publishing articles about predicting success in education on the basis of test performance. Boring labels the second decade of the century as the decade of intelligence testing (101, p. 574). The concentration on refining the concept of primary mental abilities and on developing group intelligence-testing procedures provided further useful information and approaches for schoolmen. The testing and survey movements were well established as tools for education by 1920.

Thorndike and his students staked a claim in mathematics education even prior to the recognition of the usefulness of psychology by mathematics teachers. Studies on forgetting, drill, trial-and-error learning, and transfer of training led Thorndike to evolve his common-elements paradigm for connectionism. By 1923 Thorndike's concepts for teaching mathematics were sufficiently matured for him to publish *The Psychology of Algebra* (266) and three articles in the *Mathematics Teacher*. Thorndike's use of testing as a research tool, his studies of forgetting, and his insight into transfer helped him perceive mathematics as a tool subject. His interests suggested categories of research which were to prove quite useful in providing insight into learning difficulties. His commitment to an identical-elements theory of transfer suggested the need for making a scientific analysis of the uses by typical students for mathematics.

17. The cult of efficiency and secondary school mathematics

Psychology was a fertile, established field before it began to have real impact upon school mathematics. In the same way, the imposition of ideas on the schools from the increasingly dynamic and productive world of American business developed before 1920. Support developed in the scientism of Thorndike.

In his thoroughly documented book *Education and the Cult of Efficiency*, R. E. Callahan describes the atmosphere and developments that helped to "set the stage for the spectacular debut of the efficiency expert on the American scene." He remarks (122, pp. vii–viii):

> By 1905, as James Bryce pointed out, business was King in American society, and certainly between 1910 and 1929 (if not down to the present time) the business and industrial group has had top status and power in America. On the other hand, it does not take profound knowledge of American education to know that educators are, and have been, a relatively low-status, low-power group. So I was not really surprised to find business ideas and practices being used in education.
>
> *What was not expected was the extent, not only of the power of the business industrial groups, but of the strength of the business ideology in the American culture on the one hand and the extreme weakness and unnormability of schoolmen, especially school administrators, on the other.* I had expected more professional autonomy and I was completely unprepared for the extent and degree of capitulation by administrators to whatever demands were made upon them. I was surprised and then dismayed to learn how many decisions they made or were forced to make, not on educational grounds, but as a means of appeasing their critics in order to maintain their positions in the school.

There were early indications of the potential impact of this new business orientation toward the management of schools. Bagley's book *Classroom Management*, which was written for teachers in training and enjoyed obvious success (it went through more than thirty printings between 1907 and 1927), was saturated with business terminology (122, pp. 6–7). In the Twelfth Yearbook of the National Society for the Study of Education, published in 1913, Franklin Bobbit set forth a list of basic principles to be followed in educational management (122, p. 11). The two principles listed in his first section, on standards, are illustrative:

EMERGING ISSUES 189

> Principle I—Definite qualitative and quantitative standards must be determined for the product.
>
> Principle II—Where the material that is acted upon by the labor processes passes through a number of progressive stages on its way from the raw material to the ultimate product, definite qualitative and quantitative standards must be determined for the product at each of these stages.

Educational leaders were quick to seize upon the business management–educational administration analogy. For example, Cubberly wrote the following (130, p. 338):

> Our schools are, in a sense, factories in which the raw materials (children) are to be shaped and fashioned into products to meet the various demands of life. The specifications for manufacturing come from the demands of the twentieth century civilization, and it is the business of the school to build its pupils to the specifications laid down. This demands good tools, specialized machinery, continuous measurement of production to see if it is according to specifications, the elimination of waste in manufacture, and a large variety of output.

What great implications were tied up in this one short statement!

Scientific management, standardization, efficiency, economy, cost accounting, assessment—these were the catchwords of educational reform. The focus was on results. Evaluation was the name of the game. Objectivity was the model. Education was crying out for scientific methods.

The simultaneous development of the measurement movement in psychology by Thorndike and his followers and of an orientation toward efficiency in education has to be more than historical accident. For Thorndike, measurement was a means to an end. For the educational reformer, it became both servant and master. How more appropriately scientific could you get than to specify educational goals and assess their achievement through objective tests?

But the art of educational measurement was in its infancy. The popular dictum "Anything that exists, exists in some amount and can therefore be measured" was translated as "If we can't measure it, it doesn't exist." The goals of mathematics education began to be formulated in atomistic, fragmentary terms. Any objective that could not be measured tended to be lost. The net effect of the measurement movement was to concentrate attention in the curriculum on those things that were showing up in the tests.

Although Thorndike cannot be credited with beginning the movement toward a science of education, he became perhaps its most successful advocate. His application of scientific methods to the study of educational problems set the pattern for educators and psychologists alike. He provided not only methods but answers. The educator borrowed both. Frederick McDonald made the following comment (378, p. 14):

> The story of how Thorndike slew the dragon of formal discipline is well known. His experimental work provided a scientific basis for the liberalization of the curriculum. That the curriculum would have been liberalized in any case seems apparent. . . . But when the issue was what knowledge or training was of the most use, an appeal to Thorndike would be made.
> The prevailing doctrine of "social utility" as the criterion for constructing the curriculum fitted superbly into Thorndike's general conception of learning and his analytic method of studying educational problems.

Thorndike's appeal, to a generation of educators who were looking toward the scientific methods of business and industry to solve the problems of education, must have been magnified by the quantitative nature of his system. When educators were viewing the student as raw material to be molded through a production process, it was natural that they turn to Thorndike.

The impact of the cult of efficiency on the mathematical curriculum was most pronounced when coupled with the questioning of the nature of transfer. In order to avoid the waste of time on obsolete topics, the actual use of mathematical topics in adult life became the criterion for inclusion of topics in the secondary school curriculum. During the late teens and early twenties, individuals such as Mildred Stone and Franklin Bobbit made counts of the usage of mathematical concepts in specific industries, popular magazines, cookbooks, and so forth. (See Wilson, Stone, and Dalrymple (279) for a bibliography of such surveys.) This inclination toward efficiency in the schools was an ongoing concern of the NEA's Department of Superintendence. The Department of Superintendence appointed the Committee on the Economy of Time in Education in 1911. This committee derived a list of minimum essentials for arithmetic which appeared in three of the four reports issued beginning in 1915 (23). Although concerned with the elementary school, many of the findings had import for the arithmetic component of the junior high school curriculum. The plea that topics

EMERGING ISSUES

"must minister to the social needs *common*" to children constituted the important criterion for the selection of content. This was a step toward the concept of functional competence, which was to serve as a curriculum selector during the thirties and forties.

Borrowing ideas from the business community was not inherently bad. Callahan notes that if educators had sought "the finest product at the lowest price" the results would not have been unfortunate. But he concludes that the record shows that the emphasis was on the "lowest price" (122, p. 244). At any rate, the cult of efficiency contributed to a more scientific analysis of the educational processes and helped to force more penetrating analyses of the aims of education.

The changed school population, the psychologizing of school mathematics, and the cult of efficiency provided an emphasis on utility as the goal of mathematics teaching. A new and different focus in mathematics teaching appeared in the experimental Lincoln School of Columbia University. Founded in 1916 as a result of discussions between Teachers College and the General Education Board of New York City, it provided a climate in which Harold Rugg and John R. Clark produced curriculum guides, texts, workbooks, teaching units, and achievement tests for the six-year secondary school. The school was based on the concept of "[giving] children the knowledge they need, and [developing] in them the power to handle themselves in our own world" (129, p. 280). The approach to mathematics was in terms of units that contributed to the study of larger core units. For example, in grade 8, the focus of the core was on the relation between culture and environment; a unit on mathematics contributed to an understanding of "living in a power age" (p. 286). The development of the units is consistent with the concept of unified mathematics, but it is more appropriately labeled as an example of the new concept of general mathematics. The unit approach was to prove particularly appropriate for many innovators in junior high school mathematics by providing a tenable organizational schema for planning other than one based on a logical development of mathematics. The founding of this school and its thirty-one-year existence represent a continuing concern for the utility of mathematics as perceived by the child in dealing with his environment.

Utility of mathematics was a primary objective of one of the first books to be published expressly for the junior high school. In 1919 John C. Stone of the Montclair State Normal School in New Jersey declared to the student, on the first page of *Junior High School Mathematics, Book I* (251), that our knowledge of mathematics enables us to answer questions that arise about the entire quantitative side of life, such as buying, selling, and producing. These involve questions on economy and thrift, questions of investment, and various questions upon which our prosperity depends.

This set the stage for the remainder of the chapter on computation.

In this seventh-grade text, Stone maintained the commitment to unified mathematics first shown in the 1911 Stone-Millis algebra text. He described it (p. v) as exploring mathematics used,

> as in life, to answer some necessary question arising out of some social issue being used to furnish a motive for learning mathematics.

From a second chapter, on graphic representation of data, Stone proceeded to chapters entitled "Personal, Home, and Community Interests" and "Problems of Investment" before progressing to geometrical construction and mensuration. Individual lessons on topics such as electric-meter reading, the money value of an education, and the increasing cost of living were based on 1918 statistics and provided considerable incidental information. The influence of the idea behind the Lincoln School unit approach is discernible in this text.

Stone's junior high text indicates concerns that were having impact throughout the education community. Franklin Bobbit and W. H. Kilpatrick published general curriculum books that were extensions of Deweyan ideas. Going beyond Dewey in basing the curriculum on the child, his experiences and interests, some of the generalists became so absorbed in the concept of social utility and in the child's inductive processes that they lost sight of the logical integrity of mathematics as well as of many other subject-matter areas. Although the goals and aims of learning mathematics had been written about and discussed previously, the growing influence of the social utility–child interest point of view was to lead mathematics educators to realize that the aims of education were of crucial importance.

18. *The educational generalists' view of the curriculum*

The spirit of the times is further indicated by the reports of the NEA's Commission on the Reorganization of Secondary Education

EMERGING ISSUES 193

(19; 20). One report contains the now-classic seven cardinal principles, a statement of aims which reflects the commitment to the future needs of students in designing curricular experiences. The commission recommended atttendance in elementary school for six years, to be followed by three years in a comprehensive junior high and three years in a senior high school in which specialization would be possible. The recommendation of school attendance through age eighteen was a new acceptance of responsibility by the schools. As the commission recognized individual differences in student abilities, needs and aspirations would become even more important in curriculum design. Analysis of adult activities in modern life and employment indicated that understanding of only the fundamental processes of arithmetic was not sufficient (19, p. 10).

The commission maintained that every subject taught in the high schools was in need of extensive reorganization. In response, the NEA formed a committee to examine mathematics. Chaired by W. H. Kilpatrick, it was composed of educators and no mathematicians. Its 1920 report, *The Problem of Mathematics in Secondary Education*, indicated that the disagreements among educators and psychologists prevented the development of a theoretical base from which new courses could be designed with surety (20). Although evidence was being amassed which tore at the very roots of mental discipline, nothing had yet evolved as a substitute to serve as a new basis for curricular design. The committee noted as crucial the already two-decade-old issue between mathematics for everyone and mathematics for specialists. The significant questions were what should be taught, how much of it, to whom, how, and why. The traditional logical ordering was not enough. Topics in mathematics should be selected to serve students as instruments useful in attaining ends other than mathematics itself. "No subject or item [shall] be retained in any curriculum unless its value, viewed in relation to other topics and to time involved, can be made reasonably probable." The committee proposed a three-track program based on the needs of four different groups—general readers, future mathematicians, and those entering trades or engineering (20, p. 24). Psychological concepts—such as "attention sets," "felt needs," and "satisfaction"—based on empirical study should serve as determiners of curricular content and order. The development and use of aptitude tests in mathematics was recommended.

The mathematics-education community did not welcome this report. D. E. Smith attacked the committee on the following points (444, p. 33):

1. The entire report had been written by the chairman, Kilpatrick, who was to found the Progressive Education Association.
2. There had been no meeting of the committee.
3. The committee was not representative of the teaching of mathematics or mathematics as a science.

William Betz, writing in 1923, perceived the Kilpatrick report as a negative influence. He accepted the report's statement of individual differences among students but stated that the schools were not prepared or equipped to differentiate four groups of students. Betz's and Smith's comments in the early twenties, several years after the Committee on the Economy of Time, refined the arguments and are evidence of the concerns of the mathematics-education community.

19. *Founding of the NCTM*

The National Council of Teachers of Mathematics was founded in 1920 at the spring meeting of the NEA. C. M. Austin, the first president, discussed the rationale for founding the NCTM in the first issue of the *Mathematics Teacher* published under its sponsorship, as follows (289, p. 1):

> During the same period [1910–20] high school mathematics courses have been assailed on every hand. So-called educational reformers have tinkered with the courses, and they, not knowing the subject and its values, in many cases have thrown out mathematics altogether or made it entirely elective. The individual teachers and local organizations have made a fine defense to be sure, but there could be no concerted action. Finally, the American Mathematical Association of America [*sic*] came to the rescue and appointed a committee to study the situation and to make recommendations. Already two valuable reports have been issued and others are in preparation. The pity of it is that this work, wholly in the realm of the secondary schools, should have to be done by an organization of college teachers. True they have generously called in high school teachers to help, but the fact is that it remained for the college people to initiate the work.

Austin continued that the NCTM was formed "to help remedy the situation."

As "good reasons for the National Council," Austin listed the following (p. 3):

EMERGING ISSUES

> First, it will at all times keep the values and interests of mathematics before the educational world. Instead of continual criticism at educational meetings, we intend to present constructive programs, by the friends of mathematics. We prefer that curriculum studies and reforms and adjustments come from the teachers of mathematics rather than from the educational reformers.
>
> Second, it will furnish a medium through which teachers in one part of the country may know what is going on in every other part of the country....
>
> Third, the Council through its journal will furnish a medium of expression for all of the teachers of the country....
>
> Fourth, the Council will help the progressive teacher to be more progressive. It will also arouse the conservative teacher from his satisfaction....
>
> Fifth, the splendid work of the National Committee on Mathematcal Requirements will be conserved and extended....

The Austin article set the stage for an article by J. W. Young of Dartmouth (438). Young's article appeared in the same issue (January 1921) and provides further evidence of the reaction to the Kilpatrick committee's concept of educational reform.

Austin was more emphatic about the NCTM's being founded in a spirit of reaction when talking with Glenn Hewitt on the fiftieth anniversary of the Men's Mathematics Club of Chicago in 1963 (211, p. 196).

> The early club members were all quite conservative in their thinking about educational matters.... Superintendents and principals taken up (or taken in) with this new movement were advocating the substitution of social studies and civics for algebra and geometry. The Club opposed this idea.... Some of the members believed that there should be a national organization to combat the spread of these "progressive" ideas. Accordingly at the March 1919 meeting a committee consisting of Mr. Austin, Mr. Newell and Dr. Breslich was appointed to correspond with teachers in other sections to ascertain their opinions about the formation of a national organization. A circular letter was sent to about one hundred representative teachers of secondary mathematics in various parts of the country. Encouraged by the large majority of favorable, and in many cases, enthusiastic responses, the committee issued a call for a meeting to be held in Cleveland, Ohio, on February 24, 1920, at the time of the annual meeting of the Department of Superintendence of the NEA. On that day, one hundred twenty-seven enthusiastic mathematics teachers, representing twenty states, met and

thoroughly debated the pros and cons of the question of forming a national organization. Several plans of possible organization were presented, one of them by the Chicago delegation. The group decided to proceed with forming the organization, and later that same day a constitution was adopted, specifying the name of the new organization to be the National Council of Teachers of Mathematics.

20. *Overview: 1890 to 1920*

A mathematics teacher whose career had spanned this period and who had attempted to be professional would have observed many changes in mathematics education. His younger colleagues, hired to help with the expanding school population, would have had the benefits of methods courses, professional literature, and professional organizations which had not been available to him early in his career. He would have seen the gradual rejection of the curriculum based on the concept of mental discipline and at the same time the increasing acceptance of curricular decisions based on child-centeredness and social utility. He might have participated in bringing real, applied problems into his new junior high school classroom and decided not to use one of the new unified texts because he had become committed to the correlated-mathematics curriculum. He would have remained comfortable in thinking of mathematics as a generalization from physical reality. Growing awareness of the psychology of individual differences against the lack of an adequate psychological explanation of transfer in his professional literature would have left him with a sense of frustration. He would have gained some feeling of comfort from the decreasing amount of formalism based upon excessive drill. The more realistic number and kinds of geometry theorems would have pleased his students as they faced college-entrance tests.

This teacher would have been strongly aware of the issues but would have observed that each side was represented by reputable individuals. He would have noted that many of these issues were not resolved. Indeed, he may have sensed that the issues would be subject to argument for years to come.

CHAPTER THIRTEEN

Mathematics Education on the Defensive: 1920-45

1. *"The 1923 Report"*

The first two decades of this century defined the arena for conflict over issues in mathematics education. The Kilpatrick committee hurled down the gauntlet of the needs of youth and the utility of mathematics as curriculum determiners to replace mental discipline. The subsequent jousting over the aims in teaching mathematics has continued until today. The increasing rate of failure and decreasing rate of enrollment in classical mathematics courses, the increasing recognition of and concern for individual differences, the growing criticism of instruction dominated by drill and manipulative formalism led to worried concern for the quality of mathematics education on the part of both mathematicians and professional educators. As a result, the mathematics education community assumed a defensive stance throughout the twenties and thirties and, to some extent, during the post–World War II years.

Largely in response to this state of affairs, the Mathematical Association of America formed the National Committee on Mathematical Requirements (NCMR) in 1916. The reports of this committee were collected into a volume entitled *The Reorganization of Mathematics in Secondary Education*, which is often called *The 1923 Report*. Several of the reports were published first in the *Mathematics Teacher*. The committee chose to use the *Mathematics Teacher* as a vehicle of communication rather than the *American Mathematical Monthly*, journal of the MAA, because of the nature of the reading audiences of the magazines. This report was to be cited through the thirties in the prefaces of textbooks as providing the guidance for content selection and organization.

J. W. Young stated in the *Mathematics Teacher* that the NCMR was organized by the MAA in the fall of 1916 "in response to an insistent demand that national expression be given to various movements looking towards reform in the teaching of mathematics." The committee was instructed "to investigate the whole field of mathematical education from the secondary school through the college and to make recommendations looking toward a desirable reorganization of courses and the improvement of teaching" (438, p. 5). The original members of the committee were appointed by E. R. Hedrick. Six mathematicians and three high school teachers were members of the original committee.

World War I interrupted the work. Funding of $16,000 was granted by the General Education Board of New York City to last one year (until July 1, 1920). Later $25,000 was given to complete the work. This made it possible for Young (chairman) and J. A. Foberg (vice-chairman), of Crane Technical High School in Chicago, to work full time for the committee and provided offices, equipment, clerical help, travel money, and so forth. J. W. Young said, "It is probably true that this is the first committee engaged upon a specific educational problem which has had adequate financial resources" (438, p. 6). The committee tried to make its work national in scope by soliciting "advice and constructive criticism" from teachers of mathematics. "At the present time nearly one hundred organizations of teachers are cooperating with us" (p. 7). This included 31 state teachers' associations, 25 associations and societies of teachers of mathematics or of mathematics and science, local councils or clubs in 20 cities, and others.

The reports of the committee were submitted to special committees of many of these groups for approval, comment, criticism, and advice. "The Committee is therefore acting in a very real sense as a national clearinghouse for ideas relating to its problems.... As a result, it may confidently be expected that our final recommendations will have the support of the great majority of progressive teachers throughout the country" (p. 7).

The reproduction of the table of contents of the final report, which follows copies of the title page and list of members, should be studied for the view it gives of the concerns of the period.

THE
REORGANIZATION OF MATHEMATICS
IN
SECONDARY EDUCATION

A Report by

THE NATIONAL COMMITTEE
ON
MATHEMATICAL REQUIREMENTS

under the auspices of

THE MATHEMATICAL ASSOCIATION
OF AMERICA, INC.

THE MATHEMATICAL ASSOCIATION OF AMERICA, INC.
1923

The National Committee on Mathematical Requirements

(Under the auspices of The Mathematical Association of America, Inc.)

OFFICERS.

J. W. Young, chairman, Dartmouth College, Hanover, N.H.
J. A. Foberg, vice chairman, State Department of Public Instruction, Harrisburg, Pa.

MEMBERS.

A. R. Crathorne, University of Illinois.
C. N. Moore, University of Cincinnati.[1]
E. H. Moore, University of Chicago.
David Eugene Smith, Columbia University.
H. W. Tyler, Massachusetts Institute of Technology.
J. W. Young, Dartmouth College.
W. F. Downey, English High School, Boston, Mass.,
   representing the Association of Teachers of Mathematics in New England.[2]
Vevia Blair, Horace Mann School, New York City,
   representing the Association of Teachers of Mathematics in the Middle States and Maryland.
J. A. Foberg, director of mathematical instruction, State Department, Harrisburg, Pa.,[3]
   representing the Central Association of Science and Mathematics Teachers.
A. C. Olney, Commissioner of Secondary Education, Sacramento, Calif.
Raleigh Schorling, The Lincoln School, New York City.
P. H. Underwood, Ball High School, Galveston, Tex.
Eula A. Weeks, Cleveland High School, St. Louis, Mo.

---

[1] Prof. Moore took the place vacated in 1918 by the resignation of Oswald Veblen, Princeton University.
[2] Mr. Downey took the place vacated in 1919 by the resignation of G. W. Evans, Charlestown High School, Boston, Mass.
[3] Until July, 1921, of the Crane Technical High School, Chicago, Ill.

TABLE OF CONTENTS

PART I. GENERAL PRINCIPLES AND RECOMMENDATIONS

		PAGE
CHAPTER I.	A brief outline of the report	3
CHAPTER II.	Aims of mathematical instruction—general principles	5
CHAPTER III.	Mathematics for years seven, eight and nine	19
CHAPTER IV.	Mathematics for years ten, eleven and twelve	32
CHAPTER V.	College entrance requirements	43
CHAPTER VI.	List of propositions in plane and solid geometry	55
CHAPTER VII.	The function concept in secondary school mathematics	64
CHAPTER VIII.	Terms and symbols in elementary mathematics	74

PART II. INVESTIGATIONS CONDUCTED FOR THE COMMITTEE

CHAPTER IX.	The present status of disciplinary values in education by Vevia Blair	89
CHAPTER X.	The theory of correlation applied to school grades by A. R. Crathorne	105
CHAPTER XI.	Mathematical curricula in foreign countries by J. C. Brown	129
CHAPTER XII.	Experimental courses in mathematics by Raleigh Schorling	177
CHAPTER XIII.	Standardized tests in mathematics for secondary schools by C. B. Upton	279
CHAPTER XIV.	The training of teachers of mathematics by R. C. Archibald	429
CHAPTER XV.	Certain questionnaire investigations	509
CHAPTER XVI.	Bibliography on the teaching of mathematics by D. E. Smith and J. A. Foberg	539
	Appendix: List of Co-operating Organizations	632
	Index	639

Young pleaded that the National Council of Teachers of Mathematics continue the work of the NCMR. The NCTM accepted this responsibility. During its first year of publication under the NCTM, 1921, the *Mathematics Teacher* devoted almost half of its pages to reports and discussions of the NCMR. This continued through part of 1922. Many of the speeches at the annual meetings of 1921, 1922, and 1923 were directly related to the work of the committee.

The topics covered by the report indicated an awareness of the uses of the measurement movement and of psychology in mathematics education. The attention given to reorganization in terms of smoothing the transition from elementary school to secondary school and the attention given to the problem of college entrance requirements may be interpreted in part as resulting from the interest in business management and efficiency cited in the previous chapter. Thus the scientism of psychological research and the cult of efficiency were healthy forces in education insofar as they led to well-considered changes in curriculum design.

The 1923 Report had five major areas of impact. First, the report contained a careful attempt to define and defend the purpose of mathematics in secondary education. Second, the concept of mental discipline as a psychological basis for curriculum organization was rejected in favor of the more sophisticated idea of transfer, although a theoretical construct of transfer was not defined and accepted in the report. Next, the function concept was recognized as "the one great idea which is best adapted to unify the course." (59, p. 12.) Fourth, the committee stated content requirements for college entrance which were accepted and used by the College Entrance Examination Board (232). Finally, model curricula were offered, not only those suggested by the committee but also descriptions of experimental work in the United States and of the curricula of foreign countries.

2. *Aims and "The 1923 Report"*

The first chapter of *The 1923 Report* described the aims of mathematical instruction as practical, disciplinary, and cultural. These were not mutually exclusive categories, but more specific objectives were assigned to them for convenience. Under practical aims the following were listed (59, p. 6):

1. The fundamental processes of arithmetic have an immediate and undisputed utility in the life of every individual. Accuracy and facility in numerical computation are of such vital importance to every in-

dividual that effective drill in this subject should be continued throughout the secondary school period, not as a separate topic, but in connection with the numerical problems arising in other work. In this numerical work, besides accuracy and speed, the following aims are of the greatest importance:
- a) A progressive increase in the pupil's understanding of the nature of the fundamental operations and power to apply them in new situations.
- b) Exercise of common sense and judgment in computing from approximate data, familiarity with the effect of small errors in measurements, the determination of the number of figures to be used in the computing and to be retained in the result, and the like.
- c) The development of self-reliance in the handling of numerical problems, through the consistent use of checks in all numerical work.
2. Of almost equal importance to every educated person is an understanding of the language of algebra and the ability to use this language intelligently and readily.
3. The development of the ability to understand and to use such elementary algebraic methods involves a study of the fundamental laws of algebra and at least a certain minimum of drill in algebraic technique. The essence of algebra as distinguished from arithmetic lies in the fact that algebra concerns itself with the operations upon numbers in general, while arithmetic confines itself to operations on particular numbers.
4. The ability to understand and interpret correctly graphic representations of various kinds is important.
5. The last practical aim was familiarity with the geometric forms common in nature, industry, and life; the elementary properties and relations of these forms, including their mensuration; the development of space-perception; and the exercise of spatial imagination.

The committee listed four disciplinary aims (p. 88):

1. The acquisition of those ideas or concepts in terms of which the quantitative thinking of the world is done.
2. The development of ability to think clearly in terms of such ideas and concepts. This ability involves training in:
   a) Analysis of a complex situation into simpler parts.
   b) The recognition of logical relations between interdependent factors.
   c) Generalization; that is, the discovery and formulation of a general law and an understanding of its properties and applications.
3. The acquisition of mental habits and attitudes which will make

the above training effective in the life of the individual.
4. Many of these disciplinary aims are included in the broad sense of the idea of relationship or dependence—in what the mathematician refers to as a "function" of one or more variables. Training in "functional thinking" is one of the most fundamental disciplinary aims of the teaching of mathematics.

By cultural aims, the committee meant those somewhat less tangible aims that are involved in the development of appreciation and insight and the formation of ideas of perfection. More specifically, it meant (p. 10):

1. Appreciation of beauty in the geometrical forms of nature, art, and industry
2. Ideals of perfection as to logical structure, precision of statement and of thought, logical reasoning, discrimination between the true and the false
3. Appreciation of the power of mathematics and the role that mathematics and abstract thinking have played in the development of civilization.

The exceedingly thorough and comprehensive analysis of aims in teaching mathematics was an attempt to be sufficiently broad to encompass all populations and interest groups. This, plus the care that was taken to be thoroughly reasonable, is evidence of the importance of the issues of aim or objective. Indeed, during the remainder of this decade and throughout the next decade, writers for yearbooks and the *Mathematics Teacher* wrote many articles concerned with the aims of mathematics. The continuing defensive posture that characterizes these articles attests to the significance of the NCMR's reaction to the state of affairs in the schools. The NCMR imposed a hierarchy of importance on the categories of aims by indicating practical aims "may without danger be given secondary position" by the teacher as he organizes for teaching (p. 10). The categories of aims were broad enough to satisfy almost everyone. They were subject to many interpretations. But attesting that practical aims may be given secondary position served the purpose of making the issue explicit. The gauntlet of the "seven cardinal principles" had been picked up and the battle of objectives joined in earnest.

3. *Psychology and the report*

The National Committee on Mathematical Requirements exhibited growing awareness of the uses of psychology in two ways. Vevia

Blair provided an analysis of the status of disciplinary aims in studying mathematics by reviewing and synthesizing the experimental studies of transfer in order to provide eminent psychologists a basis for reaction. Not only did this provide for a dissemination of experimental evidence, it was a vote of confidence in psychology by a set of respected mathematicians and mathematics educators. George Myers commented in 1921 that "psychological justification was hardly thought of as applicable to high school teaching of mathematics a few years since" (385, p. 60). He continued to reflect about modifying teaching strategies according to the maturity of the learner. Although the recognition afforded psychology would have transpired at any rate, it is safe to conclude that *The 1923 Report* hastened the process.

The NCMR turned to the concept of transfer of training to provide a rationale for its discussion of disciplinary aims and to rationalize the rejection of the "extreme" concepts of formal discipline (59, p. 8). Sigurdson labels the treatment of disciplinary aims as conservative (447, pp. 422-23). Transfer was discussed extensively (59, pp. 89-104), but at no place did the committee commit itself to discussing other than its existence. The comments concerning pedagogic procedures did not even hypothesize how the teacher might teach for transfer. The lack of a psychological basis for instruction to replace the concept of mental discipline was to contribute to the continuing dialogue about aims during the coming years.

In addition to helping increase the respect for psychology by mathematics educators, the NCMR exhibited models and tools for experimental work and evaluation for use by teachers and school systems. Special consideration was given to correlation, use of standardized tests, descriptions of experimental courses, and analyses of some questionnaire studies. Parts of the report were given to all superintendents of cities larger than 2,500 population, to all normal schools, to 1,500 libraries, the publishers of 300 newspapers and periodicals, and to 4,500 individuals (387, p. 33). Such a large-scale effort in disseminating ideas to an audience who had not been perusing research journals and professional literature could not fail to have impact, albeit not immediate.

4. *The function concept*

The function concept was labeled as the best single concept for unifying the curriculum. Although this idea was developed initially in a section titled "The Point of View Governing Instruction," the rationale for this statement was not in terms of teaching processes. Rather, in this section and the ten-page chapter devoted to the concept, the rationale was almost totally in terms of the almost universal incidence of functions in mathematics and science and the consequent potential for usage by students. The basic notion exhibited in examples was that a dependency relationship is a function. The use of unifying ideas for instructional purposes as described by Felix Klein and E. H. Moore twenty years earlier appears elsewhere in *The 1923 Report*, but the potential use of the function concept provided the primary unifying rationale for the NCMR. Much of the potential for the function concept at the junior high school level was seen as imbedded in the specific topics of formula, graphing, and interpretation of data.

5. Model curricula of the report

Model curricula were treated in two different ways by the NCMR. First, the NCMR designed curricula for schools with the new junior high organization (6-3-3) and for the traditional 8-4 school organization. Secondly, the NCMR reported on existing programs in foreign countries and on existing experimental programs in schools of the United States. The latter were for the most part programs that existed in single schools, many of which were experimental. There were examples of vocational programs such as the Cass Technical School in Detroit. Most of the programs exhibited a commitment to either unified or correlated mathematics. The report of the program of the Parker School in Chicago described a forerunner of team teaching. H. O. Rugg and John R. Clark used a team approach as a basis for being scientific in evaluating curriculum and teaching (59, p. 251).

The NCMR designed five model curricula for the junior high school. The committee's commitment to unified and/or correlated mathematics is evident in that each curriculum encompassed algebra, intuitive geometry, trigonometry, and the option of some demonstrative geometry, in addition to arithmetic. The committee noted in passing that the junior high school movement had encouraged the design of unified and correlated mathematics courses (p. 13).

The general description of the content of the junior high program called for the use of the formula in the sense of one variable's depending upon another to provide for much of this unification. The use of graphs and analysis of data played a major role in each of the curricula. There was a suggestion that drill could be overdone, with the note that many topics could be omitted. The selection of material to be omitted showed the impact of Bobbit, Thorndike, Stone, and other members of the usage cult. For example, attention was to be given to the "simple fractions as $\frac{1}{2}, \frac{1}{3}, \frac{2}{3}, \frac{1}{4}, \frac{3}{4}, \frac{1}{5}, \frac{1}{8}$"; other fractions were to receive less attention (p. 21). The demand for "practical" problems was to be met "insofar as the maturity and previous experience of the pupil will permit" (p. 27).

The teacher who accepted the point of view that mathematics was an empirical science would have felt comfortable in reading *The 1923 Report*. All the statements concerning variable, function, dependence, and formula would have allowed the reader to consider algebra as generalized arithmetic, indeed generalized from counting implicit in the real world. There was little to indicate that geometry had the potential of being other than a description of the physical world. The emphasis in geometry, beyond the informal introductory stage, was on proof and demonstration instead of structure. Alternative algebraic structures were not considered at all. Although modern algebras and non-Euclidean geometries had existed for seventy-five years and some leading mathematicians had been rejecting the Kantian view of the nature of mathematics, the committee did not.

The committee recommended that the senior high school allow for election of mathematics courses, in contrast to their recommendation of required course work at the junior high school level. For geometry the NCMR recommended the omission of the formal theory of limits and incommensurable magnitudes and held that more attention should be given to loci. The work of the Committee of Fifteen was noted. One section suggested an even smaller list of basal theorems for plane and solid geometry. It was recommended that the content of solid geometry should not take more than one-third of a year to cover because the aims associated with proof should have been accomplished in plane geometry. Correlation or unification was implicit in the four alternative curricular plans. Each of the plans recommended that the statistics of measures of central tendency and that trigonometry be part of either the tenth- or eleventh-grade course. The twelfth year was set aside in each of the four programs for the calculus or another elective. The content was limited to the calculus of polynomials and was to be based upon extensive application and to be highly graphical. (Pp. 32–42.) J. W. A. Young, in reviewing this section carefully, admonished that calculus was not intended for every school—that only a few schools had an appropriate precalculus program and the staff for such a course (285, pp. 430–33).

6. *Immediate reactions and responses to the report*

The reaction to the efforts of the NCMR included much praise. Individuals observed that the existence of a committee with members of such deserved repute was indeed unique. However, George Myers singled out the relation between the NCMR and the Kilpatrick committee for discussion. He indicated a feeling that the Kilpatrick committee knew of the content of *The 1923 Report* prior to its publication. He stated, "One cannot but wonder whether there was as sincere a desire to help the situation for secondary mathematics as there was to nullify the probable effects of the report of the National Committee" (444, p. 426). He added that the immediate effects were "not obvious on the curriculum of the junior or senior high school" (p. 427).

The reaction was most positive and constructive for those features pertaining to the junior high school curriculum. Reactions to the proposed junior high school programs included the publication of texts and methods books. Most books incorporated the "new" mathematics in that the authors intended to exhibit or discuss the unified or correlated character of the NCMR programs. J. W. A. Young indicated in 1924 that "the appearance . . . of eight or nine different series of textbooks intended for these grades [7, 8, 9] and purporting to embody the 'new mathematics' is convincing evidence of the vitality of the movement" (89, p. v). This appears in the introduction to Harry C. Barber's methods book for junior high school teachers, written to explain the teaching of the new mathematics. D. E. Smith and W. D. Reeve wrote a methods book (243) for the same purpose in 1927.

Insight into the reception accorded the report is given by the reaction of a panel of leaders in mathematics education in the January 1921 issue of the *Mathematics Teacher* (426) to the preliminary version of the section describing the junior high school curricula. Breslich noted that never before had such an opportunity for creating new courses existed. Betz envisioned, in the same sense, an opportunity to establish an organizational approach to curricular reform (similar to this generation's School Mathematics Study Group). Breslich recognized that the NCMR "emphasized the concept of function throughout" but apparently did not see the concept of function serving as a unifier of the curriculum. Discussion shifted to the role of intuitive geometry in the junior high school. Marie Gugle's point of view foreshadowed an important issue for the future. She remarked, "Intuitive geometry fuses perfectly with other mathematics. *Demonstrative geometry cannot, for it is really logic, not mathematics.*" (P. 28.) Today mathematics educators are questioning whether the existence of tenth-grade geometry can be justified on the basis of the aim of teaching the logic and structure of mathematics.

Among the more immediately tangible reactions to *The 1923 Report* were the College Entrance Examination Board recommendations. The description of content to be tested by the CEEB in 1923 was based on the report. Perhaps this is not too surprising because D. E. Smith and E. H. Moore were members of the CEEB committee as well as the NCMR. The 1923 CEEB committee cooperated closely with the NCMR and accepted all of the recommendations, including the testing of elementary trigonometry for entrance examinations, with one significant exception. The CEEB did not accept the function concept as appropriate for testing in elementary algebra even though graphs and graphical representation began to serve as a base for questions. (397, pp. 407–8.) Orlando Overn's study of changes since 1900 in the content of elementary algebra (397) shows *The 1923 Report* was not without influence. Table II from his report dramatically indicates how graphing was incorporated into the content of the test; the information is given here in table 13.1. Textbooks also reflected the influence of the report (440).

➢➢➢➢ 7. *The dominant forces—1920 through 1940*

The years following *The 1923 Report* were not all sweetness and light for mathematics educators. Enrollments in mathematics courses in secondary school were on the decline. Kenneth Brown and Ellsworth S. Obourn determined the ratio of students enrolled in algebra to the number graduating from high school for the four years 1915, 1922, 1928, and 1934 to be 48.8 percent, 40.2 percent, 35.2 percent, and 30.4 percent, respectively (110, p. 58). By looking at the ratio of students enrolled to students graduating, a feeling for the decrease in popularity of mathematics is acquired—the decrease is not hidden by the increases in school population. The pattern of enrollment in plane geometry was similar, with the percentage enrollment decreasing from 26.5 in 1915 to 17.5 in 1934. Frank Allen reviewed changes that took place in the curriculum from 1913 to 1963 for the semicentennial celebration of the Men's Mathematics Club of Chicago. He indicated that the years 1932 through 1938 marked the "low point of our fortunes" in

TABLE 13.1
Distribution of Material in Successive Annual Examinations of the College Entrance Examination Board in Mathematics A1

Year of Examination	Elementary Algebraic Technique	Numerical Equations, Problems	Literal Equations and Formulas	Graphs and Graphic Representation	Numerical Trigonometry	Total
Early Period						
1901	80	20	...	...	...	100
1902	60	37	3	...	...	100
1903	70	27	3	...	...	100
1904	75	19	7	...	...	100
Middle Period						
1905	62	19	19	...	...	100
1906	37	44	19	...	...	100
1907	44	25	31	...	...	100
1908	50	25	25	...	...	100
1909	29	42	29	...	...	100
1910	38	25	37	...	...	100
1911	40	54	6	...	...	100
1912	25	62	13	...	...	100
1913	31	50	19	...	...	100
1914	29	64	7	...	...	100
1915	42	50	8	...	...	100
1916	50	42	8	...	...	100
1917	52	41	17	...	...	100
1918	50	50	...	...	...	100
1919	33	50	17	...	...	100
1920	50	50	...	...	...	100
1921	50	33	17	...	...	100
1922	33	34	33	...	...	100
1923	50	33	17	...	...	100
1924[a]	50	17	33	...	...	100
Recent Period						
1924[b]	50	17	16	...	17	100
1925	42	17	25	...	16	100
1926	37	21	17	17	8	100
1927	38	17	21	16	8	100
1928	25	50	...	17	8	100
1929	23	52	7	15	3	100
1930	20	55	7	15	3	100
1931	23	40	7	15	15	100
1932	23	33	25	15	4	100
1933	24	45	8	15	8	100
1934	16	49	16	15	4	100
1935	27	54	...	13	6	100
Average	40.8	37.8	14.4	4.2	2.8	100.0

[a] Old Requirement Examination.   [b] New Requirement Examination.

mathematics education. During this period the typical four-year high school in the Chicago area cut back from a four-year mathematics course offering to an offering of three or three and one-half years (211, p. 92).

Although the efforts of the National Council of Teachers of Mathematics to disseminate *The 1923 Report* were thorough and extensive, the hope that the influence of the report would be immediate and significant was not realized. Modification of junior high school curricula awaited the creation of text materials and the education of a set of teachers in the philosophy of the report. The concern for the objectives of the mathematics curriculum provided the basis for an ongoing argument that did not lend itself to immediate resolution.

Not only had educators like Kilpatrick questioned the aims and objectives in mathematics education, but also the student population was offering evidence to mathematics educators of dissatisfaction with the nature of the curriculum. The response of mathematics educators included both a negative defensive attitude, indicating bewilderment on the part of some, and on the part of others some very positive forward-looking steps in the direction of curricular change.

The yearbook the NCTM published in 1936 was entitled *The Place of Mathematics in Modern Education*. It contained some interesting and helpful articles that opened vistas of new and interesting applications of mathematics. E. T. Bell's article (193, pp. 144–47) foreshadowed this generation's interest in mathematical systems by discussing Hilbert's postulate set in geometry and also by contending that algebra stands on its own feet as a hypothetico-deductive system as he examined the field properties. However, the tone for the volume was determined by William David Reeve's keynote article, entitled "Attacks on Mathematics and How to Meet Them."

The defensive posture Reeve assumed indicates the nature of the evolution of mathematics education after 1923. Reeve quoted three kinds of critics of mathematics education (the editorial writers in the popular press, school superintendents, and college professors) and two types of criticisms. The first criticism was that school mathematics never related to life. David Sneddon, for example, said, "Algebra ... is a nonfunctional and nearly valueless subject for 90 percent of all boys and 99 percent of all girls—and no changes in method or content will change the situation" (p. 1). The second type of criticism cited the large number of failures in secondary school mathematics. Reeve's response to the criticisms was, "I think it [the reaction to mathematics] is largely due to the stupid way in which mathematics is too often presented to the pupils" (p. 2).

The next article, a scholarly treatise by William Betz, examined the forces, issues, and prevailing philosophies of education in a much more constructive manner.

However, the issues and forces Reeve and Betz had cited were accentuated by the increased enrollment in secondary schools. The concept of universal secondary education was accepted by a greater number of families partly because of the force of the depression. School attendance laws were passed which protected the job sources for adults. The percentage of lower-ability students enrolled increased, thereby developing a need for non-college-bound mathematics courses and highlighting the problem of individual differences. Consequently, the mental-measurement movement became increasingly useful in mathematics education as the twenties and thirties progressed.

Apparently, teachers prior to 1920 had not used a wide variety of testing forms which are used today. The First Yearbook (186), published in 1926, contained an article by Reeve that indicated the newness of several test forms and test uses. The attention given to prognostic tests, to practice tests and to different forms such as completion, true-false, matching, and multiple-choice was to continue through several of the coming yearbooks (Third, Fourth, Fifth, Seventh) and was to assume a significant role in H. E. Benz's survey of research in the Eighth Yearbook.

8. *Individual differences become an issue*

The uses of refined measuring techniques of psychology and of research findings were inexorably intertwined as the problems of individual differences were explored. E. L. Thorndike's *Psychology of Algebra* advised that the child with an IQ of less than 110 could not expect success in studying algebra (266, pp. 36–37). H. E. Benz's survey of research in mathematics education for the period 1915 through 1931 (300) showed that a large proportion of the studies were of the type that provided evidence for a statement such as Thorndike's. Benz cited a large number of studies that correlated various mathematical abilities with success in mathematics and in other disciplinary areas. By 1932 the NCTM had a special committee for individual differences, chaired by Raleigh Schorling. As might be expected, there were proponents of grouping by ability and individuals who were concerned with maintaining standards.

The Schorling committee's report in 1933 (63) concentrated on the problem of the retarded pupil. The conclusion reached was at variance with recommendations of *The 1923 Report*, namely, that a special two-year training course outside the normal junior high school curriculum was a necessity if these students were to continue to a minimal high school program. The issue of how much of an individual's education should be a common experience with other prospective members of a democratic society was thus moved to the junior high school.

Curricular modification, such as recommended by the Schorling committee, was not the only approach to the problem. William Betz noted that extensive attempts at simplifying the language of mathematics were made by authors of textbooks (305). The degree of difficulty of problems was lessened, and this led to charges of watering down the curriculum. Speaking of the plan to lower requirements to reduce percentages of retardation and "failure," Betz stated: *"Its tremendous danger, however, is in the direction of such dilution of the curriculum for all pupils that very little of value remains for anybody"* (p. 93).

A more positive approach to the problem of the slow student in mathematics stemmed from the psychology of Thorndike. By the late twenties his model of human learning based upon connectionism was sufficiently sophisticated to serve as a guide for designing instructional materials. In his 1923 *Psychology of Algebra* he stated that the obvious method for improving performance in algebra was by "a general increase in the amount of practice on computation." He continued, stating, "We have not mentioned it because it is doubtful whether a general increase in the kind of practice now given is an economical means of securing mastery" (266, p. 334). Thorndike established in a subsequent chapter of the book that few mathematics educators had any feelings of how much drill was implicit in materials they used and that few possessed a well-founded judgment of how much drill should be used. Thorndike proceeded to develop a strategy for determination of appropriate amounts of drill and practice which served as a model for research. During the next few years studies of drill, practice, and retention occupied a major amount of the research energy devoted to mathematics education. Although this research provided a useful basis for the design of textbooks and for helping teachers plan, the research focused attention on the small steps to learning mathematics rather than the more pervasive, unifying concepts.

9. *Objectives, psychological theories, and progressive education become issues*

The Thorndikean approach to the psychology of learning was a wholesale commitment to mathematics as a tool. Of what use was establishing bonds of learning unless there was a payoff in usage? This Bobbit-style orientation was deeply imbedded in Thorndike's analysis of problem solving. For Thorndike a crucial factor was how genuine the problem was. In terms reminiscent of the real-applied-problem movement of an earlier era, he advocated that problems should be the types which would be met in life—if these types occurred relatively frequently, it was better for the learner.

The Thorndikean perception of mathematics as a tool subject carried with it the aura of respectability that romantically accrues to some research-based positions even today. Mathematics educators judged mathematics to be more than simply a tool and were quick to realize that in the battle of objectives individuals could enlist the aid of a scientism that extended beyond the helpful attention to the learning process in mathematics. The Third Yearbook's article by Charles Judd (359, pp. 1-10) was a counterattack entitled "The Fallacy of Treating School Subjects as 'Tool Subjects.'" Stating that mathematics is a "mode of thinking," Judd turned to an anthropological-historical analysis to argue that the tool-subject viewpoint denigrates mathematics as a field of endeavor. He further labeled the use of the survey approach to curriculum building as being shortsighted and a negative influence.

The utilitarian point of view was often combined with arguments concerning the difficulty of mathematics for secondary school students. The following excerpt from an article in the April 1924 issue of *School Science and Mathematics* is an early example of this:

> The study of math is a stumbling block to large numbers of high school students. Math is taught in the high school in a form too technical for students to comprehend. A large number of students do not like math and are therefore unsuccessful in their attempt to master the subject. Students who are not mathematically inclined should not waste their time with the study of math. Although math is considered by many as the most difficult subject, it is of the least value when judged from a utility point of view.

The arguments of individuals with points of view similar to Judd's had to be strong, indeed, to contravene such a view of mathematics in the schools.

Sophocles' remark that one must wait until evening to see how splendid the day has been is particularly appropriate when one assesses the contribution of the progressive education movement to the battle of objectives. Although the Progressive Education Association was not formed until 4 April 1919, the ideas implicit in its initial credo had been in evidence in mathematics education since the turn of this century. The unified mathematics movement, the real-applied-problem movement, the early attempts at using laboratory teaching methods, and the scientism of the early testing movement all possessed characteristics of the progressive education movement. And as the movement matured, many of the ideas were considered appropriate to secondary school mathematics by mathematics educators. Yet, as the ideas were used, the progressive education movement became more than a force; it became an issue.

The stage had been set for the progressive movement at the turn of the century in the laboratory schools of John Dewey and Colonel Parker in Chicago. The psychology of Dewey incorporated scientifically careful child study, but upon his leaving Chicago for Columbia University it matured into a more encompassing philosophy that was to serve as the operational psychology for countless teachers. Dewey's view that an aim of education must be built from a foundation of the intrinsic activities and the needs of the child was recognizable in the curricular materials produced by individuals like John C. Stone, Raleigh Schorling, and John R. Clark for the developing junior high schools. Problem solving was to provide the *modus operandi* for moving from the basis of the needs and activities of the child. It involved intelligent action. Such action was motivated by interest that resided within the individual, and it was directed toward a felt need or aim. In essence, Dewey put a human being in between Thorndike's stimulus and response. His focus was on the interaction of people and events. Human learning was purposive. To Thorndike, stimulus and response were distinguishable, and the connection was the central psychological event. To Dewey, stimulus and response were originally related, and "mediating experiences" were the central psychological events.

> Thorndike and Dewey in this early period can be seen pitted against the same foes—Dewey providing penetrating analyses, Thorndike his own analyses and overwhelming mounds of data. The unperceptive observer would have seen only the clash with a now outmoded tradition, the demolition of unscientific ideas. But Dewey caught the spirit of the times in a way that Thorndike did not, so that when differences between them became apparent, Dewey was chosen by educators. (378, p. 14.)

The psychology that was to dominate educational thought throughout this period was the pragmatic psychology of Dewey and James—not the scientific psychology of connectionism and behaviorism. Many psychologists of the more scientific persuasion withdrew to their laboratories, as the mathematicians had done, and left the field to the educators.

Psychologists in America had generally not been supportive of introspective psychology. Although the psychologists wanted to study areas such as meaning, understanding, and motivation, the prevailing spirit of the times mitigated against studies of these topics. The advent of Gestalt psychology in the late twenties, though divisive to the field of psychology, brought with it an aura of scientific respectability which was acceptable to many professional psychologists and educators. Although Max Wertheimer, K. Kohler, and W. Koffka had developed their psychology earlier, this psychology did not become available to the community of American scholars until translations were made of their original German works and as these men began to publish in American journals. The field of Gestalt psychology advanced notably in America when Hitler's racism forced these three men to America.

It again became respectable for mathematics educators to talk of meaning and understanding even when they wanted to be thought of as scientific. Mathematics educators incorporated the gestalt point of view into their writings much more rapidly than they had the precepts of connectionism or the related but new behavioristic approaches. Perhaps this was due to better communication in the academic community, but it is more likely that mathematics educators could sense psychological support for unifying concepts and felt that the discoveries of learners were more readily explained by the gestalt model of learning. Researchers apparently did not find that Gestalt psychology suggested as many problems for exploration as connectionism during the thirties. However, T. R. McConnell (376, pp. 268–89), C. H. Judd (162), William Brownell, and others made strong research efforts to explore meaning and understanding. These psychologists felt the connectionism of Thorndike de-emphasized the structured nature of mathematical thought. McConnell stated that some mathematical topics must be learned even if they are of "no immediate social utility" (376, p. 276). He labeled connectionism as stressing the product of learning rather than organization, memorization rather than understanding (pp. 276–77).

The effects of connectionism were noticeable in the textbooks of the late twenties. Authors used the error-analysis experiments and the usage surveys to design the content of problems and their ordering in texts. During the thirties some authors turned to Gestalt psychology as an organizer of the content of textbook materials. Herbert Blackhurst's *Humanized Geometry*, although not widely used, provides an example of this incorporation of the gestalt point of view. It went to the extreme of using a description of Kohler's observation of monkeys' problem solving on the island of Teneriffe as the heart of a long analysis of the problem-solving process for the students (98, pp. 186–93). The student is told incidentally that social problems are exceedingly more complex than the "simple" problems of geometry; indeed, that "the simplest problems are usually mathematical in the sense that they are based on agreements" (p. 191). Although the Blackhurst text incorporated Gestalt psychology, it is perhaps the exception rather than the rule for mathematical texts.

The significant points concerning Gestalt psychology are that it provided the mathematics educator with a better model for explaining some of the observable learning in the classroom and fit objectives other than social utility in a more comfortable manner. Gestalt psychology provided a base for an eclectic selection of arguments in the continuing battle of objectives. Perhaps Gestalt psychology would have led to an earlier exploration of discovery learning if it would not have been for the events of World War II. Both the connectionism of Thorndike and the Gestalt theory of Koffka, Kohler, and Wertheimer contributed to the evolution of the field of mathematics education but provided support for opposite sides on the issue of utility of mathematics.

The emergence of Gestalt psychology and the field theories was, in a sense, an extension of Dewey's notion of purposive behavior. Educators became acutely aware of the conflicting psychologies. By 1940 it had become perfectly clear that the controversy over learning theories was decided. Thorndike was out. Cognition was in. However, translating this decision into school curricula and teaching methods was a slow process. The drill theory did not die an easy death—as the analyses of the issues and programs throughout the period will show.

The forces that affected the battle of objectives interacted to such an extent that specific influences are difficult to separate. The inexorably increasing pressure of the expanding school populations provided the fertile soil for both the progressive education movement to grow and the psychology and measurement movements to promise fruition. Mathematicians tended to turn from the problems of the secondary school to their own problems, thus leaving the battle of objectives to be fought by the mathematics educators.

10. *The curriculum in grades 7 and 8*

The impact of the forces stemming from these psychological and philosophical debates on text and materials is more evident in junior high school texts than in materials prepared for senior high school students. Their aims, content, and methodology provide evidence of a shifting perception of what was important in the teaching of mathematics.

During the twenties most authors accepted the Bobbit point of view —mathematics was to be practical for everyday life. Walter Hart's junior high text stated, for example, "The instruction on new topics must be limited to processes and applications encountered by the average person" (154, p. iii). A second widely held aim was maintaining skill in computation. John C. Stone stated that a textbook should "furnish material that will develop a high degree of accuracy and reasonable speed in the necessary processes with whole numbers and fractions" (252, p. iii). Some authors coupled this latter aim with providing a good foundation for the subsequent mathematical courses of algebra and geometry.

The methods used typically paid lip service to teaching for meaning but in fact tended to be organized with a drill orientation. One author, Walter W. Hart, stated that in elementary school the "how" was emphasized rather than the "why" (154, p. v). Indicating that the "major aim of secondary mathematics is that of rationalizing mathematical processes" in the introduction, he proceeded to the following "rationalization" of the process of adding fractions (pp. 26–27).

> *Rule—To add or subtract fractions:*
> 1. Change the fractions into equal fractions having a common denominator.
> 2. Then add, or subtract, the numerators for the numerator of the result, and use the common denominator for the denominator of the result.

Then two illustrative examples were worked prior to a set of drill exercises.

Drill was the primary instructional method through the twenties. Toward the latter part of the decade many authors were including timed practice tests in the texts; perhaps this reflected the impact of the measurement movement. Strayer and Upton, for example, suggested to the student (257, p. 2) that:

> the teacher will usually have you do the same test on several successive days, until the class "hits the roof" by making a median score of 10. Then she will start a new test and continue with it until the class again reaches a median score of 10. If your score is not up to the class median when the class leaves a test, practice the test by yourself. Then, when the class tries that test again after a few weeks, you should be able to equal the class median.
>
> The median divides a class into two equal groups, representing the upper and lower halves of the class. In which half do you want to be? . . .
>
> Always try to be among those whose mark is above the median, so that you will be in the upper half of the class.

Some authors had different ideas. Stone indicated that a student in a new division of school has a right to expect a "new kind of mathematics in place of review and continuation" of the sixth-grade work (p. iii). The greatest freedom in departing from traditional methodologies was taken by individuals such as Marie Gugle and Ernest Breslich, each of whom incorporated nontraditional topics into their texts. Gugle's incorporation of intuitive geometry was wedded with laboratory methodology (150).

The texts of the twenties did not for the most part incorporate the content suggested by *The 1923 Report*. The compromise taken by most authors was to place any nontraditional material at the end of the book and to indicate to the teacher that it could be omitted. Most books were oriented to business arithmetic and began with a lengthy review section.

The texts of the thirties demonstrated a profound shift in emphasis. The content of junior high school texts incorporated more mathematics for purposes of socialization. This content, often of a unified nature, stressed the use of mathematics in a democratic society. A considerable number of authors turned to mathematical exercises to impart nonmathematical information. Less emphasis was placed on the mathematics of business and more attention given to consumer mathematics. The topics of intuitive geometry and elementary algebra became more popular. Meaning and understanding began to replace the words accuracy and drill in the prefaces.

The preface of Strayer and Upton's 1935 edition states the trend quite succinctly, "Throughout this work the interpretational and social aspects of arithmetic are stressed, as well as the computational features" (256, p. iv). Intuitive geometry, graphs, and formulas were incorporated in a spiral fashion in both the seventh- and eight-grade books.

The table of contents for *Mathematics and Life* (223), an eighth-grade text, exemplified the trend:

1. Mathematics and the Community
2. The Merchant and the Community
3. The Bank and the Community
4. Taxes and Other Community Funds
5. Community Planning
6. The Community and Its Neighbors
7. An Inventory of the Year's Work

Many authors included chapters such as Guy Buswell's "How a Pioneer Trading Post Became a City in 100 Years." Douglass and Kinney (139, p. 207) followed a retail mathematics discussion by asking the student to name articles of food or clothing from foreign countries which they could purchase. In these ways considerable incidental information was introduced into the mathematics classroom.

The books published during the thirties no longer contained lengthy drill and review chapters at the beginning. Many authors included prognostic tests for several chapters. The incidence of graphical explanations of new content increased. The introduction to elementary algebra became more elementary toward the close of the thirties. For example, few authors felt any necessity to develop the negative integers for purposes of solving equations.

The junior high school courses reflect the strength of the fads and forces in education during the twenties and thirties. Of particular note is the weakening of the tendency to teach mathematics for the sake of mathematics. The pressures to which the mathematics education reformers were subjected led many of them to ignore the important disciplinary aims of mathematics. Although the aim of social utility received deserved and belated attention in the design of the curriculum, it seemed to serve as a replacement rather than a companion to other important aims.

➤➤➤➤ 11. *Algebra and general mathematics*

The developments in the algebra textbooks reflect incompletely the forces impinging upon school mathematics. The aims espoused by most authors were traditional, although most prefaces through 1940 cited *The 1923 Report* and the CEEB reports. The emphasis was on computational algebra, firmly founded upon generalized arithmetic. The following sequence summarizes the method of the 1920s: definition, illustration, rule and example, drill, review, and speed tests.

Schorling and Clark seem to have reflected a very early impact of psychology when they said in 1924 (234, p. iii):

> In this book, a personal, thought-provoking, problem-solving appeal is made to the pupil. Whenever possible, the materials have been organized after the ideals of the laboratory method. There is every reason why the pupil should learn his mathematics as he learns the relations in other fields—in a truly experimental manner. It is astonishing to note the degree to which modern psychology is neglected in the construction of secondary school textbooks.

During the thirties some changes were evident. During the thirties some authors modified their approach to algebra. John A. Swenson published *Integrated Mathematics, Algebra*, which was a unified mathematics book. The function concept permeated the text. Some geometry and trigonometry were included. Analysis of Swenson's textual materials indicates that his treatment of algebra is closer to the modern structural emphasis than that of most of his contemporaries (442). Swenson was conscious, for example, of the importance of noting the replacement set for variables in discussing the distributive property (263, p. 94). Although his texts were not popular, John Swenson's professionalized subject-matter courses for teachers at Teachers College, Columbia University, were popular and contributed to his influence (442).

William Betz was the only popular author who unified his course around the function concept. Generally, authors appeared to think it necessary to defend the place of algebra in the curriculum and to convince students of its value. For example, Betz felt called upon to remark to his readers (95, p. 6):

> Unfortunately, wrong views as to the place of mathematics in the modern world are still very common. Even in the schools, many boys and girls are likely to hear that, beyond a little arithmetic in such ordinary business transactions as buying and selling, they have practically no use for the courses in mathematics that are offered to them. They are not being informed that with every day that passes, mathematics is becoming more and more interwoven with our daily lives and with familiar things of which we make daily use.

Such was the state of algebra. However, during the thirties the new unified course called general mathematics began to play a more important role in many schools. Although first in evidence in the early twenties, the course in general mathematics did not fit the sequential character of the existing program. Many respected mathematics educators such as Reeve and Schorling saw the potential of general mathematics as the continuation of the newer, unified junior high school programs, but no ground swell of support developed among teachers and no demand by students or parents was evident. Given the nature of college entrance requirements, it was not perceived by the majority as a replacement for algebra.

⇛⇛ 12. *Geometry*

The evolution of geometry in the schools proceeded differently from that of algebra or junior high school courses. Prior to 1920 geometry had evolved into being essentially a course in logic and demonstration. Marie Gugle had noted this in responding to *The 1923 Report* in the January 1921 issue of the *Mathematics Teacher*. The emphasis was not on the production of computational skills. As such (a course in logic and demonstration), the geometry course remained closer to the disciplinary aims of mathematics than the pregeometry courses.

Research associated with the more complex processes of proof did not fit the mold established by the Bobbit-Thorndike research interests. Individuals, such as Herbert Welte (269), examined minimal lists of theorems and "ideal" orderings of theorems. H. C. Christofferson (123) and Nathan Lazar (170) in the thirties provided examples of the creative analysis and use of different types of proof in plane geometry. Their emphasis on the role of counterexamples, converses, inverses, and contrapositives in geometry was perhaps closer to the spirit of mathematics for its own sake than any of the research associated with the junior high school mathematics or algebra.

The geometry texts of the twenties were different from those of the previous decade in that the emphasis shifted to the thinking through of "original" exercises rather than memorization of "book" theorems. More and more books began with an informal, intuitive geometry section rather than a dive right into proof. In the prefaces authors wrote more about the practical aims of geometry by discussing mensuration.

Although both the Committee of Fifteen and the NCMR had attacked the problems of the geometry course and had had considerable influence, the National Council of Teachers of Mathematics formed a committee on geometry which reported in 1932 and 1933. The goal of the committee was "stimulation of classroom teachers" (295). This ill-defined goal was perhaps in reaction to the growing disenchantment of students with geometry, as evidenced by the decreasing enrollments. An early report of the committee (62) seemed to favor the combination of solid and plane geometry. The committee recognized that the important facts of geometry could be mastered before grade 10 through inductive experiences and recommended the inclusion of nonmathematical transfer materials in the tenth-grade course. However, other than serving as a clearinghouse for ideas, the committee accomplished little that had lasting impact.

The chairman of the committee, Ralph Beatley, of Harvard, cooperated with George Birkhoff in authoring one of the few outstandingly innovative texts of the first half of this century. The text, *Basic Geometry* (97), was in many senses the forerunner of the SMSG geometry text. The postulate system was atypical. It was based on a postulate set first described for teachers in the 1930 yearbook, *The Teaching of Geometry* (189, pp. 86–95). The approach was based upon number and similarity rather than the typical synthetic geometry that had evolved from Euclid's *Elements*.

The aims for teaching geometry during the thirties were markedly transformed. Many authors—such as J. Herbert Blackhurst, whose *Humanized Geometry* (98) was published in 1935, and David Reichgott and Lee R. Spiller, whose *Today's Geometry* was published in 1938—wrote texts that were easier and contained fewer theorems. Texts such as these emphasized the transfer of logical reasoning forms and processes to nongeometrical contexts and the applications of geometry rather than limiting the content to the geometric structure. Many authors included a chapter on informal trigonometry.

An issue that faced curriculum designers was whether solid geometry could be justified as a separate course. It was recognized that the aim of establishing a concept of proof could be accomplished in the plane-geometry course. Many authors began to include an extensive amount of informal solid geometry in their tenth-grade texts, but a sufficient number of engineering colleges retained a solid-geometry-course entrance requirement so that the issue remained controversial beyond the thirties. As early as 1920 the CEEB had recommended combination and had set a combined test. A small proportion of the students took the combined plane- and solid-geometry test during the twenties.

Harold Fawcett, at the University School of the Ohio State University, provided a significant example of the teaching of geometry for purposes of transfer. *The Nature of Proof* (141), like the research of Christofferson and Lazar, was not in the Thorndike-Bobbit mold. It provided an existence proof that the aim of teaching mathematics for mathematics' sake was not inconsistent with the aims of social utility as held in such high esteem by the progressivists. As such, it was optimistic and forward-looking. However, this was but one experiment dealing with one mathematics course in a large country that was reeling from the depression and was in the process of becoming aware of the menace across the Atlantic.

Perhaps a more realistic view of mathematics on the defensive is acquired from a highly pessimistic statement of E. T. Bell, who wrote in the *American Mathematical Monthly* in 1935 (299, p. 559):

> It must now be obvious, even to a blind imbecile, that American mathematics and mathematicians are beginning to get their due share of those withering criticisms, motivated by a drastic revaluation of all our ideals and institutions, from the pursuit of truth for truth's sake to democratic government, which are only the first, mild zephyrs of the storm that is about to overwhelm us all. In the coming tempest only those things will be left standing that have something of demonstrable social importance to stand upon. Mathematics, we as mathematicians believe, has so much enduring worth to offer humanity on all sides from the severely practical to the ethereally cultural or spiritual, that we feel secure—until we stop to think.
>
> The arresting thought that we as mathematicians have done next to nothing to inform and convince the sweating men and sweated women, whose hard labor makes possible our own leisurely pursuit of the "science divine," that mathematics does mean something in their lives and might mean much more, may well make us apprehensive of the future, for these too patient men and women in the storm ahead of us all will cast the deciding vote.
>
> The harsh attrition has already begun. Are not mathematicians and teachers of mathematics in liberal America today facing the bitterest struggle for their continued existence in the history of our Republic? American mathematics is exactly where, by common social justice, it should be—in harnessed retreat, fighting a desperate rear-guard action to ward off annihilation. Until something more substantial than has yet been exhibited, both practical and spiritual, is shown the non-mathematical public as a justification for its continued support of mathematics and mathematicians, both the subject and its cultivators will have only themselves to thank if our immediate successors exterminate both.
>
> Taking a realistic view of the facts, anyone but an indurated bigot must admit that *mathematics has not yet made out a compelling case*

for democratic support, so that the men and women who pay the bills which make mathematics possible can see clearly what they are asked to pay for [italics added]. This must be done, and immediately, if mathematics is to survive in America.

This pessimistic tone was mirrored by William Betz in 1940 when he described the status of mathematics in the schools. He explicated the factors contributing to the poor status of mathematics thus in the *Mathematics Teacher* (303, p. 340):

(1) a general unawareness of the tremendous significance of mathematics in the modern world; (2) a one-sided emphasis on the doctrine of "social utility"; (3) mechanistic and hence ineffective methods of teaching in primary arithmetic, leading recently to such futile attempts at correction as "stepping up" the entire subject; (4) the absence of a clearly formulated and generally accepted philosophy of education; (5) the doctrines of "progressive education," with their emphasis on immediate experience, individual interests and "felt needs," and their disregard of race experience and sequential learning; (6) a policy of incoherent curriculum revision based largely on momentary interests, "social reconstruction," superficial "orientation," to the exclusion of continuity and foundational training in essential lines of work; (7) the problem of mass education, with the resulting attempts at "adaptation" to individual needs and interests, all of which attempts have been unsuccessful because they have ignored basic causes and problems, have rejected standards, and have preferred an inconsequential tinkering with opportunist expedients or surface adjustments; (8) a wrong psychology of learning based on a mechanistic conception of the mind and avoiding real understanding, thus making the ruination of mathematical instruction almost inevitable; (9) a narrowly specific and hence inadequate training of secondary teachers; (10) the uncertain economic outlook, with a resulting aimlessness and lack of enthusiasm among millions of our young people.

➤➤➤ 13. *The reports of the Progressive Education Association committee and of the Joint Commission—1940*

Two major curriculum reports for secondary school mathematics were published in 1940. Both were written during the period described in the preceeding statements by Bell and Betz. One, *Mathematics in General Education*, was a report of the PEA Committee on the Function of Mathematics in General Education. The other was a product of the Joint Commission of the MAA and the NCTM. The first was begun in 1932, the latter in 1934. The committees preparing the reports were not disjoint; Maurice L. Hartung and A. A. Bennett were members of each committee. The Joint Commission's efforts were funded in part by the PEA (50, p. ix). As might be expected, the reports were similar in many respects. However, there were basic differences in the philosophies of the two reports.

The goal of the PEA committee was to examine "the study and teaching of mathematics for their values in relation to the whole process of general education" (24, p. vi). The committee selected broad categories of mathematical behavior which they felt were extensively applicable to the problem solving of life. The categories of behavior which were to grow out of mathematical experiences are listed here:

1. *Formulation and solution.* The teacher had the responsibility to help students analyze issues in problems to determine when mathematics was applicable and when it was not. Student attention was to be focused upon the processes of formulation and the quest for generality of solution.

2. *Data.* The teacher must help students become aware of differing kinds of data and their characteristics (such as accuracy and relevancy). The student should acquire the ability to collect and record data, understand the measurement process, and be familiar with the construction and use of tables and graphs.

3. *Approximation.* The teacher must aid the student in understanding approximation in both measurement and computation. A major area of approximation involved statistical concepts with measures of central tendency, correlation, and dispersion serving as approximations of population characteristics.

4. *Function.* The student should acquire understandings of the concept of variables, dependency, and the generality and power of the function concept. (The difference between a mathematician's idea and an educator's idea of what would be a functional approach to a mathematics course was carefully discussed.)

5. *Operations.* The committee was concerned with "stressing concepts basic to operations no less than the techniques by which they may be performed" (24, p. 169). Counting, structural properties, and concepts relating to comparisons (i.e., difference, ratio, and proportionality) were considered as basic.

6. *Proof.* The report of the committee proposed that the student should be led to engage in deductive reasoning of his own in, for instance, the study of geometry. His understanding is presumably augmented when the student is led to focus his attention on the nature of proof. The student should have an understanding of the nature of proof in the broad sense, such as in cases where proof of any kind is unnecessary, impossible, or premature and as in the case of "proof" by means of induction.

Similarly, the student should have an understanding of the nature of proof in the narrow sense. He must know how to use the if-then principle, or formal implication; he must recognize necessary and sufficient conditions; he must understand the interplay of deduction and induction; he must distinguish between logical deduction, truth, and fact; he must develop skill in applying various methods of indirect proof, as well as develop an understanding of the concepts underlying these methods; he must recognize that proof, by its very nature, seeks validity rather than truth.

7. *Symbolism.* Students should be aware of the economy, clarity, and flexibility attendent to effective use of symbols. (Comparison of mathematical and nonmathematical uses of symbols was suggested.)

The report was formulated in terms of these seven conceptual areas with the hope that the very generality of the concepts would render them applicable to widely diverse but specific situations. Generality was, therefore, one key to teaching for transfer in the view of this committee. The other equally important key was to found instruction on life; in particular, to exhibit application of mathematics to the situations faced in life.

The PEA committee was concerned with the communications gap that existed between mathematics and other disciplines. Not only did it defend the relation of mathematics to the purposes of general education in a democracy, it carefully discussed the history of mathematical ideas as evidence of the evolutionary character of ideas generally.

Specific subject-matter recommendations were not made. The hope was that educators would formulate and improve curricular programs using the ideas of the report as a guide.

The Joint Commission, unlike the PEA committee, formulated its report in terms of specific subject-matter recommendations. Recognizing that there is no one perfect curricular plan, it attempted to suggest programs of sufficient merit and flexibility to meet a wide variety of needs. While recognizing the trend from authoritarian prescription to reducing or removing requirements, the commission felt that mathematics could not produce cultural return if it were offered as a disjoint sequence of isolated units.

The commission felt that there was a need to provide a list of guiding principles designed as carefully as possible to offer a definite step toward educational harmony. Excerpts from this list of guiding principles (50, pp. 55–57) are given below. (A correction has been made in the numbering.)

1. The curriculum should include the basic elements of arithmetic, algebra, geometry, graphic representation, and trigonometry.

2. A mathematical course of study must give constant attention to the "foundations," while at the same time it stresses significant applications within the learner's potential range of understanding and interest.

3. The fundamental concepts, principles, and skills of mathematics must be introduced and developed in a carefully organized pattern. Due attention must be given at all times not only to logical considerations, but also to psychological and pedagogical principles.

4. In the case of retarded pupils, modifications are needed in the rate of progress and the degree of comprehension, rather than in the choice of the basic mathematical units.

5. Psychological considerations such as those having to do with the problem of understanding, with motivation, rates of learning, and with degrees of mastery, are also of great significance in connection with the construction of modern curricula.

6. Mathematics is often described as a "hard" subject. . . . Each forward step in the subject is, as a rule, a very simple one. . . . The teacher can eliminate, to a large extent, the painful and futile struggle that is only too evident in some mathematics classrooms. In particular, the following considerations are significant:

    a) Early in each year the mathematical maturity of each pupil should be determined.

    b) Since mathematics is a cumulative subject, pupils should be made to realize that each day's work counts towards success or failure.

c) An understanding of the concepts and principles of mathematics is the key to its successful study. To teach in such a way that the concepts become clear is the hardest and the most significant task confronting the teacher of mathematics. By way of illustration, a definition should usually be the outgrowth, not the beginning, of a learning process.

d) "Overviews" and motivating discussions are valuable as directing guides, while summaries and organic reviews are effective means of creating perspective and confidence.

e) In the past much dependence was placed on mere drill. Recent psychological investigations suggest that all techniques should be based on insight.

f) Modern psychology has proved the effectiveness of "spaced learning."

The list of guiding principles was concluded with a list of principles (pp. 57–58) referring primarily to the sequence of the topics to be included in the curriculum.

1. The sequence in the curriculum should be such that each topic will contribute definitely toward an ever-growing and more significant organization of the basic concepts, principles, skills, facts, relationships, types of appreciation, and fields of application, resulting in the development of a unified mathematical picture.
2. The study should emphasize problem solving and modes of thinking.
3. It is not always advisable to attempt in each of the units a complete or exhaustive treatment of the central theme or topic under discussion.
4. A new topic should not be introduced unless there is a sufficient background of prerequisite concepts and skills to permit unhindered concentration upon the new elements.
5. A new idea or principle should not, as a rule, be introduced prior to the time at which it is needed or may be effectively applied.

The commission formulated its recommendations in terms of the following foundational fields:

1. Number and Computation
2. Geometric Form and Space Perception
3. Graphic Representation

4. Elementary Analysis
5. Logical (or Straight) Thinking
6. Relational Thinking
7. Symbolic Representation and Thinking

Two alternative curricular plans were offered for grades 7 through 12. Attention was given to the problems of retardation, acceleration, evaluation, and junior college mathematics.

The PEA report and the Joint Commission report are striking both in their similarities and in their differences. The primary difference is in the philosophical bases; the PEA turned to the student and his life, whereas the Joint Commission formulated recommendations anchored to the subject matter.

Both the PEA report and the Joint Commission report were conceived during the depression and published on the eve of war. It would seem natural to turn to these two reports as barometers of mathematics education at that time. But the surprising thing about these reports is the extent to which their authors were able to rise above the negativism surrounding mathematics in the 1930s to produce positive, forward-looking statements. The two reports did invoke all the classic arguments for the values of mathematics in the school curriculum, and the fact that they felt called upon to do so is possibly an indication that the place of mathematics was not secure. But neither report compromised on basic issues to design a program that would appeal to the forces that had placed mathematics under attack. In the face of a widespread move toward utility as a determiner of content, each committee saw a broader base for the study of mathematics. While other forces were tending to produce a fragmented curriculum of brief, specialized courses in "consumer" mathematics, these committees made impressive pleas for the cultural and disciplinary values of a curriculum built around broad, unifying concepts. Each committee constructed what they felt was a blueprint for a program in mathematics that could stand on its own merits. And they were not apologetic in their tone. Historical perspective might cause us to see these reports as briefs for the defense in the case of *The Public* v. *Mathematics*. But if that was the case, we must at least admit that the planned defense was aggressive.

Each committee had been formed at a time when the place of mathematics in the secondary school curriculum was being questioned. And as the committees worked, the attacks continued and the position of mathematics became even less secure. Those on the PEA committee might have been doubly sensitive to the mounting criticism. Not only was mathematics under attack from both public and professional sectors, but the progressive movement itself was being questioned. And it was not uncommon for spokesmen within mathematics education to make "progressivism" the scapegoat for the sorry state of affairs.

→→→ 14. *Gearing up for war*

The battle of objectives suddenly acquired secondary importance with the beginning of World War II. Teachers shifted from a preoccupation with the social well-being of the students to a concern for the existence of the American way of life. The May 1941 issue of the *Mathematics Teacher* featured "Mathematics in the Defense Program." This publication indicates the awareness of the mathematics education community of the heavy responsibility which was to be theirs during the coming years. The first article, by Marston Morse and William Hart, reported the existence of the War Preparedness Committee of the MAA and the AMS. The reflections on the crisis facing the nation led this committee of mathematicians to turn the profession's attention again to the secondary schools in a manner foreshadowing the mathematicians' involvement in the post-Sputnik revolution in school mathematics. Professor Morse recommended that "a *new definition of socialized mathematics* be adopted in the curricula for students of *all* ability levels, where we would recognize that, at least for boys, *mathematical content with military uses* is the most socialized variety of mathematics to which they can be exposed at present" (54, p. 201). The article exhibited a deep concern for the forces that were motivating students not to elect more mathematics. In a progress report of the War Preparedness Committee, published two issues later, William Hart indicated a strong concern that emergency courses of a remedial nature were not sufficient but that payoff is realized in terms of foundational courses in mathematics not specific to particular needs or industries (36, p. 298). Many committee members, such as Marshall Stone and Samuel Wilkes, were to retain a constructive interest in school mathematics through the post-Sputnik revolution.

The induction testing for World War II presented evidence that many youths were incompetent in mathematics. Admiral Nimitz's letter, referred to in chapter 5, considered the problems this established for the military. However, concern for the mathematical competence of American youth extended beyond military needs to encompass the employment and training problems of increasingly technical industries.

The NCTM and the USOE cooperated in 1943 in discussing the content necessary for preinduction courses (76). The emphasis recommended was maximal understanding as opposed to mechanical manipulation, general courses rather than several specific courses, and extensive examination of applications in many fields. The writers were concerned that any modification of sequential courses should demonstrate awareness of future civilian use of the courses.

The impact of World War II on secondary school mathematics is at least partially reflected in the trends in advertisements that appeared in the *Mathematics Teacher* during the war years. The evidence suggests that actual substantive change in the mathematics program (or at least in the texts) may have occurred much less rapidly than changes in the basis upon which the program was "sold." Perhaps the most dramatic evidence of this is in the sequence of advertisements for the Mathematics in Everyday Life series. There is nothing in the advertisements to suggest that the five units—*Finance, Health, Leisure, Geometry*, and *Drill*—enjoyed any substantive revision during the period. But, oh, how the ads changed! We give examples below.

For the *Drill* unit:

> January 1939. High School: For a one-semester "brush-up" course for seniors who are graduating into the business world and who are "rusty" on their arithmetic. As a supplementary drill book for bookkeeping and accounting courses.
> Primarily for Grades 7–9: but equally effective for any drill book needed in grades 5–6 and 10–12.

> February 1941. Today's swollen secondary-school population poses a mathematics problem. Pupils on any single grade level from 7th through 12th are in many stages of advancement or retardation where fundamental mathematics skills are concerned.

> October 1942. Now when the call of war industries and the armed services is for young men with proper mastery of fundamental arithmetic processes, you can make good use of this more scientific drill book for grades 7 to 12—Why grade 12? Now as never before, high schools must offer their graduating seniors, who have grown "rusty" in arithmetic, a brush-up course in the fundamentals.

For the *Geometry* unit:

> October 1940. Good old Euclid's "abstract" triangles have been the slaughtering pens into which hordes of non-academic pupils, and pupils with no flair for mathematics, often have been driven without warning.

April 1942. In the drive to gear mathematics classwork to wartime needs, it is recommended that indirect measurement be taught in junior and senior high school, outdoors as well as in the classroom. ... In this unit are the principles and activities of such engineering and military work as range-finding, height-finding, etc.

The advertisements shifted from emphasizing words like easy, practical, motivating, socializing, and informal to stressing preinduction needs and competencies. Indirect measure became a significant topic. Industrial, aeronautical, and nautical uses were stressed after the war began, even to the point of dramatic use of pictures. Many of the older texts tried to ride on the coattails of this emphasis. Only a few books were advertised on the basis of their conformation to the recommendations of the Joint Commission or the PEA Committee.

The recommendations of the PEA's *Mathematics in General Education* and the Joint Commission's *The Place of Mathematics in Secondary Education* were lost as the educational establishment dealt with the national crises. Claude Brown's methods book for secondary school mathematics provided in 1952 a more reasoned assessment of their impact than literature of the years immediately following the reports. Commenting about the fundamental problems that arise from conflicts between philosophies of life, of education, and of mathematics, Brown stated emphatically that teaching programs which emphasize only the theoretical in mathematics or emphasize only the applications of mathematics are incapable of meeting the needs of life (107, p. 131). Brown observed that the progressives came to a somewhat belated realization of this fact. He suggested that there may have been a break between the philosophy of the committee preparing the report and that of the parent PEA (p. 112). Because of the demands of the armed services and industries, the importance of the utilitarian aims was once more emphasized. The aims relating to social utility, held so dear by the progressivists, were not as broadly utilitarian as the era demanded. New and formerly "pure" mathematics was needed by the technicians, engineers, and scientists of an expanding wartime technology. John D. Hancock's analysis of the changing curricular patterns led him to conclude that "the recommendations of 1940 were forgotten as the schools retooled along traditional or expedient lines" (444, p. 67).

15. *Summary*

During the years following publication of *The 1923 Report* the degree of involvement of mathematicians with school mathematics decreased. They would, as a body, turn their attention again to the problems of the schools only in a new period of national crisis. They were content to leave the implementation in the hands of the able men who had helped to draft their recommendations. This produced a clear mandate for a new breed—the mathematics educator. But these able men, once identified so clearly with the community of mathematicians, soon became identified even more with the community of educators. The National Council of Teachers of Mathematics grew. And as it grew, it attracted to its membership and to its leadership those in positions much more subject to the influence and pressure of the professional reform movements—in education, in psychology, and in sociology. And so the battle of objectives which was to characterize this turbulent period in the history of mathematics education was joined.

The evolution of mathematics education from 1920 to the post–World War II years hinged primarily on one issue, namely, the usefulness of mathematics. For some, mathematics provided another tool in helping one take his place in society. A sense of desperation stemming from larger and different pupil populations and the depression helped mathematics educators lose sight of the fact that neither mathematics for its own sake nor mathematics for direct and immediate use provided a sufficient rationale for students. The progressive movement focused attention on the issue of the aims for teaching mathematics.

Many topics that appropriately might have been included in this chapter have not been discussed. The issues involved in the changes in eleventh-grade algebra or in the trigonometry course are of minor importance in comparison to this crucial issue of the utility of mathematics. The awareness of the NCTM of the plight of Negro teachers and students in separate but "equal" schools as shown in 1940 (344) was not a mature or strong force. The shift in policy of the CEEB from examining achievement for specific mathematics courses to general tests predictive of college success (144) was of negligible impact generally as the depression and World War II provided other concerns for teachers. None of these interesting facets of the history of mathematics education touches the crucial problem. The strong forces and the elemental issues for the mathematics education community were those which had the potential of being important to all American youth. The strong influences and pressures from outside of mathematics education also were concerned with all American youth. As universal education was extended upward from the elementary school, grades 7 through 10 provided the arena for conflict.

CHAPTER FOURTEEN

Reform, Revolution, and Reaction

1. *Introduction: forces and issues*

When future historians seek a bench mark for the revolution in school mathematics, the list of contenders will be long indeed. The publication of the Steelman report in 1947, the establishment of the National Science Foundation in 1950, the creation of the University of Illinois Committee on School Mathematics in 1951, the appointment of the Commission on Mathematics by the College Entrance Examination Board in 1955, the founding of the School Mathematics Study Group in 1958—any of these and more may survive the test of time to rank with other notable events that have come to mark an era in our field. However, for those who are living through this period of rapid change, it is too soon to single out any one event as the dominating force. In fact, some feel that what is past is only a prelude to an even greater revolution yet to come (137). And others see the events of the past two decades as a natural, although accelerated, evolution from the long sequence of events which has been traced throughout this book. However, few would deny that, as measured against that of any comparable period in the history of mathematics education, both the pace and the extent of change over the past twenty years have been revolutionary.

A complex coalition of forces and issues was required to create a receptive atmosphere and to supply momentum for such a dramatic revision of the curriculum. But the nature and direction of change in the early years of this period suggests that the renewed concern of mathematicians was at least a necessary condition for what transpired. Perhaps more than any other, this period has been characterized by the impact of college mathematicians on the school curriculum. Without their active participation, who can say whether mathematics education would have moved as far, as fast, or in the same direction?

In tracing the historical origins of the SMSG, William Wooton noted the following (282, p. 5):

> In the eyes of many thoughtful members of the mathematical community, the picture of mathematics education in American high schools in 1950 was not a pretty one. In particular, they were dissatisfied both with the content of the course offerings and with the spirit in which the material was presented. They were convinced that the traditional subject matter was inappropriate to the times. Worse, they were alarmed at what they felt were the implications for the future. In their opinion there was undue emphasis being placed on skills, an unnecessary preoccupation with the immediate usefulness of what was taught, and an unfortunate distortion of the students' ideas as to the nature of mathematics. They believed that these things were actually dangerous to the future welfare of the country.

In attempting to find a source of responsibility for this situation, Wooton said further:

> Such authority as the departments of education had over mathematics education in the schools fell to them primarily through the default of their colleagues in the mathematics departments.
>
> If blame has to be placed somewhere, perhaps it should be placed on the research mathematicians of the country who, as a group, abandoned any interest in high school mathematics or the training of teachers of high school mathematics in favor of concentrating entirely on research. But blaming them would not seem wholly justified either. The mathematicians had work of compelling importance to accomplish in their own specialities, work that could not be done by others.

The renewed concern of mathematicians was not a sudden thing. Beginning at least as early as the work of the Joint Commission, there

REFORM, REVOLUTION, AND REACTION 237

was growing evidence of their involvement. The war emergency produced a number of committee reports in which mathematicians addressed themselves to the problems of the secondary schools. Of particular note is the report of the Subcommittee on Education for Service of the War Preparedness Committee which represented the growing concern of the AMS and the MAA. The objectives of this subcommittee were the following (54, pp. 198-99):

1. To investigate what mathematics is of prime utility in industry and in the Army and Navy in the national defense.
2. In accordance with the results of this investigation, to make useful recommendations in regard to mathematical curricula at both the secondary and college levels.
3. To determine in what ways mathematicians may aid in the preparation of textbook material and in the teaching of those who will have mathematical duties in industry or as enlisted men or officers.

The third objective is of special historical significance as an early indication that mathematicians would break the "recommendations only" posture that their committees had adopted in the past. Professor Begle, director of the SMSG, refers to this change when discussing the impact of the CEEB Commission on Mathematics (93, p. 139).

> A second serious limitation was that the Commission, with one exception, restricted itself to making recommendations. The history of mathematics education in the United States, and attempts to reform it, show that recommendations alone often have no effect and, at best, are reflected in curriculum changes very slowly.
> In one particular case, however, the Commission went beyond a mere recommendation. As a possible topic for study in the last year of high school, the Commission recommended a course in probability. Since a serious study of this topic had never before been tried in the high schools of this country, the Commission felt that its recommendations should be accompanied by some evidence of its feasibility. Accordingly, the Commission prepared an actual textbook for high school use on this topic and tried it out in a number of classrooms, with very gratifying results.
> This text is of historical importance. It was prepared by a group of authors consisting of both research mathematicians and classroom teachers, and therefore demonstrated that such a group could not only agree on recommendations for the high school curriculum, but could also work together successfully on the preparation of such texts for the high school. The enthusiastic reception which this text re-

ceived, for example, in summer institutes . . . demonstrated that a recommendation accompanied by text materials which present the recommendation in complete detail, had a much better chance of being accepted quickly and widely than would recommendations alone.

These two facts, that classroom teachers and research mathematicians could work effectively together in the preparation of texts and that the existence of appropriate texts could drastically shorten the time span between the making of recommendations and their implementation, strongly influenced the work of the School Mathematics Study Group.

The preparation of text materials became the standard pattern of intervention, beginning with the UICSM and continuing to the present time. There had been earlier, sporadic attempts by college groups, notably at the University of Chicago, to exert a more direct influence on the secondary school curriculum by preparing texts. But these efforts never achieved popular appeal.

The almost immediate impact of such groups as the UICSM, the University of Maryland Mathematics Project (UMMaP), and the SMSG in the 1950s depended, at least in part, on a receptive climate in education. And, as the disenchantment of the college mathematicians grew, other forces were at work that would make their intervention more likely to be accepted by educators and would bring unprecedented financial support to their efforts.

World War II had focused national attention on the growing need for trained personnel to serve an emerging technological society. The needs of government and industry in the sciences and mathematics expanded dramatically after the war. Manpower surveys, such as the Steelman report (80) and subsequent studies conducted by the professional mathematics societies, increased the sensitivity of the college mathematicians to the postcollege needs of their students. A more parochial concern for their own graduate programs and for increasing the research potential within mathematics worked to bring into the undergraduate curriculum advanced topics that had previously been taught only at the graduate level. In the immediate postwar years, these concerns were concurrent with refresher courses for veterans, diminishing entrance requirements, the offering of secondary school-level courses in the freshman year (in many cases for college credit), and an increasing demand for service courses in mathematics for majors in areas not previously considered technical fields. In spite of these latter forces, the increasing demand for advanced courses—to prepare more college teachers and to meet the unprecedented demands of industry and the computer revolution—tended to widen the gap between the secondary school and college programs.

Within mathematics education there was still the backlog of criticism built up before and during the war years. The reports of the Progressive Education Association (PEA) committee and of the Joint Committee of the MAA and the NCTM, both calling for a redirection of the programs immediately preceding the war, had essentially been shelved for the duration. Although the wartime emergency had given mathematics a temporary reprieve from the attacks of the 1930s, its place in the curriculum had not been reestablished on the solid, permanent ground the PEA and the Joint Commission had envisioned. While change had occurred within the curriculum as adjustment to the crisis of war, it was not the kind of change that was called for in the prewar reports. It was a response to a new type of utilitarianism. After the war, new movements within education threatened even further the discipline-based, unified curriculum that leading mathematics educators had been seeking.

⇢⇢⇢ 2. *The Educational Policies Commission*

Even before the war was over, two major reports gave evidence of what some mathematics educators would see as emerging threats to the role of mathematics in the secondary school program. *Education for All American Youth* (33), report of the Educational Policies Commission in 1944, may well have raised questions in the minds of many mathematics educators.

In describing the high school curriculum in a hypothetical American city, the authors listed four divisions of learning—"Vocational Preparation," "Individual Interests," "Common Learnings," and "Health and Physical Education." One has to examine the pages describing this curriculum carefully if he is to find the place of mathematics. It is mentioned as one of the areas under "Vocational Preparation," but virtually no explanation is given. Science, however, is given a special, separate place in the program, allied to but not subsumed by the "Common Learnings." One gets the impression that mathematics at the high school level would be restricted to traditional programs for the college-preparatory student and to specialized vocational courses, or nothing at all, for all others. The goal of the vocational courses was apparently to supply minimum preparation for the student to take a beginner's job. Beyond this, he would rely on additional course work taken in community institutes or on-the-job training.

In reference to the work of the Educational Policies Commission (and specifically to the programs described in *Education for All American Youth*), Cremin says the following (129, p. 332):

> Education in the Commission's world of the fifties is patently the logical outcome of the progressive education movement. In effect, the Commission was projecting the "schools of tomorrow" that the United States might have if it was willing to buy the progressive dream.

The commission was only a little more explicit in describing the program for its other hypothetical locality, Farmville (33, p. 140).

> In mathematics the operations which all should master are identified during the earlier grades, and most students have learned them by the time they reach the tenth grade. For those who have not, remedial instruction is provided until accepted mastery has been achieved. After ninth grade, advanced mathematics is taught to all as needed in connection with agriculture, mechanics, business education, homemaking, and in systematic courses for those whose occupational and educational plans require it.

Apparently, the major distinction between mathematics in American City and mathematics in Farmville was in the nature of the applications the student would be likely to need. This suggestion that mathematics should properly follow the line of vocational interest posed a threat similar to that of the fragmented, consumer-oriented programs to which mathematics educators had reacted before and during the war.

The Educational Policies Commission was appointed jointly by the NEA and the American Association of School Administrators. Its report was widely circulated among school administrators. The issue labeled as most crucial for the postwar years was federal versus local control. However, a reader would have been more impressed with the commission's treatment of the guidance problem in its two utopian schools. The total commitment to expanding the guidance services and to every teacher's accepting a responsibility for guidance was repeatedly emphasized. The progressive influence was particularly evident in statements such as the following (33, p. 74):

REFORM, REVOLUTION, AND REACTION   241

> The repetition of the phrase, "they help the student to do so and so," suggests that responsibility in these matters rests finally with students. So it does. The Farmville Secondary School has no required curriculum of college preparatory studies. It helps each student plan a course adapted to his abilities and his long-range interests.

The self-direction implicit in the area of guidance also pervaded the writing concerned with the learning processes. This self-direction was often within the context of a core-curriculum approach. Although the core-curriculum concept was emphasized for the junior high school, its appropriateness for senior high school was indicated in the following passage (p. 45):

> The study of "the World at Work" is a project of the entire tenth grade teaching staff, rather than of one teacher or department. Teachers of mathematics and science, for example, undertake to acquaint students with the nature and requirements of scientific and engineering occupations, as well as to show the uses of mathematics and science in other occupations.

⇛⇛ 3. *The Harvard report*

The Harvard report (1945) found a somewhat more secure place for mathematics in the secondary school's college preparatory program. In part, it was not too inconsistent with the two major prewar reports. But earlier experiences with muddled concepts of general mathematics may have conditioned mathematics educators against any movement that seemed to emphasize general education at the expense of other concerns. In the classical triumvirate of objectives—utilitarian, cultural, and disciplinary—the Harvard report may be seen as the principal postwar advocate of cultural objectives. "Appreciation" seemed to be a key word in describing the role of mathematics in secondary education, as is illustrated by the following passages (37, pp. 162–66):

> By the end of the seventh or the middle of the eighth grade every pupil should have acquired a reasonable facility in the language of arithmetic, the beginning of an appreciation of the number system, some competence in the solution of arithmetical problems, and some appreciation of the power of mathematics in formulating and solving problems in the real world....
> By this time also every pupil should have learned the commoner

facts of geometry, either by induction from measurements, drawings and gross observations, or by intuitive reasoning. The next stage in mathematical instruction, and the last for those students who are least apt in the subject, should convey an appreciation of the use of formulas, graphs, and simple equations, and should develop some skills in solving right triangles trigonometrically. . . .

Students of relatively good mathematical endowment . . . can acquire in the ninth and higher grades a genuine appreciation of algebra . . . [and] demonstrative geometry. . . .

A further course might be given in the senior year—"an introductory survey of elementary trigonometry, statistics, precision of measurement, and the use of graphs."

To some extent, both mathematicians and mathematics educators could identify with the Harvard report. The emphasis was clearly on mathematics as an abstract, logical structure. A relatively strong program was suggested for the college preparatory student. The committee found fault with the existing program, largely on the grounds that it failed to emphasize the abstract structure of mathematics in favor of manipulative skills. Committee members recognized the greater difficulty in teaching basic concepts for understanding, and (p. 165) they felt that

> the pressure to make mathematics easier for students . . . is inclined to take the form of making it less meaningful and more technical, of developing it as a ritual of memorized formulas and procedures.

But even the Harvard report failed to support an extended program at the high school level for other than the college preparatory student. The committee summarized its position as follows (p. 167):

> Those aspects of mathematics that should be prescribed for all students can be mastered by the end of the eighth grade or by the middle of the ninth. Above this point a division must be recognized between students who can derive little profit from further instruction in pure mathematics and those with relatively good mathematical aptitude.

Thus, beyond recommending increased emphasis on fundamental concepts and logical structure, the Harvard report did not present a very far-reaching program in mathematics.

Both reports introduced an element that would plague many mathematics educators in the postwar years. Both the Harvard report, with its common learnings, and *Education for All American Youth*, with its support of the core curriculum, introduced opportunities for progressive educators to imbed mathematics instruction in a socialized setting. Many mathematics educators could support the fundamental concept of a core curriculum and could see the definite contribution mathematics could make. However, for many of them the typical core-curriculum programs in the schools were just too close to progressivism. Consequently, the role of mathematics in the core curriculum became a prime area of debate among mathematics educators in the late forties and the early fifties. As Howard Fehr expressed it, mathematics teachers were afraid of the core programs because "they [were] afraid the good ship mathematics [might] be lost in the process" (336, p. 4).

Harold Fawcett also expressed concern about the potential impact of the core movement on mathematics (334, pp. 11-12).

> There are, in fact, large elements of chance operating in the selection and conduct of these core units and since an "intelligent evaluation" of responsible citizenship in our modern industrial democracy calls for mathematical literacy, will we be faithful to our obligations if we leave to chance the development of a mathematical program appropriate to general education?
>
> The characteristic of the core which places even more serious limitations on its usefulness as an instrument for the effective teaching of mathematics is the demand that learning activities be organized "without reference to conventional subject lines." Mathematics is a system of ideas and to make it seem nothing more than a group of discrete manipulative skills, unrelated and unorganized, is to limit its usefulness and to distort its meaning.

So a movement that held the promise of breaking down the watertight compartments of the traditional program also may have created the fear that no compartment at all would remain for mathematics as a separate discipline.

→→→→ 4 *Commission on Post-War Plans*

The reports of the Commission on Post-War Plans of the NCTM, published in 1944 (15), 1945 (16), and 1947 (18), reflect the thinking of the mathematics-education community during the period in which the Harvard report and *Education for All American Youth* were written. Each of the three reports possessed features in common with these two documents.

The first report offered general rather than specific suggestions. The commission held that the school should ensure mathematical literacy for all who can possibly achieve it. This report was offered much in the spirit of the common learnings of the Educational Policies Commission. Concern for individual differences was expressed in terms of the needs of youth. A tentative proposal for a three-track program included a sequential four-year program that was to be rigorous, to have some continuity, and to be designed for college-bound students. Courses for students entering industry were to be obtained by improving the existing courses in general mathematics. The commission recognized a need for courses in social mathematics, to ensure mathematical competency in everyday affairs. Finally, the commission stated that a completely new approach to the problem of the slow learner was needed, that there was a need to improve the teaching of arithmetic, and that the sequential courses needed improvement. These suggestions were offered in the spirit of promoting dialogue and discussion.

The second report made the suggestions of the first report more specific by offering thirty-four theses embodying recommendations for improving instruction in grades 1–14. A unified mathematics program for all regular students was suggested for grades 7 and 8. Algebra was recommended for some students in grade 9, but it was suggested that the majority should take general mathematics. In the senior high the sequential courses were to be reserved for students with the requisite ability. These courses were to be organized in terms of key concepts and a few large units, with an emphasis on functional competence and mathematical power.

The third report contained a checklist of twenty-nine key concepts that, in effect, defined functional competence (18, pp. 318–19). They were not reminiscent of the unifying-concepts idea of Felix Klein but were specific objectives for junior high school mathematics. The concepts listed were the following:

1. Computation
2. Percents
3. Ratio
4. Estimating
5. Rounding numbers
6. Tables
7. Graphs
8. Statistics
9. Nature of measurement
10. Use of measuring devices
11. Square root

12. Angles
13. Geometric concepts
14. The 3-4-5 relation
15. Constructions
16. Drawings
17. Vectors
18. Metric system
19. Conversion [of units in measurement]
20. Algebraic symbolism
21. Formulas
22. Signed numbers
23. Using axioms
24. Practical formulas
25. Similar triangles and proportion
26. Trigonometry
27. First steps in business arithmetic
28. Stretching the dollar
29. Proceeding from hypothesis to conclusion

This final report was entitled "Guidance Report." It was later published in pamphlet form for use by high school students and counselors. It covered the following areas:

1. Mathematics for personal use
2. Mathematics used by trained workers
3. Mathematics for college preparation
4. Mathematics for professional workers
5. Women in mathematics
6. Mathematics used by civil service workers

A statement by the commission relating to consumer education was published by the National Association of Secondary School Principals (17, p. 23). Three common mistakes in the teaching of mathematics for consumer education were identified as follows:

1. Attempting to teach to completion in grades 7 and 8 topics for which the children are not ready
2. The use of obsolete materials
3. Too much computation, and failure to emphasize the social implications

The commission believed consumer problems in junior high school should be kept on an informational or appreciation level. A separate course was recommended for senior high school for the following reasons:

1. The mathematical part of consumer education cannot be satisfactorily completed in grade 8.

2. Consumer education cannot be fitted into any of the traditional courses.
3. It provides an excellent opportunity to reteach arithmetic skills.

The content should include statistics, consumer credit, better buymanship, budgeting, insurance, taxation, wise use of money, business dealings in the home, and proper use of scarce or precious materials. In this publication, as well as the three reports, it was pointed out that no stigmatizing of the consumer course should be allowed.

The Commission on Post-War Plans was committed to the idea of mathematics as a tool subject. This was the meaning of the word "functional" as it was used to modify competence and in listing the twenty-nine key ideas. Although perhaps tempered by the reaction to the PEA report and the Joint Commission document, the reports were basically regressive. They were more closely related to the thoughts of the Educational Policies Commission than to the Harvard report in the degree of emphasis on guidance, individual differences, and social and applied mathematics.

5. "General Education in School and College"

Discussions that evolved from the Harvard report moved toward a position most mathematics educators could support. For example, the book *General Education in School and College* reports the 1950/51 discussions of a committee representing the faculties of Andover, Exeter, and Lawrenceville preparatory schools and Harvard, Princeton, and Yale universities. This committee took a very positive position with respect to mathematics (35, p. 52):

> No subject is more properly a major part of secondary education than mathematics. None has a more distinguished history or a finer tradition of teaching. Perhaps the very excellence of the topic has helped, in recent decades, to keep the content and order of its teaching largely unexamined. One of the most remarkable of our sessions was the one in which we consulted with a group of first-rate school and college teachers of mathematics and discovered, as the evening progressed, a very high degree of consensus on the view that school offerings in mathematics are ready for drastic alteration and improvement.

How different from the following statement of the Educational Policies Commission (33, p. 142):

> There is no aristocracy of "subjects" in the Farmville curriculum. Mathematics and mechanics, art and agriculture, history and homemaking are peers. For the teachers of Farmville believe that the key to intellectual growth is found, not in the inherent virtues of particular fields of learning, but in the strong purposes of the learner which impel him to attempt the difficult and to persevere until he has accomplished that which he has undertaken to do.

As with most committees, recommendations for alteration and improvement were forthcoming from this committee of preparatory school and university faculty members. It found the traditional four-year course—two years of algebra, one of plane geometry, and one of solid geometry and trigonometry—wanting, primarily because of what was usually omitted and because "in some cases the woods of principle seem to be obscured by the trees of constant repetition and problem solving" (35, p. 53). Committee members felt that mathematics operated under a law of rapidly diminishing returns and that curricular emphasis should be placed upon fundamental notions and not on extensive elaborations of ideas already grown familiar. To them, the incorporation of solid geometry into plane geometry was a single revision that could save nearly half a year in the standard school curriculum. With other "excess fat on the body mathematical" they found the treatments of complex numbers, determinants, logarithmic solutions of triangles, and the geometry of the circle too extensive and suitable for condensation or omission. With the help of professional advisers they concluded that "much can be squeezed out, to the positive advantage of the basic notions which are now taught" (35, p. 54).

By squeezing out the excess fat, this committee hoped to find the time in the standard school curriculum to include a year of the calculus (with a minimal framework of analytic geometry) and half a year of statistics. But they did not lose sight of the need to emphasize at all levels the basic principles and central concepts of mathematics. The Harvard report had also emphasized the need to focus on basic ideas but had suggested the following (37, p. 163):

> It is unfortunately true that those aspects of algebra and geometry that are of greatest interest in general education are also more difficult to teach, and are much harder for the student to grasp, than are the technical skills of mathematical manipulation.

The committee noted this reservation stated in the Harvard report but insisted (35, p. 53) that from every point of view—that of the college mathematics teacher as well as that of general education—we are persuaded that the great business of the school's mathematics curriculum should be to communicate as many of these central concepts as it can; we think the better student can do much more of this than he has been doing, and we are certain that he should try.

This report has been discussed here out of proportion to its known impact because of its prophetic reflection of directions the revolution in secondary mathematics was to take and because it indicates that, at least in some cases, the positions of the college mathematician and of the general educator could be reconciled and could even coalesce. The nature of the schools and universities involved as well as the professional consultants the committee utilized makes it unlikely that this report reflected a general, widespread reaction to the Harvard report. But the position expressed seems close to the thinking of those who were to take the lead in the developments to follow in the 1950s.

It is difficult not to compare the state of affairs in mathematics education at midcentury with that in 1920, when the postures of the National Committee on Mathematical Requirements and of the Committee on Economy of Time were so clearly in conflict. A new skirmish in the battle of objectives began. Three separate camps, corresponding to the cultural, utilitarian, and disciplinary goals of mathematics, were already identifiable. But the new disciplinary emphases, represented by the concerns of the college mathematician, were imbedded in the subject matter rather than in learning theory. Perhaps most mathematics educators would have preferred a middle-of-the-road course. But seeing the threat of potential excesses in movements pointed in directions they had found unsuitable in the past may have helped them develop a state of mind welcoming the intervention of the college mathematician. This time, the climate was right for the mathematician.

6. *Technological needs and education of the gifted*

Many of the forces and issues that combined to set the stage for major revision in secondary school mathematics are summarized in chapter 6, Part One. Growing pressure from the federal government that reflected an emerging, national concern for excellence in education; organized efforts to provide better programs for the gifted student; an untapped (at the secondary school level) backlog of more recent developments in mathematics and its applications; a popular press that was again critical of secondary education—all of these could be added to the basic forces within the mathematics and education communities which provided a setting for dramatic change. By 1950 education, and mathematics education particularly, was ripe for a revolution. The mathematicians were ready to supply direction, and the mathematics educators were inclined to accept their leadership.

The organized concern of the mathematics community may have been delayed by the exploding college enrollments in the years immediately following the war. But experiences with the more mature needs of returning veterans—with their prewar training in mathematics—perhaps even increased the likelihood of mathematicians' involving themselves in secondary school affairs. At least the evidence is clear that by the early 1950s mathematicians were poised for an attack on the school curriculum. C. O. Oakley had communicated the nature of the coming revolution in 1942 in the *Mathematics Teacher* (391), but it was not until the early fifties, ten years later, that the need for reform was made to seem pressing and real to the readers of this journal.

One focus of the need for curricular revision was the needs of the gifted student. G. B. Price argued in 1951 (400) that slighting the education of the gifted was slighting the need for a creative cadre of people for national defense purposes. Noting that there were many examples of youths extremely creative in advanced mathematics, he argued (p. 373) that there was a profound need to (1) identify the gifted and (2) educate them

> to the limit of their abilities—in spite of the draft or war—for the sake of the safety and welfare of the nation.

Continuing on to pedagogical matters, Price stated the following (p. 376):

> Finally, the teacher of the mathematically gifted will fail if he stresses only the *usefulness* of his subject. The young are full of curiosity and easily attracted by something that is interesting and elegant. The high school student is much less attracted by an opportunity to take up the world's burdens.

Could you imagine this in the *Mathematics Teacher* in 1935? Price's article is typical of many articles appearing in the *Mathematics Teacher* during the early fifties. From his experience in government service, R. S. Burington argued that young people were beginning careers too late. He continued as follows (321):

> As many of you realize, the typical mass education, which has evolved over the last two or three generations, has been developed for the good of the larger proportion of students endowed with what might be called typical ability. In most situations this educational program is probably not the best that we could provide for the coming generations, and in particular for those students with outstanding talents.

He stated further that gearing the curriculum to the average retards the more able. He suggested a program quite similar to the advanced placement program.

The other focus for articles making the case for reform may also be construed as pertaining to the gifted. Scores of articles stressed the need for mathematically trained personnel in government service, in engineering, in industry, and so forth. However, the arguments were in terms of the average college student rather than in terms of the highly creative and exceptionally intelligent student who possessed the potential for an extremely specialized career. Kenneth Henderson and Kern Dickman (353) and S. S. Cairns (323) reflected the growing concern for the average college-bound student and looked specifically at the problem at the University of Illinois. Articles by individuals such as Daniel Lloyd (374), Allen Orth (396), and Dael Wolfle (436) documented the growing shortage of technically trained people for industry. Some authors raised the flag of patriotism by comparing the production of engineers in Russia to that in the United States. But not all of the articles were written from the standpoint of what needed to be done for and to the schools. P. D. Edwards, P. S. Jones, and B. E. Meserve wrote an article aimed at the student population for the May 1952 issue of the *Mathematics Teacher* (333). Bearing some resemblance to the guidance pamphlet of the Commission on Post-War Plans, the intent was to inform the student about what high school mathematics was needed for various college curricula. The document was informative while selling mathematics to college-aspiring youth.

In the May 1954 issue of the *Mathematics Teacher*, a section titled "Which Way Mathematics?" was devoted to the problems of the school mathematics curriculum. Harl Douglass, R. S. Burington, S. S. Cairns, and Kenneth O. May wrote articles discussing the need for reform. Cairns noted (323, p. 301) as an underlying cause of the current state of affairs

> the theory that high schools should limit their programs to those skills and manipulations that some group of individuals finds necessary to the average adult.

How different from Bobbitt and Kilpatrick! May declared the following (375, p. 303):

> The present crisis in mathematics is due not to any deterioration in the work of mathematics teachers, but to an urgent national need for more and better mathematics at a time when administrators and the public have for years slighted mathematics and, indeed, discouraged all vigorous mental effort in the high schools. . . . Excellence in scholarship is permitted, but mediocrity is considered more "democratic."

The entire section was devoted to the need for reform and offered some proposals for reform. The articles were written from the point of view of national crisis and national need.

7. The University of Illinois Committee on School Mathematics

Of all the forces cited, the mathematical needs of students entering college must be identified as triggering the first major curriculum development at the secondary school level in this period. The UICSM was formed "to investigate problems concerning the content and teaching of high school mathematics" (60, p. 57). It immediately followed a survey made by the Engineering and Education schools at Illinois which led to the pamphlet *Mathematical Needs of Prospective Students in the College of Engineering of the University of Illinois.* The motivation for this survey and the way in which the needs of prospective students were assessed is documented in a 1952 article (353). The work of the UICSM was initiated primarily as a means of correcting the weaknesses in secondary school programs which left students short of minimum needs.

Since its origin was in 1951, the UICSM has been viewed as the "progenitor of all current curriculum projects in mathematics" (155, p. 57). Several aspects of the model it provided became characteristic of subsequent development projects. The UICSM received support through the Carnegie Foundation and later from the NSF and the USOE. Extensive financial support through private foundations and governmental agencies became possibly the most critical factor in both the extent of reform and the rapidity of its implementation in the schools. The director of the UICSM, Max Beberman, reported that he and his associates decided very soon that "any realistic proposal for improvement would have to include classroom-tested instructional materials" (296, p. 374). This too became characteristic of most subsequent curriculum-development projects. That such a practice had been recommended in several earlier instances does not lessen the contribution of the UICSM in providing a concrete example of the feasibility of such an approach. The UICSM recognized that the success of its new materials and of the recommendations for teaching with them depended in large measure on a well-trained cadre of teachers. Accordingly, until 1958 it made its textbooks available in classroom lots only to teachers who had received special training in their use. Most later curriculum projects also made related teacher education one of their primary concerns. The success of the specifically oriented teacher-training institutes conducted by the UICSM may have added impetus to the summer (and later, the academic-year) programs supported first by private corporations (General Electric, Shell, etc.) and later in unprecedented amounts by the federal government. Finally, the UICSM established a pattern of curriculum revision which addressed itself not only to significant changes in mathematical content but also to the development of a teaching philosophy consistent with the new mathematical emphasis. The limited impact of subsequent projects that focused only on mathematical content may have heightened the recognition of the importance of teaching strategies. Nevertheless, the UICSM established a pattern that was followed by several major curriculum projects that made teaching methodology a central concern.

The UICSM program evolved as a joint effort of the College of Education, the College of Engineering, and the College of Liberal Arts and Sciences, but the essential character of the program was largely a reflection of the teaching philosophy of its director, Max Beberman, and his colleagues David Page, Gertrude Hendrix, and Herbert Vaughn, who worked directly in the development of the materials.

From the beginning, the UICSM was a broadly conceived program. In addition to developing a four-year high school mathematics curriculum (in recent years this effort has been extended to the elementary and junior high school levels), the staff of the UICSM (1) taught this program in the University High School; (2) taught its philosophy, program, and methodology to teachers; (3) supervised these teachers as they taught the UICSM materials in cooperating schools; (4) taught demonstration lessons before interested teacher groups; and (5) prepared a series of films illustrating the teaching of the UICSM materials to high school classes.

By 1958, after several revisions, courses for the four high school grades were being tried in a dozen pilot schools. The UICSM materials were divided into eleven units, covering essentially all the topics in the usual secondary school programs. The eleven units were the following (147, p. 130):

1. Arithmetic of the Real Numbers
2. Generalizations and Algebraic Manipulation
3. Equations and Inequations
4. Ordered Pairs and Graphs
5. Relations and Functions
6. Geometry
7. Mathematical Induction
8. Sequences
9. Elementary Functions
10. Circular Functions and Trigonometry
11. Polynomial Functions and Complex Numbers

The committee did not originally intend to designate specific units for each year of the high school program. Instead, the loose-leaf format of the original materials was intended to provide considerable flexibility in the pace and extent of coverage. Thus capable students might complete the entire sequence of eleven units during the four years while less capable students might complete only six. The first six units would be roughly comparable to one year of algebra and one of geometry. As "courses" evolved from the units, a first course might cover units 1-4 in grade 9; a second course, units 5-6 in grade 10; a third course, units 7-9 in grade 11; and a fourth course, units 10-11 in grade 12. The unit format and the refusal to use the traditional designations, such as algebra and geometry, for single-year courses were a significant break from the past and a partial realization of a recurring recommendation in mathematics education.

Professor Beberman described the philosophy and program of the UICSM in the Inglis Lecture in 1958. There he stated the mathematical objectives of the program as follows (91, p. 4):

> The curriculum developer . . . has in mind the traditional expectations of what a college-bound high school graduate should know of

mathematics. He is expected, among other things, to solve equations (singly and in systems), to use algorisms and formulas in transforming algebraic and trigonometric expressions, to deduce theorems from postulates, to find ordered pairs which belong to relations, to graph relations, and to apply his knowledge to a host of geometric and physical problems.

We think that these objectives are sensible and proper, and our curriculum is planned accordingly. But we insist upon an important qualification: the student must *understand* his mathematics. Now, the word "understand" and its close relative "meaningful" have been bandied about in educational circles to a point where just about everyone pledges allegiance to the goal of teaching meaningful and understandable mathematics. We have tried to translate these words into operational terms. We believe that a student will come to understand mathematics when his textbook and teacher use unambiguous language and when he is enabled to discover generalizations by himself.

The two facets of understanding he identifies—*precision of language* and *discovery of generalizations*—were central influences in the development of both the curriculum and the methodology of the project.

Although examination of the UICSM units reveals considerable emphasis on such contemporary topics as set terminology and notation, logical quantifiers, and deductive structure and theory, the developers felt that the introduction of contemporary mathematics was of less concern than consistency. When new topics were introduced it was for the purpose of adding clarification and precision rather than merely for the sake of beefing up the mathematics (377).

Features of the content of the UICSM materials that represented clear changes from the traditional program include (1) the move toward an integrated mathematics curriculum in which algebra is found throughout the four-year program; (2) the fact that geometry, especially solid geometry, is minimized; (3) the disappearance of trigonometry as a separate subject and the introduction of the more general circular functions; (4) the introduction of some modern concepts such as set terminology and quantifiers; and (5) the relocation of several topics, such as mathematical induction and inequalities, to lower levels in the curriculum. Of particular note is the fact that the two facets of understanding are apparent throughout the eleven units. Care was taken to ensure precision of expression, even to the extent of inventing new terms and symbols (e.g., "pronumeral"). Discovery teaching and learning became the hallmark of the UICSM program.

Beberman discussed this last feature of the program in the following excerpts from his Inglis Lecture (pp. 24, 26, 27, 38):

> A second major principle which has guided us in developing the UICSM program is that the student will come to understand mathematics if he plays an active part in developing mathematical ideas and procedures. To us this means that after we have selected a body of subject matter to be learned we must design both exposition and exercises in such a way that the student will discover principles and rules.
>
> It is important to point out here that it is unnecessary to require a student to verbalize his discovery to determine whether he is aware of a rule. The teacher can use a sequence of questions to determine whether awareness is present. In fact, immediate verbalization has the obvious disadvantage of giving the game away to other students, as well as the more serious disadvantage of compelling the student to make a statement when he may not have the linguistic capacity to do so.
>
> This technique of *delaying* the verbalization of important discoveries is characteristic of the UICSM program, and differentiates our discovery method from other methods which are also called "discovery methods" but which always involve the immediate verbalization of discoveries.
>
> Thus the discovery method develops interest in mathematics, and power in mathematical thinking. Because of the student's independence of rote rules and routines, it also develops versatility in applying mathematics.

In more recent years the UICSM materials have been modified and published in commercial form. The focus of the project has shifted to include such efforts as the development of a two-year sequence in vector geometry, with heavy emphasis on the arbitrary nature and the power of postulates and mathematical systems; the preparation of materials for low achievers in grades 7 and 8; and experimentation with programmed learning and computer-assisted instruction. In addition, a program for the elementary school has been developing under the guidance of David Page.

The evolutionary pattern in the UICSM has been paralleled in most of the curriculum development projects. The initial focus on the college-capable student at the secondary level has typically broadened into a concern for all students, often at all grade levels.

⇛⇛ 8. *The coalescence of national support*

Many sources have cited the launching of the first Soviet satellite in October 1957 as the spur to curriculum revolution in the United States. There is little doubt that this event focused public attention on educational problems. The increased awareness and the resulting furor in the popular press surely added to the pressure on governmental offices to increase financial support. Unprecedented amounts of money did become available—especially for curriculum development and teacher training in the sciences and mathematics. But the historical record shows clearly that curriculum reform had already begun (and with federal support) well before Sputnik jolted the public conscience.

Concurrent with the work of the UICSM, conferences were under way which would establish between the NSF and the mathematics community a relation that led eventually to the series of meetings from which the SMSG evolved.

One cannot examine the lists of participating mathematicians (beginning with the wartime committees and continuing through the curriculum projects of the fifties) without being struck by the frequent reappearance of the same names. S. S. Wilks, A. A. Albert, Mina Rees, C. V. Newsom, J. G. Kemeny, Albert W. Tucker, E. E. Moise, A. M. Gleason, Albert E. Meder, J. L. Kelly, E. G. Begle, Marshall Stone, Carl Allendoerfer, Frederick Mosteller, Saunders MacLane, R. H. Bing, Paul Rosenbloom—such people, with their basic professional training and their interest in research mathematics, would have been unlikely associates in school mathematics in earlier periods. Their continued participation over a number of years contributed to the consistency of direction that the reform movement took.

The NSF was established in 1950 for the purpose of developing a national policy for the promotion of basic research and education in the sciences. In this same year a small group of mathematicians was appointed by the Policy Committee for Mathematics to assess the needs of the mathematics community and to prepare a proposed budget for the NSF. This policy committee represented the AMS, the MAA, the Institute of Mathematical Statistics, and the Association for Symbolic Logic. Members of the budget-preparation committee were A. A. Albert (chairman), C. V. Newsom, Mina Rees, J. L. Walsh, and S. S. Wilks. They recommended (25, pp. 70–71)

> that the Board request the National Research Council to appoint a Special Commission of Mathematicians to survey the teaching of

mathematics and the mathematics curriculum in the secondary schools. The training at this level has long been a matter of concern to mathematicians and efforts should be made to investigate the situation and to recommend changes to improve it.

Although the amount budgeted for secondary schools ($18,000) was a very small portion of the total budget recommended for mathematics ($2,229,000), it was an official expression of concern by a committee representing the four leading professional organizations of mathematicians. However, to explore the eventual ramifications of this modest, initial expression of organized concern would be to get ahead of the story. Several very significant events were to occur between 1950 and 1958, when the SMSG was finally formed.

The UICSM had started its work, and several other local curriculum-development projects were under way, by the mid-fifties. In 1954 the NCTM published its Twenty-second Yearbook, entitled *Emerging Practices in Mathematics Education* (198). The contents of this yearbook were divided into five parts as follows:

Part 1. Various Provisions for Differentiated Mathematics Curriculums
Part 2. Laboratory Teaching in Mathematics
Part 3. Teacher Education
Part 4. New Emphases in Subject Matter
Part 5. The Evaluation of Mathematical Learning

Study of this yearbook reveals little suggestion that a major revolution in mathematics education was on the horizon and certainly none that such a revolution was under way. The guiding principles that seem to be revealed in Part 1 are essentially those of the Commission on Post-War Plans—particularly as expressed in the "Guidance Report." Some leading schools had moved beyond the double-track program recommended by the commission to a multitrack program. Two bases for tracking seem to have been used—ability grouping and vocational plans. As one of the authors of the report later put it (393, p. 56), "Two vocational slogans—'Meet the needs of the learner' and 'Provide for individual differences'—are ever present in modern educational discussions" and seem to dominate curricular decisions. Descriptions of these differentiated curricula give the impression that functional competence and consumer mathematics were still prominent theories even in these emerging practices.

Part 2, "Laboratory Teaching in Mathematics," deals almost entirely with the use of audiovisual aids. It has much the same flavor as the "Devices in the Mathematics Classroom" column in the *Mathematics Teacher* and as the Eighteenth Yearbook of the NCTM, *Multi-Sensory Aids in the Teaching of Mathematics* (195), which had been published in 1945. It gives little hint of the newer concepts of methodology such as those being tested in the UICSM project.

And Part 4, "New Emphases in Subject Matter," which one would hope would reflect the impending change, is again disappointing on this point. In one article, Jack Wilson traces the history of general mathematics with its various interpretations, and in the process he alludes to the narrow, consumer-oriented conception of general mathematics which had been a thorn in the side of many mathematics educators in the prewar years. And yet he concludes (434, p. 291):

> Textbooks devoted almost exclusively to consumer mathematics are now being published. Apparently mathematics for general education now means mathematics for use, including social mathematics and consumer mathematics.

Apparently there had been no substantial movement toward the emphasis on basic concepts and abstract structure called for by the Harvard report or even toward the unified concept of general mathematics held by the PEA and Joint Commission reports.

In two other articles in Part 4 (408, pp. 269–75; 221, pp. 276–83), the "new emphasis" in the teaching of geometry seems to be upon nongeometric exercises as they had been described by Harold Fawcett in the Thirteenth Yearbook of the NCTM, *The Nature of Proof* (141). It is true that these nongeometric exercises were being designed and incorporated primarily to clarify the logical reasoning process, and they were seen as a basis for transfer of learning in this area. That the emerging emphasis was upon proof and locial reasoning may have been an indication of things to come, but in geometry the emerging practices seem to have been guided by prewar recommendations and not to reflect more recent concerns.

There are slight indications in the yearbook that certain advanced topics were beginning to find a place earlier in the curriculum. Some elements of analytic geometry (e.g., the slope concept) were finding their way into the algebra and geometry texts (431, pp. 284–87), and probability and statistical inference were seen by at least a few schools as appropriate topics for the secondary school (373, pp. 303–9).

But the few encouraging signs (at least for those who were thinking revolutionary thoughts) must have been partially offset by the two articles concerning approximate data (414, pp. 310–22; 339, pp. 323–42). These were in the vein of Aaron Bakst's *Approximate Computation*, published in 1937 as the Twelfth Yearbook of the NCTM. Even though the authors of the Twenty-second Yearbook presented a somewhat more modern treatment, their articles still seem much more appropriate to the emphasis of the thirties and forties than to what was to come in the late fifties. As emerging practices they certainly gave no clue as to what was to happen within the next few years.

Perhaps the failure—the failure of a yearbook published by the most influential professional organization for mathematics education, and a yearbook designed specifically to reveal emerging practices—to capture almost anything of the impending change is an indication of how hard it is to discern among published recommendations and the efforts of small experimental groups the actual directions of changes to come. One might assume that what appeared in *Emerging Practices in Mathematics Education* represented the thinking and the programs of the "cream of the crop" of secondary schools. What, then, of the less progressive schools? Is there any reason to believe they had progressed any significant distance from the programs of the prewar period? The texts in use also fail to reveal any dramatic change. Can we believe that even the recommendations of the PEA and Joint Commission had received any widespread implementation? Apparently not.

In 1954 the Carnegie Foundation asked the Educational Testing Service to describe research activities that would lead to better mathematics courses and teaching in the elementary and secondary schools. A survey conducted by a committee under the chairmanship of S. S. Wilks of Princeton described problems in mathematics education—particularly in the college preparatory program. Although the report of this committee (32) was not published until 1956, the results of the survey were made immediately available to the CEEB.

9. *The Commission on Mathematics of the CEEB*

In 1955, the policy-making Committee on Examinations of the CEEB recommended that a commission on mathematics be appointed to study the "mathematics needs of today's American Youth" and report its findings and recommendations to the board. Although the final report of this commission was not published until 1959, it is appropriate to discuss it at this point because it was available in preliminary form to curriculum groups that would begin their projects before the final version was published.

The CEEB exerted an indirect influence on the secondary school program through its examinations. If its examinations remained static, it could be accused of exerting a stabilizing influence on the curriculum. If its examinations changed too much, it could be accused of trying to control the direction curriculum change might take. The establishing of the Commission on Mathematics was a new kind of open attempt by the board to influence the school curriculum. To the credit of the board, it should be pointed out, it chose a committee of professionals who represented the three groups most directly concerned with the secondary school program in mathematics—college mathematicians, high school teachers, and college teachers of mathematics education.

Albert W. Tucker of Princeton University was appointed chairman of the commission, and Dean Albert E. Meder, Jr., of Rutgers University became its executive director. Samuel S. Wilks (Princeton), George B. Thomas, Jr. (Massachusetts Institute of Technology), Frederick Mosteller (Harvard University), Carl Allendoerfer (University of Washington), Howard Fehr (Teachers College), Eugene Northrop (University of Chicago), and Henry Van Engen (Iowa State Teachers College) represented the colleges. Edwin C. Douglas (The Taft School), Martha Hildebrandt (Proviso Township High School), Morris Meister (Bronx High School of Science), and Robert E. K. Rourke (Kent School) represented the schools.

It should be noted that the members of the commission came from many parts of the country and that the commission was, in this period, the first truly national group to concern itself with the high school curriculum, although the high schools with members on the commission were obviously representative of a select group. The commission was formed as a working group combining classroom teachers, university mathematicians, and mathematics educators.

The commission summarized its recommendations in the following nine-point program for college-capable students (12, pp. 33-34):

1. Strong preparation, *both* in concepts *and* in skills, for college mathematics at the level of calculus and analytic geometry
2. Understanding of the nature and role of deductive reasoning—in algebra, as well as in geometry
3. Appreciation of mathematical structure ("patterns")—for example, properties of natural, rational, real, and complex numbers

4. Judicious use of unifying ideas—sets, variables, functions and relations
5. Treatment of inequalities along with equations
6. Incorporation with plane geometry of some coordinate geometry, and essentials of solid geometry and space perception
7. Introduction in grade 11 of fundamental trigonometry—centered on coordinates, vectors, and complex numbers
8. Emphasis in grade 12 on elementary functions (polynomial, exponential, circular)
9. Recommendation of additional alternative units for grade 12: *either* introductory probability with statistical applications *or* an introduction to modern algebra.

The commission did not view its recommendations as calling for major changes in basic content. It asserted (p. 34):

> As a close scrutiny of the full report will show, the Commission's recommendations embody relatively minor changes in content, but tremendously important changes in the points of view of instruction, and major changes in teaching emphases. None of these changes is simply for the sake of change. The Commission, as stated before, has tried to produce a curriculum suitable for students and oriented to the needs of mathematics, natural science, social science, business, technology, and industry in the second half of the twentieth century. This has been the overriding objective. Whatever of the old has disappeared, whatever of the traditional yet remains, whatever of the new appears, is in or out of the curriculum solely to effect necessary modification and improvement.

The commission report did not devote a lot of space to teaching methods. And yet, imbedded throughout the report are indications that it recognized the importance of this phase of the problems facing mathematics education. The following excerpts are examples (pp. 6, 7, 10, 13, 14, 17, 18):

> A poor curriculum well taught is better than a good curriculum badly taught. A good curriculum well taught is the only acceptable goal.... The quality of the curriculum and the skill of the teacher both are vital.
>
> If the nation is indeed faced with low levels of mathematical competence—and in fact it is . . . a complete solution demands improvements in the effectiveness of instruction and in the appropriateness of

course content. . . . Individual differences among human beings are the rule; these differences can be neglected only with peril.

Our program is a college preparatory program, designed for students who can profit from it. We believe the secondary school must meet the needs of this group, as well as the needs of all other groups. . . . All students need not be taught at the same pace, in the same order, or to the same extent, or with the same emphasis.

Students studying college preparatory mathematics should, in our opinion, be taught in groups with similar interests and similar intellectual abilities.

The Commission believes also that content in mathematics or any other subject, for that matter, must be appropriate to the level of maturity of the student. Otherwise there can be no meaningful learning. . . . Even for traditional subject matter, psychological research has barely scratched the surface.

This flexibility of the recommended program includes its manner of presentation. Members of the Commission would decry an authoritarian approach to method and practice, but a teacher who believes that such an approach is most effective may present this material in the same way that he has, presumably, taught the traditional content. Most if not all of the Commission members would prefer to see a developmental approach, which would encourage the student to discover as much of the mathematical subject matter for himself as his ability and the time available (for this is a time-consuming method) will permit.

Questions about methods of teaching and patterns of organization . . . have no ideal answers, valid at all times and in all schools.

The nine-point summary offered by the commission does not do justice to the level of specificity achieved in its recommendations. Detailed outlines of recommended courses were presented for each of the grade levels 9-12. And for areas that were somewhat new or that differed from the traditional treatment, the commission expanded further on these outlines in illustrative appendices to their report and in classroom units such as "Concepts of Equation and Inequality" and "Informal Deduction in Algebra." The recommended programs for each grade level are summarized below:

Mathematics for grade 9 (Elementary Mathematics I)

1. Operations with simple algebraic expressions. The distinctive feature of this section was its heavy emphasis on set concepts

and terminology and upon the extension of the basic laws of operations for the nonnegative rational numbers—the commutative, associative, and distributive laws—to the transformation of simple algebraic expressions.

2. Positive and negative numbers. This section was distinguished by use of the number line and by absolute value, concepts of additive inverse and multiplicative inverse, and the arithmetic of the rationals interpreted on the number line.
3. Linear equations and inequalities in one variable. The commission prepared an illustrative unit for this section because the topic of inequalities was not standard in the curriculum and the principles of solution based upon equivalent sentences as preserving a solution set was an innovation for most teachers.
4. Variation (optional). This section dealt with direct and inverse variation with related verbal problems.
5. Linear equations and inequalities in two variables. Again, there was a heavy use of set concepts and graphical methods.
6. Polynomial expressions. Factoring was based on application of the distributive principle rather than on the standard-form or trial-and-error methods of the traditional program.
7. Rational (fractional) expressions. Transformation to equivalent expressions emphasized concept of multiplicative inverse.
8. Informal deduction in algebra. Algebra was not typically approached deductively, and so the commission again supplied an illustrative unit.
9. Quadratic equations. This unit was characterized by an attempt to provide a meaningful concept of the real numbers via nonterminating, nonrepeating decimals as filling in holes in the number line.
10. Descriptive statistics (optional).
11. Numerical trigonometry of the right triangle (optional).

Mathematics for grade 10 (Elementary Mathematics II)

1. Informal geometry. This unit was intended to provide the kind of intuitive, informal background in geometry that would ideally be covered in a strong junior high school program.
2. Deductive reasoning.
3. Sequence of theorems culminating in the Pythagorean theorem. This section utilized conventional assumptions (but *not* superposition) and developed a much-abbreviated sequence of the-

orems in order to introduce the Pythagorean relation more quickly.

4. Coordinate geometry. The introduction of coordinate methods in the tenth-grade course was a definite innovation from the standard program and was made possible by taking as direct a route as possible to the Pythagorean theorem. The standard coordinate geometry of the line and circle was included.

5. Additional theorems and originals. This section covered the additional standard topics involving circles and loci.

6. Solid geometry. Again, an illustrative unit was prepared for this section.

Mathematics for grade 11 (Intermediate Mathematics)

1. Basic concepts and skills. This section covered a careful review of the development of the real number system via extensions and review of the operations in each system.

2. Linear functions. A set-theoretic approach to function was supplemented by formula, table, and graph approaches.

3. Radicals.

4. Quadratic functions.

5. Quadratic equations. The complex numbers were introduced in this section.

6. Systems of equations.

7. Exponents and logarithms.

8. Series.

9. Number fields. This section gave a more rigorous treatment of the field properties as defining an abstract algebraic structure.

10. Plane vectors. This was another uncommon topic in the standard program.

11. Coordinate trigonometry. This section introduced both rectangular and polar coordinates; it treated complex numbers as vectors and expressed them in polar form.

12. Trigonometric formulas.

Mathematics for grade 12 (Advanced Mathematics)

Three possible programs were suggested. Each included in the first semester a course in elementary functions, as given below.

1. Sets and combinations—review and extension of set concepts leading to permutations, combinations, the binomial theorem, and mathematical induction.
2. Functions and relations from a set-theoretic approach.
3. Polynomial functions.
4. Exponential functions.
5. Logarithmic functions.
6. Circular functions, utilizing the wrapping function.

Second-semester alternatives included a course in introductory probability with statistical applications, an introduction to modern algebra (fields and groups), and a course made up of selected topics that largely included extensions of topics from the first-semester course. This third option was seen as providing flexibility, especially for those classes that could not complete the elementary functions course during the first half of the year.

The probability and statistics course the commission proposed represented an area that had never been studied seriously at the high school level. Consequently, the commission felt its recommendation should be accompanied by a demonstration of its feasibility; members of the commission prepared a textbook for this course and taught it in experimental classes. As was noted earlier, in Professor Begle's comment, this text was of historical significance as an existing proof of the feasibility of mathematicians' working together with teachers to exert a direct influence on the curriculum by preparing a sample text.

The topical outlines of the commission's recommended courses do not appear dramatically different from leading texts of the day, but the treatments of the topics were substantially different—and what new material was added was consistently in the direction of more abstract and higher level topics. There was absolutely no "consumer mathematics" flavor in the report. It came much closer to capturing the spirit of contemporary mathematics than did even the best of the previously existing programs.

In addition to preparing recommendations and illustrating these recommendations in appendices, sample units, and a new text, the commission also was quite effective in publicizing its results widely about the country. It helped to create interest in curriculum revision not only on the part of the teachers and mathematicians but also among school administrators, parents, and others. Its success in these efforts contributed positively to the entire reform movement.

Of course, not everyone appreciated their work (369, p. 62).

> After hundreds of speeches and articles which dealt with symbolic logic, topology, abstract algebra, and sets and after creating uneasiness and alarm among teachers over all the country, the Commission had ended up with few real changes and these are undesirable. Of all the new topics only the notion of sets is retained and this is used to make the solution of equations, the concept of function, coordinate geometry, and a few other topics more abstract and hence less teachable.

But Begle's feeling, that the formation of the Commission on Mathematics was "probably the most important step in the improvement of the mathematics curriculum in the United States" (93, p. 137), was probably a much more common reaction.

As a creature of the CEEB, the commission restricted its attention to the program for the college-capable student. Perhaps it was the climate of the times more than the narrow focus of this highly influential group, but in the early years of the reform movement virtually every major curriculum-development project was similarly restricted. And all of the major curriculum-development projects until after 1960 were directed toward the secondary level.

10. *The NCTM's support of the reform movement*

The *Mathematics Teacher* served as a forum for those who supported the views enunciated by the commission The many articles relating to the need for revolution in school mathematics and the nature of modern mathematics had helped to ready teachers for implementing changes in the schools. In addition to providing this forum, the NCTM had made its own attempt at a curricular reform by appointing the Secondary-School Curriculum Committee. Its report (65), published in the May 1959 issue of the *Mathematics Teacher*, was of relatively minor influence. The curricular modifications suggested in this report were essentially a rubber stamp of those suggested by the commission. The report was markedly different, however, in that the pedagogical context and implications of content modification were explored to a greater extent. In particular, the concerns of the committee extended from the academically talented to the below-average pupils. Problems of administration of the curricular program were also considered.

The committee's lack of influence may safely be attributed to the fact that its thunder had been stolen. It cited the commission, the

SMSG, the Ball State Group, and the UICSM (p. 407). These groups were all active in making the reform happen by the time the NCTM committee published its report.

The NCTM Secondary-School Curriculum Committee noted that European school systems generally possessed good programs for the intellectually elite but that they had not yet developed a program for the nontalented student. Noting that "in the United States we have a good program for the large mass of able pupils" (p. 394), the committee proceeded to develop a rationale for a program for the gifted. The arguments were quite similar to those involved in the passage of the National Defense Education Act of 1958. Indeed, one wonders if the reform movement would have been as successful and would have received such substantial financial support if the event of Sputnik had not been preceded by the McCarthy era. Albeit an unhealthy force in American political life, McCarthyism led to an attitude that made arguments for funds for education more attractive to legislators and the American public.

The NCTM provided substantial aid to the cause of changing the curriculum in school mathematics through the publication of two yearbooks. Although the Twenty-third Yearbook, *Insights into Modern Mathematics* (199), and the Twenty-fourth Yearbook, *The Growth of Mathematical Ideas, Grades K–12* (200), were planned and written independently, they were complementary to the extent that there was overlap in the titles of chapters. *Insights into Modern Mathematics* was an explication of the nature of modern mathematics. Not only did mathematicians explore topics such as topology which seemed a bit distant from the school curriculum of the day, but they also looked at the mathematics currently being taught in the classroom. This coverage was acceptable both in language and style to most modern mathematicians.

The intent of the authors of *The Growth of Mathematical Ideas* was not so much to explain modern mathematics as it was to highlight "the most basic mathematical themes which should be central to the entirety of a modern mathematics curriculum, and . . . the similarly key concepts of modern teaching techniques" (p. vi). The yearbook, published in 1959 five years after its conception, captured the essence of Felix Klein's unifying-concepts theme. The tone for the book was established in the first paragraph by the following two axioms:

> Axiom 1. *The best learning is that in which the learned facts, concepts, and processes are meaningful to and understood by the learner.*

> Axiom 2. *Understanding and meaningfulness are rarely if ever "all or none" insights in either the sense of being achieved instantaneously or in the sense of embracing the whole of a concept and its implications at any one time.*

Arguing that these axioms entailed teachers' providing for recurring but varied contacts with fundamental concepts and processes and that understandings grow within children throughout their school careers, the book proceeded to explore major concepts of mathematics by careful explication of the concepts and by providing examples appropriate to a variety of grade levels for each concept. The major concepts explored were the following:

1. Number and operation
2. Relations and functions
3. Proof
4. Measurement and approximation
5. Probability
6. Statistics
7. Language and symbolism in mathematics

The Twenty-fourth Yearbook possessed conceptual similarities to both the PEA's *Mathematics in General Education* and the Joint Commission's report of an earlier era. Fortunately, the mathematics-education community was in a more receptive mood. Teachers who found modern mathematics to be new and different found the extensive examples helpful. The last section of the final chapter, "A Flow Chart of Basic Mathematical Ideas," provided an example of an approach to curricular design which transcended grade levels.

In many respects the Twenty-fourth Yearbook was the most singularly helpful act of the NCTM in promoting the new mathematics. The fact that the authors held a brief for sound pedagogy as well as sound mathematics helped to maintain a healthy state of affairs in curricular reform.

⇛⇛ 11. *Early curriculum development projects*

Many other curricular projects were initiated during the mid-fifties (60; 250). It is impossible to discuss even a half of them here. Many of them were restricted by their local character, and each reflected the idiosyncrasies of its leaders. None had the national impact that was awarded the commission report or would later derive from the SMSG, but each made significant, and in some cases unique, contributions. Discussions of a few of them will illustrate the type of concern and effort that was spreading across the nation.

The Ball State Teachers College Experimental Program began in 1955. The materials were developed under the leadership of Merrill Shanks of Purdue University and Charles Brumfiel and Robert Eicholz of Ball State, and they were tested largely in the laboratory school at Ball State. The program was characterized by its emphasis on the axiomatic structure of mathematics. First to be developed was a geometry course that was a radical departure from the traditional program in that it utilized a modified version of the Hilbert postulates. It contained a substantial unit on symbolic logic and was a positive attempt to present an abstract mathematical system. The algebra was a much more precise and structured version of the classical program which emphasized structural concepts and minimized drill. Eventually a complete secondary school program was developed. Although it never dominated the textbook market, it did constitute an existence proof that a substantial program of abstract mathematics could be developed and taught successfully at the secondary level.

The Developmental Project in Secondary Mathematics of Southern Illinois University was funded specifically to implement the recommendations of the Commission on Mathematics—in 1958, a year before the commission report was published. This is dramatic evidence of the success with which the commission's recommendations were publicized even in their preliminary forms.

The University of Maryland Mathematics Project (UMMaP) approached the construction of a modernized junior high school program by recruiting a substantial number of local teachers, who studied mathematical topics in an in-service program for a term before joining with the project's staff in designing new text materials. They then taught these materials in their schools. The effect of this project on the SMSG program will be noted in the next section.

12. *The School Mathematics Project*

The School Mathematics Study Group (SMSG) was organized by mathematicians. It was, in a way, the natural consequence of a growing concern dating back at least to the mid-forties. Professional mathematicians were moving more and more toward direct involvement in the affairs of the schools. In the final analysis, the catalytic agent leading to its formation may have been the promise of substantial financial support for such an effort through the NSF. However, all the elements necessary to the reaction were already present.

The SMSG grew directly out of two conferences, both sponsored by the NSF. On 21 February 1958 the Chicago Conference on Research Potential and Training met to survey the problem of supply and demand with respect to research mathematicians. This conference had evolved over a period of years from the initial work of a subcommittee of the Policy Committee for Mathematics which in 1950 had attempted to assess the needs of the mathematical community in preparing a proposed budget for mathematics for the NSF. We have already pointed out that this initial group included in their projected budget a small amount of money for a survey of the needs at the secondary school level. In 1953/54 the officers of the AMS, executive officers of the Division of Mathematics of the National Research Council (NRC), and the program director for the NSF discussed the need for a comprehensive survey, again as a potential basis for budget decisions. In May 1954 at the annual meeting of the Division of Mathematics of the NRC, the chairman appointed the membership of the division to serve as a committee to discuss the proposed survey. It was at that meeting that the full scope of the survey developed.

In November 1954 the Committee on the Survey was appointed, with A. A. Albert as its chairman. Among the familiar names on this committee is that of S. S. Wilks, who was at this same time chairing a committee sponsored by the Carnegie Foundation and working with the Educational Testing Service to describe research activities that would lead to better mathematics courses and teaching at the elementary and secondary school levels (32). During the period of the survey, Wilks was also to become a member of the Commission on Mathematics. E. G. Begle, who became and has remained the director of the SMSG, was also a member of the survey committee.

While the survey was planned as a committee activity, it was finally set up as a research contract with the University of Chicago under the direction of A. A. Albert. Funding was by the NSF. The final report of the survey was published in June 1957 (25), and the Chicago conference was based on this report.

Although on the surface the problem under consideration at the Chicago conference would seem to have been restricted to graduate and postdoctoral training in mathematics, the participants at the conference apparently felt otherwise. Wooton made the following comment (282, p. 10):

They took the view that concentrating effort on the training of mathematical personnel in the colleges at either the undergraduate or graduate level was a short-range attack on the long-range problem, and that one of the causes of the shortage of adequately trained persons was inadequate early schooling.

The participants were also aware of the budding drive to improve school mathematics. They knew of the curriculum-development projects that were already under way, and they were sensitive to the fact that these were local in a scope. They also had knowledge, in some cases very direct knowledge, of the recommendations of the Commission on Mathematics. Many of them must have been very familiar with the newer texts that had been evolving at the University of Chicago over a number of years. Finally, they must have been impressed with the efforts in a sister field which had obtained substantial support from the NSF for the Physical Science Study Committee (PSSC) project.

With this complex of knowledge and concern, it is not surprising that the Chicago conference adopted a resolution requesting that the president of the AMS, after consulting with the presidents of the MAA and the NCTM, appoint a committee of mathematicians to seek funds from suitable sources and proceed toward a solution of the problems of the school mathematics curriculum.

The other conference leading to the SMSG had already been scheduled for 28 February 1958. This second meeting, just one week after the Chicago conference, was held at the Massachusetts Institute of Technology in Cambridge. The meeting was called the Mathematics Meeting of the NSF, and it was arranged and presided over by Dean Mina Rees of Hunter College.

The second meeting was held at Cambridge for the express purpose of allowing the participants to confer with the physicists who had founded the PSSC in 1956 and who had already had two years of experience in developing materials for the secondary school. This meeting came to be called the Cambridge conference. The participants were primarily research mathematicians. After conferring with the physicists and hearing a report of the recommendations of the Commission on Mathematics, the conference reaffirmed the resolution of the Chicago conference. They followed this with two specific recommendations for action: (1) that a four- or five-week writing session be held that summer (1958) to prepare a detailed syllabus for a model secondary school program beginning with the seventh grade and (2) that a series of monographs on mathematical topics of interest and value to secondary students be published.

To appoint a committee to intervene in the secondary school curriculum was a new venture for the AMS. Historically, it had been so devoted to research in mathematics that it had helped create the MAA to take care of the more mundane concerns of college teachers. But the resolutions of the Chicago and Cambridge conferences were realized. The committee was appointed. After conferring with the presidents of the MAA and the NCTM, Richard Brauer, president of the AMS, named a committee of eight mathematicians to act in accordance with the Chicago and Cambridge resolutions. This committee included A. A. Albert, E. G. Begle, Lipman Bers, A. E. Meder, G. B. Price, Henry Van Engen, R. L. Wilder, and S. S. Wilks.

Wooton notes the following in his history of the SMSG (282, pp. 12–13):

> It is difficult to overstate the importance of this move on the part of the Council and the President of the Society. For more than thirty years, the AMS had held itself aloof from the elementary and secondary school level of mathematics and had contributed very little to the teaching of it. With the appointment of the Committee of Eight, it officially expressed an interest in the mathematics curriculum of the schools, and the approval of the Society made it possible for a large number of distinguished college teachers and research mathematicians to enter wholeheartedly into cooperation with high school teachers in a concerted effort to improve the quality and presentation of school mathematics.

The stamp of respectability had finally been placed on working with the schools!

Yale University expressed a willingness to provide institutional leadership to the project, and E. G. Begle of its department of mathematics took the individual responsibility for directing the work. The Committee of Eight had been appointed on 3 April. A name had been selected—the School Mathematics Study Group—a proposal prepared, and an initial grant of $100,000 received from the NSF by 7 May.

When the initial grant was received, the Committee of Eight appointed twenty-six members to an advisory committee for the project. This group included persons, of widespread geographical distribution, from both high schools and colleges.

Within six weeks of the date of the initial grant, a writing group of forty-five persons had been formed and was at work at the Yale campus. Twenty-one were college teachers of mathematics; twenty-one were high school teachers and supervisors; and there was one representative each from the Rand Corporation, Bell Telephone Laboratories, and the American Association for the Advancement of Science (AAAS). It was a distinguished group, and the type of balance it represented became characteristic of all subsequent writing groups for the SMSG.

Professor Begle stated as follows that three specific objectives guided the work of the SMSG (93, p. 140):

> The first . . . was the provision for an improved curriculum for the schools, a curriculum which would, on the one hand, preserve important skills and mathematical techniques which experience has shown to be important and useful, and, at the same time, provide students with a deeper understanding of the mathematics underlying these skills and techniques.
>
> The second objective was to provide materials for the preparation of teachers to enable them to teach such an improved curriculum.
>
> The third objective was that of making mathematics more interesting in order to attract more students to the subject and hold them for a longer time.

To ensure that the first writing group would not go too far afield, and to achieve some degree of uniformity and continuity, the as-yet-unpublished recommendations of the Commission on Mathematics of the CEEB were made available to the members, as were the works of the UICSM and the UMMaP. Professor Begle pointed out at the opening session that it was *not* the function of the SMSG to attempt to establish a single curriculum for the schools of the United States. One of the things the group *was* to do was to design a detailed outline for a series of textbooks in mathematics for grades 7–12, textbooks that could serve as a sample of what the group considered a curriculum suitable for a college-capable student of today. The reason for concentrating on college-capable students (upper third of each grade) was that these students, with their college potential, were most in need of an improved mathematics curriculum (282, pp. 18–19). By the time this first writing session had concluded, a considerable amount of material had been produced: the group for grades 7 and 8 had produced thirteen units of supplementary material to strengthen the program in those grades, while each of the other committees had produced either a preliminary text or an outline of one for their respective grades.

These materials were tried out in schools during the academic year 1958/59 and edited and revised during the summer of 1959.

The SMSG was to adhere to this process. It produced materials in trial form, submitted them to classroom tryouts, revised them at a subsequent writing session in the light of such trials, and then published them for nationwide distribution. It should be added that during preliminary trials, the SMSG went to great lengths to provide assistance to the teachers. This included the setting up of several consultation centers at each grade level in strategic locations around the country.

Since that first writing session in 1958, literally hundreds of persons have been involved in the SMSG writing sessions. Contributors have come and gone, many of them to serve as authors of contemporary texts for commercial publishers. This phenomenon, strange as it may seem, had the blessing of the SMSG. The SMSG envisioned from the beginning that its texts would serve as guidelines to the mathematics community until such time as a sufficient number of commercial publishers presented texts incorporating the SMSG program. At that time, plans called for SMSG to withdraw its texts from the market.

To underline this point, Edwin E. Moise, originally a member of the SMSG geometry writing team and presently an author for Addison-Wesley Publishing Company, wrote the following in 1962 (180):

> The SMSG is now beginning a different sort of work. Its "crash" program is finished. It is expected that its high school books will be withdrawn from circulation in another two or three years, when similar books become available through commercial publishers. From now on, SMSG's main job will be long range experimentation with courses and programs that are not necessarily suitable for wide use in the near future.

The work of the SMSG continues. New textbooks have been added, including a series for the elementary grades (1964), a one-semester, senior-level course on analytic geometry (1964), a senior-level course on calculus (1965), and a senior-level, one-semester course on computer mathematics (1966). A senior-level course covering the elementary functions and approximating a semester of calculus is in preparation.

Texts for the below-average seventh-, eighth-, and ninth-grade students were published in 1962. In 1967 the SMSG advisory board decided to give careful attention to programs and textual materials for gifted students. A conference was held in October 1967 to formulate recommendations of specific actions for the advisory board to consider. What will become of these recommendations is yet to be decided.

Given the temper of the times in which the SMSG was inaugurated, it is not at all surprising that the products of these writing sessions have enjoyed extensive use.

In the beginning, the SMSG's sole aim was spelled out by the AMS, which set it in operation. That goal, succinctly stated, was to seek a solution to the problem of the inadequacy of the mathematics curriculum (282, p. 10). Somewhat later, after considerable writing had been completed, the SMSG published in March 1959 a "progress report to the mathematicians of this country" (230) in which the objectives of the group were set forth. This statement follows (p. 4):

> The world of today demands more mathematical knowledge on the part of more people than the world of yesterday and the world of tomorrow will make still greater demands. Our society leans more and more heavily on science and technology. The number of our citizens skilled in mathematics must be greatly increased; and understanding of the role of mathematics in our society is now a prerequisite for intelligent citizenship. Since no one can predict with certainty his future profession, much less foretell which mathematical skills will be required in the future by a given profession, it is important that mathematics be so taught that students will be able in later life to learn the new mathematical skills which the future will surely demand of many of them.
>
> To achieve this objective in the teaching of school mathematics, three things are required. First, we need an improved curriculum which will offer students not only the basic mathematical skills but also a deeper understanding of the basic concepts and structure of mathematics. Second, mathematics programs must attract and train more of the students who are capable of studying mathematics with profit. Finally, all help possible must be provided for teachers who are preparing themselves to teach these challenging and interesting courses.
>
> Each project undertaken by the School Mathematics Study Group is concerned with one or more of these three needs.

On the other hand, it is also true that each writing team developed its own philosophy with respect to the objectives it was seeking to attain. These have been set forth in a 1965 SMSG publication entitled *Philosophies and Procedures of the SMSG Writing Teams*. Here we have another instance of the SMSG's not deciding on the course for the entire group but rather allowing each segment to plot its own course. It would certainly appear that each writing group was allowed considerable latitude in choosing the direction it wished to follow.

Discussing the SMSG series, one high school teacher voiced the opinion that "within its limits can be found all of the traditional topics, albeit somewhat transformed" (174, p. 476). The transformations referred to were, for the most part, those suggested by the CEEB in its recommendations. Ninth-grade mathematics was still the first course in algebra, and all the usual topics were discussed. The tenth-grade geometry course as originally produced had some notable innovations, some of which were suggested by the Commission on Mathematics. The eleventh-grade course, Intermediate Mathematics, comprised the usual topics of intermediate algebra and plane trigonometry but with a reduced emphasis on their computational aspects. Elementary Functions was designed for a part of a twelfth-grade course, as was Introduction to Matrix Algebra, a follow-up to the commission's recommendations and a companion or alternate to its book on probability and statistics for the twelfth grade.

Other innovations included the use of the notion and notation of sets, stress on the function concept, and a rather careful development of the properties of the real numbers. It should be noted that none of this content was revolutionary from a mathematician's point of view. All of the mathematics recommended by the commission and incorporated into the SMSG texts was well known to mathematicians before the year 1900 (180, p. 28).

The manner in which the SMSG produced its texts was bound to give rise to some lack of continuity in its program. On each committee were mathematicians of some reputation who would certainly have their own ideas about the way mathematics should be taught. In addition, the high school teachers and supervisors who were present with their front-line experience could be counted upon to interject their opinions. It became then a matter of whose argument would carry the day. It is true that the material in the texts represented the consensus of a writing team, but possibly of that team alone.

The booklet *Philosophies and Procedures of the SMSG Writing Teams* provides interesting examples of the free interchange of ideas among the members of a single team. The lack of a single guiding philosophy directing all the teams was apparent. Each team apparently worked on the basis of consensus, and the alternatives that were rejected are clear evidence that no unique pattern for a desirable program had achieved universal acceptance.

The following passage from the report of the group for grades 7 and 8 indicates some decisions this particular group made (229, p. 2):

> The idea of a course in algebra or a course in geometry, as such, was rejected in favor of courses for grades 7 and 8 in which there

would be as much emphasis as possible on mathematical structure and in which materials would be selected from arithmetic, algebra, geometry, and trigonometry. It was agreed that the work in social mathematics was greatly overemphasized in the seventh and eighth grades and, if this were to be included at all, it should come as applications of mathematical ideas and procedures. It was further agreed that there would be no review or drill sections on topics previously studied, but that maintenance of skills would be provided for in new settings, such as the system of rational numbers or metric and non-metric relations in geometry. From the beginning and throughout the material mathematical ideas have been associated with their applications, but the applications have been secondary, not an end in themselves. It is fruitless to train students in applications that will soon be outmoded. They must have the basic knowledge from which to make whatever applications are appropriate to their time.

The group also accepted the hypothesis that at this level experience with and appreciation of abstract concepts, the role of definition, the development of precise vocabulary and thought, experimentation and proof, were essential and appropriate. Experience in teaching the materials and the sample texts has also confirmed that this is a sound hypothesis.

During the first summer, there was close cooperation between the UMMaP and the SMSG writing group for the junior high school level. In fact John Mayor, who was director of the Maryland project, served as chairman of the SMSG's subgroup for the seventh and eighth grades. Except for editorial changes, some of the chapters in the seventh-grade books of the two projects were almost identical. Some of these chapters were written by the group working at Yale and others by the group at Maryland. Two special characteristics of the Maryland courses were the following (229, p. 4):

1. Most of the material is developed from the point of view of number systems—much more than in the SMSG development—and,

2. The grade 7 and 8 courses are written so that a student finishing these two courses will have completed a first year in algebra.

Subsequent SMSG writing teams rejected both of these emphases. It was felt that mathematical systems could be overemphasized at the expense of some important related topics, applications, and materials from geometry. And, because SMSG had developed a substantial first course in algebra for the ninth grade, it seemed undesirable to duplicate this material in the seventh- and eighth-grade courses.

In the reports from the various writing groups it became clear that the basic guideline was the set of recommendations of the Commission on Mathematics, as was stated in the following passage from the SMSG booklet (p. 23):

> When the SMSG began its work, at Yale, in the summer of 1958, the total writing group was split into four teams, one for each of the high school grades. As a provisional basis for this division of labor, the writing teams agreed that they would cover approximately the material recommended in the report of the Commission on Mathematics of the College Entrance Examination Board. In the case of the tenth grade, the approximation was extremely close. With minor exceptions, all of the Commission's topics are covered in the SMSG book. (The only exceptions that seem worthy of mention are spherical geometry and solution sets of linear inequalities.) In fact, the only major difference between the two programs, as far as content is concerned, is that the SMSG gives proofs for many theorems for which the Commission suggested merely informal indications of proof.

However, it was precisely with respect to geometry that the SMSG initially ignored the most radical suggestions of the commission: that geometry be taught as a series of deductive sequences linked by more informal and intuitive sections to lay a stress on postulational systems; that analytic methods be used extensively after proceeding synthetically as rapidly as possible to the Pythagorean theorem; and that solid geometry be unified with plane. Considerable attention was paid to this latter recommendation, but continued suggestions from persons favoring the analytic-geometry approach led the SMSG in later years to appoint a new writing team to prepare its *Geometry with Coordinates*. The original SMSG geometry was distinguished by its use of ruler and protractor postulates, which had been suggested earlier by G. D. Birkhoff and incorporated by him and Ralph Beatley into their *Basic Geometry* (97) as a device for simplifying a more careful treatment of limits, continuity, and betweenness.

As has been noted, the commission's recommendations did not call for radical changes in content. One of the factors that led the SMSG to settle essentially for the modest change recommended in the commission's report was the expected ability and preparation of the teachers who would have to implement the change. Professor Begle discussed this aspect of the program as follows (93, pp. 141-42):

It was agreed that, for the time being, it would be best not to make such major changes that a great deal of time would have to be invested by teachers in learning this new way of looking at mathematics. Specifically, the aim was to prepare texts which would require of the teacher no more than what could be learned in a single six week summer course or a course meeting once a week during the academic year the first time the teacher taught the text.

During the initial tryout period, the SMSG procedure was to bring small groups of teachers, all teaching the same course, together about once each week. At this session a subject-matter expert would discuss with the teachers the mathematics they were then teaching to their students. Questions of pedagogy were left to the teacher in these in-service sessions.

The SMSG did not refrain from comments on methodology, but the nature and amount of attention paid to methodology also varied from writing group to writing group. In fact, for some groups the methodology advocated was perhaps as dramatic a departure from the traditional program as the content changes they built into the materials. They were aware that teachers in the high schools still tended to teach mathematics in much the same way as they had been exposed to it in college—that is, through the lecture or "ground to be covered" method. This, they felt, was undoubtedly one of the major reasons for the pupils' lack of enthusiasm for mathematics.

Accordingly, they began to stress the discovery approach (especially in grades 7 and 8), the spiral curriculum, the importance of structure, and the role of intuition. These ideas were by no means new to educationists, but they were a revelation to many mathematics teachers. The basic aim in these new emphases was that the pupil should play an active role in the development of mathematics.

These ideas have their foundation in theories of learning. The Twenty-first Yearbook of the NCTM listed elements derived from various learning theories. This list includes the areas of agreement among the various theories, and it was suggested as a point of departure for all those interested in the teaching of mathematics. The following are the essential elements from that list (197, pp. 30–31):

1. There must be a *goal* on the part of the student to learn.
2. All cognitive learning involves *association*.
3. We recognize trial and error or analysis in most learning.
4. Learning is complete to the extent to which the relationships and their implications have been understood.

5. The learner must be in action, mentally and/or physically.
6. Intrinsic reward of success and awareness of progress toward a goal strengthens the learning and the motivation for further learning.
7. Discrimination of attributes (abstraction) and generalization are essential to effective learning.
8. New learning is in part a matter of transference of past learning.
9. We learn facts and skills and we also learn how to learn.
10. We also learn feelings (attitudes).

This list could be used as a rationale for the importance of structure, guided discovery, and so on.

How aware the authors of the SMSG materials were of these considerations and to what extent such ideas influenced their work are open questions. It is difficult to find any reference made to the theories of learning per se in the publications of the SMSG. One remark heard not infrequently was that the new curricular projects decided to get right down to work on the important matters (the discipline concerned) and to leave the rest to the theorists, who would probably never decide anyway.

On the other hand, Begle was present at the Woods Hole Conference in 1959, and the *Teacher's Commentaries* of the SMSG do reflect the aforementioned notions from the theories of learning. This fact would indicate that they may have been a matter of some concern to the authors. Certainly, the approaches advocated in Jerome Bruner's *The Process of Education* (112) are among those recommended to teachers of the SMSG material.

The SMSG program has expanded in several directions. Writing in 1966, John Goodlad noted the following (147, p. 26):

> With the task of creating sample curricula for grades K-12 largely finished, SMSG now plans to concentrate on three major concerns: to provide a closer connection between mathematics and the various areas in which mathematics is used; to continue research on how students learn mathematics; and to devise curriculum materials that are suitable for students whose achievement in mathematics is below average.

Tentative outlines for a new secondary school program, viewing it as a whole rather than as a collection of six separate courses, have been prepared and implemented. In contrast to the earlier curricular work of the SMSG, the present effort is being carried out more experimentally, and careful evaluation will accompany rather than follow the process of writing and revision. It is not expected that the concrete results of this effort will appear in the very near future (298, pp. 241-42).

The list of SMSG publications presently available is lengthy. It includes not only textbooks and teacher commentaries but also programmed materials, computer-programming instruction, monographs, and in-service-training material. The SMSG publications, without doubt, constitute the most extensively used experimental materials in school mathematics at the present time.

It is difficult to assess the number of pupils using SMSG materials. Makoff (173, p. 3) says that in the year 1961/62 some 5 million copies of SMSG materials were purchased, and one can only assume that this number has continued to grow. However, the fact is that, until very recently, the revolution in school mathematics was an upper-middle-class phenomenon. The small, wealthy, suburban schools made the transition well before the larger urban ones.

The SMSG has, from its inception, been concerned with the evaluation of its materials. In the first year of its existence it cooperated with the Minnesota National Laboratory for the Improvement of Secondary School Mathematics in a preliminary evaluation of the original fourteen units in the seventh- and eighth-grade program. The SMSG contributed part of the financial support to this evaluation program. Subsequent studies have reported comparisons of the SMSG with other experimental and conventional programs. In 1962, under a grant from the NSF, the SMSG inaugurated a National Longitudinal Study of Mathematical Abilities. This was a five-year study involving some 120,000 students. Only a preliminary analysis of the data from this study had been completed when this was written.

⇶⇶ 13. *A summary of the curriculum-reform projects*

By 1961 the reform in mathematics education was of sufficient proportions to be labeled officially a revolution by the NCTM. The pamphlet in which the NCTM saw fit to do so was the outgrowth of a series of regional orientation conferences financed by the NSF in 1960.

The following information appeared in the pamphlet just mentioned (64, p. 17):

The table below shows the grades for which material is now available from some of the improved programs.

Textbooks Available

	7th	8th	9th	10th	11th	12th
SMSG	x	x	x	x	x	x
UICSM (Univ. of Illinois)			x	x	x	
Univ. of Southern Ill.			x	x		
Ball State T. C.		x	x	x		
Boston Series		x				
University of Maryland	x	x				

Outlines of these programs were given in the pamphlet. Each of them had distinguishing characteristics, but a pattern of common elements had begun to emerge. Because of the long history of the continuing struggle to build a unified curriculum, the fact that the authors of *The Revolution in School Mathematics* could identify a common emphasis on certain unifying themes in the programs was most encouraging. The set of unifying themes identified is somewhat broader even than that in the Twenty-fourth Yearbook, but it reflects the evolution of a focus on central concepts that has been traced throughout this book. The pamphlet stated the following (p. 22):

> All the programs we have discussed attempt to avoid the presentation of new material as a string of unrelated topics. Indeed, they stress unifying themes or ideas in mathematics such as the following:
> Structure
> Operations and their inverses
> Measurement
> Extensive use of graphical representation
> Systems of numeration
> Properties of numbers, development of the real number system
> Statistical inference, probability
> Sets—language and elementary theory
> Logical deductions
> Valid generalizations.

In the early years of the revolution, the hallmark of the new programs became their extensive use of the concepts, terminology, and symbolism of sets. This was a brand-new area in school mathematics. In some of the programs the early presentations of set theory were sporadic. It was not uncommon for all the ideas to be squeezed into one isolated unit—at almost any grade level, from 7 through 12. As long as that was the case, sets could hardly serve as a unifying concept. But as the programs matured the use of sets served as a fundamental thread to tie all elements of the program together. By 1961, and to a lesser extent even today, a program could not receive the label "modern mathematics" unless it included significant portions of set notation and vocabulary.

Structure was another unifying theme common to all the new programs. Many of the elements of mathematical structure and its role as a course organizer were old, but the use of these elements in teaching and the stress on structures as a whole were new. Further, in the new programs the emphasis was not only on the logical structure of a single system, such as algebra or geometry, but rather upon abstract mathematical structures as generalizations. This was described as follows (pp. 25–26):

> For many years high school mathematics has consisted of the study of . . . models, and pupils have failed to see the basic properties common to all [models]. In the improved programs the pupils look at the mathematical system itself. The properties of the abstract system . . . apply to the models. Properties, in fact, may be obvious in the abstract system that are hidden by the physical objects in the models. The properties of the mathematical system are fundamental and enduring; the models or applications change as the needs of our society change.

No longer was algebra only generalized arithmetic.

To the builders of the new program this emphasis may have seemed the better way to teach applications. Rather than presenting isolated, physical models and studying their properties separately, the move was toward abstracting a mathematical model (or models), studying the abstract system, and then using information about the abstract system to apply to physical representations or models of the system. But this particular innovation generated considerable criticism of the new programs on the basis that they did not relate to the real world—that they failed to teach the youth to apply the principles as they should. This was true of the several new programs to varying degrees—not infrequently because the teacher did not understand the ultimate purpose of studying the abstract structure.

Systems of numeration became another hallmark of the new programs—primarily because the study of other number bases was involved. This was a dramatic change. To the layman this was a new arithmetic, almost iconoclastic in its impact. Although other number bases were in the program primarily to clarify concepts of numeration and the algorithms in the base-ten system, they became the focal point of the popular press, of PTA groups, and even of satirical nightclub acts. Mathematics educators must share the responsibility for the gross misinterpretation of this element of the new programs. Other number bases were a dramatic new topic and made an excellent subject for talks at professional meetings or to lay groups. Fortunately, with the passage of time the correct emphasis apparently has predominated, and the topic of numeration systems has become almost standard in newer elementary school texts.

The new emphasis on operations was largely a means of providing a systematic, logical rationale for the operations of algebra. For example, $7a + 2a = 9a$ not because of the fact that 7 apples together with 2 apples amounts to 9 apples but because of the distributive property of multiplication over addition. And $(^-2)(^-3) = {}^+6$ because the operations on the negative numbers were invented in such a way as to preserve familiar properties of the nonnegative numbers.

Measurement, graphical representation, logical deductions, and the remaining unifying concepts listed had all been parts of the program in the past. But in the new programs there was a much more conscious effort to utilize these concepts in tying the various branches of the program together. Perhaps for the first time, there was a widespread effort to realize in the secondary school program the kind of dream Felix Klein had for mathematics so many years before.

⇛⇛ 14. *Criticisms of reforms*

Two years later, in 1963, these new programs had reached such a state of maturity that they seemed fair game for analysis and comparison. The NCTM booklet *An Analysis of New Mathematics Programs* (60) reviewed the following eight curriculum-revision projects:

1. The Boston College Mathematics Institute
2. The Greater Cleveland Mathematics Program
3. The Syracuse University–Webster College Madison Project
4. The University of Maryland Mathematics Project
5. The Ontario Mathematics Commission
6. The School Mathematics Study Group
7. The Developmental Project in Secondary Mathematics at Southern Illinois University
8. The University of Illinois Committee on School Mathematics

Each of these projects had produced materials at the secondary school level, although projects 2 and 3 had concentrated on work in elementary schools. The kind of questions that were being raised concerning these new programs is indicated in the following excerpts (pp. 2–4) from the list of issues on which the NCTM committee based its analysis:

> Social Applications. *How much emphasis should be placed on the social applications of mathematics? What should be the purpose and nature of these applications?*
>
> Placement. *At a particular grade level, what topics can be most effectively developed and which are most appropriate?*
>
> Structure. *What emphasis should be placed on the study of mathematical structures to being about a better understanding and use of mathematics?*
>
> Vocabulary. *How rapidly should the student be led from the use of the general unsophisticated language of mathematics to the very precise and sophisticated use of it?*
>
> Methods. *What is the relative merit of presenting a sequence of activities from which a student may independently come to recognize the desired knowledge as opposed to presenting the knowledge and helping students rationalize it?*
>
> Concepts vs. Skills. *What relationship should exist in the mathematics programs between the function of developing concepts and that of developing skill in the manipulation of symbols?*
>
> Proof. *At what level should proof be introduced and with what degree of rigor? How rapidly should a student be led to make proofs independently?*
>
> Evaluation. *Are there available measures of the changes taking place that can be applied at this time, and what provisions can be made for evaluating the same changes in the future?*

Apparently neither evolution, revolution, nor the simple passage of time can alter the fundamental issues in mathematics education!

Virtually these same issues served as focal points in a continuing debate concerning the value of the new programs. Morris Kline—the earliest and most bitter, vocal, and persistent of the critics—at various times characterized aspects of the programs as "wholly misguided," "sheer nonsense," "hastily produced and untested," and "peripheral to the body of mathematics" and as replacing the "fruitful and rich essence of mathematics with sterile, peripheral, pedantic details" (329). The polemical character of Kline's criticism should not disguise the fact that his significant questions contributed to a healthy examination of the values and purposes of learning mathematics. A somewhat more reserved position was taken by Lucien B. Kinney when he noted the following shortcomings in the current curriculum projects (364, pp. 453-54):

> *Disregard of the Purposes of Secondary Education.* This is well illustrated in the criterion for grade placement of topics and for introduction of new topics typically used in the several projects, namely, the ability of pupils to master the topic at any given level. No consideration is given to future needs of the pupil, or what contributions society will require from him. . . . Data on what can be taught need to be supplemented by information on what should be taught, in the light of the purposes of the secondary schools, before the program of curriculum development can be completed.
>
> *Neglect of Important Concomitant Outcomes.* Perhaps because of the preoccupation with the structure of mathematics, a variety of concomitant outcomes whose importance has been recognized over the years have been overlooked. One of these is development of skill in the techniques of problem solving in a real rather than an abstract problem situation. While we do not know what problems a given pupil will encounter, or even in what area he will encounter them, we know that he should learn the techniques of finding and testing the solution to his problem. Mathematics does not carry the sole responsibility for developing this ability, but the nature of the field is such that it offers the most effective opportunity for learning the techniques of problem solving. Emphasis on the structure of mathematics, however, has led to de-emphasis on applications. Such applications as occur are largely from the physical sciences and are primarily designed as occasions for introducing mathematical concepts or computations. Thus, while discovery and generalization in the area of abstract mathematics are encouraged, the development of systematically applied techniques of problem solving, in the sense advocated, for example, by Polya, is neglected. . . .
>
> *Neglect of Differential Needs of Various Pupil Groups.* The purposes for teaching mathematics must take into account the abilities, interests, and vocational needs of various groups of pupils, not only as a service to the pupils, but also for the benefit of society, which needs the fully developed resources of each group. Development of these resources cannot be achieved by focusing attention on the technically oriented group and assuming that the study of mathematics for its own sake will meet the needs of the rest. The questionable assumptions on which experimentation with gifted groups is based have been previously mentioned. Provision for the slower pupils, on the other hand, is based on the premise that, given more time and

a less formal approach, slower pupils can cover the same materials as the more rapid pupils. This is in contradiction to research findings as well as to the experience of classroom teachers.

Those who took issue with the new developments were objecting only to the nature of the change—not to the fact that change was occurring. The need for reform seems never to have been at issue during this period. The fact that the revolution in mathematics had so many points in common with similar developments in the other curricular areas is quite possibly a symptom of common cause as much as common need. The forces in our society which helped to create our revolution were felt throughout the school program.

→»→» 15. *Similarities among reform movements*

Evans Clinchy (326, pp. 221-37) identified a number of striking common characteristics, principally in science and mathematics, in the new curricula that had evolved prior to 1964. Excerpts and comments are given below.

> 1. The new curricular programs typically evolve—and in most cases have actually been started by—men who are among the best minds a particular discipline has to offer.

The involvement of first-rate scholars and their commitment to their task is seen by Clinchy as perhaps the single most striking feature of the new programs. The developments of the late fifties broke a long period of isolation of the university scholars from the schools. The resulting alliance of school and university personnel brought an aura of intellectual respectability to the field of curriculum design. Moreover, because of this alliance the resulting programs were intellectually respectable. The university scholar, embedded in school affairs initially because of his interests in the discipline, often broadened his concern to encompass the problems of teaching and learning as well.

> 2. The new programs tend to be national in scope and to be supported on a large scale.

The unprecedented level of financial support for curriculum development not only speeded the impact but broadened it as well. There was fear in some parts that the new programs might move toward a national curriculum, but no locally supported project could utilize the extensive resources, personal and physical, that were made possible by federal support.

> 3. The first step in the important reforms has been for the scholars to decide what is to be taught.

The tendency in all recent curriculum reform has been for the scholars to attempt to organize the program around what Jerome Bruner, in his *Process of Education*, has termed the "structure" of the subject. Mathematics may have progressed most rapidly partly because of its well-defined structure. The arguments in mathematics (among mathematicians) usually focused on priorities, not substance. In a less structured discipline—social studies, for example—the framework, or structure, was much less clear.

> 4. Every significant reform has introduced a deliberate effort to bring the curriculum up to date.

There was a tendency of scholars in the field to want to expose youth to the more recent developments in the subject. This led in some cases to the criticism that the emphasis was on the discipline at the expense of the needs of the child—a perennial issue.

> 5. The current reforms almost always involve not only a radical approach to the content but also explorations into new and different ways of teaching and learning.

Clinchy made the point that discovery methods became a part of virtually *all* curriculum-development projects in *all* fields. He attributed this in part to the fact that scholars held the faith that students —all kinds of students at all ages—should and could be scholars and scientists themselves. To enable them to do so, students should be treated with respect and allowed to work through the materials as the scholar or scientist would work through new materials himself.

Clinchy cited a very telling quotation on this point.

> "Teach your scholar to observe the phenomena of nature, you will soon raise his curiosity, but if you would have it grow, do not be in too great a hurry to satisfy the curiosity. Put the problems before him and let him solve them himself. Let him know nothing because you have told him, but because he has learnt it for himself. If ever

you substitute authority for reason, he will cease to reason, he will be a mere plaything of other people's thoughts....

"Undoubtedly the notions of things thus acquired for oneself are clearer and much more convincing than those acquired from the teaching of others: and not only is our reason not accustomed to slavish submission to authority, but we develop greater ingenuity in discovering relations, connecting ideas and inventing apparatus, than when we merely accept what is given us and allow our minds to be enfeebled by indifference."

No, this did not come from Jerrold Zacharias or Max Beberman, nor from a Jerome Bruner or John Dewey. Rather it came from Rousseau's *Emile*, published in 1762 (222, pp. 228–29).

6. The new programs almost always include the production of actual educational materials or specific directions for building instructional "models," and the exhaustive trial of these materials or models in the classroom before they are made widely available to the schools.
7. There is a tendency in the new programs to develop a greatly expanded range of integrated materials designed to foster the inductive, "work through the problem yourself" approach to instruction.
8. The new programs and the material and methods they have produced tend to cast the teacher in a new and different role.

Many of the new programs, even in mathematics, have attempted to transfer some of the teacher's responsibility to the materials. Not that they attempted to eliminate the teacher from the scene—far from it. The teacher has become more important than ever, but not as a simple dispenser of knowledge.

9. Most of the major revisions have undertaken programs of training teachers to handle the new materials and new methods.
10. Most of the people involved in curriculum revision are aware of the fact that the present programs are only the first step in a large, long-range effort.

The above ten statements might have been written to characterize only the developments in mathematics education in the decade 1955–65. They certainly are an accurate depiction of major aspects in the development of the new mathematics curricula. But they were not written as descriptive only of the revolution in school mathematics. They were written as a characterization of a general phenomenon in the schools. Although the evolutionary events that readied mathematics education for change can be traced, and a chain of forces and issues leading to such a pattern of intervention can be identified, it must be admitted that mathematics educators were creatures of their time. The forces that acted on mathematics influenced all curricular areas in the schools. The issues in mathematics were paralleled in the other disciplines. Perhaps the failure of mathematics education to enjoy major revisions along the lines recommended in earlier decades can be attributed to the absence of some of Clinchy's characteristics at the time the recommendations were made.

As the mid-sixties approached, the direction of reform in mathematics education at the secondary school level was reasonably well established—at least for the college-preparatory students. Many exemplary experimental programs had evolved. The pattern of emphasis had become clear. Commercial publishers rushed to take advantage of the new market, and many texts incorporating the new materials appeared. Many of those who had developed texts for the emerging programs allied themselves with a commercial concern and produced modified versions of their earlier work for publication. The reform movement looked for new fields to conquer.

Many of the major curriculum-development projects turned their attention toward the elementary field. Some, reacting to the biting criticism first from professional circles and later from the popular press, began to reexamine their materials and to modify them to remove excess abstractness and to increase emphasis on such areas as applications and skill development. Partly because the slow learner and the disadvantaged youth had been virtually ignored in the first round of revision and largely because new pressures in our society created a dramatic shift in national concern and federal support, several existing projects and some new projects turned their attention to these students. As new technology became available—the computer, for example—curriculum innovators began to redesign their programs to capitalize on it. A new revolution—or perhaps a second round in the existing revolution—began. Attention shifted from content to methodology. Educators and mathematicians-turned-educators began to concern themselves more and more with questions of how mathematics is learned and how it can be taught to increase the likelihood that it will be learned.

Clinchy's tenth statement, "Most of the people involved in curriculum revision are aware of the fact that the present programs are only the first step in a large, long-range effort," certainly is true in mathematics education. Even before the first round of curriculum revision was complete, a major conference had been called to project change well into the future.

16. *The Cambridge conference*

In the summer of 1962, Professors Zacharias and Martin of the Massachusetts Institute of Technology invited several Cambridge mathematicians and representatives of the NSF to an informal discussion of the state of mathematics in both the elementary and secondary schools of the United States. At this meeting it was decided to organize a conference to deal with radical revisions in the mathematics curriculum. Financial support was obtained from the NSF, and Professors Martin and Gleason (Harvard) became directors of the project.

The resulting Cambridge Conference on School Mathematics drafted a report, *Goals for School Mathematics* (11), which was published in 1963. The conference very consciously directed its attention to exploratory thinking with a view to a long-range future. Members did not intend to describe a curriculum suitable for the next few years —they were looking toward 1990 or 2000. As a consequence, they refused to be shackled by the realities of today. They ignored the problem of teacher training, they ignored the fine points of pedagogical technique, and they did not take account of recent research in cognitive learning. They agreed to be bound only by the limits of their own imagination. The participants were twenty-five well-trained mathematicians. Most had been closely involved in the new developments over the past few years. Their imaginations had apparently been well stimulated; they produced an ambitious report.

The subject matter that the conference proposed was roughly described by them as follows (p. 7):

> A student who has worked through the full thirteen years of mathematics in grades K to 12 should have a level of training comparable to three years of top-level college training today; that is, we shall expect him to have the equivalent of two years of calculus, and one semester each of modern algebra and probability theory.

The members recognized the necessity of omitting something in order to accomplish the feat of adding so much content to the existing mathematics program. Drill for drill's sake was the first target—

not that the members considered drill unimportant, but they felt it could be accomplished along with more mathematics.

Some of the key ideas about which the members were in unanimous agreement included the following: (1) The goal of the program was to be "familiarity with mathematics," which they hoped could be accomplished through a spiral curriculum. (2) A parallel development of geometry and arithmetic was recommended for the elementary grades. (3) Some "feeling" for probability and statistics was considered important for all students as well as a "nodding acquaintance" with calculus. The report stated (p. 9) that

> liberal education requires the contemplation of the works of genius, and the calculus is one of the grandest edifices constructed by mankind.

The members agreed that the authoritarian method of teaching, besides stifling creativity, suggested that one is helpless if he forgets the formula. They considered the role of modern mathematics as supplying concepts useful in organizing material. No dichotomy was made between pure and applied mathematics except to recognize that there are more users of mathematics than makers. They suggested that a balance between rigor and guesswork was represented by problems like this (p. 11):

"Here is a situation—think about it—what can you say?"

It was considered important that the students understand what mathematics is and recognize both its powers and its limitations.

The conference attached great importance to teaching methods (p. 13):

> An omission of a subject from a student's curriculum can be made up readily later, in college or adult education courses, if the student has previously developed a sound approach to mathematics. On the other hand, improperly taught material may confuse the student's understanding of the facts, inhibit good mathematical reasoning, and lead to dislike of the whole subject.

The spiral curriculum could be used to keep the proper balance between intuition and rigor. Concepts could first be presented heuristically, and opportunities then could be provided for the students to use these concepts in appropriate mathematical contexts. The caution, however, was given that the premathematical ideas be mathematically correct. Later developments could then lead to greater rigor, but not to the neglect of the intuition that should always accompany any mathematical endeavor. The spiral curriculum was also thought to be useful in developing concepts with equal degrees of rigor but with different approaches. The coordinated development of algebra and geometry was stressed again in this context.

As was mentioned earlier, drill was de-emphasized (p. 16):

> The conference felt strongly that the understanding of the algorithms justifying the manipulations will in the end lead to better skills while opening the door to deeper and more advanced mathematics. The last allows more advanced skills to evolve.

Discovery techniques were recognized as valuable, but because of the time element it was suggested that most discovery be guided by the teacher. This discovery learning could be accomplished in the earlier grades through class discussions and after about grade 7 mostly through independent exercises. This guidance should be as free as possible from authoritarianism, so that the students would be free to arrive at their own solutions. In these free discussions the students could often help each other in the formation of concepts.

The conference considered the exercises the most important part of the prepared course material, and it suggested that they be written immediately after the theme of a section was formulated, making the textual discussions only an illumination of thematic matter not wholly developed in the exercises. Problems should be so devised as to foster discovery and creativity and also to supply the variability necessary to provide for individual differences.

Motivation could be developed by means of historical discussions, by looking into the possible future uses of mathematics, and by setting aside some time for a mathematics laboratory.

The problem of evaluation was cited because of the difficulty in formulating tests that measure understanding and creative ability. It was recommended that a continuing committee work toward developing such tests. The conference had no sympathy for theorists who maintain that objectives that cannot be subjected to the available means of evaluation are meaningless. They made the following comment (p. 29):

> We are shocked by the callow empiricism which confers honorary validity on whatever measurement techniques it has managed

to devise, and confers honorary nonexistence on all aspects of the human psyche that have not yet been explained to an IBM punching machine.

Recognition was given to the importance of allowing for nonverbal awareness of concepts. When words can be associated with the concepts, this should be done; a superfluous vocabulary should be avoided and only words that are clear and useful chosen. (Appropriate terms are no more difficult to learn than inappropriate ones.)

Applications of mathematics were divided into two categories—internal (relating to mathematics itself) and external. External applications, such as in the physical sciences, were recommended only if they served to clarify the concept—not if the physical applications were more unfamiliar to the student than the concepts being developed. In regard to professional and business applications, the report may be paraphrased by saying that students should be prepared to "use mathematicians" as well as to use mathematics.

The program set forth by the conference gives greater respect to the intellectual ability of children than do the current programs. In this regard, it was not ignoring psychological studies in child development such as those of Piaget, but rather was recognizing that these studies were made with children educated in the traditional manner and thus did not necessarily imply that the difficulties were intrinsic.

The importance of the correctness of whatever mathematics is taught was stressed (p. 25):

> To avoid major errors of presentation, we believe that the serious thought of our best mathematical minds will be required in the design of even the kindergarten curriculum.

The report included curriculum plans for grades K–2 and grades 3–6 and two proposals for grades 7–12. Generally, the objectives for grades K–6 included familiarity with the real number system and with the ideas of geometry. Through the use of the number line the children could be introduced to negative as well as to positive whole numbers. By crossed number lines they were to be introduced to Cartesian coordinates. In geometry, the emphasis was on spatial intuition. The notions of function and sets were unifying concepts. The program for grades 7–12 included a more rigorous development of the algebra and geometry begun in the earlier grades. For students electing mathematics through grade 12 the program would include calculus, linear algebra, and probability.

→→→→→ 17. *Reactions to the Cambridge report*

The Cambridge Conference on School Mathematics created a noticeable stir in academic and educational circles. The conference explicitly stated that the proposals were tentative and provisional; nevertheless, the recommendations marked such a radical departure from current practice in the United States that they were bound to arouse debate and controversy.

In reading the articles written concerning the Cambridge report, one is confronted with various degrees of acceptance or rejection of the report. One type of reaction is exemplified in the following comment by Fred Weaver (428, pp. 209–10):

> The Cambridge Conference recommendations can serve us well as a basis for formulating numerous relevant hypotheses to be tested through suitable research. From this point of view the significance of the Cambridge Conference lies in the questions it raises—some deep and profound ones which should challenge us to new and profitable research ventures.

Marshall Stone reviewed the Cambridge report for the book-review section in the *Mathematics Teacher* (422). Stone professed to be "profoundly disturbed" by the report as he considered present needs and potentialities in the schools.

Stone was disturbed because he felt that the goals proposed by the Cambridge report fell short of those already formulated and already on the way to realization in Europe. He was reluctant to believe that the Cambridge report represented the best thinking of those in the United States who are collectively capable in the field of mathematics education.

In the discussion of the secondary school mathematics program, which included "college subjects," Stone criticized the report as follows (p. 357):

> The detailed descriptions given in the Report of these segments of college mathematics could have been lifted with little change from almost any good college announcement. Thus, in essence, the Cambridge Report just shifts downward by three years the existing college material which it proposes to incorporate in the secondary school curriculum without raising any question as to whether the prevailing college curriculum is also in need of some revision and improvement!

Some commentators were bothered by the attention given to the superelite, by the apparent lack of concern for the student who was academically not so fortunate (288), and by the failure to recognize constraints imposed by what was known of cognitive processes (287). Irving Adler was optimistic concerning the teachability of the program but cited the low level of teacher preparation as a limitation. He noted (287, p. 215) the following "fallacious educational theories" that could operate against the successful operation of the program:

1. [A child's] I.Q. signifies an upper limit to his ability to learn.
2. The norm of a standardized test represents a satisfactory level of performance.
3. The growth of a child from one stage of learning to another is a process of unfolding from within that cannot be accelerated by educational influences.
4. The child must discover by himself, without teacher guidance, everything that he must learn.

Adler felt that the prevalence of these ideas implied the necessity of nationwide discussion of educational philosophy for the reeducation not only of teachers but also of those who train teachers.

While the Cambridge report was being criticized, Burt Kaufman (165) initiated the recommended curriculum at Nova High School in Fort Lauderdale, Florida. This long-term curriculum-development project was moved to the University of Southern Illinois under the sponsorship of the Central Midwestern Regional Educational Laboratory. The curriculum that evolved there is designed for the bright, highly verbal student and is organized around a highly individualized instructional strategy.

→»→» 18. *New directions*

The reform movement was most in evidence in the curriculum for the college-capable student. As the sixties progressed, initial enthusiasm for reform matured in two different directions. First, the problem of individual differences again became crucial as more students aspired to college and as it was realized that the new curricula did not adequately serve students with lower ability. As the problems of inner-city schools have been accentuated by protest, racism, and riot, educators have again examined the aims of teaching mathematics. But dialogue concerning aims has been in terms of special populations, such as the low achiever, rather than in terms of educating all American youth, and it has been as concerned with methods as with content.

The second direction of the maturation of the reform movement has been toward more careful analysis of teaching methodology. In particular, discovery teaching has captured the imagination of teacher and researcher alike. Psychologists have provided penetrating analyses of discovery in mathematics (239) as well as of other aspects of the teaching-learning process. Major modifications of curricula are seldom undertaken today by mathematicians or mathematics teachers operating in a vacuum. Typically scientists, such as psychologists and evaluators, are incorporated into the planning process.

The dialogue in these revolutionary years has been dominated by the same issues that occupied mathematics educators of earlier generations. The materials, writing, and conversation during this revolutionary period indicated a willingness to perceive mathematics differently; many do not hold it to be a science. Newer concepts and processes, such as mathematical-model building, are acquiring significance for the schools. However, *the problem of what mathematics is appropriate for whom remains the overriding concern.* If the objectives or aims have been of insufficient scope and have been applied to markedly diverse populations, healthy argumentation and debate have resulted in curricular modification. Beyond a doubt this will remain the state of the art of teaching mathematics through the coming years. Mathematics for the schools will be debated in terms of its potential for use and its appeal on its own merits to students. Teaching strategies may change, but the continuing dialogue of mathematics educators will concern aims and objectives.

THE

LOGIC AND UTILITY

OF

MATHEMATICS,

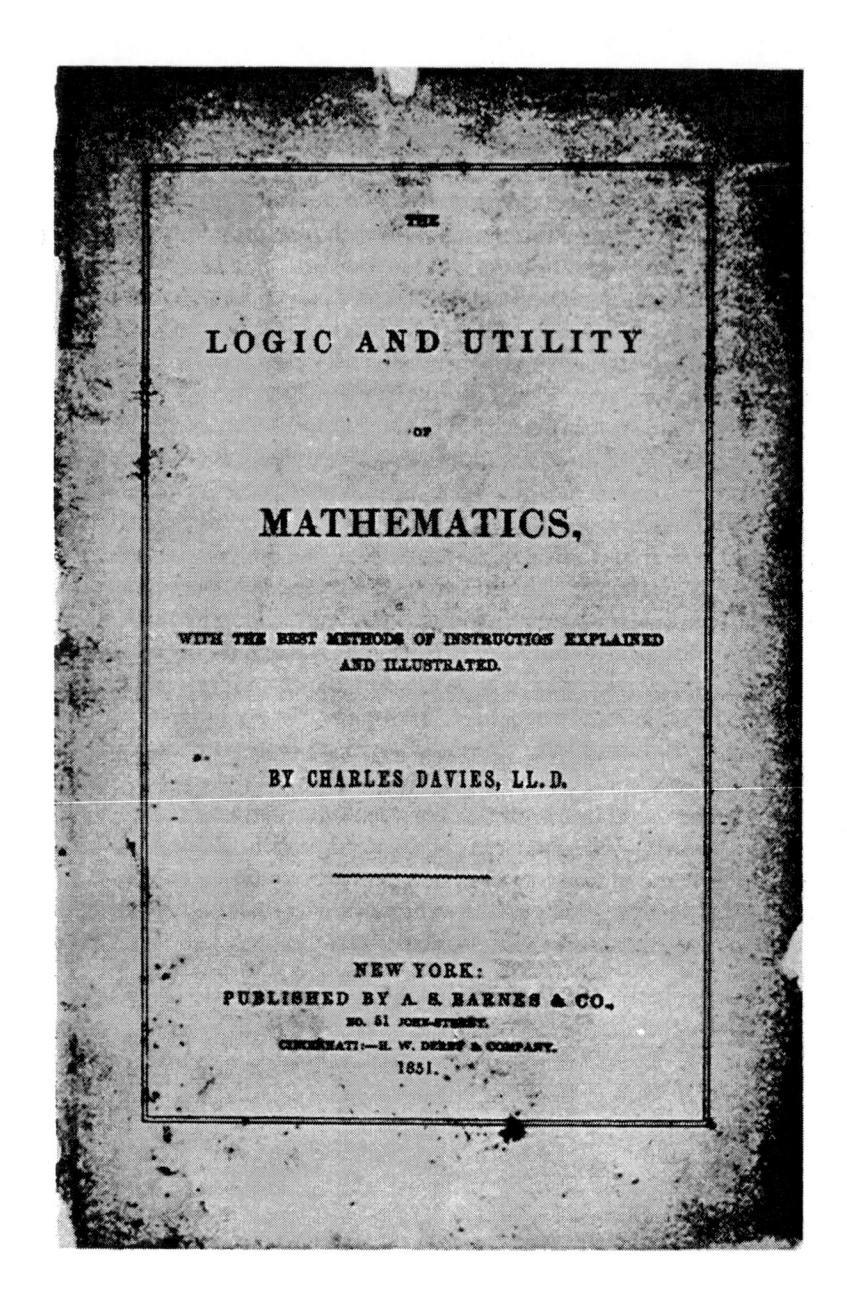

WITH THE BEST METHODS OF INSTRUCTION EXPLAINED
AND ILLUSTRATED.

BY CHARLES DAVIES, LL.D.

NEW YORK:
PUBLISHED BY A. S. BARNES & CO.,
NO. 51 JOHN-STREET.
CINCINNATI:—H. W. DERBY & COMPANY.
1851.

FIRST BOOK ON THE TEACHING OF MATHEMATICS IN THE UNITED STATES. There is a copy of the first printing, dated 1850, in the University of Michigan Library.

*The Education
of Teachers of Mathematics*

PART FOUR

*E. Glenadine Gibb
Houston T. Karnes
F. Lynwood Wren*

THE
PHILOSOPHY OF ARITHMETIC

AS DEVELOPED FROM THE

THREE FUNDAMENTAL PROCESSES

OF

SYNTHESIS, ANALYSIS, AND COMPARISON

CONTAINING ALSO

A HISTORY OF ARITHMETIC

BY

EDWARD BROOKS, A. M., Ph. D.,

SUPERINTENDENT OF PUBLIC SCHOOLS OF PHILADELPHIA,
PRINCIPAL OF PENNSYLVANIA STATE NORMAL SCHOOL, AND AUTHOR OF A
NORMAL SERIES OF MATHEMATICS.

"The highest Science is the greatest simplicity."

LANCASTER, PA.:
NORMAL PUBLISHING COMPANY.
1880.

FIRST BOOK ON THE TEACHING OF ARITHMETIC PUBLISHED IN THE UNITED STATES

CHAPTER FIFTEEN

Teacher Education in the United States through 1945

1. *Introduction*

From the early nineteenth century up to the present time, the need for better-qualified teachers has been a critical issue in the minds of parents and educators. The story of teacher education has evolved as a consequence of issues and forces that directed educators in their efforts to meet demands for intelligent planning and action in the interest of an effective professional program. The desire to provide such a program for both elementary teachers and secondary teachers has been accompanied by such impelling questions as these: What are the essential characteristics of a professional program for teachers? Should a program for teachers differ from a liberal arts program, and, if so, what should be the differences? How much subject matter should be contained in the program for elementary teachers and for secondary teachers? What should be the distinctive features of the treatment of subject matter in each type of program? What types of courses in professional education should be required of prospective teachers? Should there be separate schools for teacher education, and, if so, how should they differ from established colleges and universities? Discussions of such critical issues led to the formulation of the normal school program that became the foundation of subsequent teacher-education programs.

The further desire to establish teaching as a bona fide profession soon created new issues concerning degree recognition for the completion of qualified training programs and necessary standards for certification of teachers. From these issues there evolved a recognition of the need for the degree-granting teachers college and of the desirability of combining the efforts of subject-matter departments and schools of education to provide both in-service and preservice programs for teachers. The concept of teaching as a profession soon became a significant force. It has, through the years, exercised a strong influence in shaping programs of teacher education and also in determining a solution to the issue of the proper balance between academic and professional courses in such programs.

A comparison of different editions of books on the teaching of mathematics reveals the importance of such changing forces and issues in shaping the program for the professional education of mathematics teachers (117; 149; 184; 185; 249). The problems of appropriate preservice education, continuing in-service education, scholarly research, the growing challenges of the expanding domain of mathematical knowledge, the changing emphases in basic learning theory, the demands of an increasing school population in a technological era—all have combined to create new crises and to foster new forces. Only by intelligent thinking and careful planning can these forces be directed to form effective professional programs for the better preparation of the mathematics teachers of our elementary and secondary schools. Thus the interaction of critical issues and professional forces has served from early frontier days to shape the education of teachers in the field of mathematics. This story, which is of major importance in the history of mathematics education, is traced here from the founding of the first American normal school in the early nineteenth century through the disturbing controversies of the war years to the challenge sounded by the projection of the school mathematics program into the impending technological future of the late twentieth century.

⇛⇛ 2. *The first normal school*

The years 1823, 1825, and 1839 are of great significance in the history of teacher education. Long before these dates, the need for more competent teachers had been recognized as critical. In 1823 efforts to meet this need resulted in the opening of the first American school for the preparation of teachers. This school was founded in Concord, Vermont, by the Reverend Samuel R. Hall, as a private academy much like any other academy of the time except for two distinguishing features in its program: (1) provision for a series of lectures on "schoolkeeping" and (2) admission of a limited number of children to be used as a class in which good teaching techniques could be demonstrated for prospective teachers (153, p. 13).

The year 1825 was still more eventful for the cause of teacher education. During that year three influential public-spirited men spoke out for state-supported programs for the training of teachers (153, pp. 14-17). Gov. DeWitt Clinton of New York recommended to the state legislature that it work on the problem of staffing the schools of the state with competent teachers. In Connecticut the Reverend Thomas H. Gallaudet publicized his *Plan of a Seminary for the Education of the Instructors of Youth*. Because of the specific nature of its proposals, this plan received a great deal of support throughout New England. A third person to espouse the cause of a government-supported program of teacher education was James G. Carter, a member of the Massachusetts legislature. He is known as the "father of the American normal school." In a series of articles published in a Boston newspaper, he stressed the state's responsibility for the preparation of teachers. It was largely through his efforts that legislation was passed creating the first state board of education and authorizing the first state-supported normal school in the United States.

Although the movement to establish state-supported institutions to educate teachers was a native product and was distinctly American in its development in the hundred years after 1839, the experiences of other countries influenced the movement here by furnishing and strengthening arguments for it during the period of 1825-39. "The success of France and Holland and more especially Prussia in establishing normal schools converted many people in this country to the practicability of the plan" (153, p. 17).

The influence of Clinton, Gallaudet, and Carter, together with the foreign successes, became a strong force in the interest of teacher education which led finally to the opening on 3 July 1839 of the first state-supported institution whose sole purpose was the preparation of teachers. On this date in Lexington, Massachusetts, three young ladies were admitted as students to the first state normal school.

The principal of this first state normal school was the Reverend Cyrus Peirce of Nantucket, who worked untiringly to ensure the success of his school. The normal school was moved to West Newton in September 1844 and remained there until December 1853, when it was moved to Framingham. It has continued in Framingham to the present time. The second normal school in Massachusetts opened on 4 September 1839 at Barre and later was moved to Westfield. A third school opened on 9 September 1840 at Bridgewater, and a fourth on 13 September 1854 at Salem.

The curriculum of these early Massachusetts schools consisted of reading, writing, *arithmetic*, geography, grammar, spelling, composition, vocal music, drawing, physiology, *algebra*, *geometry*, philosophy, methods of teaching, and reading of the Scriptures. There was a very thorough treatment of subjects that were to be taught in the district schools, and the normal schools took joy in glorifying the branches of common everyday learning. As far as difficulty was concerned, the quality of the work in *arithmetic*, grammar, and geography was on the college level. It was the belief in these normal schools that the educational value of a study was proportional to its difficulty. Thus, it is evident that the early normal schools in Massachusetts maintained a high level of quality in mathematics study (pp. 25–27, 29–31).

From this meager beginning, and in spite of great indifference and frequent opposition, support for such schools continued to grow. The program was designed not only to prepare teachers for the common (elementary) schools but also to elevate teaching to the level of a true profession. By 1875 the movement had spread westward and southward so effectively that the state normal school was recognized throughout the country as the principal agency for the training of teachers, although city and private normal schools and liberal arts colleges and universities also provided such programs (pp. 39, 96).

3. *The normal school program*

Once it was accepted that there should be state-supported schools for the education of teachers, new issues began to present themselves. What kind of program was most effective in preparing teachers? How should individuals be selected and admitted to this program? What should be its duration? How should satisfactory completion of the requirements be recognized? Should academic departments of liberal arts colleges and universities assume any responsibility for such programs? Should there be programs for high school teachers as well as elementary teachers? If so. who should organize and direct them?

From the beginning, the program of the normal school was trichotomous in nature, consisting of academic curriculum, professional curriculum on methods of teaching, and laboratory experiences. The academic curriculum was designed to give a thorough treatment of the subjects that were taught in the schools. The professional training was designed to provide knowledge of teaching. In some schools such knowledge was provided by scattered weekly lectures; in others, through one or more regularly scheduled courses. In both patterns experienced teachers were used, and the emphasis was on the "science of pedagogy" or the "art of teaching." The third distinct characteristic of most normal school programs was the laboratory school where, by precept and example, experienced teachers could demonstrate for those preparing to teach a subject the most effective procedures for teaching it.

Admission to the normal school program was, in general, by examination, and the attendance was for a short period of time. By the end of the century most of these teacher-training institutions were recognizing, by diploma or degree, graduation from either a two-year or a four-year program. Also, regional accrediting associations were beginning to have indirect impact on teacher education programs through their interest in high standards of professional preparation of teachers (53, pp. 45-47).

Another force that had impact in shaping the program of the normal school was a pragmatic philosophy that demanded that the program be kept closely related to the needs of the people and that the curriculum contain everything that might contribute toward making the prospective or in-service teacher a better teacher. At the time, the arithmetic program of the elementary school consisted primarily of the fundamental operations with whole numbers and common fractions. Thus pragmatism dictated that the mathematical training for teachers consist basically of arithmetic with some algebra and geometry.

While some student texts reflected a Herbartian influence by stressing the need for meanings, the prevailing design for learning was that prescribed by faculty psychology. Thus teachers were expected to know the rules of computation and know how to conduct drill sessions. This, however, was but one aspect of the real issue that had developed by this time in teacher education. The question "What type of education does the teacher need?" had become a topic for lively debate in professional circles, with a great deal of active support given to each of three distinct positions:

1. Knowing what to teach is of little value unless one knows how to teach the subject matter to children.
2. If one knows thoroughly what to teach, the "how" comes naturally.
3. The "what" and the "how" are both essential, and the teacher education program must provide adequately for each of them.

Colleges and universities, both public and private—having become conscious of the distinct service rendered by the professional programs of the normal schools—began to establish departments or schools of education. In many cases these departments and schools were established only for the purpose of preparing high school teachers. The preparation of teachers for the elementary schools continued to be the responsibility of the normal school.

The normal school, being the seat of teacher training, was in the midst of pressures for the improvement of teaching which began with the wave of reform in educational theory and practice that took place between 1886 and 1900. The movement, known as Herbartianism, had produced the textbooks referred to earlier. It began at the University of Königsberg when Herbart established a pedagogical seminary in which his ideas might be exemplified. Americans absorbed this foreign influence in the eighties when a group of young Americans journeyed to Germany and those interested in the problems of schoolteaching took graduate courses at Jena, Halle, and Leipzig.

The American Herbartian movement was not just an imitation or a direct importation of ideas and practices, although the movement was largely due to the efforts of Charles De Garmo, Frank M. and Charles A. McMurry, and C. C. Van Liew, who were among those who went to Germany. The movement in the United States was a direct attack on the system of method and subject matter that was entrenched in the public schools. It preached the doctrine of interest, the organization of subject matter around fundamental meanings, and the inclusion of vital and interesting materials in the curriculum. The young leaders of the movement kept in close touch with the public schools and succeeded in getting their ideas into the actual day-by-day work of the classroom through their instruction of the teachers in normal schools (153, pp. 124-25).

The foreign influence in American teacher education, as exemplified by the Herbartian movement and by Pestalozzi's influence on Warren Colburn, was quite extensive. It has already been pointed out in Part One that many of the textbooks used by students of mathematics, at the school and college level, were foreign or of foreign inspiration. The same situation obtained with books on methods of teaching mathematics.

Both D. E. Smith and J. W. A. Young documented this state of affairs prior to 1900 by including lists of important books on pedagogy in their methods books. Smith's book *The Teaching of Elementary Mathematics* (241) preceded Young's *The Teaching of Mathematics* (285) by seven years. In his last chapter, "The Teacher's Book-shelf" (pp. 297-305), Smith cited works indispensable to a teacher. With regard to arithmetic he suggested that there were no methods books devoted to elementary school mathematics by noting that "the teacher of primary arithmetic needs to consult works on the science of education rather than those upon the subject itself, both because all of our special writers seem to hold a brief for some particular device, and because the mathematical phase of the question is exceedingly limited" (p. 298). The American books mentioned were by De Garmo, the McMurrys, and McLellan and Dewey. In the areas of algebra and geometry, nearly all the books mentioned were German, French, or Italian.

In J. W. A. Young's bibliography for his chapter "The Study of the Pedagogy of Mathematics" (285, pp. 1-8), thirteen foreign entries were included, but only four American ones—one of which was the work by Smith. Moreover, Young credited Germany with pedagogic leadership by calling Germany the home of pedagogy (p. 3). Thus it is apparent that prior to 1900 most influential ideas on mathematics teaching had been imported to America from abroad.

However, as the twentieth century progressed, the foreign influence became less noticeable. American authors prepared methods books in increasing numbers as the need for them increased in the teacher-training institutions. Examples are the works of Ernest Breslich, C. Butler and F. Wren, Clarence McCormick, and N. B. Rosenberger on the secondary level and of F. Grossnickle and L. Brueckner, R. Morton, H. Spitzer, J. Stone and V. Mallory, H. Wheat, and Guy Wilson at the elementary level. The rapid proliferation of methods books in the twentieth century documents the acceptance of instruction in methodology as an integral part of a teacher-education program.

Near 1900 still another force, in the form of committee action, began to express itself in the interest of improved programs of teacher education. Two influential committees, the Committee of Ten on Secondary School Studies (72, pp. 105-16) and the Committee on

College Entrance Requirements (74, pp. 648–51), recommended a substantial program of algebra and geometry for the curriculum of the common schools. The educational trend that motivated these reports also lent support to the inclusion of content from these areas among the academic courses of the normal schools. As a consequence the academic program of the normal school, with its seemingly elementary content, came under severe scrutiny by the faculties of the classical liberal arts colleges and universities. The criticism became particularly serious when the normal schools began to consider it their legal and professional responsibility to provide programs for the preparation of teachers for the public high schools as well as for the elementary schools.

⇢⇢⇢ 4. *The first two decades of the twentieth century*

By the turn of the century the tremendous growth of the public high schools had created new issues in teacher education. Should the normal schools become degree-granting teachers colleges with full academic stature so that they might train secondary teachers as well as elementary teachers? What implementation should be given to the teacher-preparation program in order to recognize and emphasize teaching as an important profession? What should be the proper balance between professional courses and content courses in the program for elementary teachers as well as for secondary teachers? Should academic departments combine forces with education departments in colleges and universities to shape and promote a professional program of teacher preparation? Should there be separate professional departments, oriented to subject matter, that would be fully staffed and recognized as responsible for programs for undergraduate and graduate degrees, with majors on academic parity with all other degrees? How could the most effective patterns for in-service education of elementary school teachers and of secondary school teachers be designed and implemented? Responses to these issues have continued through the years to be the principal forces shaping the professional programs of teacher education, whether in normal school, teachers college, liberal arts college, or university.

The effort of the normal schools to convert to teachers colleges was a force that continued to grow and to have a great deal of influence in shaping the overall pattern of teacher education. The three-pronged program of academic subject matter, professional education, and supervised teaching in a laboratory school, which had been inaugurated and developed by the early normal schools, was established as an approved pattern for professional training of teachers. Both state and private colleges and universities began to show greater recognition of teaching as a profession. Evidence of this recognition is seen in their increased efforts to provide approved four-year programs, and in a few cases graduate programs, which combined liberal arts and professional education courses.

There was also developing in the early 1900s a definite pattern of summer sessions with courses and schedules designed specifically for in-service teachers. The normal schools played a major role in popularizing these summer sessions, which they considered to be a natural extension of their in-service or follow-up work. For example, in 1879 Dr. Edwin Hewett, president of Illinois State Normal University (ISNU), reduced the school year at Normal from forty to thirty-six weeks, and he provided for a summer session of four weeks with ISNU faculty members as instructors. Although the summer sessions at ISNU were not held every year, in 1900 the summer session was expanded to six weeks and college credit for summer study was first given (158, pp. 29, 35). Summer school sessions proved to be quite beneficial to teachers, and they were attended accordingly. "By 1900 the summer school enrollment in most of the normals equalled or exceeded their regular enrollment" (153, p. 117). The fact that teachers came back to school voluntarily encouraged some liberal arts departments to inaugurate professional programs within their jurisdiction.

In an effort to secure firsthand information on the effect of issues and forces on teacher education in mathematics, especially from 1920 to the present, a questionnaire was sent during the spring of 1968 to individuals in 132 representative colleges and universities throughout the United States and Canada, including at least one institution from each state and selected province. Responses were received from universities and colleges in thirty-five states, leaving only fifteen states unrepresented, and from one university in Canada. Since sixty-one questionnaires were returned, obviously more than one institution responded from some states. Even though a greater percentage of the responses came from the eastern section of the United States, the responses to the questionnaire were representative of progress in teacher education throughout the United States. Figure 15.1 shows the distribution of responding institutions. (See following page.)

Of the sixty-one schools responding to the questionnaire, forty-six were universities, thirteen were colleges, and two were teachers colleges. Seventeen of those schools which are now universities or colleges were at one time teachers colleges or normal schools. Although no information for the period before 1920 was given in some of the replies, the training of teachers of mathematics for the public high schools in the programs reported consisted of a liberal arts major (or possibly a minor) in mathematics and some further credits in the teaching of mathematics. Such professional courses were categorized by some as mathematical pedagogy, by others as methods of teaching mathematics, and by still others merely as teachers' courses. The mathematics major was generally restricted to college (or higher) algebra, trigonometry, analytic geometry, differential and integral calculus. Variations from this outline included one or more courses in bookkeeping, history of mathematics, or statistics. According to information on the questionnaires, at least one institution included review work in arithmetic, algebra, and plane geometry. One of the greatest departures from this program, by a state university, was one designed "after the normal-school pattern," to offer courses of six weeks' duration "in secondary school mathematics and a methods course in the teaching of arithmetic." This program was more service-

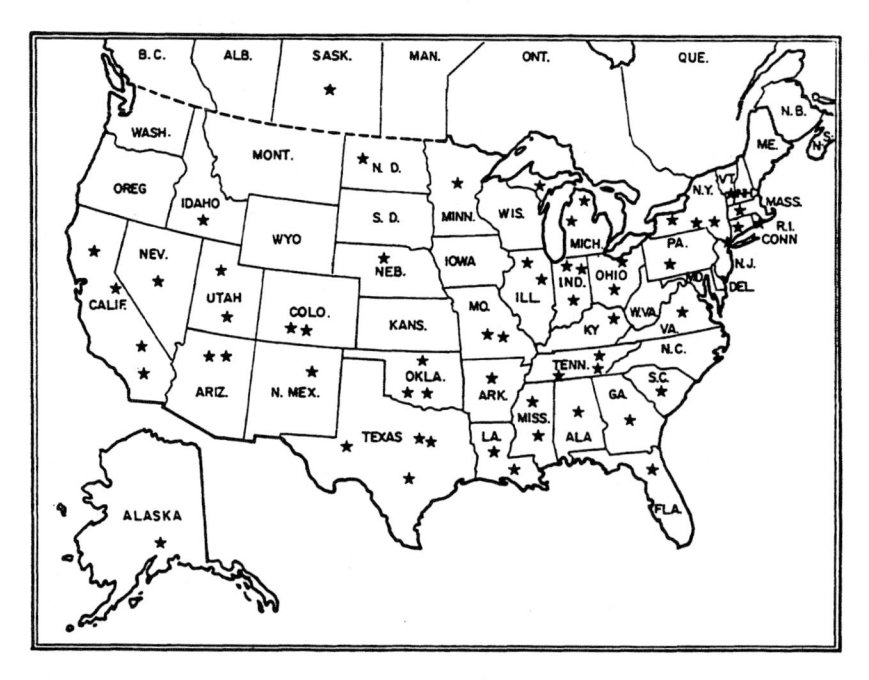

Fig. 15.1. Each star represents an institution that responded to the questionnaire on teacher education.

oriented than degree-oriented. It was designed "so that a teacher in a short term school could come to school six weeks, teach a term, and return for another six weeks term." Another major departure was a program first instituted in 1890, in which the students "completed the first two years of the curriculum offered in their major subject. Their last two years included ten terms (quarters) of technical work . . . intended to ground the student in the philosophy of teaching and training pupils and the management of schools." This program was designed to lead to the degree of bachelor of literature.

Three distinct patterns seemed to characterize the evolutionary process that was taking place in the educational programs designed to prepare teachers of mathematics. The normal schools, in their interpretation of the philosophy of professionalized subject matter, tended to lean too heavily on courses of the refresher type or containing liberal arts material of a rather elementary nature. The liberal arts colleges and universities, while recognizing the need to give the program a professional flavor, sought to accomplish this by supplementing a prescribed liberal arts major in mathematics by a limited number of courses from the new departments of education. Overpowered by the fast growth of the secondary schools, neither of these programs provided for the mathematics education of those preparing to teach in the elementary schools. The "special" training of teachers of arithmetic was confined almost entirely to one course of limited credit. In most cases this was a course in general methods, with some specific applications to arithmetic. In a few cases it was designed specifically as a course in methods of teaching arithmetic but was extended to include subject matter almost entirely of a review or refresher type.

The liberal arts pattern for the training of teachers at the secondary level of instruction was characteristic of recommendations of the two committee reports resulting from rather intensive studies made during the period 1900–1920. At the fourth International Congress of Mathematicians, which met in Rome in 1908, the International Commission on the Teaching of Mathematics was appointed. The American commissioners sponsored several subcommittees, one of them on the teaching of mathematics in elementary and secondary schools of the United States. In its report, published in 1911, it made these recommendations (43, pp. 13–14):

> The ideal preparation for teaching in the secondary schools and the first two years of college should be something more complete than that now generally found. . . .

On the side of pure mathematics we may expect the calculus, differential equations, solid analytic geometry, theory of equations, theory of functions, theory of curves and surfaces, theory of numbers, and some group theory. On the applied side we should demand a strong course in mechanics, theoretical and practical astronomy, descriptive geometry, and some mathematical physics with a thorough course in experimental physics. To this should be added special courses on surveying and general applications of mathematics that the student may see to what all of the above work is leading. As pedagogical training there should be included a strong course on the teaching of secondary mathematics with observation and practice teaching under expert supervision, a course on the history of mathematics, at least one graduate course on the history and teaching of mathematics, and a course of an encyclopedic nature dealing critically with the field of elementary mathematics from the higher standpoint. A foundation in psychology and the history of education is also necessary. Such a preparation may at first seem excessive, but it is the ideal, and, with the exception of about half of the pedagogic training outlines, it is no more severe than the requirements in France today for the secondary teaching license known as the *aggrégation*.

The International Commission stimulated follow-up study into the war years. In 1918 a study of the mathematics programs in the secondary schools of the countries participating in the commission was published. This report incorporated a recommended minimum course of study for prospective teachers of secondary mathematics (5, pp. 206–7). In outline the course is as follows, semester hours being given in parentheses: plane trigonometry (3), higher algebra (3), solid geometry (3), plane analytic geometry (4), differential and integral calculus (8), teachers' course in algebra (6), and teachers' course in geometry (6). The teachers' course in algebra constituted an introduction to some of the concepts of modern analysis. Among the topics treated were the number system with special reference to irrational numbers, limits, infinite series, the fundamental operations, and determinants.

It was recommended that in the teachers' course in elementary geometry the student should be taught methods for attacking Euclidean problems; discussions of famous problems; the existence of transcendental numbers and the proofs of the transcendence of e and π; means of rigorous discussion of the more delicate and difficult parts of the subject, such as the systems of axioms; something about (1) the history and literature of elementary geometry (2) the most important French, German, and Italian texts, and (3) non-Euclidean geometry.

It was further recommended that students preparing to teach in secondary schools should constantly elect further mathematical work, such as (1) a 2-hour course in differential equations, (2) a 6-hour course in the theory of functions of a real variable (text, first part of Goursat-Hedrick's *Mathematical Analysis*), (3) a 6-hour course in functions of a complex variable (text, Pierpont or Burkhardt-Rasor); (4) a 6-hour course in differential geometry (text, latter part of Goursat-Hedrick, and Gauss's memoir); (5) a 6-hour course in projective geometry; (6) a 3-hour course in tangential coordinates (French text by Papelier); (8) a 3-hour course in algebra (German text by Weber, vol. 1).

Although by the time of publication of this report the curriculum followed by secondary school teachers was a four-year program, the curriculum followed by elementary teachers continued to be primarily a two-year program. Yet during these first two decades of the twentieth century there was an increasing awareness of the need to improve the mathematical competence of the elementary teacher. Review courses in arithmetic were offered, usually a mixture of methods and subject matter with arithmetic serving as the material to be mastered and the medium through which proper methods of instruction were presented. Although the old faculty psychology was giving away to the theories and philosophies of Dewey, Thorndike, and others, drill continued to be a primary means of instruction.

There had evolved a point of view concerning the type of education needed by elementary teachers which had a definite effect on the amount of arithmetic or arithmetic methods in the teacher-education curriculum. This philosophy prescribed that primary teachers needed no special training in arithmetic and methods of teaching arithmetic, intermediate grade teachers needed some work in subject matter and in methods, particularly verbal problems and percentages, and teachers of upper elementary grades (those forming the junior high school) needed some academic training in mathematics. This point of view, combined with the standardized testing movement, the developing influence of the connectionist theory, and reports from committees concerned with problems of preparation of elementary school teachers, underscored a need for greater separation of professional education and mathematics content in the education of elementary school teachers.

It was during this period of rapid development in mathematics and growing interest in and concern for the problems of teacher preparation that three organizations interested in mathmatics education came into existence. In April 1903 the Central Association of Science and Mathematics Teachers was organized to develop and encourage interest in science and mathematics among the teachers and students of the secondary schools of the United States. In December 1915 a small group of college and university professors formed the Mathematical Association of America as an organization to further the cause of improved content and more effective instruction in college mathematics. Finally, in February 1920, the National Council of Teachers of Mathematics was officially organized as a professional group whose purpose was to promote programs for the improvement of instruction in junior and senior high school mathematics. These three professional organizations, originally concerned only with secondary school and collegiate mathematics instruction, were destined to become tremendous forces in shaping mathematics programs in the elementary school and in improving educational programs for the preparation of mathematics teachers for all these schools.

5. *In-service teacher education*

Two related forces of great influence in the continuing education of teachers have been supervision and institutes. The development of supervision was simultaneous with the emergence of the public schools. At the very beginning, supervision was directed toward the selection and screening of teachers according to the strict religious and moral standards of the colonies. Though the responsibility for supervision passed from the church to committees composed of laymen and clergy and finally, in the early 1800s, to the superintendent of schools, the function of supervisors was still to enforce conformity of rules and to transmit their superior knowledge to teachers.

Throughout the early 1900s this authoritative attitude persisted. With emphasis on product, measurement, and testing by scientific management theories, the supervisor assumed responsibility for setting the standards to be "attained" by both students and teachers and for seeing that desired practices were implemented. The administrative levels were the central sources of knowledge, and the teachers were expected to carry out orders and not to generate new ideas. In 1914 Elliot made the first attempt to define the goals of supervision, and during the quiet years between the world wars those concerned with supervision concentrated on defining their policies and setting clear, straightforward objectives for their program. In one study William Burton aimed to improve teaching through directed teaching, demonstration teaching, classroom visits, group and individual conferences, and proposed standards of improvement. He also stressed the supervisor's role in the selection and organization of subject matter and instructional materials. However, his objectives still carried the stigma of authoritative rule by supervisors over teaching personnel.

The 1920s also failed to produce a cooperative effort by teachers and supervisors toward self-evaluation. The rising popularity and overestimated significance of standardized testing reinforced the concept of conformity that had been fostered by supervision of teachers since the very early stages. Thus the period just after World War I was an active period in the examination of teacher and school supervision but not necessarily a progressive one. It produced a set of clarified and well-defined objectives, but it failed in two important aspects: first, supervisors did not realize the value of cooperative efforts by supervisors and teachers and, second, they failed to utilize the valuable resource of individual teacher creativity and innovation.

The trend toward a much more productive role for supervisors began in the 1930s, when there emerged two important attitudes: a feeling for democratic living and an acceptance of growth and change. The new period in supervision worked on a premise that previous periods had ignored. There was a reevaluation of what teaching actually was: "a non-repetitive act involving judgment and creativity rather than automatic application of rules" (262, p. 23). Supervisors became consultants, assistants, or advisors, in reaction to the earlier attitude of superiority of supervisor over teacher and in hope of stressing cooperative efforts.

Some concrete advances in supervision included growing responsibility of the school principal in the supervision of teachers and a great extension in the role of the superintendent of schools. Supervisory objectives, which had earlier concentrated on directing procedure in specific classroom situations, were reorganized into broader categories that allowed more teacher creativity and innovation in classroom planning. The emphasis was on increasing the teacher's knowledge of his instructional field, relating extracurricular activities to learning, improving morale, and stressing the importance of professional activities in the development of the individual teacher.

At the heart of the supervisory program is in-service education. The supervisor must see that instructional improvements of significance improve the behavior patterns of teachers. He can best do this, and thus ensure accomplishment on the part of the teacher, through in-service training.

Teacher institutes, which have contributed so much in recent years to the program of in-service education, actually came into existence during the latter part of the nineteenth century. Their original purpose was to make and/or revise school laws and to establish uniformity in textbooks, rather than to educate teachers. However, teacher education soon became the dominant emphasis of teacher institutes.

By 1898 twenty-nine states recognized professional preparation as the basis for granting teacher certification. In conjunction with the inclusion of more professional preparation for teachers, the idea was abandoned that normal schools and teachers colleges could prepare a person to teach forever. The need for continuing and in-service education for teachers was recognized. Nonetheless, in 1900 only one state had set up state control of teacher preparation, whereas by 1926 ten states were exercising such control, and life teaching certificates were being issued on the basis of in-service education.

World War I brought many changes to the educational systems in the United States; among these was an increase in in-service education. During this period 39.2 percent of the renewable certificates were contingent on some form of in-service education and 54.6 percent of the different kinds of life certificates were awarded on "bases involving some form of in-service education" (217 p. 134). In 1923 the principal methods of such education in the smaller school systems were personal conferences, classroom visitations, regular teachers' meetings, group conferences, observation of expert teaching, use of supervisory bulletins, teacher rating, and course-of-study work. The larger school systems used most of these as well as professional supervision, merit salary increments, extension work, and summer school attendance.

The year 1936 was characterized by the study of professional literature, and in the summer of that year the first workshop was instituted. As the need for in-service education became more and more apparent, institutes became increasingly prominent throughout the United States. The trend was toward subject specialization, and scholarly knowledge in a particular teaching field was emphasized. As a consequence of this development the first mathematics institute was held at Duke University during the summer of 1941.

➤➤➤ 6. *"The 1923 Report"* and its consequences

Among the first important acts of the newly organized Mathematical Association of America was to appoint, in 1916, a Committee on Mathematical Requirements. The mandate to this committee was to study the needs for the reorganization of the mathematics programs in the nation's secondary schools. The report, *The Reorganization of Mathematics in Secondary Education*, was made in 1923. In addition to pointed suggestions for improvement of the mathematics program within the schools, this committee made some rather important recommendations for the preparation of teachers.

In making their recommendations, the committee considered the training required of teachers in seventeen foreign countries. It was found that the United States was far behind Europe in the scientific and professional training required of its secondary school teachers. Though the standard would still be far below the standards of several European countries, the recommended requirements would raise standards to a reasonable level—a level which reflected an attempt to approximate European standards (59).

> To receive permanent appointment as a teacher of mathematics in a senior high school a candidate should satisfy the following requirements, or their equivalent:
>
> 1. Graduation from a standard four-year college, or university, or from an institution offering courses of at least equal difficulty and educational value
> 2. Credit for at least the following mathematical courses (given by teachers of mathematics in colleges or universities):
>   a) Plane and spherical trigonometry
>   b) Plane analytic geometry and the elements of analytic geometry of three dimensions
>   c) College algebra (1 semester) [here, and in what follows, the term "semester" implying about 45 lectures or recitations—3 hours a week for 15 weeks]
>   d) Differential and integral calculus, with applications to geometry and mechanics (3 semesters)
>   e) Synthetic projective geometry (1 semester)
>   f) Scientific training in geometry (2 semesters)
>   g) Scientific training in algebra (2 semesters)
> 3. Credit for at least the following scientific courses: Theoretical and practical physics (3 semesters), chemistry (2 semesters)
> 4. Credit for at least the following theoretical professional courses (4 semesters; given by teachers of education): History of education, principles of education, methods of teaching (including the teaching of elementary algebra and geometry), educational psychology, organization and function of secondary education
> 5. Satisfactory performance of the duties of a teacher of mathematics in a secondary school for a period of not less than 10 years, or

20 semester hours (It is considered by many competent authorities that the most satisfactory conditions for this practical professional training are in connection with a year of postgraduate work in a school of education organized so that continuous directed teaching of classes in public schools throughout the year is available to students.)

It is believed that college semester-courses in rational solid geometry, descriptive geometry, analytic projective geometry, theory of statistics, mathematics of investment, surveying, practical and descriptive astronomy, and in as many other mathematical topics as possible, are also desirable.

It is generally conceded as further desirable that the prospective teacher should have studied during the college course the following subjects: History, economics, sociology, political science, general psychology, philosophy, and ethics.

Finally, it is suggested to state departments of education that the best interests of its teachers, and their charges, would be conserved, if during the first twenty years of service, an appreciable portion of periodic salary increases of the teacher were made dependent upon scientific development (for example, by means of summer-school courses), and upon active cooperation with colleagues in promoting the interests of mathematics and the ideals and purposes of mathematical organizations.

The training of teachers of arithmetic was still regarded as not being of any concern to college or university departments of mathematics. Any efforts to improve instruction in arithmetic were left to departments of education. This, of course, meant that the program consisted only of methods courses, few of which gave much attention to subject matter. Some institutions continued to recognize that there were subject-matter deficiencies that needed attention, but the efforts to meet these needs consisted almost entirely of review or refresher courses with a rather elementary content. Furthermore, the postwar uncertainty concerning the goals of arithmetic was one of the greatest forces against an improved program of arithmetic in the preparation of elementary teachers. With the decline of the connectionist theory and the increased recognition of the need to develop the total child, a theory of "incidental learning" became popular. Thus, in many teacher education programs for elementary teachers, methodology overshadowed content. The prevailing philosophy held that the teacher should teach the child, not teach arithmetic. To put this theory into practice, teachers needed to be trained to develop and use well-planned series of social experiences that would give the learner many contacts with the important applications and uses of arithmetic in the affairs of daily life. The new issues created by the incidental-learning theory became crucial not only to the fundamental concerns in curriculum construction but also to the basic psychology of teacher education. While their impact was felt most severely at the elementary level, they had an effect on the secondary program as well.

The emergence of the junior high school introduced into mathematics education two other issues, those of the curriculum and the instructional pattern of such schools. It was through this new unit in the school organization that the incidental-learning theory had its strongest effect on the mathematics of the secondary school and the programs for the preparation of teachers of secondary mathematics. The desirability of a general mathematics program for the junior high school was first clearly and extensively stated in *The 1923 Report*.

Information from the replies to the questionnaire to which reference was made in section 4 provides evidence of the effect this report had on teacher education in mathematics. From the sixty-one replies it became quite clear that *The 1923 Report* exerted a very strong influence on the shaping of programs for the education of teachers of secondary school mathematics in the United States. These replies indicated that the sampled institutions were following rather closely the recommended programs in mathematics and professional education, in both type of content and units of credit. Titles of courses indicated some variation in content and reflected a slight tendency not to include much, if any, material above the level of the calculus. While not all institutions followed the recommendations concerning physics and chemistry, a small minority went beyond the specifications of the report and required a substantial minor in one or the other, preferably physics. Also, there was a tendency to follow the committee proposal for "possibly desirable" courses by including courses in statistics, mathematics of finance, field work (surveying), or "tools of geometry" (descriptive geometry). One variant pattern that seemed to have fairly general approval was to permit a minor in any area representing a subject taught in the secondary school rather than to require a science minor as recommended by the report. The replies also reflected a newly developing policy of offering a fifth-year program that, in most cases, provided only additional opportunity for professional education courses with a particular emphasis on practice teaching. However, at least four institutions used this fifth year as one leading to a graduate degree. Summer institutes began to offer opportunities for in-service teachers to seek further schooling in mathematics.

→»→» 7. *Further developments: 1923–45*

Two developments of the period, not incorporated within the recommendations of the report, were revealed by the questionnaire survey:

1. *Adoption of a policy, by at least seven institutions, of creating joint professorships between the departments of mathematics and education.* Individuals appointed to these professorships were to have a strong background combining both mathematical content and professional training. Among the responsibilities of an appointment to such a position were to advise prospective teachers, assist in supervising student teachers, teach methods courses dealing with problems of instruction at the secondary level of instruction, and teach pertinent content courses of professional import. In some cases these professorships carried the additional responsibility of organizing and supervising programs leading to graduate degrees.

2. *Increase in content and methods requirements for prospective elementary teachers.* Some institutions increased the requirements to six semester hours in content plus three semester hours in methods. This seemed to be in accord with state specifications for certification. At least one institution required prospective elementary school teachers to have a major of twenty semester hours in an academic area. Neither the area nor the pattern of courses within any area was specified. At a later date this same institution stipulated that such a major in mathematics must include trigonometry, college algebra, arithmetic for teachers, and twelve semester hours of electives. An additional condition was that one-third of the credits acquired for an elementary major must be from the upper-division level of instruction.

It was at this time that the professional literature began to emphasize that the teaching of mathematics was a dignified and demanding profession that called for a professional pattern of preparation. Forces created by this solution to the issue of professional status now began to prescribe that the teacher education program be threefold in character, consisting of (1) *general knowledge* to provide a broad cultural orientation; (2) *professionalized knowledge* to develop a deeper appreciation for the history, philosophy, and psychology of education; and (3) *specialized knowledge* to provide a professionalized background in mathematics as a foundation on which to build an informed pattern of instruction (56; 117; 283; 293; 361; 369; 411; 437).

The emphasis on the need for a professionalized subject-matter program for prospective elementary teachers was based on the feeling that any inexperienced teacher would be most likely to teach after the fashion in which he was taught. It was felt that academic instructors had only slight acquaintance with the program and the problems of the elementary schools and, consequently, little appreciation for the tasks of the teachers in these schools. On the other hand, the education specialist too often was inclined to deal in instructional generalities, with little or no adaptation to the specific problems of arithmetic. Similarly it was felt that the prospective teacher of secondary mathematics would profit more from study and learning experiences in a professional atmosphere in which the emphasis of instruction was on developing a background for enriched and confident interpretation for the inexperienced learner rather than on building a foundation for research or industrial application.

The years from 1923 through 1945 were also problem years for mathematics. The prevalent educational philosophy of the period fostered a somewhat negative attitude toward mathematics which brought about a reevaluation of the content of instruction, particularly at the elementary and junior high school levels. The rather limited interpretation of values induced by the pragmatism of the period led in many cases both to a lowering in the amount of mathematics required and to a modification of the content of instruction. The events of the latter part of this period, leading up to and including World War II, not only affected the high school programs but also caused major changes at the college and university levels.

In 1933 the trustees of the MAA authorized the appointment of a Commission on the Training and Utilization of Advanced Students of Mathematics. The commission report, published in 1935, was divided into two parts. Part 1 was entitled "Graduate Training for Teaching Secondary Mathematics." Its recommendations seem to be the first on record to recognize programs for teachers of mathematics that were to lead to the doctorate (21, pp. 267-74). The recommendations of part 2 (pp. 275-76) advocated threefold subject-matter preparation: general knowledge, professionalized knowledge, and specialized knowledge. The emphasis was on specialized knowledge with strong suggestions that no more work in educational theory be taken than was legally required to obtain a certificate. Following is the outline for this portion of the report:

Recommendations Concerning Preparation for Major Teaching of Secondary Mathematics

1. Minimum training in mathematics
    a) Courses in mathematics including complete treatments of trigonometry, college algebra, analytic geometry, and 6 semester hours of calculus
    b) A college treatment of synthetic Euclidean geometry, or possibly descriptive geometry (3 semester hours)
    c) Advanced algebra, such as theory of equations (3 semester hours)
    d) Either directed reading or a formal course in the history of mathematics and the fundamental concepts of mathematics
2. Minimum college training in fields related to mathematics
    a) Introductory courses in physics and in another science (12 semester hours)
    b) A course in mathematics of investment (3 semester hours)
    c) An introductory course in economics
    d) A first course in statistics, with a mathematical viewpoint (3 semester hours)
3. Desirable additional training in mathematics and related fields
    a) Advanced calculus and differential equations or mechanics (6 semester hours)
    b) Additional work in geometry, such as projective geometry, solid analytic geometry, etc. (3 semester hours)
    c) Additional study in algebra (3 semester hours)
    d) Introduction to astronomy
    e) Additional study of physics and other sciences to complete a background in three or more sciences (9 semester hours)
4. Adequate training in English composition and cultural training outside of mathematics and related fields; work in languages, literature, fine arts, and the social sciences in preference to increased specialization in mathematics and related fields, and in preference to elective work in the theory of education beyond the legal requirements
5. Training in the theory of education and practice teaching
    a) One-year course in methods of teaching and practice teaching in secondary mathematics, together with any distinctively pertinent material concerning educational measurements and other content from educational theory (10 semester hours)
    It is our belief that this essential part of the student's training should, if possible, be under the direction of professors who have had graduate mathematical training, who have taught mathematics at the secondary level, and who have maintained contacts with the secondary field.

b) Study of methods of teaching in the principal minor field selected by the student, and any additional material relating to the history, psychology, or administration of education which can be objectively justified in the training of a teacher (not more than 5 semester hours)

Because of the acute situation in mathematics education caused by the untoward events of this period, the NCTM and the MAA joined forces to appoint the Joint Commission on the Place of Mathematics in Secondary Education. Its report was published in 1940 as the Fifteenth Yearbook of the NCTM. In addition to making extensive recommendations concerning the programs of instruction in the secondary schools, and supporting the need for a "general culture program" as recommended in *The 1923 Report*, the report suggested programs for training prospective teachers of mathematics in these schools, beginning with an outline for those preparing to teach mathematics and a second subject (50, pp. 201–3):

The teacher's training should include:
1. In mathematics
    a) Courses including complete treatments of college algebra, analytic geometry (including a little solid analytics), and 6 semester hours of calculus
    b) A course that examines somewhat critically Euclidean geometry and gives a brief introduction to projective geometry and non-Euclidean geometry, using synthetic methods (3 semester hours)
    c) Advanced algebra, including work in theory of equations, mathematics of finance, and statistics (6 semester hours)
        This course should give some careful attention to the basic laws of algebra, to the nature of irrational and complex numbers, and operations with them. It should be throughout somewhat critical and not purely manipulative.
    d) Either directed reading or a formal course in the history of mathematics and its concepts
2. In related fields
    An introductory course in physics, astronomy, or chemistry that makes use of some mathematics
3. In professional preparation
    a) A course in methods (2 or 3 semester hours)
        This work should be given by a person who has had a good mathematical education and also experience in high school teaching.

b) A course in secondary education (3 semester hours)
    Some consideration of educational philosophy and of the history of education can be given in this course.
c) A course in psychology, with emphasis on its educational bearing and on the problem of learning (3 semester hours)
d) A course in educational tests and measurements that employs some statistical material (2 semester hours)
e) Practice teaching
    It is not usually possible for a student to have practice teaching in two fields. If mathematics is his major he should do his practice teaching in that subject.

The report continued, under the heading "High School Teachers of Mathematics Alone":

A teacher whose full time is devoted to mathematics and who is in a school that provides courses in more advanced secondary mathematics should have, in addition to the training previously described, as much as possible of the following work.
1. Advanced calculus and differential equations or mechanics (6 semester hours)
2. Additional work in geometry, such as projective geometry, descriptive geometry, etc. (3 semester hours)
3. Additional work in algebra, including some modern algebra (3 semester hours)
4. At least one more of the three sciences of physics, chemistry, and astronomy

During World War II the technical demands of the training programs for military inductees exposed many serious deficiencies in the mathematical training they had received in their elementary and secondary school programs of instruction. The situation became so serious that the AMS, the MAA, and the NCTM made individual and joint efforts to find solutions to the various training problems. One important outcome of these investigations was the appointment by the NCTM of the Commission on Post-War Plans. This commission was not only to give serious study to the problems of methods and content of instruction in the postwar school programs but also to lay the foundation for improved programs for teacher education in mathematics. In 1945 the "Second Report" of the commission presented its recommendations for the improvement of instruction in mathematics in the form of thirty-four theses, of which theses 24 through 32 were concerned with teacher education. The proposals were directed toward the existing situation and toward the serious implications for needed change which military experiences and committee studies had brought to the public's attention. Excerpts from the report are given below (16, pp. 215–19):

Grades 1–8

[These recommendations are made with recognition of the duties and subjects which the elementary teacher must be capable of teaching and performing.]

Thesis 24. *All students who are likely to teach mathematics in grades 1–8 should, as a minimum, demonstrate competence over the whole range of subject matter which may be taught in these grades.*

[For each teacher in grades 1–6 this criterion should be satisfied individually, if necessary, without course credit. An acceptable score on some acceptable standard examination would indicate competence. . . . This criterion is not enough for teachers of grades 7 and 8. The teacher in these grades needs work] beyond the elements of algebra, geometry, and trigonometry.

Thesis 25. *Teachers of mathematics in grades 1–8 should have special course work relating to subject matter* [that he is going to teach] *as well as to the teaching process.*

Grades 9–12

Thesis 26. *The teacher of mathematics should have a wide background in the subjects he will be called upon to teach.*

Thesis 27. *The mathematics teacher should have a sound background in related fields.* [Related fields are physics, mechanics, astronomy, economics, etc.]

Thesis 28. *The mathematics teacher should have adequate training in the teaching of mathematics, including arithmetic.*

Thesis 29. *The course in mathematical subject matter for the prospective mathematics teacher should be professionalized.*

Thesis 30. *It is desirable that a mathematics teacher acquire a background of experience in practical fields where mathematics is used.*

Thesis 31. *The minimum training for mathematics teachers in small high schools should be a college minor in mathematics.*

Thesis 32. *Provision should be made for the continuous education of teachers in service.*

Leaders in the area of elementary teacher education were beginning to accept the fact that much of the difficulty that teachers of the primary grades were having with arithmetic was due to inadequate subject-matter background. Incidental-learning theory was recognized as providing an inefficient pattern of instruction for a subject area as sequentially structured as mathematics. Teachers needed not only proficiency in the fundamental operations with number but also a strong supporting background to give meaning to the content of instruction. Inadequacies in both content of instruction and teaching efficiency began to focus very critical attention on the standards of certification at both the elementary and secondary levels of instruction. The end of the war period found the total program of mathematical education under very severe scrutiny.

CHAPTER SIXTEEN

The Modern Era: 1945–Present

1. Introduction

The recognition of grave deficiencies in the school mathematics program, as first exposed by World War II and later highlighted dramatically by the spectacular performance of Sputnik, sparked a new era of thought and action concerning the instructional program in school mathematics. The federal government and private industry began to provide liberal support for significant experimentation in curriculum content at both elementary and secondary levels of instruction; the GI Bill provided funds for many veterans to return to their interrupted college educational programs; private corporations supported valuable scholarships to encourage high school graduates to continue their schooling; and scattered studies reemphasized the basic need for a stronger program for the better preparation of teachers of mathematics at both the elementary and the secondary levels of instruction.

In 1946 the Cooperative Committee on the Teaching of Science and Mathematics of the American Association for the Advancement of Science (AAAS) published, as a report, "The Preparation of High School Science and Mathematics Teachers" (2). Although less specific in its recommendations for the training of mathematics teachers than the Commission on Post-War Plans, the committee made some concrete suggestions:

Approximately half of the prospective teacher's four-year college program should be devoted to courses in the sciences. . . . Colleges and certification authorities should work toward a five-year program for the preparation of high school teachers. . . . Curriculum improvements in the small high school should go hand in hand with improvement in teacher preparation.

In a 1947 report this committee suggested, "We should gear the financial support of public education to our economy," and it recommended not only higher teacher salaries but also that "higher institutions as well as public school systems, should provide strong in-service programs for teachers" to include "workshops, maintained through grants-in-aid providing for teacher subsistence" and "science and mathematics counselors throughout the country."

2. *Status surveys*

In a comparative analysis of several independent studies that were concerned with the status of the mathematics preparation of elementary teachers, Ruddell, Dutton, and Reckzek (224, pp. 296–306) found in 1960 that, although the amount of college training required for certification of elementary teachers had increased significantly, there had been practically no change in the amount of prescribed mathematics. Only twelve states required any specified mathematics, and this requirement was an inadequate minimum which consisted of a course in general mathematics or a methods course in arithmetic. While thirty-five states required college graduation for certification, this did not imply very high standards for preparation in mathematics. Approximately two-thirds of the institutions studied would admit prospective elementary teachers whose programs showed no high school mathematics. However, some of these schools did require for admission a minimum proficiency level in arithmetic. A typical graduate from the four-year program for certification to teach in the elementary school had completed two years of high school mathematics, one 3-semester-unit course in general mathematics, and one 2-semester-unit course in methods of teaching mathematics.

The U.S. Office of Education (USOE), in a 1959 survey of 799 teachers of high school mathematics, found that 7.1 percent had taken no college mathematics and that only 61 percent had studied calculus or more advanced courses. Approximately 87 percent of the mathematics and science teachers had taken some college mathematics. The average preparation of those who were teaching one or more courses in mathematics was 23 semester hours, much of it at a level below calculus, and for those teaching a combination of mathematics and science the average was only 17.3 semester hours. Much of the mathematics had been studied prior to 1940, and only 20.2 percent of the teachers had taken a course in calculus or more advanced mathematics since 1950. Approximately two-thirds of the mathematics teachers had had student (practice) teaching but very little work in the methods of teaching mathematics. The average amount of credit in mathematics methods courses was 2.6 semester hours, and only 15.1 percent of the teachers had taken any such work since 1950. About one-third of the group studied had a master's degree, but the major area of concentration was not mathematics (8, p. 29).

As a result of a detailed study of the programs for teachers of secondary school mathematics offered by 140 institutional members of the American Association of Colleges for Teacher Education, Schumaker, in 1961, reported these findings (411):

1. The median minimum of semester hours required for a major in mathematics increased from 24 to 27 between the academic years 1920/21 and 1957/58; for a minor the increase was from 12 to 18 semester hours; and, in professional courses, the increase was from 21 to 24 semester hours.

2. The course outline of the required program was rather uniform through calculus, but there were many variations in the upper division program.

3. The most frequently occurring upper division courses were, roughly in the order listed, differential equations, college geometry, theory of equations, mathematics of finance, elementary statistics, advanced calculus, history of mathematics, and solid analytic geometry.

4. For state certification as a teacher of mathematics in the senior high school the median number of semester hours required in mathematics was 15 (slightly less than the minimum requirements for a minor).

3. *In-service education*

The second half of the twentieth century has seen an unprecedented series of forces directing the attention of educators to the need for improving the background and effectiveness of in-service teachers. These forces include the following:

1. Development of new content and new curricula, or "modern

mathematics" (for example, in the early years of its development the University of Illinois project would not permit its materials to be used by teachers who had not had special training on that campus)

2. Development of new forms of "discovery teaching," and stress upon such attempts to stimulate creativity and appreciation of the nature and beauty of mathematics

3. Greater emphasis on the need for education beyond high school and hence the need to prepare the better-qualified students of the eleventh and twelfth grades for college courses

4. Inclusion of new and higher-level mathematics, analytic geometry, calculus, linear algebra, and probability and statistics in some twelfth-grade programs

Duke University had operated a summer institute for mathematics teachers as early as 1941, and the General Electric Company, Westinghouse Educational Foundation, E. I. Du Pont de Nemours and Company, Shell Companies Foundation, and Crown Zellerbach Foundation had supported institutes for science and mathematics teachers in the 1940s and 1950s. However, the most important programs in teacher education have been those supported by the National Science Foundation (NSF) since it was established by Congress in 1950. NSF activities have taken the form of summer institutes, in-service institutes, academic year institutes, fellowships, and cooperative programs between colleges or universities and school districts or systems.

A program of institutes for college teachers was started by NSF in 1953 at the University of Colorado (201, p. 7). It was designed initially for teachers in four-year liberal arts colleges who had lost contact with current mathematical research. Later these institutes were redesigned to serve junior college teachers. College teacher institutes were administered by the same office as the program for high school teachers until 1961. Since that time the two programs have been separated, and now they function under the jurisdiction of distinct offices.

The first NSF-supported summer institute for high school teachers was in mathematics. It was held in 1954 at the University of Washington (201, p. 1). This was followed in 1955 with six institutes: one each in physics and chemistry and two each in science and mathematics. From this meager beginning the program grew to a peak of 458 institutes during the summer of 1968. Approximately 110,000 secondary school teachers have been involved in 222,634 participations in summer institutes. In 1967, 36.3 percent of those participating were teachers of mathematics; in 1968, 36.8 percent were teachers of mathematics; and in earlier years approximately 35 percent of those involved were teachers of mathematics.

The first summer institutes for elementary school personnel were held in 1959, although an experimental institute in science was held at the University of Rochester in 1958. Of the institutes held in 1959, those in mathematics were held at the University of Michigan and at Rutgers, and those in mathematics and science combined were held at DePauw and at the State University of New York College at Plattsburg. There were eight other institutes held in science only. The maximum number of summer institutes for elementary school teachers in the peak year of 1965 was thirty-nine. Approximately 7,088 elementary school personnel, including supervisors, principals, and teachers, were involved in summer institutes. This program has been discontinued.

Academic-year institutes for secondary school teachers were first held in 1956/57. These two were held at Oklahoma A. and M. and at the University of Wisconsin and were both multiple-field, including mathematics. The first mathematics-only institutes were held in 1957/58 at the University of Chicago and at the University of Illinois. There were also fourteen other multiple-field institutes that included mathematics. The maximum number of academic-year institutes for secondary school teachers in the peak year of 1969 was 67. Approximately 18,971 have attended these institutes. In 1967/68, 39.4 percent were teachers of mathematics; in 1969/70, 39.7 percent were teachers of mathematics; and in earlier years approximately 40 percent of those involved were teachers of mathematics.

The first in-service institutes for secondary school teachers were held in the spring semester of 1957 at Reed College and at Antioch College. They were both multiple-field, including mathematics. The maximum number of in-service institutes in the peak year of 1965/66 was 313. Approximately 70,000 to 80,000 secondary school teachers have been involved in 141,616 participations in in-service institutes. In 1967/68, 49.7 percent of those participating were teachers of mathematics; in 1968/69, 48.7 percent of those participating were teachers of mathematics, and in earlier years usually just over 50 percent were teachers of mathematics.

In-service institutes for elementary school personnel began in 1959/60, although there was a pilot project in 1957/58 at the University of Colorado in science. The first eleven institutes included mathematics only at Emory University, Northwestern University, the

College of St. Catherine, and Montana State College and mixed mathematics and science at Shaw University and the State College at Salem. The maximum number of in-service institutes in the peak year of 1964/65 was 70. This program has been discontinued.

The first fellowship program for high school teachers was established in 1959. In this program teachers were awarded fellowships to attend the college or university of their choice and pursue the program indicated on their applications. Most of these awards were for a period of three years. The fellowship program was discontinued in 1965. Although the NSF did not insist on it, most of the institutes they supported carried graduate credit, and many led to advanced degrees.

The possibility of teaching higher-level mathematics (including calculus) in high school meant that the existing institutes needed to be revamped. The USOE saw the need to go beyond institutes and workshops for in-service education. Both elementary and high school mathematics teachers needed to be educated at the graduate level. The Higher Education Act of 1965 commissioned the Prospective and Experienced Teacher Fellowship Program to assist teachers to undertake such advanced study. Under the Experienced Teacher Fellowship Program teachers with three years of experience could qualify for federal assistance to return to graduate school and work toward a master's degree.

Public school systems are currently doing much to encourage teacher participation in various in-service education projects. More released time is allowed; compensation is given for time spent on in-service projects outside the workday; teachers are employed for an extended time, with additional time being used for in-service education; professional help is increasingly available for teachers to use; and non-college programs are conducted by school personnel. Financial support from outside sources and from the schools themselves is making in-service education more feasible.

A trend that seems to be developing now is to prepare high school teachers to be leaders of in-service education programs for teachers of elementary school mathematics. This plan has great potential for helping elementary teachers become better qualified for their responsibilities in teaching mathematics.

When the "new math" hit in the early 1960s, the demand for guidelines for in-service education became particularly strong. The NCTM and the USOE recognized the need and provided two conferences dealing with the problem.

The first conference was held in Washington, D.C., on 17–19 March 1960. This conference was devoted to in-service education for high school teachers of mathematics. The participants were fifty leaders in mathematics education drawn from high schools, state departments of education, colleges, universities, and the USOE (111). The second was held in Washington, D.C., on 7-8 March 1963. The emphasis of this conference was on "promising practices" for in-service education of elementary and secondary school teachers. The forty-five participants in this conference came from backgrounds similar to those of participants in the earlier conference (236).

The In-Service Education Committee of the NCTM participated in the 1963 conference on a consultation basis. In 1967 the NCTM published a bulletin on in-service education for elementary school teachers that could be used in school systems as a guide in planning appropriate programs. More specifically, the bulletin had the following purposes: (1) to aid those involved in conducting in-service education courses for elementary school teachers by providing resource assistance, (2) to provide information on the range of current in-service activities throughout the nation, (3) to stimulate the increased effort that must be made to meet the great need which still exists, and (4) to supply schools and school systems with information to help them determine their present status and the appropriate next steps in mathematics in-service education (38, p. iii).

The material compiled to fulfill these purposes was divided into three parts in the bulletin. Part 1 presented valuable information on the elementary school, the elementary school teacher, the philosophy of the elementary school as stated by leaders in elementary school education, and implications for mathematics in-service education.

Descriptions of various types of in-service procedures and programs that would benefit teachers, principals, and supervisors were included in part 2. The procedures and programs were divided into three categories: (1) efforts to stimulate informal self-directed study, (2) institutes, workshops, and courses emphasizing both content and method, and (3) courses carrying college credit with the major emphasis on content necessary to the more modern mathematics programs.

Part 3 (pp. 36-44) was devoted to contemporary in-service programs of promise, to the factors that encourage participation in in-service programs, and to the future challenge to in-service education resulting from the changes in elementary school mathematics.

Leadership in in-service education was provided initially by college teacher-trainers. Recently some of the leadership responsibility has shifted to state, county, and city mathematics coordinators and supervisors. In 1958 only five states and the District of Columbia had special supervisors responsible for state-level mathematics programs, but by 1968 more than eighty persons held comparable positions. In-service education is a major responsibility of these people, but the range of their responsibilities and accomplishments is as varied as the needs of the teachers in the various states. There is no doubt that supervisory personnel will continue to play an important role in all phases of school life, including in-service education (90; 237; 262; 347).

4. Recommendations for improvement in teacher education

As a result of experience with institutes and studies of the status of teacher education, it became quite evident that a large proportion of the experienced teachers, as well as those who were just starting their teaching career, were not prepared to teach the mathematics of the newly developing curricula. Professional organizations became more acutely concerned with the program of teacher preparation. Committees appointed to study the new problems of mathematics education were asked to give careful attention also to teacher education. Four of the first committees to make their reports were the Commission on Mathematics of the CEEB (1959), the Secondary School Curriculum Committee of the NCTM (1959), the Subcommittee on Teacher Certification of the Cooperative Committee on the Teaching of Science and Mathematics of the AAAS (1959), and the Committee on the Undergraduate Program in Mathematics of the MAA (1961).

After a rather detailed presentation of its proposals for revision of the secondary school curriculum in mathematics, the report of the Commission on Mathematics gave token attention to the problem of the mathematical education of elementary teachers. Recognizing that "all secondary school instruction in mathematics rests upon the foundation laid in the elementary school," the commission made these recommendations concerning the program for elementary teachers (12, pp. 48–50):

> On the sound principle that one cannot teach any subject well unless his knowledge exceeds the material he is expected to teach, [teachers of arithmetic should be required to complete at least three years of secondary mathematics comparable to that outlined in the report. Additional work in college mathematics would be highly desirable.] . . . Teachers should be acquainted with the findings of psychological research concerning grade placement of topics, methods of dealing with individual strengths and weaknesses, and the uses of

tests. Teachers should also understand the methodology ... the use of concrete materials [to aid in developing more meaningful understanding of abstractions. ... A program of in-service training should be followed.]

The recommendations for the training of secondary teachers (pp. 50–58) can be summarized as follows:

A different program of college mathematics for the experienced teacher is needed. The departments of education and mathematics must cooperate in designing new courses to meet the needs in this area. College and university mathematics faculties have a responsibility for cooperating fully with the mathematics teacher in bringing this training up to date.
1. Short summer conferences are good regional projects.
2. Regular study group meetings can be regional or even neighborhood in their organization.
3. Special university lecture series can be offered by university faculties at convenient times for secondary school teachers.
4. Professional society meetings offer many opportunities for educating the teacher in a particular area.

Programs of continued study should be followed.

It is imperative that the undergraduate program be modified at once to provide a sound background of study of contemporary mathematical material, and to produce teachers adequately equipped to deal with the new curricular patterns.

A sound teacher education program can be developed around a major of 24 hours beyond the calculus (i.e., differential equations, probability and statistics, modern algebra, non-Euclidean geometry, advanced calculus, logic, history of mathematics, and number theory).

It is desirable for the teacher to have a strong minor in at least one field that uses mathematical methods extensively.

Certainly all mathematics majors should have courses in such subjects as psychology, foundations of education, methods of teaching mathematics, and student teaching.

The report of the Secondary-School Curriculum Committee concerned itself entirely with the mathematics program of the secondary school and the education considered necessary to prepare teachers for this program. The proposals from this group (65, pp. 414-15) are given below. They were in close agreement with those of the contemporaneous commission report.

In view of current curriculum demands teachers of mathematics in grades 7 through 12 will need to have competence in (1) analysis—

trigonometry, plane and solid analytic geometry, and calculus; (2) foundations of mathematics—theory of sets, mathematical or symbolic logic, postulational systems, real and complex number systems; (3) algebra—matrices and determinants, theory of numbers, theory of equations, and structure of algebra; (4) geometry—Euclidean and non-Euclidean, metric and projective, synthetic and analytic; (5) statistics—probability and statistical inference; (6) applications—mechanics, theory of games, linear programming, and operations research.

Ideally, every teacher of secondary mathematics should have completed successfully a five-year program, emphasizing the above areas and culminating in the master's degree. As a minimum, teachers of mathematics at the seventh- and eighth-grade levels should have completed successfully a program of at least eighteen semester hours, including six semester hours of calculus, in courses selected from the above areas. Also as a minimum, teacher of mathematics in grades 9 through 12 should have completed successfully a program of at least twenty-four semester hours, including a full-year program in calculus, in courses selected from the above areas. Both programs should contain fundamental treatments of relevant topics from the foundations of mathematics and probability and statistics. These programs in mathematics should be supplemented by a basic program in education and psychology. As a minimum, a teacher should have completed successfully eighteen semester hours, including student teaching in mathematics, in such courses as: a methods course in the teaching of mathematics; psychology of learning (with particular reference to adolescents); psychology of adjustment (mental hygiene); and tests and measurements. This total program of specialization should be based on a strong program of general education.

The subcommittee of the AAAS Cooperative Committee summarized its recommendations for the preparation of teachers of secondary mathematics in a preliminary report in 1959 (3, pp. 287–88) and a final report that appeared in 1960 (4, pp. 1027–28). For this purpose they separated the teachers into two categories—I, teachers of mathematics only in grades 7–12, and II, teachers of mathematics as a second subject—and the subject matter of mathematics into six categories as follows:

> A. Analysis. Trigonometry, plane and solid analytic geometry, calculus are a minimum, some of which may have been done in high school. Electives to make a total of at least 12 hours should be chosen from advanced calculus, differential equations, infinite series.
> B. Algebra. Courses selected from abstract algebra, matrices, theory of equations, and number theory.

C. Geometry. Courses selected from metric and other geometries, non-Euclidean geometry, differential geometry, topology.

D. Foundations of mathematics. Sets, logic, postulational systems.

E. Probability and statistics.

F. Applications. To physics, astronomy, actuarial science, and behavioral sciences.

Their recommended education programs are summarized in table 16.1, the course areas being identified as above.

TABLE 16.1
AAAS Mathematics and Science Requirements in Semester Hours

Level	Course Areas						Four-Year Total			Fifth Year			Five-Year Total		
	A	B	C	D	E	F	Math	Phys.	Sup. areas*	Math	Phys.	Sup. areas*	Math	Phys.	Sup. areas*
I	12	3	3	6	3	3	30	8	22	15		15	45	8	37
II	12	3	3				18	18†	24	12	12†	6	30	30†	30

* Supporting areas
† Physics, chemistry, or other second subject

One of the most persistently promoted reports in the interest of teacher education has been that of the Panel on Teacher Training of the Committee on the Undergraduate Program in Mathematics (CUPM). In their report, originally published in 1961, revised in 1964 and 1966, this group specified five levels of teaching responsibility, in terms of which their recommendations would be made, namely, teachers of (I) elementary school mathematics, (II) elements of algebra and geometry, (III) high school mathematics, (IV) elements of calculus, linear algebra, probability, and so forth, and (V) college mathematics.

Minimum numbers of college courses were then described and recommended for each of the levels except level V, which has continued as an area of study. These recommendations follow (26):

Recommendations for Level I:

As a prerequisite for the college training of elementary school teachers, we recommend at least two years of college preparatory mathematics, consisting of a year of algebra and a year of geometry, or the same material in integrated courses. It must also be assured that these teachers are competent in the basic techniques of arithmetic.

The exact length of the training program will depend on the strength of their preparation. For their college training, we recommend the equivalent of:

A. A two-course sequence devoted to the structure of the real number system and its subsystems. ...
B. A course devoted to the basic concepts of algebra. ...
C. A course in informal geometry. ...

The material in these courses might, in a sense, duplicate material studied in high school by the prospective teacher, but we urge that this material be covered again, this time from a more sophisticated, college-level point of view. Whether the material suggested in A above can be covered in one or two courses will depend upon the previous preparation of the student.

We strongly recommend that at least 20 percent of the level I teachers in each school have stronger preparation in mathematics, comparable to level II preparation but not necessarily including calculus. Such teachers would clearly strengthen the elementry program by their very presence within the school faculty. This additional preparation is certainly required for elementary teachers who are called upon to teach an introduction to algebra or geometry.

Recommendations for Level II:

Prospective teachers of the elements of algebra and geometry should enter this program ready for a mathematics course at the level of a beginning course in analytic geometry and calculus (requiring a minimum of three years in college preparatory mathematics). It is recognized that many students will have to correct high school deficiencies in college. (However, such courses as trigonometry and college algebra should not count toward the fulfillment of minimum requirements at the college level.) Their college mathematics should then include:

A. Three courses in elementary analysis (including or presupposing the fundamentals of analytic geometry). ...

This introduction to analysis should stress basic concepts. However, prospective teachers should be qualified to take more advanced mathematics courses requiring a year of the calculus, and hence calculus courses especially designed for teachers are normally not desirable.

B. Four other courses: a course in abstract algebra, a course in geometry, a course in probability from a set-theoretic point of view, and one elective. One of these courses should contain an introduction to the language of logic and sets. The panel strongly recommends that a course in applied mathematics or statistics be included. [This last sentence was added in the 1966 revision.]

Recommendations for Level III:

Prospective teachers of high school mathematics beyond the elements of algebra and geometry should complete a major in mathematics and a minor in some field in which a substantial amount of mathematics is used. This latter should be selected from the areas in the physical sciences, biological sciences, and the social studies, but the minor in each case should be pursued to the extent that the student will have encountered substantial applications of mathematics.

The major in mathematics should include, in addition to the work listed under level II, at least an additional course in each of algebra, geometry, and probability-statistics, and one more elective [cut from two to one in the 1966 revision].

Thus the minimum requirements for high school mathematics teachers should consist of the following (the requirements for level II preparation have been included in this list):

A. Three courses in analysis [analytic geometry and calculus].
B. Two courses in abstract algebra [introduction to algebraic structures; finite-dimensional linear algebra].
C. Two courses in geometry beyond analytic geometry [emphasizing a "higher understanding of the geometry of the school curriculum"].
D. Two courses in probability and statistics. . . .
E. In view of the introduction of computing courses in the secondary school, a course in computer science is highly recommended [added in 1966 revision].
F. Two upper-class elective courses. A course in the applications of mathematics is particularly desirable [added in 1966]. Other courses suggested are introduction to real variables, number theory, topology, or history of mathematics. Particular attention should be given here to laying groundwork for later graduate study.

One of these courses should contain an introduction to the language of logic and sets, which can be used in a variety of courses.

Recommendations for Level IV:

For level IV high school teachers we recommend a master's degree, with at least two-thirds of the courses being in mathematics, and for which an undergraduate program at least as strong as level III training is a prerequisite. A teacher who has completed the recommendations for level III should use the additional mathematics courses to acquire greater mathematical breadth.

Since these teachers will be called upon to teach calculus, we recommend that the program include the equivalent of at least two courses of theoretical analysis in the spirit of the theory of functions of real and complex variables.

It is important that universities have graduate programs available which can be entered with level III preparation, recognizing that these students substitute greater breadth for lack of depth in analysis as compared with an ordinary B.A. with a major in mathematics. In other respects, graduate schools should have great freedom in designing the M.A. program for teachers.

Recommendations for Level V:

These teachers should be qualified to teach all basic courses offered in a strong undergraduate college curriculum. We believe this requires the knowledge and talents of a person holding the Ph.D. in mathematics or at least having the training corresponding to the subject-matter competence of the Ph.D. [This paragraph substituted in 1966 revision.]
Curriculum–Study Courses

. . . Effective mathematics teachers must be familiar with such items as:

A. The objectives and content of the many proposals for change in our curriculum and texts.
B. The techniques, relative merits, and roles of such teaching procedures as the inductive and deductive approaches to new ideas.
C. The literature of mathematics and its teaching.
D. The underlying ideas of elementary mathematics and the manner in which they may provide a rational basis for teaching. . . .
E. The chief applications which have given rise to various mathematical subjects. These applications will depend upon the level of mathematics to be taught, and are an essential part of the equipment for all mathematics teachers.

Such topics are properly taught in so-called "methods" courses. We would like to stress that adequate teaching of such courses can be done only by persons who are well informed *both* as to the basic mathematical concepts and as to the nature of American public schools—and as to the concepts, problems, and literature of mathematics education. In particular, we do not feel that this can be done effectively at either the elementary level in the context of "general" methods courses, or by persons who have not had at least the training of level IV.

In 1963, after a study of the educational background of teachers in American schools, James Bryant Conant recommended that prospective elementary teachers have three years of high school mathematics on entering college. He suggested that they then be required to take 6 semester hours of mathematics in their general education programs. He thought that teachers of grades K–3 should include additional mathematics in a 30-semester-hour requirement in mathematics, English, and social studies, with mastery being tested by a compre-

THE MODERN ERA: 1945-PRESENT 341

hensive examination. Teachers in grades 4-6 were urged to take 30 semester hours for specialization in one of four areas (mathematics, English, social studies, or science), mastery being tested by a comprehensive examination. As part of the professional program Conant suggested 8 semester hours of practice teaching—eight weeks of 3 hours a day in the classroom, including three weeks of full responsibility in the classroom (128, pp. 154-60).

For mathematics teachers in the secondary schools Conant recommended 6 semester hours of mathematics in the general education program which should be supplemented by 39 semester hours in mathematics and 6 semester hours in physics or chemistry. This program also should include among the professional education courses 9 semester hours of practice teaching and special methods (pp. 171-72).

It is interesting to observe that in recent years concern for the preparation of elementary teachers almost invariably accompanies concern for the preparation of secondary school teachers. This parallels the development of "middle schools" as administrative and educational units as well as the shifting of subject-matter content to different grade levels with its accompanying articulation problems: elementary-secondary, junior high–senior high, senior high–college (junior college, technical school).

5. *The implementation of recommendations*

The Panel on Teacher Training of the MAA's Committee on the Undergraduate Program was further charged with the implementation of its report. This was attempted through various publications and conferences (27; 28; 29; 30; 31). This program has, to some extent, been evaluated by objective study and has been found to be effective in a very positive way. J. J. Fisher made a study of catalog descriptions of course offerings in 117 colleges and universities "chosen by random sampling from 822 institutions listed in *Guide to Undergraduate Programs in Mathematics* as offering programs for preparing secondary school teachers." He found that during the years 1960-65 there was a significant increase in the amount of mathematics required in the preservice program for elementary teachers: from a mean of 1.97 semester hours in 1960 to 4.15 semester hours in 1965. This increase has been confined almost entirely to the study of the structure of number systems, with very little attention being given either to algebra or to geometry (337). The same survey revealed a significant increase in the preservice program for secondary school teachers of mathematics "in

CUPM-type mathematics, abstract algebra, geometry, and probability-statistics." It was clearly evident, however, that there was a long distance yet to be traveled before complete implementation of CUPM level III mathematics would be accomplished (338).

Fisher's findings are in agreement with those revealed by a CUPM survey conducted at approximately the same time. Each of 911 colleges known to be engaged in teacher education was asked to indicate the number of semester hours in mathematics (exclusive of courses in methods) that were required of elementary education majors for graduation. From 887 replies it was found that, as of January 1966, the percentage of colleges requiring no mathematics had dropped to 8.1 from the value 22.7 found in a similar survey in 1962. Also, in the same period, the percentage of colleges requiring five or more semester hours of mathematics of elementary majors had increased from 32.8 to 50.1 (30).

Colleges responding to the questionnaire cited in chapter 15 were almost unanimous in stating that since 1960 there had been significant changes in their teacher-training programs and that such changes had been influenced largely by the CUPM recommendations. These changes were reflected partially in the increase in mathematics courses required of elementary teachers as well as of secondary teachers and in the number of courses offered. The term "progress" used in replies to the questionnaire was ambiguous, and the failure of some replies to differentiate changes in the elementary and secondary programs

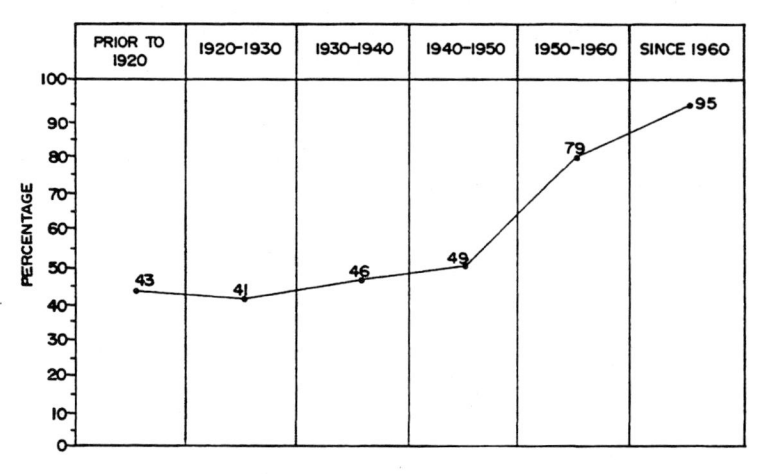

Fig. 16.1. Percentage of responding institutions that reported progress in any phase of their mathematics teacher education program.

THE MODERN ERA: 1945–PRESENT 343

forced the addition of an awkward "unspecified" category to the analysis. In spite of this, the three charts on these pages give an interesting view of changes in mathematics education since 1920. (See figs. 16.1–3.)

The questionnaires also included reports of several new graduate degrees for secondary teachers, some of which were sponsored cooperatively by departments of mathematics and education, also of bachelor's and master's degrees, with a strong content minor in mathe-

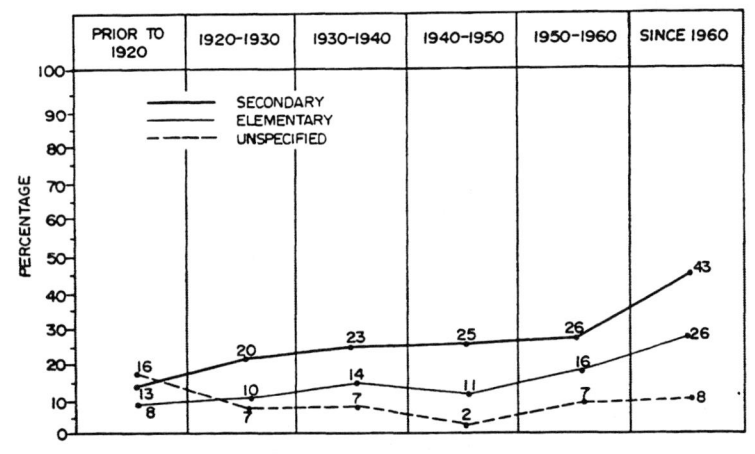

Fig. 16.2. Percentage of responding institutions that reported progress in mathematics courses.

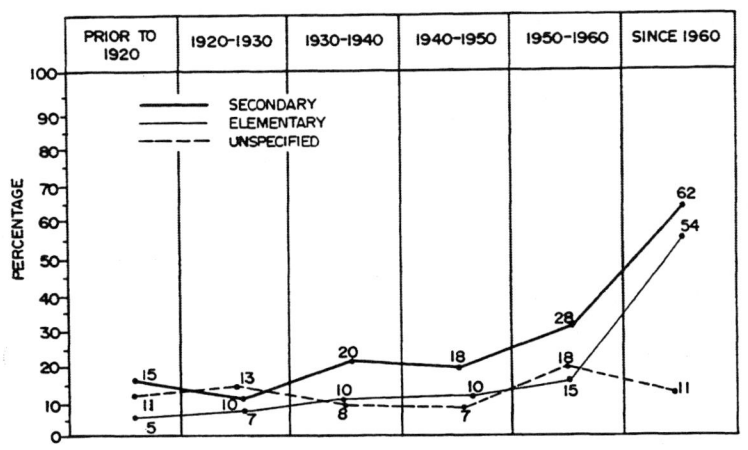

Fig. 16.3. Percentage of responding institutions that reported progress in methods courses in mathematics.

matics, promoted by departments or schools of education. In a few cases programs specifically designed for preservice or in-service training of junior high school teachers were described. Some institutions reported teaching options to the master's degree under the direction of the mathematics department. One such program with distinct professional emphasis states that the content "is of graduate level and emphasizes rigorous development of concepts selected for their relevance to candidates planning educational careers." Other professional features of this program are an interpretive course in the history of mathematics, a course in which the study of carefully selected mathematical models is pursued, a seminar on problem solving, and a credit plan in which each student will pursue individual study of a problem in either a mathematical or an educational context. Furthermore, there is provision for six units of elective work that may be in mathematics or related professional studies.

The responses also indicated that the content requirements for teachers of arithmetic were being increased, with several schools reporting a two-course requirement supplemented by a methods course with increased credit. At least two schools reported an academic minor of eighteen units required by schools of education for elementary majors, with mathematics as one of the suggested minor areas. Two institutions reported a four-course requirement modeled after the CUPM level I recommendations. All content curricula for elementary teachers, and many for secondary teachers, claimed the CUPM model for their selection and organization of materials. Almost every response indicated a decided increase in the ratio of content to professional courses, with the increase favoring mathematics. Similar reports were being made concerning the various state requirements for certification at both the elementary level and the secondary level. There was also an increasing tendency to include in the teacher-education program requirements some form of computer mathematics as well as experimentation in the use of various types of instructional media such as closed-circuit television, films, filmstrips, and programmed materials. The content of instruction was reflecting the revised demands of the modern era of mathematics on the elementary and secondary curriculum. There was more emphasis on set concepts and language; structure of number systems, of algebra, and of geometry; non-Euclidean geometry and a clearer concept of measurement; linear algebra; and probability and statistics. In a few instances new independent departments of mathematics education had been or were being established for the purpose of promoting both undergraduate and graduate programs of teacher training. More and more emphasis was being placed on the fifth year, which in most cases was designed for the major portion of the professional part of the program. Also, there was rapidly developing a strong trend toward required internship as an important component of the teacher-education program.

A survey conducted by the Organization for European Economic Cooperation, later known as the Organization for Economic Cooperation and Development (OECD), revealed the following information concerning the status of teacher education in the United States at the time of the report, which was published in 1961 (204, pp. 155–62):

1. For the prospective elementary teacher entrance to a four-year training college requires graduation from the high school with one year of mathematics study. Usually only one course in arithmetic is required in college. About half the colleges have a special methods course in teaching arithmetic.
2. For permanent certification to teach in secondary schools the requirements are graduation from a four-year university with 24 semester hours in mathematics and 18 to 28 semester hours in education, including 90 clock hours in practice teaching.

No additional in-service training is required. Some states, however, do have such a requirement for salary increases. Opportunities for in-service programs are provided by colleges and universities with financial support from industry and the National Science Foundation. Universities also offer consultant service and provide extension courses as community projects.

6. *What of the future?*

In the summer of 1963, under the joint sponsorship of Educational Services Incorporated and the NSF, a group of mathematicians gathered in Cambridge, Massachusetts, for the expressed purpose of considering the current and future state of mathematics in the elementary and secondary schools of the United States. The report of the Cambridge conference, published later in the year under the title *Goals for School Mathematics* (11) and commonly referred to as the "Cambridge Report," has provoked a great deal of professional debate and discussion. In the introductory statement of the report the group made it clear that the report was to be "a discussion document, and not a prescription"; and that, due to the purpose for which the conference was called, the report would ignore "the whole problem of teacher training, and proceed on the assumption that if a teachable program were developed, teachers would be trained to handle it." The proposals made in the report were designed "for the mathematics curricula of two or three decades hence, from kindergarten through grade 12."

After the publication of the report, the steering committee of the conference called another group to Cambridge in 1965. This group designed experimental units in line with the report and proposed still a third conference for the purpose of studying the problems of preparation of teachers to implement the proposed programs. This third conference, the Cambridge Conference on Teacher Training, was convened during the summer of 1966. Its report (10), published in 1967, followed somewhat the same pattern as that of the previous Cambridge conference. No claim was made for prescription but, rather, the expressed desire was that it "should be regarded only as a tentative and, hopefully, thought-provoking document." The conference made two proposals, each a two-year sequence of courses, for the training of elementary teachers to deal with the proposals of the *Goals* report for the K–6 mathematics curriculum. As a prefatory remark in introducing the proposals, attention was called to the fact that they are "aimed (hopefully) at a time when the CUPM recommendations will have been strongly implemented." In essence, the outline of the two proposals is as follows (10, pp. 15–24):

Proposal I
  Course A (one year)
    Analytic geometry (lines and their properties, circles, triangles, inequalities, convexity)
    Matrices and their operations (up to 3×3)
    Group properties of matrix multiplication (emphasis on 2×2)
    Systems of linear equations
    Study of certain linear transformations of the plane, using matrices (enlargements, translations, reflections)
    Sensed angles, sine and cosine, measurement of angles
    Composition of transformations and the associated matrix multiplication
    Transformations of equations, with application to the development of ellipses and their equation from the distortions of circles
    Elements of vectors (via Cartesian coordinates)
  Course B (one-half year)
    Functions (concept, examples, representation, operations with, inverses)
    Linear functions (graph and slope)
    Quadratic functions (examples and motivation, graphs, zeros)

THE MODERN ERA: 1945–PRESENT

  Quadratic formula
  Polynomial functions and polynomial algebra
  Integral domains
  Elementary number theory
Course C (one-half year)
  Systems of linear equations and optimization
  Intuitive calculus
  Probability and statistics
  Logic (if time permits)

Proposal II

(Under this proposal there are two alternates. In each case the number in parentheses indicates a rough approximation to the number of class hours.)

Alternate I

Course 1
  A. Number theory (16)
  B. Vectors in the line and plane (8)
  C. Transformations and functions (12)
Course 2
  A. The real number system (25)
  B. Counting problems and probability (22)
Course 3
  A. Intuitive differential calculus (22)
  B. Linear transformations and matrices (15)
Course 4
  A. Isometries and symmetry groups (15)
  B. Quadratic forms and conics (10)
  C. Intuitive integral calculus (15)

Alternate II

Course 1
  A. Circular functions and complex numbers (10)
  B. The real number system (16)
  C. Counting problems and induction (8); functions (6)
Course 2
  A. Vectors in line, plane, and space (20)
  B. Intuitive differential calculus (20)
Course 3
  A. Rings and unique factorization (20)
  B. Computational matrix theory and applications (20)

Course 4
  A. Intuitive integral calculus (15)
  B. Probability (15)
  C_1. Statistics (10)
  or
  C_2. Impossibility of angle trisection (10)

No proposals have, as yet, been made concerning a teacher-training program to prepare teachers to meet the instructional responsibilities of the 7–12 program proposed in the *Goals* report. It is not difficult to project from the quality of the present report the high quality of mathematical content that will characterize the proposals for the preparation of secondary teachers. Whether or not one agrees with the content of these reports, it must be admitted that they provoke intelligent discussion and debate.

Whatever may be the future recommendations for teacher training in mathematics, whether they result from the Cambridge Conference reports or from other responsible and informed sources, it seems safe to predict that they may be evaluated scientifically if they are subjected to the guidelines proposed jointly by the National Association of State Directors of Teacher Education and Certification and the AAAS. These guidelines were published in the form of two pamphlets under the auspices of the two cooperating organizations. *Guidelines for Science and Mathematics in the Preparation Program of Elementary School Teachers* gives the guidelines as follows (56, pp. viii–ix):

> Guideline 1. The faculty of each institution should design its program for the preparation of the elementary teacher after careful analysis of the role of (1) the elementary school in American society, (2) the elementary school teacher, and (3) the institutions preparing teachers.
>
> Guideline 2. The program of preparation for the elementary school teacher should include a broad general education with attention to human growth, learning, and behavior.
>
> Guideline 3. Instruction in science and mathematics should be conducted in ways that will develop in teachers an understanding of processes and in scientific inquiry and mathematical thinking.
>
> Guideline 4. The program of preparation for the elementary school teacher should include breadth of preparation in the sciences and in mathematics most appropriate as background for the elementary school program, with emphasis on concept development and interdisciplinary treatment.

Guideline 5. The program of preparation for the elementary school teacher should include study of the aims and methods of teaching science and mathematics in the elementary school.

Guideline 6. Professional laboratory experiences, including observation and student teaching, should provide opportunities for the prospective teacher to work with experienced elementary school teachers who are competent in the subject area, skilled in nurturing the spirit of inquiry, and effective in helping children benefit from the study of science and mathematics.

Guideline 7. The program for the preparation of the elementary school teacher should provide opportunities for pursuit of additional undergraduate study in a carefully planned program in science and mathematics.

Guideline 8. Fifth-year and sixth-year programs for the elementary school teacher should offer appropriate science courses and mathematics courses which might be applied toward an advanced degree.

Guideline 9. In-service education should provide opportunities for the elementary school teacher continuously to improve and extend the competencies required for effective teaching of science and mathematics.

Guidelines for Preparation Programs of Teachers of Secondary School Science and Mathematics gives proposals as follows (55, pp. 5–6):

Guideline 1. The program should include a thorough, college-level study of the aspects of the subject that are included in the high school curriculum.

Guideline 2. The program should take into account the sequential nature of the subject to be taught, and in particular should provide the prospective teacher with an understanding of the aspects of the subject which his students will meet in subsequent courses.

Guideline 3. The program should include a major in the subject to be taught, with courses chosen for their relevance to the high school curriculum.

Guideline 4. The major should include sufficient preparation for the later pursuit of graduate work in one of the sciences or in mathematics.

Guideline 5. A fifth-year program should include work in areas related to the subject to be taught.

Guideline 6. The program should include preparation in the methods especially appropriate to the subject to be taught.

Guideline 7. The program should include work in areas related to the subject to be taught.

Guideline 8. The program should take into account the recommendations for curriculum improvement currently being made by various national groups.

Each distinct era of mathematics education has been characterized by its individual problems of curriculum content, instructional patterns, and teacher preparation. As in the past, curriculum and instructional problems will continue to be shaped by two distinct but not independent influences: an intrinsic influence arising from the evolution of mathematical knowledge and an extrinsic influence arising from the demands of a changing environment. The problem of teacher education will continue to be current as critical educational issues are debated, as professional and societal forces continue to motivate and to mold informed effort, and as educators attempt to shape teacher education programs to meet the demands of the present and the challenges of the future.

*School Mathematics
in Canada*

PART FIVE

*Douglas J. Potvin
Douglas H. Crawford
Solberg E. Sigurdson*

CHAPTER SEVENTEEN

Mathematics Education in French-speaking Canada

Douglas J. Potvin

1. *Two cultures*

The educational structure in Quebec is different from that of any other province or state in North America. In order to appreciate the development and the present state of the teaching of mathematics in French Canada, it is necessary to comprehend the significance of the educational structure. Not many people outside of the Province of Quebec understand the educational organization. Therefore, a review of some of the more significant historical events in education and in the cultural development of two different types of people—the French-speaking majority and the English-speaking minority—is essential to an understanding of the two philosophies of the teaching of mathematics in French Canada. Much of the meaning would be lost if attention were paid only to a succession of events as they occurred in a sequence of time. It will be far more meaningful to consider a succession of ideas that impart a meaning and form the basis for all succeeding educational reform.

In the Province of Quebec there are two distinct systems of education which operate under a common law. One system is for Roman Catholics, who constitute approximately 87 percent of the population, and the other system is for Protestants and other non–Roman Catholics. W. P. Percival, in his book *Across the Years*, says (92*, p. 1):

> The story of the development of Education in Quebec is fascinating because it contains the record of the struggle of two cultures for freedom to expand and hand down their own traditions to succeeding generations. The solution reached after almost a century of deep and continued thought following the cession of New France contains the elements of genius. That the solution is effective and satisfactory is a tribute to the goodwill of the government and the inhabitants of the Province who avail themselves of the two systems that have been worked out within a common framework of legislation.

An outline of the historical evolution in Quebec is essential to an understanding of the three mathematics curricula that have existed for so long in the Province. Although it is true that in most parts of North America early education was introduced by missionaries, there are very few other areas in which the religious influence has been maintained to the extent that it has in Quebec—among the French Catholics, the English Catholics, and the English Protestants, all under one public system of education and all with individual curricula.

2. *The historical development*

Samuel de Champlain arrived in Quebec in 1608. The first attempts to initiate an educational program were provided to meet the needs of some of the early French explorers and to begin a program of conversion of the Indians.

On 24 April 1615 Fathers Denis Jamay, Jean Dolbeau, and Joseph LeCaron and Brother Pacifique Duplessis landed at Tadoussac. Duplessis appears to have been the first teacher in New France, although some claims are made for the Jesuit fathers Biard and Massé.

The Récollets built the first monastery in Canada near the St. Charles River. When the Récollets were unable to meet all of the demands of the colonists, they invited the Jesuits to help them. The first classical college was opened by the Jesuits in 1635, and humanities, mathematics, and hydrography were taught.

---

* The references in Part Five are to Bibliography B.

In 1639 the education of girls was begun through the founding in Quebec of the Ursuline Convent by Mme. Marie Madeleine de Le Peltrie. The first superior was the Venerable Marie de L'Incarnation. These pioneers in education were followed by Sister Marguerite Bourgeois, who came to Ville Marie (the original name for Montreal) to found the Congregation of Notre Dame. The Grand Séminaire de Quebec was founded by Monseigneur de Laval in 1663, and two centuries later this institution became Laval University.

Though no regular system of education was organized throughout New France during the French régime, a good deal of education was carried on privately. Following the British conquest an effort was made to furnish education for English-speaking children. Teachers were very scarce, and salaries were low. The Reverend John Stuart, who opened an academy in 1781, wrote the following message to Governor Haldimand about his assistant:

> I could have dispensed with his ignorance of the English language and faulty accent, but when I found him unacquainted with the rules of common arithmetic and often obliged to apply to me (in the presence of the pupils) for the solution of the most simple question, I could no longer doubt of his inefficiency.

Just prior to 1790, there were two schools in the Province which received government grants. Private schools were established, and tuition fees were charged. Some of the monthly charges were: Latin, half a guinea; English and arithmetic, two pounds.

In 1801, a law was passed entitled "An Act for the establishment of free schools and the advancement of learning in the Province." The act made provision for the creation of the Royal Institution for the Advancement of Learning. The act provided for the establishment of free schools in a parish or township. The engagement of the teachers was the responsibility of the governor, lieutenant governor, or administration. The teachers would determine the medium of instruction. Teachers from England were recommended, and it was made clear that the language of instruction was to be English. As a result, an attempt was made to anglicize the French-speaking students.

Led by Monseigneur Plessis, the bishop of Quebec, the Roman Catholics became openly rebellious because they knew that their language and religion would suffer if the Royal Institution were allowed to flourish. The English-speaking people of the Province, who were predominantly of the Protestant faith, were also apathetic to the situation. The Reverend Mr. Mills, secretary of the Royal Institution, recognized the folly of trying to force the French Canadians to attend English-language schools. He suggested that a similar institution be established for them.

The years 1824-46 were years of educational experiment. In 1824 the conditions of the previous legislation were repeated and the Fabrique Act was passed. The Fabrique Act initiated the first move toward democratic education in Quebec. The Fabrique Act appealed to the French-speaking population. It provided that each "fabrique," or church council, was authorized to acquire land and property for school purposes. The system was a voluntary one, and no outside interference was to be tolerated. This meant that each fabrique was empowered to employ its own teachers and form its own course of studies.

In 1829 the Act for the Encouragement of Elementary Education was passed. Subsidies were granted by the government to schools that were visited by government-appointed inspectors and met specified standards. As a result, political influence in education reached an intolerable level.

The report of the Standing Committee on Education and Schools in 1831 revealed that about 25 percent of the child population was attending school. In 1837 the Christian Brothers came from France to establish elementary schools, and their activities in education in Quebec have influenced both French-speaking and English-speaking students to the present day.

Education at this time was far different from what it is today. Motivation, which is now considered an essential of sound pedagogy, consisted only of securing effort by threats and punishment. The teachers of the day were men and women of varied accomplishment. Although some were highly cultured people, others were lazy or incompetent or became teachers only because they were physically unfit to work on the land.

In 1838 Lord Durham came from England as Governor General and made a report on conditions following the Rebellion of 1837. This report has been challenged by historians who claim that Durham did not carry out a sufficiently complete investigation.

As a result of Durham's report, the Education Act of 1841 was passed. Some of the main provisions of the legislation were—

Appointment of a superintendent of education
Granting of authority to municipal corporations to be boards of

education that might levy taxes for the construction and maintenance of schools

Authorisation allowing the minority to dissent

In 1846 all previous acts were repealed. New legislation (the Education Act of 1846) gave the people, the clergy, and the government a more equitable control over the public schools. Most of the subsequent legislation in education in the Province of Quebec has been based upon this act.

Each municipality was to establish one or more common schools, and these were to be managed by school commissioners who were to be completely independent of municipal authorities.

School boards engaged teachers, regulated the course of study, levied taxes, and generally managed the schools. It was also enacted that, on a simple declaration of dissidence, Protestants would not be subject to the authority of the school commissioners. They were entitled to establish corporations of trustees and empowered to manage their schools and appoint teachers of their own faith. Other provisions of the legislation allowed the use of only those textbooks that were recommended by the Board of Examiners.

In 1857 the Jacques Cartier and the McGill normal schools were founded in Montreal and the Laval Normal School was opened in the city of Quebec. With the opening of these teacher-training colleges, the first attempt was made to establish teaching as a profession practiced by skilled people. To the present day, McGill is the only English university in the province which has a faculty of education to provide for the training of teachers for the Protestant elementary and secondary schools. There are a number of normal schools and teachers colleges that prepare Catholic teachers for the elementary and secondary levels. All of these schools are under the jurisdiction of the department of education. Licences or teaching diplomas are granted only through the department of education.

In 1859 the Council of Education was established, and in 1875 Roman Catholics and Protestants were given the freedom to govern their own schools.

Part of the legislation reads as follows:

> Everything which, within the scope of the functions of the Council of Public Instruction respects especially the schools, and public instruction generally, of Roman Catholics shall be within the exclusive jurisdiction of the Roman Catholic Committee of such Council. In

the same manner, everything which, within the scope of such functions respects especially the schools and public instruction generally of Protestants, shall be within the exclusive jurisdiction of the Protestant Committee.

With the passage of this legislation the Quebec educational system came under the supervision of the Superior Council of Public Instruction, with two subcommittees, one Catholic and one Protestant. Each subcommittee had control over its own schools including programmes and textbooks.

As a consequence of the foregoing educational evolution, there developed the unique situation in Quebec in which there were approximately fifteen hundred Roman Catholic school boards and about fifty Protestant school boards. All Roman Catholic school boards in the Province are French, but many of them have a separate English curriculum.

It may be interesting at this point to consider part of the programme for the elementary schools under the Protestant Committee in 1883.

Grade 1, Mental arithmetic. Counting, addition and subtraction of numbers with three digits, reading and writing numbers to 1,000, multiplication table to 6×9

Grade 2, Mental arithmetic. Arithmetic—4 simple rules to long division, multiplication table, avoirdupois weight, long and liquid measure

Grade 3, Mental arithmetic. Long division, compound rules, simple examples in fractions, dry measure, square and cubic measures

Grade 4, Mental arithmetic. Fractions, decimals, elementary interest, and percentage

3. *The classical colleges*

Apart from the public schools, there were approximately one hundred classical colleges that were not subject to the supervision of the Council of Education or the government.

The French classical colleges exerted the greatest influence upon the formation of French-speaking students. Until 1920, the only French-speaking schools under the Council of Education were the elementary schools. All post-elementary education was conducted by the classical colleges and the seminaries.

The classical colleges were, from the first, intensely literary and classical. Belles lettres was considered an elegant and beneficial discipline, training students to think and helping them to give adequate expression to their ideas. French Canada has recently heard several expressions of alarm concerning its shortcomings in the teaching of mathematics and science. Today there are approximately fifteen thousand engineers in the Province of Quebec, of whom about four thousand were trained in the French-speaking universities. On a per capita basis, in comparison to the North American population, there should be approximately thirty thousand French-speaking engineers. It has also been claimed in the *Report of the Royal Commission of Inquiry on Education*, volume 3, published in 1965, that

> students entering the university are often incapable of independent thought. They shrink from applying the simplest of reasoning processes and avoid discussion of the validity of results obtained through calculation or from measurement. Such an attitude is opposed to the most elementary principles of scientific philosophy. . . . The role of the scientist consists precisely in checking the area of validity of scientific laws, in improving them and in discovering new ones. He cannot succeed in this without having both a critical and creative attitude.

In recent years, the Université de Montréal and Laval University have made an earnest attempt to interest French Canadians in commercial, economic, and technical subjects. Prior to this change, the universities were conceived as being the means of preserving the best traditions of the past rather than being a laboratory for new ideas. The emphasis on training in the classics, philosophy, and metaphysics served to differentiate the graduates of French-Canadian schools from those of the English schools.

Both the classical colleges and the secondary schools in French Canada were subject to clerical dominance. The teachers were largely members of religious orders, and there was a distinct preference for the traditional classical curriculum that led to the favorite French-Canadian careers of medicine, law, and the church.

4. *Mathematics in New France*

François de Dainville completed a study of the history of mathematics in the Jesuit colleges of France during the sixteenth and seventeenth centuries, and the result of his findings has shed a new light on the teaching of mathematics in Canada. Two books used by the Jesuits in the seventeenth century in Canada were *L'Arithmétique ou l'art de compter toutes sortes de nombres avec la plume et les jettons*, by Father Jean François—the fourth edition, published in Rennes in 1661—and *Trigonométrie canonique* by Jean-Baptiste Morin, published in Paris in 1633. These two books were for a long time in the possession of the Congregation of Notre Dame and were sent to Collège Charles-Garnier at the time of the fourth centennial celebration of the Society of Jesus—the Jesuits.

Most of the early manuscripts are catalogued in the Saint-Sulpice library. At the present time, many of the early texts and manuscripts belong to the government of the Province of Quebec.

Father Houdet, a Sulpician, arrived in Canada in 1796 and taught at the Collège de Montréal until 1830. His manuscripts contain 100 pages of algebra, 110 pages of geometry and trigonometry, and 221 problems.

The first theses were written by students at the University of Quebec in 1775. They were listed as shown below:

> *Thèses de Mathématique qui seront soutenues au Séminaire de Québec vendredi, 26 mai, depuis neuf heures jusqu'à midi par M. M. Bernard, Claude Panet, Charles Perrault, Charles Chauvaux, étudiants en Physique sous Mr. Thomas Bédard, Diacre, Professeur de Philosophie à Québec, chez Guillaume Brown, derrière l'Eglise Cathédrale M,DCC,LXXV.*

Subtitles showed that the theses dealt with arithmetic; algebra; proportion; problems with one unknown, two unknowns, three unknowns, or four unknowns; increasing geometric progressions, decreasing geometric progressions; direct discount; inverse discount; geometry; lines, angles, and triangles; surfaces and proportional lines; solids; practical geometry; trigonometry.

The catalogue of the Gagnon collection contains the front page of the nine-page syllabus indicated as the first schoolbook printed in Quebec. In reality this was not a text but only the programme of the oral examination held in public by the students Panet, Perrault, and Chauvaux.

At the end of the eighteenth century there appeared a second collection of theses on physics and mathematics listed as shown:

> *Thèses de Mathématiques et de Physique qui seront soutenues au Séminaire de Québec, mardi, 5 octobre, depuis 9 heures du matin jusqu'à 3 heures après-midi, par MM. Michel Brunel, Jérôme Raisenne,*

Augustin Chaboillez, Denys Denechau, Louis Bédard, Eustache Dumont, Etudiants en Physique, sous Mr. Edmund Burke, prêtre, professeur de Philosophie, chez C. Neilson, Rue de la Montagne (Québec) (vers 1790).

This ten-page syllabus begins with a few geometric and algebraic propositions. The subsequent propositions deal with rectilinear and spherical trigonometry, conical sections, parabolas, mechanics, statics, hydrostatics, hydraulics, optics, and astronomy. In all, 112 propositions had to be demonstrated by the six students undergoing the public examination.

Edmund Burke, an Irish father, exerted a profound influence and brought new blood through his teachings at the Séminaire de Québec. This influence was not only felt at the Séminaire but was transmitted to Laval University. The program indicated by the theses presented under him shows an improvement over the program of 1775 and resembles the program of 1841.

The first work printed in Quebec—probably the first in Canada—as a manual used by the students (prior to this, only the teacher had a text) is titled as shown below.

Traité d'Arithmétique pour l'usage des Ecoles par Jean Antoine Bouthillier. A Québec, chez Jean Neilson, Imprimeur, Libraire, Rue de la Montagne, No. 3, 1809, 144 pages.

In the preface, the author writes:

> The necessity of a Text of Arithmetic for use in French schools has spurred the author to undertake this work. The scarcity of this type of book in this country has until now obliged teachers to have the students copy the lengthy principles and rules of arithmetic in their copy books.
>
> This resulted in a considerable waste of time; this small book will remedy that inconvenience.

For a long time this, or one of its later editions, was the only manual used in Quebec.

In 1816 Michel Bibaud published a manual entitled

L'Arithmétique en quatre parties savoir: l'arithmétique vulgaire, l'arithmétique marchande, l'arithmétique scientifique, l'arithmétique curieuse, suivie d'un précis sur la tenue des livres de comptes par M. Bibaud. Imprimé pour l'auteur par Nahum Mower, Montréal, 1816, 200 pages.

In the preface the author notes that his book is designed for those people who wish to learn mathematics by themselves. Although written in the same lines as Bouthillier's manual, Bibaud's is more complete and much more general.

In 1832 Bibaud published a second manual, and to these two popular manuals were soon added those of Casimir Ladreyt and Joseph Laurin in 1836. In contrast to that of Ladreyt, which was full of clear definitions, Laurin's work appears quite dry and contains mostly tables, problems, and rare examples.

Arriving in Canada in 1837, the following year, the Frères des Écoles Chrétiennes published *Nouveau traité d'arithmétique à l'usage des Écoles Chrétiennes des Frères, chez C. P. Leprohon, Montréal, 1838, 140 pages*. This manual was purposely made for Canadian use; it contains tables for converting shillings into francs and English measures into French, and numerous problems utilizing the pound and shilling.

The first work done in English was

> *Adam's New Arithmetic suited to Halifax currency in which the principles of operating by numbers are analytically explained and synthetically applied, thus combining the advantages to be derived both from the inductive and synthetic mode for instruction, etc. Designed for the use of schools and academies in the British Provinces. By Daniel Adams, M.D. Stanstead, L.C. Published by Walton & Gaylord, 1833, 258 pages.*

The author was an American from Mount Vernon, New Hampshire, who was very well informed and knew the inductive method introduced by Pestalozzi in Switzerland.

Another work in English which is worthy of note is *First Book of Arithmetic for the Use of Schools*, Dublin, "published by Direction of the Commissioners of National Education and Re-printed by express Permission at Montreal by Armour and Ramsay, 1847." This work is part of the collection of the National School books and was printed in Montreal because of the large number of Irish immigrants who came to Canada at the time. This was to be the last publication of elementary manuals, since the needs of the schools were satisfied by the work of the Frères des Écoles Chrétiennes, who through adaptations of French works almost totally discouraged competition from Canadian authors.

Subsequent publications dealt with special work designed for advanced students at the college level. An example is the work attributed to Isaac Le Sieur Désaulniers, who taught at the Seminary of Nicolet,

> *Nouveau Traité abrégé de la Sphère d'après le système de Copernic, par demandes et par réponses. Nouvelle édition à l'Usage du Séminaire de Nicolet, Trois-Rivières, chez Ludger Duvernay. Imprimeur, Libraire et Relieur. 1824, 24 pages.*

An inventory of the collection also includes books on mensuration, interest, solution of triangles, and logarithms published in English, although by French authors, since the English clientele was larger than the French.

Another most interesting publication of the collection is

> *Traité élémentaire de calcul différentiel et de calcul intégral Québec, Imprimerie d'Aug. Côté et Cie. 1848, 118 pages et une planche horstexte, gravée par T. Ireland, Montreal.*

The author of this treatise, the first to be published in Canada, is Father Jean-Pierre François Laforce-Langevin, who taught mathematics at the Séminaire de Québec. The work is excellent, and the author (who knows and cites Lagrange) utilizes Leibnitz's notation.

Although there were a few later works dealing with trigonometry and stereometry, 1850 marked the end of the Golden Age of the teaching of mathematics in Quebec. Several reasons may be given for the almost total eclipse in the publication and teaching of mathematics in Quebec after 1850. Two of them are that the difficult situation faced by mathematicians in finding jobs in Quebec forced many to find employment in the United States and, secondly, the growing belief that the French Canadians were better endowed for philosophy, literature, and the arts in general left the sciences and commercial field almost totally in the hands of the English Canadians.

As a consequence, not only mathematics, but also the other sciences (biology, chemistry, and physics) suffered an eclipse. Only a few amateurs kept alive the tradition that lost itself in the classical colleges and in the universities of French Canada.

The year 1960 marked a reform in the evolution of French-Canadian schooling, especially with respect to the sciences. Before that period, the curriculum and texts used in the collèges classiques were mainly determined by each institution as it saw fit.

Before the year 1930 the only texts available were those imported from France or those compiled from notes given in lectures by some outstanding professor. This held true in the fields of physics, chemistry, and especially mathematics.

After 1930, in the field of mathematics all branches were taught from several texts compiled by the Fédération de l'Instruction Chrétienne (F.I.C.) under the Fédération des Écoles Chrétiennes (F.E.C.). The texts were contained in a volume called *Manuel des Écoles Chrétiennes*. Some of the texts, which were used as late as 1962/63, were F.I.C. *Géométrie Analytique* (Laprairie) and F.E.C. *Cours d'Algèbre Elémentaire* No. 264.

L'Abbé Robert distinguished himself with numerous publications such as *Complements d'Algèbre*, dating back to 1945 and still in use today. Other recent publications include:

> LaRue and Risi, *Mathématiques Intermédiare* (Les Presses de l'Université Laval (P.U.L.) 1962/63)
> Garand, *Cours d'Algèbre* (Beauchemin 1962/63)
> LaRue, *Mathématiques Générales* (P.U.L. 1962/63)
> LaRue, *Trigonométrie rectiligne* (P.U.L. 1962/63)

In recent years, in addition to these, English and American texts have largely been used at the suggestion of la faculté des arts of the affiliated university. The scope of secondary and collegiate studies underwent a change in perspective after the reform, especially with respect to mathematics. As quoted in the introduction to the mathematics curriculum of the Cours Collégial Classique, Faculté des Arts, Université de Montréal:

> The aim of classical studies is to give the students the culture which will permit them to be at ease, both in the fields of Science and Arts and to furnish them with the basis which will enable them to learn, as the need arises, that which they might not have learned while pursuing their formal studies.
>
> To achieve this, and while eliminating the over-burdening of the Programmes, it is necessary to consider only the essential of the fundamental disciplines.
>
> In Mathematics, we must condition the learning process to mathematical reasoning and accustom it to its rigor. The objective will therefore never be to induce the student to develop automated calculations and use non-proven formulas.

5. *Mathematics in the English schools*

The English Catholic schools developed their own curriculum and used textbooks printed in either England or Ontario. As recently as 1963 such texts as *Intermediate Mathematics* (Copp and Clark) were used in grades 8 and 9, and *A New Algebra for High Schools* by Crawford, Dean, and Jackson was used in grades 10 and 11. The Algebra II course was covered by the text *Intermediate Algebra* by Tate, and *Elementary Trigonometry* by Hall and Knight was used. The program for the Protestant schools was somewhat similar in content, but *Progressive High School Algebra* by Hart was used in grades 9 to 11, and *A New Analytic Geometry* by Durrant et al. was used for analytical geometry. Students in the English schools—both Protestant and Catholic—were obliged to complete four years of algebra and at least two years of geometry to meet the requirements for college entrance. Provincial examinations were set by the Protestant Committee, and different examinations were set by the Catholic Committee. Each committee hired a set of teachers who marked examinations for students of all schools under their jurisdiction.

6. *New trends in mathematics education*

In 1961 the teaching of mathematics was greatly influenced by the changes that were taking place in the United States. The three affiliates of the National Council of Teachers of Mathematics—L'Association Mathématique de Québec, the Provincial Association of Mathematics Teachers, and the Association of Mathematics Teachers of the Province of Quebec—encouraged teachers in the province to adopt the new approach to the teaching of mathematics. It should be noted that the differences between the three groups of teachers and the differences in the curriculum and administration of the segments of education warranted the continuation of the three associations. It is also interesting to note that the 1967 Montreal meeting of the NCTM set a precedent in that some section meetings were conducted entirely in the French language.

The following is a description of the mathematics program as outlined in the *Report of the Royal Commission of Inquiry on Education in the Province of Quebec*, volume 3, 1965.

> At the present time arithmetic is taught in the Catholic and Protestant schools for seven years; the students receive three and one-half hours of instruction in their first two years, four and one-half hours in their third year, and five hours in the remaining four years. Fractions are introduced in the fourth year, and then in the following years the ideas of surface, volume, time, capacity weight as well as the reading of graphs and the elements of commercial arithmetic, cheques, bookkeeping, and banking.

Starting in 1960, some Catholic and Protestant schools began to use the Cuisenaire-Gattegno method. Some English schools tried methods suggested in the work of Maurice Hartung and Henry Van Engen, now known by the name "Seeing through Arithmetic" (STA); this method, which is used in the Alberta public schools, has now been introduced in the English Catholic schools. The seventh-year programme contains material that would be difficult for university-level students educated according to traditional methods.

In the French Catholic secondary schools, a student had five or six hours of mathematics in grades 8 and 9, depending on whether he was in the general or the scientific section; in grades 10 and 11 there were five hours a week in the science or science-letters options and seven hours a week in the science-mathematics option. Arithmetic and intuitive geometry were given in grade 8, algebra and plane geometry in grade 9. Algebra and plane geometry were given in the science-letters option and algebra, plane geometry, analytic geometry, and trigonometry in the science-mathematics option in grades 10 and 11. Commercial arithmetic, including accounting, was given in grades 10 and 11 of the commercial course (six hours in grade 10 and five hours in grade 11 for the boys, two and three hours of optional courses for future stenographers and office clerks). The course leading to advanced work contained three compulsory periods of mathematics a week and an extra course of three other periods.

In the English Catholic schools, algebra and geometry are begun only in grades 8 and 9; these subjects are continued in grades 10 and 11, but some students take an accelerated course at this stage and start intermediate algebra and intermediate trigonometry in grades 10 and 11. Since 1961 the new type of mathematics has been given in elementary English Catholic schools, and it has also been tested in grades 8 and 9.

The Quebec Protestant schools followed a rather traditional programme: two years were devoted to arithmetic, algebra, and geometry; trigonometry and graphs were sometimes added. Optional courses in algebra and geometry were offered in the two last years of high school, and the majority of pupils took these courses because the universities generally required two mathematics examinations for admission. In 1960 one-third of the students who finished high school took trigonometry, and about one-sixth took advanced algebra. The Canadian Mathematical Congress has suggested that mathematics be taught at two levels, one for the majority of students and the other for future university students. There were general complaints that too much time was spent on sums and problems to the detriment of an understanding of basic ideas, that there were too many theorems to memorise, and that there was no attempt to show the unity of the diverse branches of mathematics taught at school. McGill University has organised mathematics courses at the request of the Protestant School Board of Greater Montreal. Canadian and American television has been used for mathematical instruction since 1959. Students at the Institute of Education at McGill are urged to take courses in modern algebra and statistics. Teachers who have never taken special courses in this subject are, however, still teaching in the high schools. (56, pp. 277-95.)

⇢⇢⇢ 7. *Uniformity in the curriculum*

As a result of educational reform and through Bill 60, a "Ministry of Education" was formed and a "Minister of Education" took office. This was a radical change from the previous structure in that the minister of education was selected from elected members of Parliament. Hence he was responsible not only to the government and his party, but also to the electorate. The first minister of education was Paul Guerin-Lajoie, who assumed office in 1964. Under the minister of education there is a deputy minister for Catholic education and a deputy minister for Protestant education. Although the schools remain separate in administration, there is a strong tendency to implement a uniform curriculum in areas where this is possible. The Superior Council (consisting of twenty-four members chosen from educators, parents, and businessmen) acts as a consulting body to the minister. The Catholic Committee and the Protestant Committee are now subcommittees of the Superior Council.

In recent years textbooks published in the United States or Ontario have been used in the English schools. Some textbooks were translated into the French lanaguage and used in the elementary and secondary schools. Difficulties were found in translating many examples, and during the past few years great strides have been made by French-speaking authors in writing textbooks for their own schools. Some of these textbooks are now being used not only in the Province of Quebec, but also in the Province of New Brunswick.

Difficulties have always been encountered in equating the number of years of study to degrees obtained in the French institutions. English-speaking institutions required seven years of elementary school, four years of secondary school, and four additional years for a bachelor's degree. Students in the French institutions were separated into two distinct classes insofar as university entrance was concerned. Students from the public schools were admitted to university after the twelfth grade. Students from the collèges classiques were admitted after fifteen years of study. One of the major reforms in education in the province was the introduction of the Collèges d'Enseignement Général et Professionnel, often referred to as C.E.G.E.P. or Colleges for Professional and Vocational Training.

In 1968, thirty-two French-speaking C.E.G.E.P.'s were opened in the Province. These replaced the classical colleges. In 1969, the first English-speaking C.E.G.E.P. was opened, and McGill University, Sir George Williams University, Bishop's University, and Loyola College introduced a two-year C.E.G.E.P. parallel program. In the future, a uniform structure of education will be available to all students in the province. This structure will consist of

Elementary—Grades 1–6
Secondary—Grades 7–11
C.E.G.E.P.—2 years
University—3 years

Along with these changes, two significant developments have occurred in the area of mathematics education. In April 1969 the Association of Mathematics Teachers of the Province of Quebec and the Provincial Association of Mathematics Teachers amalgamated to form one affiliate of the NCTM. After so many years, the need for separate associations was no longer apparent. Also in April 1969 the Catholic Committee and the Protestant Committee of the Superior Council of Education approved a curriculum in mathematics for all students of secondary schools in the Province.

The new program was introduced in fifty classes in September 1967, and modifications were made for the courses starting in 1968. This program will be tried, revised, and implemented progressively.

The organisation of the programs consists of a streaming in which students are grouped according to ability. At the time of writing there are four basic streams, as follows:

1. *Mathematics—Slow Stream*. The programme is limited to a definition of the specific objectives pupils following this stream should attain, on the average, during the first four years of secondary education. It is for pupils who would not generally continue their studies beyond the secondary level, and its aim is to give them information adapted to their needs and interests.

2. *Algebra, Geometry, and Functions—Regular Stream*. The programmes in algebra and geometry list the specific objectives to be

attained, on the average, by pupils in the regular stream during the first four years of secondary school. The functions course follows the one in algebra and geometry. These three courses are designed primarily for students wishing to continue their studies beyond the secondary school. The admission requirements of the C.E.G.E.P.'s specify which of these three courses are required, depending on the programme selected for the higher level.

3. *Enriched Stream.* The programme for the enriched stream is not defined in this particular curriculum. Nevertheless, any eventual definition of the programme for this stream must include the regular stream programme. Local school authorities may use the optional topics foreseen in the courses of the regular stream to establish courses for the enriched stream.

4. *Optional Course in Secondary V.* The course entitled "Functions—Regular Stream" is the only one that has been defined for the Secondary V level. Any additional course that might be designed for pupils at this level is subject to the approval of the General Directorate of Elementary and Secondary Education.

In Secondary I and Secondary II, generally speaking, pupils should follow the same programme, defined locally and presented in three different forms corresponding to the slow, regular, and enriched streams. So conceived, the programme for these two years will facilitate the transferring of pupils from one stream to another.

Nevertheless, in order to minimise inconveniences caused by pupils' moving to a different school or different region, efforts must be made to ensure that every pupil, upon completion of Secondary II, has been introduced to (1) basic ideas concerning sets, (2) sets of numbers (natural, integers, positive rationals, and positive reals), (3) elementary constructions in geometry, and (4) the usual weights and measures.

In Secondary III and Secondary IV, the basic programmes designed locally for Secondary I and Secondary II will lead into the course "Mathematics—Slow Stream" or the regular stream or enriched courses.

The school boards might therefore allow their pupils to follow one of the following alternatives: (1) complete the course "Mathematics—Slow Stream" in Secondary III, in exceptional cases, or in Secondary IV, or (2) complete algebra (regular or enriched) and geometry (regular or enriched) in succession in Secondary III and IV or simultaneously in Secondary II; special conditions may even warrant one or both these courses to be completed only in Secondary V if this does not prevent students from taking the course normally designed for Secondary V.

8. *Forces and issues*

An attempt has been made to trace the evolution of mathematics education in French Canada and to indicate the legislation that led to the implementation of three distinct programmes of study. It has been a source of embarrassment to try to explain to people outside of the Province that there was an English Catholic mathematics programme, a French Catholic mathematics programme, and an English Protestant mathematics programme. This situation resulted from the fact that the French schools were dominated by religious orders, and the philosophy of education characterised by the classical colleges prevented the development of a rigourous program in mathematics and science. As a result of the educational philosophy of the French-speaking people, there is a dearth of technical and scientific personnel in the province. The introduction of the C.E.G.E.P.'s is an attempt to provide a different form of education in the hope that a greater emphasis will be placed upon technical and vocational training.

It must be stated (to the credit of the French majority in the province) that allowances were made for English Catholic curricula to be developed. Since 1875, Protestant school boards have been controlled by their own board of trustees and allowed to develop their own curriculum. The evolution of a common curriculum in mathematics is a very recent development. The introduction of the C.E.G.E.P.'s played an important role in bringing about this common curriculum. Teachers and school administrators of the Province of Quebec are looking forward with much enthusiasm to the eventual fulfillment of their efforts towards uniformity of curriculum and educational standards.

CHAPTER EIGHTEEN

School Mathematics in Ontario 1763–1894 From Settlement to System

Douglas H. Crawford

1. *Introduction*

Before 1763 there were few settlers in the part of Quebec province known then as Western Canada (now called Ontario). However, this part of Canada developed rapidly during the last decades of the eighteenth century. In 1784 over ten thousand citizens of the New England states emigrated there so that they might remain loyal to the British flag. These United Empire Loyalists, as they were called, settled around the north shore of Lake Ontario as far west as the Niagara peninsula and as far east as Kingston. In addition, many other settlers were attracted by the liberal land-grant policy of Lord Simcoe, the first governor appointed under the Constitutional Act of 1791, which divided Quebec into the two provinces of Upper and Lower Canada (now southern Ontario and southern Quebec, respectively).

Education in mathematics during the next century or so may be conveniently divided into periods: (1) The pioneer period (1790–1841), during which public education emerged in the form of common schools and academies, and some degree of uniformity in curriculum developed. (2) The period of the influence of the Reverend Egerton Ryerson (1841–76) followed. In 1844 Ryerson made a systematic study of education in twenty European countries. He then proceeded to revolutionise education by a series of school acts enforcing uniformity in regulations, training, teachers, books, equipment, buildings, and fees. When he ended his career as superintendent of education in 1876 he left behind not only a well-coordinated system from the public school to the university, but also the legacy of the free school so that every child was given the opportunity to receive an elementary school education. (3) The period from 1876–94 took much of its character from the influence of Dr. J. A. McLellan, a high school inspector and later principal of the Ontario School of Pedagogy, who believed strongly in the value of mathematics as an instrument in education and in the importance of sound methodology.

2. *The pioneer period: 1790–1841*

The first schools to appear in Upper Canada were private schools, agitated for by the more aristocratic and wealthy families eager to prepare their sons for their expected positions as leaders. They appeared in and around the main towns—York (Toronto), Kingston, and Newark (Niagara)—and were patterned after the corresponding private secondary schools of England. They provided both elementary and secondary instruction. In the early years arithmetic, bookkeeping, and practical mathematics were taught, as well as reading and writing, while the secondary curriculum consisted of classics and mathematics.

Due to the efforts of Lord Simcoe, the District Public School Act passed in 1807 provided that a public or grammar school be established in each of the eight districts of the province. However, these schools were not received with great enthusiasm by the majority of citizens, who clamoured for common schools. This dissatisfaction culminated in the founding of such schools via the Common Schools Act of 1816.

In the private schools of the early 1800s, arithmetic was studied by means of the ciphering book because of the scarcity of texts. This ciphering book was a workbook compiled by dictation from the teacher. Often the teacher himself did much of the writing. According to Campbell (161, p. 128), "A uniform method was followed, viz., a definition of the topic for study, rules of procedure, illustrative examples to show the application of the rules followed by exercises for pupil's work."

The Reverend Dr. Strachan, a Scot who was influential in education in the early 1800s (67, p. 25), published his famous *Arithmetic* in 1809. In it, he enumerated thirteen special features (mainly related to the rules of arithmetic) which he felt should make it more acceptable than any other contemporary text. Like most arithmetic texts then in use it was pure "rule arithmetic." However, Bonnycastle's *Arithmetic*, published in 1799, and the arithmetic texts of the American writers Colburn in 1821 and Daniel Adams in 1841 had an increasing influence toward the end of the period. These texts all attempted to introduce a measure of understanding into the learning of arithmetic.

The first attempt to regulate the scope of work covered in the schools was made in 1816 by the Reverend Dr. Strachan in his suggested course of study for the district grammar schools. The mathematical content for Years III–V (ages eleven to fifteen, approximately) was specified as:

Year III	Ages eleven to thirteen	Commence Algebra
Year IV	Ages thirteen to fifteen	Algebra continued Begin Euclid
Year V	Algebra, Euclid, Trigonometry and its application to heights and distances, Surveying, Navigation, Dialling, Elements of Astronomy.	

However, *no detail other than the names of the subjects was given.* This order of the subjects continued for many years.

In 1828 a further course of study was prepared by the General Board of Education. It covered Years I–V and ages seven onwards. It agreed in essence with the 1816 proposals for Years III–V but stated that arithmetic—mental arithmetic, initially—was to be studied in grades 1 and 2 (162, p. 13).

Further elaboration of the curriculum in mathematics took place in 1830 and 1839. In 1830 Upper Canada College, a more advanced type of grammar school, was opened in York. The importance ascribed to mathematics in its curriculum can be judged by the fact that classics and mathematics masters were paid the same salary (£300), although in Form IV there were seventeen hours of classics weekly as opposed to eight hours of mathematics! Arithmetic was taught in Forms I, II, and III and mathematics in Forms IV, V, and VI. The mathematics textbooks to be used in Forms III and IV in this college and other grammar schools were named in the 1839 report of the committee of the commissioners of education. They were Form III, Bonnycastle's *Arithmetic*, and Form IV, Bridge's *Algebra* and Blakelock's *Symbolical Euclid*.

Apparently the study included only the simplest topics in algebra and the first two books of Euclid (162, p. 16).

A seventh form, which subsequently was replaced by the first year of the provincial university, was also established; in it plane trigonometry, logarithms, and elementary conic sections were studied.

During this period, the influence of the Reverend Dr. Strachan is obvious. Some degree of uniformity was achieved by the beginnings of curricular and textbook specifications, but in many grammar schools teachers were weak, and most schools continued to be inefficient and unable to offer the curriculum adequately.

3. *The Ryerson regime: 1841–76*

According to Phillips (94, p. 224), "The period of expansion between 1841 and 1871 was a time of improvements in communications, of rapid growth by immigration, and of newly achieved democracy, provincial and municipal."

The 1830s and 1840s saw the development of a network of canals, so that by 1849 (after the expenditure of about 20 million dollars) vessels drawing 9 feet could move between Lake Huron and Montreal. The focus in transport shifted in the 1850s to the railways. By 1859 the Grand Trunk Railway had been built all the way to Levis, opposite the city of Quebec, from the foot of Lake Huron through Toronto and Montreal. However, financial difficulties due to mismanagement and the British depression of 1857 were experienced soon afterwards.

As for population, the economic distress and social unrest in Great Britain after the Napoleonic wars resulted in the emigration of hundreds of thousands to Canada during the period 1825–55. Population statistics show a growth in the number of residents in Ontario from 952,000 in 1851 to nearly 1,621,000 in 1871.

Equally significant was the movement toward democracy. The entrenchment of the ruling class, predominantly Anglicans, was challenged by the dissenters who formed a majority of the more recent immigrants. Men such as William Lyon Mackenzie "constantly attacked the relatively high governmental expenditures on a few schools which were useless to most of the people" (95, p. 36).

Uprisings that took place in both Upper and Lower Canada in 1837 led to the appointment of Earl Durham as governor general of Canada to investigate the state of the country. The two essential recommendations of his famous report of 1839 were that responsible government be freely conceded and that the "two Canadas" be reunited to allay the racial discord in Quebec. The Union Act of 1840 resulted, the salient feature being the transfer of political power to an assembly chosen on a very democratic basis. Although there were imperfections in the act, it allowed the party system to mature, and education received increasing attention politically.

It was against this background of change and development that Egerton Ryerson exercised his influence on education in Ontario. He made his famous tour of the United States, Great Britain, and continental Europe in 1844 and reported to the legislature in 1846. The report was a very comprehensive document in which he expressed his views on education. J. D. Campbell reports (161, p. 185):

> It was his desire to see education for all in Upper Canada suited to the needs of a new country. It should have a religious foundation with a broad curriculum to include the three R's together with subjects as music, art, history, civics, nature study, geography, agriculture, etc. He stated the books used in the schools were unsuitable and recommended uniform textbooks throughout the province with one text for each subject.

Ryerson strongly advised the adoption of the Irish National series of textbooks, claiming that "these books [had been] prepared by experienced teachers and with great care and [were] suitable and appropriate textbooks for Upper Canada" (p. 189).

The mathematical subjects included in the series were arithmetic, mensuration, and geometry.

The composition and extent of the mathematics studied in the Ryerson era can be ascertained to some degree by a consideration of the courses of studies, while the quality of the teaching is best illustrated by looking briefly at other developments in education initiated by Ryerson. Let us first examine the courses of study.

Although a new curriculum had been proposed in 1839, a course of study for use in grammar schools was not issued until 1841. The members of the Council of Public Instruction showed their degree of interest in this course by the fact that a quorum could not be mustered in four consecutive meetings during the period of its production!

The mathematical content appeared similar to that in previous use.

Arithmetic was to be the only subject of study in Forms I–III; algebra and geometry appeared in Forms IV–VI with arithmetic remaining till Form V, in which form mensuration also was taught. No details other than the specification of certain texts were included, and—suprisingly, in view of the earlier popularity of trigonometry—no specific mention was made of that subject.

Although no estimate of the time allotted to mathematics can be made, a simple count shows that eleven year-long courses out of a total of fifty-eight over the six forms dealt with mathematics (19 percent), while twenty-six of them were classical in nature (45 percent). Clearly, the main emphasis was now upon the classical subjects.

The continuation of arithmetic to Form V as compared with Form III in the 1839 curriculum seems to indicate a recognition of "the increasing social importance of numerical ability" (162, p. 25).

An event of considerable educational significance ushered in the next course of study some twelve years later. In 1853 the grammar schools (together with the common schools and the normal schools) came under the control of the Council of Public Instruction.

Perhaps a digression at this point is in order, to point out that the first normal school for the training of teachers in Ontario was opened in Toronto in 1847. More will be said of this later. Here it is enough to note that the students there "received more from the course given than academic and professional training. They were inspired with a love for teaching, with high ideals and with an urge for service in a high calling which was reflected in their teaching and the management of their school." (161, p. 196.)

The significance of this Act of 1853 was that "it established a realistic foundation for a new concept of secondary education as an extension of elementary education" (95, p. 40).

By this act the grammar schools came under the control of local trustees appointed by county councils instead of by the crown. These trustees were authorised to certificate and appoint the masters.

The new mathematical course of study of 1854—the first to be centrally controlled—shows some definite reference to content and its sequence of development. The general pattern is much as before, but with some variations. Arithmetic was taught in Forms I–III, being described as practical in Form II and commercial in Form III. Algebra now appeared in Form I and paralleled the study of arithmetic in Forms I–III, being developed as far as quadratic equations. Geometry began in Form III with the study of Euclid (Books I and II) and concluded (with Books III–VI) in Form IV, where it was taught along with algebra. Form V was devoted to plane trigonometry, mensuration, and a review of previous subjects.

Thus algebra was now studied earlier, concurrently with arithmetic, allowing more opportunity for integration of the two, while both arithmetic and geometry were reduced in time coverage, allowing the introduction of the "new" subjects of trigonometry and surveying in Form V.

A count of year-long courses reveals a relative emphasis of nearly two to one in favour of classical subjects (24 percent of the total) as opposed to mathematics (14 percent of the total). Both disciplines show decreased percentages, a change accounted for by the introduction of various new subjects such as composition.

In many cases one teacher provided the entire instruction in the school, and this after only a limited academic training in any given subject, as can be seen by reading the formidable array of subjects of instruction student masters were required to study—for some ten hours daily! (159, p. 29.) The actual efficiency of instruction must therefore be seen in this perspective.

Another development of economic significance which had its repercussion in the mathematics taught in the school was the adoption of a decimal currency in 1858. This marked the recognition of the geographical proximity of the United States and the growing importance of trade with it. Henceforth, all government accounts were kept in decimal currency.

Ryerson requested Herbert Sangster, mathematical master in the Toronto Normal School, to revise the *Irish National Arithmetic* accordingly. The result of this was a "practically new arithmetic" (161, p. 200). According to Campbell, this "treatise was a superior book and, along with the *National Arithmetic* by the same author, received liberal praise throughout the province in the public press" (p. 202).

Among the claims made for Sangster's new *Arithmetic* was that the pupil was required to think for himself. This same trend was evidenced in the first report of George Paxton Young in 1864, soon after his appointment as grammar school inspector. His report was more specific than those of his predecessors and asserted that the development of understanding should be an objective of the schools. Young's philosophy can be judged by the fact that during the next few years he tried, although unsuccessfully, to have teachers limit the amount of science content to be learned "in order to give pupils practice in observation and reasoning" (94, p. 489).

Young's report resulted in yet another education act in 1865; this divorced the grammar schools from the common schools and prevented "any further dissipation of the grammar school fund on giving instruction in what is properly common school work" (98, p. 79).

The act above provided two new courses of study—a classical course that continued the traditional curriculum for those intending to follow careers in law, medicine, and arts and a nonclassical course for intending surveyors, engineers, and other nonclassicists.

The classical course did not differ greatly from the previous one. Algebra was studied in Forms II–V, and it proceeded perhaps a little further. Geometry remained much as before, while trigonometry disappeared entirely, presumably because of its inclusion in the nonclassical curriculum. However, it had reappeared by 1870. More details of the content were given, together with a note on prescribed texts. Mathematical subjects represented 12 percent of the total number of year-long courses and classical subjects 29 percent, indicating a swing toward the classics. By 1870, this increased emphasis was quite noticeable. It was clearly due to the fact that the grant received by a school was based directly on the number of students of Latin and Greek.

This change was balanced by the fact that the nonclassical course was predominantly mathematical. This course covered two years only, comprising arithmetic, algebra, and geometry in the first year and algebra (including the conditional study of logarithms), geometry, and plane trigonometry (optional for nonengineering students) in the second.

Unfortunately the public reaction to this course was one of indifference, and in 1867 only seven boys in the province were in it. Young therefore recommended its removal. Here we seem to recognise the well-known modern stigma attached to the conflict of the "vocational" vis-à-vis the "academic."

Much had been achieved thus far during the Ryerson regime. A strong central authority had been established, opportunity had been given at the local level to raise money by taxation and to improve schools, and schedules of courses, texts, and teachers' qualifications had been drawn up. By 1871, however, school enrollment had increased twice as fast as population. This increase, coupled with the lack of mastery in mathematics of the masters and the "unreasonable load and diversity of work" thrown on them, resulted in a particularly low standing of the schools in mathematics.

In his inspector's report for 1871, Young recommended that an assistant be appointed to the one-teacher schools and that "more enthusiasm among the teachers of mathematics should be encouraged" (162, p. 21).

Many worthwhile and significant reforms ensued in the 1871 act, among them the setting up of a two-tier system of free schools (some schools did charge small fees until about 1900). The common schools became known as public schools, and the grammar schools as high schools and collegiate institutes. Other reforms included the appointment of county inspectors by county councils and the authorisation of the Council of Public Instruction to prepare "examination papers on which candidates for a teacher's certificate were to be examined . . . [and] a course of studies for public schools and for the training of teachers" (99, p. 22).

As in 1865, the act provided for two courses of instruction, an English course and a classical course. The mathematics included in both courses was practically identical. The course covered four years, not five as in the past. Arithmetic, algebra, and geometry were studied in all four years, mensuration in the first two, and trigonometry in the last two. The course content, though still somewhat vaguely defined, was more clearly indicated than before, both by way of topic prescription and by the naming of the authorised texts, noted below:

Advanced Arithmetic for Canadian Schools: Smith and McMurchy
Elements of Algebra: Todhunter or Sangster
Euclid's Elements of Geometry: Potts or Todhunter
National Mensuration
Elementary Arithmetic for Canadian Schools: Smith and McMurchy

The main changes seem to be the doubling (to four) of the number of subjects studied each year, the addition of mensuration, and the reintroduction of trigonometry with increased emphasis and coverage that included the study of astronomy and some elementary aspects of spherical trigonometry. This implied a very broadly trained and able master for satisfactory teaching of what must be considered an imposing programme.

However, it seems that the course of study was not translated into reality, as apparently it was too pretentious to be adequately handled by a two-master school. According to Gray (162, p. 39),

> Not only was it impossible for the teachers to provide instruction in all of the courses offered, but the pupils did not want to be subjected to all of the courses prescribed for them. The multiplicity of studies was leading to a mechanical and unintelligent style of teaching

and learning. Bishop Fraser in his report as Imperial Commissioner stated the difficulty to be a confusion of thought between the processes that convey knowledge and the processes that develop mental power. As a consequence the imposing but unworkable programme of 1871 collapsed as had its predecessors.

However, it should be noted that by 1878 there was an average of three masters to each of the 103 high schools, whereas in 1871 few of the total of 107 employed more than one master.

Ryerson died in 1876. His last years in office coincided with the introduction of "payments by results" in the form of an intermediate examination given at the end of the second high school year, "to determine the efficiency of the school and the grant it should receive" (94, p. 224).

Other written examinations were introduced for various purposes. Inspector Seath condemned those administered by bodies external to the school and went on to state that the examinations were destroying teaching, making it a "lost art."

One consequence of this was the decline in the emphasis on classics, with a resulting predominance of mathematics in the course of study.

To sum up: By the end of the period in question a free system of public education had been established, centralised in terms of curriculum, teacher training, and texts but locally taxed and administered. In mathematics, noticeable improvements in content and in teaching method had occurred, although these were far from being universal.

⋙⋙ 4. *McLellan and subsequent reaction: 1876–94*

J. A. McLellan was appointed a high school inspector in 1871 but exerted his greatest influence in the years following the introduction of the 1878 course of study. He was a firm believer in the value of mathematics as an instrument in education, and in 1879 he gave an able, learned, but largely unintelligible address on the subject as president of the Ontario Association of Teachers of Mathematics and Physics. He strongly denounced the introduction of new subjects such as art and bookkeeping into the curriculum, contending in his report for 1883, "The sooner we return to a judicious fixed course with comparatively few options, the better it will be for the cause of education in this province" (162, p. 42). His greatest contribution lay in improving methodology. Among several texts written by him were *Elements of Algebra*, published in 1886, and *The Psychology of Number*, pub-

EGERTON RYERSON
Founder of the Ontario Educational System
(From a painting by Theophile Hammel)

JAMES A. McLELLAN

lished in 1897, on which he collaborated with the great John Dewey.

The major development that dominated this period of education in Ontario was, as already indicated, the opening of secondary schools to more than the select few. (Incidentally, until 1871 only boys were admitted!) "Payment by results" and the introduction of written examinations controlling entry to various levels, together with the nonclassical curriculum, were essentially devices used to control this trend to mass secondary education.

The Act of 1871 aimed at broadening the curriculum of the high schools; but the new program included too many subjects, and this tended to reduce its effectiveness. Nearly two-thirds of the 106 schools operating in 1873 were united with elementary schools, a move that was considered highly detrimental to the best interests of the pupils. McLellan strongly condemned this "union school plan," and it was in fact abandoned in 1874 (75, p. 159).

The criticism and failure of the overpretentious program of 1871 finally resulted in its replacement by a new program in 1878.

The new mathematical syllabus was defined in a fair amount of detail, and authorised texts in arithmetic, algebra, and geometry were specified. The syllabus is notable in several ways, among them the following:

1. It consisted of two divisions, lower school and upper school, because of the existence of the intermediate examination.
2. There was a fair degree of flexibility in what was studied in a given year in each division.
3. Improvements in arithmetic stressed less review and put more emphasis on advanced theory and commercial application.
4. Trigonometry was taught in the upper school only.
5. For the first time, analytical geometry was added to the curriculum.

Gray regarded this as very significant, stating (162, p. 47):

> Analytical geometry, while possessing all the advantages of Euclidean geometry as a "disciplinary" subject, has the added advantage that it provides a necessary basis upon which to build more advanced mathematical experiences. Consequently, the inclusion of this phase of geometry on the secondary level indicates a significant advance.

Mathematics continued to enjoy a prominent place in the overall curriculum, as is evidenced by the numerical value assigned to it in the matriculation examinations for the University of Toronto at that time (p. 47). In effect, mathematics was assigned the same weight as the classics, and more than twice the weight of English, at both junior and senior matriculation level.

However, the greatest influence of McLellan is to be found in the realm of methodology. Young, in his penetrating report of 1864, had criticised the slavish adherence to rules and formulae. This contributed greatly to the subsequent shift toward the use of the inductive method, which can be seen in algebra texts such as Hamblin Smith's (published in 1871) and that of Loudon (published in 1878), both of which were authorised in the 1878 course of study.

McLellan was a strong believer in rational methods of teaching. Included in his philosophy was a belief in the effectiveness of mental arithmetic. In 1878, he published *Mental Arithmetic, Fundamental Rules, Fractions, Analysis,* in the preface to which he stated, "Mental Arithmetic leads the pupil into an intelligent possession of principles, and renders him expert and logical in their application." The questions were well graded, and "of the kind which require the pupils to think" (161, p. 228).

His *Elements of Algebra* was published somewhat later, in 1886, and, strangely enough, reverted to a deductive development. It is just possible that McLellan himself may have been reacting to the emerging views of teachers who, "while admitting the excellence of the inductive method of teaching, ... stated that it was of no use if time was not granted in which to apply it" (162, p. 43). (How modern the above comment sounds. It might have been made in the 1960s by Ausubel!)

McLellan's text did contain other worthwhile innovations. Unnecessarily complicated problems and puzzles were omitted, questions were stated in simple language, provision was made for individual differences by difficulty gradings of A, B, and C, and mental algebraic exercises were included for the first time.

A very graphic picture of the heyday of the period is given by I. J. Birchard, himself the author of a trigonometry text published in 1891 (55, p. 98).

> On January 7, 1881, I became Principal of the Perth Collegiate, and in May of that year the late J. M. Buchan made his inspectoral visit. He made careful examinations of the organization, timetables and equipment; nothing escaped his eye. He visited the various classes and noted the methods of instruction employed, but he did much more than sit as a spectator. He would take charge of a class, ask a few questions to get in sympathetic touch with the students, and then teach a lesson

which was an inspiration to the class and a model for the instruction of the teacher. After all had been completed, he invited me to take a quiet walk with him while he might talk over school affairs with me. He noted first the strong points of my work, and then showed me how I might improve where he found a weakness. He was an accomplished scholar, and experienced teacher, enthusiastic in his work; his advice was acceptable and profitable accordingly.

A revised course of study was adopted in 1885. It is notable in that it reverts to description in terms of Form I through Form IV and appears to be a modification agreed on by the minister of education in consultation with the University of Toronto to fit in with a simplification of the department of education's academic examination for public school teachers.

The revision was, if anything, a regressive change in mathematics. The study of arithmetic was restricted and analytic geometry dropped. There was also less flexibility, and a less extensive course in algebra. Yet John Seath saw in this latest curriculum revision the opportunity for "the proper correlation of the different subjects"—indeed a worthwhile objective, currently in vogue in Ontario but still far from being achieved.

Although the revised mathematics syllabus did not seem educationally an improvement, other encouraging mathematical developments were occurring. In 1887 some very important textbook authorisations were made which underscored the changes in method taking place in mathematics and presaged further improvement in geometry methods, in particular. McKay's *Elements of Euclid* contained a good collection of suitable exercises, while later editions included historical notes and more adequate treatment of definitions, postulates, and axioms. In the minister of education's report for 1889 this text was credited with leading to an improvement in the ability of pupils to make deductions.

Further evidence of improvement in school mathematics comes from a comparison of the intermediate algebra examinations of 1876 with that for junior matriculation in 1899. Gray states (162, p. 52) that in the earlier one the main interest was

> upon complicated applications of the simple rules of operations. It would seem that the primary aim was to provide an opportunity to demonstrate the ability in numerical gymnastics, regardless of whether or not such situations had any real application to later developments of the subject.

In contrast, Gray describes the paper of 1889 as follows (p. 53):

The actual make up of the questions is sufficiently complex as to provide a real test of the student's ability. However, they are not complicated for the sole purpose of testing facility in the fundamental operations. Each question asked represents a phase of algebra that has definite application to subsequent advance in the subject. In contrast with earlier examinations, this [examination] tests knowledge of those skills which represent the line of direct advance from elementary to more advanced areas of the subject.

Looked at as a whole, the period was one of considerable change. Due to the influence of McLellan and his followers, significant progress was made methodologically. At the same time, the coming into being of a new administration lacking mathematical representatives (99, p. 116) and the reorganisation of examinations that gave a key position to university matriculation with a consequent reemphasis on Latin (in 1891 less than 40 percent of Ontario high school students studied Latin; in 1896 more than 60 percent did) combined to produce a relative decline in the earlier emphasis on mathematics.

5. Summary

In a century and a quarter education in Ontario had, therefore, developed from a few private secondary schools catering to only the affluent and the aristocratic to a fully developed system of public education.

In mathematics, both curriculum and methodology saw continual, though uneven, growth and development. From 1816 onwards a series of revisions in the mathematics curriculum took place, with a definite movement toward specifying it in more detail and providing more than one programme. These revisions and changes represented serious attempts to adapt the mathematics curriculum to the needs of the times and to provide textbooks of good quality. A definite trend from learning by rule toward the use of inductive approaches and much improved motivation generally is evident over the period in question.

Some decline in the earlier favourable position of mathematics did occur in the last decade or so of the period, yet the improvements noted in curricula, tests, methods, and examinations were very significant. One may, therefore, conclude that in 1894 the level of school mathematics instruction was relatively satisfactory (for the times in question) and, of course, decidedly superior to that of the late eighteenth century.

CHAPTER NINETEEN

School Mathematics in Ontario 1894-1959 Expansion and Moderate Reform

Douglas H. Crawford

1. Introduction

In the years spanning the period from 1894 through 1959, the year 1896 was of great significance for Ontario and Canada. It saw the fall of the long-lived Canadian government of Sir John A. MacDonald and the revival of world trade. From then until the first world war times were prosperous. It was a time of increasing demand from Europe for food—a demand that led to the settlement of the Canadian West by immigrants from Britain, the United States, and continental Europe. Between 1896 and 1914, 2.5 million persons entered Canada, and of these almost 1 million went to the prairie provinces and British Columbia in the peak period of 1901-11.

Thereafter Canada grew to Dominion status in 1931, partly as a result of its participation as an ally of Britain in World War I. Although its economy and way of life became tied more and more to those of the United States and conscription in both world wars tended to produce opposition in Quebec, overall the commercial and political realities of interplay with the outside world had combined to corrode defensive separation and deepen Canada's sense of internal identity by the 1950s, when its population had grown to some 16 million.

With an increase in population from 2.2 million in 1901 to 5.4 million in 1956, interrupted only by the two world wars, Ontario's major problem was how to deal with growing industrialisation and urbanisation. In its abundance of natural resources, land, water, and minerals lay the key to progress. It shared in the great age of railway building which "bound all the regions of Canada together in a far stronger web of steel" and helped to hasten the mining boom in gold, silver, copper, and nickel which developed in northern Ontario. It was also fortunate in the plentifulness of its water resources, which enabled it to create hydroelectric power on a vast scale to support its burgeoning manufacturing industries.

A synopsis of developments in education covering the period 1900 to 1955 has been given by Phillips (94, p. 226) and is worth reproducing here as setting the scene for our more specific examination of mathematics education. Writing in the mid-fifties, he states that the period

> was characterized in Ontario as elsewhere by decreasing confidence in the forms of the past and more concern for the needs of the individual pupil here and now. We have seen that the years of compulsory schooling were extended and that some attendance at high school became almost universal. There was a striking development of vocational eduction. In the period between the two great wars, the number of pupils in vocational schools and courses increased from a negligible proportion to thirty per cent of the total secondary school enrollment. New school services included free textbooks, medical and dental inspection, and transportation to school.
>
> Gradually, throughout the period measures have been taken to make the system less rigid and more elastic. More and more pupils were excused from the high school entrance examination until in 1950 it was abolished. Recommendation by teachers was accepted from 1932 as an alternative to passing Grade XI and XII departmental examinations, which were abandoned altogether a few years later. Since 1950 experimental efforts have been under way to overcome retardation resulting from a lockstep system of grading, to encourage the adaptation of the school program to local needs, and to have teachers take over responsibility for curriculum planning.

For our purposes, the period 1894–1959 can be thought of as occurring in three stages or periods. The first was 1894–1920; during this interval reform in school mathematics came to the fore, sparked by the report of the Committee of Ten in the United States. The second was 1920–45; during this period the major emphasis was on revising curricula to meet the requirements of life more adequately. The third was 1945–59; the trend towards programs appropriate for the ordinary pupil continued, and traditional demands on the college-bound student were gradually reduced.

2. The period of reform movements: 1894–1920

As indicated previously, the closing years of the McLellan period showed a lessening of emphasis on mathematics as a subject in the curriculum. Various reasons were advanced for this state of affairs. W. J. Robertson, for example, speaking in 1893, blamed it on increased emphasis on English and science and on an overcrowded curriculum (162, pp. 55–56). A. H. McDougall (later to be principal of Ottawa, now Lisgar, Collegiate) delivered a noteworthy address entitled "Mathematical Education in Ontario" in 1895, at the annual meeting of the Mathematics and Physics Association of Ontario, which had been formed four years earlier. In this address McDougall was equally forthright in attributing the changed attitude in part to the increase of female teachers—from 49 percent of the total of 4,890 in 1867 to 67 percent of the total of 8,480 in 1892! McDougall cited other causes, also, and gave a most candid summary (88, pp. 7–8) of the state of things as he saw them then. This makes interesting reading some seventy-five years later.

> There is a growing tendency to introduce the Yankee idea of getting over difficulties by leaving them out. For example our Public School arithmetic has left out everything in the shape of complicated fractional expressions, and it has become somewhat fashionable to sneer at anything of that kind. As a natural consequence there is a growing tendency in our classes in the High School to shirk algebraic problems that involve complicated expressions. Our pupils have not had the old-time training that made such work easy. Recurring decimals have disappeared from Public School work. . . . The High School arithmetic has a well graded set of examples on annuities . . . but here again the Yankee idea has prevailed and henceforth we are to have arithmetic omitting annuities.

The study of mathematics, he believed, was no longer progressive, with advance and expansion into new lines. He proceeded to suggest a new outline in geometry for Forms II, III, and IV which, if adopted, might result in greater interest and supply a connecting link between the elementary geometry it covered and the conic sections and modern geometry as taught in universities.

Not only was the curriculum being "watered down," apparently, but "students were beginning to go back to the old vice of dependence upon rules and formulae" (42, p. 118).

According to W. B. Gray, the first concrete outcome of the widespread dissatisfaction with the teaching of mathematics was the report of the Committee of Ten in the United States, published in 1894 (see chap. 3, sec. 6, and chap. 12, sec. 7). Its recommendations were primarily pedagogical in nature. Apart from recommendations relating to arithmetic and algebra content and emphasis, the report reaffirmed that "the [arithmetic] rules should be arrived at inductively and the textbook should be subordinate to the teacher."

Also, significantly for the times, the Committee of Ten recommended that geometry be introduced by means of a practical course.

A new course of study for Ontario schools was issued in 1896, but the mathematics curriculum showed relatively minor changes from that of 1885, and the committee's recommendations were largely ignored. The main changes in content were specific additions. For example, simultaneous quadratics were now part of third-form algebra, while in the fourth form the mathematics of investment was included after the binomial theorem.

A more radical movement in the teaching of mathematics originated in 1902 when John Perry presented a paper at Glasgow, Scotland, to the Educational Science Section of the British association. The major reform advocated by Perry was to allow the study of many "essential notions of trigonometry, algebra, geometry and even calculus, without proofs" (162, p. 60). In this way the pupil was to be provided with a varied collection of mathematical tools with which he could analyse and solve problems. Gray comments further (pp. 60–61):

> Perry could see no harm in permitting the pupil to assume the truths of many propositions or to determine them experimentally. He believed that teachers of demonstrative geometry were destroying the inherent power to think and were producing a dislike for all computations and therefore for all scientific study of nature and were therefore doing incalculable harm.

Perry's views were expounded and elaborated in America by Professor E. H. Moore (see chap. 4, sec. 3, and chap. 12, sec. 10). Moore aimed to put more emphasis on the practical side of mathematics and its relation to physics, chemistry, and engineering, so that by using the best available tools the student would be motivated to achieve and hence to explore the theory behind the tools.

This early attempt to "psychologise" mathematics faced as its major problem the unification of pure and applied mathematics and the correlation of the various subjects of the curriculum. Today Ontario is still wrestling with the same problems, as can be seen by careful reading of the Hall-Dennis report, *Living and Learning* (24).

The main immediate effects were to stimulate the teaching of intuitive geometry and to reduce the strict formalism that prevailed in the teaching of algebra.

Reliable evidence of the movement toward modifying the slavish adherence to Euclid is found in the fact that "The Study of Euclid" appeared annually from 1900 to 1904 on the program of the Mathematical and Physical Section of the Ontario Education Association. In 1903 the Committee on Geometrical Study presented a resolution endorsing changes in geometry for the lower school that was being proposed by the provincial department and resolving further "that this Section is of the opinion that in the Middle and Upper Schools some work in Geometry more practical and harmonious than Euclid, with the applied mathematics taught in these forms, is desirable, if such work can be secured without sacrificing the rigor of Euclid's demonstrations" (88, pp. 10–11).

The curriculum was in fact revised in 1904. Although it had been supposed to usher in great reforms, namely, to reduce "excessive unification of the courses of study and the undue pressure of examinations" (162, p. 63), this revision achieved neither of these worthy aims.

The course was divided into lower-, middle-, and upper-school sections, with corresponding time allotments of 2 or 3, 1 or 2, and 1 or 2 years. Thus the overall time span could vary from 4 to 7 years, which in theory allowed for some provision for individual differences.

The influence of the Committee of Ten and of the Perry-Moore movement is evident in this new mathematics program. The following note from the 1904 *Regulations* of the Ontario Department of Education (162, p. 65) gave official blessing to the recommendations of the 1894 Committee of Ten report suggesting emphasis on familiar objects, concrete problems, and skill and accuracy.

> *Note:* The processes and problems in commercial work should be such as find direct application in ordinary business life. Accuracy,

rapidity and neatness of work should be aimed at. Proofs of the more difficult formulae in mensuration are not required. During the first year, the study of arithmetic should be an intensive one, the work of the public schools being thoroughly reviewed. After the first year the stress should be placed on algebra.

Most significant, however, was that for the first time the geometry course was defined without reference to Euclid. The lower-school course was to emphasise physical accuracy and include "some leading propositions of Euclidean geometry reached by induction as the result of accurate construction of figures" (162, p. 64).

However, deduction was to be employed as principles were developed and understood. In the middle school modifications in the method of proof were allowed according to certain stated specifications—for example, free employment of the method of superposition. (How does this sound when one considers the continuing changes in geometry of the 1960s?) A further noteworthy example was the permission to use algebraic methods relating to ratio and proportion for commensurable quantities.

Finally, the upper-school course included an introductory course in the coordinate geometry of the point, straight line, and circle.

The details of these new courses in geometry were set forth in the minutes of the 1904 meeting of the Ontario Education Association's Mathematical and Physical Section.

The year 1909 saw yet a further revision of the course of study. The upper-school curriculum continued unchanged, but there were important additions at lower levels. These included the discussion of common banking and business forms in lower-school arithmetic and the study of graphical solutions in middle-school algebra.

It will be evident that education was now breaking national boundaries so that events and movements in individual countries began to influence those in others. This increased interaction is clearly to be seen in the discussions on school mathematics in Ontario from 1900 on. For example, papers on mathematics by mathematicians from Norway, England, Germany, France, and the United States were presented at the professional association meetings during the period 1901 to 1905.

This trend continued with the setting up of the International Commission on the Teaching of Mathematics in 1911. In its report, published in 1918, it made several important recommendations. Gray notes seven (162, p. 71). Several are reiterations of the reforms advocated earlier: reduction of the numbers of geometrical proofs and of complex algebraic manipulations and introduction of more problems from physics, other sciences, and practical life. Another suggested that more prominence be given to the equation in algebra. This had already been achieved some years earlier, according to Gray.

Two of the seven recommendations related to long-term problems in education. Firstly, a specific program which intending teachers of mathematics might undergo was suggested. The program in its entirety is given below.

Trigonometry
College algebra
Analytic geometry
Surveying or descriptive geometry or elementary astronomy
Differential and integral calculus with applications to geometry
Mechanics and physics
Modern geometry
Elements of analytical geometry
Elements of theoretical and laboratory physics
Algebra from the modern standpoint
History of mathematics
Teaching of mathematics

Its comprehensive nature is evident. Even today many teachers of secondary school mathematics in Ontario tend to be less well prepared. Particularly notable when compared with some of the emphasis in Ontario curricula fifty years later are the courses relating to algebra from the modern standpoint and the history of mathematics.

A further major recommendation was, "There should be a more equitable division between elementary and secondary education. The pupils of grades VII, VIII, and IX form a more or less homogeneous group" (162, p. 71).

This suggestion, that grades 7, 8, and 9 become the junior high school, did not find favour in Ontario, in part at least because of the question of separate schools. In its majority report the Hope Commission (appointed in 1945 and finally reporting in 1950) did advocate a restructuring of the Ontario school system on a 6-4-3 plan—a six-year elementary school, a four-year secondary school, and a three-year junior college. But this was a politically unrealistic proposal at the time and stirred up religious acrimony as it implied a contraction of the separate school system from eight to six grades (67, p. 170).

The period under discussion coincided largely with the influence of Dr. John Seath, first as inspector of high schools (1884–1906) and later (1906–19) as superintendent of education, an advisory position only. Many problems had arisen and been tackled energetically, among them textbook authorisation, unrealistic examination policies, and the improvement of teacher training. Yet Seath's critics, while acknowledging the many achievements of the period, were critical of some of the restrictive features still to be found in the system. Thus the system was described by Watson Kirkconnel in 1920 as "at once one of the most uniformly efficient in the world and one of the most paralysing to individual initiative in teacher or school" (75, p. 171).

As far as school mathematics is concerned, the period is significant for the breakdown of "provincial isolation" and for the growing recognition that pedagogy is at least as important as content, hence that the teaching of mathematics requires a teacher well trained in both these respects.

⇶⇶ 3. *Adapting curricula to life: 1920–45*

The 1920s in Canada have been referred to by Careless (60, p. 35) as the "booming twenties." Until 1929, when the "great crash" occurred, Canada in general enjoyed a period of renewed prosperity. The advance to the West was over, and the greatest developments occurred in manufacturing, minerals, pulpwood, and newsprint, especially in the semibarren Shield. Also, the majority of Canadians were becoming a race of townsmen, most of them to be found in Ontario and Quebec. By 1931 the population of Ontario had grown to nearly 3.5 million, of whom over half were classed as urban dwellers. In particular, statistics show that whereas 45.8 percent of all male working Canadians were involved in agriculture in 1901, this percentage had declined to 33.9 in 1931, and to 31.7 in 1941.

According to Careless (60, p. 352–54, 300),

> These post-war developments were of high importance. They gave Canada a more balanced, stable way of life, less dependent on the ups and downs of the world market. They gave her new staple exports besides wheat....
> Yet much of this post-war growth tended to cut across the east-west unity of Canada and was felt unevenly in the different regions....
> The northern development, for example, chiefly benefited the provinces of Ontario and Quebec and the powerful business interests

concentrated there. Toronto built a great mining empire in northern Ontario, but its connections generally ran north and south, strengthening regionalism not the east-west system of Canada. . . .

Then in the 1930's came the blackest depression ever to hit Canada. In its long hard years the demand for social changes arose with new force across the nation.

In addition, these years of stress encouraged the emergence of a variety of sectional movements at the expense of national political parties. In Ontario, a long Conservative reign was replaced in 1934 by a Liberal administration following a campaign to reduce government spending during the depression.

The effect of increased population in Ontario was felt especially in the areas of secondary and vocational education. The average daily attendance in all secondary schools doubled between 1919/20 and 1924/25. One factor in this increase was raising of the school-leaving age to sixteen years in 1921 by the Adolescent School Attendance Act. Another factor was the steadily rising proportion of the population attending school. (By 1939/40 average attendance was proportionately three times greater than in 1900.) It should be noted also that 30 percent of pupils were in vocational education by 1939, compared with a negligible proportion in 1919.

An overall review of the educational system occurred in the early 1920s. The functions of the high school were defined by the minister of education in his 1920 report (162, p. 75) as—

1. To provide a broad, general education for the average boy or girl
2. To prepare candidates for entrance into the universities
3. To give the necessary academic training to those who propose becoming public school teachers

He also appointed a committee in 1920 "to devise a system which would suitably provide for modern educational needs, without causing undue pressure on the pupils and teachers, and which would enable local authorities to choose courses suitable to special local needs" (p. 76).

Many of the resulting changes and expansions are described in some detail by McCutcheon (75, pp. 113–16, 172–74) and in the Hope Commission report (44, pp. 18–22). It is enough to note here that significant efforts were made to improve the physical and social environment of education via such measures (among others relating to social education and teacher training) as the abolition of school fees in secondary schools and the development of dental and medical inspection and of improved heating, lighting, ventilating, and sanitary systems.

In actual fact, the mathematical content of the revised course of study of 1924 showed few changes. The work in arithmetic was limited to a single year, with the suggestion that it be studied in the second high school year. The topic of approximate computation was deleted—a retrograde step, according to Gray (162, p. 79). Most if not all of us would surely agree with him today, in this computer age.

Algebra revisions included some downward movement of content, the deletion of the discussion of cube roots in the middle school, and a greater stress on factoring and the theory of quadratics.

Perhaps the most important feature of the revision was the reorganisation of the length and structure of the secondary school program, which, according to McCutcheon (75, p. 173) "lightened the burden and permitted better organisation and more thorough teaching."

The course itself was reduced to five years, the number of subjects studied in the lower and middle school was to be from five through eight, compulsory subjects were reduced in number and prescribed, and there was a flexible list of optional subjects with provision for local needs.

A further course revision took place in 1928. Again, not many changes in mathematics occurred. Geometry remained the same as in 1904, as did algebra for the most part. However, the trigonometry course was redefined, for the first time since 1896, and extended to include discussion of inverse functions. Also, some valuable new business topics, particularly compound interest and the use of interest tables, were added to the course in arithmetic.

During the late twenties and early thirties lively discussions regarding both method and content were continuing among the members of the O.E.A. Mathematical and Physical section. The 1928 annual meeting included separate papers entitled "Teaching Arithmetic" (S. Wightman), "Teaching Algebra" (C. W. Robb), and "Teaching Geometry" (J. G. Workman). Wightman was concerned about the decline in arithmetic, while Robb explained his special methods in connection with the factoring and index laws. Among the points made by Workman were (1) the importance of a good introduction to geometry, with less emphasis on teaching definitions and formal recitations, (2) the need to teach pupils that geometry is valuable because it trains us to come to sound conclusions under circumstances of different kinds, and (3) the importance of broad understanding of geometry by the teacher so that pupils with new solutions will get full credit for their originality.

The desirability and possibility of introducing calculus into the school curriculum was also debated from 1931 onwards. In 1931 the president, R. N. McKenzie, pointed out that modern research workers tended to express their results in this form and that commercially developing fields such as wireless and aeronautics demanded a knowledge of it. Ontario was behind several European countries and the more progressive schools in the United States, and thus Ontario boys were being handicapped. In 1933 the following motions were adopted (88, p. 21):

> That this section *endorses the proposal to substitute an extension of the course in Analytical Geometry and an elementary course in Calculus for the present course in Synthetic Geometry of the Upper School.* That this suggestion be brought to the attention of the Department of Education. That a committee be appointed to draw up a definite course to be submitted to this section at the session of 1934 along the following lines: (a) Revision of Pass Geometry to include part of Synthetic Geometry of Upper Schools; (b) Extension of Analytical Geometry to include easier parts of the ellipse, parabola and hyperbola; (c) An introduction to the Calculus.

However, a much weaker amendment, "That this meeting look forward to the introduction of Calculus and appoint a committee to interview the Department of Education" (p. 21) won the day! This committee was duly appointed and reported in 1934. Its chairman, James Jenkins, indicated that a possible course had been prepared but only part of it had so far appeared in the magazine *The School*. Discussion of this continued in 1935 and in fact was extended to the desirability of reviewing the entire secondary school mathematics curriculum. The 1936 meeting was devoted entirely to these themes. In the discussion on the Tuesday, the necessity for continuity in the teaching of a subject and the advantages of a certain amount of correlation where possible were pointed out. The main concern was to work out a course better suited to the average pupil's needs. On the Wednesday, Jenkins outlined some experimental teaching of calculus which he had carried out, and Professor Beatty reviewed the topics treated in the calculus text just completed. In Jenkins's view, there would be a sufficient number of keen students of mathematics in the larger schools to justify the teaching of calculus.

These discussions reflect the concern and points of view of mathematics teachers in Ontario during the period in question. It was indeed a time of change and unrest.

The early thirties saw a temporary end to the expansion and prosperity of the twenties with the advent of the Great Depression. According to McCutcheon, the momentum gained in the twenties enabled educational standards to be maintained in the elementary schools, though not always in the secondary ones. At both elementary and secondary levels, expenditures generally and teaching-staff salaries in particular were reduced, and severe overcrowding resulted in many cases. By 1935, however, economic conditions had improved noticeably, and the time was nearly ripe for the most drastic revision of the entire school program since the times of Ryerson.

As has been indicated, dramatic increases had been taking place in the school population, particularly at the high school level, not only in Ontario but in the other Canadian provinces and the United States. This changed the very nature of the high school. As Johnson notes (67, p. 144):

> The high school students were becoming much more of a cross-section of the adolescent population. No longer were they a select group. No longer were their interests or abilities all academic. Every man's son and daughter were now in high school and it behooved the educators to find courses and programs suited to the needs of the vocationally-oriented as well as the professionally-bound.

In the United States the philosophy called progressive education now held sway. The basic tenets of this philosophy have been well summarised by Johnson (pp. 133–34) and might be briefly described by the phrases "child-centred," "learn by doing," "teach meaningfully," and "democratic development." (See also pp. 174–94.)

The combined influences of increased enrollment and progressivism led to the introduction of the junior high school in the United States as early as 1909 in an attempt to provide more suitable education for the adolescent. This was based on the belief that a 6-3-3 system was psychologically more appropriate, with the intermediate stage from grade 7 to grade 9 conceived of as exploratory in nature and as preparation for high school.

This movement spread to British Columbia in the late twenties and to Alberta and Nova Scotia by 1936. However, the situation in Ontario was complicated by the regulations guaranteeing Roman Catholic schools in the first ten grades.

The 1937 revision of the Ontario program of studies took due account of these forces, and of developments elsewhere, and tried to link education more closely than before to the actual problems of living. The school was divided into grades instead of forms (elementary, grades 1–8; secondary, grades 9–13). While it retained the best features and objectives of former courses, the new program attempted "to place the emphasis upon the things that really matter in the education of school children" (75, p. 119).

The character of the new secondary curriculum was "influenced by the view that a practical child should not be less well provided for than an intellectual child and by the fact that too much emphasis was placed in the past upon the traditional and so-called cultural subjects" (p. 178). In particular the grade 9 course was "designed specifically to enable the pupils to explore their abilities, inclinations, and aptitudes" (p. 178).

It was in this climate that the revision of the mathematics program took place. At the elementary level the key note was education through and by activities, with a reduction from fifteen subjects to seven, and a much-increased emphasis on social development. Arithmetic, which had received the greatest time allotment in the old course, was simplified and now received half an hour daily, dropping to fifth place in order of importance.

At the secondary school level numerous changes occurred, though they were less extensive than the professional discussions and reports up to 1936 seemed to presage. The major change was the introduction of a two-year general mathematics course for grades 9 and 10. The grade 9 course included elements of arithmetic, algebra, practical geometry, and graphs, while the grade 10 course dealt with algebra, theoretical geometry, graphical representation, and numerical trigonometry.

The idea of such an approach had grown over the years in connection with the junior high school. It had begun with papers by Perry and Newell in 1902 and by Nunn in 1914. Gray describes how content is approached and integrated in accordance with the philosophy as follows (162, p. 85):

> In this [the junior high] school it was possible to introduce intuitive geometry in grade seven. Algebra was allowed to grow out of the evident need for formulae in connection with this geometry. Simple numerical trigonometry was the obvious result of this earlier fusion of algebra and geometry. Also some knowledge of the significance of demonstration in formal geometry was given to the pupils of these

grades. It is only natural that some sort of integration of these elementary phases of various mathematical subjects should result.

He then goes on to outline the psychology and purpose of general mathematics (p. 86):

> General mathematics has resulted in less formal arrangements and more concrete beginnings. The treatment is less rigorous but more explanatory and illustrative material is included. The exercises are made as practical as possible and the development is influenced by psychology. General mathematics serves as an instrument for motivation, articulation and exploration. Motivation is provided through applications of one subject to the development of another. It articulates the arithmetic of the elementary school with the mathematics of the senior high school. It affords exploration of the pupil's aptitude for future work.

The minutes of the Ontario Association of Teachers of Mathematics and Physics (O.A.T.M.P.) for the following years contain discussions of the innovation. One successful part of it was the emphasis on graphs. In 1938 Miss J. Kinnear demonstrated how graphs caught the interests of pupils and how they could be used in cooperation with other subjects, while in 1940 James McQueen claimed that this use was necessary because of common occurrence in the business world but that much time could be wasted in the making of elaborate graphs. The topic's chief justification, in his view, was the "formula" graph that developed the concept of related variables.

The main criticisms of the course advanced by Gray were that the elements lacked integration and that there was too much material. This second criticism was also voiced to the O.A.T.M.P. by J. E. Dean in 1938—and more forcibly in subsequent years, when a plea was made for increasing the available time.

There was little change in the courses for grades 11 and 12. However, at the level for grade 13 (formerly upper school), the old half-year courses in synthetic and solid geometry were replaced by an enlarged course in analytical geometry which now included the parabola, ellipse, and hyperbola.

Moreover, in algebra, the function concept and its unifying influence were given attention in grade 13. The values of such an approach had been advocated at the 1939 O.E.A. section meeting by R. E. K. Rourke in a speech entitled "A Unifying Principle in Secondary School Algebra." He stated (43) that criticisms of algebra centred around it "as a manipulation and drill subject with litttle appeal for the average pupil." It appeared to be fundamental to develop the functional method of thinking in algebra, and he suggested that "a study of related variables by means of formulae, graphs, tables and practical problems should be developed throughout the course in algebra" to culminate in explicit attention to functions in grade 13. In 1941, in a paper-discussing a new grade 13 text (77), Dr. Johns, of McMaster University, stated he found it fresh, stimulating, and interesting: "Algebra has been changed from a cut-and-dried subject to a subject alive and interesting. . . . The equation formerly dominated our algebra but in the new book it is put in its proper place." (88, p. 23.)

The war years brought with them an increased need for applied mathematics, particularly the mathematics of navigation. Many teachers gave their time voluntarily to instruct potential pilots. A most interesting address, "Practical Air Navigation," was given at the professional meeting in 1942. The speaker, Flight Lieutenant Vanstone, formerly a Toronto high school teacher, stated that while the initial mathematics required was very low, accuracy in all calculations was essential.

By 1945, the end of the period under discussion, the revised program of studies was in full swing. It had been an eventful quarter-century economically, politically, and with respect to leaping school enrollments. Much thinking had gone on in the area of school mathematics in attempts to meet the changing needs. Clearly, the reaction in Ontario had been slower than elsewhere. The main issues of concern seemed to be (1) the time allotment and philosophy of arithmetic, (2) the question of whether calculus should be introduced in the last year of high school, and (3) the finding of a better solution in time allotment and approach to general mathematics. It will be seen that these issues were to continue to cause debate. On the positive side, the teaching of both geometry and algebra was receiving a good deal of thought, and reforms in general were such as to emphasise the need to consider not just the academically able pupils but also those of only average ability. Education in mathematics is not the whole of education, by a long way.

4. *Postwar reform and the "rebirth" of school mathematics: 1945–59*

The period 1945–59 was one of considerable change in Canada and Ontario. By the end of World War II Canada was a vigorous industrial nation, fourth in world importance. She was one of the four nations with a large surplus of food and industrial goods available for restoring prosperity. She was young and possessed vast resources and regions available for development, yet she had achieved a measure of stability and maturity through facing the problems of expansion, depression, and two world wars.

The period of reconstruction and readjustment following the war developed into a postwar boom of great proportions. Population rose from about 14 million in 1950 to about 18 million in 1960. Among the major contributing factors were the favourable world trade due to her strength in 1945, her greatly increased productive and manufacturing capacity, the continuing opening up of her natural resources such as oil, aluminum, and uranium, the flow of foreign capital, and last but not least the remarkable increase in her population.

Although urbanisation continued apace so that metropolitan government was set up for Toronto as early as 1954, there was also a steady pushing back of the northern frontiers. In addition, the gigantic oil developments in the prairie provinces led to the laying of pipelines both to Ontario in the East and Vancouver in the West. Thus were created important new communication links, to be accompanied by many other developments in communications, culminating in the opening of the St. Lawrence Seaway jointly with the United States in 1959.

However, it has to be said that problems accompanied the period of boom. Among these were the recurring seasonal unemployment natural to a northernly situated country like Canada and so-called technological unemployment—the result of automation. In addition, with the recovery of Germany and Japan, Canadian producers lost some of their markets by relative inefficiency and possibly excessive wage levels. Moreover, the pattern of unemployment was not even across the country.

Another problem, possibly more serious in the long run, was the close way Canada became tied into the American market during the boom. United States corporations set up many branch plants across Canada or bought out Canadian firms. The influence of increasing trade with the United States, of mass media, and of "military integration" all combined to tighten the already close bond between the two countries and make Canada increasingly dependent on her southern neighbor.

Furthermore, the government's financial policy of tight money had the effect of dampening business enterprise in the late fifties when the boom was beginning to disappear. The Diefenbaker government of 1958 did not deal adequately with the economic problems of these years; capital began to flow out of Canada, and there was a mild reaction toward Liberalism with neither major political party having a clear mandate to govern. Such a structure led Careless to conclude that Canada "had entered the sixties politically confused and considerably disunited" (60, p. 421).

Ontario had a major share in the postwar boom by virtue of its combination of natural and industrial resources and its burgeoning population, which jumped from 4.6 million in 1951 to 6.2 million in 1961. Of 1.5 million immigrants from 1945–57, one-third settled in Toronto.

Educationally, the period began with the appointment in 1945 of the Hope Commission, which received 258 briefs and 44 memoranda, held innumerable hearings and committee meetings, and finally reported in 1950. The mathematics community responded by means of a brief submitted in 1946 by three members of the executive committee of the Mathematics and Physics section of the O.E.A. on behalf of the section. The chief recommendations show how much thought went into its preparation. They were as follows (88, p. 24):

(1) that a Programme Revision Committee be set up;
(2) that a Unified Course in Mathematics through the elementary and secondary schools be provided;
(3) that a Mathematical Utility survey be made;
(4) that equipment and accommodation be increased in order that mathematics might be taught as a science;
(5) that literacy in mathematics be stressed, particularly in Grades IX and X;
(6) that provision be made for in-service training of teachers.

Another very significant event had occurred the previous year, namely, the founding of the Canadian Mathematical Congress. Its chief aims were enumerated by R. E. K. Rourke, in an address to the section the same year (88, p. 24):

(1) to maintain a professional attitude among teachers of Mathematics by discarding the "Isolationism in Mathematics" which now exists between Canada and the U.S., and even between the different provinces of Canada;
(2) to keep our mathematics alive;
(3) to help us with the development of superior students.

In 1948 under the editorship of Dr. Norman Miller, of Queen's University, an excellent booklet entitled *Why Study Mathematics?* was produced at the instigation of the congress.

We have already seen that in the 1938 revisions, arithmetic had suffered both in time allotment and importance. A strong movement to reverse this situation developed in 1946 via regional conferences and committees studying lower- and middle-school mathematics. In reporting to the annual meeting of the section in 1947, Professor Petrie stated (43):

> It is idle to build a superstructure on a weak foundation. Therefore I think that in elementary school arithmetic we should appeal for at least a partial restoration of the time taken from the subject in 1938.

A meeting to discuss the problem was subsequently arranged with Dr. Althouse, the chief director of education. Although sympathetic, Dr. Althouse pointed out that there would be no curricular revision conducted by the department until the report of the Royal Commission had been presented. The executive then proposed a plan for cooperating with the department in the meantime by setting up a mathematics curriculum research committee and carrying out approved experimental work locally. By this means it was hoped to have plans for necessary course revisions ready for presentation to Dr. Althouse soon after the Royal Commission reported.

That changes were coming was pointed out by Inspector J. E. Durrant that same year in a luncheon address in which he surveyed how the present courses had worked out in the previous eight years. In actual fact, the revisions did not seem to have achieved the stated purpose. For example, according to Horne, "In *General Mathematics II*, the grade ten textbook, little exposition was used in presenting geometrical subject matter as a series of propositions, i.e. theorems or problems" (163). In grade 12, pupils were expected to be able to reproduce formal proofs of thirty starred propositions from a list of eighty, and also had to study similar polygons, extensions of Pythagoras' theorem, and the theorems of Ceva and Menelaus and their converses. It can hardly be said that this was a "practical" content course.

In 1948 Harold Fawcett (an expatriated Nova Scotian who achieved fame in the United States, particularly in Ohio) gave a foretaste of things to come in an inspiring speech entitled "Unifying Concepts in Mathematics." In turn, he discussed *number* (embodied in the ideas of exact and approximate numbers, the latter of which led to increasing stress upon precision of measurement); *relationship* (embodied in the formula, graph, and table); *operation* (the fundamental one is counting); and *symbolism* (the economical language of mathematics which accelerates the transfer of ideas).

The changes referred to by Inspector Durrant came sooner than expected. In December 1949 the minister of education, the Honorable Dana Porter, announced a major experiment in curriculum revision known as the Porter Plan. Grades 1-13 were now conceived of as comprising four divisions: primary, 1-3; junior, 4-6; intermediate, 7-10; and senior, 11-13. Reorganisation was to take place in the primary division to enable pupils to stay longer with one teacher, to lessen wastage from retardation, and to allow for acceleration. The creation of the intermediate division was designed to foster articulation between elementary and secondary education, to enable the operation of a well-rounded course for those leaving at age sixteen, and to introduce an exploratory phase for students to find where their interests and abilities lay.

An interesting commentary on school mathematics as it appeared to one observer in 1950 is provided by the presidential address of J. A. Sonley of Ottawa to the O.E.A. Mathematics and Physics Section Annual Meeting of that year. Sonley first reviewed changes in education within the teaching experience of those present. He referred to the raising of the school age to sixteen as of "major importance" in that it brought into the secondary school "a group for which our academic type of curriculum is not entirely suited to their innate abilities."

Standards had been adjusted to graduate those of this type who did not drop out at age sixteen. He went on to note that a theory adverse to drill had arisen and claimed that this had contributed largely to inaccuracy in mathematical solutions, both time-wasting and discouraging for the students. He also discussed the reduction in time allowed for the teaching of mathematics in lower school, and stated (43) that the course in the elementary schools

> has been "watered down" until the Grades 7 and 8 mathematics texts resemble a book in Social Studies with a few fractions thrown in to separate the topics. . . . One of the dangers which must be guarded against in our [present] re-adjustment is not to swing too far to either extreme or to follow blindly experiments which have not been tested sufficiently.

He then outlined three objectives in mathematics for "education today" (the theme of the session):

(1) Accuracy in our calculations and modes of thinking

(2) The development of the student's reasoning ability and his ability to express his ideas clearly and concisely

(3) The application of facts learned and techniques acquired to the problems of everyday life

He concluded,

> Irrespective of whatever type of education is developed, or curriculum evolved, little can be accomplished unless we develop in our students a healthy attitude to work. Let us not become obsessed with the educative importance of too many extra-curricular activities so that little time is left to be devoted to the prime purpose of education.

At the same meeting, Dr. Carl N. Shuster spoke interestingly on two topics, "Field Work in Mathematics" and "Constructing a Modern Curriculum in Mathematics." Dr. Shuster attacked the "compartment" method of teaching mathematics: "The students are taught algebra for a year; then it is 'put into a deep freeze for a year and two months'; then it is 'dragged out' and six months are spent in review to thaw it out!" He referred to his article "A Call for Reform in High School Mathematics" (151), asserted that field work in mathematics, approximate data, and the reform movement with regard to integrated mathematics were "going over," and suggested that Canadians "watch the United States in the next ten years."

The significant new feature in the revisions of 1950 (63) was that the province shared the curriculum responsibility for grades 7–10 with local committees. For the first time, local coordinating committees were given freedom to revise curriculum.

Some insights as to how mathematics figured in the Porter Plan can be gained by considering a very comprehensive luncheon address given by the Honorable Dana Porter himself to the Mathematics and Physics Section at the O.E.A. meetings of 1951 (43, pp. 242–49). After indicating why mathematics was such an important subject, he reported that for these reasons local curriculum committees had made the tackling of the revision in mathematics one of their first duties. The resulting cooperative effort and increased mutual understanding between the elementary and secondary school was success in itself. The minister went on to outline the aims of the revision and gave a brief résumé of progress to date. He then made some general observations regarding the changes in mathematics proposed in the newly revised department courses. We quote from the *Minutes*, cited above, and give comments.

> (1) At the Grade VII and VIII level, more time had been found to develop and reinforce fundamental skills and provide for diagnostic and remedial work by deleting obsolescent or non-practical topics and deferring others to later grades.

According to Pullen (166, p. 183) most of the items dropped were the practical problems related to the wartime activities of the people (rationing and salvage, for example). Furthermore, the calculations of interest and board measure, circumference of the circle, measurement and construction of angles, study of triangles and the making of circle graphs had been moved to grade 9, placing them at a level much more in line with the pupil's experience.

> (2) The program for Grades VII, VIII, IX had been modified to include the mathematical concepts which all pupils of these grades should know—with the hope that the varying mathematical needs and abilities of different groups of students would be met by different emphases and time distribution. Parallel courses to meet these needs might follow. In Grade X, the Minister specified four groups ranging from those going on to Grade XIII mathematics to those expecting to leave at age 16, or not to proceed beyond Grade X.

The grade 10 course as revised showed changes mainly in arrangement. Much less detail was given, "teachers simply being asked to bridge the gap between the compulsory Grade IX course and the prescriptive one of Grade XI" (166, p. 185). However, the synthetic geometry part was lightened, "only twenty-two propositions being suggested as opposed to the thirty prescribed by the 1948 course" (166, p. 185). In addition, trigonometry and mensuration, which appeared in the old course, were not specifically mentioned.

> (3) Experimentation was proceeding in three different schools with suggested re-allocations of subject matter in Grade XI or XII with a view to implementation generally in September 1951.

He asked teachers to note that by requiring only three instead of four optional subjects for the secondary school graduation there would tend to be a greater time allotment to each option. Also, the average calibre of student should rise, since not all students who formerly took mathematics as one of four options would now do so.

In his concluding remarks the minister expressed the hope that "as a result of the present committee activity, curriculum study will not only spread to other localities but will become a permanent feature of our educational system." He also reminded his audience that with the increase in the number of optional subjects, mathematics faced keen competition, and suggested that, to ensure that mathematics continued to hold its own,

> you all, as professional people and teachers of the subject, do some intensive heart-searching as to the function of mathematics in our educational system, as to its value for different types of pupil, and as to its most effective teaching techniques.

Another significant development occurred at the same time as the revision work in curriculum. This was the discontinuing by the provincial department of its policy of prescribing one textbook per subject. Pullen states (166, p. 136):

> Before the 1950 pronouncement the prescription of books for Grades I–VI had been dropped and in 1950 the prescription of Grades VII and VIII was lifted. By 1952 all authorization of books from Grades I–X was done away with and local authorities thus were forced to choose from books placed on a recommendation list. Further, every encouragement was given to local committees to make suggestions to the Department in order that the list might be as extensive as possible.

Thus, of necessity, local groups had to make their own decisions as to whether to accept or reject a particular book for use in their locality. The discipline of reading texts carefully and making such decisions has been described by Pullen as "in itself a salutary educational experience and a real part of local curriculum participation" (p. 136).

The next few years saw the Ontario Curriculum Revision Experiment in action. Pullen made a comprehensive study of it as the main thrust of his D.Ed. dissertation of 1955, entitled "Secondary School Curricular Change in Canada with Special Emphasis on an Ontario Experiment," from which we have already quoted.

According to him the Porter Plan or "Operation Curriculum," as it has also been called, was introduced first through the five largest cities and later with the help of elementary school inspectors into many other parts of Ontario. He attempted by means of interviews, questionnaires, and the analysis of course revisions in mathematics and social studies in six centres to ascertain what revisions had taken place and what had been accomplished.

He concluded (p. 185):

> An examination of revised courses in a limited number of centres showed that, although greatly influenced by the new Department Courses, local committees really did make adaptations which suited local conditions or reflected the independent thinking of the revisers.

The most interesting and extensive adaptation in mathematics was that in the city of Hamilton, which took advantage of the opportunity to put special emphasis on topics not stressed by the department and to add other items regarded as necessary. For example, in grade 8 the local committee added an entirely new section on timekeeping, foremen's cards, varying wage rates, and master payrolls. Equally interesting were the innovations in the business arithmetic topics for grade 9.

By 1955, 51 of the 111 committees established during the experiment had been discontinued. Pullen listed this among other disturbing facts about the local curriculum revision. These facts included the apparent withdrawal of department support after the appointment of a new minister and the negative effect of the release of revised department courses just after local committees were established. On the whole, Pullen assessed the experiment as having far-reaching and vitalising effects, since other educational improvement followed in many areas and teachers' federations had been encouraged to launch vigorous programmes of teacher and curriculum improvement.

At the senior division, experiments in mathematics revision continued through 1951/52. In a talk at Easter 1952, Inspector Laing outlined these experiments and intimated that the results had been incorporated into revised courses of study for the algebra and geometry of grades 11 and 12. These would be issued shortly. The program in upper-school algebra was to be lightened by correlating topics and bringing down geometric series and arithmetic topics. More adequate preparation was also being included for trigonometry and statics by increased emphasis on logarithms, introduction to trigonometric ratios, and the solution of right-angled triangles. Some topics in the grade 11 and 12 courses were now optional. Provision should be made for individual differences in various ways such as extended (rather than daily) assignments, and assignments of differing length or difficulty. He noted that some schools were taking the geometry in grade 11 and the algebra in grade 12, feeling that it led more effectively to the work of grade 13. If the opposite order were to be used, he advocated a brief review of quadratics and logarithms in May of grade 12.

A further area of concern was considered at the same meeting when Dr. A. E. Johns spoke on the topic "The New Trend of the Matriculation Problems Paper." He produced statistics showing that in recent years the paper had been much too hard. The markers of the papers had been instrumental in having the 1951 paper made easier, with encouraging improvements. He cited two main purposes of the paper: (1) to stimulate and challenge student and teacher and (2) to separate the sheep from the goats. From this he went on to discuss the kind of paper which should be set and the use of the results by the universities and to say he hoped that free discussion would result from his talk. Discussion of the value of the problems paper continued in later years. In 1955 Dr. S. Beatty, by then chancellor of the University of Toronto, made some excellent comments and suggestions and stressed the great value of doing problems. He made the following points:

1. Teachers should prepare their own problems. The whole class can do some of this as a venture. Much more interest and intimacy is provided, and the feeling that all the influences come from outside is diminished.
2. Students should realise the important part played by intuition in understanding and in the production of results.
3. We should break down the idea that all problems should be done at once, that is, on the first try.

The problem of unifying the mathematics of grades 11 and 12 also continued to receive attention. At the Easter 1955 O.E.A. meetings, there was a panel discussion on this theme. It was agreed that the study of alternative plans be continued by the executive and that a report be presented the following year. In 1956, Del Grande reported on "surveys taken on the arrangements now in vogue over Ontario of taking Grades 11 and 12 Mathematics." The *Minutes* (43) go on to state: "It has been found impossible, because a majority for any particular plan cannot be found, to reach a conclusive recommendation."

The matter was therefore shelved by general agreement. However, the situation was finally resolved officially by the provincial department when in 1958 the order of geometry in grade 11, followed by algebra in grade 12, was adopted for a trial period of five years.

Changes in provincial department policy also affected school mathematics in the late 1950s. In late 1956 the policy of appointing staff inspectors for academic subjects was adopted. The first appointment for 1957 included two for mathematics, A. W. Bishop and J. F. Kinlin. According to Kinlin (135), there was "no doubt that mathematics in Ontario profited from this concentration of attention." A second new department policy was the decision to move towards integration of elementary and secondary education. The fact that Kinlin was the first *elementary* inspector to become an inspector of academic subjects in the secondary schools meant that mathematics was in the vanguard in this respect.

Speakers from south of the border continued to bring news of developments there throughout the fifties. Those who came included prominent contributors to NCTM yearbooks (Yates and Fehr, 1954, and Fawcett, 1955) and others who were pioneering reforms. In 1956, Maurice Hartung of the University of Chicago spoke on the topic "Can Elementary Algebra Be Taught as a Deductive System?" He claimed that although it could not be presented as such to beginners, in the strict sense of logical reasoning, "it might and should be taught as a sequence of developments based upon a few very simple arrangements" (43). On such a basis he felt that the distributive laws in themselves could broaden algebraic concepts. Professor Tucker, of Princeton, spoke in 1958 on the topic "Why Sets?" as well as on new emphases in trigonometry. It is noteworthy that he, Canadian by birth, was chairman of the Commission on Mathematics of the CEEB, convened in 1955 to study possible reforms.

In 1959, the culminating year of the period under discussion, the guest speaker was Dr. Kenneth O. May of Carleton College, Minnesota, who is now on the faculty of the University of Toronto. Dr. May centered his major address around "the life and times of N. Bourbaki"—N. Bourbaki being a pseudonym for a group of young French mathematicians who banded together in 1930 to attempt to write a logical synthesis of mathematics. According to the minutes of the O.E.A. section meeting, "The Bourbaki group is trying to make mathematics coherent again. They are trying to define all Mathematics in terms of sets. No such organisation has occurred since the time of Euclid."

He stated that a crisis of communication existed in mathematics, and that the world of mathematics was incoherent because a great deal of work was going off on tangents. The search was now for some method, some set language, for unifying these unrelated fields. In his view,

Sets should be started at the elementary school level. In Europe, the idea of sets for the high school is now being discussed. There are several research programs now operating in the U.S.A. We must leave in the curriculum those things that are useful and meaningful.

In his second talk, Dr. May discussed the idea of function. After giving the more popular definitions of function, including (1) dependence, (2) graph, (3) formula, and (4) correspondence, and indicating the difficulties associated with them, he ended up with the one he thought was correct: namely, "[A] function is the set of ordered pairs (x,y) in which no first element belongs to more than one pair."

The *Toronto Globe and Mail* of 2 April 1959 carried an account of Dr. May's Bourbaki talk, together with the views of Bruce MacLean, of the University of Toronto schools. Professor MacLean is quoted as saying:

> As far as any re-evaluation of mathematics is concerned, it will be in the realm of how it is to be taught, rather than material that is to be taught. There is no substitute for creative teaching. No change in the curriculum can ever be substituted. . . . Courses must be designed so that we don't impede the progress of the quick or confuse the slow.

In the postwar period of some fifteen years, the activity, study, and discussion in school mathematics reflected the changes in education and society. In this period the population of Ontario grew from about 4 million to over 6.2 million. Rapid population growth brought with it a corresponding increase in the school population. The major attempt to meet the diverse needs of pupils was clearly the Porter Plan. Although the innovations were successful in some respects, in general, teachers and boards were unprepared for the innovation, while the authorised courses issued by the provincial department very soon after the first announcement acted as a deterrent to original work by committees. There was, in fact, a general lack of liaison between the department, the teachers' federations, and the local committees.

Clearly, the leaders in school mathematics took these matters seriously, as is witnessed by the brief of 1946 to the Hope Commission (with its emphasis not just on programme revision but on the need for equipment and continuing teacher education) and the fact that both Dr. Althouse and the Honorable Dana Porter were invited to address the professional association.

Throughout the fifties the discussion moved naturally enough to the senior-division curricula and the problems paper. In addition, the whole

Department of Education, Ontario.

Annual Examinations, 1914.

ENTRANCE INTO THE MODEL SCHOOLS.

ALGEBRA AND GEOMETRY.

A.

1. Factor, showing in each case the steps in the process:—
   (a) $a^2 + 2ac - b^2 + 2bd + c^2 - d^2$.
   (b) $(x^2 - a^2)(x^2 + a^2) + ax^3 - a^3x$.
   (c) $a^6 - b^6$.

2. Simplify:—
   (a) $\dfrac{a-c}{(a-b)(x-a)} - \dfrac{b-c}{(b-a)(b-x)}$.
   (b) $\left(x + \dfrac{xy}{x-y}\right)\left(x - \dfrac{xy}{x+y}\right) \div \dfrac{x^2+y^2}{x^2-y^2}$.

3. Find the L. C. M. of
   $x^3 + 2x^2 - 13x + 10$ and $3x^3 + 3x^2 - 30x + 24$.

4. Solve:—
   (a) $x - 7(4x - 11) = 14(x - 5) - 19(8 - x) - 61$.
   (b) $\dfrac{2}{2x-3} + \dfrac{1}{x-2} = \dfrac{6}{3x+2}$.

5. A person bought a piece of land at $80 an acre. Retaining 25 acres for himself, he divided the balance into lots and was thus enabled to sell this portion at three times as much per acre as it cost him, and to realize for it $400 more than he paid for the whole piece. How many acres did he buy?

6. A man bought 30 pounds of sugar of two different grades, and paid for the whole $2.94. The better grade cost 10 cents a pound, and the poorer grade 7 cents a pound. How many pounds were there of each grade?

[OVER]

B.
PRACTICAL GEOMETRY.

7. Using only ruler, compasses, and pencil, make accurately the following constructions. A description of the method of construction is to accompany the drawing, and all construction lines must be shown, but proof is not required:—

(a) Draw a straight line, take a point in it, and from this point draw another straight line making an angle of 45° with the first straight line.

(b) Draw a straight line two inches long, and on this straight line as base construct a quadrilateral having each of its sides which are adjacent to the base 1½ inches long and making with the base an angle of 120°.

THEORETICAL GEOMETRY.

PROBLEMS.

8. The particular enunciation, construction, and proof are required in the following problems:—

(a) Bisect a given straight line.

(b) On a given base describe an isosceles triangle having its altitude equal to a given straight line.

THEOREMS.

9. If two triangles have two angles and a side of one respectively equal to two angles and the corresponding side of the other, the triangles are congruent.

10. Straight lines which join the ends of two equal and parallel straight lines towards the same parts are themselves equal and parallel.

ONTARIO ALGEBRA AND GEOMETRY EXAMINATION, 1914. (See illustration facing page 410 for beginning of examination.)

spectrum of problems in secondary school mathematics was covered by the annual guest speakers from the United States—from "aims in mathematics" and "laboratory methods" to significant discussions on sets and the need to unify mathematics itself as well as school mathematics.

For all the discussion, however, the actual changes made in the senior-division curricula laid down by the 1937 revision were not great (163, pp. 18–22). The difficulty over deciding the grade 11–12 algebra and geometry issue indicates the resistance of the teachers themselves to change. Yet the pressure of international events, such as Sputnik and the growing experimentation in the United States, was inescapable. In April 1959, the month when Dr. May gave his powerful speeches in Toronto, the CEEB Commission on School Mathematics published its influential report. The stage was now really set for further significant developments.

CHAPTER TWENTY

Mathematics Education in Western Canada

Solberg E. Sigurdson

1. A survey

The British North American Act of 1867 established Canada as a Dominion and detailed the division of powers of the provincial and federal governments. Education was placed under provincial jurisdiction, so one of the first responsibilities of the newly formed western provinces was to set up systems of education.

Even though the land west of Ontario was largely empty when Egerton Ryerson died in 1876, this man was to have a profound influence on the educational systems of the western provinces. As the provinces joined the confederation in turn—Manitoba in 1870, British Columbia in 1871, and Alberta and Saskatchewan in 1905—they patterned their educational systems after that established by Ryerson for Ontario.

As in Ontario, the custom was for provinces to authorize single textbooks for each subject and to administer examinations in all grades from 8 through 12. Inspectors were appointed to supervise instruction and to see that regulations of provincial departments of education were strictly observed. The extent of the provincial control is revealed in the following excerpt from a 1917 issue of the *Western School Journal* (128):

> It is reported to us that some teachers are having their pupils keep special books in which only the corrected work will appear. . . . Books prepared in this way will not be accepted. We shall require the books containing the work done from day to day, showing the original mistake of the pupils, their corrections, and their general progress in these subjects through the term.

Before 1900 the curriculum in the missionary schools of the Northwest Territories (now Alberta and Saskatchewan) "included reading, writing, small amounts of art and music, and farming" (167, p. 3). The high school curriculum, however, was dominated by mathematical subjects. In British Columbia in 1884 a set of high school examinations consisted of fourteen tests, seven of which dealt with mathematical subjects—mental arithmetic, arithmetic, mensuration, algebra, Euclid, trigonometry, and bookkeeping (13).

The thirty years after the turn of the century marked a rapid development of the western frontier. Waves of settlers moving into the areas put great strain on the educational facilities. Then, too, during this period the proportion of students who stayed for a high school education increased steadily. Only 3 percent of students of high school age were attending high school in Alberta in 1912. By 1932 this had increased to 17 percent. (3, p. 213.) The period saw the high school divided into grades, high school courses divided into units, and the variety of high school and elementary courses increase. It witnessed a change from a mental-discipline view of education to a view that regarded knowledge, not discipline, as the end of education and recommended adoption of the drill method of teaching to achieve that goal. Although the status of mathematics in the curriculum did not change appreciably during this period, some adjustments occurred: Geometry lost its place in the upper elementary school, analytical geometry found a place in the senior year of high school, and arithmetic and mathematics teachers were having more and more to defend arithmetic as a course in high school.

Not much effort was made in this period to adapt the mathematics program to the interests and abilities of the learner. In 1932 one irate mathematics teacher had this to say (150, p. 7):

> Come to high school, young people. . . . True the material we shall teach you will be completely useless to most of you. . . . We shall teach it to you anyhow, even if we make incurable bluffers out of you in the process. Our duty in this new day is to train you for citizenship and we propose to perform that duty by administering to you exactly the same training as was given to an entirely different class for an entirely different purpose a generation ago.

By 1930 almost 100 percent of the students in high school were following a mathematics program leading to university matriculation, even though the number of graduates subsequently attending a university was negligible.

The period from 1930 to 1959 was characterized by a continuously decreasing number of mathematics courses in the high school and a corresponding decrease in formal arithmetic in the elementary grades. In the late thirties, instructors in Alberta's normal schools established both formal and informal ties with leaders of the progressive education movement in the United States and began to advocate a more incidental approach to the teaching of mathematics in the elementary and junior high school grades. An enterprise, or project, method of teaching was officially endorsed by the Alberta Department of Education. This method suggested the integration of all subjects of the elementary curriculum, including mathematics. Then, by the mid-fifties, integrated mathematics tended to disappear. The official statement in 1957 that "the amount of time to be devoted to arithmetic [in the primary grades] has been increased to 30 minutes per day" (50, p. 12) must indeed have been welcome to many teachers.

Although provincial curricula made provision for a diversity of programs in high school mathematics in this period—such as technical, agricultural, and commercial mathematics—a large percentage of high school pupils registered in the program designed for university matriculation. In 1959, for example, 80 percent of Alberta pupils in all years of the high school were pursuing mathematics courses leading to matriculation (2, p. 210). It has been a tradition in the western provinces to hold vocational mathematics in low esteem. One result was that the number of grade 12 mathematics courses leading to matriculation decreased in number from two or three in the thirties to one by the mid-fifties.

The balance of this chapter will trace in more detail the development of school mathematics in western Canada under the following headings:

ALBERTA MATRICULATION EXAMINATION, 1939

HIGH SCHOOL AND UNIVERSITY MATRICULATION EXAMINATIONS BOARD
DEPARTMENTAL EXAMINATIONS, 1939

ALGEBRA 2

Time—2½ hours.

Note—Show all steps and explanations.
Graph paper and sets of mathematical tables will be supplied by the presiding examiner.

Candidates will attempt *all* of Section A, and *one* question of Section B.

SECTION A

Values

4 1. (a) If $2x = 4y$, and $2z = 5x$, find integers to complete the statement $x : y : z =$

4 (b) The first, second and fourth terms of a proportion are, respectively, $\sqrt{2}-1$, -1, and $3 + 2\sqrt{2}$. Find the third term.

8 2. The illumination of a surface varies inversely as the square of the distance from the source and directly as the power of the light. If a 100-candle-power light produces an illumination of 6 foot-candles at a certain distance, what will be the illumination produced at two-thirds this distance by a 125-candle-power light?

3. (a) By examining the factors find for what range of values of x

3 (1) $x^2 - 5x + 6$ is negative;

3 (2) $9 - x^2$ is positive.

2 (b) Check your results in (1) and (2) by freehand graphs.

4. x represents the number of linear units in the side of a variable square and A represents the number of square units in the area.

2 (a) In relation to the square of side 7 inches, what is the meaning of $(7 + \Delta x)^2 - 49$?

3 (b) In the graph of A against x what is the meaning of the expression $\dfrac{(x + \Delta x)^2 - x^2}{\Delta x}$?

3 (c) Simplify the expression
$$\lim_{\Delta x \to 0} \dfrac{(x + \Delta x)^2 - x^2}{\Delta x}.$$

2 5. (a) Differentiate with respect to x:
$$2x^3 + \dfrac{b}{\sqrt{x}} - \dfrac{2}{x}$$

5 (b) Evaluate $\int_0^4 (2 - 5x^4)dx$.

5 6. (a) Find the area between the curve $y = 4x^2$, the x-axis, and the ordinates $x = 1$ and $x = 3$.

6 (b) Find the volume of the solid generated by the rotation, about the axis of x, of the portion of the figure considered in (a).

5 7. (a) Use the formula to express the sum of the first 20 terms of the geometric progression $-\tfrac{1}{3}, \tfrac{1}{6}, \ldots$ but do not simplify. Is this sum positive or negative?

5 (b) By using the binomial theorem find $\sqrt{0.98}$ to five decimal places.

3 8. (a) How many different parties of eight men can be chosen from fifteen men?

3 (b) In how many of these will two particular men, A and B, be found?

3 (c) In how many would A be found, but neither B nor C?

10 9. Write the first three and the last two terms of the series which expresses the accumulated amount, at the end of fifteen years, of ten annual payments of $400, interest at 4% per annum, compounded semi-annually, the first payment being made immediately.

10. The relation between the velocity, V feet per second, and the head of water, H feet, is suggested by the following pairs of values:

H	4	16	25	36
V	15.7	32.7	39.3	49.1

4 (a) Plot V against $\sqrt{H}$.

2 (b) By inspection draw among the points $(\sqrt{H}, V)$ the "best fitting" straight line.

2 (c) Use this graph to express V as a function of H.

2 (d) Express H as a function of V.

(See illustration facing page 415 for continuation of examination.)

ALBERTA MATRICULATION EXAMINATION, 1939

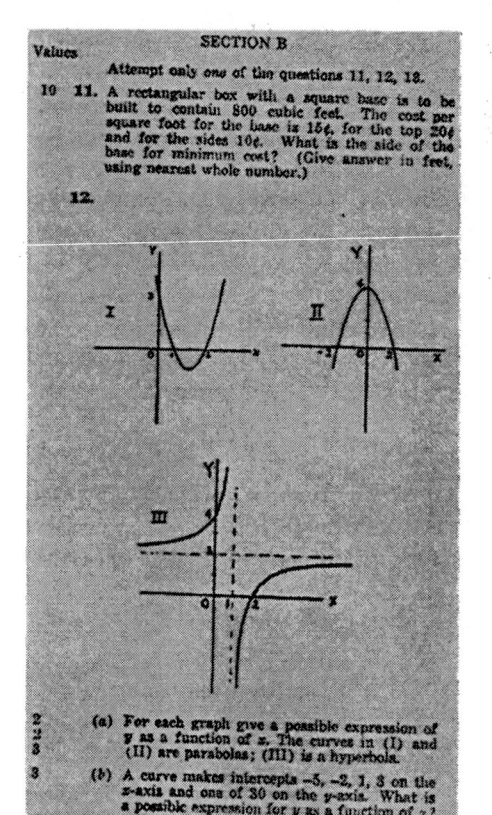

Values

SECTION B

Attempt only *one* of the questions 11, 12, 13.

10   11. A rectangular box with a square base is to be built to contain 800 cubic feet. The cost per square foot for the base is 15¢, for the top 20¢ and for the sides 10¢. What is the side of the base for minimum cost? (Give answer in feet, using nearest whole number.)

12.

[Graphs I, II, III shown]

2
4 (a) For each graph give a possible expression of
3   y as a function of x. The curves in (I) and
        (II) are parabolas; (III) is a hyperbola.

3   (b) A curve makes intercepts −5, −2, 1, 3 on the
        x-axis and one of 30 on the y-axis. What is
        a possible expression for y as a function of x?

Values

10   13. Describe the function $y = \frac{k}{x}$, dealing with *any five* of the following:

(a) Is y defined for every value of x? What is the name of the graph? How many branches has it?

(b) In what quadrants is the graph? Is the graph rising or falling as x increases?

(c) Relation to Boyle's Law, $pv = c$.

(d) Relation to the theory of variation.

(e) The gradient of the graph at any point.

(f) The volume $\pi \int_a^b \frac{1}{x^2} \, dx$.

(g) What is the difficulty in finding the area $\int_a^b \frac{1}{x} \, dx$?

(h) How could you find an approximation to the value of the integral in (g)?

___

100

(See illustration facing page 414 for beginning of examination.)

2. *Elementary school arithmetic*
3. *Intermediate school mathematics*
4. *Unifying mathematics*
5. *Decline of high school arithmetic*

⇶⇶ 2. *Elementary school arithmetic*

In 1902 the Department of Education of the Northwest Territories authorized for teacher use Wentworth's *Primary Arithmetic*. The course of studies for the first two Standards (equivalent to grades 1–4) included the following (35, pp. 75–76):

Addition, subtraction, multiplication, and division of numbers up to 100
Addition, subtraction, multiplication, and division of fractions (halves to twenty-fifths)
Use and meaning of fractions to hundredths
Percentage
Use and meaning of measurement units
Reading roman numerals to C

In grades 5 and 6 the work of the first four grades was extended and included common fractions, decimal fractions, application of percentage (simple interest, profit and loss), and use of weights and measures in practical problems. A similar program of studies was followed in Manitoba (28, pp. 1–11).

The method of teaching advocated in this period emphasized the logical aspect of arithmetic. The main objective was "training the power of attention and . . . the reasoning faculty" (34, p. 42). There was considerable interest in improving methods of teaching arithmetic, which led to some rather modern-sounding statements. A book reviewer for the *Educational Journal of Western Canada* had this to say in 1899 (131, pp. 30–31): "Every subject has an immortal inherent rationality which should determine in some measure its method of presentation."

An example of the logical approach (54, p. 248) is given below.

First Lesson on 20

(Introductory remark: Base 10 is so common and important that some teachers think it could be the basis for our teaching. Pupils should be required to use their knowledge of the basal group as the basis of further thinking.)

Q. What is 20?
A. 20 is 2 tens.
Q. Think 20 into nines.
A. 20 is 2 nines and 2 over.
Q. How did you think that?
A. 20 is 2 tens. In each 10 there is a 9 and a 1 so in 2 tens there is 2 nines and 2 ones.
Q. Show that 2 nines and 2 ones are 20.
A. Put a 1 in each 9 and that makes 2 tens, so 2 nines and 2 ones are 20.
Q. Think 20 into eights.
A. 20 is two eights and 4 over.

Those who defended the logical approach to the teaching of number argued against the use of objects as advocated by Pestalozzi and others. The reason, according to them, was that handling objects could "only result in the exercise of the faculty of perception" (133, p. 82), whereas the logical approach exercised the reasoning faculty.

Defenders of the logical approach, however, had their adversaries in western Canada. I. I. Currie, writing in the *Educational Journal of Western Canada* in 1899 (122), claimed that "analysis of number has been pushed to an extreme, even to stultification." He contended that it is wasteful of the pupil's time to make a new analysis every time he forgets a combination. Besides, he continued, pupils do not have a lot of time to acquire a knowledge of arithmetic which has a practical value, and if the system were made more efficient more time might be "devoted to other subjects of higher educational value."

After the first ten or twelve years of this century, west Canadian educators began promoting mental arithmetic. In order to obtain the "highest educational value in the delicacy and accuracy of the thought involved," it was claimed, the pupil should be provided with mental drill in a great number of exercises in simple calculations (125, p. 127). Also, it was alleged that "mental arithmetic secured greater speed and accuracy in less time" (33, p. 57). It was suggested that much time was wasted in "writing arithmetic in the earlier grades, because much more practice can be obtained in mental arithmetic" (148, p. 185).

By 1913 an observer in Manitoba was pleased to report the following (33, p. 57):

> The pendulum is swinging toward centre, and pupils are being drilled on the facts of numbers as well as on the logical study. . . . For a time teachers became so absorbed in the teaching of numbers from the logical standpoint that all else was forgotten.

Stimulus-response learning, which was advocated by Thorndike and which first appeared in the form of mental arithmetic, became a firmly established influence by 1920. The views of an Edmonton teacher writing about this time reveal this influence (160, p. 31).

> It would be far more practical to refer to first principles only at the very beginning of any topic in arithmetic and even then very sparingly and purely as a means of obtaining a "rule" or tool for use. Then we should go ahead and use the tools at once, paying no further attention to their origin. It is useless to try to teach little children the philosophy of number—as the present admittedly indifferent results in arithmetic eloquently testify.

The Number Highway series of texts (71), prepared for elementary pupils by two prominent Alberta educators and officially adopted by the province in 1932, could have served as a model for learning as advocated by Thorndike. Facts and processes were reduced to their elements, and a carefully worked-out program of drill was provided.

The preoccupation with the psychologizing of arithmetic infected west Canadian educators as it had done others in North America. The following statement from a western educational publication indicates the intensity of this preoccupation (137, p. 338):

> Years ago it was assumed that there were 45 simple addition facts and that the mastery of these, accompanied by an understanding of addition by endings, was sufficient preparation for all work in addition. Later, investigations showed that children who knew $7 + 3 = 10$, for example, might not know $3 + 7 = 10$. The reverse combinations have therefore to be taught, and 36 new combinations were added to give a total of 81 facts. Further investigations proved that the zero combinations provided peculiar difficulties, and the addition combinations to be taught grew from 81 to 100 to accommodate the nineteen zero facts. More recently it has been shown that the knowledge of $4 + 3 = 7$ does not guarantee the knowledge of $14 + 3 = 17$, $24 + 3 = 27$, and so on. . . . The original 45 addition combinations have now become 500.
>
> It has been demonstrated that there are 55 skills required in the process of division of common fractions. If learning is to be successful, then, the basis must be meaning and understanding.

To accompany the trend toward accuracy and detailed analysis of arithmetical ideas, arithmetic in western Canada as elsewhere was replete with diagnostic tests, standardized tests, remedial exercises, and systematic analysis of student errors.

For a period during the thirties attempts were made to render drill more palatable through the use of games. In 1936, the *Programme of Studies* for British Columbia listed thirty-five such games (18, pp. 11–14). A Manitoba outline not only listed games but also listed the following criteria for the selection and management of such games (26, p. 165):

1. It should keep all the pupils busy most of the time or most of the pupils busy all of the time.
2. There should be an intrinsic arithmetic value in the game itself. The scoring should afford a real use in arithmetic.
3. The game should put a premium on accuracy and usually on speed.
4. The game should be designed to be played without confusion.

As the Great Depression of the thirties wore on, curriculum makers began to promote "the growth of the view that an aim in education is to help the child in adjusting himself to society (18, p. 6). Just prior to 1940, the Saskatchewan Department of Education recommended that there be no formal arithmetic in grade 1 but still demanded 100 percent mastery of the addition and subtraction combinations in grade 2 (49, pp. 233–37). The change was reflected also in the Alberta curriculum, where it was claimed that "problem solving is not a topic in Arithmetic; it is the curriculum of the subject" (4, p. 252). And finally the change in emphasis was attested to by the textbooks of the day, in which almost every new or at least different learning experience was introduced around some topic socially or personally significant for children: for example, "Joe Wilson Learns How to Make a Model Glider"; "Learning to Fly"; "Conquering the Seas"; and "Wonders of the Past" (69, pp. 16–51).

A word might be said here about the changes in the mathematical preparation of elementary teachers in the western provinces. In 1943 the Alberta legislature set up the Post-War Reconstruction Committee. The *Report of the Subcommittee on Education* was published in 1945 (9). Its main recommendation was to make the preparation of both elementary and secondary teachers the sole responsibility of the University of Alberta. The normal schools closed in 1944, and the faculty of education took over the recommended responsibility in 1945. The basic program is four years in duration and culminates in the B.Ed. degree. Provision is made for elementary teachers interested in specializing in mathematics teaching to take a major in the subject. This has proven to be an unusually fine preparation for mathematics teachers in the elementary school, and the leadership provided by those with this specialty is of the highest quality. Similar moves have been made by the other western provinces, but the normal schools in eastern Canada still operate as the main agent for the preparation of elementary school teachers.

3. Intermediate school mathematics

The intermediate school consisted of grades 7 and 8 in 1900 but later included grade 9. In 1902 the grade 8 level of arithmetical and mathematical education presented quite a varied picture, including arithmetic and mensuration, geometry, and algebra. The following examples from the 1902 "Public School Leaving Examination" of the Northwest Territories (35, pp. 103–4) indicate the caliber of work in this grade:

> A school district is 4 miles wide and 5 miles long and wishes to raise $487.50 in taxes. If there are 5 quarter sections free from taxation what is the tax rate per acre?
> A plate of metal 3½ inches thick and 21 feet long is rolled to form a hollow cylinder having an outer circumference of 3 feet 8 inches. What will it cost to paint its lateral surface at 15 cents a square foot?
> Multiply together $a^2 + ax + x^2$, $a + x$, $a^2 - ax + x^2$, $a - x$, and divide by $a^3 - x^3$.
> A person bought oranges at the rate of 36 cents a dozen; had he received 6 more for the same money they would have cost him 6 cents a dozen less. How many did he buy?
> Prove that a perpendicular is the shortest distance from a point to a straight line.
> (a) Define tangent.
> (b) Draw a tangent to a given circle through a given point. Let the point be outside the given circle.

A reviewer of the results of the examination commented (35, p. 23) that, to do the proof about perpendiculars, many candidates used Euclid's method of proof instead of Hill's, which the reviewer preferred. Hill's *Lessons in Geometry* had just been introduced into the grade 8 program in the Northwest Territories (160, p. 17). A geometry course based on Euclid's Book I would clearly be more rigorous and more amenable to demonstration than Hill's *Geometry*, which emphasized constructional geometry. In fact, the use of Hill's

Geometry was a departure from the usual Euclidean geometry, and "strange to say, a great many of the teachers in the Territories are strongly opposed to this preparatory course" (132, p. 144). By 1912 algebra had vanished, and in geometry more emphasis was being placed on "problems in construction and measurement only" (29, p. 23). Arithmetic, apart from mensuration, concentrated on the application of decimals and percentages to insurance, commission and brokerage, profit and loss, duties, and interest and discount (28, p. 11). The following is a typical problem from a 1912 arithmetic examination: "On May 10th, 1912, Wm. Foster gave F. Jones his note for $425 for four months, with interest at 8 per cent per annum. Write the note and find the value when due." (1, p. 167.)

In 1913 the grade 8 diploma in Saskatchewan still required credit in arithmetic, geometry, and business forms (48, p. 33). That year bookkeeping was removed from the diploma requirement in Manitoba, and one teacher was prompted to remark (129, p. 438):

> What a splendid educational game it is to "make the set come out". When children of eleven and twelve years ask permission to remain after hours to search for a mistake, and then, glowing with success, search for you half over town to let you know that "It came out all right" where are you to find a study that will better develop the inhibition powers as well as develop accuracy? Where can we better teach penmanship and neatness than in the lessons on bookkeeping?

In 1921 the Manitoba entrance examinations at the end of grade 8 included a test for geometry, but geometry was not offered as a separate course in grade 8 after that. By 1923 Smith and Roberts's *Arithmetic* (103) was used in British Columbia, and it contained no geometry. The demise of geometry in grade 8 may have been partly the result of crowding when other subjects were introduced, but there was considerable pressure from high school teachers to leave geometry out of the intermediate grades. A prominent Alberta high school mathematics teacher claimed that teaching geometry in these grades was a "positive injury" and that "it was put there according to my recollection because so many students left school before entering High School and hence got no training in Geometry" (154, p. 15).

The junior high school movement reached the western provinces just prior to 1930 and resulted in the first major provincial authorization of American textbooks for student use. The texts were Thorndike's Junior Mathematics series. The adoption of this series resulted in a great increase in algebra content and a corresponding decrease in geometry and arithmetic. These changes caused some agitation on the part of teachers, particularly in Manitoba and British Columbia (138, p. 167). Modifications were made six years later when *Mathematics for Everyday Use* was adopted.

The objection raised to the Thorndike texts resulted in even greater changes at the grade 9 level. In British Columbia in 1940 a new provincial authorization put arithmetic back into grade 9. An analysis of the text, which remained the provincial authorization from 1940 to 1957, indicated that arithmetical topics appeared on 51 percent of the pages, algebra on 24 percent, and geometry on 20 percent (163, p. 14). Algebra as the sole study for grade 9 was a drastic failure, probably because such content could not meet the curricular demands of the day—namely, the demand that all topics be socialized. A note of apology for including algebra and geometry in the grade 9 course claimed that, because so many pupils leave school at the end of grade 9, "It has been necessary to include in Grade IX material of no immediate value which will enable these pupils to adjust themselves more adequately to their future environment" (19, p. 366). An important claim made in the British Columbia textbook was that the "social aspects of arithmetic are based upon information obtained through questionnaires addressed to representative individuals and business firms in Western Canada" (130, p. x). Around 1940 Saskatchewan authorized Cooper's *Socialized Mathematics*, which apparently lived up to its name.

In half a century of concern for mathematics teaching in western Canada at the junior high school level, the program had become much different from that offered in 1900. For one thing, it had to serve a clientele of much wider abilities and interests. The social concerns of the times resulted in an emphasis on applications rather than on the development of new mathematical ideas at these levels.

4. *Unifying mathematics*

In 1880, wherever a high school curriculum existed in western Canada as many as seven or eight subjects in each grade were mathematical in nature. By 1912 the typical pattern of mathematics courses was as follows:

Grade 9 . . . Arithmetic and mensuration
            Algebra—up to simple equations and simple factoring
            Geometry—constructional and some deductions, Book I

Grade 10 . . . Arithmetic and mensuration
Algebra—H.C.F., L.C.M., fractions, simple equations in one, two, and three unknowns

Grade 11 . . . Algebra—Theory of indices and surds and quadratics
Geometry—Books I, II, and III

Grade 12 . . . Algebra—complete textbook
Geometry—Euclid, Books I, II, III, IV; definitions in Book V
Trigonometry (Hall and Knight's *Trigonometry*)

In addition to the mathematics courses listed for grade 10, a student in Manitoba would also be studying literature, composition, spelling, science, bookkeeping, history, drawing, and music. With so many mathematics courses in the program, it would seem that some attempt would have been made to integrate topics. One important factor working against this was that a student studying mathematics was expected to master a book (Hall and Knight's *Algebra*, Todhunter and Loney's *Euclid*, or Baker's *Theoretical Geometry*) or a section of a book, and the external examination was based directly on the specific contents of that book. Any attempt to integrate topics would have ruined a student's chance of passing the provincial examination.

The increasing demand for more subjects in the curriculum and the trend toward a unit system of six or seven courses per grade began to force integration about 1930. It was quite an undertaking to reduce the fourteen or fifteen courses in a grade to only six or seven, and as one critic complained the unit idea was pushing five years of work into a four-year high school program (156, p. 22).

An interesting controversy arose in Alberta as to how the three mathematics courses of grade 12 could be reduced to one. Many teachers were against unification. One of them explained, "They are furnishing a certain school of educationists in this province with the very chance they crave to depress our mathematical standards to even a lower level than they occupy now" (149). And still another stated his position more clearly by saying, "We might just as well bind together Physics and Biology and call it 'popular science' . . . or put all the subjects in one book and label it 'Hash' " (152, p. 24).

Prior to 1939 there were three grade 12 mathematics courses—algebra (Durrell and Wright's *Senior Algebra*), analytic geometry, and trigonometry—each of which was examined externally by a department of education examination. It is interesting to note that the Durrell and

Wright text contained an introduction to differential and integral calculus. In 1939 it was agreed that the offerings in mathematics should be reduced to two courses—one in algebra and the other in trigonometry and analytic geometry. Finally in 1953 a single course in algebra, called Mathematics 30, replaced the two courses. However, there was still some demand for trigonometry by certain faculties of Canadian universities, so a supplementary half-course, Mathematics 31, was offered on an elective, no-examination basis. It was only a year or two before the elective in trigonometry was made a requirement for students entering the bachelor of science programs of Alberta universities (160, p. 78).

In British Columbia the problem was solved by adding a fifth year (grade 13) to the high school program and placing a course containing trigonometry and analytic geometry in this last year (17, pp. 113–15).

The attempt to design single mathematics courses for grades 10 and 11 has an interesting history. In Manitoba the Thorndike books had been used in the junior high school, and geometry and algebra were restricted to grade 10 and grade 11, respectively (31, pp. 51–68). However, by 1933 the grade 10 course was a unit consisting of one-half algebra and one-half geometry. The algebra and geometry came from two different texts, and they were usually taught on an alternate-day basis with little or no attempt to unify (32, pp. 49–54).

In 1939, a year of extensive curriculum revision, Alberta students in grades 10 and 11 could elect to take either geometry or algebra—but not both—in each of the years (5, pp. 10–13). The grade 9 course was made up of about equal weights of geometry and algebra. This arrangement did not meet with great favor, and committees to offer a solution were set up by both the Alberta Teachers' Association and the curriculum branch of the provincial Department of Education (114, p. 33). By 1945 Alberta students were studying a unified version of algebra and geometry in grades 10 and 11.

In 1946, pupils in grades 10 and 11 in British Columbia began using the text *Education through Mathematics*, which attempted to integrate mathematics completely. One observer noted the following (163, p. 17):

> The style of the geometry sections is radically different from the traditional . . . in that the theorems are imbedded in extensive discussions of applications. These applications include: finding the latitude from the pole star or the sun, measuring the earth's diameter, the pantograph and the trigonometric functions.

424 HISTORY OF MATHEMATICS EDUCATION

However, by 1954 this province again authorized separate algebra and geometry texts in grades 10 and 11.

It is unfortunate that the debates of those days have not been better preserved, because western Canada, which adopted so many features of American education, completely rejected the algebra-geometry-algebra sequence typical of mathematics organization in American schools. Whatever the real reason, one teacher claimed that in learning subjects like algebra and geometry "the time element cannot be ignored in the question of mental adjustments, any more than it can be in purely physical adjustments" (153, p. 3). Apparently he had evidence that exposure to these courses in smaller doses over a longer period of time would facilitate pupil learning.

⇶⇶ 5. *The decline of high school arithmetic*

The development of high school mathematics programs in western Canada can be better appreciated if the role played by arithmetic is clearly understood. J. Hamblin Smith's *A Treatise on Arithmetic* was adapted to Canadian schools and was available as early as 1890. The following excerpts from the first few pages (105, pp. 1–22) will give some idea of the nature of this book:

> Arithmetic is the science which treats the use of number. The number one, or unity, is taken as the foundation of all numbers. To write in words the meaning of a number expressed in figures is called NUMERATION.
>
> To represent by figures a number expressed in words is called NOTATION.
>
> Multiplication is the process by which we find the sum of two, four or more numbers, which are equal.
>
> Division is the process by which, when a product is given, and we know one of the factors, the other factor is determined.

About 100 pages were devoted to the development of arithmetic rules, while the remaining 200 pages contained applications of the rules to problems in currency, measures, simple and compound interest, present worth and discount, equation of payments, profit and loss, stocks and shares, proportional parts, alligation, exchange, and mensuration. A revision (106) came out in 1900 in which the number of "extra problems" in the book was increased from 325 to 528.

By 1912 arithmetic was still taught in grades 9, 10, and 11 in

Saskatchewan and in grades 9 and 10 in the other western provinces. Somewhat later the courses were usually accompanied by a course in mental arithmetic, and a separate examination was provided on the mental arithmetic section by the provincial authorities (30, p. 67). A special text was usually provided from which the teacher could dictate the mental arithmetic examples (100, p. iii). In 1925 the provincial examination for arithmetic in Saskatchewan was a three-hour test, while the tests for algebra and geometry were only two hours each. Up to 1925 there had been no appreciable change in the content of the high school arithmetic program.

In 1925 a curriculum revision in Alberta provided one course in arithmetic in the high school, and that was in grade 11 (160, p. 47). This move stirred up considerable controversy, not only because it reduced the time devoted to arithmetic but also because it created a gap of two years and thus a lack of continuity in the arithmetic program (146, p. 13). The 1936 and 1939 curriculum revisions in Alberta eliminated arithmetic as a high school subject completely except that some arithmetic was retained in the general mathematics course designed for students in vocational patterns and for students needing remedial work (5, p. 35).

The general mathematics course was never popular and was used mainly by low-achieving pupils to gain entrance to the mathematics program for university-bound students.

Partly as a result of the rigor of the provincial examination program, the percentage of students who actually enter the university is not large. Yet any attempt to design mathematics courses more in line with the interests and abilities of students not bound for the university has met with very limited success. Students consider courses not on the academic route to be inferior, and so they are not interested in taking them. Soon after arithmetic was removed as an academic subject it disappeared from the high school program.

There is, finally, a report of a panel of Alberta teachers who in 1942 unanimously agreed upon the following resolution (114, p. 33):

> That a course in arithmetic should be placed on the Senior High School Curriculum, that this course should be in addition to the existing course in mathematics, and should be taken by all students in the school.

It is not easy, anymore, to find anyone to mourn the passing of arithmetic.

CHAPTER TWENTY-ONE

Rethinking School Mathematics 1959–Present

Douglas H. Crawford

◡

1. *The socioeconomic status of Canada in 1960*

As Canada entered the 1960s emphasis turned toward the celebrations of 1967, when confederation would be one hundred years old. Outwardly, then, it was a time of joyful planning and anticipation. Yet it was an uneasy world—one that "faced possibilities of mass destruction quite inconceivable to previous ages" (60, p. 427). Successive federal governments strove to promote nuclear disarmament while wrestling with the problem of whether Canada should arm herself technologically to defend herself from possible bomb or missile attack. The potentialities of technological advances were enormous: "jet flight that whittled down the vast Canadian land mass; atomic power, already applied to a pilot project in Ontario to produce electricity; and advances in electronics that made intricate computers and automated factories increasingly a part of the Canadian business scene" (pp. 427–28).

However, many Canadians were preoccupied with the fact that the unemployment rate in Canada was becoming one of the highest in all the Western world. The flow of capital from the postwar boom had died off, "leaving Canada with much larger productive capacities but facing the need to adjust her production and prices to a strongly competitive new era" (p. 428).

In spite of being tied increasingly to the United States—industrially, commercially, militarily, and even psychologically through the mass media—sectional differences grew because of the strongly regional basis of economic developments. In particular, the Maritimes and the provinces of Saskatchewan and Manitoba felt that they were being left behind commercially.

The results of the 1962 federal election reflected the uncertainties and sectionalism, and no party gained a majority. This continued to be the political situation for the next few years. Ontario was dissatisfied with the Conservative fiscal policies that culminated in the devaluation of the Canadian dollar just before the 1962 election, while Quebec enjoyed a resurgence of French-Canadian idealism and self-pride. The rush of educational and social reforms which swept through the province after the iron rule of Duplessis ended in 1959 was virtually social emancipation and reevaluation. Although separation did not immediately enter the political arena as the goal of a specific political party, it flourished as "a mixture of heady optimism, idealistic nationalism, and long cherished resentments." Its overall grip on Quebec ebbed and flowed to a great extent with the measure of goodwill and understanding that the province received from the rest of Canada. By centennial year, with its joyful and successful Expo '67, the more extreme elements had failed to convince the majority of Quebecers of the wisdom of such a drastic course of action.

2. *The commissions on education*

The same years were years of reexamination of education across Canada. In the year 1958/59, there were royal commissions on education scrutinising the school systems of the western provinces of Manitoba, Alberta, and British Columbia. All these commissions had reported by early 1960. Their major recommendations have been summarised by F. Henry Johnson (67). They show a general trend toward reorganising postelementary education in order to provide more adequately for individual differences and a concern with raising the standards of admission and minimum preparation of teachers, particularly those of the elementary school. The aim here in two of the provinces was to require all those intending to be teachers to have a university degree as soon as this could be achieved. The sixties saw the spotlight swing from west to east, so that every province from Ontario eastwards has had in operation commissions concerned with all or part of education. In Quebec, the parent commission investigated school systems not only in Canada but in many other countries. Its report was issued in five volumes between 1963 and 1966 and, according to Johnson, represented "the boldest attempt yet by a commission to restructure totally a very complex tradition-bound system." The crucial change was the establishment of a ministry of education to centralise previously scattered educational services. Other changes were that fifty-five regional commissions were established to administer suitably large, consolidated school districts; the elementary school was reformed along activist (i.e., Progressivist) lines with the goal of "formation more than information"; and all students were to receive secondary school education via the "polyvalent," or composite, school. As in the West, teacher training was to be at the university level. The same goal was stated for Ontario elementary school teachers with the publication of the McLeod report in 1966 (41).

In Ontario the Commission on Aims and Objectives of Education in Ontario—known informally as the Hall-Dennis commission—was constituted in 1966 to report on the aims and objectives of elementary education. Its terms of reference were extended to include the secondary school, and it finally reported in the spring of 1968. Its report, entitled *Living and Learning* (24), focused strongly on providing a student-centred education appropriate to the technological, fast-changing world of the sixties and seventies. It recommended the elimination of lockstep education, the breaking down of rigid barriers between subjects at the secondary level, a strong de-emphasis of year-end examinations as prime determinants of promotion, and reaffirmed the centrality of the teacher in the educational process—but as a guide to learning by the student.

In Canadian school mathematics, the period under discussion was one of intense activity. Clearly, the place of mathematics in education was being greatly affected by the scrutiny of education as a whole. However, independently of this general scrutiny, worldwide developments were occurring which ushered in an era of unprecedented examination and study of mathematics education in all its aspects.

3. *The 1960 Ottawa seminar*

Three events of significance occurred in 1959. Two originated in the United States—the report of the Commission on Mathematics of the College Entrance Examination Board (CEEB), issued in April 1959, and the Twenty-fourth Yearbook of the NCTM, entitled *The Growth of Mathematical Ideas, Grades K–12*, which was published very soon afterwards. The third was the Seminar on New Thinking in School Mathematics held at Royaumont, France, from 23 November to 5 December 1959, under the auspices of the Organization for European Economic Cooperation.

These events precipitated action at the national level, even though Canada possessed no federal office of education. The Canadian Teachers' Federation was aware of its responsibilities and was fortunate in having as its research director Dr. F. G. Robinson, a graduate in mathematics who in his doctoral work had turned to the psychology of learning mathematics. The federation sent a delegate to the Royaumont seminar and planned a similar seminar in Ottawa in April 1960. To this seminar came some sixty representatives from all the provinces and from all levels and aspects of education in mathematics.

As the foreword to its report stated, the seminar was convened "to give those Canadians most closely involved and interested in school mathematics a starting point on the long road to accurate assessment and possible revisions of their programs and methods" (22, p. iii).

The presentations that had the greatest impact were probably those of Robert Rourke and Hugh Burwell. Rourke devoted his speech to discussing his impressions of a recent visit to the Soviet Union and to outlining recent changes in the United States. He noted that the Russians had excellent in-service training facilities and that they enjoyed tremendous cooperation from top mathematicians. He summarised the new CEEB proposals, noting that they recommended a de-emphasis on Euclid and a move toward developing appreciation of algebraic structure. On the basis of his wide experience, he made the following suggestions for updating Canadian school mathematics:

1. We must think in terms of many programmes.
2. Texts and materials must be written by teams.
3. Never forget the difference between what *can* and what *should* be taught.
4. We must start with a teacher-training programme.

Rourke then discussed areas of broad agreement in the United States regarding the reform of school mathematics.

Burwell spoke on the topic "School Mathematics in Europe," particularly as it related to the Royaumont seminar, where he represented Canada.

He gave a summary of the main ideas presented there and noted that the seminar had underscored the need "to construct a curriculum that emphasises the building of mathematical concepts, structure and understanding just as much as the development of manipulative skills" (22, p. 28).

In concluding, Burwell suggested, "We in Canada should consider introduction of intuitive geometry and inclusion of the study of vectors at the high school level," and he called on "those with the best knowledge of mathematics to give leadership in curricular change," noting that such change would require a solution to the problem of streaming pupils by ability.

The seminar participants obviously felt the need to take further action, for they passed a number of resolutions. The central one was the following (22, p. 161):

> The Seminar recommends to the Canadian Teachers' Federation that it consider ways and means of organizing a Canadian Association of Teachers of Mathematics with member groups comprised of associations of mathematics teachers from the several provinces and others interested in the teaching of mathematics.

In addition, a further resolution spelled out some of the first considerations thought appropriate for such an association. It specified the need to consider the establishment of writing groups at the provincial and national levels.

4. *The Canadian Association of Mathematics Teachers*

In actual fact, the interprovincial developments which seemed imminent in 1960 did not materialize until March 1967, when, again at the instigation of the Canadian Teachers' Federation, a conference was held in Ottawa with the following purpose (21):

> to afford an opportunity for communication among mathematics teachers in various provinces, and between them and mathematicians working outside the classroom. The program was designed to suggest the kind of topic which might fruitfully be studied by later conferences of a national association of mathematics teachers.

The Canadian Association of Mathematics Teachers grew out of this conference. A planning committee established at the time of the conference wrote a constitution and organised a first meeting to be held in December 1967—a fitting climax to centennial year in Canada.

Developments in school mathematics in Canada between 1960 and 1967 thus took place at the province-wide level, with each province making changes and reforms independently of others. Nonetheless, there was a good deal of intercommunication and consultation—some of it at official levels through visits, discussions, and studies of what other provinces were doing, some of it informally by individuals with common or similar problems to solve. In addition, at different points throughout the period various assessments of trends and current reforms in Canada and elsewhere appeared in the form of speeches, articles, books, theses, and reports (90; 117; 121; 123; 155; 163).

Perhaps the best perspective on this period of reappraisal and change can be gained by looking at the ways in which individual provinces approached the problem. Let us look in turn, then, at Alberta, Ontario, and Nova Scotia, as representative of Canada.

→>>→>> 5. *Alberta*

Alberta was among the first provinces to realise the need to "plan and restructure the entire program [in mathematics], Grade I through College." These were the words of her associate director of curriculum, A. B. Evenson, who in his address (124) to the NCTM's 1960 annual meeting in Buffalo, spoke comprehensively about his views on the changing curriculum in mathematics. He explained how, because of the centralisation of education systems in Canada, great care must be exercised in the development of new courses. He outlined what he felt to be desirable features of a new programme in school mathematics. The basic aim was to restructure the entire programme, although to avoid a long and tedious procedure progress might be made on a broken front. Some of its features should be diversification and an emphasis on understanding and insight, on structure, and on deductive methods. He went on to outline urgent needs in building such a programme, pointing out things like the judicious use of resources, particularly teamwork with the master classroom teacher as a vital member of the team; the centrality and complexity of teacher training; the need to try out many things experimentally in regular classrooms; and the importance of public education and public relations. In addition, he pointed out how many of the new ideas and notations—such as placeholders, open sentences, and so on—needed to be clarified before they could be incorporated into a programme. Finally, he spoke briefly of developments in Canada (see also 120 and 123) and predicted that within the next three or four years improvement programmes in mathematics would be greatly accelerated in Canada.

This restructuring of the entire programme began in 1959 with a three-year study of the elementary school programme in arithmetic "to be fairly certain that the foundation programme . . . is as good as we can make it before seriously considering a revision of the secondary school programme in mathematics" (120).

In the same year, a programme of summer institutes for high school teachers was begun at the University of Alberta, and it continued for a number of years. Stimulated partly by the personal nature of these institutes and also in large measure by the forward-looking attitude of the Alberta Teachers' Association in promoting articles and monographs on the new mathematics, the Mathematics Council of the A.T.A. came into being in 1961. A very successful inaugural conference was held in August of that year, and this council has continued to play a significant role in the reshaping of school mathematics in the province. It became one of the first Canadian affiliates of the NCTM, and in August 1966 it acted as a cohost to a summer meeting of the NCTM in Calgary and published a special annual containing a sample of the papers presented at the meetings. A quick count reveals that of twelve contributors to the annual, nine were deeply involved in mathematics education in Canada—three from Alberta, one from Manitoba, four from Ontario, and one from Quebec. Topics ranged from how Manitoba was meeting the challenge of retraining teachers via TV and regional services to an outline of an experimental course in Ontario which was using computer methods to further the student's knowledge of mathematics.

In 1961/62 the provincial department of education experimented in thirty-one classrooms with the grade 7 text from the Seeing through Mathematics series—a series that is essentially student-centred, with very precise mathematical language. The seventh-grade text includes topics such as sets and variables, intersection and union of sets, sets of ordered pairs and graphs, and the conditions involving rate-pairs.

A questionnaire was sent out to educators in the western United States who had some experience with the same mathematics programme. Thirty-four completed questionnaires were returned. Although conclusions drawn from such a survey are clearly tenuous, certain inferences seemed reasonably valid. These included the following:

1. The length was suitable only for superior students.
2. There was doubt as to whether there was sufficient review and

reinforcement of basic skills for other than superior students.
3. Teacher reaction to the discovery approach and to the inclusion of most new concepts was good.
4. In the main, student reaction by superior students was enthusiastic, by average students satisfactory, and by poorer students variable.

In the 1962/63 school year, further experiments were carried out at grade 7 and grade 8 levels, with three texts in each case. Of these, one of the grade 7 texts was Canadian-produced. Control groups and experimental groups were set up to compare growth of mathematical abilities.

As a result of such experiments, it appeared that by 1967/68 the content had been updated in all the mathematics programmes in the matriculation (college preparatory) sequence with the exception of the grade 12 trigonometry (Mathematics 31) course (21, p. 44). In 1966/67 an experiment was tried in Mathematics 31: half a year of trigonometry was followed by half a year of either calculus, linear algebra, or probability. Student reactions to all three variations were similar and favourable. Teacher reaction to the probability course was quite positive, but that portion of the experiment was not continued in 1967/68, as there is now a unit on probability in the revised Mathematics 30 course.

In assessing the situation current in Alberta in 1967/68, Dr. J. Hrabi, provincial director of curriculum, noted that the programme for grades 1–9 was the same for virtually all students and that the "Seeing through Arithmetic" programme was dominant for grades 1–6. The province has accepted the principle of multiple authorisation of texts and is heading in that direction at all levels. Furthermore, another cycle of analysis has started at the elementary level, where "virtually every mathematics program that exists" is being scrutinised.

Hrabi also identified some of the issues that, in his view, mathematics educators have to face. (Are any of them new?)

1. Attempts have to be made to meet individual differences at various stages in the 6–3–3 Alberta programme, and not much provision is made at the junior high school level.
2. The integration of the various fields of mathematics is a problem, and at the high school level the programme "more closely resembles a mixture than it does a compound."
3. How and where to deal with geometry is an important question,

and Canada seems very strongly wedded to Euclidean geometry.
4. The place of computers, calculators, and mathematics laboratories has to be considered.
5. Methodology in mathematics instruction varies widely: "I have a feeling that if you took five or six or seven different teachers, those five or six or seven different teachers could achieve what they all agree upon as the significant objectives of mathematics by five or six or seven different kinds of methodology."

6. *Ontario*

In August 1959 a historic conference took place at Lakefield School, near Peterborough. "There, thirty university professors and high school teachers spent six days exchanging opinions and finally produced a preliminary outline for a total reorganization of the high school mathematics curriculum" (113). The group in question was the Mathematics Commission of the Ontario Teachers' Federation, formed in February 1959 at the instigation of Professor D. T. Faught, of Assumption University (now the University of Windsor), and Howard Mulligan, a teacher at Central Technical School in Toronto. The proposed reorganisation was based largely on the recommendation of the Commission on Mathematics of the CEEB. There was agreement that the present Ontario curriculum was generally sound and that its central core should be incorporated in any new curriculum.

Rigid barriers between algebra, geometry, and trigonometry should be broken down, and much greater care should be taken "to explicitly set forth the set in which various relations are valid." To achieve these desiderata, grade 9 was to include coordinate geometry as well as algebra; certain less important material, particularly the number of stated theorems and memorised proofs, was to be reduced or discarded; and grade 13 was to be reorganised to have one terminal course and two specialised courses, for future mathematical practitioners. (113, p. 206.)

The cooperation of the department of education was secured early in 1960 by Dr. A. J. Coleman, of Queen's University, in negotiation with the chief director of education. As a result, departmental personnel became full-fledged members of the commission (which was renamed the Ontario Mathematics Commission, the O.M.C.), and the department made annual grants to it for experimental purposes. It was a time of great delicacy, according to Kinlin. He attributes much of the success in overcoming the internal consternation of some of the senior departmental officials to the "good judgment and policy of frank and improved consultation" of Frank Asbury, a former mathematics teacher, inspector, and assistant superintendent who was the commission's executive secretary-treasurer (135, p. 5).

This cooperation, among all concerned with school mathematics in the province, bore plentiful fruit in the next few years. Grade 13 problem materials and experimental texts for grades 9–12 were written and tested in the field with the help of the department. Details of the operation, which lasted until 1965/66 have been given by Kinlin (p. 6).

Significant steps in the process of reform were the listing of the experimental texts for grades 9 and 10 in department circulars of 1962 and 1963, respectively, and their coming into widespread use throughout the school systems. The first official action toward course revision at the provincial level took place in January 1963, when curriculum revision committees for the senior division (grades 11–13) and the intermediate division (grades 7–10) were set up.

The new courses for the senior division were introduced in September of 1964, 1965, and 1966, respectively. The main change in the grade 11 course was in approach rather than content, so that it became a course in mathematics rather than in algebra, geometry, or trigonometry. In essence the course is a study of the straight line, with an emphasis on graphs and the use of set language where desirable for the sake of clarity or conciseness. The grade 12 course extends the work of grade 11 to the study of functions and the mathematics of the simpler curves, particularly the quadratic function and its graph. In the grade 13 course the study of functions is further extended "with emphasis on the mapping concept which will be found recurring throughout to the extent that it may be considered the unifying concept of the course" (83, p. 1).

The revised grade 13 course consists of Mathematics A and Mathematics B, not three courses as originally conceived by the O.M.C. Mathematics A and B are equal in instruction time, which remains unchanged at a total of nine hours. Mathematics A is a terminal course in analysis built around the idea of a function as a mapping. It treats the basic ideas of differentiation, has a unit on trigonometric functions, and includes work on second-degree relations and transformations in the plane. Mathematics B is an algebra course with the main emphasis on vectors, matrices, and the algebraic structure of field and group. It also includes a discussion of permutations and probability from the point of view of sets. This course is intended to be more difficult and is suitable for students planning to pursue further studies in mathematics.

The revisions in the intermediate division began in September 1964 with the introduction of a new grade 7 course on an optional basis. This course became compulsory in 1965, at the same time that an optional grade 8 course became available. Here again it is the approach and emphasis that have changed most. Set language is introduced gradually, discovery by the student is emphasised, and there is a movement away from procedural or mechanical rules toward reliance on the more basic number relationships or properties. Some new content (e.g., numeration systems, inequalities, and statistics and probability) appears at the expense of what was regarded as an undue emphasis on computation.

The subsequent revisions in grades 9 and 10 carry these changes further—to the study of real numbers and to the inductive treatment of the basic geometrical relationships associated with angles, triangles, quadrilaterals, and circles at the grade 9 level; and to the introduction of vectors and three-dimensional geometry at the grade 10 level. Also introduced for pupils in the four-year programmes were modified parallel courses that make liberal use of practical problems from business and industry.

Several features of the revisions are noteworthy. They include the following:

1. Acceptance of the integrated (spiral) development of topics
2. Provision of optional topics that offer an opportunity for specialisation in topics of particular interest and simultaneously enable less able students to spend more time on the core, if desirable
3. Phasing of the change from optional to compulsory over a period of one or two years to allow for students' transitional problems and for teacher preparation

The part played by the O.M.C. in bringing about these revisions was a significant one. Through its elementary and secondary committees it discussed new ideas and formulated suggestions that found their way to the appropriate curriculum committees, often because of common membership. In addition, from 1965 onward its summer-study committees, financed originally by the Ontario Curriculum Institute and subsequently by its successor, the Ontario Institute for Studies in Education, examined developments elsewhere and with the help of consultants suggested guidelines for reform in the four-year programme (38) and in the study of high school geometry (39). The work of such committees is continuing strongly and is being extended to other aspects of mathematics curricula. Particularly striking was the movement toward approaching geometry from various points of view—via vectors and transformations as well as by the traditional synthetic and analytic methods. Furthermore, as a result of its 1965 study committee dealing with the four-year programme, the O.M.C. initiated an experimental programme beginning at the grade 10 level. Materials for grades 10, 11, and 12 were tried out in sequence from 1966 onward and were important criteria in the development of the relevant curricular revisions of the department of education.

Yet another revision occurred in September 1966—the introduction of Curriculum P1, J1, Interim Revision Mathematics for K-6. This was largely the outgrowth of the work of the Elementary Education Committee of the O.M.C., which from its early days encouraged experimentation in elementary classes and acted as an agency for fostering better communication of modern ideas. A subcommittee's production in 1965 of a suggested course outline for grades K-8 led to the appointment of a K-6 study group, which met for a month in July 1965 and produced an excellent report (37).

The report recommended a study of various interrelated sequences of topics, stemming from an initial consideration of sets of real objects. Stress was placed on teaching mathematics, not just arithmetic; a strong case was made for teaching geometry from kindergarten through grade 6, beginning with a study of objects in three dimensions; and relations and functions were seen as central ideas in mathematics which demanded attention in the K-6 curriculum.

In the provincial K-6 revision, the emphasis is on three main streams of experience in mathematics—namely, number and operations, measurement and relationships, and shapes and space.

No specific assignment of topics to grade levels is given, although experiences are listed as following each other in preferred sequences. Graphing and geometry are considered as items to be included from the earliest grades, and the entire revision is based on the centrality of children's actual experiences with real objects from which they can abstract mathematical ideas.

Experimentation has also been going on in the areas of computer science and data processing. According to Bonham (20, p. 3), a course of study has evolved in the business and commerce branch which introduces the student to data processing through a study of manual, electromechanical, and finally electronic means. The student is also introduced to commercial programming and to systems analysis, either of which represents a potential career for him if he chooses to follow up these introductory courses with further study.

In mathematics, computer-science courses based on material prepared by the School Mathematics Study Group (SMSG) were taught experimentally in a number of schools in 1965/66 and 1966/67. The committee in charge of the experiment decided that the problems employed to develop understanding of computers and problem solving should not be limited to mathematical ones only, and it began to compile a set of such wide-ranging problems. In 1967/68 the committee continued to meet, with a view to deciding whether to recommend to the department the establishment of a computer-science curriculum committee.

By the end of 1967 revision work in grades 11 and 12 leading toward a full implementation of the new grade 13 curriculum (83) was under way (20). In addition, a minor revision of the revisions at grades 7 and 8 was contemplated, mainly to reduce duplication and give more flexibility.

Finally, it should be emphasised that no courses of study are being published for those not intending to complete, or not capable of completing, the two-year secondary programme, as it is felt that the needs of such students are best met by the local development of flexible, individual curricula.

In this set of revisions of the 1960s, several changes in department policy have been pointed out by Kinlin (135). They include the following:

1. Acceptance of the principle of field pretrials of curriculum materials
2. Growing acceptance of consultation with teachers and other educators while a curriculum revision committee is deliberating
3. General acceptance of the idea that courses should be designed to be of short duration to allow for flexibility of change
4. Breaking down of traditional, internal dividing lines in the department of education to enable the pooling of resources for in-service education

Both the K–6 and the K–13 geometry study committees of the O.M.C. continued their work subsequently. That of the K–6 committee took the form of an experimental project, which was set up in January 1966. This group prepared materials for the study of geometry in grades 1, 2, and 3 and for the study of graphs, mappings, and relations in grades 4, 5, and 6. These materials were then tried out across the province, in a three-phase experiment in 1966/67, by teachers specially selected and trained in the summer of 1966. Evaluation and further experimentation in 1967/68 ensued, with particular emphasis on the laboratory approach in grades 2 and 5.

An outgrowth of the emphasis of the project on laboratory learning was the visit of Edith Biggs from England to conduct a concentrated series of workshops in the fall of 1967. The objective was to have teachers "learn by doing" and so develop techniques that encourage active learning by the student. The organisation of the workshops was unusual and worthy of note, and in the author's view they were generally successful. In particular, elementary and high school teachers worked together in the same groups, and so they developed understanding for each other by personal encounter.

Some further significant changes in the department's view of its role in curriculum development (probably resulting from the K–6 developments since 1965) were spelled out in December 1967 by Garth Kaye (20). He cited horizontal and vertical integration of the school system as two of the main aims of the curriculum section. He also stated that the department had to move away from a directive role to providing leadership and resources. This required a belief in teachers' willingness to accept an extended responsibility. It might take a long time for some teachers to be ready for this shift in emphasis. Most significantly, his final remarks were on the subject of textbooks:

> I don't think there is anything more limiting to the development of a curriculum than a single textbook concept. We are working right now towards an elimination of the textbook. We are encouraging publishers to publish booklets to segment the material for courses of study in a small handy type of pamphlet or booklet. But I think we must relegate the textbook to what I claim is its proper place as one—and *only* one—of a wide variety of aids to the teacher to develop a programme in his or her classroom. And for too long it has been *the* aid. For too long it has meant that we as teachers have not really accepted our responsibility.

Other developments, such as the use of TV and the trend toward the concept of the ungraded school, also occurred. In the area of curricula and curriculum development, the developments and trends might be summed up as movements toward (1) greater flexibility in curricula, in use of texts and methods, and in school organisation and (2) a comprehensive research-development-implementation type of curriculum development intended to be self-modifying and self-correcting.

7. *Nova Scotia*

The Nova Scotia high school curriculum before the recent revision is discussed by Frank E. Milne (164). A reexamination of curricula in mathematics at both the elementary and the high school levels was initiated in 1961. The procedure followed was to form two committees —one for grades 1–6, the other for grades 7–12—broadly representative of teachers, university people, and departmental officials.

Major curriculum developments in other Canadian provinces, in the United States, and in the O.E.E.C. countries were studied first, and then the SMSG materials were scrutinised in some detail. The next step was to initiate pilot studies across the province, using commercial texts chosen as embodying the SMSG philosophy. About forty schools were involved in pilot programmes, which were still going on at the senior high school level in 1967/68.

Two developments of major significance in the carrying out of reforms occurred in 1962. One was the founding of the Nova Scotia Mathematics Teachers' Association under the sponsorship of the Nova Scotia Teachers' Union; the other was the pioneer use of television to overcome the alarming need for qualified high school teachers in the field of science and mathematics.

For those contemplating reform, much food for thought was provided at the inaugural conference of the Mathematics Teachers' Association in April 1962, attended by over a hundred mathematics teachers and educators (36). The key speaker was Professor D. T. Faught, of the O.M.C. He pleaded not for a more difficult curriculum but for one that "could be easier and certainly more vital, stimulating and challenging to the student of today." He first discussed the need for reform and pointed out that it existed also in physics, where reforms initiated at MIT, bypassing the high school teachers, should act as a warning against proceeding in a similar manner with mathematics. He then considered the subjects of algebra and geometry and the way in which they had developed toward abstraction. Algebra was just as deductive as geometry, while geometry itself was pulled into algebra on the one hand and into analysis on the other. He stressed the modern unity of mathematics and indicated how trigonometry could become a very unifying subject if emphasis were placed on periodicity, vectors, De Moivre's theorem, and polar coordinates.

In the final part of his address, Father Faught identified four groups of people (teachers, university professors, civil servants, inspectors and local school boards) who should be deeply involved in curriculum instruction at the high school level, and he discussed the part being played in Ontario by the Mathematics Commission there, citing not only its successes but some of its failures! Among the latter was the key one of not keeping all the teachers of the province informed of suggested changes. The result of this had been to generate a good deal of resistance to any idea that had its genesis in the commission. However, the commission did have accomplishments to its credit. It had been successful in establishing summer schools and night courses to allow teachers to update themselves, and it was making good progress with its programme of writing and testing experimental texts. In addition, it had just begun to publish the *Ontario Mathematics Gazette*, a periodical devoted to high school teaching.

Other significant parts of the conference were the symposium entitled "Some Questions regarding Modern Mathematics" and the evaluation address given by Floyd Robinson. Dr. Robinson gave it as his view that there is "a genuine sense of urgency" in proposals for change across Canada. He noted common elements in such proposals and the fact that a few Canadian mathematicians appeared to think that no change in either content or emphasis was required in the secondary school programme. Two areas of apparent controversy were the fruitfulness of strict axiomatic approaches and the battle over the traditional synthetic geometry course. He felt that these differences of opinion were being resolved, at least at the provincial level.

He also raised the following questions (as he had done in 1960 at the National Seminar):

1. What content should be taught and when?
2. How should it be taught?
3. To whom should it be taught?

The first question tied in with the study of mathematical development in students; for example, with Piaget's stages of concrete and formal operations. One of the emerging possibilities with respect to the second was the use of programmed learning for both student and teacher, especially as the SMSG materials were about to be rewritten in the form of programmed textbooks. The third was the thorniest of all. Dr. Robinson pointed out the following (36):

> We should not indulge in extravagant claims to advance the importance of mathematics education. . . . We may as well concede the fact

that study after study has revealed that the total extent of the typical adult's usage of mathematics is confined to the very straightforward parts of arithmetic. What I am saying is that it is not-at-all obvious why the vast majority of students need much mathematics, either of the traditional or modern variety.

He also disclaimed

the supreme faith of many teachers that mathematics courses, no matter how violently disliked by students, can miraculously develop the student's ability to solve real-life problems.

In presuming to offer some proposals for future action, he concurred with the need for a team approach and made a special plea for the inclusion of psychologists "where their special interests indicate the possibility of a contribution to the problems of mathematical education."

Some of his other important points were the following:

1. The need for at least a measure of national consideration and stimulation in developing mathematics curricula, in view of the fact of the increasing interprovincial mobility of school and university students.
2. The lack of real experimentation with respect to new Canadian mathematics programmes. Such experimentation would be valuable in answering various questions, such as, Will there be any deterioration in sheer manipulative skills if an emphasis is put on underlying structure and unifying concepts?
3. The continuing problem of in-service training. He compared the Canadian teacher's fifty-hour weekly workload of teaching, preparation, supervision, and clerical duties with the provision made for one full day per week devoted to in-service training for his Russian counterpart.

Subsequent annual conferences give up-to-date reports of tryout programmes and feature excellent articles on various aspects of updated school mathematics, such as the concepts of group and inverse.

Educational television began operating in the province in September 1962. Initially, in mathematics, five 20-minute programmes per week were screened in grade 11 geometry and algebra. "These programs of direct instruction, supplemented occasionally by enrichment programs, were an attempt to assist teachers and pupils by providing a continuing and well-organized mathematics program via television" (21). The total number of pupils receiving instruction by television climbed from about 5,000 in 1962/63 to something like 100,000 in 1966/67, when telecasts of grade 7 and 9 mathematics were offered as two of the nine courses available.

In addition, for several years a series of Saturday morning, in-service programmes have been telecast for teachers. Among other materials used have been the SMSG, SRA, and Holt, Rinehart, and Winston teacher-training films. According to W. F. Garth, supervisor of television instruction for the Nova Scotia Department of Education, the extra stimulus and specialised aid of ETV provide a basis for the work of the nonspecialist teacher and assist him "more efficiently than textbooks did in the past."

Another major influence in school mathematics reform was the part played by the Canadian Mathematics Congress. In cooperation with the department of education and through the Nova Scotia Summer School for Teachers, it has offered a four-summer block programme designed for high school teachers. In 1967 there were eighty-six teachers enrolled in the junior high school block programme and forty-four in the one for senior high school. At the elementary level well-known mathematics educators have acted as instructors in modern school arithmetic since 1964.

The pilot programmes begun in 1962 covered the whole area of school mathematics, including proposals for change in grade 12 mathematics. Particular texts were normally given a year's tryout, after which the teachers involved met with the relevant curriculum committee to report their experiences. On the basis of their reports and discussions, relevant text materials were then authorised by the department. Among the materials tried out at the elementary levels were Cuisenaire rods and Unifix cubes, while programmed learning materials in grade 10 algebra and geometry were used with a class of boys and a class of girls. However, the teachers involved did not feel the programme was effective, and it was dropped after one year of use.

As a result, a Canadian version of the Addison-Wesley Elementary Mathematics series was finally authorised for grades 1–6. At the senior high school level, the Houghton Mifflin texts were viewed favourably, but the programme was still experimental in 1967/68 with geometry in grades 10 and 11 still in the tryout phase. At the grade 12 level, a "home produced" programme was agreed upon, consisting of half a year of coordinate geometry and trigonometry and half a year of algebra with an optional calculus unit. The algebra and calculus were in the process of being taught experimentally in 1967/68.

→→→→→ 8. *An overview*

The period in question was clearly one of intense activity, not only in those provinces just considered but equally in all the other provinces.

The main trends at the elementary level might be seen as including the following:

1. Acceptance of the principle of teaching mathematics, not just arithmetic. This implies integrating geometrical and algebraic experiences with traditional arithmetic.
2. Downward movement of certain content and concepts implied by item 1 and also by revisions at the secondary level.
3. Emergence on the one hand of structured materials such as those of Cuisenaire, Stern, and Dienes.
4. Emergence on the other hand of the environmental approach associated with the Nuffield project.
5. A general emphasis on the activist approach and the use of guided discovery (implied by both items 3 and 4).

Surveying trends and development at this level in the report of the 1967 Canadian Teachers' Federation (C.T.F.) conference, *Mathematics and the Teacher*, Norman France reminded his audience that mathematics in the elementary school involves teachers and students just as much as content. In considering on what basis a topic should be included, he made the following comment (21, p. 17):

> We should not seek to justify the inclusion of a topic by the claim that children are thereby enabled to do more complicated operations at an earlier age. Rather should we apply the test: "Can the pupil appreciate and enjoy the experience?" In fact, the constructors of the curriculum need to go a step further and ask: "Can the teacher appreciate and enjoy the experience of teaching this topic?"

He went on to discuss the experimental, environmental approach of the British (later adopted in the 1966 Ontario revisions) and the trend towards structural apparatus. He stated (p. 20):

> All in all, the structured approach through the use of this kind of apparatus will provide a valuable complement to the work done in

environmental studies. The skills and understanding which result from the use of the apparatus can be applied to solve the problems met in the experimental field. Which particular piece of apparatus proves to be most effective in the long run will be more a function of the teacher and of the child than of the concrete analogy which the apparatus provides.

In his view, we want variety in our approach—a multiplicity of method, not an automatic, universal approach. Teachers are not in actual fact shackled, and it is our job to persuade them to enjoy their freedom. In a cogent passage near the end of his talk, he spoke the following words (p. 22), which seem to sum up the essence of what we should strive for at the elementary level.

> After all the programmes and materials have been reviewed, the fundamental truth emerges once more—the teacher, not the method nor the content, really determines the effectiveness of what is being done. So let us remember first and foremost to cater for her needs. We must be realists. We cannot advocate something which is beyond her powers. She needs help but she doesn't need cosseting. The more we spell out what we think has to be done the more the average teacher will feel she has to conform. The "new" mathematics can be just as restrictive, academic, formal and dull as the old if we try to prescribe what has to be done and how it shall be done. But the best "new" mathematics has these features: (1) structure and order; (2) greater stress on concept relationships; (3) concepts learned at an earlier age; (4) discovery enhances learning and retention; (5) creative thinking encouraged; (6) concrete materials complement symbolic manipulation for ground of understanding; (7) teaching skills tidies up after discovery; (8) practical applications, reinforced learning.

What of trends and developments at the secondary level? Among the main ones are the following:

1. A strong movement towards treating mathematics as a unity and eliminating compartmentation
2. Permeation of the curriculum with the idea of set and relation (or function)
3. Strong emphasis on the structural aspects of mathematics as opposed to the computational aspects
4. Growing recognition that flexibility must be greater, both in content and approach, to meet the great variety of needs among students of differing aptitudes and abilities

The evidence collated by Edgar B. Horne (163) on change in college-preparatory curricula up to 1965 is worth noting also. He compared the content of provincial revisions with the CEEB proposals of 1959, finding noticeable differences in content and major differences in sequence and organisation.

> British Columbia's new program was most like the C.E.E.B. program, but New Brunswick's experimental program, with its inclusion of transformations of the plane and extensive work with vectors, showed the greatest change from traditional content and presentation.

He also found that

> no one pattern adequately described the mechanism of change. Individuals were more influential than groups, although the relative importance of individuals and groups varied. Nevertheless, a significant factor in all the revisions was the active participation of university mathematicians.

Horne proposed a national committee "as the most practical way of bringing about greater communication and co-ordination of effort among the provinces" and recommended a multiple-textbook-authorisation policy instead of a single-textbook one. Soon after, the Canadian Mathematics Congress reconvened its Secondary School Committee to study the problems of curricula coordination and common curricula.

Much has indeed been achieved. An updating of content, with needed restructuring to emphasise basic ideas so that students get a proper view of what mathematics is and how it operates, has certainly occurred. Also, progress has been made in the realm of adopting more flexible methods.

Perhaps the first flush of enthusiastic reform is now over, and some of the issues that require continued attention are being seen more clearly. Those identified earlier by Hrabi certainly demand attention. It would appear that the level requiring the most study and experiment now is the junior high school level, say ages twelve to sixteen, for this is the transitional period during which students test their abilities and interests and so need every help in making decisions that will affect their future significantly.

It has to be said that, notwithstanding a fair amount of effort directed towards the needs of the average and below-average pupil, the predominant effort at the secondary level has catered to the needs of the college-bound students. Probably reform had to proceed in this way, initially, because of the pressures of exploding knowledge and technological progress. However, the time has come when much more effort must be focused on the problems of appropriate mathematical experiences for the other-than-superior student. One seemingly accepted approach to this is by way of the principle of the core curriculum adopted in several provinces.

Some further insights into areas needing continued examination can be gained from the contributions made at the 1967 C.T.F. conference on the theme "What Should the Schools Be Doing?" George Duff made a number of interesting points (21, p. 3). Among them were the following:

1. The importance of fitting drill intelligently into both the elementary and the high school grades by approaches using such things as patterns, arithmetic in solving applied problems, and calculating aids.
2. The need to include plenty of specific examples and lots of graphical work from which to build up the notion of function.
3. Replacement in mathematics of "rigour" by "adaptability." By this Duff meant emphasis on how to analyse, elaborate upon, and generally respond to new situations. "One should play down the notion that the idea is just to get 'the answer,' and concentrate on developing skill and endurance, as opportunity is afforded by the growth of the child."

In his contribution (p. 6), Dr. Gwilliam spoke of developments in vocational and technical education at the federal and provincial levels, and reported the following as the main complaint from technical institutions:

> Most of the students coming into these institutions after twelve years of schooling have never really thought in an applied sense about mathematics; never been asked to translate a physical situation into mathematical terms then to do something with the mathematical model— resolve, modify it or improve it, then change it back into a physical situation. Their learning has been too axiomatic, not intuitive.

Representing the business world, Nazla Dane of the Canadian Life Assurance Association spoke very urgently about the need to retain the how as well as the why in school mathematics. She gave details of a survey she made in supermarkets, department stores, and in the head office of a life insurance company. Her firm conclusion (p. 12) was that "although the 'why' of mathematics is very necessary to the proper use of the manipulative functions of the subject if someone is to advance, the 'how' is of great importance because of accuracy requirements."

In the course of making this survey, she became concerned about the need for better teacher-student-employer relationships. She wondered if employers should demand more in the way of basic computational knowledge from new employees and pleaded with the schools to teach basic economic concepts in more exciting ways.

Clearly, important problems await further and continued study.

Lastly, what of the teacher in this period of change, upheaval, and reassessment? Provision for updating teachers seems to have varied from province to province, according to particular needs, facilities, and appreciation by those in authority of the importance of such updating. It is certain that a major effort has been made by every obvious means—summer courses, winter courses, seminars, workshops, TV programmes, and so on. In the first years of reform, the emphasis was on an updating of content, particularly because of the influence of the major reform movements in the United States. However, the importance of approach as well as of content has been increasingly recognised, through the growing knowledge and awareness of studies and projects like those of Piaget, Dienes, the University of Illinois Committee on School Mathematics, and the Nuffield project (21, p. 34).

What other developments have been affecting the teacher? Notably, developments in teaching resources resulting from technology. These include the use of TV, film in various forms, programmed learning, and the computer. Experimentation in using some or all of these together in the form of computer-assisted instruction is also well under way.

Also discussed at the 1967 C.T.F. conference was the effect of these developments on the role of the teacher and on those needs of the teacher which must be met if school mathematics teaching is not to continue to be "sterile, stagnant, and seventeenth century." In Crawford's view (p. 39):

> The changes in content and approach resulting from knowledge explosion, population explosion, teacher shortage, and modern technology all point generally not to a diminution in your role but to a definite shift in it from a relatively isolated individual to becoming the key

member in a team of various specialists. More and more your role will tend to become, in my view, that of a resource person, coordinator, and personal tutor, freed from much routine work, but still exerting a vital personal influence on students.

Dr. Elliott pointed out a number of basic things which the teacher and public must realise (p. 41). Among them were the need to convey a liking of mathematics to students and the need to be forward-looking in our preparation of teachers in the future. These factors implied the design of special courses at the universities and colleges of education. In Elliott's view, the needs of high school teachers included the following: "The pedagogical courses must include suggestions for teaching new topics not yet in the curriculum as well as the established topics. Any topics which seem likely to enter the curriculum at any level in the next five to ten years *must* be included."

Moreover, since in his judgment teachers will need updating in content and methods about every five years, "the terms of professional employment of teachers must be changed by the teachers' organizations, the departments of education and the school boards."

At least one half-day a week for elementary teachers and two half-days a week for high school teachers should be available for professional study and discussion. In addition, it was argued (p. 43) that auxiliary staff should be provided.

> No business organisation would employ its professional and executive personnel in menial clerical and manual tasks; secretaries and clerks are employed at lower salaries to do these tasks. Use of these auxiliary personnel for reproduction services to prepare teaching materials, and for routine supervision of playgrounds, luncheons, study areas will free teachers for more essential work.

Crawford's conclusions, stated in the background paper prepared for the Commonwealth Conference on Mathematics in Schools in September 1968 (121, p. 3), seem to provide an apt summing-up of recent developments in Canada.

> Two main conclusions seem in order. The first is that every province now realises that curriculum development is an unending process. The second is that sound development without well-planned teacher education and updating is impossible.
>
> Clearly, sound improvements in the teaching of Mathematics are best achieved by the continued cooperation of all involved in the edu-

cational process, and should always be aimed at helping the child to learn optimally.

We end, therefore, as we began, by realising that sound development in school mathematics is inextricably bound up with the evolution of education and society. School mathematics in Canada since 1959 has surely helped to indicate strongly where change in content and in the teaching and learning environment is needed. In doing so, it has pointed up the fact that the role and status of the teacher must change significantly if education in mathematics is to match the challenge of the complex technological environment of the twentieth and twenty-first centuries.

Epilogue: Summary and Forecast

PART SIX

Phillip S. Jones

CHAPTER TWENTY-TWO

Present-Day Issues and Forces

1. *Persons and personalities*

In any activity so concerned with individuals as education should be, the personal influence of persuasive, thoughtful, kindly, concerned teachers and leaders will always be present. We have noted earlier, for example, the possible effect of overlapping committee memberships. To try to analyze or carefully portray personal factors, such as those related to the influence of E. H. Moore, J. W. A. Young, David Eugene Smith, E. G. Begle, or Max Beberman, is far from easy. It is difficult enough with respect to those belonging to earlier eras; with respect to those of the present day it is nearly impossible, for we lack the perspective of time. Nevertheless, although we could not mention all important people nor expand on the personal achievements of any, we have for the sake of bibliographical reference, for the identification of writers with their projects, and for clarity and concreteness, mentioned many persons. We regret the apparent unfairness of this. The inclusion or exclusion of a name may appear to imply a judgment that we did not make and would not wish to imply.

As partial compensation, and as an aid to persons who may wish to explore further these facets of mathematics education, Appendix A gives a list of members of the major committees whose reports have been discussed and a list of the officers of the National Council of Teachers of Mathematics and the editors of its journals and yearbooks.

Even this listing has an unwelcome implication that some were chosen and others not. The NCTM has had many hardworking and useful committees not included here. We listed the members of those committees that appear in the report section of Bibliography A. In general, these are the committees whose reports, published separately or circulated widely as offprints from the journals, seemed to call for some extensive discussion in the body of the text.

2. *Research in mathematics education*

Throughout this book many studies have been mentioned, some of which would properly be labeled "research." They were mentioned, for example, in connection with the history of theories of the learning of mathematics and with the so-called battle of the objectives between those stressing directly utilitarian goals and those believing in the more general values associated with mental discipline. Much of this research was done by persons who thought of themselves as psychologists rather than mathematics educators. In fact, the concept of mathematics education as a separate professional area, in the United States at least, is definitely a twentieth-century development. It probably should be dated from the period of David Eugene Smith's incumbency as professor of mathematics at Teachers College, Columbia University (he served from 1901 through 1926), and that of J. W. A. Young as "associate" and then as assistant professor and then associate professor of the pedagogy of mathematics in the mathematics department of the University of Chicago (1892–1926). Young had gone to Chicago immediately after his completion of a Ph.D. in group theory at Clark University in 1892. Smith, after receiving a doctor's degree from Syracuse University, served as professor of mathematics at Michigan State Normal College from 1891 to 1898, and then as principal of the State Normal School at Brockport, New York, before going to Teachers College. Both Columbia and Chicago were universities with rapidly developing traditions of graduate study and research. The first doctoral theses in mathematics education at Teachers College were those of L. L. Jackson and A. W. Stamper, submitted in 1906 and dealing with the history of the teaching of arithmetic and geometry, respectively. C. W. Stone, in 1912, wrote on factors determining arithmetical abilities.

The development of advanced degrees and research specializing in mathematics education is, therefore, even more a child of the twentieth century than the field itself. The changing patterns of the topics subjected to careful study and the amount of research being done in mathematics education are now of historical interest. We asked Helen B. Smiler to begin a study of research in the field of mathematics education. Her data is incomplete, and she herself warns against certain hasty interpretations. However, we thought her approach interesting enough in itself, and sufficiently indicative of further possible approaches to the recent history of mathematics education, to merit being included as Appendix B. She points out that, as would be expected, her data shows that the topics for research studies reflect changing issues and forces, such as a period of considerable interest in test construction and standardization and a shift from studies of computational ability to ones dealing with the understanding of concepts.

The most recent developments in the area of research in mathematics education include the setting up of positions largely or solely devoted to research in this area and the training of specialists to fill them, the work of several research centers, and the founding of three new specialized journals (*Educational Studies in Mathematics*, Reidel, Holland; *Investigations in Mathematics Education*, SMSG; and *Journal for Research in Mathematics Education*, NCTM).

⇢⇢⇢ 3. *Recurring issues and continuing themes*

To this writer, who has also been a reader of the previous pages, it seems again that one of the lessons of history is that much about human beings changes only very slowly. Consequently activities, such as education, that are closely involved with the minds, drives, and emotions of human beings, change very slowly in their basic issues. In fact, the perspective of history often shows that what were thought to be significant changes in issues were more nearly mere variations in the relative emphasis or prominence accorded to them.

This view that the real issues in mathematics education are continuing over time, changing slowly if at all, would of course be trivial and agreed to by all were we to state our issues so globally as to ask, "Should we provide a better education in mathematics?" or even "Should we teach mathematics, in some form, to all students?" This view would be false were we to state our issues so narrowly and in such time-related terms as to ask, "Should we set up computer-assisted-instruction units in every school?" This view that the fundamental issues have a high degree of permanence would be dangerous if we were to conclude from it either that "there is nothing new under the sun" or that "there is no hope for continuing improvement and growth and therefore no point to continuing effort or study." Neither of these conclusions expresses our belief or intent.

The analysis of issues set up in Part Two and represented by figure 7.1, although designed as a framework for discussing mathematics in the elementary school, is also valid for the secondary school and college. It displays the interconnections between the issues expressed by the simple words *why, what,* and *how.* (How sequence the content? How conduct instruction?) This writer might have added two other interrogatives: *to whom* and *when.* However, these are closely tied to the first three. For example, your answers to *why, what,* and *how* may depend in part on whom you are teaching—college-bound students from the upper socioeconomic group or potential college students from disadvantaged areas with uncertain motivations. In other words, the question *How do you accommodate instruction to individual and class differences?* is a continuing issue that has grown in prominence as the school population has grown and changed. It must be considered in seeking answers to all four of these issues: Why? What? How organize and sequence content? How organize and implement instruction?

Each current issue in mathematics education suggests projects for further experimentation and research. For example, the question of how we should deal with individual differences suggests:

1. Do different individuals respond to different learning-teaching strategies? If so, how are the proper strategies for any particular individual determined and brought to bear?
2. Is there a set of learning strategies that is common to significant subgroups of the school population, such as disadvantaged youths?
3. How can educational technology be combined with other techniques to individualize mathematical instruction effectively?

It is an oversimplification to state educational issues as dichotomies, even though it helps to focus the debates that swirl around them. The issue *Why should we teach mathematics?* naturally leads to dichotomies. Because it is practical, useful in vocations, in everyday life, and in forming decisions as citizens? Or because it is an art the appreciation of which can enrich everyone's life? In 1925 J. W. N. Sullivan, in his *History of Mathematics in Europe,* wrote: "It is convenient to keep the old classification of mathematics as one of the sciences, but it is more just to call it an art or a game. . . . Unlike the sciences but like the art of music or the game of chess, mathematics is a free creation of the mind." In 1960 the mathematical physicist E. P. Wigner, in

Commentaries on Pure and Applied Mathematics, described mathematics as "the science of skillful operations with concepts and rules invented for just this purpose. . . . [Although] the concepts of elementary mathematics . . . were formulated to describe entities which were suggested by the actual world, the same does not seem to be true of more advanced concepts."

Both mathematics and its practitioners are Janus-headed, with one face looking toward the physical world for problems, inspirations, and applications, and the other looking at pure logic and the hypothetical structures it builds. Wigner felt that advanced mathematics is not so clearly based in the physical world as is elementary mathematics. However, many pure mathematicians claim a physical or geometric intuition as the source of their theoretical ideas, even as many applied mathematicians urge teachers to stress structure and axiomatics by beginning and ending instruction with the study of mathematical models.

The concept of a mathematical model serves to highlight the fact that dichotomies in education are artificial and incomplete statements of problems. The real world may inspire and use mathematics, but it is not identical with mathematics. To use mathematics, one first analyzes the real-world situation for its essential elements and relations and then seeks a mathematical system with corresponding elements and relations—in other words, a mathematical structure that is isomorphic to our idea of the real-world system. The mathematical system is then studied and manipulated. Its results are reinterpreted into the physical world. The critical step here is the selection of a mathematical model that fits the problem. Is it a system of inequalities rather than equations? Is it a finite geometry or arithmetic rather than a Euclidean or infinite projective space? Knowledge of a variety of mathematical structures, systems, and theories has become essential to persons in modern operations analysis, physics, computer design and operation, psychology, and other fields. The pure-applied, theoretical-practical, art-tool dichotomies no longer exist for many people. Theory is highly practical! However, not all students will easily understand the nature of mathematical models. Even fewer will consciously make extensive use of this concept in their daily work, although the concept applies even to computing one's sales tax or income tax, the family budget, and the proper mixtures for sprays and fertilizers. But structure and theory seem unnecessary and unimportant to many persons who need mathematics on these levels and for these purposes.

The issue of *What are the goals of mathematics instruction?* has been neglected recently. It should probably receive renewed attention.

It is no longer sufficient merely to claim mathematics should be learned by every one either for its utility or for its aesthetic values. Persons fully aware of current social, scientific, political, economic, and mathematical trends must share in the development of a new consensus as to the proper goals for mathematics education today.

Here, again, a current issue suggests needed research and experimentation. For example, two questions with respect to mathematical models which should be investigated are:

1. How can students be taught or exposed to experiences such that they learn how to create and use mathematical models in problem solving?
2. At each grade or maturity level, what real-world problems or modeling situations can be made into appropriate examples and exercises?

Some psychologists hold that students will learn their needed skills and routines more easily, for longer retention and simpler extension, if they understand the "why," the reasoning and the structure of the system. In this case an understanding of proof and structure becomes a goal of instruction, not merely because in it one sees the beauties of the art that is mathematics nor because through it one can find the proper structure to use in applying mathematics, but because it creates the "understanding" or "meaning" that is needed.

All this leads to the questions *How do we teach mathematics?* and *How do we help students to become mathematicians?* More specifically, we need research and experimentation that will develop both teaching and testing devices associated with meaning and understanding. Do we stress discovery teaching and hope to encourage creativity as well as develop insight? Do we stress precise terminology and complete, careful deduction with the hope that children thus learn to be modern mathematicians? Some mathematicians would use the analogy that one must learn to walk before he can run. He must learn some facts and manipulations before he can have a mind free to reach for more imaginative things. He must be able to test his conjectures quickly and accurately before he can take advantage of the ideas brought to him by a soaring imagination. Oliver Heaviside, the somewhat eccentric, largely self-taught English scientist-mathematician, stated at a conference on the teaching of mathematics in 1901:

> Boys are not philosophers and logicians. . . . Now the prevalent idea of mathematical works is that you must understand the reason

first before you practice. This is fuss and fiddlesticks. . . . I know mathematical processes that I have used with success for a very long time of which neither I nor anyone else understands the scholastic logic. . . . There is something wanting, no matter how logical people may pretend. . . . Geometry should be entirely observational and experimental at first.

Here, then, are issues that are still alive, although they are not exactly the same now as they were years ago. For emphasis and clarity we state them as overly simplified dichotomies:

1. *What are the goals of mathematical instruction?*—Utility or aesthetic appreciation? Problem solving or theorem proving? Manipulative mastery, creative conjecturing, or deductive dilettantism? The question is old, the answer is changing. The need is to reexamine the issue, to define the *educational* utilities of all the elements of our dichotomies, and to associate with them the students, topics, and methods that will lead to achieving the goals that are appropriate for the students.

2. *What should we teach at each grade level?*—Facts or the formulation of conjectures? Manipulative processes or mathematical structures? The solving of equations or the properties of a field? Clearly answers to these questions about the content of our program will be influenced by our assessment of the goals. Again, a likely conclusion is that we must have all—that the problem is what doses to administer to what patients.

However, insofar as our task is to teach *mathematics*, the curriculum planner must continually reckon with two facts and two implications. The body of mathematics is growing at a phenomenal rate. So are the applications of mathematics. These facts imply that more people must learn more mathematics earlier. Thus they must either begin to learn it earlier or learn it more rapidly. The trend of the day is to move topics downward to earlier grades in the belief that the organizing and generalizing function of a knowledge of structure will enable students to learn more with less problem solving and drill. Is this a sound trend? Can we rely on structure and understanding to reduce the need for drill? Are there maturity levels below which it is impossible to teach some topics? These questions need research.

3. *How can we organize our content and classroom methods to achieve these goals in a rapidly growing and diverse school population?*

The following statement by C. A. Laisant, a Belgian mathematics educator of the turn of the century, appears on the title page of the Alexander-Dewey arithmetic book: "The problem is always the same: to interest the pupil, to induce research, to give him continually the illusion, if you please, that he is discovering for himself, that which is being taught to him" (Bib. A, 85). However, discovery is an individual activity. Should all individuals "discover" the same things at the same time? Can they?

Again the issue and even some proposed solutions are old; but new methods (programmed materials, computer-assisted instruction), new versions of old methods (laboratory and discovery teaching), and new administrative organization (team teaching, modular scheduling) produce exciting and strenuous new challenges to improve the quality of our instruction and its adaptation to individual differences in interests, abilities, and needs.

4. *Forces*

The forces playing upon mathematics education are "where the action is." It is they that make issues come to the fore. They direct discussion and research. They function to produce at least a temporary resolution of the issues at any given time. The broad analysis of forces represented by figure 7.2 applies well at all levels, not merely at that of the elementary school. This analysis classifies forces as derived from mathematics itself, from psychology, from society, and from curriculum theory. The forces are due to changed situations. For example, the forces derived from mathematics are the rapid growth of its content, the phenomenal expansion of its applications (both in their number and in the fields to which mathematics is applied), and the changing nature of the subject or of mathematicians' view of it. All these forces from mathematics were among the stimuli that produced the "revolution" of the decade from 1952 to 1962.

This revolution was strongly guided by the late-nineteenth- and twentieth-century emphases on generalization, extension, abstraction, and axiomatization in mathematics itself. By the same token much of the reaction to the revolution also came from mathematicians (many, but not all, of them applied mathematicians) who felt that too early a stress on abstraction and axiomatization, too great a departure from real-world roots and applications, might produce a loss of interest among students as well as a lessening of intuitive insight and creativity. Some said, "Rigor!" Others replied, "Rigor mortis!"

These forces continue to bring pressures to bear on the curriculum, causing a continuing downward movement of content. The elementary school program is expanding to include much more geometric material, probability, and more advanced number ideas such as negative numbers. The secondary school program is receiving not only parts of the classical college algebra, analytic geometry, and calculus, but also simple linear algebra (perhaps not under that name or as a separate course), matrices, and probability and statistics.

These forces have also encouraged research, in and out of classrooms, such as the work of Piaget on stages in learning and the readiness of children for new generalizations, or research concerning the nature and importance of properly sequencing subsidiary ideas in constructing a new curriculum, or study of the effect of content, teachers, and instructional methods on student attitudes.

The psychological-curricular research and development just listed should not, however, be associated entirely with mathematical forces or mathematicians. The recently developed teamwork between psychologists and mathematicians has, of course, partially grown out of concern about the effects of introducing more abstraction, more study of meaning and structure, and less drill into school instruction. This has been a concern of educators and school boards, but mathematicians have shared it. However, mathematics education is also being subjected to forces generated by changing interests and theories in psychology. Recent psychological interest in the nature and encouragement of creativity has been consistent with new goals in mathematics education. Recent psychological investigations of learning seem sometimes to return to an added stress on stimulus-response psychology, as in the work on programmed learning; at other times they seem to be rehabilitating mental discipline in a new and scientific guise. These matters have been discussed in earlier chapters. Here we merely point out that changing theories and research results in psychology are increasingly recognized as strong forces affecting mathematics education. In the past the psychological forces have substantially affected elementary school content and method. They are now exerting an increasing influence on the secondary school. The influence is increasing because of the involvement of psychologists with mathematicians and mathematics educators in recent curriculum development and innovation. Their involvement and help with further research and learning-theory development is urgently needed because the mathematical forces directed toward abstraction and the downward movement of advanced content are immediately opposed by questions about the development of students' rate of learning and of students' capacity for and interest in abstraction.

We must also look at the societal forces. Immediately after World War II there was broad concern for growing technical manpower needs as well as criticism of the schools for anti-intellectualism. These forces, embodied in government-sponsored reports and in tirades in the public press, directed the attention of educators toward developing programs of excellence for superior, motivated, college-bound students. In fact, the solid scholastic efforts of returning veterans and the spirit of the press of the day increased the prestige of the scholar—especially the scientist—and added to the motivation of the student.

It is now increasingly being realized that these motivating forces and new school programs missed a large and important segment of the school population. Newer social forces are redirecting research and development toward programs for the less able or less well motivated or culturally deprived student. At the moment it appears that the combination of mathematical and societal forces will produce continuing change in the programs for both groups, but at different rates and perhaps in different directions.

Further and new societal forces are the beliefs and emotions of the youthful activists of today with their concern for a narrowly defined "relevance." Their interests tend to be directed more toward the social sciences than toward technical areas such as engineering. Theoretical physics and mathematics may have felt the shift of interest less than engineering, but they remain difficult subjects that have become a little less glamorous.

The effect on mathematics of the forces generated by new curricular theories will probably again be greater at the elementary than at the secondary level. College and vocational requirements and accreditation standards still tend to produce a substantial inertia in the high school. However, even here team teaching may improve instruction, and modular scheduling with team teaching may make for better adaptation to individual differences.

In the past many committee reports have not led to new developments so much as they have revealed beliefs that were already generally accepted. However, the very advanced "dreaming" of the Cambridge Conference reports may encourage not only the downward movement of course content but also the development of less compartmentalized, more integrated and spiraled, courses. If history can be trusted, more experimental texts and teaching, more evaluation, and more ballyhoo will be needed to turn this into a general movement.

Similarly, SMSG's attempts to develop courses or units stressing the use of applications and mathematical models in teaching deserve more success than they appear to have been able to achieve.

5. *Teacher education*

It is scarcely necessary to point out that all the movements suggested above call for changes in the teacher-education program. At all levels teachers will need to know more, such as geometry and simple algebra in the elementary school, computer programming, linear algebra, vectors, and the geometry of transformations in the secondary school. They also need more experience with programs functioning at different levels of the curriculum, of student capacity, and of teaching method (e.g., discovery and laboratory teaching) and classroom organization (e.g., team teaching).

It may seem that a continuing provision of institutes and in-service programs to update teachers should be unnecessary if teacher-training institutions modify their programs properly. However, if our statements about the continuing curricular change required to keep up with continuing changes in mathematics and its uses are accepted, then some provision must be made for stimulating the continuing education of in-service teachers.

6. *Similarities and differences*

It is illuminating to compare the problems and trends in the United States with those in Canada. An interesting view of the nature of a church-dominated system appears in the chapter on mathematics education in Quebec. Other chapters of Part Five give some insight into the advantages and disadvantages of a centrally supported and controlled school system with external examinations. The system of one province, for example, has been characterized as "at once one of the most uniformly efficient in the world and one of the most paralysing to individual initiative in teacher or school" (Bib. B, 75, p. 171).

It appears that from as far back as the report of the Committee of Ten, Canadian educators have been influenced by developments in the United States. However, they have not always accepted the conclusions reached south of their border; and when they have, not every Canadian has approved. Witness A. H. McDougall's statement that "there is a growing tendency to introduce the Yankee idea of getting over difficulties by leaving them out" (Bib. B, 88, p. 7). In similar vein but with no mention of Yankees, a Canadian comment dated 1950 shows that the progressive stress on felt needs and social utility affected the Canadian curriculum too—perhaps arriving a little later than in the United States. At that time J. A. Sonley said that the mathematics course in the elementary schools "has been 'watered down' until the Grades 7 and 8 mathematics texts resemble a book in Social Studies with a few fractions thrown in to separate the topics" (Bib. B, 44).

Not only do Canadian educators have a pleasantly pithy way of expressing themselves, but we who are their neighbors may find the differences between their curriculum and ours more interesting than the similarities. The Canadian schools have been much more receptive to the idea of integrating rather than compartmentalizing their curriculum, to the idea of spiraling the treatment of topics and subjects, and to the use of inductive approaches to instruction. Particularly in teaching geometry their use of induction has been prominent, but it is currently associated with a stress on the use of an "environmental approach" in the elementary schools.

It likewise appears that Canadian educators, in facing many of the same issues ("knowledge" versus "power" as a goal, the fruitfulness of strict axiomatic approaches, the replacement of "rigour" by "adaptability"), may have stated the issues and made their choices a little more clearly and sharply than their American colleagues. This may be an illusion due to the style of the writers of Part Five and the compression of their story into fewer pages. In any event this makes Part Five good reading and further stresses the generality and continuity of the basic issues in mathematics education.

7. "L'Envoi"

Whether or not we have had a "revolution" in mathematics education in the last two decades is a moot question. We need more and better data on exactly what has been accomplished and what the effect has been on our students. Robert B. Davis states, "The 'new mathematics' revolution has not taken place, but . . . it probably will, possibly within the next ten years" (137). He bases his argument largely upon the forces generated by the educational potential and needs of computer technology. Certainly the societal, mathematical, and psychological forces we have cited above will continue to exert pressure for change. As teachers we must learn to enjoy the prospect of continued learning, experimentation, evaluation—and to be content with the feeling of discontent that accompanies the perception of new goals, and with progress that falls short of perfection.

The report of the superintendent of public instruction for the state of Michigan for 1899 includes a talk given by E. C. Goddard at the state teachers meeting. This address, entitled "The Distribution of Mathematics through the Twelve Grades," recommended that *mathematics*, not merely *arithmetic*, be taught in the elementary school. It called for teaching that would consider the capacity of the young child and use concrete and constructive methods in teaching him geometry, for the inclusion of algebra in grades 6–12 along with some arithmetic and geometry, and for the introduction of trigonometry into the high school. Then Goddard turned to a consideration of the goals of mathematical instruction, pleading that teaching develop "the power to think closely, to reason clearly, to see things through to their end." He closed with the following anecdote. (Remember that he came from a college town, with many rooms to rent to students, at a time when electricity was being introduced into some homes.)

> Said a business man to me: "My boy is in the high school and yet he could not tell me where the Charity Islands are." And pity if he could! It is no part of an education to lumber up the mind with such useless facts. This boy was educated if, when he needed that knowledge, he knew how to find where the Charity Islands, or any other islands are. There is a suggestive sign [on homes in Ann Arbor]—"Rooms to let in the upper story, unfurnished." No doubt our schoolboys' and girls' upper stories ought, when ready to let, to be furnished. And yet I had rather their condition be expressed by that other sign, so often used in modern blocks in these days of machinery—"Room to let, with power."

This comment still epitomizes the problem, the joys, the frustrations, and the rewards of the teacher. We still deal with persons who come to us with "room to let, with power." Helping them to furnish the room, to harness and apply the power, is the challenge! When we see that it has been done, we have the reward.

APPENDIX A

Members of Cited Committees and NCTM Officers, Directors, and Editors

The effect of different persons as individuals on the development of mathematics education is impossible to dispute, although the effect is almost impossible to define and measure, especially in a work of this size. The same person serving as a member of two committees not only impresses his own views and beliefs on two reports but also serves to convey the germs of ideas from one to another. (As a counterexample, however, two rather radically different reports that appeared in 1940 were produced by committees that shared the services of Albert A. Bennett and Maurice L. Hartung.) Further, the "visibility" of any one person as author, speaker, or officer has real but unmeasurable effect on the extent of his influence.

These difficulties, together with the danger of unfairness as a result of omissions, have led to the policy of holding personal mention to a relative minimum in our text. However, the importance of individual influence has led us to feel that some recognition should be extended—hence the decision to include in this Appendix a list of persons active in mathematical education. The list and its cross-referenced alphabetical index were compiled by Helen B. Smiler, a mathematics teacher and graduate student at the University of Michigan.

Committees and subcommittees are listed in the chronological order of their reports. In some cases the extensiveness of subcommittees necessitated listing only their chairmen, but every effort has been made to include all the members of the principal comittees, together with their place of employment at the time the committee report was published. We call the attention of readers to the facts that (1) often committees changed in composition during their period of existence, (2) often committees co-opted the services of others not originally or officially on the committee, and (3) some committees, such as the Panel on Teacher Training of CUPM, have had a continuing existence and a correspondingly changing membership. We urge users to check these matters in the original records, which can be traced through Bibliography A.

The officers, directors, and editors of the National Council of Teachers of Mathematics are also listed chronologically.

Committees are labeled numerically, with subcommittees identified by a second number, and a "subsubcommittee" by a third. To illustrate: The American Commissioners of the International Commission on the Teaching of Mathematics are identified as "6." Subcommittee 1 of Committee I of the Commission is identified by "6.1.1." Similarly, the officers, directors, and editors of the NCTM are identified by "24" as the preliminary number and then by another one that identifies the area of service.

CITED COMMITTEES

1. *Committee of Ten on Secondary School Studies* (NEA)— 1893

Charles W. Eliot, Chairman	President of Harvard University
James B. Angell	President, University of Michigan
James D. Baker	President, University of Colorado
William T. Harris	U.S. Commissioner of Education
Richard H. Jesse	President, University of Missouri
Henry C. King	Oberlin College
James C. Mackenzie	Headmaster, Lawrenceville School, Lawrenceville, N.J.
Oscar D. Robinson	Principal of high school, Albany, N.Y.
James M. Taylor	President, Vassar College
John Tetlow	Headmaster, Girls' High School and Girls' Latin School, Boston, Mass.

1.1 *Subcommittee on Mathematics of the Committee of Ten on Secondary School Studies*

Simon Newcomb, Chairman	Johns Hopkins University
William E. Byerly, Vice-Chairman	Harvard University
Arthur H. Cutler, Secretary	Principal of a private school for boys, New York, N.Y.
Florian Cajori	Colorado College
Henry B. Fine	College of New Jersey (now Princeton University)
W. A. Greeson	Principal of high school, Grand Rapids, Mich.
Andrew Ingraham	Swain Free School, New Bedford, Mass.
George D. Olds	Amherst College
James L. Patterson	Lawrenceville School, Lawrenceville, N.J.
T. H. Safford	Williams College

MEMBERS OF CITED COMMITTEES

2. *Committee of Fifteen on Elementary Education* (NEA)—1895

William H. Maxwell, Chairman	Superintendent, Brooklyn, N.Y.
T. M. Balliet	Superintendent, Springfield, Mass.
Edward Brooks	Superintendent, Philadelphia, Pa.
Oscar H. Cooper	Superintendent, Galveston, Tex.
N. C. Dougherty	Superintendent, Peoria, Ill.
Andrew S. Draper	President, University of Illinois
Charles B. Gilbert	Superintendent, Saint Paul, Minn.
J. M. Greenwood	Superintendent, Kansas City, Mo.
William T. Harris	U.S. Commissioner of Education
L. H. Jones	Superintendent, Indianapolis, Ind.
A. G. Lane	Superintendent, Chicago, Ill.
A. B. Poland	State Superintendent, New Jersey
W. B. Powell	Superintendent, Washington, D.C.
E. P. Seaver	Superintendent, Boston, Mass.
H. S. Tarbell	Superintendent, Providence, R.I.

3. *Committee on College Entrance Requirements* (NEA)—1895-99

A. F. Nightingale, Chairman	Superintendent of High Schools, Chicago, Ill.
William H. Smiley, Secretary	Principal, High School Dist. 1, Denver, Colo.
George B. Aiton	Inspector of High Schools, Minnesota
J. Remsen Bishop	Principal, Walnut Hills High School, Cincinnati, Ohio
John T. Buchanan	Kansas City, Mo., high school
Paul H. Hanus	Harvard University
Burke A. Hinsdale	University of Michigan
Ray Greene Huling	Principal, English High School, Cambridge, Mass.
Edmund J. James	University of Chicago
William Carey Jones	University of California
James E. Russell	University of Colorado
Charles H. Thurber	Morgan Park Academy and University of Chicago

3.1 *Conference on Mathematics of Committee on College Entrance Requirements*—1896

Professors:

William E. Byerly	Harvard University
Doolittle	University of Pennsylvania
Henry B. Fine	Princeton University
A. W. Phillips	Yale University
J. H. Van Amringe	Columbia University
L. A. Wait	Cornell University

Schoolmasters:

W. F. Bradbury	Latin School, Cambridge, Mass.
A. H. Cutler	Cutler School, New York, N.Y.
Fletcher Durell	Lawrenceville School, Lawrenceville, N.J.
J. G. Estill	Hotchkins School, Lakeville, Conn.
S. A. Farrand	Newark Academy, Newark, N.J.
L. R. Hunt	Free Academy, Corning, N.Y.

4. *Committee on the Definition of College Entrance Requirements in Mathematics* (AMS)—1903
H. W. Tyler, Chairman	Massachusetts Institute of Technology
T. S. Fiske	Columbia University
W. F. Osgood	Harvard University
J. W. A. Young	University of Chicago
Alexander Ziwet	University of Michigan

5. *National Committee of Fifteen on the Geometry Syllabus* (NEA)—1911
Herbert E. Slaught, Chairman	University of Chicago
Charles L. Bouton	Harvard University
Edward L. Brown	North High School, Denver, Colo.
Florian Cajori	Colorado College
William Fuller	Mechanic Arts High School, Boston, Mass.
Walter W. Hart	Shortridge High School, Indianapolis, Ind.
Herbert E. Hawkes	Yale University (to Columbia University)
Earle R. Hedrick	University of Missouri
Frederick E. Newton	Andover Academy, Andover, Mass.
Henry L. Rietz	University of Illinois
Robert L. Short	Technical High School, Cleveland, Ohio
David Eugene Smith	Teachers College, Columbia University
Eugene R. Smith	Polytechnic Preparatory School, Brooklyn, N.Y.
Mabel Sykes	Bowen High School, Chicago, Ill.

6. *International Commission on the Teaching of Mathematics—American Commissioners*—1911–12
David Eugene Smith, Chairman	Teachers College, Columbia University
W. F. Osgood	Harvard University
J. W. A. Young	University of Chicago

Chairmen of committees and subcommittees are listed below. The members are not included here, but they are named in the index, where numerical listings identify the committee or subcommittee for which each worked.

6.1 *Committee I, Mathematics in the Elementary Schools*
C. N. Kendall	State Commissioner of Education, New Jersey

6.1.1 *Subcommittee 1, Schematic Survey of American Educational Institutions: Their Sequence and Interrelation*
David Snedder	Commissioner of Education, Massachusetts

6.1.2 *Subcommittee 2, Mathematics in the Kindergarten*
Patty Hill	Teachers College, Columbia University

6.1.3 *Subcommittee 3, Mathematics in Grades K–6*
Theda Gildemeister	State Normal School, Winona, Minn.

MEMBERS OF CITED COMMITTEES 471

6.1.4	*Subcommittee 4, Preparation of Teachers for Grades 1–6*	
	F. G. Bonser	Teachers College, Columbia University
6.1.5	*Subcommittee 5, Mathematics in Grades 7 and 8*	
	Walter W. Hart	University of Wisconsin
6.1.6	*Subcommittee 6, Preparation of Teachers for Grades 7 and 8*	
	Ira S. Condit	Iowa State Teachers College
6.2	*Committee II, Special Kinds of Elementary Schools*	
	George D. Strayer	Teachers College, Columbia University
6.2.1	*Subcommittee 1, Industrial Classes in Public Schools*	
	H. S. Yonker	State Normal School, Oshkosh, Wis.
6.2.2	*Subcommittee 2, Corporation Industrial Schools*	
	Henry Gardner	Assistant Superintendent of Apprentices, New York Central
6.2.3	*Subcommittee 3, Preparation of Teachers of Mathematics for Trade and Industrial Schools*	
	W. A. Baldwin	State Normal School, Hyannis, Mass.
6.3	*Committee III, Mathematics in the Public General Secondary Schools*	
	George W. Evans	Charlestown High School, Boston, Mass.
6.3.1	*Subcommittee 1, Boys' Schools*	
	Henry M. Wright	English High School, Boston, Mass.
6.3.2	*Subcommittee 2, Girls' Schools*	
	Ernest G. Hapgood	Girls' Latin School, Boston, Mass.
6.3.3	*Subcommittee 3, Coeducational High Schools in the East*	
	Charles D. Meserve	Newton High School, Newton, Mass.
6.3.4	*Subcommittee 4, Coeducational High Schools in the Middle West*	
	Charles Ammerman	McKinley High School, Saint Louis, Mo.
6.3.5	*Subcommittee 5, Coeducational High Schools in the South*	
	George W. Evans	Charlestown High School, Boston, Mass.
6.3.6	*Subcommittee 6, Coeducational High Schools on the Pacific Coast*	
	H. D. Gaylord	Cambridge, Mass.
6.3.7	*Subcommittee 7, The Preparation of Teachers of Mathematics for the Public High Schools*	
	L. C. Ames	University of Missouri
6.3.8	*Subcommittee 8, The Six-Year Curriculum*	
	Arthur Sullivan Gale	University of Rochester
6.3.9	*Subcommittee 9, Failures in the Technique of Secondary Teaching of Mathematics: Their Causes and Remedies*	
	William Betz	East High School, Rochester, N.Y.
6.4	*Committee IV, Mathematics in the Private General Secondary Schools*	
	William E. Stark	Superintendent, Hackensack, N.J.

6.4.1 *Subcommittee 1, Boys' Schools, Including Religious and Military Schools*
John S. French   Morris Heights School, Providence, R.I.

6.4.2 *Subcommittee 2, Girls' Schools, Including Religious Schools*
S. A. Courtis   Detroit Home and Day School, Detroit, Mich.

6.4.3 *Subcommittee 3, Coeducational Schools*
C. W. Newhall   Shattuck School, Faribault, Minn.

Appendices

6.4.a *Report on Mathematics in Evening Technical Schools*
A. D. Dean   State Education Department, New York

6.4.b *Report on Private Correspondence Schools*
W. F. Rocheleau   Interstate School of Correspondence, Chicago, Ill.

6.4.c *Report on Mathematics in Schools and Colleges for Negroes*
W. T. B. Williams   Hampton Institute

6.5 *Committee V, The Training of Teachers of Elementary and Secondary Mathematics in the United States*
E. H. Taylor   State Normal School, Charleston, Ill.

6.5.1 *Subcommittee 1, The Training of Teachers of Mathematics in Professional Schools of Collegiate Grade, Separated from or Connected with Colleges or Universities*
Clifford B. Upton   Teachers College, Columbia University

6.5.2 *Subcommittee 2, State Normal Schools*
H. Clay Harvey   State Normal School, Kirksville, Mo.

6.5.3 *Subcommittee 3, Private Normal Schools*
M. E. Bogarte   Normal University

6.5.4 *Subcommittee 4, Teachers for Normal Schools*
J. C. Brown   Horace Mann School, New York, N.Y.

6.6 *Committee VI, Mathematics in the Technical Secondary Schools in the United States*
C. N. Haskins   Dartmouth College

6.6.1 *Subcommittee 1, Public, Private, and Corporation Trade Schools*
F. D. Crawshaw   University of Wisconsin

6.6.2 *Subcommittee 2, Public and Private Commercial Schools*
J. E. Downey   High School of Commerce, Boston, Mass.

6.6.3 *Subcommittee 3, Agricultural Schools*
J. E. Ostrander   Massachusetts Agricultural College

Supplementary Report: *The Industrial School of Secondary and Intermediate Grade*
Nathan N. Dickler   Manual Training High School, Brooklyn, N.Y.

MEMBERS OF CITED COMMITTEES 473

6.7 *Committee VII, Examinations in Mathematics Other than Those Set by the Teacher for His Own Classes*
    T. S. Fiske   Columbia University

6.7.1 *Subcommittee 1, Nature of Promotion in Elementary Schools and Admission*
    H. C. Pearson   Horace Mann School, New York, N.Y.

6.7.2 *Subcommittee 2, Entrance to College by College Examinations*
    H. D. Thompson   Princeton University

6.7.3 *Subcommittee 3, Entrance to College by College Entrance Board Examinations*
    Virgil Snyder   Cornell University

6.7.4 *Subcommittee 4, Entrance to College by State Examinations*
    C. F. Wheelock   State Education Department, New York

6.7.5 *Subcommittee 5, Entrance to College by Certification*
    N. F. Davis   Brown University

6.7.6 *Subcommittee 6, State and Local Examination of Teachers*
    Robert J. Aley   President, University of Maine

6.7.7 *Subcommittee 7, Examination of Actuaries*
    J. K. Gore   President of the Actuarial Society of America

6.8 *Committee VIII, Influences Tending to Improve the Work of the Teacher in Mathematics*
    E. P. Cubberly   Leland Stanford University

6.8.1 *Subcommittee 1, Scientific Societies and Periodical Literature*
    F. N. Cole   Columbia University

6.8.2 *Subcommittee 2, Teachers' Associations and Reading Circles*
    Gustave LeGras   College of the City of New York

6.8.3 *Subcommittee 3, Teachers' Institutes*
    A. W. Stamper   State Normal School, Chico, Calif.

6.8.4 *Subcommittee 4, State Inspection and Supervisors of Instruction*
    E. B. Skinner   University of Wisconsin

6.8.5 *Subcommittee 5, Activities of Publishers and Their Agents*
    L. L. Jackson   New York, N.Y.

6.8.6 *Subcommittee 6, The Teaching of Mathematics in Summer Sessions of Universities and Normal Schools*
    Herbert E. Slaught   University of Chicago

6.9 *Committee IX, Math in Technological Schools of Collegiate Grade*
    H. W. Tyler   Massachusetts Institute of Technology

6.9.1 *Subcommittee 1, Independent Technological Schools*
    C. S. Howe   Case School of Applied Science, Cleveland, Ohio

6.9.2	Subcommittee 2, Technological Departments of Colleges and Universities	
	S. E. Slocum	University of Cincinnati
6.10	Committee X, Undergraduate Work in Mathematics in Colleges of Liberal Arts Universities	
	H. S. White	Vassar College
6.10.1	Subcommittee 1, Men's Colleges	
	F. C. Ferry	Williams College
6.10.2	Subcommittee 2, Women's Colleges	
	W. H. Maltbie	Baltimore, Md.
6.10.3	Subcommittee 3, Coeducational Colleges	
	Thomas F. Holgate	Northwestern University
6.11	Committee XI, Mathematics at West Point and Annapolis	
	Clifford B. Upton	Teachers College, Columbia University
6.11.1	Subcommittee 1, The Training of Army Officers, Including Schools for Graduates of West Point	
	C. P. Echols	U.S. Military Academy
6.11.2	Subcommittee 2, The Training of Naval Officers, Including Schools for Graduates of Annapolis	
	W. J. King	U.S. Naval Academy
6.12	Committee XII, Graduate Work in Universities and in Other Institutions of Like Grade in the United States	
	Maxime Bocher	Harvard University
6.12.1	Subcommittee 1, Course of Study and Master's Degree	
	D. R. Curtiss	Northwestern University
6.12.2	Subcommittee 2, Preparation for Research and the Doctor's Degree	
	Percy F. Smith	Yale University
6.12.3	Subcommittee 3, Preparation of Instructors for Colleges and Universities	
	E. B. Van Vleck	University of Wisconsin
7.	National Committee on Mathematical Requirements (MAA)—1920	
	J. W. Young, Chairman	Dartmouth College
	J. A. Foberg, Vice-Chairman	State Department of Public Instruction, Pennsylvania
	Vevia Blair	Horace Mann School, New York, N.Y.
	A. R. Crathorne	University of Illinois
	Walter F. Downey	English High School, Boston, Mass.
	C. N. Moore	University of Cincinnati
	E. H. Moore	University of Chicago
	A. C. Olney	Commissioner of Secondary Education, Sacramento, Calif.
	Raleigh Schorling	Lincoln School, New York, N.Y.
	David Eugene Smith	Columbia University
	H. W. Tyler	Massachusetts Institute of Technology
	P. H. Underwood	Ball High School, Galveston, Tex.
	Eula A. Weeks	Cleveland High School, Saint Louis, Mo.

MEMBERS OF CITED COMMITTEES 475

8. *Subcommittee on Training of Teachers of Mathematics of Commission on the Training and Utilization of Advanced Students of Mathematics (MAA)*—1935

William L. Hart, Chairman	University of Minnesota
J. O. Hassler	University of Oklahoma
Earle R. Hedrick	University of California at Los Angeles
M. H. Ingraham	University of Wisconsin
E. J. Moulton	Northwestern University
Herbert E. Slaught	University of Chicago

9. *Committee of Seven on Grade-Placement in Arithmetic* (Northern Illinois Conference on Supervision)

Carleton Washburne, Chairman	Superintendent of Schools, Winnetka, Ill.
Orville T. Bright	Superintendent of Schools, Flossmoor, Ill.
Harry O. Gillet	Principal, University of Chicago Elementary School
J. R. Harper	Superintendent of Schools, Wilmette, Ill.
Raymond Osborne	Principal, Francis W. Parker School, Chicago, Ill.
O. E. Peterson	Head of Department of Education, Northern Illinois State Teachers College
Howard C. Storm	Superintendent of Schools, Batavia, Ill.

Associates:

Mabel Vogel Morphett	Director of Research, Public Schools, Winnetka, Ill.
William Voas	Psychologist, Public Schools, Winnetka, Ill.

10. *Committee on the Function of Mathematics in General Education of the Commission on the Secondary School Curriculum of the Progressive Education Association*—1940

Albert A. Bennett	Brown University
Cuthbert Daniel	Editorial Consultant, Radio Research Project, Princeton University
Harold Fawcett	Ohio State University School
Maurice L. Hartung	University of Chicago
Robert J. Havighurst	Director for General Education, General Education Board
Joseph Jablonower	Board of Examiners, New York, N.Y.
Ruth Kotinsky	Secretary of Commission on Secondary School Curriculum, PEA
V. T. Thayer	Educational Director of Ethical Culture Schools; Chairman of Commission on Secondary School Curriculum, PEA

11. *Joint Commission on the Place of Mathematics in the Secondary Schools (MAA and NCTM)*—1940

Representing the Association:

K. P. Williams, Chairman	Indiana University
Albert A. Bennett	Brown University

11. *Joint Commission on the Place of Mathematics in the Secondary Schools (MAA and NCTM)—1940 (continued)*

H. E. Buchanan	Tulane University
F. L. Griffin	Reed College
C. A. Hutchinson	University of Colorado
H. F. MacNeish	Brooklyn College
U. G. Mitchell	University of Kansas

Representing the Council:

William Betz	Public Schools, Rochester, N.Y.
Maurice L. Hartung	University of Chicago
G. H. Jamison	State Teachers College, Kirksville, Mo.
Ruth Lane	State University of Iowa
J. A. Nyberg	Hyde Park High School, Chicago, Ill.
Mary A. Potter	Supervisor of Mathematics, Racine, Wis.
W. D. Reeve	Teachers College, Columbia University

12. *Subcommittee on Education for Service of the War Preparedness Committee of the AMS and the MAA—1941*

R. S. Burington	Case School of Applied Science
H. B. Curry	Pennsylvania State College
E. C. Goldsworthy	
F. L. Griffin	Reed College
William L. Hart	University of Minnesota
M. H. Ingraham	University of Wisconsin
E. J. Moulton	Northwestern University

13. *Committee on Arithmetic of the NCTM—1941*

R. L. Morton, Chairman	Ohio University
Harry E. Benz	Ohio University
A. E. Bond	Western Washington College of Education
William A. Brownell	Duke University
Guy T. Buswell	University of Chicago
Paul R. Hanna	Stanford University
Lorena B. Stretch	Baylor University
Ben A. Sueltz	State Normal School, Cortland, N.Y.
C. Louis Thiele	Board of Education, Detroit, Mich.
Harry G. Wheat	West Virginia University

14. *Essential Mathematics for Minimum Army Needs—1943*

Virgil S. Mallory, Chairman	State Teachers College, Montclair, N.J.
William A. Brownell	Duke University
John Lund	U.S. Office of Education
Giles M. Ruch	U.S. Office of Education
Rolland R. Smith	Public Schools, Springfield, Mass.
C. Louis Thiele	Public Schools, Detroit, Mich.
F. Lynwood Wren	George Peabody College for Teachers

15. *Committee on Pre-Induction Courses in Mathematics—1943*

Rolland R. Smith, Chairman	Specialist in Mathematics, Public Schools, Springfield, Mass.
Virgil S. Mallory	Teachers College, Columbia University
Giles M. Ruch	U.S. Office of Education
Raleigh Schorling	University of Michigan

MEMBERS OF CITED COMMITTEES 477

16. *Commission on Post-War Plans* (NCTM)—1944

16.1 *First Report*
    Raleigh Schorling, Chairman — University High School, Ann Arbor, Mich.
    William Betz — Specialist in Mathematics, Public Schools, Rochester, N.Y.
    Eugenie C. Hausle — James Monroe High School, Bronx, N.Y.
    Rolland R. Smith — Coordinator of Mathematics, Public Schools, Springfield, Mass.
    F. Lynwood Wren — George Peabody College for Teachers

16.2 *Second Report*
The above, also:
    William A. Brownell — Duke University
    Virgil S. Mallory — State Teachers College, Montclair, N.J.
    Mary Potter — Supervisor of Mathematics, Racine, Wis.
    William L. Schaaf — Brooklyn College
    Ruth Sumner — President, Mathematics Section, State Teachers Association, Oakland, Calif.
    James H. Zant — Oklahoma State University of Agriculture and Applied Science

17. *Subcommittee of War Policy Committee of MAA, Universal Military Training in Peace Time*—1945
    William L. Hart, Chairman — University of Minnesota
    Saunders MacLane — University of Chicago
    C. B. Morrey, Jr.

18. *Committee on Mathematics, School and College Study of Admission with Advanced Standing* (See Bibliography A, entry 6.)—1954
    H. W. Brinkman, Chairman — Swarthmore College
    Julius Hlavaty — Bronx High School of Science, New York, N.Y.
    Elsie Parker Johnson — Oak Park and River Forest High School, Oak Park, Ill.
    Charles Mergendahl — Newton High School, Newton, Mass.
    George B. Thomas, Jr. — Massachusetts Institute of Technology
    Elbridge P. Vance — Oberlin College
    Volney H. Wells — Williams College

19. *Commission on Mathematics* (CEEB)—1959
    Albert W. Tucker, Chairman — Princeton University
    Carl B. Allendoerfer — University of Washington
    Edwin C. Douglas (*ex officio*) — Taft High School, Watertown, Conn.
    Howard F. Fehr — Teachers College, Columbia University
    Martha Hildebrandt — Proviso Township High School, Maywood, Ill.
    Albert E. Meder, Jr. — Rutgers—The State University
    Morris Meister (*ex officio*) — Bronx High School of Science, New York, N.Y.

APPENDIX A

19. *Commission on Mathematics* (CEEB)—1959 *(continued)*
Frederick Mosteller	Harvard University
Eugene P. Northrop	University of Chicago
Ernest R. Ranucci	Weequahich High School, Newark, N.J.
Robert E. K. Rourke	Kent School, Kent, Conn.
George B. Thomas, Jr.	Massachusetts Institute of Technology
Henry Van Engen	Iowa State Teachers College
Samuel S. Wilks	Princeton University

20. *Elementary-School Curriculum Committee* (NCTM)—1959
J. Fred Weaver, Chairman	Boston University
Joyce Benbrook	University of Houston
Laura K. Eads	Bureau of Curriculum Research, Public Schools, New York, N.Y.
Ann C. Peters	State Teachers College, Keene, N.H.
Irene Sauble	Division of Instruction, Public Schools, Detroit, Mich.
Henry Van Engen	University of Wisconsin

21. *Secondary School Curriculum Committee* (NCTM)—1959
Frank B. Allen, Chairman	Lyons Township High School and Junior College, La Grange, Ill.
F. Lynwood Wren, Editor	George Peabody College for Teachers
Jackson B. Adkins	Phillips Exeter Academy, Exeter, N.H.
Kenneth E. Brown	U.S. Office of Education
Harold P. Fawcett	College of Education, Ohio State University
Howard F. Fehr	Teachers College, Columbia University
Maurice L. Hartung	School of Education, University of Chicago
Magnus R. Hestenes	University of California at Los Angeles
A. S. Householder	Chief, Mathematics Panel, Oak Ridge National Laboratory
Lottchen L. Hunter	Supervisor of Mathematics, Public Schools, Wichita, Kans.
Burton W. Jones	University of Colorado
John R. Mayor	Director of Education, AAAS
Bruce E. Meserve	Montclair State College
Sheldon S. Myers	Head of Mathematics Section in Test Development, Educational Testing Service
E. B. Newell	Allison Division, General Motors Corporation
Alfred E. Putnam	University of Chicago
Elizabeth Roudebush	Director of Mathematics, Public Schools, Seattle, Wash.
Marie S. Wilcox	Thomas Carr Howe High School, Indianapolis, Ind.

    Chairmen of subcommittees are listed below.

    21.1 *The Place of Mathematics in a Changing Society*
J. D. Williams	Rand Corporation

MEMBERS OF CITED COMMITTEES

21.2 *The Aims of Mathematics Education and the Pedagogy of Mathematics*
    Maurice L. Hartung   University of Chicago

21.3 *The Nature of Mathematical Thought for Grades 7–12*
    Burton W. Jones   University of Colorado

21.4 *How Geometry Should Be Introduced and Developed*
    E. H. C. Hildebrandt   Northwestern University

21.5 *The Content and Organization for Junior High School Mathematics*
    John R. Mayor   AAAS

21.6 *Foreign Mathematics Programs for Pupils of Ages 12–18*
    Howard F. Fehr   Teachers College, Columbia University

21.7 *Adjustment of the Mathematics Program to Pupils of Average and Below-Average Ability*
    Max A. Sobel   Montclair State College

21.8 *Aids to Teaching*
    Emil J. Berger   University of Minnesota and Monroe High School, Saint Paul, Minn.

21.9 *Organization of the Mathematics Program*
    Marie S. Wilcox   Thomas Carr Howe High School, Indianapolis, Ind.

21.10 *The Administration of the Mathematics Program*
    Veryl Schult   Supervising Director, Mathematics Curriculum, Public Schools, Washington, D.C.

21.11 *Mathematics for the Academically Gifted Pupils*
    Harry Ruderman   Hunter College

22. *Committee on the Undergraduate Program in Mathematics—Panel on Teacher Training (MAA)—1961–66*

Edwin E. Moise, Chairman	Harvard University
Edward G. Begle	SMSG, Stanford University
Roy Dubisch	University of Washington
Mary Folsom	University of Miami
Clarence Ethel Hardgrove	Northern Illinois University
Bruce E. Meserve	Montclair State College
Rothwell Stephens	Knox College
Gail S. Young, Jr.	Tulane University

23. *Cambridge Conference on School Mathematics—1963*

Maurice Auslander	Brandeis University
*Edward G. Begle	SMSG, Stanford University
*Jerome S. Bruner	Harvard University
R. Creighton Buck	University of Wisconsin
George Francis Carrier	Harvard University

*Members of Steering Committee.

23. *Cambridge Conference on School Mathematics—1963 (continued)*

Julian D. Cole	California Institute of Technology
Robert Davis	Syracuse University
Robert P. Dilworth	California Institute of Technology
Bernard Friedman	University of California
H. L. Frisch	Yeshiva University and Bell Telephone Laboratories
*Andrew M. Gleason	Harvard University
Peter J. Hilton	Cornell University
J. L. Hodges, Jr.	University of California
*Mark Kac	Rockefeller Institute
Seymour H. Koenig	IBM Watson Laboratories and Columbia University
A. H. Laub	University of Illinois
C. C. Lin	Massachusetts Institute of Technology
Earle L. Lomon	Massachusetts Institute of Technology
*William Ted Martin	Massachusetts Institute of Technology
*Edwin E. Moise	Harvard University
Frederick Mosteller	Harvard University
Henry O. Pollak	Bell Telephone Laboratories
*Mina S. Rees	City University of New York
Max M. Schiffer	Stanford University
George Springer	University of Kansas
*Patrick Suppes	Stanford University
*Stephen White	Educational Services Incorporated
*Samuel S. Wilks	Princeton University
*Jerrold R. Zacharias	Massachusetts Institute of Technology

NATIONAL COUNCIL OF TEACHERS OF MATHEMATICS

24. *Officers, Directors, and Editors*

24.1 *Honorary Presidents*

Herbert E. Slaught, 1936–38	Chicago, Ill.
W. S. Schlauch, 1948–53	Dumont, N.J.

24.2 *Presidents*

C. M. Austin, 1920–21	Oak Park, Ill.
J. H. Minnick, 1921–24	Philadelphia, Pa.
Raleigh Schorling, 1924–26	Ann Arbor, Mich.
Marie Gugle, 1926–28	Columbus, Ohio
Harry C. Barber, 1928–30	Exeter, N.H.
John P. Everett, 1930–32	Kalamazoo, Mich.
William Betz, 1932–34	Rochester, N.Y.
J. O. Hassler, 1934–36	Norman, Okla.
Martha Hildebrandt, 1936–38	Maywood, Ill.
H. C. Christofferson, 1938–40	Oxford, Ohio
Mary A. Potter, 1940–42	Racine, Wis.
Rolland R. Smith, 1942–44	Springfield, Mass.
F. Lynwood Wren, 1944–46	Nashville, Tenn.
Carl N. Shuster, 1946–48	Trenton, N.J.
E. H. C. Hildebrandt, 1948–50	Evanston, Ill.

*Members of Steering Committee.

MEMBERS OF CITED COMMITTEES 481

    H. W. Charlesworth, 1950–52   Denver, Colo.
    John R. Mayor, 1952–54   Madison, Wis.
    Marie S. Wilcox, 1954–56   Indianapolis, Ind.
    Howard F. Fehr, 1956–58   New York, N. Y.
    Harold P. Fawcett, 1958–60   Columbus, Ohio
    Phillip S. Jones, 1960–62   Ann Arbor, Mich.
    Frank B. Allen, 1962–64   La Grange, Ill.
    Bruce E. Meserve, 1964–66   Burlington, Vt.
    Donovan A. Johnson, 1966–68   Minneapolis, Minn.
    Julius H. Hlavaty, 1968–70   New Rochelle, N.Y.
    H. Vernon Price, 1970–72   Iowa City, Iowa

24.3 *Vice-Presidents*

    Harold O. Rugg, 1920–21   New York, N.Y.
    E. H. Taylor, 1921–22   Charleston, Ill.
    Eula A. Weeks, 1922–23   Saint Louis, Mo.
    Mabel Sykes, 1923–24   Chicago, Ill.
    Florence Bixby, 1924–25   Milwaukee, Wis.
    Winnie Daley, 1925–26   New Orleans, La.
    Walter W. Hart, 1926–27   Madison, Wis.
    C. M. Austin, 1927–29   Oak Park, Ill.
    Mary S. Sabin, 1928–30   Denver, Colo.
    Hallie S. Poole, 1929–31   Buffalo, N.Y.
    W. S. Schlauch, 1930–32   New York, N.Y.
    Martha Hildebrandt, 1931–33   Maywood, Ill.
    Mary A. Potter, 1932–34   Racine, Wis.
    Ralph Beatley, 1933–35   Cambridge, Mass.
    Allan R. Congdon, 1934–36   Lincoln, Nebr.
    Florence Brooks Miller, 1935–37   Shaker Heights, Ohio
    Mary Kelly, 1936–38   Wichita, Kans.
    John T. Johnson, 1936–39   Chicago, Ill.
    Ruth Lane, 1938–40   Iowa City, Iowa
    E. R. Breslich, 1939–41   Chicago, Ill.
    F. Lynwood Wren, 1940–42   Nashville, Tenn.
    R. L. Morton, 1941–43   Athens, Ohio
    Dorothy S. Wheeler, 1942–44   Hartford, Conn.
    Edwin G. Olds, 1943–45   Pittsburgh, Pa.
    Edith Woolsey, 1944–46   Minneapolis, Minn.
    L. H. Whitcraft, 1945–47   Muncie, Ind.
    H. W. Charlesworth, 1946–48   Denver, Colo.
    E. H. C. Hildebrandt, 1947–49   Evanston, Ill.
    Vera Sanford, 1948–50   Oneonta, N.Y.
    Charles H. Butler, 1949–51   Kalamazoo, Mich.
    Dale Carpenter, 1950–52   Los Angeles, Calif.
    Lenore S. John, 1950–52   Chicago, Ill.
    James H. Zant, 1951–53   Stillwater, Okla.
    Agnes Herbert, 1952–53   Baltimore, Md.
    Marie S. Wilcox, 1952–54   Indianapolis, Ind.
    Irene Sauble, 1952–54   Detroit, Mich.
    H. Glenn Ayre, 1953–55   Macomb, Ill.
    Mary C. Rogers, 1953–55   Westfield, N. J.
    Charlotte W. Junge, 1954–56   Detroit, Mich.
    H. Vernon Price, 1954–56   Iowa City, Iowa
    Milton W. Beckmann, 1955–57   Lincoln, Nebr.

APPENDIX A

24.3 *Vice Presidents (continued)*

Francis G. Lankford, Jr., 1955–57	Farmville, Va.
Laura K. Eads, 1956–58	New York, N.Y.
Donovan A. Johnson, 1956–58	Minneapolis, Minn.
Alice M. Hach, 1957–59	Racine, Wis.
Robert E. Pingry, 1957–59	Urbana, Ill.
Ida May (Bernhard) Puett, 1958–60	Atlanta, Ga.
E. Glenadine Gibb, 1958–60	Cedar Falls, Iowa
Phillip S. Jones, 1959–60	Ann Arbor, Mich.
Mildred B. Cole, 1959–61	Hyattsville, Md.
Clifford Bell, 1960–62	Los Angeles, Calif.
William H. Glenn, 1960–61	Pasadena, Calif.
Clarence Ethel Hardgrove, 1960–62	De Kalb, Ill.
Eunice Lewis, 1961–62	Norman, Okla.
Mildred Keiffer, 1961–63	Cincinnati, Ohio
Bruce E. Meserve, 1961–63	Upper Montclair, N.J.
Marguerite Brydegaard, 1962–64	San Diego, Calif.
Eugene P. Smith, 1962–64	Detroit, Mich.
Roy Dubisch, 1963–65	Seattle, Wash.
Emma M. Lewis, 1963–65	Washington, D.C.
Donald F. Marshall, 1964–66	Dearborn, Mich.
Edith Steanson, 1964–66	Norman, Okla.
Earle F. Myers, 1965–67	Pittsburgh, Pa.
Oscar F. Schaaf, 1965–67	Eugene, Oreg.
George S. Cunningham, 1966–68	Cleveland, Ohio
Henry W. Syer, 1966–68	Kent, Conn.
Sarah Greenholz, 1967–69	Cincinnati, Ohio
Kenneth C. Skeen, 1967–69	Concord, Calif.
David W. Wells, 1968–70	Pontiac, Mich.
James K. Whitney, 1968–70	Hopkins, Minn.
Mary E. Stine, 1969–70	Fairfax, Va.
Jack E. Forbes, 1969–70	Flossmoor, Ill.

24.4 *Secretary-Treasurers*

J. A. Foberg, 1920–23, 1923–27, 1927–28, 1928–29	Chicago, Ill.
Edwin W. Schreiber, 1929–51	Macomb, Ill.

24.5 *Executive Secretaries*

H. W. Charlesworth, 1950–51	Washington, D.C.
M. H. Ahrendt, 1951–54, 1954–57, 1957–64	Washington, D.C.
James D. Gates, 1964–67, 1967–70	Washington, D.C.

24.6 *Recording Secretaries*

Agnes Herbert, 1953–54	Baltimore, Md.
Houston T. Karnes, 1954–55, 1955–56, 1956–57, 1957–58, 1958–59, 1959–60, 1960–61, 1961–62, 1962–63, 1963–64, 1964–65, 1965–66	Baton Rouge, La.
Robert E. Pingry, 1966–67	Urbana, Ill.
Lenore S. John, 1967–69	Chicago, Ill.

24.7 *Editors, "Mathematics Teacher"*

John R. Clark, 1921–29	New York, N.Y.

MEMBERS OF CITED COMMITTEES 483

        W. D. Reeve, 1928–50   New York, N.Y.
        E. H. C. Hildebrandt, 1950–53   Evanston, Ill.
        Henry Van Engen, 1953–56, 1956–59   Madison, Wis.
        Robert E. Pingry, 1959–62, 1962–64   Urbana, Ill.
        Irvin H. Brune, 1964–70   Bowling Green, Ohio

24.8   *Editors, "Arithmetic Teacher"*
        Ben A. Sueltz, 1954–57, 1957–60   Cortland, N.Y.
        E. Glenadine Gibb, 1960–63, 1963–66   Cedar Falls, Iowa
        Marguerite Brydegaard, 1966–69, 1969–70   San Diego, Calif.

24.9   *Editors, "Mathematics Student Journal"*
        H. D. Larsen, 1954–56   Albion, Mich.
        Max Beberman, 1956–58   Urbana, Ill.
        W. Warwick Sawyer, 1958–61   Middletown, Conn.
        Myron F. Rosskopf, 1961–64   New York, N.Y.
        Stephen S. Willoughby, 1964–67   New York, N.Y.
        Thomas J. Hill, 1967–69   Norman, Okla.

24.10   *Editor, "Journal of Research for Mathematics Education"*
        David C. Johnson, 1968–71   Minneapolis, Minn.

24.11   *Directors*
        Marie Gugle, 1920–23, 1928–31, 1931–34   Columbus, Ohio
        Jonathan T. Rorer, 1920–23   Philadelphia, Pa.
        A. Harry Wheeler, 1920–22   Worcester, Mass.
        W. A. Austin, 1920–22   Fresno, Calif.
        W. D. Reeve, 1920–21, 1926–28   Minneapolis, Minn.
        W. D. Beck, 1920–21   Iowa City, Iowa
        Orpha Worden, 1921–24, 1924–28   Detroit, Mich.
        C. M. Austin, 1921–24, 1924–27, 1930–33,   Oak Park, Ill.
            1940–43
        Gertrude Allen, 1922–25   Oakland, Calif.
        W. W. Rankin, 1922–25   Durham, N.C.
        Eula A. Weeks, 1923–26   Saint Louis, Mo.
        W. C. Eells, 1923–26   Walla Walla, Wash.
        Harry English, 1925–28, 1928–31   Washington, D.C.
        Harry C. Barber, 1925–28, 1930–33, 1933–36   Boston, Mass.
        Frank C. Touton, 1926–29   Los Angeles, Calif.
        Vera Sanford, 1927–29   New York, N.Y.
        William Betz, 1927–30, 1930–32, 1934–37,   Rochester, N.Y.
            1937–40
        Walter F. Downey, 1928–30   Boston, Mass.
        Edwin W. Schreiber, 1928–30   Ann Arbor, Mich.
        Elizabeth Dice, 1928–29, 1929–32   Dallas, Tex.
        J. O. Hassler, 1928–29, 1929–32, 1933–34,   Norman, Okla.
            1941–44
        John R. Clark, 1929–32   New York, N.Y.
        Mary S. Sabin, 1929–31, 1931–34   Denver, Colo.
        J. A. Foberg, 1929–30   California, Pa.
        C. Louis Thiele, 1931–34   Detroit, Mich.
        Mary Kelly, 1932–33   Wichita, Kans.
        John P. Everett, 1932–35   Kalamazoo, Mich.
        Elsie Parker Johnson, 1932–35   Oak Park, Ill.
        Raleigh Schorling, 1932–35   Ann Arbor, Mich.

APPENDIX A

24.11   *Directors (continued)*

W. S. Schlauch, 1933–36	New York, N.Y.
H. C. Christofferson, 1934–37, 1937–38	Oxford, Ohio
Edith Woolsey, 1934–37, 1937–40	Minneapolis, Minn.
Martha Hildebrandt, 1934–36, 1938–40	Maywood, Ill.
Maurice L. Hartung, 1935–38, 1938–41	Madison, Wis.
Mary L. Potter, 1935–38	Racine, Wis.
Rolland R. Smith, 1935–38, 1938–41	Springfield, Mass.
E. R. Breslich, 1936–39	Chicago, Ill.
L. D. Haertter, 1936–39	Clayton, Mo.
Virgil S. Mallory, 1936–39, 1939–42	Montclair, N.J.
Katherine Bell, 1938–41, 1941–44	Spokane, Wash.
A. Brown Miller, 1939–42, 1942–45	Shaker Heights, Ohio
Dorothy S. Wheeler, 1939–42	Hartford, Conn.
Hildegarde Beck, 1940–43, 1943–46	Detroit, Mich.
H. W. Charlesworth, 1940–43, 1943–46	Denver, Colo.
L. H. Whitcraft, 1941–44	Muncie, Ind.
Allan R. Congdon, 1942–45	Lincoln, Nebr.
Ina R. Holroyd, 1942–45	Manhattan, Kans.
Veryl Schult, 1943–46, 1946–49, 1949–50	Washington, D.C.
E. H. C. Hildebrandt, 1944–47	Evanston, Ill.
Carl N. Shuster, 1944–47	Trenton, N.J.
Ruth W. Stokes, 1944–47	Rock Hill, S.C.
Lorena Cassidy, 1945–48	Wichita, Kans.
Harold B. Garland, 1945–48	Boston, Mass.
George E. Hawkins, 1945–48, 1948–51	La Grange, Ill.
Ona Kraft, 1946–47, 1947–50	Cleveland, Ohio
Lee Boyer, 1946–49	Millersville, Pa.
Walter H. Carnahan, 1946–49	Lafayette, Ind.
Charles H. Butler, 1947–49	Kalamazoo, Mich.
Emma Hesse, 1947–48	Berkeley, Calif.
Elenore M. Lazansky, 1948–50	Berkeley, Calif.
Marie S. Wilcox, 1948–51	Indianapolis, Ind.
James H. Zant, 1948–51	Stillwater, Okla.
Agnes Herbert, 1949–52	Baltimore, Md.
John R. Mayor, 1949–52	Washington, D. C.
Henry W. Syer, 1949–52	Kent, Conn.
Ida Mae Heard, 1950–53	Lafayette, La.
Donovan A. Johnson, 1950–53	Minneapolis, Minn.
Mary C. Rodgers, 1950–53	Westfield, N.J.
William A. Gager, 1951–54, 1954–57	Gainesville, Fla.
Lucy E. Hall, 1951–54	Wichita, Kans.
Henry Van Engen, 1951–53, 1959–62	Madison, Wis.
Allene Archer, 1952–55	Richmond, Va.
Ida May (Bernhard) Puett, 1952–55, 1955–58	Atlanta, Ga.
Harold P. Fawcett, 1952–55	Columbus, Ohio
Houston T. Karnes, 1953–54	Baton Rouge, La.
Howard F. Fehr, 1953–56	New York, N.Y.
Phillip S. Jones, 1953–56, 1956–59	Ann Arbor, Mich.
Elizabeth J. Roudebush, 1953–56	Seattle, Wash.
Clifford Bell, 1954–57, 1957–60	Los Angeles, Calif.
Catherine A. V. Lyons, 1954–57	Pittsburgh, Pa.
Jackson B. Adkins, 1955–58	Exeter, N.H.

MEMBERS OF CITED COMMITTEES

Henry Swain, 1955–58 — Winnetka, Ill.
H. Vernon Price, 1956–59 — Iowa City, Iowa
Philip Peak, 1956–59, 1959–62 — Bloomington, Ind.
Robert E. K. Rourke, 1957–60, 1960–63 — Kent, Conn.
Annie John Williams, 1957–60 — Durham, N.C.
Frank B. Allen, 1958–61 — La Grange, Ill.
Burton W. Jones, 1958–61, 1962–65 — Boulder, Colo.
Bruce E. Meserve, 1958–61 — Upper Montclair, N.J.
Oscar F. Schaaf, 1959–62 — Eugene, Oreg.
J. Houston Banks, 1960–63 — Nashville, Tenn.
Irvin H. Brune, 1960–63 — Cedar Falls, Iowa
Max Beberman, 1961–64 — Urbana, Ill.
W. T. Guy, Jr., 1961–64 — Austin, Tex.
Julius H. Hlavaty, 1961–64 — New York, N.Y.
Edward G. Begle, 1962–65 — Stanford, Calif.
Emil J. Berger, 1962–65 — Saint Paul, Minn.
Stanley J. Bezuszka, S.J., 1963–66 — Chestnut Hill, Mass.
Harold C. Trimble, 1963–66 — Columbus, Ohio
Helen Warren, 1963–66 — Salisbury, Md.
Kenneth E. Brown, 1964–67 — Washington, D.C.
Kenneth B. Henderson, 1964–67 — Urbana, Ill.
Louis F. Scholl, 1964–67 — Buffalo, N.Y.
Elden B. Egbers, 1965–68 — Olympia, Wash.
John C. Egsgard, C.S.B., 1965–68 — Toronto, Ont.
Lenore S. John, 1965–68 — Chicago, Ill.
Clarence H. Heinke, 1966–69 — Columbus, Ohio
Houston T. Karnes, 1966–69 — Baton Rouge, La.
William K. McNabb, 1966–69 — Dallas, Tex.
W. Eugene Ferguson, 1967–70 — Newtonville, Mass.
Juanita S. Tolson, 1967–70 — Washington, D.C.
Lauren G. Woodby, 1967–70 — East Lansing, Mich.
Eugene D. Nichols, 1968–71 — Tallahassee, Fla.
Joseph J. Stipanowich, 1968–71 — Macomb, Ill.
Stephen S. Willoughby, 1968–71 — New York, N.Y.
John F. Devlin, 1969–72 — East Norwich, N.Y.
Lehi T. Smith, 1969–72 — Tempe, Ariz.
Helen F. Kriegsman, 1969–72 — Pittsburg, Kans.
Mary E. Stine, 1970–72 — Fairfax, Va.
Jack E. Forbes, 1970–71 — Flossmoor, Ill.

24.12 *Yearbook Editors and Authors*

First Yearbook (1926). *A General Survey of Progress in the Last Twenty-Five Years.* Raleigh Schorling, ed.

Second Yearbook (1927). *Curriculum Problems in Teaching Mathematics.* W. D. Reeve, ed.

Third Yearbook (1928). *Selected Topics in the Teaching of Mathematics.* John R. Clark and W. D. Reeve, eds.

Fourth Yearbook (1929). *Significant Trends and Changes in the Teaching of Mathematics throughout the World since 1910.* W. D. Reeve, ed.

Fifth Yearbook (1930). *The Teaching of Geometry.* W. D. Reeve, ed.

Sixth Yearbook (1931). *Mathematics in Modern Life.* W. D. Reeve, ed.

Seventh Yearbook (1932). *The Teaching of Algebra.* W. D. Reeve, ed.

Eighth Yearbook (1933). *The Teaching of Mathematics in the Secondary School.* W. D. Reeve, ed.

24.12 *Yearbook Editors and Authors (continued)*

Ninth Yearbook (1934). *Relational and Functional Thinking in Mathematics.* W. D. Reeve, ed.; Herbert R. Hamley, au.

Tenth Yearbook (1935). *The Teaching of Arithmetic.* W. D. Reeve, ed.

Eleventh Yearbook (1936). *The Place of Mathematics in Modern Education.* W. D. Reeve, ed.

Twelfth Yearbook (1937). *Approximate Computation.* W. D. Reeve, ed.; Aaron Bakst, au.

Thirteenth Yearbook (1938). *The Nature of Proof.* W. D. Reeve, ed.; Harold P. Fawcett, au.

Fourteenth Yearbook (1939). *The Training of Mathematics Teachers for Secondary Schools in England and Wales and in the United States.* W. D. Reeve, ed.; Ivan Stewart Turner, au.

Fifteenth Yearbook (1940). *The Place of Mathematics in Secondary Education* (Final report of the Joint Commission of the MAA and the NCTM). W. D. Reeve, ed.; K. P. Williams, commission chm.

Sixteenth Yearbook (1941). *Arithmetic in General Education* (Final report of the NCTM Committee on Arithmetic). W. D. Reeve, ed.; R. L. Morton, committee chm.

Seventeenth Yearbook (1942). *A Source Book of Mathematical Applications.* W. D. Reeve, ed.; Edwin G. Olds, committee chm.

Eighteenth Yearbook (1945). *Multi-Sensory Aids in the Teaching of Mathematics.* W. D. Reeve, ed.; E. H. C. Hildebrandt, committee chm.

Nineteenth Yearbook (1947). *Surveying Instruments: Their History and Classroom Use.* W. D. Reeve, ed.; Edmond R. Kiely, au.

Twentieth Yearbook (1948). *The Metric System of Weights and Measures.* W. D. Reeve, ed.; John T. Johnson, committee chm.

Twenty-first Yearbook (1953). *The Learning of Mathematics: Its Theory and Practice.* Howard F. Fehr, ed.

Twenty-second Yearbook (1954). *Emerging Practices in Mathematical Education.* John R. Clark, ed.

Twenty-third Yearbook (1957). *Insights into Modern Mathematics.* F. Lynwood Wren, ed.

Twenty-fourth Yearbook (1959). *The Growth of Mathematical Ideas, Grades K–12.* Phillip S. Jones, ed.

Twenty-fifth Yearbook (1960). *Instruction in Arithmetic.* Foster E. Grossnickle, ed.

Twenty-sixth Yearbook (1961). *Evaluation in Mathematics.* Donovan A. Johnson, ed.

Twenty-seventh Yearbook (1963). *Enrichment Mathematics for the Grades.* Julius H. Hlavaty, ed.

Twenty-eighth Yearbook (1963). *Enrichment Mathematics for High School.* Julius H. Hlavaty, ed.

Twenty-ninth Yearbook (1964). *Topics in Mathematics for Elementary School Teachers.* Lenore S. John, ed.

Thirtieth Yearbook (1969). *More Topics in Mathematics for Elementary School Teachers.* Edwin F. Beckenbach, ed.

Thirty-first Yearbook (1969). *Historical Topics for the Mathematics Classroom.* Arthur E. Hallerberg, ed.

Thirty-second Yearbook (1970). *A History of Mathematics Education in the United States and Canada.* Phillip S. Jones, ed.

Index of Names

Adkins, Jackson B., 21; 24.11
Aiton, George B., 3
Ahrendt, M. H., 24.5
Albright, G. H., 6.4.3
Alden, Grace A., 6.3.2
Aley, Robert J., 6.7.6
Allen, Frank B., 21; 24.2; 24.11
Allen, Gertrude, 24.11
Allen, Lucie B., 6.3.4
Allendoerfer, Carl B., 19
Ames, L. C., 6.3; 6.3.7
Ammerman, Charles, 6.3.4
Angell, James B., 1
Anthony, Oscar W., 6.3.7
Archer, Allene, 24.1
Auslander, Maurice, 23
Austin, C. M., 24.2; 24.3; 24.11
Austin, W. A., 24.11
Ayre, H. Glenn, 24.3

Bakst, Aaron, 24.12
Bagley, W. C., 6.1.6
Baker, James D., 1
Baldwin, W. A., 6.2.3
Balliet, T. M., 2
Banks, J. Houston, 24.11
Barber, Harry C., 24.2; 24.11
Barker, E. C., 6.6.1
Bartlett, Josiah, 6.4.1
Batt, A. Laura, 6.3.2
Beatley, Ralph, 24.3
Beberman, Max, 24.9; 24.11
Beck, Hildegarde, 24.11
Beck, W. D., 24.11
Beckenbach, Edwin F., 24.12
Beckmann, Milton W., 24.3
Beetle, Ralph D., 6.6.2
Begle, Edward G., 22; 23; 24.11
Bell, Clifford, 24.3; 24.11
Bell, Katherine, 6.3.8; 24.11
Beman, W. W., 6.7.5
Benbrook, Joyce, 20
Benitz, William L., 6.1.5
Bennett, Albert A., 10; 11
Bennett, C. A., 6.6.1
Berger, Emil J., 21.8; 24.11
Berry, C. F., 6.6.1
Benz, Harry E., 13
Betz, William, 5; 6.3.9; 11; 15.1; 15.2; 16.1; 24.2; 24.11
Bezuszka, Stanley J., S.J., 24.11

Birkhoff, G. D., 6.12.2
Bishop, J. Remsen, 3
Bixby, Florence, 24.3
Blair, Vevia, 6.4.2; 7
Bocher, Maxime, 6.12
Bogarte, M. E., 6.5.3
Bohannan, R. D., 6.5.1
Bond, A. E., 13
Bonser, F. G., 6.1.4
Bouton, Charles L., 5; 6.12.3
Boyer, Lee, 24.11
Boynton, F. D., 6.7.4
Bradbury, W. F., 3.1
Breckenridge, William E., 6.8.2; 6.11
Breslich, E. R., 6.4.3; 24.3; 24.11
Bright, Orville T., 9
Brinkman, H. W., 18
Brookman, Miss T. A., 6.3.6
Brooks, Edward, 2
Brown, Edward L., 5
Brown, J. C., 6.5.4
Brown, Kenneth E., 21; 24.11
Brownell, William A., 13; 14; 16.2
Brueckner, Leo J., 13
Brune, Irvin H., 24.7; 24.11
Bruner, Jerome S., 23
Brydegaard, Marguerite, 24.3; 24.8
Buchanan, H. E., 11
Buchanan, John T., 3
Buck, R. Creighton, 23
Buckingham, Harriet D., 6.4.2
Burington, R. S., 12
Buswell, Guy T., 13
Butler, Charles H., 24.3; 24.11
Butler, Tait, 6.6.3
Byerly, William E., 1.1; 3.1
Byrnes, J. C., 6.7.6

Cajori, Florian, 1.1; 5
Campbell, D. F., 6.9.1
Candy, A. L., 6.5.1
Carnahan, Walter H., 24.11
Carpenter, Dale, 24.3
Carrier, George Frances, 23
Carroll, Emma H., 6.3.2
Cassidy, Lorena, 24.11
Chandler, Turner C., 9
Charlesworth, H. W., 24.2; 24.3; 24.5; 24.11
Christofferson, H. C., 24.2; 24.11
Clark, John R., 24.7; 24.11; 24.12

Clarke, John E., 6.8.4
Cole, F. N., 6.8.1
Cole, Julian D., 23
Cole, Mildred B., 24.3
Collins, Joseph V., 6.5.4
Condit, Ira S., 6.1; 6.1.6
Congdon, Allan R., 24.3; 24.11
Coolidge, J. L., 6.7.2
Cooney, Annie E., 6.3.5
Cooper, Oscar H., 2
Cornish, W. A., 6.5.2
Courtis, S. A., 6.4.2
Cowles, Emma M., 6.4.2
Crathorne, A. R., 7
Crawley, E. S., 6.7.5
Crawshaw, F. D., 6.6.1
Cubberly, E. R., 6.8
Cunningham, George S., 24.3
Curry, H. B., 12
Curtiss, D. R., 6.12.1
Cutler, Arthur H., 1.1; 3.1

Daley, Winnie, 24.3
Daniel, Cuthbert, 10
Davis, N. F., 6.7.5
Davis, Robert, 23
Dean, A. D., 6.4.a
DeCou, E. E., 6.3.6
Devlin, John F., 24.11
Dewey, C. O., 6.1.6
Dickler, Nathan N., 6.6
Dice, Elizabeth, 24.11
Dickson, Tracy C., 6.11.1
Dilworth, Robert P., 23
Doolittle, 3.1
Dougherty, N. C., 2
Douglas, Edwin C., 19
Dow, 6.7.7
Downey, J. E., 6.6.2
Downey, Walter F., 7; 24.11
Draper, Andrew S., 2
Dubisch, Roy, 22; 24.3
Durell, Fletcher, 3.1

Eads, Laura K., 20; 24.3
Earnest, William D., 6.2.2
Eaton, Clara F., 6.6.2
Echols, C. P., 6.11.1
Edwards, George C., 6.7.5
Eells, W. C., 24.11
Egbers, Elden B., 24.11
Egsgard, John, C. S. B., 24.11
Eisenhart, L. P., 6.10.1
Eliot, Charles W., 1

Elliott, E. C., 6.1.1
English, Harry, 6.3.1; 6.7.6; 24.11
Estill, J. G., 3.1
Evans, George W., 6.3.5
Everett, John P., 24.2; 24.11

Farrand, S. A., 3.1
Faught, J. D., 6.5.2
Fawcett, Harold P.,
   10; 21; 24.2; 24.11; 24.12
Fehr, Howard F.,
   19; 21; 21.6; 24.2; 24.11; 24.12
Feldman, Daniel D., 6.3.3
Ferguson, W. Eugene, 24.11
Ferry, F. C., 6.10.1
Fine, Henry B., 1.1; 3.1
Fiske, T. S., 4; 6.7
Fletcher, William, 6.8.3
Foberg, J. A., 7; 24.4; 24.11
Folsom, Mary, 22
Forbes, Jack E., 24.3; 24.11
French, John S., 6.4.1
Friedman, Bernard, 23
Frisch, H. L., 23
Fuller, William, 5

Gager, William A., 24.11
Gale, Arthur Sullivan, 6.3.8
Gardner, Henry, 6.2.2
Garland, Harold B., 24.11
Garrett, T. H., 6.3.2
Gates, James D., 24.5
Gaylord, H. D., 6.3.6
Gibb, E. Glenadine, 24.3; 24.8
Gilbert, Charles B., 2
Gildemeister, Theda, 6.1.3
Gillet, Harry O., 9
Gleason, Andrew M., 23
Glenn, William H., 24.3
Glover, James W., 6.10.3
Goldsworthy, E. C., 12
Gore, J. K., 6.7.7
Gould, J. E., 6.8.1
Gould, Mary F., 6.3.3
Greenholz, Sarah, 24.3
Greenwood, J. M., 2
Greeson, W. A., 1.1
Griffin, F. L., 11; 12
Grossnickle, Foster E., 24.12
Gugle, Marie, 6.3.4; 24.2; 24.11
Gummere, Henry V., 6.1.5
Guy, W. T., Jr., 24.11

Hach, Alice M., 24.3

MEMBERS OF CITED COMMITTEES

Haertter, L. D., 24.11
Hall, D. W., 6.8.5
Hall, Lucy E., 24.11
Hallerberg, Arthur E., 24.12
Hamilton, Alston, 6.11.1
Hamley, H. R., 24.12
Hanna, Paul R., 13
Hanus, Paul H., 3
Hapgood, Ernest G., 6.3.2
Hardgrove, Clarence Ethel, 22; 24.3
Harper, J. R., 9
Harpman, Albert J., 6.5.3
Harris, William T., 1; 2
Harrison, Elizabeth, 6.1.2
Hart, C. A., 6.7.3
Hart, Walter W., 5; 6.1.5; 24.3
Hart, William L., 8; 12; 17
Hartung, Maurice L., 10; 11; 21; 21.2; 24.11
Harvey, H. Clay, 6.5.2
Haskins, C. N., 6.6
Hassler, J. O., 8; 24.2; 24.11
Hausle, Eugenie C., 16.1; 16.2
Havighurst, Robert J., 10
Hawkes, Herbert E., 5; 6.12.3
Hawkins, George E., 24.11
Heard, Ida Mae, 24.11
Hedrick, Earle R., 5; 8
Heinke, Clarence H., 24.11
Henderson, Kenneth W., 24.11
Herbert, Agnes, 24.3; 24.6; 24.11
Hesse, Emma, 24.11
Hestenes, Magnus R., 21
Hildebrandt, E. H. C., 21; 21.4; 24.2; 24.3; 24.7; 24.11; 24.12
Hildebrandt, Martha, 19; 24.2; 24.3; 24.11
Hill, Patty, 6.1.2
Hill, Thomas J., 24.9
Hilton, Peter J., 23
Hinsdale, Burke A., 3
Hlavaty, Julius H., 18; 24.2; 24.11; 24.12
Hodges, J. L., Jr., 23
Holgate, Thomas F., 6.10.3
Holland, E., 6.1.1
Holroyd, Ina A., 24.11
Householder, A. S., 21
Howe, C. S., 6.9.1
Hubbard, T. O., 6.2.1
Hughes, William, 6.4.1
Hulburt, L. S., 6.7.2; 6.10.1
Huling, Ray Greene, 3
Hull, George W., 6.5.4
Hunt, L. R., 3.1

Hunter, Lottchen L., 21
Huntington, E. V., 6.9.2
Hutchinson, C. A., 11
Hutchinson, J. I., 6.12.2

Ingraham, Andrew, 1.1
Ingraham, M. H., 8; 12

Jablonower, Joseph, 10
Jackson, L. L., 6.8.5
James, Edmund J., 3
Jamison, G. H., 11
Jesse, Richard H., 1
John, Lenore S., 24.3; 24.6; 24.11; 24.12
Johnson, 6.2.3
Johnson, David C., 24.10
Johnson, Donovan A., 21; 24.2; 24.3; 24.11; 24.12
Johnson, Elsie Parker, 18; 24.11
Johnson, John T., 24.3; 24.12
Jones, Burton W., 21.3; 24.11
Jones, Franklin T., 6.3.9; 6.4.1
Jones, L. H., 2
Jones, Phillip S., 24.2; 24.3; 24.11; 24.12
Jones, William Carey, 3
Jordan, W. Lee, 6.3.4
Junge, Charlotte W., 24.3

Kac, Mark, 23
Karnes, Houston T., 24.6; 24.11
Karpinski, L. C., 6.3.7
Kasner, Edward, 6.12.1
Keenan, Thomas W., 6.5.3
Keiffer, Mildred, 24.3
Keith, J. C., 6.3.6
Kelly, Mary, 24.3; 24.11
Kendall, C. N., 6.1
Kenyon, A. M., 6.9.1
Keppel, H. G., 6.10.3
Kiely, Edmond R., 24.12
King, Henry C., 1
King, W. J., 6.11.2
Koenig, Seymour H., 23
Kotinsky, Ruth, 10
Kraft, Ona, 24.11
Kriegsman, Helen F., 24.11

Laird, Raymond G., 6.6.2
Lake, Sarah M., 6.4.2
Lane, A. G., 2
Lane, Ruth, 11; 24.3
Lankford, Francis G., Jr., 24.3
Larsen, H. D., 24.9
Laub, A. H., 23

Lazansky, Elenore M., 24.11
Leadbetter, Maud, 6.3.3
LeGras, Gustave, 6.8.2
Lewis, Emma M., 24.3
Lewis, Eunice, 24.3
Lin, C. C., 23
Livingston, Alfred, 6.3.5
Lomon, Earle L., 23
Long, Edith, 6.3.4
Loomis, H. B., 6.7.1
Lowe, A. W., 6.2.2
Lund, John, 14
Lunn, A. C., 6.12.1
Lyons, Catherine A. V., 24.11
Lyttle, E. W., 6.8.4

Mackenzie, James C., 1
MacLane, Saunders, 17
MacNeish, H. F., 11
Mahoney, J. O., 6.1.6
Mallory, Virgil S., 14; 15; 16.2; 24.11
Maltbie, W. H., 6.10.2
Maritz, R. E., 6.3.6
Marsh, John A., 6.3.1
Marsh, Walter R., 6.4.1
Marshall, Donald F., 24.3
Martin, Julia, 6.1.3
Martin, William Ted, 23
Masen, Max, 6.12.2
Mathews, Jane, 6.2.1
Mayor, John R., 21; 21.5; 24.2; 24.11
Maxwell, William H., 2
McAuliffe, William J., 6.1.4
McFarlane, C. T., 6.3.8
McKinney, T. E., 6.10.3
McNabb, William K., 24.11
Meder, Albert E., Jr., 19
Meister, Morris, 19
Melcher, George, 6.1.6
Mergendahl, Charles, 18
Merrill, Helen A., 6.10.2
Meserve, Bruce E.,
    21; 22; 24.2; 24.3; 24.11
Meserve, Charles D., 6.3.3
Messenger, H. J., 6.7.7
Metzler, W. H., 6.8.1
Miller, A. Brown, 24.11
Miller, Florence Brooks, 24.3
Minnick, J. H., 24.2
Mitchell, U. G., 11
Moise, Edwin E., 22; 23
Moore, C. L. E., 6.7.3
Moore, C. N., 7
Moore, E. H., 7

Morphett, Mabel Vogel, 9
Morrey, C. B., Jr., 17
Morrison, Gibbert B., 6.3.8
Morton, R. L., 13; 24.3; 24.12
Mosteller, Frederick, 19; 23
Moulton, E. J., 8; 12
Myers, Earle F., 24.3
Myers, Sheldon S., 21

Newcomb, Simon, 1.1
Newell, E. B., 21
Newhall, C. W., 6.4.3
Newton, Frederick E., 5
Nichols, Eugene D., 24.11
Nightingale, A. F., 3
Noble, C. A., 6.3.6
Northrop, Eugene P., 19
Norton, William H., 6.3.8
Nyberg, J. A., 11

Olds, Edwin G., 24.3; 24.12
Olds, George D., 1.1; 6.12.3
Olney, A. C., 7
Osborne, Raymond, 9
Osgood, W. F., 4; 6
Ostrander, J. E., 6.6.3
Owen, E. J., 6.4.3

Parsons, S. F., 6.5.2
Patterson, James L., 1.1; 6.4.1
Pauly, Fred L., 6.5.3
Peak, Philip, 24.11
Pearson, H. C., 6.7.1
Peat, Harriet, 6.1.3
Peters, Ann C., 20
Peterson, O. E., 9
Phillips, A. W., 3.1
Pingry, Robert E., 24.3; 24.6; 24.7
Poland, A. B., 2
Pollak, Henry O., 23
Poole, Hallie, S., 24.3
Potamian, Rev. Brother, 6.4.2
Potter, Mary A., 11; 24.2; 24.3; 24.11
Powell, W. B., 2
Prentill, R. W., 6.7.3
Price, H. Vernon, 24.2; 24.3; 24.11
Prince, John T., 6.2.3
Puett, Ida May (Bernhard), 24.3
Putnam, Alfred E., 21

Rackliffe, John S., 6.7.1
Ragsdale, Virginia, 6.4.2
Rankin, W. W., 24.11
Ranucci, Ernest R., 19

MEMBERS OF CITED COMMITTEES

Rees, Mina S., 23
Reeve, W. D., 11; 14; 24.7; 24.11; 24.12
Regan, John W., 6.2; 6.3.3
Rice, C. D., 6.5.1
Rietz, Henry L., 5
Riggs, N. C., 6.6.1
Robinson, Oscar D., 1
Rocheleau, W. F., 6.4.6
Rogers, Mary C., 24.3; 24.11
Rorer, Jonathan T., 6.6.2; 24.11
Rosskopf, Myron F., 24.9; 24.12
Roudebush, Elizabeth, 21; 24.11
Rourke, Robert E. K., 19; 24.11
Ruch, Giles M., 14; 15
Ruderman, Harry, 21.11
Rugg, Harold O., 24.3
Russell, James E., 3
Russell, W. B., 6.22

Sabin, Mary S., 24.3; 24.11
Sachs, Julius, 6.7.2
Safford, T. H., 1.1
Sanford, Vera, 24.3; 24.11
Sauble, Irene, 20; 24.3
Sawyer, W. Warwick, 24.9
Scarborough, J. H., 6.5.4
Schaaf, Oscar F., 24.3; 24.11
Schaaf, William L., 16.2
Schiffer, Max M., 23
Schlauch, W. S., 24.1; 24.3; 24.11
Schobinger, J. B., 6.7.2
Scholl, Louis F., 24.11
Schorling, Raleigh,
  7; 15; 16.1; 16.2; 24.2; 24.11; 24.12
Schreiber, Edwin W., 24.4; 24.11
Schult, Veryl, 21.10; 24.11
Schwarz, William, 6.4.1
Seaver, E. P., 2
Sellew, George T., 6.10.3
Shea, Miss M. E., 6.3.9
Sherrard, R. M., 6.7.1
Short, Robert L., 5
Shuster, Carl N., 24.2; 24.11
Shutts, G. C., 6.5.2
Simons, Lao G., 6.1.4
Sisam, C. H., 6.11.2
Skeen, Kenneth C., 24.3
Skinner, E. B., 6.8.4
Slaught, Herbert E.,
  5; 6.8.6; 6.12.3; 8; 24.1
Slocum, S. E., 6.9.2
Smiley, William H., 3
Smith, David Eugene, 5; 6; 7
Smith, Eugene P., 24.3

Smith, Eugene R., 5; 6.6.1
Smith, Lehi T., 24.11
Smith, Percy F., 6.12.2
Smith, Rolland R.,
  14; 15; 16.1; 16.2; 24.2; 24.11
Snedder, David, 6.1.1
Snyder, Virgil, 6.7.3
Sobel, Max A., 21.7
Springer, George, 23
Stamper, A. W., 6.8.3
Stark, William E., 6.4
Steanson, Edith, 24.3
Stephens, Rothwell, 22
Stevens, D. L., 6.6.3
Stewart, I. S., 24.12
Stine, Mary E., 24.3; 24.11
Stipanowich, Joseph J., 24.11
Stokes, Ruth W., 24.11
Stone, C. W., 6.1.3; 6.7.1
Stone, J. C., 6.5.2
Storm, Howard C., 9
Strayer, George D., 6.2
Stretch, Lorena B., 13
Strong, William M., 6.7.7
Sueltz, Ben A., 13; 24.8
Sumner, Ruth, 16.2
Suppes, Patrick, 23
Suzzallo, Henry, 6.1.3
Swain, Henry, 24.11
Syer, Henry W., 24.3; 24.11
Sykes, Mabel, 5; 6.3.4; 24.3

Tanner, J. H., 6.1.1
Tarbell, H. S., 2
Taub, A. H., 23
Taylor, A. R., 6.3.3
Taylor, E. H., 6.5; 24.3
Taylor, James M., 1; 6.7.4
Temple, Alice, 6.1.2
Tetlow, John, 1
Thayer, V. T., 10
Thiele, C. Louis, 13; 14; 24.11
Thomas, George B., 18; 19
Thompson, H. D., 6.7.2
Thornton, William M., 6.7.5
Thurber, Charles H., 3
Tibbetts, George P., 6.4.3
Tinsley, Samuel B., 6.3.1
Tolson, Juanita S., 24.11
Touton, Frank C., 6.3.7; 24.11
Trimble, Harold C., 24.11
Tucker, Albert W., 19
Turner, Ivan Stewart, 12.4
Tyler, H. W., 4; 6.9; 7

Underwood, P. H., 6.3.5; 7
Upton, Clifford B., 6.5.1; 6.11

Van Amringe, J. H., 3.1
Vance, Elbridge P., 18
Van Engen, Henry, 19; 20; 24.7; 24.11
Van Vleck, E. B., 6.12.1
Vernon, W. C., 6.5.2
Voas, William H., 9

Wait, L. A., 3.1
Walter, Sarah J., 6.2.3
Wardwell, Mary M., 6.3.9
Warner, Charles F., 6.2.3
Warren, Helen, 24.11
Washburne, Carleton, 9
Weaver, J. Fred, 20
Webb, H. E., 6.3.8
Weeks, Eula A., 7; 24.3; 24.11
Weld, L. G., 6.5.1
Wells, Volney H., 18
Wills, David W., 24.3
Wheat, Harry G., 13
Wheeler, A. Harry, 6.8.2; 24.11
Wheeler, Dorothy S., 24.3; 24.11
Wheelock, C. F., 6.7.4
Whitcraft, L. H., 24.3; 24.11
White, H. S., 6.10
White, Stephen, 23
Whitney, James K., 24.3

Whyte, Laura A., 6.4.3
Wilcox, Marie S.,
  21; 21.9; 24.2; 24.3; 24.11
Wilczynski, E. J., 6.12.2
Wilks, Samuel S., 19; 23
Williams, Annie John, 24.11
Williams, J. D., 21.1
Williams, K. P., 11; 24.12
Williams, W. T. B., 6.4.c
Willoughby, Stephen S., 24.9; 24.11
Wood, Ruth G., 6.4.2
Woodby, Lauren G., 24.11
Woodley, O. I., 6.8.3
Woolsey, Edith, 24.3; 24.11
Worden, Orpha, 24.11
Wren, F. Lynwood,
  14; 16.1; 16.2; 21; 24.2; 24.3; 24.12
Wright, Henry M., 6.3.1
Wright, Sands, 6.5.4

Yocum, A. Duncan, 6.7.1
Yonker, H. S., 6.2.1
Young, Gail S., Jr., 22
Young, J. W., 7
Young, J. W. A., 4; 6
Yowell, E. J., 6.11.2

Zacharias, Jerrold R., 23
Zant, James H., 16.2; 24.3; 24.11
Ziwet, Alexander, 4

APPENDIX B

A Survey of Research in Mathematics Education

By Helen B. Smiler

The chart that accompanies this Appendix is an attempt to categorize some of the research in mathematics education which has been done in the United States. The data were collected from several sources. Studies prior to 1930 are reported by Buswell and Judd and by the Department of Superintendence of the National Education Association. The remaining studies are listed in the *Review of Educational Research*, in publications of the United States Office of Education, and in *Doctoral Dissertations Accepted by American Universities*. (These references are listed at the end of this Appendix.)

An attempt has been made to include only research studies and omit articles that are primarily expressions of opinion or are based on results reported elsewhere. Also excluded are master's theses and theses that deal mainly with historical topics and comparative education. Because several of the sources report only selected studies, the chart cannot be considered to be a complete listing of research. The sources cover only the period before 1964. Thus the numerous studies done recently are not considered, and several areas of major concern today are not adequately represented. Modern technology does not appear at all, and only the first studies of programmed instruction and of modern programs are included.

The problem of categorizing research is a difficult one. Even if the categories were so wide as to be almost meaningless, some investigations would not fit precisely into one particular slot. For example, most studies of programmed instruction use an advanced topic that the class is certain not to have studied previously, and thus they often show that students are capable of mastering topics usually

CATEGORIZING OF RESEARCH STUDIES IN MATHEMATICS EDUCATION

Studies Made in the U.S. from 1880 through 1963

Categories	1880–1900	1901–1905	1906–1910	1911–1915	1916–1920	1921–1925	1926–1930	1931–1935	1936–1940	1941–1945	1946–1950	1951–1955	1956–1960	1961–1963	Total
Methods															
Materials															
Drill................	...	...	2	6	5	8	11	5	6	...	1	...	2	1	47
Textbooks and exercises..	...	...	...	...	2	4	14	13	7	6	5	5	4	16	76
Games, devices, activities.	...	...	...	...	1	1	1	2	8	11	5	8	9	4	50
Programmed instruction ..	...	...	...	...	...	...	...	...	...	...	...	...	...	10	10
Radio, TV, movies........	...	...	...	...	...	...	1	...	...	1	...	2	6	7	17
Mechanics															
Time................	...	...	...	4	1	1	1	1	2	...	...	1	2	2	16
Homework and supervised study.	...	...	...	1	...	1	2	3	4	1	...	...	...	...	12
Grouping.............	...	...	...	...	...	...	...	...	1	...	...	2	1	3	7
Teaching approach	...	...	...	2	2	2	6	6	14	13	22	22	17	16	120
Processes	1	...	...	3	6	5	14	13	6	7	8	10	5	...	81
Problem solving	...	...	...	...	...	3	20	13	7	3	3	3	6	5	63
Individual differences......	2	...	...	2	1	8	9	1	4	2	1	...	...	...	32
Curriculum															
Social utility	...	1	...	...	8	9	5	10	13	8	10	3	...	...	67
Functional competency and general education........	...	...	...	...	...	...	...	...	3	3	1	9	4	1	21
Math in special fields......	...	...	...	...	...	2	3	...	4	3	6	12	4	1	35
Effect on thinking........	...	...	...	1	...	...	...	...	3	2	3	2	...	1	12
Grade placement.........	...	...	...	3	1	...	5	3	6	5	2	3	3	6	37

Category															Total
Enrichment	...	...	...	...	...	...	...	...	1	2	1	1	2	2	9
Trends and current practices	...	...	...	2	...	2	1	3	2	5	7	6	5		34
Integrated courses	...	...	...	...	...	...	2	...	1	1	...	2	2		8
Other recommendations	...	...	3	2	3	1	4	6	2	4	17	10	4		56
Psychology															
Testing and measurement															
Analysis and validation of tests	...	...	1	1	...	2	3	5	1	1	3	...	...		22
Diagnostic testing	...	...	1	3	10	13	21	13	9	20	7	8	1	...	103
Factors related to mathematics achievement and prediction	2	2	1	6	10	11	7	15	27	19	20	16	20	10	166
Development and use of achievement tests	2	1	...	20	17	1	5	9	4	8	1	4	4	5	81
Relative difficulty of facts and topics	...	...	...	...	1	2	3	6	2	5	4	3	1	...	27
Transfer	...	...	1	3	...	1	1	3	2	...	...	...	...	...	11
Development of concepts (readiness)	8	3	2	1	1	3	9	9	7	6	10	5	2	3	69
Attitudes and motivation	...	...	...	1	1	...	1	...	1	4	3	2	2	5	20
Retention	...	...	...	1	1	...	2	2	...	1	2	1	1	...	8
Thought processes	...	1	...	...	1	2	2	1	4	1	1	...	...	...	13
Teacher training															
Professional and mathematics courses	...	...	...	...	...	...	1	1	5	1	5	15	12	5	45
Skills of preservice teachers	...	...	...	...	...	1	...	1	1	1	...	4	4	6	18
Miscellaneous	...	...	...	...	...	1	...	1	1	2	3	4	2	5	19
Miscellaneous	2	...	1	1	...	...	5	1	3	10	7	5	7	2	44
Total	17	7	13	64	69	86	154	140	169	152	142	177	139	127	1,456

taught later. Also, the whole area of remedial work deserves a category of its own. However, content goals must be determined and mastery of them tested before the necessity of remedial work becomes apparent. At that point a particular method or approach is often tested. Thus studies dealing with remedial work are scattered throughout the chart.

Such considerations have led to an attempt to classify each study according to its major emphasis. The classifications chosen are certainly not the only ones possible. There are several categories that have been studied frequently enough to warrant inclusion, even though they could also be considered as a part of a larger category. Although many of the categories seem quite obvious, explanation is necessary in several cases.

The early studies of drill deal primarily with the relative effectiveness of various patterns of drill, while the more recent studies question the necessity of any drill at all. The earliest studies of texts are usually analyses of the drill or of the reading material they contain. More recently, modern programs are compared with those in traditional texts, so perhaps such studies should be classified under curriculum. Studies dealing with time investigate such questions as time allotment and the effects of time pressure.

The category of teaching approach includes a number of different types of studies. In most cases the conventional approach is compared with an alternative such as more student participation, discovery, inductive development of concepts, or the application of a particular theory of learning. It would be difficult to refine the classification any further, since in most cases several variables are involved, in different combinations.

Studies of processes include all those that compare the effectiveness of different mechanical or theoretical approaches to a particular topic. Over the years there has been a definite shift here from the mechanical to the theoretical. Early studies consider such items as the relative desirability of adding columns of figures from the top or from the bottom, while a more recent study might deal with a vector approach to analytic geometry or might emphasize the structure of the number system. Problem solving has been included under methods, since most studies deal with efforts to improve problem-solving ability. The category of individual differences has an incomplete listing, since many studies concerned with handling individual differences appear in such categories as teaching approach and programmed instruction.

The first two categories under curriculum are closely related. Most studies in the first group are concerned with determining the mathematics actually used by the average person. The second class contains proposals for programs designed to bring students to a minimum level of mathematical competence, such as that suggested by the Commission on Post-War Plans. Studies of grade placement deal with the introduction of material at a higher or lower level than it is usually taught. There is some overlap with the idea of readiness, although the latter category has been reserved for studies that attempt to determine the child's level of understanding of certain concepts and thus his readiness for related instruction. The final category contains studies dealing with the curriculum which do not fit elsewhere, such as an investigation of an experimental statistics course for high school students.

Much of the early work in testing is related to the development of testing in general. Tests were developed and given to large numbers of students in order to establish norms and then to evaluate local programs. Many such studies are reported by Buswell and Judd (see reference following this Appendix). Most studies dealing with diagnostic testing also report attempts to deal with various deficiencies. Correlations between mathematical skills of various types and other factors has been an area of major interest. Intelligence, sex, and reading ability are some of the factors studied. Several studies compare the achievements of rural and urban students just as, more recently, social and economic factors are considered. A number of studies attempt to develop procedures for predicting success in various courses. Since in most cases this is done by correlating certain measures with final achievement, these studies are included in the factors category.

A number of dissertations deal with the courses necessary for elementary teachers who will be teaching mathematics. There are also several studies that test the skills of teachers-in-training (and generally find them to be below desired standards). The miscellaneous category includes studies of certification requirements and evaluations of student teaching. There are also two studies of the role of the administrator in mathematics education and, more recently, four studies of the effects of institutes for experienced teachers.

The final miscellaneous category contains a number of studies that could not be classified otherwise. In some cases there are only one or two studies in an area where further research is needed. Examples from this category are a study of the effect on pupil achievement of teacher attitudes toward learning theories and two studies following up students from particular schools. Other studies are concerned with such topics as math clubs, cooperation between education and industry, and the methods of research in mathematics education.

In some cases it would be misleading to draw conclusions from the chart. A change in numbers does not necessarily represent a trend. In addition to the problem of data collection, previously mentioned, in several instances one source was interested in a particular area and reported several studies in close succession. For example, Brownell reports, around 1947, a number of studies that deal with meaningful learning. This became an area of major concern and a number of articles were published, although very little further research was done. Other examples would be Guiler's analyses of errors in 1945 or the cluster of dissertations on factor analysis from Catholic University around 1959. (For more details, see *Doctoral Dissertations*.)

The chart also cannot show the general educational research that has affected mathematics teaching.

There have been some obvious changes in research in mathematics education since its beginnings. Early studies are primarily concerned with computational ability, while the more recent emphasis is on an understanding of concepts. Early researchers were educators interested in the entire educational spectrum, whereas most current research is being carried on by specialists who usually have had considerable mathematical training. Certainly the amount of research has increased; no doubt it will continue to increase as the large number of questions that are yet unanswered are studied.

REFERENCES

The abbreviations used in Bibliographies A and B are used here also.

Brown, Kenneth E. *Analysis of Research in the Teaching of Mathematics, 1955 and 1956.* USOE Bulletin 1958, no. 4. Washington, D.C.: GPO, 1958.

———. *Mathematics Education Research Studies, 1952–.* USOE Circular 377. Washington, D.C.: GPO, 1953.

Brown, Kenneth E., and Theodore L. Abell. *Analysis of Research in the Teaching of Mathematics.* USOE Bulletin 1965, no. 28. Washington, D.C.: GPO, 1965.

Brown, Kenneth E., and John J. Kinsella. *Analysis of Research in the Teaching of Mathematics of 1957 and 1958.* USOE Bulletin 1965, no. 28. Washington, D. C.: GPO, 1960.

Brown, Kenneth E., et al. *Analysis of Research in the Teaching of Mathematics, 1959 and 1960.* USOE Bulletin 1963, no. 12. Washington, D.C.: GPO, 1963.

Buswell, Guy Thomas, and Charles Hubbard Judd. *Summary of Educational Investigations Relating to Arithmetic.* Supplementary Educational Monographs, no. 27. Chicago: University of Chicago, Department of Education, 1925.

Doctoral Dissertations Accepted by American Universities. New York: H. W. Wilson Co., 1934–56.

NEA, American Educational Research Association. *Review of Educational Research* 1, 2, 4, 5, 7, 8, 12, 15, 18, 21. Washington, D.C.: American Educational Research Association.

NEA, Department of Superintendence. Chap. 3, "Arithmetic." In *Research in Constructing the Elementary School Curriculum.* Third Yearbook of the American Association of School Administrators. Washington, D.C.: American Association of School Administrators, 1925.

BIBLIOGRAPHY A

The United States of America

Organizations, agencies, and periodicals to which frequent reference is made are indicated in both Bibliographies as follows:

    AAAS American Association for the Advancement of Science
    AMM *American Mathematical Monthly*
    AMS American Mathematical Society
    AT *Arithmetic Teacher*
    CEEB College Entrance Examination Board
    GPO Government Printing Office
    MAA Mathematical Association of America
    MT *Mathematics Teacher*
    NCTM National Council of Teachers of Mathematics
    NEA National Education Association
    NSSE National Society for the Study of Education
    SMSG School Mathematics Study Group
    SSM *School Science and Mathematics*
    USBE United States Bureau of Education
    USOE United States Office of Education

COMMITTEE REPORTS AND STATUS STUDIES

1. AAAS, Cooperative Committee on the Teaching of Science and Mathematics. "High School Science and Mathematics in Relation to the Manpower Problem." *SSM* 43 (February 1943): 126–56.
2. ———. "The Preparation of High School Science and Mathematics Teachers." *SSM* 46 (February 1946): 107–18.
3. AAAS (by Alfred B. Garrett). "Recommendations for the Preparation of High School Teachers of Science and Mathematics—1959." *SSM* 59 (April 1959): 281–89.
4. AAAS. "Preparation of High School Science Teachers." *Science* 131 (8 April 1960): 1024–29.
5. Archibald, Raymond Clare. *The Training of Teachers of Mathematics for the Secondary Schools of the Countries Represented in the International Commission on the Teaching of Mathematics.* USBE Bulletin 1917, no. 27. Washington, D.C.: GPO, 1918.
6. Brinkman, H. N. "Mathematics in the Secondary Schools for the Exceptional Student." *AMM* 61 (May 1954): 319–23.
7. Brown, Joseph Clifton. *Curricula in Mathematics: A Comparison of Courses in the Countries Represented in the International Commission on the Teaching of Mathematics.* USBE Bulletin 1914, no. 45. Washington, D.C.: GPO, 1915.

8. Brown, Kenneth E., and Ellsworth S. Obourn. *Qualifications and Teaching Loads of Mathematics and Science Teachers.* USOE Circular no. 575. Washington D.C.: GPO, 1959.
9. California State-wide Mathematics Advisory Committee. "Mathematics Program, K–8, 1967–1968, Strands Report." *Bulletin of the California Mathematics Council* 25 (October 1967): 5–17.
10. Cambridge Conference on Teacher Training. *Goals for Mathematical Education of Elementary School Teachers.* Boston: Houghton Mifflin Co., 1967.
11. Cambridge Conference on School Mathematics. *Goals for School Mathematics.* Boston: Houghton Mifflin Co., 1963.
12. CEEB, Commission on Mathematics. *Program for College Preparatory Mathematics.* New York: CEEB, 1959.
13. ———. *Appendices.* New York: CEEB, 1959.
14. CEEB. "Report of the Commission on Examinations in Mathematics." *MT* 28 (March 1935): 154–66.
Commission on Mathematics. *See* entries 12 and 13.
15. Commission on Post-War Plans of the NCTM. "First Report of the Commission on Post-War Plans." *MT* 37 (May 1944): 225–32.
16. ———. "Second Report of the Commission on Post-War Plans." *MT* 38 (May 1945): 195–221.
17. ———. *The Role of Mathematics in Consumer Education.* Washington, D.C.: Consumer Education Study, 1945.
18. ———. "Guidance Report of the Commission on Post-War Plans." *MT* 40 (July 1947): 315–39.
19. Commission on the Reorganization of Secondary Education. *Cardinal Principles of Secondary Education.* USBE Bulletin 1918, no. 35. Washington, D.C.: GPO, 1918.
20. ———, Committee on the Problem of Mathematics in Secondary Education. *The Problem of Mathematics in Secondary Education.* USBE Bulletin 1920, no. 1. Washington, D.C.: GPO, 1920.
21. Commission on the Training and Utilization of Advanced Students in Mathematics. "Report on the Training of Teachers of Mathematics." *AMM* 42 (1935): 263–77.
22. Committee on the Definitions of College Entrance Requirements. "Committee of 1903." *Bulletin* of the AMS 10 (October 1903–July 1904): 74–77.
23. Committee on the Economy of Time in Education. *Fourth Report of the Committee on the Economy of Time in Education.* Eighteenth Yearbook of the NSSE, pt. 2. Bloomington, Ill.: Public School Publishing Co., 1919.
24. Committee on the Function of Mathematics in General Education of the Commission on the Secondary School Curriculum of the Progressive Education Association. *Mathematics in General Education.* New York: D. Appleton-Century Co., 1940.

25. Committee on the Survey. *A Survey of Research Potential and Training in the Mathematical Sciences.* Final report. Chicago: University of Chicago Press, 1957.
26. Committee on the Undergraduate Program in Mathematics of the MAA, Panel on Teacher Training. *Recommendations for the Training of Teachers of Mathematics.* Berkeley, Calif.: CUPM, 1961. Rev. ed., 1966. This also appeared in *MT* 53 (December 1960): 632–38, 643.
27. ———. *Course Guides for the Training of Teachers of Junior High and High School Mathematics.* Berkeley, Calif.: 1961.
28. ———. *Course Guides for the Training of Teachers of Elementary School Mathematics.* Berkeley, Calif.: CUPM, 1964. Rev. ed., 1968.
29. ———. *Forty-one Conferences on the Training of Teachers of Elementary School Mathematics.* Berkeley, Calif.: CUPM, 1966.
30. ———. *Eleven Conferences on the Training of Teachers of Elementary School Mathematics.* Berkeley, Calif.: CUPM, 1966.
31. ———. *Panel on Teacher Training.* Berkeley, Calif.: CUPM, 1966.

Cooperative Committee on the Teaching of Science and Mathematics. *See* entries 1–2.

32. Dyer, Henry S., Robert Kalin, and Frederick M. Lord. *Problems in Mathematics Education.* Princeton, N.J.: Educational Testing Service, 1956.
33. Educational Policies Commission. *Education for All American Youth.* Washington, D.C.: NEA, 1948.
34. "Essential Mathematics for Minimum Army Needs." *MT* 36 (October 1943): 243–82.
35. *General Education in School and College.* A committee report by the faculties of Andover, Exeter, Lawrenceville, Harvard, Princeton, and Yale. Cambridge, Mass.: Harvard University Press, 1952.
36. Hart, William L. "Progress Report of the Subcommittee on Education for Service of the War Preparedness Committee of the American Mathematical Society and the Mathematical Association of America." *MT* 34 (November 1941): 297–304; *AMM* 48 (1941): 353–62; *SSM* 41 (November 1941): 779–87.
37. Harvard Committee. *General Education in a Free Society.* Cambridge, Mass.: Harvard University Press, 1945.
38. In-Service Education Committee of the NCTM. *In-Service Education in Elementary School Mathematics.* Washington, D.C.: NCTM, 1967.
39. International Commission on the Teaching of Mathematics. The American Report. *Graduate Work in Mathematics in Universities and in Other Institutions of Like Grade in the United States.* Committee no. 12. USBE Bulletin 1911, no. 6. Washington, D.C.: GPO, 1911.

40. ———. *Undergraduate Work in Mathematics in Colleges of Liberal Arts and Universities.* Committee no. 10. USBE Bulletin 1911, no. 7. Washington, D.C.: GPO, 1911.
41. ———. *Examinations in Mathematics Other than Those Set by the Teacher for His Own Classes.* Committee no. 7. USBE Bulletin 1911, no. 8.
42. ———. *Mathematics in the Technological Schools of Collegiate Grade in the United States.* Committee no. 9. USBE Bulletin 1911, no. 9. Washington, D.C.: GPO, 1911.
43. ———. *The Training of Teachers of Elementary and Secondary Mathematics.* Committee no. 5. USBE Bulletin 1911, no. 12. Washington, D.C.: GPO, 1911.
44. ———. *Mathematics in the Elementary Schools of the United States.* Committees 1 and 2. USBE Bulletin 1911, no. 13. Washington, D.C.: GPO, 1911.
45. ———. *Mathematics in the Public and Private Secondary Schools of the United States.* Committees 3 and 4. USBE Bulletin 1911, no. 16. Washington, D.C.: GPO, 1911.
46. ———. *Mathematics at West Point and Annapolis.* Committee no. 11. USBE Bulletin 1912, no. 2. Washington, D.C.: GPO, 1912.
47. ———. *Mathematics in the Technical Secondary Schools in the United States.* Committee no. 6. USBE Bulletin 1912, no. 4. Washington, D.C.: GPO, 1912.
48. ———. *Influences Tending to Improve the Work of the Teacher of Mathematics.* Committee no. 8. USBE Bulletin 1912, no. 13. Washington, D.C.: GPO, 1912.
49. ———. *Report of the American Commissioners of the International Commission on the Teaching of Mathematics.* USBE Bulletin 1912, no. 14. Washington, D.C.: GPO, 1912.
50. Joint Commission of the MAA and the NCTM. *The Place of Mathematics in Secondary Education.* Fifteenth Yearbook of the NCTM. New York: Bureau of Publications, Teachers College, Columbia University, 1940.
51. MAA. "College Mathematics Needed in the Social Sciences." Report of a committee of the MAA. *AMM* 39 (1932): 569–77.
    MAA. *See also* the following entries: 21, 26–31, 36, 50, 54, 57–59, 77, 82.
52. "Mathematics Instruction for Purposes of General Education." From a preliminary report of a committee of the AAAS on the improvement of science teaching in the schools. *AMM* 48 (March 1941): 189–97.
53. Mayor, John R., and Willis G. Swartz. *Accreditation in Teacher Education.* Washington, D.C.: National Commission on Accrediting, 1965.
54. Morse, Marston, and William L. Hart. "Mathematics in the Defense Program." *MT* 34 (May 1941): 195–202.

55. National Association of State Directors of Teacher Education and Certification and the AAAS. *Guidelines for Preparation Programs of Teachers of Secondary School Science and Mathematics.* Washington, D.C.: AAAS, 1961.
56. ———. *Guidelines for Science and Mathematics in the Preparation Program of Elementary School Teachers.* Washington, D.C.: AAAS, 1961.
57. National Committee on Mathematical Requirements of the MAA. *The Reorganization of the First Courses in Secondary School Mathematics.* USBE Secondary School Circular no. 5. Washington, D.C.: GPO, 1920.
58. ———. *The Reorganization of Mathematics in Secondary Education.* USBE Bulletin 1921, no. 32. Washington, D.C.: GPO, 1922.
59. ———. *The Reorganization of Mathematics in Secondary Education.* MAA, 1923.
60. NCTM. *An Analysis of New Mathematics Programs.* Washington, D.C.: NCTM, 1963.
61. ———, Committee on Arithmetic. *Arithmetic in General Education.* Sixteenth Yearbook of the NCTM. New York: Bureau of Publications, Teachers College, Columbia University, 1941.
62. ———. "Report of the Committee on Geometry." *MT* 24 (May 1931): 298–302.
63. ———. "Report of the Committee on Individual Differences." *MT* 26 (October 1933): 350–65.
64. ———. *The Revolution in School Mathematics.* A report of regional orientation conferences in mathematics. Washington, D.C.: NCTM, 1961.
65. ———. Secondary Curriculum Committee. "The Secondary Mathematics Curriculum." *MT* 52 (May 1959): 389–417.

NCTM. *See also* the listings under BOOKS AND PAMPHLETS and the following entries: 15–18, 34, 38, 50, 76, 295.

66. NEA. "Provisional Report of the National Committee of Fifteen on the Geometry Syllabus." *SSM* 11 (April, May, June 1911).
67. ———. *Journal of Addresses and Proceedings, Session of the Year 1895.* Saint Paul: NEA, 1895.
68. ———. *Report of the Committee of Fifteen on Elementary Education.* New York: American Book Co., 1895.
69. ———. *Report of the Committee on College Entrance Requirements.* Chicago: University of Chicago Press, 1899. *See also* entry 74.
70. ———. "The Committee on College-Entrance Requirements: Report of the Chairman." *School Review* (June 1897): 321–31.
71. ———. *Report of the Committee on Secondary School Studies.* Document 205. Washington, D.C.: NEA, 1893.
72. ———. *Report of the Committee of Ten on Secondary School Studies with the Reports of the Conferences Arranged by the Committees.* New York: American Book Co., 1894.

73. *National Survey of the Education of Teachers.* USBE Bulletin 1935, no. 10. Washington, D.C.: GPO, 1935.
74. Nightingale, A. F. "Report of the Committee on College Entrance Requirements." In *Journal of Proceedings and Addresses of the Thirty-eighth Annual Meeting.* Chicago: NEA, 1899.
75. North Central Association of Colleges and Secondary Schools. *Proceedings.* Ann Arbor, Mich.: The Association. Published annually, 1896–1925.
76. "Pre-Induction Courses in Mathematics." Report of a committee appointed by the USOE with the cooperation of the NCTM. *MT* 36 (March 1943): 114–24.
77. "Report on the Training of Teachers of Mathematics." *AMM* 42 (1935): 263–77.
78. Secondary School Curriculum Committee of the NCTM. "The Secondary Mathematics Curriculum." *MT* 52 (May 1959): 389–417.
79. Social Research Council. *Items* 9 (May 1955): 13–16.
80. Steelman, John R. *Manpower for Research.* Vol. 4 of *Science and Public Policy: A Report to the President.* Washington, D.C.: GPO, 1947.
81. Tarbell, H. S. "Report of the Sub-Committee on the Training of Teachers." In *Journal of Proceedings and Addresses, Session of the Year 1895.* Saint Paul: NEA, 1895.
82. "Universal Military Training in Peace Time." Report of a subcommittee of the War Policy Committee of the AMS and the MAA, prepared in July 1945. *MT* 39 (January 1946): 17–23.
83. Washburne, Carleton. "The Grade Placement of Arithmetic Topics." In *Report of the Society's Committee on Arithmetic.* Twenty-ninth Yearbook of the NSSE. Bloomington, Ill.: Public School Publishing Co., 1930.
84. ———. "The Work of the Committee of Seven on Grade-Placement in Arithmetic." In *Child Development and the Curriculum.* Thirty-eighth Yearbook of the NSSE, pt. 1. Bloomington, Ill.: Public School Publishing Co., 1939.

Books and Pamphlets

85. Alexander, Georgia. *Arithmetic: Elementary, Intermediate, Advanced.* Edited by John Dewey. 3 vols. New York: Longmans, Green & Co., 1920.
86. Archibald, Raymond Clare. *A Semicentennial History of the American Mathematical Society, 1888–1938.* New York: AMS, 1938.
87. Atwell, Robert K. *First Book in General Mathematics.* New York: Parker P. Simmons Co., 1917.
88. Bakst, Aaron. *Approximate Computation.* Twelfth Yearbook of the NCTM. New York: Bureau of Publications, Teachers College, Columbia University, 1937.

89. Barber, Harry C. *Teaching Junior High School Mathematics.* Boston: Houghton Mifflin Co., 1924.
90. Barr, A. S., William H. Burton, and Leo J. Brueckner. "The Emerging Concept of Supervision." In *Supervision.* New York: D. Appleton-Century Co., 1938.
91. Beberman, Max. *An Emerging Program of Secondary School Mathematics.* Cambridge, Mass.: Harvard University Press, 1958.
92. Begle, E. G. "Curriculum Research in Mathematics." In *Research and Development toward the Improvement of Education.* Madison, Wis.: Dembar Educational Research Services, 1969.
93. ———. "The Reform of Mathematics Education in the United States of America." In *Mathematical Education in the Americas,* edited by Howard Fehr. New York: Bureau of Publications, Teachers College, Columbia University, 1963.
94. Bestor, Arthur E. *Educational Wastelands: The Retreat from Learning in Our Public Schools.* Urbana: University of Illinois Press, 1953.
95. Betz, William. *Algebra for Today: First Course.* Boston: Ginn & Co., 1937.
96. Biggs, Edith E., and James R. MacLean. *Freedom to Learn: An Active Learning Approach to Mathematics.* Don Mills, Ont.: Addison-Wesley (Canada), 1969.
97. Birkhoff, George David, and Ralph Beatley. *Basic Geometry.* Chicago: Scott, Foresman & Co., 1941; New York: Chelsea Publishing Co., 1959.
98. Blackhurst, J. Herbert. *Humanized Geometry: An Introduction to Thinking.* Des Moines: University of Iowa Press, 1935.
99. Bobbit, Franklin. *The Curriculum.* Boston: Houghton Mifflin Co., 1918.
100. ———. *The Curriculum of Modern Education.* New York: McGraw-Hill Book Co., 1941.
101. Boring, Edwin G. *A History of Experimental Psychology.* 2d ed. New York: Appleton-Century-Crofts, 1957.
102. Breslich, Ernst R. *Senior Mathematics,* bk. 1. Chicago: University of Chicago Press, 1928.
103. ———. *The Technique of Teaching Secondary-School Mathematics.* Chicago: University of Chicago Press, 1930.
104. Brooks, Edward. *Mental Science and Methods of Mental Culture.* Lancaster, Pa.: Normal Publishing Co., 1883.
105. ———. *Normal Methods of Teaching.* Lancaster, Pa.: Normal Publishing Co., 1883.
106. ———. *The Philosophy of Arithmetic.* Lancaster, Pa.: Normal Publishing Co., 1880.
107. Brown, Claude H. *The Teaching of Secondary Mathematics.* New York: Harper & Bros., 1952.

108. Brown, Kenneth E. *Mathematics in Public High Schools.* USOE Bulletin 1953, no. 5. Washington, D.C.: GPO, 1953.
109. ———. *Offerings and Enrollments in Science and Mathematics in Public High Schools.* USOE Pamphlet no. 118. Washington, D.C.: GPO, 1956.
110. Brown, Kenneth E., and Ellsworth S. Obourn. *Offerings and Enrollments in Science and Mathematics in Public High Schools.* USOE Bulletin 1961, no. 5. Washington, D.C.: GPO, 1961.
111. Brown, Kenneth E., and Daniel Snader. *Inservice Education of High School Mathematics Teachers.* USOE Bulletin 1961, no. 10. Washington, D.C.: GPO, 1961.
112. Bruner, Jerome S. *The Process of Education.* Cambridge, Mass.: Harvard University Press, 1960.
113. ———. *Toward a Theory of Instruction.* Cambridge, Mass.: Harvard University Press, 1966.
114. Bruner, Jerome S., and Helen J. Kenney. "Representation and Mathematics Learning." In *Mathematical Learning.* Monographs of the Society for Research in Child Development, serial no. 99, no. 1. Chicago: University of Chicago Press, 1965.
115. Bruner, Jerome S., ed. *Learning about Learning.* USOE Cooperative Research Monograph no. 15. Washington, D.C.: GPO, 1966.
116. Buswell, Guy Thomas, William A. Brownell, and Lenore John. *Living Arithmetic, Grade Eight.* Boston: Ginn & Co., 1938, 1943.
117. Butler, Charles H., and F. Lynwood Wren. *The Teaching of Secondary Mathematics.* New York: McGraw-Hill Book Co., 1941, 1951, 1960, 1965.
118. Butts, R. Freeman. *A Cultural History of Western Education.* New York: McGraw-Hill Book Co., 1955.
119. Butts, R. Freeman, and Lawrence A. Cremin. *A History of Education in American Culture.* New York: Henry Holt & Co., 1955.
120. Cajori, Florian. *The Early Mathematical Sciences in North and South America.* Boston: Richard G. Badger, Publisher, 1928.
121. ———. *The Teaching and History of Mathematics in the United States.* USBE. Washington, D.C.: GPO, 1890.
122. Callahan, R. E. *Education and the Cult of Efficiency.* Chicago: University of Chicago Press, 1962.
123. Christofferson, Halbert C. *Geometry Professionalized for Teachers.* Oxford, Ohio: H. C. Christofferson, 1933.
124. Clapp, F. L. *The Number Combinations: Their Relative Difficulty and the Frequency of Their Appearance in Text-Books.* Bureau of Educational Research Bulletin nos. 1 and 2. Madison: University of Wisconsin Press, 1924.

125. Colburn, Warren. *An Arithmetic on the Plan of Pestalozzi, with Some Improvements.* Boston: 1821. Later editions had various titles, including *First Lessons in Arithmetic on the Plan of Pestalozzi* (1822) and *Intellectual Arithmetic upon the Inductive Method of Instruction* (1826). See also entry 164: 236–39.

126. ———. *An Introduction to Algebra upon the Inductive Method of Instruction.* Boston: Cummings, Hilliard, & Co., 1825.

127. Coleman, Robert. *The Development of Informal Geometry.* Contributions to Education, no. 865. New York: Bureau of Publications, Teachers College, Columbia University, 1942.

128. Conant, James B. *The Education of American Teachers.* New York: McGraw-Hill Book Co., 1963.

129. Cremin, Lawrence A. *The Transformation of the School: Progressivism in American Education, 1876–1957.* New York: Alfred A. Knopf, 1961.

130. Cubberly, Elwood P. *Changing Conceptions of Education.* Boston: Houghton Mifflin Co., 1909.

131. ———. *Public School Administration.* Boston: Houghton Mifflin Co., 1929.

132. Cuisenaire, G., and C. Gattegno. *Numbers in Colour.* London: William Heinemann, 1954.

133. Davies, Charles. *The Logic and Utility of Mathematics with the Best Methods of Instruction Explained and Illustrated.* New York: A. S. Barnes & Co., 1850.

134. ———. *Elements of Geometry and Trigonometry.* From the works of A. M. Legendre. New York: A. S. Barnes & Co., 1869.

135. Davis, E. F. *Practical Book-keeping and Arithmetic.* Philadelphia: J. B. Lippincott Co., 1859.

136. Davis, Robert B. *A Modern Mathematics Program as It Pertains to the Interrelationships of Mathematical Content, Teaching Methods and Classroom Atmosphere.* Final report, USOE Project no. D-233. Syracuse University and Webster College, October 1967.

137. ———. *The Changing Curriculum: Mathematics.* Washington, D.C.: Association for Supervision and Curriculum Development, NEA, 1967.

138. Dienes, Zoltan P. *Building Up Mathematics.* Rev. ed. London: Hutchinson Educational, 1965.

139. Douglass, Harl R., and Lucien B. Kinney. *Junior Mathematics*, bk. 2. New York: Henry Holt & Co., 1940.

140. Elicker, Paul. Letter, 23 January 1962. "To Officers in the State Principals' Associations and Selected Leaders in Secondary Education."

141. Fawcett, Harold P. *The Nature of Proof.* Thirteenth Yearbook of the NCTM. New York: Bureau of Publications, Teachers College, Columbia University, 1938.

142. Fields, Ralph R. *The Community College Movement*. New York: McGraw-Hill Book Co., 1962.
143. Flavell, John H. *The Developmental Psychology of Jean Piaget*. Princeton, N.J.: D. Van Nostrand Co., 1963.
144. Fuess, Claude M. *The College Board: Its First Fifty Years*. New York: CEEB, 1967.
145. Gagné, Robert M. *The Conditions of Learning*. New York: Holt, Rinehart & Winston, 1965.
146. Gagné, Robert M., et al. "Some Factors in Learning Non-Metric Geometry." In *Mathematical Learning*. Monographs of the Society for Research in Child Development, vol. 30, serial no. 99, no. 1. Chicago: University of Chicago Press, 1965.
147. Goodlad, John I. *The Changing School Curriculum*. New York: Fund for the Advancement of Education, 1966.
148. Griffin, William M. *Grammar-School Algebra*. New York: American Book Co., 1899.
149. Grossnickle, Foster E., et al. *How to Make Arithmetic Meaningful*. 5th ed. New York: Holt, Rinehart & Winston, 1968. Previous editions published with titles *Discovering Meanings in Arithmetic* and *Discovering Meanings in Elementary School Mathematics*.
150. Gugle, Marie. *Modern Junior Mathematics*, bk. 2. New York: Gregg Publishing Co., 1920.
151. Halsted, George B. *Rational Geometry; A Text-book for the Science of Space; Based on Hilbert's Foundations*. New York: John Wiley & Sons, 1904.
152. Hamley, Herbert Russell. *Relational and Functional Thinking in Mathematics*. Ninth Yearbook of the NCTM. New York: Bureau of Publications, Teachers College, Columbia University, 1934.
153. Harper, Charles A. *A Century of Public Teacher Education*. Washington, D.C.: American Association of Teachers Colleges, 1939; NEA, 1967.
154. Hart, Walter W. *Junior High School Mathematics*, bk. 1. Boston: D.C. Heath & Co., 1921.
155. Henderson, Kenneth B. "Mathematics." In *Using Current Curriculum Developments*. Washington, D.C.: Association for Supervision and Curriculum Development, NEA, 1963.
156. Hofstadter, Richard. *The Age of Reform*. New York: Random House, 1955.
157. Holloway, G. E. T. *An Introduction to the Child's Conception of Geometry*. London: Routledge & Kegan Paul, 1967.
158. Hurst, Homer. *Illinois State Normal University and the Public Normal School Movement*. Contribution to Education, no. 390. Nashville: George Peabody College for Teachers, 1948.
159. Hutchins, Robert M. *The Conflict in Education in a Democratic Society*. New York: Harper & Bros., 1953.

160. Inhelder, B., and Jean Piaget. *The Growth of Logical Thinking from Childhood to Adolescence.* New York: Basic Books, Publishers, 1958.
161. Jessen, Carl A. *Offerings and Registrations in High School Subjects.* USOE Bulletin 1938, no. 6. Washington, D.C.: GPO, 1938.
162. Judd, Charles H. *Education as Cultivation of Higher Mental Processes.* New York: Macmillan Co., 1936.
163. Kandel, Isaac Leon. *The Training of Elementary School Teachers in Mathematics in the Countries Represented in the International Commission on the Teaching of Mathematics.* USBE Bulletin 1915, no. 39. Washington, D.C.: GPO, 1915.
164. Karpinski, Louis C. *Bibliography of Mathematical Works Printed in America through 1850.* Ann Arbor: University of Michigan Press, 1940.
165. Kaufman, Burt A., and Hans G. Steiner. "The CSMP Approach to a Content-Oriented, Highly Individualized Mathematics Education." Mimeographed. Carbondale, Ill.: Central Midwestern Educational Laboratory, 1968.
166. Kinsella, John J. *Secondary School Mathematics.* New York: Center for Applied Research in Education, 1965.
167. Klein, Felix. *Elementary Mathematics from an Advanced Standpoint: Geometry.* Translated from 3d German edition by E. R. Hedrick and C. A. Noble. New York: Dover Publications, 1932, 1939.
168. Kolesnik, Walter B. *Mental Discipline in Modern Education.* Madison: University of Wisconsin Press, 1958.
169. Koos, Leonard V. *The Junior High School.* Boston: Ginn & Co., 1927.
170. Lazar, Nathan. *The Importance of Certain Concepts and Laws of Logic for the Study and Teaching of Geometry.* New York: Nathan Lazar, 1938.
171. Lide, Edwin S. *Instruction in Mathematics.* National Survey of Secondary Education. USOE Bulletin 1932, no. 17. Washington, D.C.: GPO, 1933.
172. Lynd, Albert. *Quackery in the Public Schools.* Boston: Little, Brown & Co., 1953.
173. Makoff, Lester M. "Why the New Math?" *Journal of Secondary Education* 41 (March 1966): 134–41.
174. Marlin, Lillian. "SMSG—One Point of View." *MT* 55 (October 1962): 476–78.
175. Marsh, Paul E., and Ross A. Gartner. *Federal Aid to Science Education: Two Programs.* Syracuse, N.Y.: Syracuse University Press, 1963.
176. Mayor, John R. "The Regional Accrediting Associations." In *Accreditation in Teacher Education.* Washington, D.C.: National Commission on Accrediting, 1965.

177. McCormick, Clarence. *The Teaching of General Mathematics in the Secondary Schools of the United States.* New York: Bureau of Publications, Teachers College, Columbia University, 1929.
178. McLellan, James A., and John Dewey. *The Psychology of Number and Its Applications to Methods of Teaching Arithmetic.* New York: D. Appleton & Co., 1895.
179. Milne, William J. *High School Algebra.* New York: American Book Co., 1892.
180. Moise, Edwin. "The New Mathematics Programs." *Education Digest* 28 (September 1962): 28–31.
181. Monroe, Walter S. *Development of Arithmetic as a School Subject.* USBE Bulletin 1917, no. 10. Washington, D.C.: GPO, 1917.
182. Morison, Samuel Eliot. *The Oxford History of the American People.* New York: Oxford University Press, 1965.
183. Morrisett, Lloyd N., and John Vinsonhaler, eds. *Mathematical Learning.* Monographs of the Society for Research in Child Development, serial no. 99, no. 1. Chicago: University of Chicago Press, 1965.
184. Morton, Robert Lee. *Teaching Arithmetic in the Elementary School.* 3 vols. 2d ed. New York: Silver Burdett Co., 1939.
185. ———. *Teaching Children Arithmetic.* New York: Silver Burdett Co., 1953.
186. NCTM. *A General Survey of Progress in the Last Twenty-five Years.* First Yearbook. New York: Bureau of Publications, Teachers College, Columbia University, 1926.
187. ———. *Selected Topics in the Teaching of Mathematics.* Third Yearbook. New York: Bureau of Publications, Teachers College, Columbia University, 1928.
188. ———. *Significant Changes and Trends in the Teaching of Secondary Mathematics throughout the World since 1910.* Fourth Yearbook. New York: Bureau of Publications, Teachers College, Columbia University, 1929.
189. ———. *The Teaching of Geometry.* Fifth Yearbook. New York: Bureau of Publications, Teachers College, Columbia University, 1930.
190. ———. *Mathematics in Modern Life.* Sixth Yearbook. New York: Bureau of Publications, Teachers College, Columbia University, 1931.
191. ———. *The Teaching of Algebra.* Seventh Yearbook. New York: Bureau of Publications, Teachers College, Columbia University, 1932.
192. ———. *The Teaching of Mathematics in the Secondary School.* Eighth Yearbook. New York: Bureau of Publications, Teachers College, Columbia University, 1933.

THE UNITED STATES OF AMERICA 513

193. ———. *The Place of Mathematics in Modern Education*. Eleventh Yearbook. New York: Bureau of Publications, Teachers College, Columbia University, 1936.

194. ———. *A Source Book of Mathematical Applications*. Seventeenth Yearbook. New York: Bureau of Publications, Teachers College, Columbia University, 1942.

195. ———. *Multi-Sensory Aids in the Teaching of Mathematics*. Eighteenth Yearbook. New York: Bureau of Publications, Teachers College, Columbia University, 1945.

196. ———. *Surveying Instruments: Their History and Classroom Use*. Nineteenth Yearbook. New York: Bureau of Publications, Teachers College, Columbia University, 1947.

197. ———. *The Learning of Mathematics: Its Theory and Practice*. Twenty-first Yearbook. Washington, D.C.: NCTM, 1953.

198. ———. *Emerging Practices in Mathematics Education*. Twenty-second Yearbook. Washington, D.C.: NCTM, 1954.

199. ———. *Insights into Modern Mathematics*. Twenty-third Yearbook. Washington, D.C.: NCTM, 1957.

200. ———. *The Growth of Mathematical Ideas: Grades K–12*. Twenty-fourth Yearbook. Washington, D.C.: NCTM, 1959.

NCTM. *See also* listings under COMMITTEE REPORTS AND STATUS STUDIES and the following numbered entries: 88, 141, 152, 224, 295, 376.

201. NSF. *To Improve Secondary School Science and Mathematics Teaching*. Washington, D.C.: GPO, 1968.

202. NSSE. *Some Aspects of High School Instruction and Administration*, pt. 1; *Plans for Organizing School Surveys*, pt. 2. Thirteenth Yearbook. Chicago: University of Chicago Press, 1914.

203. Nietz, John A. *Old Textbooks*. Pittsburgh: University of Pittsburgh Press, 1961.

204. Organization for Economic Cooperation and Development. *New Thinking in School Mathematics*. Washington, D.C.: The Organization, 1961.

205. Paddock, C. E., and E. E. Holton. *Vocational Arithmetic*. New York: D. Appleton & Co., 1920.

206. Palmer, C. I. *Practical Mathematics, Part 3: Algebra with Application*. 2d ed. New York: McGraw-Hill Co., 1918.

207. Perkins, George R. *The Practical Arithmetic*. New York: D. Appleton & Co., 1851.

208. Piaget, Jean. *The Child's Conception of Number*. New York: Humanities Press, 1952.

209. Piaget, Jean, Barbel Inhelder, and Alina Szeminska. *The Child's Conception of Geometry*. New York: Basic Books, Publishers, 1960.

210. Price, G. Baley. "Progress in Mathematics and Its Implications for Schools." In *The Revolution in School Mathematics.* Washington, D.C.: NCTM, 1961.
211. Rappaport, David, ed. *A Half Century of Mathematics Progress.* Chicago: Men's Mathematics Club of Chicago and Metropolitan Area, 1965.
212. Ray, Joseph. *Intellectual Arithmetic.* Cincinnati: Wilson, Hinkle & Co., 1857.
213. ———. *New Practical Arithmetic.* Cincinnati: Van Antwerp Bragg & Co., 1877.
214. ———. *The Rudiments of Arithmetic.* Cincinnati: Wilson, Hinkle & Co., 1866.
215. Reeve, William D. *General Mathematics,* bk. 2. Boston: Ginn & Co., 1922.
216. ———. *Mathematics for the Secondary School.* New York: Henry Holt & Co., 1954.
217. "Relation of Pre-Service Education of Teachers to In-Service Education of Teachers." USOE Bulletin 1933, no. 10, vol. 6. Washington, D.C.: GPO, 1933.
218. Rice, Howard C., Jr. *The Rittenhouse Orrery.* Princeton, N.J.: Princeton University Library, 1954.
219. Rickover, H. G. *Education and Freedom.* New York: E. P. Dutton & Co., 1959.
220. Rosenberger, Noah Bryan. *The Place of the Elementary Calculus in the Senior High School Mathematics.* New York: Bureau of Publications, Teachers College, Columbia University, 1921.
221. Rosskopf, Myron F. "Nongeometric Exercises in Geometry." In *Emerging Practices in Mathematics Education.* Twenty-second Yearbook of the NCTM. Washington, D.C.: NCTM, 1954.
222. Rousseau, Jean Jacques. *Émile.* Translated by Barbara Foxley. London: J. M. Dent & Sons, 1911.
223. Ruch, G. M., F. B. Knight, and J. W. Studebaker. *Mathematics and Life,* bk. 2. Chicago: Scott, Foresman & Co., 1937, 1942.
224. Ruddell, Arden K., Wilbur Dutton, and John Reckzek. "Background Mathematics for Elementary Teachers." In *Instruction in Arithmetic.* Twenty-fifth Yearbook of the NCTM. Washington, D.C.: NCTM, 1960.
225. Rudolph, Frederick. *The American College and University.* New York: Vintage Books, 1962.
226. Safford, Truman H. *Mathematical Teaching and Its Modern Methods.* Monographs on Education. Boston: D.C. Heath & Co., 1887.
227. Sandiford, Peter. *Educational Psychology.* New York: Longmans, Green & Co., 1934.
228. SMSG. *Report of a Conference on Future Responsibilities for School Mathematics.* Stanford, Calif.: SMSG, 1961.

229. ———. *Philosophies and Procedures of SMSG Writing Teams.* Stanford, Calif.: Stanford University Press, 1965.
230. ———. *Newsletter No. 1.* SMSG progress report, March 1959. New Haven: Yale University Press, 1959.
231. Schorling, Raleigh. *A Tentative List of Objectives in the Teaching of Junior High School Mathematics with Investigations for Determining Their Validity.* Ann Arbor, Mich.: George Wahr, 1925.
232. ———. *The Teaching of Mathematics.* Ann Arbor, Mich.: Ann Arbor Press, 1936.
233. Schorling, Raleigh, and John R. Clark. *Mathematics in Life: Basic Course.* Yonkers-on-Hudson, N.Y.: World Book Co., 1946.
234. ———. *Modern Algebra: Ninth School Year.* Yonkers-on-Hudson, N.Y.: World Book Co., 1924.
235. Schorling, Raleigh, John R. Clark, and Rolland R. Smith. *Modern-School Algebra: First Course.* Modern School Mathematics. Yonkers-on-Hudson, N.Y.: World Book Co., 1936.
236. Schult, Veryl, and Theodore Abell. *Inservice Mathematics Education.* USOE Bulletin 1964, no. 36. Washington, D.C.: GPO, 1964.
237. Shafer, Harold T. "Roles of Supervisors and Curriculum Workers." In *Toward Professional Maturity of Supervisors and Curriculum Workers.* Washington, D.C.: Association for Supervision and Curriculum Development, NEA, 1967.
238. Shibli, Jabir. *Recent Developments in the Teaching of Geometry.* York, Pa.: Maple Press, 1932.
239. Shulman, Lee S., and Evan R. Keislar, eds. *Learning by Discovery: A Critical Appraisal.* Chicago: Rand McNally & Co., 1966.
240. Simons, Lao G. *Introduction of Algebra into American Schools in the Eighteenth Century.* USBE Bulletin 1924, no. 18. Washington, D.C.: GPO, 1924.
241. Smith, David Eugene. *The Teaching of Elementary Mathematics.* New York: Macmillan Co., 1900, 1908.
242. Smith, David Eugene, and Howard G. Burdge. *The Smith-Burdge Arithmetics, Advanced Book.* Boston: Ginn & Co., 1926.
243. Smith, David Eugene, and William D. Reeve. *The Teaching of Junior High Mathematics.* Boston: Ginn & Co., 1927.
244. Smith, David Eugene, and Jekuthiel Ginsburg. *A History of Mathematics in America before 1900.* MAA Carus Mathematical Monographs, no. 5. Chicago: Open Court Publishing Co., 1934.
245. Smith, David Eugene, and Charles Goldziher. *Bibliography of the Teaching of Mathematics, 1900–1912.* USBE Bulletin 1912, no. 29. Washington, D.C.: GPO, 1912.
246. Speer, William W. *Primary Arithmetic: First Year for the Use of Teachers.* Boston: Ginn & Co., 1897.

247. Spencer, William George. *Inventional Geometry: A Series of Problems, Intended to Familiarize the Pupil with Geometrical Conceptions, and to Exercise His Inventive Faculty.* Prefatory note by Herbert Spencer. New York: D. Appleton & Co., 1877.
248. Spiller, L. R., and D. Reichgott. *Today's Geometry.* New York: Prentice-Hall, 1938.
249. Spitzer, Herbert F. *Teaching Elementary School Mathematics.* Boston: Houghton Mifflin Co., 1948, 1954, 1961, 1967.
250. *Studies in Mathematics Education.* Chicago: Scott, Foresman & Co., 1960.
251. Stone, John C. *Junior High School Mathematics,* bk. 1. New York: Benjamin H. Sanborn & Co., 1919.
252. ———. *The New Mathematics,* bk. 1. Chicago: Benjamin H. Sanborn & Co., 1926.
253. ———. *The Stone Arithmetic, Advanced.* Chicago: Benjamin H. Sanborn & Co., 1926.
254. Stone, John C., and Virgil S. Mallory. *New Higher Arithmetic.* Chicago: Benjamin H. Sanborn & Co., 1938.
255. Stone, John C., and James F. Millis. *Elementary Algebra, First Course.* Boston: Benjamin J. Sanborn & Co., 1911.
256. Strayer, George D., and Clifford B. Upton. *Practical Junior Mathematics,* bk. 2. New York: American Book Co., 1935.
257. ———. *Strayer-Upton Arithmetics, Higher Grades.* New York: American Book Co., 1928.
258. Sullivan, Edmund V. *Piaget and the School Curriculum: A Critical Appraisal.* Bulletin no. 2. Ontario Institute for Studies in Education, 1967.
259. Suppes, Patrick. "On the Behavioral Foundations of Mathematical Concepts." In *Mathematical Learning.* Monographs of the Society for Research in Child Development, serial no. 99, no. 1. Chicago: University of Chicago Press, 1965.
260. ———. "Towards a Behavioral Psychology of Mathematical Thinking" and "The Psychology of Arithmetic." In *Learning about Learning.* Washington, D.C.: GPO, 1966.
261. Suppes, Patrick, et al. *Computer-Assisted Instruction: Stanford's 1965–66 Arithmetic Program.* New York: Academic Press, 1968.
262. Swearinger, Mildred E. "An Evolving Concept of Supervision." In *Supervision of Instruction: Foundations and Dimensions.* Boston: Allyn & Bacon, 1962.
263. Swenson, John A. *Integrated Mathematics,* bk. 1. Ann Arbor, Mich.: Edwards Bros., 1935.
264. Taylor, Edson Homer. *Mathematics in the Lower and Middle Commercial and Industrial Schools of Various Countries Represented in the International Commission on the Teaching of Mathematics.* USBE Bulletin 1915, no. 35. Washington, D.C.: GPO, 1915.

265. Thorndike, Edward L. *The Psychology of Arithmetic.* New York: Macmillan Co., 1922.
266. ———. *The Psychology of Algebra.* New York: Macmillan Co., 1923.
267. Van Engen, Henry, and E. Glenadine Gibb. *General Mental Functions Associated with Division.* Educational Service Studies, no. 2. Cedar Falls: Iowa State Teachers College, 1956.
268. Waples, Douglas, and Charles A. Stone. *The Teaching Unit: A Type Study.* New York: D. Appleton & Co., 1929.
269. Welte, Herbert D. *A Psychological Analysis of Plane Geometry.* University of Iowa Monographs in Education, ser. 1, no. 1. Iowa City: University of Iowa Press, 1926.
270. Wentworth, G. A. *Grammar School Arithmetic.* Rev. ed. Boston: Ginn & Co., 1891.
271. ———. *A Textbook of Geometry.* Rev. ed. Boston: Ginn & Co., 1891.
272. ———. *Primary Arithmetic.* Boston: Ginn & Co., 1890.
273. Wentworth, G. A., and E. M. Reed. *The First Steps in Number.* Boston: Ginn & Co., 1891.
274. Wheat, Harry Grove. *The Psychology and Teaching of Arithmetic.* Boston: D. C. Heath & Co., 1937.
275. ———. *How to Teach Arithmetic.* Evanston, Ill.: Row, Peterson & Co., 1951.
276. Whitcraft, Leslie Harper. *Some Influences of the Requirements and Examinations of the College Entrance Examination Board on Mathematics in Secondary Schools of the United States.* Contributions to Education, no. 557. New York: Bureau of Publications, Teachers College, Columbia University, 1933.
277. White, E. E. *A Complete Arithmetic, Uniting Mental and Written Exercises in a Natural System of Instruction.* Cincinnati: Wilson, Hinkle & Co., 1870.
278. Wilson, Guy M., et al. *Course of Study in Elementary Mathematics.* Connersville, Ind.: 1911. Rev. ed. Baltimore: Warwick & York, 1922.
279. Wilson, Guy M., Mildred B. Stone, and Charles O. Dalrymple. *Teaching the New Arithmetic.* New York: McGraw-Hill Book Co., 1939.
280. Wolff, Christian. *Psychologia Rationalis.* Francofurti & Lipsiae, 1740.
281. Woodring, Paul. *Let's Talk Sense about Our Schools.* New York: McGraw-Hill Book Co., 1953.
282. Wooton, William. *SMSG: The Making of a Curriculum.* New Haven: Yale University Press, 1965.
283. Wren, F. Lynwood. "The Professional Preparation of Teachers of Arithmetic." In *Arithmetic 1948.* Supplementary Education Monographs, no. 66. Chicago: University of Chicago Press, 1948.

284. Young, John Wesley. *Lectures on Fundamental Concepts of Algebra and Geometry*. New York: Macmillan Co., 1911.
285. Young, Jacob William Albert. *The Teaching of Mathematics in the Elementary and Secondary School*. New York: Longmans, Green & Co., 1907, 1914, 1931.
286. ———, ed. *Monographs on Topics in Modern Mathematics, Relevant to the Elementary Field*. New York: Longmans, Green & Co., 1911, 1924, 1927.

Journal and Yearbook Articles

287. Adler, Irving. "The Cambridge Conference Report: Blueprint or Fantasy?" *AT* 12 (March 1966): 179–86.
288. Allendoerfer, Carl B. "The Second Revolution in Mathematics." *MT* 58 (December 1965): 690–95.
289. Austin, C. M. "The National Council of Teachers of Mathematics." *MT* 14 (January 1921): 1–4.
290. Ausubel, David P. "Learning by Discovery: Rationale and Mystique." *Bulletin of the National Association of Secondary School Principals* 45 (December 1961): 18–58.
291. ———. "In Defense of Verbal Learning." *Educational Theory* 11 (1961): 15–25.
292. ———. "Some Psychological and Educational Limitations of Learning by Discovery." *AT* 11 (May 1964): 290–302.
293. Bagley, William C. "The Teacher's Professional Study of Subject Matter." *MT* 31 (October 1938): 273–77.
294. Baird, George H. "The Greater Cleveland Mathematics Program." *MT* 54 (January 1961): 31.
295. Beatley, Ralph. "Third Report of the Committee on Geometry." *MT* 28 (October, November 1935): 329–79, 401–50.
296. Beberman, Max. "The Old Mathematics in the New Curriculum." *Educational Leadership* 19 (March 1962): 373–75.
297. Begle, Edward G. "Some Remarks on 'On the Mathematics Curriculum of the High School.'" *MT* 55 (March 1962): 195–96.
298. ———. "SMSG: The First Decade." *MT* 61 (March 1968): 239–45.
299. Bell, Eric T. Review of David Eugene Smith's *Poetry of Mathematics*. *AMM* 42 (November 1935): 558.
300. Benz, H. E. "A Summary of Some Scientific Investigations of the Teaching of High School Mathematics." In *The Teaching of Mathematics in the Secondary School*. Eighth Yearbook of the NCTM. New York: Bureau of Publications, Teachers College, Columbia University, 1933.
301. Bestor, Arthur E. "Aimlessness in Education." *Scientific Monthly* 75 (August 1952): 109–16.

THE UNITED STATES OF AMERICA

302. Betz, William. "The Confusion of Objectives in Secondary Mathematics." *MT* 16 (December 1923): 449–69.
303. ———. "The Present Situation in Secondary Mathematics, with Particular Reference to the New National Reports on the Place of Mathematics in Education." *MT* 33 (December 1940): 339–60.
304. ———. "Five Decades of Mathematical Reform—Evaluation and Challenge." *MT* 43 (December 1950): 377–87.
305. ———. "The Reorganization of Secondary Education." In *The Place of Mathematics in Modern Education*. Eleventh Yearbook of the NCTM. New York: Bureau of Publications, Teachers College, Columbia University, 1936.
306. Bidwell, James K. "A New Look at Old Committee Reports." *MT* 61 (April 1968): 383–87.
307. Birkhoff, George D., and Ralph Beatley. "A New Approach to Elementary Geometry." In *The Teaching of Geometry*. Fifth Yearbook of the NCTM. New York: Bureau of Publications, Teachers College, Columbia University, 1930.
308. Bittinger, Marvin L. "A Review of Discovery." *MT* 61 (February 1968): 140–46.
309. ———. *The Supervision of City Schools: Some General Principles of Management Applied to the Problems of City School Systems*. Twelfth Yearbook of the NSSE, pt. 1. Bloomington, Ill.: Public School Publishing Co., 1913.
310. Breslich, Ernest R. "The Articulation of Junior and Senior High School Mathematics." In *The Teaching of Mathematics in the Secondary School*. Eighth Yearbook of the NCTM. New York: Bureau of Publications, Teachers College, Columbia University, 1933.
311. ———. "Mathematics." In *A Half Century of Science and Mathematics Teaching*. Oak Park, Ill.: Central Association of Science and Mathematics Teachers, 1950.
312. Brownell, William A. "Psychological Considerations in the Learning and the Teaching of Arithmetic." In *The Teaching of Arithmetic*. Tenth Yearbook of the NCTM. New York: Bureau of Publications, Teachers College, Columbia University, 1935.
313. ———. "Readiness and the Arithmetic Curriculum." *Elementary School Journal* 38 (January 1938): 344–54.
314. ———. "A Critique of the Committee of Seven's Investigations on the Grade Placement of Arithmetic Topics." *Elementary School Journal* 38 (March 1938): 495–508.
315. ———. "The Progressive Nature of Learning in Mathematics." *MT* 37 (April 1944): 147–57.
316. ———. "When Is Arithmetic Meaningful?" *Journal of Educational Research* 38 (March 1945): 481–98.
317. ———. "The Place of Meaning in the Teaching of Arithmetic." *Elementary School Journal* 47 (January 1947): 256–65.

318. Brueckner, Leo J. "The Development of Ability in Arithmetic." In *Child Development and the Curriculum*. Thirty-eighth Yearbook of the NSSE, pt. 1. Bloomington, Ill.: Public School Publishing Co., 1939.
319. ———. "The Social Phase of Arithmetic Instruction." In *Arithmetic in General Education*. Sixteenth Yearbook of the NCTM. New York: Bureau of Publications, Teachers College, Columbia University, 1941.
320. Buckingham, B. R. "Significance, Meaning, Insight—These Three." *MT* 31 (January 1938): 24–30.
321. Burington, Richard S. "Mathematics for Our Time." *MT* 47 (May 1954): 295–98.
322. Cairns, Stewart S. "The Educational Octopus." *Scientific Monthly*, April 1953, pp. 231–40.
323. ———. "Elementary and Secondary School Training in Mathematics." *MT* 47 (May 1954): 299–302.
324. Cave, A. J. "Common Objections to the Study of Mathematics." *SSM* 24 (April 1924).
325. Christofferson, Halbert C. "Geometry a Way of Thinking." *MT* 31 (October 1938): 147–55.
326. Clinchy, Evans. "The New Curricula." In *The Revolution in the Schools*, edited by Ronald Gross and Judith Murphy. New York: Harcourt, Brace & World, 1964.
327. Coar, Henry L. "When and How Geometry Should Be Taught." *Academy: A Journal of Secondary Education* 5 (1890): 231–38.
328. Davis, Robert B. "The 'Madison Project' of Syracuse University." *MT* 53 (November 1960): 571–75.
329. De Mott, Benjamin. "The Math Wars." *American Scholar* 31 (Spring 1962): 296–310.
330. Dienes, Zoltan P. "On the Learning of Mathematics." *AT* 10 (March 1933): 115–26.
331. Douglass, Harl R. "Issues in Elementary and Secondary School Mathematics." *MT* 47 (May 1954): 290–94.
332. Dunbar, Ruth. "Why Johnny Can't Add." *Saturday Review* 39 (8 September 1956): 28, 54.
333. Edwards, P. D., Phillip S. Jones, and Bruce E. Meserve. "Mathematical Preparation for College." *MT* 47 (May 1952): 321–30.
334. Fawcett, Harold P. "Mathematics and the Core Curriculum." *MT* 42 (January 1949): 6–13.
335. Fehr, Howard F. "General Ways to Identify Students with Scientific and Mathematical Potential." *MT* 46 (April 1953): 230–34.
336. ———. "Socializing Mathematics Instruction." *MT* 41 (January 1948): 3–7.
337. Fisher, J. J. "The Extent of Implementation of CUPM Level I Recommendations." *AT* 14 (1967): 194–97.

338. ——. "The Extent of Implementation of Level I and Level III CUPM Recommendations, Panel on Teacher Training." *AMM* 75 (1968): 290–92.
339. Gager, William A. "Approximate Data—Terminology and Computation." In *Emerging Practices in Mathematics Education.* Twenty-second Yearbook of the NCTM. Washington, D. C.: NCTM, 1954.
340. Gagné, Robert M. "The Acquisition of Knowledge." *Psychological Review* 69 (July 1962): 355–65.
341. Glass, James M. "The Present Status of the Junior High School in Cities of More than 100,000 Population." *School Review* 32 (October 1924): 598–602.
342. Graham, Patricia A. "Joseph Mayer Rice as a Founder of the Progressive Education Movement." *Journal of Educational Measurement* 3 (Summer 1966): 29–34.
343. Greenwood, J. M. "Conference Report on Mathematics." *Education* 15 (October 1894): 65–74.
344. Grubbs, Ethel Harris. "How the National Council of Teachers of Mathematics May Serve Negro Teachers and How They May Serve the Council." *MT* 34 (October 1941): 251–57.
345. Hall, G. Stanley. "The Contents of Children's Minds." *Princeton Review* 11 (1883): 249–72.
346. Harap, Henry, and Charlotte E. Mapes. "The Learning of Fundamentals in an Arithmetic-Activity Program." *Elementary School Journal* 34 (March 1934): 515–25.
347. Harris, Ben M. "Emergence of Technical Supervision." *Educational Leadership*, April 1969, pp. 494–95.
348. Hart, William L. "The Need for a Reorganization of Secondary Mathematics from the College Viewpoint." *MT* 48 (February 1935): 69–79.
349. Hartung, Maurice L. "High School Algebra for Bright Students." *MT* 46 (May 1953): 316–21.
350. ——. "Modern Methods and Current Criticisms of Mathematical Education." *SSM* 55 (February 1955): 85–90.
351. Hawley, Newton S., and Patrick Suppes. "Geometry in the First Grade." *AMM* 66 (June-July 1959): 505–6.
352. Hedrick, Earle R. "On the Selection of Topics for Elementary Algebra." *SSM* 11 (January 1911).
353. Henderson, Kenneth B., and Kern Dickman. "Minimum Mathematical Needs of Prospective Students in a College of Engineering." *MT* 45 (February 1952): 89–93.
354. Hill, Thomas. "The True Order of Studies." In *Report to the Regents of Normal Schools on the Teachers Institutes, Held in Wisconsin in 1859,* edited by Henry Barnard. Madison, Wis.: James Ross, State Printer, 1860.

355. Johnson, Donovan A. "Let's Do Something for the Gifted in Mathematics." *MT* 46 (May 1953): 322-25.
356. Jones, Phillip S. "America's First Mathematician." *MT* 48 (May 1955): 333-38.
357. ———. "Angular Measure—Enough of Its History to Improve Its Teaching." *MT* 46 (October 1953): 419-26.
358. ———. "Early American Geometry." *MT* 37 (January 1944): 3-11.
359. Judd, Charles H. "The Fallacy of Treating School Subjects as 'Tool Subjects.'" In *Selected Topics in the Teaching of Mathematics*. Third Yearbook of the NCTM. New York: Bureau of Publications, Teachers College, Columbia University, 1928.
360. Kac, Mark. "Can High Schools Handle 'Abstract' Math?" *National Observer*, 11 March 1962.
361. Karnes, Houston T. "Preparation of Teachers of Secondary Mathematics." *MT* 38 (January 1945): 3-10.
362. Keller, Jacob W. "Warren Colburn's Mental Arithmetic." *Pedagogical Seminary* 30 (June 1923): 163.
363. Kempner, A. J. "College Entrance Requirements in Mathematics." *AMM* 55 (September 1948): 414-18.
364. Kinney, Lucien B. "Mathematics." In *The High School Curriculum*, edited by Harl R. Douglass. New York: Ronald Press Co., 1964.
365. Kline, Morris. "The Ancients versus the Moderns, a New Battle of the Books." *MT* 51 (October 1958): 418-27.
366. ———. "Math Teaching Assailed as Peril to U.S. Scientific Progress." *New York University Alumni News*, October 1961.
367. ———. "Mathematical Teaching Past and Present." *ACCE Reporter* 5 (December 1967-January 1968): 191-98.
368. ———. "A Proposal for the High School Mathematics Curriculum." *MT* 59 (April 1966): 322-30.
369. ———. "New Curriculum or New Pedagogy?" *New York State Mathematics Teachers Journal* 10 (April 1960): 62.
370. Knight, F. B. "Introduction." In *Report of the Society's Committee on Arithmetic*. Twenty-ninth Yearbook of the NSSE, pt. 1. Bloomington, Ill.: Public School Publishing Co., 1930.
371. ———. "Some Aspects of Elementary Arithmetic." In *Curriculum Problems in Teaching Mathematics*. Second Yearbook of the NCTM. New York: Bureau of Publications, Teachers College, Columbia University, 1927.
372. Koerner, James D. "How to Teach Teachers." *Atlantic Monthly* 211 (February 1963): 59-63.
373. Kramer, Edna E. "Einstein vs. Heisenberg—Shall We Discuss Current Mathematics?" In *Emerging Practices in Mathematics Education*. Twenty-second Yearbook of the NTCM. Washington, D. C.: NCTM, 1954.

374. Lloyd, Daniel B. "Mathematically Trained Personnel Needed in Government Service." *MT* 44 (May 1951): 292–96.
375. May, Kenneth O. "Which Way Precollege Mathematics?" *MT* 47 (May 1954): 303–7.
376. McConnell, T. R. "Recent Trends in Learning Theory: Their Application to the Psychology of Arithmetic." In *Arithmetic in General Education*. Sixteenth Yearbook of the NCTM. New York: Bureau of Publications, Teachers College, Columbia University, 1941.
377. McCoy, M. E. "A Secondary School Mathematics Program." *Bulletin of the Association of Secondary School Principles* 43 (May 1959): 12–18.
378. McDonald, Frederick J. "The Influence of Learning Theories on Education." In *Theories of Learning and Instruction*, edited by E. R. Hilgard. Sixty-third Yearbook of the NSSE, pt. 1. Chicago: University of Chicago Press, 1964.
379. McMurry, Frank. "What Omissions Are Desirable in the Present Course of Study and What Should Be the Basis for the Same? In *Journal of Proceedings and Addresses of the Forty-third Annual Meeting*. Winona, Minn.: NEA, 1904.
380. Meder, Albert E., Jr. "The Ancients versus the Moderns—A Reply." *MT* 51 (October 1958): 428–33.
381. Moore, Eliakim Hastings. "On the Foundations of Mathematics." *MT* 60 (April 1967): 360–74. A reprinting of the 1902 address, first published in *Science*, 1903, and later included in *A General Survey of Progress in the Last Twenty-five Years*, First Yearbook of the NCTM, 1926.
382. ———. "The Cross Section Paper as a Mathematical Instrument." *School Review* 15 (1906): 317–38.
383. Mulcrone, T. F. "Benjamin Banneker, Pioneer Negro Mathematician." *MT* 54 (January 1961): 32–37.
384. Myers, George. "Two Years' Progress in Mathematics in the University School." *SSM* 11 (January 1911): 64–72.
385. ———. "Outstanding Pedagogical Principles Now Functioning in High School Mathematics." *MT* 14 (February 1921): 57–63.
386. NEA. "Problems Confronting the Commission on the Reorganization of Secondary Education." In *Journal of Proceedings and Addresses of the Fifty-second Annual Meeting*. Ann Arbor, Mich.: NEA, 1914.
387. "Notes and News." *MT* 12 (March 1920): 133–34.
388. Nimitz, Admiral C. W. Letter to Louis I. Bredvold, University Advisory Committee on Military Affairs. *MT* 35 (February 1942): 88–89.
389. Northrop, E. P. "Mathematics in a Liberal Education." *AMM* 52 (March 1945): 132–37.
390. ———. "The Mathematics Program in the College of the University of Chicago." *AMM* 55 (January 1948): 1–7.

391. Oakley, C. O. "The Coming Revolution in Mathematics." *MT* 35 (November 1942): 307–9.
392. O'Brien, F. P. *The High School Failures*. Contributions to Education, no. 2. New York: Bureau of Publications, Teachers College, Columbia University, 1919.
393. Oliver, Albert I., Jr. "In Small High Schools, Many Purposes—Many Curriculums." In *Emerging Practices in Mathematics Education*. Twenty-second Yearbook of the NCTM. Washington, D. C.: NCTM, 1954.
394. "On the Mathematics Curriculum of the High School." *MT* 55 (March 1962): 191–94; *AMM* 69 (1962): 189–93.
395. Orleans, Joseph B. "The Present Situation in Mathematics in New York City." *Junior-Senior High School Clearing House* 5 (February 1931): 354 ff.
396. Orth, Allen. "Mathematics and Manpower." *MT* 45 (October 1952): 416–22.
397. Overn, Orlando E. "Changes in Curriculum in Elementary Algebra since 1900 as Reflected by the Requirements and Examinations of the College Entrance Examination Board." *Journal of Experimental Education* 5 (June 1937): 373–468.
398. Page, David A. "The University of Illinois Arithmetic Project." *AMM* 66 (May 1959): 412–22.
399. Phillips, D. E. "Number and Its Application Psychologically Considered." *Pedagogical Seminary* 5 (October 1897): 270.
400. Price, G. Baley. "A Mathematics Program for the Able." *MT* 44 (October 1951): 369–76.
401. ———. "Progress in Mathematics and Its Implications for the Schools." In *The Revolution in School Mathematics*. Washington, D. C.: NCTM, 1961.
402. Reeve, William David. "Attacks on Mathematics and How to Meet Them." In *The Place of Mathematics in Modern Education*. Eleventh Yearbook of the NCTM. New York: Bureau of Publications, Teachers College, Columbia University, 1936.
403. ———. "The Case for General Mathematics." *MT* 15 (November 1922): 381–91.
404. ———. "The Teaching of Geometry." In *The Teaching of Geometry*. Fifth Yearbook of the NCTM. New York: Bureau of Publications, Teachers College, Columbia University, 1930.
405. Rice, J. M. "Educational Research: Causes of Success and Failure in Arithmetic." *Forum* 34 (1903): 437–52.
406. ———. "Educational Research: A Test in Arithmetic." *Forum* 34 (1902): 281–97.
407. ———. "The Public Schools of New York City." *Epoch* 9 (1891): 390–91, 406–8.

408. Schnell, Leroy H. "The New Emphasis in Teaching Geometry." In *Emerging Practices in Mathematics Education.* Twenty-second Yearbook of the NCTM. Washington, D.C.: NCTM, 1954.
409. Schorling, Raleigh. "The Need for Cooperative Action in Mathematics Education." *AMM* 52 (April 1945): 194-201.
410. ———. "Trends in Junior High School Mathematics." *MT* 35 (December 1942): 339-43.
411. Schumaker, John A. "Trends in the Education of Secondary School Mathematics Teachers." *MT* 54 (1961): 413-22.
412. Seerly, H. H. "The Report of the Committee of Ten." *Education* 15 (December 1894): 239-41.
413. Shuster, Carl N. "A Call for Reform in High School Mathematics." *AMM* 55 (October 1948): 472-75.
414. ———. "Working with Approximate Data." In *Emerging Practices in Mathematics Education.* Twenty-second Yearbook of the NCTM. Washington, D. C.: NCTM, 1954.
415. Smith, David Eugene. "Movements in Mathematics Teaching." *SSM* 5 (February 1905): 136-38.
416. ———. "A General Survey of the Progress of Mathematics in Our High Schools in the Last Twenty-five Years." In *A General Survey of Progress in the Last Twenty-five Years.* First Yearbook of the NCTM. New York: Bureau of Publications, Teachers College, Columbia University, 1926.
417. ———. "Thomas Jefferson and Mathematics." *Scripta Mathematica* 1 (1932): 2-16.
418. Social Science Research Council. *Items* 9 (May 1955): 13-16.
419. Stalnaker, John M. "Report on the Mathematics Attainment Test of June, 1936." *Research Bulletin*, no 7. New York: CEEB, 1936.
420. Stanley, J. C. "Rice as a Pioneer Educational Researcher." *Journal of Educational Measurement* 3 (Summer 1966): 135-39.
421. Stokes, C. N., and Joseph B. Orleans. "A Tentative Program for the Sub-Committee on Administrative Phases of the Individual Differences Problem." *MT* 26 (January 1933): 57-59.
422. Stone, Marshall H. Review of *Goals for School Mathematics. MT* 58 (April 1965): 353-60.
423. Thorndike, Edward L., and Robert S. Woodworth. "The Influence of Improvement in One Mental Function upon the Efficiency of Other Functions." *Psychological Review* 8 (May, July, November 1901): 247-61, 384-95, 553-64.
424. *Time*, 8 June 1956, p. 74. "Least Popular Subject."
425. Townsend, E. J. "Analysis of Failures in Freshman Mathematics." *School Review* 10 (1902): 675-86.
426. Walsh, C. B., et al. "A Symposium of Discussion on the National Committee Report on Junior High School Mathematics." *MT* 14 (January 1921): 16-41.

427. Weaver, J. Fred. "The School Mathematics Study Group Project on Elementary School Mathematics." *AT* 8 (January 1961): 32–35.
428. ———. "The Cambridge Conference on School Mathematics." *AT* 11 (March 1964): 207–10.
429. ———. "Differentiated Instruction and School-Class Organization for Mathematical Learning within the Elementary Grades." *AT* 13 (October 1966): 495–506.
430. Wheat, Harry G. "The Nature and Sequences of Learning Activities in Arithmetic." In *The Teaching of Arithmetic*. Fiftieth Yearbook of the NSSE, pt. 2. Chicago: University of Chicago Press, 1951.
431. White, W. B. "The Slope Concept via Experimental Data." In *Emerging Practices in Mathematics Education*. Twenty-second Yearbook of the NCTM. Washington, D.C.: NCTM, 1954.
432. Wilson, Guy M. "A Survey of the Social and Business Uses of Arithmetic." In *Second Report of the Committee on Minimal Essentials in Elementary-School Subjects*. Sixteenth Yearbook of the NSSE, pt. 1. Bloomington, Ill.: Public School Publishing Co., 1917.
433. ———. "The Social Utility Theory as Applied to Arithmetic: Its Research Basis and Some of Its Implications." *Journal of Educational Research* 41 (January 1948): 321–37.
434. Wilson, Jack D. "Mathematics in General Education at a State College." In *Emerging Practices in Mathematics Education*. Twenty-second Yearbook of the NCTM. Washington, D.C.: NCTM, 1954.
435. Wise, Carl T. "Survey of Arithmetical Problems Arising in Various Occupations." *Elementary School Journal* 20 (October 1919): 118–36.
436. Wolfle, Dael. "Future Supply of Science and Mathematics Students." *MT* 46 (April 1953): 225–29, 240.
437. Wren, F. Lynwood. "The Professional Preparation of Teachers." *MT* 32 (1939): 99–105.
438. Young, John Wesley. "The Work of the National Committee on Mathematical Requirements." *MT* 14 (January 1921): 5–15.

Dissertations

439. Berenson, Lewis J. "The Adaptation of High School Mathematics to Mass Education: 1915–1925." Teachers College, Columbia University, 1961.
440. Chateauneuf, Amy Olive. "Changes in the Content of Elementary Algebra since the Beginning of the High School Movement as Revealed by the Textbooks of the Period." University of Pennsylvania, 1929.
441. Clason, Robert. "Number Ideas of Arithmetic Texts of the United States from 1880 to 1966 with Related Psychological and Mathematical Developments." University of Michigan, 1968.

442. Elbrink, Larry C. "The Life and Works of Dr. John August Swenson, Mathematics Educator, 1880–1944." Ohio State University, 1969.
443. Fishman, Joseph. "Trends in Secondary School Mathematics in Relation to Educational Theories and Social Changes: 1893–1964." New York University, 1965.
444. Hancock, John D. "The Evaluation of the Secondary Mathematics Curriculum: A Critique." Stanford University, 1961.
445. Izzo, Joseph Anthony. "A History of the Use of Certain Types of Graphical Representation in Mathematics Education in Secondary Schools of the United States." Teachers College, Columbia University, 1957.
446. Oakes, Herbert I. "Objectives of Mathematics Education in the United States from 1920 to 1960." Columbia University, 1965.
447. Sigurdson, Solberg Einar. "The Development of the Idea of Unified Mathematics in the Secondary School Curriculum: 1890–1930." University of Wisconsin, 1962.

BIBLIOGRAPHY B

Canada

The abbreviations used in both Bibliographies are given on page 501.

REPORTS, STATUS STUDIES, PROGRAMMES

1. Alberta Department of Education. *Annual Report.* Edmonton: 1912.
2. ———. *Annual Report.* Edmonton: 1959.
3. ———. *Annual Report.* Edmonton: 1966.
4. ———. *Programme of Studies for the Elementary School, Grades I to VI.* Edmonton: 1940.
5. ———. *Programme of Studies for the High School.* Bulletin 1. Edmonton: 1939.
6. ———. *Programme of Studies for the High School.* Bulletin A. Edmonton: 1944.
7. ———. *Programme of Studies for the Intermediate School (Grades VII, VIII, IX).* Edmonton: 1936.
8. ———. *Second Interim Report of the Committee on High School Education.* Edmonton: 1923.
9. Alberta Post-War Reconstruction Committee. *Report of the Subcommittee on Education.* Edmonton: March 1945.
10. Alberta Teachers' Association. "Mathematics Council, Inaugural Conference." *Newsletter* 1 (August 1961).
11. ———. Mathematics Council. *1966 Annual.* NCTM Calgary Summer Meeting.
12. Asbury, F. C. "The Ontario Mathematics Commission." Mimeographed. Toronto: September 1963.
13. British Columbia Department of Education. *Annual Report, Ninth, 1879/80.* Victoria: 1881.
14. ———. *Annual Report, Thirteenth, 1883/84.* Victoria: 1885.
15. ———. *Annual Report, Forty-seventh, 1917/18.* Victoria: 1919.
16. ———. *Courses of Study for the Public, High, and Normal Schools, Intermediate Grades.* Victoria: 1921.
17. ———. *Mathematics.* Victoria: 1950.
18. ———. "Programme of Studies for the Elementary Schools." *Bulletin* 3 (1936).

CANADA 529

19. ———. *Programme of Studies for the Junior High Schools.* Victoria: 1948.
20. Canadian Association of Mathematics Teachers. *Mathematics in Canadian Schools.* Ottawa: The Association, 1967.
21. Canadian Teachers' Federation. *Mathematics and the Teacher: Report of a Conference.* Ottawa: The Federation, 1967.
22. ———. *New Thinking in School Mathematics: Report of a Seminar.* Ottawa: 1960.
23. CEEB, Commission on Mathematics. *Program for College Preparatory Mathematics and Appendices.* New York: The Board, 1959.
24. Commission on Aims and Objectives of Education in Ontario. *Living and Learning.* Toronto: Newton Publishing Co., 1968.
25. Dominion Bureau of Statistics. *Census of Canada: Population—Counties and Subdivisions, Ontario.* Ottawa: The Bureau, 1966.

Hall-Dennis Commission. See entry 24.

26. Manitoba Department of Education. *Interim Programme of Studies for the Elementary School, Grades I-VI.* Winnipeg: 1939.
27. ———. *Midsummer Examinations.* Winnipeg: 1921.
28. ———. *Programme of Studies for the Public Schools of Manitoba.* Rev. ed. Winnipeg: 1896.
29. ———. *Programme of Studies for the Schools of Manitoba, Grades I-XII.* Winnipeg: 1912.
30. ———. *Programme of Studies for the Schools of Manitoba.* Winnipeg: 1917.
31. ———. *Programme of Studies for the Schools of Manitoba, Grades VII to XII, Inclusive.* Winnipeg: 1930.
32. ———. Rev. ed. Winnipeg: 1933.
33. ———. *Report.* Winnipeg: 1913.
34. ———. *Report of the Superintendent of Education for the Protestant Schools of Manitoba.* Winnipeg: 1887.
35. Northwest Territories Department of Education. *Annual Report, 1902.* Regina: 1903.
36. Nova Scotia Teachers Union. *Outline of Report of Inaugural Conference on Mathematics.* Halifax: 1962.
37. Ontario Curriculum Institute, Committee Considering the Mathematics Programme (K to 6). *Mathematics.* Toronto: 1965.
38. ———, Committee Considering the Mathematics of the Four Year Programme. *Mathematics: The Four Year Programme.* Toronto: 1965.
39. Ontario Institute for Studies and Education, K-13 Geometry Committee of the Development Division. *Geometry: Kindergarten to Grade Thirteen.* Toronto: 1967.
40. Ontario Department of Education. *Report of the Minister's Committee on the Training of Elementary School Teachers.* Toronto: 1966.

41. ———. *Report of the Minister's Committee on the Training of Secondary School Teachers.* Toronto: 1962.
42. Ontario Education Association. "Mathematical Condition of Our Schools." *Proceedings* (1893).
43. ———. *Minutes of the Ontario Association of Teachers of Mathematics and Physics* (1927–60).
44. Royal Commission on Education in Ontario. *Report.* Toronto: Baptist Johnson, 1950.
45. Royal Commission of Inquiry on Education in the Province of Quebec. *Report,* vol. 1. Quebec: 1963.
46. Saskatchewan Department of Education. *Circular for Teachers and Students, 1931/32.* Regina: n.d.
47. ———. *Circular of Information for Students and Teachers, 1914/15.* Regina: n.d.
48. ———. *Course of Study for the Public Schools.* Regina: 1913.
49. ———. *Elementary School Curriculum, Grades I–VIII.* Regina: 1941.
50. ———. *Elementary School Curriculum, Guide III for Arithmetic.* Regina: 1957.
51. ———. *Public School Curriculum and Teachers Guide, Grades I–III.* Regina: 1931.
52. *Studies in Mathematics Education: A Brief Survey of Improvement Programs for School Mathematics.* Chicago: Scott, Foresman & Co., 1959.

Books and Pamphlets

53. Althouse, J. G. *Structure and Aims of Canadian Education.* Toronto: W. J. Gage, 1949.
54. Bell, Walter N. *The Development of the Ontario High School.* Toronto: University of Toronto Press, 1918.
55. Birchard, Isaac B. "Flashback." In *Education.* Toronto: W. J. Gage.
56. Bracq, Jean Charlemagne. *The Evolution of French Canada.* Toronto: Macmillan Co. of Canada, 1924.
57. Campbell, H. L. *Curriculum Trends in Canadian Education* (Quance Lectures, 1952). Toronto: W. J. Gage, 1953.
58. "Canada." In *Encyclopedia Americana,* vol. 5. Toronto: Americana Corp. of Canada, 1958.
59. Canadian Education Association. *The New Look in Mathematics at the Elementary School Level.* Toronto: The Association, 1964.
60. Careless, James Maurice Stockford. *Canada, a Story of Challenge.* Rev. and enl. ed. Toronto: Macmillan Co. of Canada, 1965.
61. Coulson, W. F. *Modern Concepts in Elementary Mathematics.* Improvement of Instruction, no. 4. Edmonton: Barnett House, Alberta Teachers' Association, 1963.

CANADA 531

62. Crawford, D. H. *Modern Mathematics and the High School*. Problems in Education, no. 1. Edmonton: Barnett House, Alberta Teachers' Association, 1960.
63. *Curriculum 2*. Department of Education, March 1950.
64. Guillet, Edwin C. *In the Cause of Education: Centennial History of the Ontario Education Association, 1861–1960*. Toronto: University of Toronto Press, 1967.
65. Harris, Robin S. *Quiet Evolution: A Study of the Ontario Educational System*. Toronto: University of Toronto Press, 1967.
66. Jackson, W. A., et al. *General Mathematics*, bk. 1. Toronto: Macmillan Co. of Canada, 1938.
67. Johnson, Francis Henry. *A Brief History of Canadian Education*. Toronto: McGraw-Hill Co. of Canada, 1968.
68. Kilbourn, William. *The Making of a Nation: A Century of Challenge*. Toronto: Canadian Centennial Publishing Co., 1965.
69. Knight, F. B., J. W. Studebaker, and G. M. Ruch, *Study Arithmetics*, bk. 6. Toronto: W. J. Gage, c. 1947.
70. Lazerte, M. E. *Teacher Education in Canada*. Toronto: W. J. Gage, 1951.
71. Lazerte, M. E., and G. S. Lord. *Number Highways*, bk. 4. Toronto: Clarke, Irwin & Co., 1932.
72. Lindstedt, S. A. *Mathematical Meanings in Elementary Arithmetic*. Problems in Education, no. 2. Edmonton: Barnett House, Alberta Teachers' Association, 1960.
73. Lougheed, W. J., and J. G. Workman. *General Mathematics*, bk. 2. Toronto: Macmillan Co. of Canada, 1939.
74. ———. *A Modern Geometry for High Schools*. Toronto: Macmillan Co. of Canada, 1940.
75. McCutcheon, J. M. *Public Education in Ontario*. Toronto: Macmillan Co. of Canada, 1941.
76. Miller, Norman, ed. *Why Study Mathematics?* Montreal: Cambridge Press, 1948.
77. Miller, Norman, and R. E. K. Rourke. *An Advanced Course in High School Algebra*. Toronto: Macmillan Co. of Canada, 1940.
78. Nova Scotia Department of Education. *The Scope and Sequence of Courses in Science and Mathematics, Primary to Grade 12*. Halifax: 1966.
79. "Ontario." In *Encyclopedia Americana*, vol. 20. Toronto: Americana Corp. of Canada, 1958.
80. Ontario Department of Education. *Courses of Study, Grades IX, X, XI and XII, Mathematics*. Toronto: 1943.
81. ———. *Programme of Studies for Grades 1 to 6 of the Public Schools*. Toronto: 1960.

82. ———. *Curriculum I:1—Intermediate Division, Outlines of Courses for Experimental Use.* Toronto: 1951.
83. ———. *Curriculum S.12—Senior Division Mathematics, Grades 11, 12, 13.* Toronto: 1961.
84. ———. *Curricula I, 12B, S,12A, S,12B Mathematics (Grades 7, 8, 11, 12).* Toronto: 1963, 1964.
85. ———. *Text-books Approved or Recommended for Use in Elementary and Secondary Schools.* Circular 14. Toronto: 1964.
86. ———. *Curriculum P1, J1 Interim Revision Mathematics.* Toronto: 1966.
87. ———. *A Suggested Adaptation of Curriculum S.12A* (Grade 11 Mathematics). Toronto: 1968.
88. Ontario Association of Teachers of Mathematics and Physics. *Historical Highlights, 1891–1960.* Toronto: Copp Clark Publishing Co., 1962.
89. Organization for European Economic Cooperation. *New Thinking in School Mathematics.* Paris: 1961.
90. Organization for Economic Cooperation and Development. *Mathematics To-day, a Guide for Teachers.* Paris: 1964.
91. Parvin, Viola. *Authorization of Textbooks for the Schools of Ontario, 1846–1950.* Toronto: University of Toronto Press, 1964.
92. Percival, Walter P. *Across the Years.* Montreal: Gazette Printing Co., 1946.
93. Petrie, P. A., et al. *Deductive Geometry and Introduction to Trigonometry.* Toronto: Copp Clark Publishing Co., 1957.
94. Phillips, C. E. *The Development of Education in Canada.* Toronto: W. J. Gage, 1957.
95. ———. *Public Secondary Education in Canada.* Toronto: W. J. Gage, 1957.
96. Quebec Minister of Education. *Projet de programme moderne (Secondaire I à V).* Quebec: January 1969.
97. ———. *Nouveau programme de mathématique pour l'enseignement secondaire.* Quebec: March 1969.
98. *Report of Education.* Upper Canada: 1864.
99. Ross, George W. *The School System of Ontario.* New York: D. Appleton & Co., 1896.
100. Scott, William. *Modern Mental Arithmetic.* Toronto: Educational Book Co., 1911.
101. Shortt, Adam, and A. G. Doughty. *Canada and Its Provinces.* Vols. 17 and 18. Toronto: Glasgow, Brook & Co., 1914.
102. Smith, J. A., and R. H. Roberts. *Arithmetic,* bk. 1. Toronto: W. J. Gage, 1921.
103. ———. *Arithmetic,* bk. 2. Toronto: W. J. Gage, 1924.
104. Smith, J. Hamblin. *The New Hamblin Smith Arithmetic.* Toronto: W. J. Gage, 1907.

105. ———. *A Treatise on Arithmetic.* Toronto: W. J. Gage, 1890.
106. ———. Rev. ed. Toronto: W. J .Gage, 1900.
107. Swift, W. H. *Trends in Canadian Education.* Toronto: W. J. Gage, 1958.
108. Thorndike, E. L. *Junior Mathematics,* bk. 1. Toronto: W. J. Gage, 1931.
109. Wirtz, Robert W., and Morton Botel. *Math Workshop for Children.* Montreal: Encyclopaedia Britannica Films, 1961.

Journal and Yearbook Articles

110. Allen, Harold D. "Nineteenth-Century Canadian School Mathematics." *McGill Journal of Education.*
111. Association Mathématique du Québec. *Bulletin* 11 (November 1968).
112. ———. *Bulletin* 11 (January 1969).
113. Coleman, A. J. "Reforming the High School Mathematics Curriculum." *Canadian Mathematical Bulletin* 3 (1960).
114. Cook, A. J., and Stanley Clarke. "The Math-Sci Corner, Highlights of a Discussion on Mathematics." *ATA Magazine* 23 (December 1942): 33-36.
115. Crawford, D. H. "An Analysis of Trends in School Mathematics in Ontario." Paper read at the annual convention of the Provincial Association of Protestant Teachers of Quebec, 18 November 1966. Mimeographed.
116. ———. "Developments in School Mathematics in Canada: A Survey." *Canadian Education and Research Digest* 4 (December 1964).
117. ———. "Junior High Schools Trends—Comments and Cautions from Canada." Paper read at annual meeting of Association of Mathematics Teachers of New York State, May 1963. Mimeographed.
118. ———. "Practical Aspects of the New Mathematics." *Canadian School Journal* 44 (July-August 1966).
119. ———. "Present Practices and Recent and Planned Developments in Mathematical Education: Canada." In *Commonwealth Conference on Mathematics in Schools, Trinidad.* London: Marlborough House, 1968.
120. ———. "Recent Developments in School Mathematics." *Canadian College of Teachers* 3 (1960).
121. ———. "Recent Developments in School Mathematics—Further Trends in the U.S.A." *Mathematics Teaching* 19 (Summer 1962).
122. Currie, I. I. "Mechanical Accuracy in Arithmetic." *Educational Journal of Western Canada* 1 (May 1899): 74-75.

123. Evenson, A. B. "Mathematics Improvement Programs: A Survey." *Canadian Research Digest* 5 (Winter 1960).
124. ———. "A Canadian Point of View of the Changing Curriculum in Mathematics." Paper read at NCTM annual meeting, April 1960.
125. Gall, M. "Arithmetic in the Junior Grades." *Western School Journal* 8 (April 1913): 127–32.
126. Gaulin, Claude. Personal communication to D. H Crawford. June 1969.
127. Girard, Michel. "Organisations des classes pilotes en première année du cours secondaire." *Bulletin* of the Association Mathématique du Québec 11 (January 1969).
128. "Grade VIII Drawing, Bookkeeping, and Geometry." *Western School Journal* 12 (February 1917): 45.
129. "Grade VIII Programme." *Western School Journal* 8 (February 1914): 438–39.
130. Gray, William, and E. W. Reid. *Dent's Junior Mathematics*. Don Mills, Ont.: J. M. Dent & Sons, 1940.
131. H. C. A. "Book Review." *Educational Journal of Western Canada* 1 (March 1899): 29–31.
132. Hugg, J. G. "The Introduction to Geometry." *Educational Journal of Western Canada* 1 (August-September 1899): 144–45.
133. ———. "Pure and Applied Arithmetic." *Educational Journal of Western Canada* 1 (May 1899): 80–82.
134. Kaye, G. A. "A New Role for the Teacher." Paper read to the Ontario Association of Teachers of Mathematics, Toronto, March 1968.
135. Kinlin, J. F. "Eight Years in Mathematics with the Department of Education." *Ontario Mathematics Gazette* 4 (March 1966).
136. Lemire, Lévis. "Le cours de recyclage et de perfectionnement en mathématique." *Bulletin* of the Association Mathématique du Québec 11 (January 1969).
137. Low, H. R. "Psychology and the Elementary School." *Modern Instructor* 6 (April 1938): 338–40.
138. "Mathematics Section." *Western School Journal* 29 (May 1914): 166–68.
139. Mathematics Teachers Association of the Nova Scotia Teachers Union. *Mathematics Teachers Bulletin* 1 (February 1964).
140. ———. *Mathematics Teachers Bulletin* 2 (June 1964).
141. ———. *Mathematics Teachers Association Bulletin* 3 (December 1965).
142. ———. *Mathematics Teachers Association Bulletin* 2 (December 1964).
143. Paquette, Gilbert. "La mathématique au C.E.G.E.P." *Bulletin* of the Association Mathématique du Québec 11 (November 1968).

144. Richard, Guy W. "Mathématique et formation professionnelle au C.E.G.E.P." *Bulletin* of the Association Mathématique du Québec 11 (January 1969).
145. Robarts, John. Address by the Honourable John Robarts, prime minister of Ontario, at the dedication of an addition to Southwood Secondary School, Galt, Ontario, 14 November 1967.
146. Robinson, G. "The Co-ordination of the Teaching of Algebra and Arithmetic." *ATA Magazine* 7 (March 1927): 11-13.
147. Rose, A. S. "Inspection Notes." *Educational Journal of Western Canada* 1 (December 1899): 247-48.
148. "Saskatchewan Teachers Convention." *Western School Journal* 8 (May 1913): 182-87.
149. Shortliffe, D. L. "Should We Have Unified Mathematics in High Schools?" *ATA Magazine* 10 (December 1929): 79.
150. ———. "Thoughts on Secondary Education." *ATA Magazine* 10 (July 1930): 5-7.
151. Shuster, Carl N. "A Call for Reform in High School Mathematics." *AMM* 55 (October 1948): 472-75.
152. Stanley, T. E. A. "Grade XII Mathematics." *ATA Magazine* 12 (June (1932): 24-26.
153. ———. "The New Course of Study in a Calgary High School." *ATA Magazine* 7 (February 1927): 1-7.
154. ———. "The Public School Course of Study from the High School Point of View." *ATA Magazine* 1 (November 1920): 15-16.
155. Stein, H. L. "Recent Views on Mathematics of the Secondary School." *Canadian Research Digest* 6 (Spring 1960).
156. Watson, A. J. "Senior Matriculation Requirements." *ATA Magazine* 12 (June 1932): 21-24.
157. Worth, Walter H. "Critical Issues in Elementary Education." *Canadian Education and Research Digest* 2 (September 1962).
158. ———. "The Changing Curriculum of the Elementary Schools." *Canadian Education and Research Digest* 6 (September 1958).

Theses and Dissertations

159. Althouse, J. G. *The Ontario Teacher*. Toronto: W. J. Gage, 1967.
160. Buckles, Irene E. "The Evolution of the Mathematics Programme in Alberta High Schools." University of Alberta, 1956.
161. Campbell, J. D. "The Arithmetic of the Elementary Schools of Ontario." University of Toronto, 1943.
162. Gray, W. B. "The Teaching of Mathematics in Ontario." University of Toronto, 1948.
163. Horne, Edgar B. "A Comparative Study of College Preparatory Mathematics Curricula in Canada in 1964-1965." University of Illinois, 1966.

164. Milne, Frank E. "Possible Effects of Modern Mathematics on the Mathematics Curriculum of Nova Scotia." Saint Mary's University, 1962.
165. Plourde, C. G. "A Survey of the Current Trends in Secondary School Geometry." Queen's University, 1964.
166. Pullen, Harry. "Secondary School Curricular Change in Canada with Special Emphasis on an Ontario Experiment." University of Toronto, 1955.
167. Selinger, Alphonse Daniel. "The Contribution of D. J. Goggin to the Education in the North-West Territories, 1893–1902." University of Alberta, 1960.

Index

Ability grouping, 257, 262, 368–70
Abstraction, 69, 290, 440
Academies, 18, 372
Acceleration, 71
Accrediting associations, 29, 305
Across the Years (Percival), 354
Activist approach, 397, 444
Acts, legislative
  Act for the Encouragement of Elementary Education, 356
  Act for the establishment of free schools . . . , 355
  British North American Act of 1867, 412
  Common Schools Act, 23, 372
  Compulsory attendance laws, 109, 184, 386, 393, 403
  District Public School Act (Ontario), 372
  Education Act of 1841, 356–57
  Education Act of 1846, 357
  Fabrique Act, 356
  GI Bill, 327
  Higher Education Act, 332
  Massachusetts law of 1642, 17
  National Defense Education Act, 143, 267
  Union Act of 1840, 375
Adams, Daniel, 22, 373
  Adam's New Arithmetic, 362
  Arithmetic in which the Principles of Operating by Numbers are Analytically Explained, and Synthetically applied, 22
Adams, John, 21
Adam's New Arithmetic (Adams), 362
Addison-Wesley Elementary Mathematics textbook series, 443
Adler, Irving, 146, 296
Advanced Arithmetic for Canadian Schools (Smith and McMurchy), 379
Advanced placement programs, 250

Agassiz, Louis, 31
Albert, A. A., 256, 270, 272
Alberta Teachers' Association (A.T.A.), 423, 432
Alcott, Bronson, 13
Algebra, 27, 28, 32, 33, 37, 40, 41, 47, 48, 51–55, 78, 82, 158–61, 163, 165–66, 167, 168, 170–72, 176–77, 183, 187, 203, 206, 209, 211, 218–20, 222, 228, 234, 244, 247, 253, 254, 269, 276, 277, 278, 283, 293, 304, 308, 310, 366, 368, 374, 376, 377, 378, 383, 389, 394, 397, 404, 408, 413, 420, 421, 423, 424, 434, 435, 440, 444
  Boolean, 82
  difference between arithmetic and, 203
  as generalized arithmetic, 160, 178, 207, 221
  as general mathematics, 220–22
  linear, 294, 330, 344, 433
  matrix, 276
  modern, 78, 261, 265
  utility of, 178
Algebra (Bridge), 374
Algebra (Hall and Knight), 422
Allen, Frank B., 80, 209
Allendoerfer, Carl, 256, 260
Althouse, Dr., 402, 410
American Association for the Advancement of Science (AAAS), 62, 80, 273
  guidelines (with NASDTEC), 348–50
  Works: "Mathematics Instruction for Purposes of General Education," 62; "The Preparation of High School Science and Mathematics Teachers," 327–28
American Association of School Administrators (AASA), 240
American Federation of Teachers of the Mathematical and Natural Sciences, 39, 180

American Historical Association, 169
American Journal of Mathematics (Sylvester and Story), 30
American Mathematical Society (AMS), 4, 30, 39, 42, 75, 169, 170, 175, 231, 237, 256, 270, 271, 272, 275, 324. *See also* Committee *subentries*
Chicago section, 30
American Philological Association, 169
American Practical Navigator, The (Bowditch), 21
Analysis of New Mathematics Programs, An (NCTM), 76, 284–85
Analytic method of discovering proofs, 167
Angell, James Burrill, 29
Applications, 290, 294, 423. *See also* Social utility
Appreciation of mathematics, 62, 204, 241, 260
Approximate Computation (Bakst), 259
Archibald, R. C., 40
Arithmetic, 27, 37, 41, 49, 52, 55, 93, 98, 99, 102, 104–5, 121, 130–31, 157–58, 164–67, 206, 228, 253, 304, 355, 366, 372, 373, 375, 376, 383, 394, 397, 402, 413, 414, 415–19, 420, 421, 424–25, 464. *See also* Number, science of
  aims of, 51
  ciphering books for, 13–14, 105, 372
  commercial, 13, 52, 219, 366, 376, 390, 394, 407
  difference between algebra and, 203
  generalized, 221
  goals of, 318
  grade placement of topics in, 127, 165
  integrated study of, 47
  intellectual, 25
  mental, 25, 382, 413, 416, 425
  minimum essentials for, 190
  postponement of topics in, 48, 50
  as preparation for algebra, 158
  rote procedures in, 104
  segmented approach to, 185
  theories of instruction in, 125 (*see also* Meaning theory of arithmetic)
  unit as fundamental idea of, 102
Arithmetic in which the Principles of Operating by Numbers are Analytically Explained, and Synthetically applied (Adams), 22

Arithmetic (Bonnycastle), 373, 374
Arithmetic (Davies), 29
Arithmetic (Smith and Roberts), 420
Arithmetica of Cyffer-Konst . . . Als Mede Een kort ontwerp van de Algebra (Venema), 16
Arithmetick, Vulgar and Decimal (Greenwood), 12, 23
Arithmetic Made Easy to Children (Kimber), 103
Arithmetic on the Plan of Pestalozzi with Some Improvements, An (Colburn), 22, 103
Arithmetic Primer for Young Masters and Misses, An (Temple), 103
Arithmétique ou l'art de compter toutes sortes de nombres avec la plume et les jettons, L' (Father Jean François), 360
Articulation, 29, 33, 53, 61, 71, 78, 398
Art without Science (Eaton), 29
Arte para aprender todo el menor del arithmetica sin maestro (Paz), 12
Asbury, Frank, 435
Association
  Alberta Teachers', Association, 423, 432
  American, of School Administrators, 240
  American, for the Advancement of Science (*see main entry*)
  American Historical Association, 169
  American Philological Association, 169
  Canadian, of Mathematics Teachers, 430–31
  Central, of Science and Mathematics Teachers, 39, 176, 314 (see also *School Science and Mathematics*)
  of Colleges and Secondary Schools of the Middle States and Maryland, 169, 171
  Mathematics and Physics, of Ontario, 387
  National Education Association (*see main entry*)
  National, of Secondary School Principals, 245
  National, of State Directors of Teacher Education and Certification, 80, 348–50
  National Teachers Association, 33
  New England, of Colleges and Secondary Schools, 169

New England, of Teachers of
Mathematics, 80
North Central, of Colleges and
Secondary Schools, 169, 171, 175
Nova Scotia Mathematics Teachers'
Association, 440
Ontario, of Teachers of Mathematics
and Physics, 380, 398
Ontario Education Association, 389,
390, 394, 401, 403, 404
Progressive Education Association
(see main entry)
Southern, of Colleges and Secondary
Schools, 169
for Symbolic Logic, 256
of Teachers of Mathematics in the
Middle States and Maryland, 43
of Teachers of Mathematics in New
England, 43
Astronomy, 19
Audiovisual aids, 68, 78, 258, 448
Austin, C. M., 6, 194–95
Ausubel, David, 85
Axiomatic development of theorems,
159, 161, 167, 174, 180–81, 441
Axiomization, 41, 447
Axioms for problem solving, 179

"Background Mathematics for Elementary Teachers" (Ruddell, Dutton, and Reckzek), 328
Ball State Teachers College Experimental Program, 267, 269
Banneker, Benjamin, 20
Barber, Harry C., 208
Basic Geometry (Birkhoff and Beatley), 41, 223, 278
Beatley, Ralph, 41, 223
Basic Geometry, 41, 223, 278
Beatty, Dr. S., 395, 408
Beberman, Max, 69, 252, 253–54, 289, 453
Bédard, Louis, 361
Begle, Edward G., 75, 82, 139, 146, 237, 256, 265, 266, 270, 272, 273, 279, 280, 453
Behaviorism, 113, 216
Bell, E. T., 211, 224–25
Bennett, A. A., 55, 226
Benz, H. E., 212
Bernard, M. M., 360
Bers, Lipman, 272
Bestor, Arthur E., 71, 134
Betz, William, 50, 51, 180, 194, 208,
211–12, 213, 221, 225
Biard, Father, 354
Bibaud, Michel, 361–62
Biggs, Edith, 439
Binet, Alfred, 118
Bing, R. H., 256
Birchard, I. J., 382–83
Birkhoff, George David, 41, 42
Bishop, A. W., 409
Bittinger, Marvin L., 143
Blair, Vevia, 43, 200
Bledsoe, Albert Taylor, 31
The Philosophy of Mathematics, 31
Bobbit, Franklin, 188–89, 190, 192, 207, 214, 218, 224, 251
Bolyai, Janos, 178
Bonds. See Connectionism
Bonham, G. C., 437–38
Boring, Edwin, 186, 187
History of Experimental Psychology, 185
Bourdon's Algebra (Davies), 29
Bourgeois, Sister Marguerite, 355
Bouthillier, Jean Antoine, 361, 362
Bowditch, Nathaniel, 20, 21, 30
The American Practical Navigator, 21
translation of Laplace's *Mécanique Céleste*, 30
Brauer, Richard, 75, 272
Breslich, Ernest R., 51, 176, 195, 208, 219, 307
British Columbia *Programme of Studies*, 418
British North American Act of 1867, 412
Brooks, Edward, 26–27, 102, 110–11
Brown, Claude H., 233
Brown, Guillaume, 360
Brown, Kenneth E., 209
Brownell, William A., 49, 120, 123–24, 126, 128–29, 137, 216
Brueckner, Leo J., 50, 120–21, 307
Brumfiel, Charles F., 76, 269
Brunel, Michel, 360
Bruner, Jerome, 84–85, 136–37, 143, 145, 288, 289
The Process of Education, 84, 280, 288
Buchan, Earl of, 21
Buchan, J. M., 382
Burington, R. S., 249–50
Burke, Edmund, 361
Burton, William, 314–15

Burwell, Hugh, 429–30
Business, influence of, on mathematics education, 188–92, 202
Buswell, Guy, 220
Butler, C., 307
Butler, Nicholas M., 177
Butts, Freeman, 164

Cairns, Stewart S., 71–72, 250–51
Cajori, Florian, 11, 21, 160, 175, 180
Calculus, the, 31, 55, 78, 207, 247, 260, 274, 292, 294, 310, 330, 395, 423, 433, 444
Callahan, R. E., 188, 191
  Education and the Cult of Efficiency, 188
Cambridge Conference, 79, 82, 271–72, 291–94, 295–96, 348, 462
  on School Mathematics, 57, 145, 146–52, 345–46
  on Teacher Training, 78, 346–48
Campbell, J. D., 372, 375, 377
Canadian Association of Mathematics Teachers, 430–31
Canadian Mathematics Congress, 336, 401–2, 443, 446
  Why Study Mathematics? 402
Canadian Teachers' Federation, 429, 430, 444, 447, 448
  Mathematics and the Teacher, 444
  Ottawa seminar (1960), 428–30
Careless, J. M. S., 392–93, 401
Carnegie Foundation, 72, 74, 76, 251, 259, 270
Carter, James G., 303
Cartesian coordinates, 294
Cartier, Jacques, 357
Cavalieri, Bonaventura, 31
Central Association of Science and Mathematics Teachers, 39, 43, 176, 177
  founding of, 314
  School Science and Mathematics, 39, 43, 177
Chaboillez, Augustin, 361
Chateauneuf, Amy Olive, 158, 159
Chauvaux, Charles, 360
Christofferson, Halbert C., 222, 224
Chicago, 176
  Conference on Research Potential and Training, 270, 271, 272
  Men's Mathematics Club of, 43, 195, 210
  World's Fair, 41

Child-study movement, 116, 117, 119, 133
  expressionism in the, 119
  child-centeredness in the, 119, 131–32, 196
Christian Brothers, 356, 362
Chronology of events, 23, 34–35, 44–45, 65–66, 88–89
Chute, H. N., 177
Clapp, F. L., 114
Clark, John R., 191, 206, 215, 221
Clason, Robert, 13, 38
Classical colleges, 354, 358–59, 368
Classroom Management (Bagley), 188
Clinchy, Evans, 287–89, 290–91
Clinton, DeWitt, 303
Coar, Henry, 173
Cognition, 217
Colburn, Warren, 2, 4, 21, 25–26, 32, 306–7, 373
  An Arithmetic on the Plan of Pestalozzi with Some Improvements, 22, 103
  First Lessons, 26, 105
  inductive approach of, 32
  inductive discovery of, 26
  An Introduction to Algebra on the Inductive Method of Instruction, 32
Coleman, A. J., 434
College Entrance Examination Board (CEEB), 42, 73–74, 168, 171, 202, 209, 221, 235, 259, 260, 266, 446. See also Commission and Committee *subentries*
  Advanced Placement Program, 71
  examinations, 171, 234, 260
  Report of the Commission on Mathematics, 74
College entrance requirements, 18, 29, 37, 53, 54, 61, 68, 168–73, 180, 201, 202, 366
College preparatory programs, 53, 69, 239, 241, 242, 260–61, 262, 414, 433, 446
Colleges
  Antioch College, 331
  Ball State Teachers College, 76, 267, 269
  Collège Charles-Carnier, 360
  Collège de Montréal, 360
  College of St. Catherine, 332
  College of William and Mary, 18
  Loyola College, 368

INDEX 541

Montana State College, 332
Reed College, 331
Upper Canada College, 373
Yale College, 15
Collèges d'Enseignement Général et Professionnel (C.E.G.E.P.), 368
Colleges for Professional and Vocational Training, 368
Commentaries on Pure and Applied Mathematics (Wigner), 457
Commission
  on Accredited Schools of the North Central Association, 171
  on Aims and Objectives of Education in Ontario, 428
  Educational Policies Commission (NEA and AASA), 240, 244, 246 (see also *Education for All American Youth*)
  Hall-Dennis Commission (*see* Commission, on Aims and Objectives of Education in Ontario)
  Hope Commission, 391, 393, 401, 410
  International, on the Teaching of Mathematics (International Congress of Mathematicians), 39, 46, 167, 182–83, 311–12, 390–91
  Joint Commission (MAA and NCTM), 54, 55, 58, 61, 62, 227–31, 233, 236, 239, 259, 268, 323–24
  on Mathematics (CEEB), 73, 76, 235, 237, 259–66, 268, 270, 271, 273, 276, 334–35, 409, 411, 428, 434
  Ontario Mathematics Commission (O.M.C.), 284, 434, 435, 436, 441
  Royal, of Inquiry on Education in the Province of Quebec, 365, 402
  on Post-War Plans (NCTM), 6, 50, 54, 58, 60, 61, 67, 243–46, 250, 257, 324–25, 327
  on the Reorganization of Secondary Education (NEA), 192
  on the Secondary School Curriculum (PEA), 54-55
  on the Training and Utilization of Advanced Students of Mathematics (MAA), 62, 321–23
Committee
  on Advanced Placement (CEEB), 71
  on College Entrance Requirements (NEA), 33, 42, 46, 168–69, 170, 175, 307–8
  Cooperative, on the Teaching of Science and Mathematics (AAAS), 62, 68, 80, 327–28, 336–37
  on Economy of Time (NEA), 168, 190, 194, 248
  of Eight (SMSG), 272
  Elementary Education Committee (O.M.C.), 437, 438–39
  of Fifteen on Elementary Education (NEA), 37, 108, 168
  of Fifteen on the Geometry Syllabus, National (American Federation of Teachers of the Mathematical and Natural Sciences and the NEA), 39, 180, 207, 222
  on the Function of Mathematics in General Education (PEA), 225–27, 230–31, 233, 239
  on Geometry (NCTM), 223
  In-Service Education Committee (NCTM), 333
  National, on Mathematical Requirements (MAA), 5, 40–43, 46–47, 52, 53, 57, 62, 197–209, 219, 221, 222, 223, 248, 316–19
  Physical Science Study Committee (PSSC), 74, 75, 271
  Policy, for Mathematics, 270
  on the Problem of Mathematics in Secondary Education (NEA's Commission on the Reorganization of Secondary Education), 62, 193
  Secondary School Committee (Canadian Mathematics Congress), 446
  Secondary School Curriculum Committee (NCTM), 266–67, 335–36
  of Seven (National Society for the Study of Education), 125–27
  Standing, on Education and Schools, 356
  Subcommittee on Education for Service of the War Preparedness Committee (AMS and MAA), 237
  of Ten on Secondary School Studies (NEA), 4, 33, 46, 163–68, 170, 173, 186, 307–8, 387, 388, 389, 463
  on the Undergraduate Program (CUP), 81
  on the Undergraduate Program in Mathematics (CUPM) (MAA), 81, 337–40, 341–45
  War Policy Committee (AMS and MAA), 60
  War Preparedness Committee (AMS and MAA), 58, 231, 237

Common learnings, 239, 243, 244
Common Schools Act, 372
Commonwealth Conference on Mathematics in Schools, 449
Commutativity, 49
Competence, 6, 47, 244
  functional, 58, 60, 63, 68, 69, 191, 244–45, 246, 257
Complex numbers, 247
Compulsory attendance laws, 109, 184, 386, 393, 403
Computation, 48, 52, 229
  from approximate data, 203
  skill in, 127, 218, 222
Computer-programming instruction, 281, 437
Computers, 135, 144, 290, 448
Comte, Auguste, 32
Conant, James Bryant, 340–41
Concepts
  nonverbal awareness of, 294
  versus skills, 285
Conference Board of the Mathematical Sciences, 80
Conference on Mathematics of the Committee of Ten, 164–68
Congregation of Notre Dame, 355, 360
Connectionism, 38, 49, 113, 115, 128, 129, 133, 216, 313, 318, 417. *See also* Learning theory
  common-element paradigm for, 187
"Contents of Children's Minds, The" (Hall) 108
Continuity, 78
Correlated mathematics, 166, 173, 176, 178, 196, 205, 206, 207, 395
Council of Education (Quebec), 357, 358
Council of Public Instruction (Ontario), 375, 376, 379
Counts, George S., 119
  Dare the School Build a New Social Order? 119
Cours d'Algèbre (Garand), 364
Cours d'Algèbre Elémentaire (F.E.C.), 364
Cousin, Victor, 31
Crathorne, A. R., 43, 200
Cremin, Lawrence A., 108, 118, 119–20, 157, 164, 184, 240
Cubberly, Elwood P., 189
Cuisenaire-Gattegno method, 365
Cuisenaire rods, 143, 443, 444
Cult of efficiency, 188–92, 202

Cultural values, 63, 204
Curriculum, 228, 375, 376, 439–40
  college, 19–20, 28, 81
  core, 191, 241, 243, 447
  differentiated, 257
  elective approach to building of, 164
  elementary school, 164
  experimentation with the, 327
  four divisions of learning in, 239
  grade placement of topics in, 122, 127, 165, 459
  high school, 413
  integrated, 409, 414
  junior high school, 208, 211, 218
  model, 206–7
  spiral, 38, 78, 79, 116, 220, 279, 292, 436
  traditional, 243, 247, 378
  unified, 239 (*see also* Unification movement; Unified mathematics)
  watering down the, 213
Currie, I. I., 416

Daboll, David A., 15
Daboll, Nathan, 15
Daboll's Schoolmaster's Assistant, Being a Plain Practical System of Arithmetic; Adapted to the United States (Daboll), 15
Dainville, François de, 359
Dalrymple, Charles O., 190
Dane, Nazala, 447–48
Dare the School Build a New Social Order? (Counts), 119
Data, 57, 226
  analysis of, 160
Davies, Charles, 29, 31, 42, 161
  Arithmetic, 29
  Bourdon's Algebra, 29
  Descriptive Geometry, 29
  Legendre's Geometry, 29
  The Logic and Utility of Mathematics with the Best Methods Explained and Illustrated, 34
  Surveying, 29
Davis, Robert B., 77, 139
Dean, J. E., 398
Decimal currency in Canada, 377
Deductive thinking, 26, 73, 260, 262, 382, 390, 431
De Garmo, Charles, 306, 307
Del Grande, J. J., 418
De Moivre's theorem, 440
Denechau, Denys, 361
Depression

INDEX

the British, of 1857, 374
the Great, 53, 393, 396, 418
Désaulniers, Isaac Le Sieur, 362
Descartes, René, 31
Descriptive Geometry (Davies), 29
Determinants, 247
Developmental Project in Secondary Mathematics of Southern Illinois University, 269, 284, 296
Developmental Psychology of Jean Piaget, The (Flavell), 142
Dewey, John, 38, 39, 48, 94, 111, 116, 117, 119, 176, 186, 192, 215, 216, 217, 289, 307, 313
The Psychology of Number, 111, 381
Dickman, Kern, 250
Dienes, Zoltan P., 78, 144, 444, 448
Discovery approach to instruction, 32, 72, 143, 254, 255, 279, 288, 293, 297, 444. *See also* Heuristic approach
Discovery learning, 254, 255, 262, 293, 436
Discovery teaching, 2, 84, 85, 330
Distributive law, 178-79, 284
District Public School Act (Ontario), 372
Dolbeau, Jean, 354
Dominion status for Canada, 385
Douglas, Edwin C., 260
Douglass, Harl R., 220, 250
Downey, W. F., 43, 200
Drill, 48, 49, 131, 213, 218-19, 220, 229, 232, 277, 291, 293, 305, 403, 413, 416, 417, 418, 447
Duff, George, 447
Dumont, Eustache, 361
Dunbar, Ruth, 134
Duplessis, Pacifique, 354
Durham, Lord, 356, 375
Durrant, J. E., 402, 403
Duvernay, Ludger, 363

Eaton, Amos, 29
Art without Science, 29
Education
departments of, 306
of girls, 355
schools of, 306
Education Act of 1841, 356-57
Education Act of 1846, 357
Educational Services Incorporated, 345
Educational Testing Service (ETS), 73, 259, 270
Education and the Cult of Efficiency (Callahan), 188
Education for All American Youth (Educational Policies Commission), 239, 243
Education through Mathematics, 423
Edwards, P. D., 250
Eicholz, Robert, 269
Elective courses, 28, 29
Elementary Algebra, First Course (Millis), 178
Elementary Arithmetic for Canadian Schools (Smith and McMurchy), 379
Elementary Mathematics from an Advanced Standpoint: Geometry (Klein, tr. by Hedrick and Noble), 41, 183
Elementary school, 25-27, 37-38, 48-51, 76-78, 137, 307, 358, 372, 437, 444, 445. *See also* Curriculum, elementary school
algebra in, 37, 164, 169
geometry in, 2, 77, 164, 181, 292, 437
Elementary Trigonometry (Hall and Knight), 365, 422
Elements of Algebra (McLellan), 380-81, 382
Elements of Algebra (Sangster and Todhunter), 379
Elements of Euclid (McKay), 383
Elements of Geometry (Legendre), 16
Elicker, Paul, 83
Eliot, Charles William, 28, 164
Elliott, Edward Charles, 314
Elliott, H. A., 449
Emerging Practices in Mathematics Education (Twenty-second Yearbook, NCTM), 257-59
Enrichment materials, 72, 78
Enrollment, 184, 217, 378, 393, 396
in algebra, 209
college, 249
in geometry, 54, 209, 223
in mathematics, 48, 53-54, 58, 197, 209
in secondary schools, 212, 413
Equation, concept of, 166
Equation solving, 179, 242, 253
Euclid, 161, 180, 373, 374, 376, 389, 390, 409, 419
Euclid (Todhunter and Loney), 422
Euclid's Elements of Geometry (Potts and Todhunter), 379
Eudoxus, 167
Evaluation, 257, 285, 293

Evenson, A. B., 431-32
Experimental courses, 201, 205

Fabrique Act, 356
Faculty psychology, 28, 99, 102, 113, 133, 156, 161, 162, 164, 166, 305, 313, 415-16
Failure rates, 53, 163, 177, 197, 211, 213
Faught, D. T., 434, 440-41
Fawcett, Harold P., 58, 75, 223-24, 243, 258, 402-3, 409
Fédération des Écoles Chrétiennes (F.E.C.), 364
  Cours d'Algèbre Élémentaire, 364
Fédération de l'Instruction Chrétienne (F.I.C.), 364
  Géométrie Analytique, 364
  Manuel des Écoles Chrétiennes, 364
Fehr, Howard, 243, 260, 409
Fellowship programs for teachers, 332
First Book of Arithmetic for the Use of Schools (Dublin), 362
First Lessons (Colburn), 26, 105
Fisher, J. J., 341-42
Flexible scheduling, 143
Foberg, J. A., 43, 198, 200
Forces, 8, 12-13, 20, 22-23, 24-25, 34, 36, 44, 48, 64-65, 67-72, 78, 87-88, 95-97, 98, 118-20, 156-57, 162-63, 184, 191, 209-12, 235-39, 370, 460-62
Foreign influences, 12, 202, 303, 306-7, 312-13, 318, 390
  European influences, 166
  French influences, 16, 28, 29
Formal instruction, postponement of, 67
Formulas, 52, 206, 220, 242
Foundations of Geometry (Hilbert, tr. by Townsend), 41
Fractions, 52, 415
Franklin, Benjamin, 18, 20
Fraser, Bishop, 380
Frères des Écoles Chrétiennes, 356, 362
Freud, Sigmund, 119
Freyle, Juan Diez, 12, 13, 16
Frobel, Friedrich, 25, 31, 104
Functions, 226, 253, 261, 264, 274, 276, 368, 410, 435
  concept of, 41, 47, 57, 73, 158, 160, 174, 178, 180, 201, 202, 204, 205-6, 208, 209, 221, 398
Fundamental operations, 203
Fused mathematics, 176-77, 179

Gagné, Robert M., 84, 140-41, 145
Gagnon collection, 360
Garth, W. F., 443
General Board of Education (Ontario), 373
General education, 58, 60, 61, 62, 63, 248
General Education Board (New York City), 198
General Education in School and College, 246-48
General mathematics, 41, 47, 51, 52, 53, 55, 191, 222, 241, 244, 258, 319, 397, 398, 399, 425
Geometric construction, 52, 192
Géométrie Analytique (F.I.C.), 364
Géométrie Spontanée de l'Enfant, La (Piaget), 83
Geometry (Greenleaf), 161-62
Geometry, 27, 28, 33, 39, 40, 41, 47, 51, 54, 55, 71, 73, 78, 82, 158, 161-62, 163, 165, 166, 168, 170, 174, 176-77, 178, 179-82, 183, 196, 201, 203, 207, 218, 221, 222-25, 228, 232-33, 242, 247, 253, 254, 258, 276, 277, 278, 293, 294, 304, 308, 368, 375, 376, 378, 388, 390, 394, 397, 405, 408, 413, 419-20, 421, 423, 424, 434, 436, 437, 440, 441
  algebraic methods in, 390
  analytic, 31, 55, 78, 247, 258, 260, 274, 310, 330, 366, 381, 383, 395, 398
  applications of, 223
  concrete, 168, 169
  of conic sections, 162, 388
  coordinate, 261, 264, 390
  demonstrative, 169, 206
  elementary school, 2, 77, 164, 181, 292, 413, 437
  goals of, 167
  intuitive, 33, 41, 138, 206, 208-9, 219, 220, 222, 366, 389, 397, 430
  loci in, 207
  logic in, 167, 222
  nonmetric, 140
  omission of formal theories in, 207
  original exercises in, 161, 162, 167, 222
  plane, 172, 207, 261, 366
  proof in, 167, 207, 222
  real, applied problems in, 178, 179, 182
  solid, 54, 55, 162, 172, 181, 182, 207, 223, 261
  space perception in, 181, 229, 261
  utilitarian features of solid, 181
Geometry Project (Hawley's), 140

INDEX

Geometry with Coordinates (SMSG), 278
Gestalt psychology, 49, 128, 216, 217
Gibb, E. Glenadine, 299
GI Bill, 327
Gillespie, William Mitchell, 31
The Philosophy of Mathematics, 31–32
Ginsburg, Jekuthiel, 19
Gleason, A. M., 256, 291
Goals for School Mathematics (Cambridge Conference), 57, 291, 345–46
Goddard, E. C., 465
Goodlad, John, 280
Graduate education, 30
Grammar-School Algebra (Griffin), 174
Grammar School Arithmetic (Wentworth), 156
Graphic representation, 55, 192, 203, 209, 228, 229
Graphs, 41, 52, 158, 174, 206, 209, 220, 242, 253, 366, 390, 397, 398, 435, 437
Grassmann, Hermann Günther, 165
Gray, W. B., 379–80, 381, 383–84, 388, 390, 391, 394, 397–98
Greater Cleveland Mathematics Program (GCMP), 77, 139, 284
Greenwood, Isaac, 12, 19, 21
Arithmetick, Vulgar and Decimal, 12, 23
Greenwood, James, 167
Grossnickle, Foster E., 307
Growth of Logical Thinking from Childhood to Adolescence, The (Piaget), 83
Growth of Mathematical Ideas, Grades K–12, The (Twenty-fourth Yearbook, NCTM), 267, 429
Grube system, 103
Guerin-Lajoie, Paul, 367
Gugle, Marie, 209, 219, 222
Guidance, 67, 68, 240–41, 246
Guidance Pamphlet in Mathematics for High School Students (NCTM), 58, 67, 245
"Guidance Report" (Commission on Post-War Plans), 245, 250
Gundlach, B. H., 77
Gwilliam, Robert B., 447

Hall, G. Stanley, 108, 109, 117, 119, 177
"The Contents of Children's Minds," 108

Hall, Samuel R., 303
Hall-Dennis report, *Living and Learning*, 389, 428
Halsted, G. B., 41, 175, 178
Rational Geometry, 41
Hamilton, Sir William Rowan, 31, 161, 165
Hancock, John D., 233
Hanna, Paul R., 50
Hart, Walter W., 180, 218
Hart, William L., 58, 231
Hartung, Maurice L., 55, 226, 365, 409
Harvard report, the, 241–43, 247, 248
Hawley, Newton S., 77, 140
Hawney's Complete Measurer, 16
Heaviside, Oliver, 458–59
Hedrick, Earle R., 43, 175, 180, 186–87, 198
Elementary Mathematics from an Advanced Standpoint, 41
Heidbreder, Edna, 185
Henderson, Kenneth B., 250
Hendrix, Gertrude, 252
Herbart, Johann Friedrich, 25, 31, 110, 115
Herbartian movement, 305, 306
doctrine of interest in the, 306
fundamental meanings in the, 306
Heuristic approach, 32, 292. See also Discovery approach
Hewett, Edwin, 309
Hewitt, Glenn, 195
High School Algebra (Milne), 159
High school entrance examinations, 386
Higher Education Act, 332
Hilbert, David, 41, 178, 211, 269
Foundations of Geometry, 41
Hildebrandt, Martha, 260
Hill, Thomas, 161, 166
History of Experimental Psychology (Boring), 185
History of Mathematics in Europe (Sullivan), 456
Hofstadter, Richard, 168
Hornbook, 13
Horne, Edgar B., 402, 446
Houdet, Father, 360
Houghton Mifflin textbooks, 443
Hrabi, Dr. J., 433–34, 446
Hull House, 168
Humanized Geometry, An Introduction to Thinking (Blackhurst), 217, 223
Huntington, Edward V., 41, 42, 180

Hutchins, Robert M., 134

Immigration, 184, 362, 374
Incidental learning, 48, 50, 67, 122, 125, 318, 319
Incommensurability, 162, 182
Individual differences, 6, 28, 51, 56, 193, 194, 196, 197, 212-13, 244, 246, 257, 262, 286-87, 293, 407, 413
Individual needs. *See* Social utility
Inductive thinking, 26, 32, 160, 165-66, 192, 253, 382, 390
Industrial education. *See* Vocational education
Inequalities, 261
In-service teacher education, 30, 80, 281, 308, 309, 313, 314-16, 319, 328, 329-34, 401, 441, 442, 463. *See also* Institutes
  in Russia, 429
  supervision as factor in, 314-15, 333-34
  television courses for, 443
Insights into Modern Mathematics (Twenty-third Yearbook, NCTM), 267
Institutes, 74, 77, 80, 81, 252, 314, 316, 319, 330-32, 432, 463
  Boston College Mathematics Institute, 284
  Institute of Mathematical Statistics, 256
Instruction, 83-85. *See also* Learning theory
  adapting, to the individual, 25, 413
  colonial, 13
  computer-assisted, 142, 144
  environmetal approach to, 444-445
  individualized, 144
  integrated materials for, 289
  spiraling of, 55, 78
Instructional media, 344
Integrated mathematics. *See* Unified mathematics
Intelligence testing, 187, 189, 202, 212, 217
Intermediate Algebra (Tate), 365
Intermediate Mathematics, 364
International Congress of Mathematicians, 39-40, 182, 311. *See also* Commission, International, on the Teaching of Mathematics
  American commissioners, 42

Introduction to Algebra on the Inductive Method of Instruction, An (Colburn), 32
Intuition, 85, 279, 292-93, 408, 447
Irish National textbook series, 375, 377
Issues, 7-8, 17, 22, 34, 36, 43-44, 47, 48, 63-64, 76, 86, 94-95, 156-57, 169-70, 213-18, 370, 455-60
Izzo, J. A., 174

Jackson, Andrew, 25
Jamay, Denis, 354
James, William, 186, 216
Jefferson, Thomas, 20
Jenkins, James, 395
Johns, A. E., 399, 408
Johnson, Francis Henry, 396, 427, 428
Joint professorships, 320
Jones, Phillip S., 250
Jones, W. C., 168-69
Judd, Charles H., 120, 176, 214, 216
  The Measurement of Educational Products, 118
Junior college, 39, 56, 60-61, 62
Junior high school, 37, 39, 47, 51-53, 184, 206, 209, 230, 319, 391, 396, 397, 420, 446. *See also* Curriculum, junior high school

Kandel, I. L., 40
Kant, Immanuel, 31
Karnes, Houston T., 299
Karpinski, Louis C., 14
Kaufman, Burt, 296
Kaye, Garth, 439
Kelly, J. L., 256
Kemeny, J. G., 256
Kempner, A. J., 68
Kilpatrick, William Heard, 192, 193, 194, 195, 197, 208, 211, 251
Kinlin, J. F., 409, 434-35, 438
Kinnear, Miss J., 398
Kinney, Lucien B., 220, 286
Kirkconnel, Watson, 392
Klein, Felix, 41, 174, 183, 206, 244, 267, 284
  Elementary Mathematics from an Advanced Standpoint: Geometry (tr. by Hedrick and Noble), 41, 183
Kline, Morris, 82-83, 285, 286
Knight, F. B., 111
Koffka, W., 216, 217

INDEX 547

Kohler, Kaufmann, 216, 217
Koos, Leonard V., 51

Laboratory teaching, 144, 174, 215, 219, 257, 258, 293, 410, 439
Ladreyt, Casimir, 362
Laforce-Langevin, Jean-Pierre François, 363
Laing, Inspector, 407-8
Laisant, C. A., 460
Lancasterian system, 97, 104
Laurin, Joseph, 362
Laval, Monseigneur de, 355
Lazar, Nathan, 222, 224
Learning
  programmed, 441, 448
  rate of, 228
  spaced, 229
  spiral, 38, 57
  stimulus-response (*see* Connectionism)
  transfer of (*see* Transfer of training)
"Learning of Fundamentals in an Arithmetic-Activity Program, The" (Mapes and Harap), 122
Learning theory, 36, 83-85, 115, 213, 279-80
  association, 128
  field, 128, 129, 130
LeCaron, Joseph, 354
Lectures on Fundamental Concepts of Algebra and Geometry (Young), 42
Legendre, Adrien Marie, 17, 161, 180
  Elements of Geometry, 16
Legendre's Geometry (Davies), 29
Leibnitz, Gottfried Wilhelm von, 31, 363
Le Peltrie, Mme. Marie Madeleine de, 355
Lephrohon, C. P., 362
Lessons in Geometry (Hill), 419-20
Linear Associative Algebra (Peirce), 30
Living and Learning (Commission on Aims and Objectives of Education in Ontario), 389, 428
Lloyd, Daniel, 250
Lobachevsky, Nikolai Ivanovich, 41, 178
Locke, John, 24, 31
Logic, 204, 222, 223, 230
Logic and Utility of Mathematics with the Best Methods Explained and Illustrated, The (Davies), 34
Lynd, Albert, 134

McConnell, T. R., 129, 130-31, 216
McCormick, Clarence, 307
McCutcheon, J. M., 393, 394, 396
McDonald, Frederick, 190
MacDonald, John A., 385
McDougall, A. H., 387-88, 463
McGuffey Readers, 157
McKenzie, R. N., 395
Mackenzie, William Lyon, 374
MacLane, Saunders, 256
MacLean, Bruce, 410
McLellan, James A., 38, 111, 307, 372, 380, 382, 384, 387
  Elements of Algebra, 380-81, 382
  Mental Arithmetic, Fundamental Rules, Fractions, Analysis, 382
  The Psychology of Number, 111, 381
McLeod report, 428
McMurry, Charles A., 306, 307
McMurry, Frank M., 110, 306, 307
McQueen, James, 398
Madison Project, 139, 143, 284
Makoff, Lester M., 281
Mallory, V., 307
Manipulation, 47, 160, 242
Mann, Horace, 30, 31, 43
Manpower for Research (Steelman), 68, 235, 238
Manpower needs, 67, 68, 69, 238
Manuel des Écoles Chrétiennes (F.I.C.), 364
Marie de L'Incarnation, the Venerable, 355
Martin, Professor, 291
Massachusetts Institute of Technology, 74, 440
Massé, Father, 354
Mastery of topics, 127, 418
Mathematical Analysis (Goursat-Hedrick), 313
Mathematical Association of America (MAA), 5, 40, 42, 43, 53, 54, 63, 197, 231, 237, 256, 271, 272, 316, 323, 324. See also Commission *and* Committee *subentries*
  founding of, 314
  Symposium on College Entrance Requirements, 68
  Symposium on Teacher Education in Mathematics, 79

Works: *The Place of Mathematics in Secondary Education* (with NCTM), 226, 227–31; *The Reorganization of Mathematics in Secondary Education (The 1923 Report)*, 40–41, 46–47, 197–209, 219, 221, 222, 233, 316–19; *Universal Mathematics* (CUP), 81
Mathematical models, 283, 289, 297, 447, 457, 463
Mathematical Reviews, 70
Mathematical vs. social
 aims, 51
 meaning, 50
Mathematicians, 134, 237, 242
 college, 236, 238, 248, 260
 research, 238
Mathematics
 applications of, 68, 69–70, 79, 82, 170, 181, 227, 228, 233, 463 (*see also* Utilitarian aims in mathematics education)
 applied, 175, 246, 399
 business, 56, 219, 319, 372, 389, 447–48
 colonial, 13–17
 computer, 274, 344, 437–38
 consumer, 56, 60, 219, 245–46, 257, 258, 265
 early development of, in Western Hemisphere, 11–13
 field work in, 404
 grade-placement of topics in, 285, 399
 history of, 181, 310
 literacy in, 244, 285, 401, 404
 logic and structure of, 63, 209, 228
 purpose of, in secondary education, 202
 science of, 177, 401
 shop, 56
 as a tool subject, 214, 246
 unit approach to, 191
Mathematics and Physics Association of Ontario, 387
Mathematics and the Teacher (C.T.F.), 444
Mathematics educator, the, 234, 242, 454
Mathematics for Everyday Use, 421
Mathematics in Everyday Life textbook series, 232
Mathematics in General Education (PEA), 56–57, 225–27, 230–31, 268
"Mathematics Instruction for Purposes of General Education" (AAAS), 62

Mathematics Teacher (NCTM), 6, 43, 82, 194, 266
Mathématiques Générales (LaRue), 364
Mathématiques Intermédiares (LaRue and Risi), 364
Matrices, 78, 82
Matriculation examinations, 382, 384, 408, 410
May, Kenneth O., 250, 251, 409–10, 411
Mayor, John R., 76, 277
Meaning, 48, 51, 71, 216, 219
 teaching for, 218
Meaning theory of arithmetic, 49, 120, 123–25, 127, 130, 138, 139
Measurement movement. *See* Mental measurement
Measurement of Educational Products, The (Judd), 118
Mécanique Céleste (Laplace, tr. by Bowditch), 21, 30
Meder, Albert E., Jr., 256, 260, 272
Meister, Morris, 260
Memorization, 47
Menelaus, 402
Mensuration, 28, 52, 161, 192, 375, 376, 377, 405, 413, 437
Mental Arithmetic, Fundamental Rules, Fractions, Analysis (McLellan), 382
Mental discipline, 22, 27, 28, 32, 36, 38, 57, 99, 104, 113, 155, 156, 158, 160, 162, 163, 165, 166–67, 173, 186, 187, 193, 196, 197, 202, 205, 413
Mental measurement, 187, 189, 202, 212, 217
Meserve, B. E., 250
Methods, 382, 384
 books on, 31
 courses in, 31, 310
Michelson, Albert Abraham, 177
Miller, Norman, 401
 Why Study Mathematics? 402
Millikan, Robert H., 177
Mills, the Reverend Mr., 356
Milne, Frank E., 440
Milne, William J., 160
 High School Algebra, 159
Minnesota National Laboratory, 281
Minnesota School Mathematics and Science Teaching Project (MINNEMAST), 139
Minto, Walter, 21
Moise, Edwin E., 256, 274
Modern mathematics

INDEX 549

essence of, 69
as new subject matter, 77, 80, 124
Monographs on Topics in Modern Mathematics (Young), 42, 178
Moore, C. N., 43, 200
Moore, Eliakim Hastings, 4, 39, 62, 174–75, 176, 178, 179, 183, 200, 206, 209, 388–89, 453
Morison, Samuel Eliot, 27
Morse, Marston, 58, 231
Morton, R., 307
Mosteller, Frederick, 256, 260
Motivation, 28, 56, 85, 183, 216, 228, 229, 293, 356, 398
Mulligan, Howard, 434
Multisensory aids, 68, 78, 258, 448
Myers, George, 176, 177, 178, 205, 208

National Academy of Sciences, 30
National Association of Secondary School Principals (NASSP), 245
National Association of State Directors of Teacher Education and Certification (NASDTEC), 80, 348–50
National Council of Teachers of Mathematics, 5, 42, 43, 75, 80, 194–96, 202, 211, 222–23, 232, 234, 266–68, 271, 284, 323, 324, 332, 365, 432, 453. *See also* Commission *and* Committee *subentries*
 Canadian affiliates: Association of Mathematics Teachers of the Province of Quebec, 365, 368; L'Association Mathématique de Québec, 365; Provincial Association of Mathematics Teachers, 365, 368
 founding of, 314
 regional orientation conferences in mathematics, 80, 281
 Works: *An Analysis of New Mathematics Programs*, 76, 284–85; *Emerging Practices in Mathematics Education* (Twenty-second Yearbook), 257–59; *The Growth of Mathematical Ideas, Grades K–12* (Twenty-fourth Yearbook), 267, 429; *Guidance Pamphlet in Mathematics for High School Students*, 58, 67, 245; "Guidance Report" (Commission on Post-War Plans), 245, 250; *Insights into Modern Mathematics* (Twenty-third Yearbook), 267; *Mathematics Teacher*, 6, 43, 82, 194, 266; *The Nature of Proof* (Thirteenth Yearbook), 58, 224, 258; *The Place of Mathematics in Secondary Education* (with MAA), 226, 227–31; "Pre-Induction Courses in Mathematics" (with USOE), 59, 232; *The Revolution in Mathematics*, 76, 81, 282; *The Teaching of Geometry* (Fifth Yearbook), 223
National Defense Education Act, 143, 267
National Education Association (NEA), 5, 33, 163, 168, 171, 180, 193. *See also* Commission *and* Committee *subentries*
 Department of Child Study, 108
 Department of Superintendence, 52, 190
 mathematics committee (Dept. of Superintendence), 52
National Council on Education, 163
National Herbartian Society, 110, 115
National Mensuration, 379
National Research Council (NRC), 256, 270
National Science Foundation (NSF), 72, 74, 75, 76, 81, 139, 235, 251, 256, 270, 271, 291, 330, 345
National Society for the Scientific Study of Education, 110
National Society for the Study of Education, 50
National Teachers Association, 33
Nature of Proof, The (Thirteenth Yearbook, NCTM), 58, 258
Nautical Almanac Office, 30
Negro teachers and students, plight of, 234
New Algebra for High Schools, A (Crawford, Dean, and Jackson), 364
New Analytic Geometry, A (Durrant et al.), 365
New and Complete System of Arithmetic Composed for the Use of the Citizens of the United States, A (Pike), 15–16
Newcomb, Simon, 30
Newell, 397
Newell, M. J., 195
New England Association of Colleges and Secondary Schools, 169

New England Association of Teachers of Mathematics, 80
Newsom, C. V., 256
Newton, Isaac, 31
New York Mathematical Society, 4, 30
Bulletin, 30
Nimitz, C. W., 58–59, 231
1923 Report, The. See *Reorganization of Mathematics in Secondary Education, The*
Normal schools, 30–31, 37, 301–2, 302–8, 310, 376, 414, 418. See also subentries, by name, under Schools
North Central Association of Colleges and Secondary Schools, 169, 171, 175
Northrop, Eugene P., 63, 260
Nova Scotia Mathematics Teachers' Association, 440
Nova Scotia Summer School for Teachers, 443
Nuffield Mathematics Project, 144, 444, 448
Number, 229, 437
  as ratio, 38
  familiar properties of, 284
  ideas of, 26, 130
  logical approach to the teaching of, 416
  science of, 26, 38, 107, 157
  structural properties of, 49, 226, 344
Number Highway textbook series, 417
Numeration systems, 283
  bases for, 111, 284
  Mayan system, 11
Nunn, T. Percy, 397

Oakley, C. O., 249
Objectives in mathematics education, 6, 98–99, 109–10, 120–21, 134–35, 173, 189, 193, 201, 202–4, 297, 403–4, 406, 411, 415, 457–58. See also Articulation; Utilitarian aims in mathematics education
  battle of, 193, 197, 214, 217, 218, 231, 234, 241, 248
  disciplinary objectives, 201, 202, 203, 220
  in the secondary school, 55, 155
Obourn, Ellsworth S., 209
Occupational training. See Vocational education
Olney, A. C., 43, 200

Ontario
  course of study of 1841, 375–76; of 1854, 376–77; of 1865, 377–78; of 1871, 379–80, 381; of 1878, 380, 381–82; of 1885, 383; of 1896, 388; of 1904, 389–90; of 1909, 390; of 1924, 394; of 1928, 394; of 1936, 397; of 1938, 398, 402; of 1952, 407–8
  Curriculum Revision Experiment (Porter Plan), 403, 404, 406, 410
Ontario Curriculum Institute, 436
Ontario Institute for Studies in Education, 436
Ontario Teachers' Federation, 434 (see also Commission, Ontario Mathematics)
Ontario Association of Teachers of Mathematics and Physics (O.A.T.M.P.), 380, 398
Ontario Education Association (O.E.A.), 389, 390, 394, 401, 403, 404
Ontario Mathematics Gazette (O.M.C.), 441
Operations, 57, 226, 284
Organization for European Economic Cooperation (OEEC), 345, 429
Orleans, Joseph B., 51
Orth, Allen, 250
Overn, Orlando, 158, 159, 209

Page, David A., 77, 78, 140, 252, 255
Panet, Claude, 360
Parallel courses, 173, 292, 405, 436
Parker, Colonel, 215
Pasch's postulate, 181
Patterns in Arithmetic project, 139
"Payment by results," 380, 381
Peano, Giuseppe, 180
Pedagogy, 31
Peirce, Benjamin, 30, 165
  Linear Associative Algebra, 30
Peirce, Cyrus, 303–4
Perrault, Charles, 360
Perry, John, 39, 174, 183, 388, 389, 397
Perry movement, 39, 179, 389
Pestalozzi, Johann Heinrich, 21, 22, 24, 25, 31, 32, 97, 103, 104–5, 306, 362, 416
Petrie, Professor, 402
Phillips, C. E., 374, 386
Phillips, D. E., 111
Philosophy, natural, 19

INDEX 551

Philosophy of Arithmetic, The (Brooks), 31
Philosophy of Mathematics, The (Bledsoe), 31
Philosophy of Mathematics, The, Translated from the Cours de Philosophie Positive of Auguste Comte (Gillespie), 31–32
Piaget, Jean, 83, 142, 145, 294, 441, 448, 461
  The Child's Conception of Number, 83
  developmental stages, 142
  La Géométrie Spontanée de l'Enfant, 83
  The Growth of Logical Thinking from Childhood to Adolescence, 83
  La Représentation de l'Espace Chez l'Enfant, 83
Pieri, M., 180
Place of Mathematics in Secondary Education, The (NCTM and MAA), 226, 227–31
Plan of a Seminary for the Education of the Instructors of Youth (Gallaudet), 303
Playfair, John, 16
Plessis, Monseigneur, 355
Porter, Dana, 403, 404–5, 410
Porter Plan, 403, 404, 406, 410
Postulates, 181, 223, 269
Practical Arithmetic, The (Perkins), 100
Practical Mathematics (Palmer), 185
"Pre-Induction Courses in Mathematics" (NCTM and USOE), 59, 232
"Preparation of High School Science and Mathematics Teachers, The" (AAAS), 327–28
Price, G. Baley, 75, 249, 272
Primary Arithmetic (Wentworth), 415
Probability, 78, 237, 276, 292, 294, 330, 344, 433, 435
  with statistical applications, 258, 261, 265 (*see also* Statistics)
Problems, 408
  engineering, in vocational schools, 185
  practical, 207
  real, applied, 178, 179, 182, 183, 196, 214, 215
  from science, 177
Problem solving, 57, 84, 85, 226, 229, 418

accuracy in, 166, 389, 399, 403, 404
approximation in, 57, 226, 394, 404
Process of Education, The (Bruner), 84, 280, 288
Programmed materials, 281, 443
Progressive education, 94, 140, 213, 225, 396
  activity unit in, 140
  movement, 215, 217, 234, 240, 414
Progressive Education (PEA), 119
Progressive Education Association (PEA), 55, 56, 118, 119, 194, 215, 225, 233, 259. *See also* Commission *and* Committee *subentries*
  Works: *Mathematics in General Education,* 56–57, 225–27, 230–31, 268; *Progressive Education,* 119
Progressive High School Algebra (Hart), 365
Proof, 57, 69, 166, 224, 227, 285, 390. *See also* Geometry, proof in
Proportion, 52
Protestant School Board of Greater Montreal, 367
Psychologia Rationalis (Wolff), 99
Psychological research, 36, 213
Psychologists, 78, 442
  European, 186
  task-analysis work of, 142
Psychologizing, 33, 39, 417
Psychology, 3, 83–85, 97, 102, 103, 104, 106, 113, 117, 132, 140, 145, 185–87, 204–5, 212, 213, 216, 217, 228, 234. *See also* Behaviorism; Connectionism; Faculty psychology; Gestalt psychology; Learning theory; Mental discipline; Transfer of training
  field theories of, 217
  functional approach to, 186
Psychology of Number, The (Dewey and McLellan), 111, 381
PTA, 77, 284
"Public School Leaving Examination" (Northwest Territories), 419
Pullen, Harry, 405–7

Quantifiers, 254
Quebec
  Christian Brothers in, 356
  Frères des Écoles Chrétiennes in, 362
  Jesuits in, 354, 359–60
  Rebellion of 1837 in, 356
  Récollets in, 354

Quebec (*Continued*)
  religious influence in, 354
  Roman Catholics in, 355
  struggle of two cultures in, 353–54
Questionnaire studies, 205

Raisenne, Jérôme, 360
Rankin, W. W., 80
Ratio, 38, 52
Rational Geometry (Halsted), 41
Ray, Joseph, 157, 158
  Intellectual Arithmetic, 157
  The Little Arithmetic, 157
  New Practical Arithmetic, 157
Readiness, 48, 49–50, 85
Real number system, 294
Reed, E. M., 103–4
Rees, Mina, 256, 271
Reeve, William David, 184, 208, 211, 212, 222
Reform, 33, 72–76, 81–83, 94, 250, 251, 281–84, 287–91, 387–92, 399–411
Relational thinking, 230
Rensselaer Polytechnic Institute, 20, 29
Reorganization of Mathematics in Secondary Education, The (MAA), 40–41, 46–47, 197–209, 211, 219, 221, 222, 233, 316–19
Report of the Commission on Mathematics (CEEB), 74
Report of the Subcommittee on Education (Alberta Post-War Reconstruction Committee), 418
Représentation de l'Espace Chez l'Enfant, La (Piaget), 83
Research in mathematics education, 41–42, 130, 454–55
Revolution, 78, 79, 81, 249, 281, 290, 460
Revolution in Mathematics, The (NCTM), 76, 81, 282
Rice, Joseph Mayer, 108–9, 114–15
  "Educational Research: Causes of Success and Failure in Arithmetic," 109
Rickover, Hyman, 134
Rigor, 166, 180, 292–93, 447
Rittenhouse, David, 20–21
Robb, C. W., 394
Robert, l'Abbé, 364
  Complements d'Algèbre, 364
Robertson, W. J., 387
Robinson, Floyd G., 429, 441–42
Rosenberger, N. B., 307
Rosenbloom, Paul, 256

Rourke, R. E. K., 260, 398–99, 401, 429
Rousseau, Jean Jacques, 25, 104, 119
  Émile, 289
Royal Commission of Inquiry on Education in the Province of Quebec, 365, 402
Royal Institution for the Advancement of Learning, 355–56
Royaumont seminar, 429
Rugg, Harold O., 191, 206
Russell, Bertrand, 180
Ryerson, Egerton, 372, 375, 377, 378, 380, 396, 412

Safford, Truman, 173
Saint-Sulpice library, 360
Sandiford, Peter, 114, 117
Sangster, Herbert, 377
  Elements of Algebra, 379
  Irish National Arithmetic (rev.), 377
  National Arithmetic, 377
Sawyer, W. W., 77
School administration, analogy of, to business management, 188–89
School and College Study of Admission with Advanced Standing, 71
Schoolmaster's Assistant, The: Being a Compendium of Arithmetic Both Practical and Theoretical, (Dilworth), 14–15
School Mathematics Study Group (SMSG), 74–76, 79, 81–82, 83, 139, 146, 208, 223, 235, 236, 237, 238, 256, 257, 267, 268, 269–81, 284, 438, 440, 441, 443, 463
  National Longitudinal Study of Mathematical Abilities, 75, 281
  Panel on Elementary School Mathematics, 77
  self-evaluation, 281
  textbooks, 82
  Work: *Geometry with Coordinates*, 278
Schools
  accreditation of, 171
  Boston Latin Grammar School, 18
  Cass Technical School (Detroit), 206
  colonial, 13, 94, 98
  criticism of, 134
  common, 357, 371, 378, 379
  elementary (*see* Elementary school)
  English High School, 27
  federal versus local control of, 240

INDEX 553

free, 372, 379
Girls High School, 27
grammar, 376, 378, 379
Horace Mann School, 43
Jacques Cartier Normal School, 357
Latin grammar, 17, 18
Laval Normal School, 357
Lincoln School (Columbia University), 43, 191
McGill Normal School, 357
media in, 143
Michigan State Normal School, 31
missionary, 413
nongraded, 143, 439
Nova High School (Fort Lauderdale, Fla.), 296
Nova Scotia Summer School for Teachers, 443
Ontario School of Pedagogy, 372
Parker School (Chicago), 176, 206, 215
private, 372
secondary, 27-28, 39-41, 51, 78-79, 162-63, 188-92, 231-33, 307, 312, 445-46 (*see also* Junior high school; Senior high school; Teacher training)
Toronto Normal School, 377
School Science and Mathematics (CASMT), 39, 43, 177
Schorling, Raleigh, 43, 47, 68, 200, 212, 213, 215, 221, 222
Science of education, 190
Scientism, 93-94, 106, 107-17, 118, 188, 202, 214, 215
Sectional movements in Canada, 393
Seeing through Arithmetic textbook series, 366, 433
Seeing through Mathematics textbook series, 432
Self-instruction, 12, 20, 362
Seminar on New Thinking in School Mathematics (OEEC), 429
Seminary
 Grand Séminaire de Québec, 355 (*see also* University, Laval University)
 of Nicolet, 362
 Séminaire de Québec, 361, 363
Senior Algebra (Durrell and Wright), 422-23
Senior high school, 53-58
 election of mathematics courses in, 207

Sequences, 253
Sets, 73, 82, 254, 276, 282, 283, 344, 410, 435, 436
Shuster, Carl N., 68, 404
Seath, John, 380, 383, 392
Seerly, H. H., 173
Shanks, Merrill, 269
Shibli, Jabir, 161
Sigurdson, Solberg, 167, 173, 178, 205
Simcoe, Lord, 371, 372
Simon, Theodore, 118
Simson, Robert, 16, 17
Skills, 62, 166, 170, 218, 222, 260, 290, 405
 manipulative, 47, 160, 242
Slaught, H. E., 180
Slow learner, the, 212, 213, 228, 244, 290
Smiler, Helen B., 455
Smith, David Eugene, 19, 38, 42, 43, 158-59, 168, 175, 180, 182, 193-94, 200, 208, 209, 307, 453, 454
 The Teaching of Elementary Mathematics, 42, 307
Smith, J. Hamblin, 382
 A Treatise on Arithmetic, 424
SMSG, *The Making of a Curriculum* (Wooton), 75
SMSG textbooks, 82
Sneddon, David, 211
Socialized Mathematics (Cooper), 421
Social Science Research Council, 81
Social utility, 6, 48, 58, 98-99, 110, 120, 122-24, 125, 131-32, 133, 135-36, 183, 190-92, 193-94, 196, 197, 214, 215, 220, 224, 225, 227, 243, 244, 246, 257, 277, 290, 294, 318-19, 386, 395, 404, 405, 418, 442
Society
 needs of (*see* Utilitarian aims in mathematics education)
 needs of individual in (*see* Social utility)
Sonley, J. A., 403-4, 464
Southern Association of Colleges and Secondary Schools, 169
Specialists, 143
Speer, William W., 38, 111
Spencer, Herbert, 31, 32, 38
Spitzer, H., 307
Sputnik, 135, 231, 256, 267, 327
Stamper, A. W., 454
Stanford University Institute for Mathematical Studies in the Social Sciences, 139

Statistical inference, 258
Statistics, 41, 47, 51, 78, 207, 242, 246, 247, 276, 292, 310, 319, 330, 344
Steelman, John R., 68–69, 235, 238
  Manpower for Research, 68–69
Stern, Catherine, 444
Stimulus-response. *See* Connectionism
Stone, C. W., 454
Stone, John C., 191–92, 215, 218, 219, 307
  Elementary Algebra, First Course, 178
  Junior High School Mathematics, Book I, 191–92
Stone, Marshall, 146, 231, 256, 295
Stone, Mildred, 190
Stowe, Calvin E., 31
Strachan, the Reverend Dr., 373, 374
  Arithmetic, 373
Strayer-Upton Arithmetics, Higher Grades, 219
Streaming, 257, 262, 368–70
Structural properties of number, 49, 226, 344
Structure of mathematics, 6, 69, 73, 85, 137, 140, 216, 242, 260, 277, 279, 283, 285, 288, 431
  as an abstract system, 283
  axiomatic, 269
  importance of, in teaching, 84
Stuart, John, 355
Students
  below-average, 274
  college-capable, 266, 273, 296
  gifted, 71, 248–50, 267, 274
Superior Council of Public Instruction, 358
Superposition, 390
Suppes, Patrick, 77, 85, 139, 143, 144, 145
Surveying, 19
Surveying (Davies), 29
Swenson, John A., 221
Sylvester, James Joseph, 30, 165–66
  American Journal of Mathematics, 30
Symbolic logic, 82
Symbolical Euclid (Blakelock), 374
Symbolism, 57, 187, 227, 230
Syracuse University–Webster College Madison Mathematics Project, 139, 143, 284

Teacher certification, 80, 305, 316, 328, 344

Teacher preparation for new programs, 278–79, 289, 296
Teachers
  college, 260
  counselors for, 328
  high school, 260
  modern algebra courses for, 80
  probability courses for, 80
  statistics courses for, 80, 310
  summer sessions for, 309
Teachers colleges, 302, 308, 310. *See also* Normal schools
Teacher training, 30–32, 37, 39, 42–43, 61–63, 79–80, 201, 252, 257, 378, 428, 463. *See also* Normal schools; Commission, International, on the Teaching of Mathematics; Committee, National, on Mathematical Requirements
  of college teachers, 340 (*see also* Committee, on the Undergraduate Program in Mathematics)
  of elementary school teachers, 37, 311, 313, 318, 320, 321, 325–26, 333, 340–41, 348–49, 418–19 (*see also* Commission, on Mathematics; Committee, on the Undergraduate Program in Mathematics)
  fifth-year program in, 319, 345
  films for, 443
  implementation of recommendations for, 341–45
  internships, 345
  of junior college teachers, 56, 62
  professional courses in, 310
  recommendations for, 334–41
  of secondary school teachers, 62, 79–80, 311–12, 321, 341, 349–50, 449 (*see also* Canadian Mathematics Congress; Commission, Joint; Commission, on Mathematics; Commission, on Post-War Plans; Commission, on the Training and Utilization of Advanced Students of Mathematics; Committee, Cooperative, on the Teaching of Science and Mathematics; Committee, Secondary School Curriculum; Committee, on the Undergraduate Program in Mathematics)
  survey of teachers of high school mathematics, 328
Teaching
  demonstration, 315

INDEX

methods, 285, 414
as a profession, 302, 308, 309, 311, 320–21, 357
Teaching of Elementary Mathematics, The (Smith), 42, 307
Teaching of Geometry, The (Fifth Yearbook, NCTM), 223
Teaching of Mathematics in the Elementary and Secondary School, The (Young), 42, 307
Teaching the New Arithmetic (Wilson), 120
Technology, 135, 248
Team teaching, 143, 176, 206, 215
Television courses, 80, 367, 432, 439, 440, 442–43, 448
Terman, Lewis Madison, 118
Tests, 215, 389, 413, 418, 420, 425
 intelligence (*see* Mental measurement)
 standardized, 201, 205, 313, 315, 380, 381, 412, 419
Textbook of Geometry, A (Wentworth), 162
Textbooks, 134, 156–57, 185, 217, 218, 238, 357, 367, 406. *See also under title or author's name*
 catechetical question-and-answer format in, 17
 in French-speaking Canada, 360–65
 fusion, 176–77, 179
 graded, 116
 nineteenth-century arithmetic 31
 non-Euclidean geometry, 178
 as teaching devices, 160
Theoretical Geometry (Baker), 422
Theory of Games and Economic Behavior, The (Morgenstern and von Neumann), 70
Thomas, George B., Jr., 260
Thorndike, Edward L., 38, 43, 47, 49, 115–16, 117, 118, 186–90, 207, 213–14, 215, 217, 224, 313, 417, 420, 421, 423. *See also* Connectionism
 Junior Mathematics series, 420
 The Psychology of Algebra, 38, 187, 213
 The Psychology of Arithmetic, 38, 113–14
 The Thorndike Arithmetics, 38
Today's Geometry (Reichgott and Spiller), 223
Tracks
 two-track programs, 7, 54, 55, 60, 257

555

 three-track programs, 56, 193
 multitrack programs, 257
Transfer of training, 38, 56, 58, 84, 137, 187, 190, 196, 202, 205, 223, 227, 258
Treatise on Arithmetic, A (Smith), 424
"Trends in the Education of Secondary School Mathematics Teachers" (Schumaker), 329
Trigonométrie canonique (Morin), 360
Trigonométrie rectiligne (LaRue), 364
Trigonometry, 28, 51, 54, 55, 73, 78, 82, 172, 182, 206, 207, 221, 223, 228, 234, 242, 247, 254, 261, 276, 310, 366, 374, 377, 378, 394, 397, 405, 413, 423, 434, 440
 in college entrance examinations, 209
 numerical, 41, 47, 55
Tucker, Albert W., 256, 260, 409
Tyler, H. W., 43, 200

Understanding, 48, 62, 71, 72, 85, 131, 137, 177, 203, 216, 219, 225, 228, 229, 232, 242, 254, 255, 260, 408, 431, 458
Underwood, P. H., 43, 200
Unification movement, 173–77, 207, 421–24
 reaction to, 177–79
 in science and mathematics, 177
Unified mathematics, 33, 55, 78, 172–73, 174, 176–77, 179, 185, 192, 206, 219, 221, 244, 254, 389, 398, 401, 404, 411, 444
 movement, 179, 215
 textbooks for, 179
Unifix cubes, 443
Unifying concepts, 57, 73, 138, 160, 166, 174, 178, 216, 230, 248, 260, 261, 267, 282, 283, 284, 402–3
Unifying strands, 138, 140
Union Act of 1840, 375
Universal Mathematics (CUPM), 81
University
 of Alberta, 432
 Bishop's University, 368
 Brown University, 18, 31
 of California at Los Angeles, 80
 of Chicago, 63, 176, 238, 270, 271, 331, 454
 of Colorado, 74, 330, 331
 Columbia University, 18, 43, 62, 81, 186; Teachers College, 31, 42, 454
 Cornell University, 27
 Dartmouth University, 15, 16, 18

University (*Continued*)
  DePauw University, 331
  Duke University, 80, 316, 330
  Emory University, 331
  Harvard University, 15, 16, 18, 19, 21, 27, 28, 31, 158
  of Illinois, 72, 331
  of Illinois Arithmetic Project, 77, 140
  of Illinois Committee on School Mathematics (UICSM), 72–73, 74, 76, 235, 238, 251–55, 256, 257, 258, 267, 273, 284, 448
  Illinois State Normal University, 309
  Johns Hopkins University, 30
  Laval University, 355, 359, 361
  Louisiana State University, 80
  McGill University, 367, 368
  McMaster University, 399
  of Maryland Mathematics Project (UMMaP), 76, 83, 238, 269, 273, 277, 284
  of Michigan, 27, 29, 31, 80, 331
  Université de Montréal, 359, 364
  New York University, 31
  Northwestern University, 41, 331
  Oklahoma A. and M. University, 331
  of Pennsylvania, 18, 20, 21
  of Philadelphia, 18, 20
  Princeton University, 18, 20, 21, 27
  of Quebec, 360
  Queens University, 401–2
  of Rochester, 331
  Rutgers—the State University, 18, 331
  Shaw University, 332
  Sir George Williams University, 368
  State, of New York College at Plattsburg, 331
  of Toronto, 382, 383
  of Virginia, 20
  of Wisconsin, 79, 331
  Yale University, 16, 18, 19, 27, 28, 75, 272
Ursuline Convent, 355
U.S. Bureau of Education, 40
U.S. Coast and Geodetic Survey, 30
U.S. Office of Education, 72, 74, 232, 251, 328, 332. *See also* U.S. Bureau of Education
  survey of teachers of high school mathematics, 328
  Work: "Pre-Induction Courses in Mathematics" (with NCTM), 59, 232
Usage cult, 207
Utilitarian aims in mathematics education, 6, 28, 48, 67, 78, 95, 98–99, 105, 110, 116, 120, 131–32, 133, 144, 183, 190–92, 197, 219, 230, 231–33, 234, 237, 239, 240, 258, 285, 321, 389, 401, 418

Van Engen, Henry, 139, 260, 272, 365
Van Liew, C. C., 306
Variables
  as quantities, 178
  as unknowns, 160
Vaughn, Herbert, 252
Veblen, Oswald, 41, 42, 180
Verbalization, 255, 294
Ville Marie (Montreal), 355
Vocational Arithmetic (Holton and Paddock), 185
Vocational education, 28, 51, 157, 184–85, 206, 378, 386, 393, 414
Vocational needs, 53, 58, 158, 257

Wallis, John, 19
Walsh, J. L., 256
Washburne, Carleton, 125–26, 127
Washington, George, 21
Weaver, Fred, 295
Weeks, Eula A., 43, 200
Welte, Herbert, 222
Wertheimer, Max, 216, 217
West Point, 20, 28, 29
Wheat, Harry G., 121, 307
Why Study Mathematics? (Canadian Mathematics Congress), 402
Why Study Mathematics? (Miller), 402
Wightman, S., 394
Wigner, E. P., 456
Wilder, R. L., 272
Wilks, Samuel S., 231, 256, 259, 260, 270, 272
William and Mary, College of, 18
Williams, S., 15
Wilson, Guy M., 110, 122–23, 125, 190, 307
Wilson, Jack, 258
Winthrop, John, 19, 21
Wolff, Christian, 99
  Psychologia Rationalis, 99
Wolfle, Dael, 250
Woodring, Paul, 134
Woods Hole Conference, 136, 280
Woodward, B., 15, 157

INDEX 557

Woodworth, R. S., 113
Wooton, William, 236, 270, 271, 272
Workman, J. G., 394–95
Workshops, 316, 328
World War II, 238, 327
   the effect on mathematics of, 58–60, 231–33
   the effect on secondary schools of, 231–33
Wren, F. Lynwood, 299, 307
Wurteen, Nathaniel, 14

Yates, Robert C., 409

Yerkes, Robert M., 118–19
Young, George Paxton, 377–79, 382
Young, Jacob William Albert, 42, 169, 175, 176, 178, 207, 208, 307, 453, 454
   Monographs on Topics in Modern Mathematics, 42, 178
Young, John Wesley, 42, 43, 195, 198, 200, 202
Young Secretary's Assistant, The (Hill), 12

Zacharias, Jerrold R., 74, 289, 291
Zenger, J. Peter, 16